JESUS
AND THE
GOSPELS

—— SECOND EDITION ——

CRAIG L. BLOMBERG

NEW TESTAMENT
INTRODUCTION AND SURVEY
VOLUME 1

APOLLOS (an imprint of Inter-Varsity Press)
Norton Street, Nottingham NG7 3HR, England
Email: ivp@ivpbooks.com
Website: www.ivpbooks.com

First published 2009
Reprinted in this format 2011, 2014

British Library Cataloguing in Publication Data
A catalogue record for this book is available from the British Library.

ISBN: 978-1-84474-574-6

Typeset in the United States of America

for Elizabeth

and Rachel

Contents

List of Abbreviations

Standard abbreviations for books of the Bible, apocrypha, pseudepigrapha, and Dead Sea Scrolls are used. Other ancient sources are written out in full. In addition, the following abbreviations are utilized.

ABD	*Anchor Bible Dictionary*
Abod. Zar.	*Avodah Zarah*
Adv. Haer.	*Against Heresies,* Irenaeus
Ag. Cels.	*Against Celsus,* Origen
AJT	*Asia Journal of Theology*
Ann.	*Annales,* Tacitus
Ant.	*Jewish Antiquities,* Josephus
ANTC	Abingdon New Testament Commentary
AshTJ	*Ashland Theological Journal*
b.	*Babylonian Talmud*
BA	*Biblical Archaeologist*
BAR	*Biblical Archaeology Review*
BBR	*Bulletin for Biblical Research*
BECNT	Baker Exegetical Commentary on the New Testament
Bib	*Biblica*
BI	*Biblical Interpretation*
BIP	Biblical Institute Press
BJRL	*Bulletin of the John Rylands Library*
BNTC	Black's New Testament Commentary
BSac	*Bibliotheca Sacra*
BSC	Bible Student's Commentary
BST	Bible Speaks Today
BT	*Bible Translator*
BTB	*Biblical Theology Bulletin*
BZ	*Biblische Zeitschrift*
CBQ	*Catholic Biblical Quarterly*
CBR	*Currents in Biblical Research*
CC	Concordia Commentary
chap(s).	chapter(s)

Claud.	*Claudius,* Suetonius
CSR	*Christian Scholar's Review*
CTJ	*Calvin Theological Journal*
CTM	*Currents in Theology and Mission*
CTR	*Criswell Theological Review*
CUP	Cambridge University Press
De virib. illustr.	*Lives of Illustrious Men,* Jerome
Dial.	*Dialogues,* Justin Martyr
DJG	*Dictionary of Jesus and the Gospels,* ed. Joel B. Green, Scot McKnight, I. Howard Marshall (Leicester and Downers Grove: IVP, 1992)
DNTB	*Dictionary of New Testament Background,* ed. Craig A. Evans and Stanley E. Porter (Leicester and Downers Grove: IVP, 2000)
DPL	*Dictionary of Paul and His Letters,* ed. Gerald F. Hawthorne, Ralph P. Martin and Daniel G. Reid (Downers Grove and Leicester: IVP, 1993)
EC	Epworth Commentaries
EJ	*Evangelical Journal*
EJT	*European Journal of Theology*
Ep.	*Epistle*
EQ	*Evangelical Quarterly*
ERT	*Evangelical Review of Theology*
ESV	English Standard Version
ExpT	*Expository Times*
FN	*Filología Neotestamentaria*
Fr.	French
Germ.	German
Git.	*Gittin*
Gk.	Greek
GTJ	*Grace Theological Journal*
Gos. Pet.	*Gospel of Peter*
Hb.	Hebrew
HBT	*Horizons in Biblical Theology*
HCSB	Holman Christian Standard Bible
Hist. eccl.	*Church History,* Eusebius
HTR	*Harvard Theological Review*
IBR	Institute of Biblical Research
IBS	*Irish Biblical Studies*
ICC	International Critical Commentary
IDB	*Interpreter's Dictionary of the Bible*
ISBE	*International Standard Bible Encyclopedia Revised*
Int	*Interpretation*
IVP	InterVarsity Press

IVPNTC	InterVarsity Press New Testament Commentary
JAAR	*Journal of the American Academy of Religion*
JBL	*Journal of Biblical Literature*
JETS	*Journal of the Evangelical Theological Society*
JJS	*Journal of Jewish Studies*
JPC	*Journal of Psychology and Christianity*
JR	*Journal of Religion*
JRH	*Journal of Religious History*
JRS	*Journal of Roman Studies*
JSHJ	*Journal for the Study of the Historical Jesus*
JSJ	*Journal for the Study of Judaism*
JSNT	*Journal for the Study of the New Testament*
JSOT	Journal for the Society of the Old Testament Press
JSP	*Journal for the Study of the Pseudepigrapha*
JTS	*Journal of Theological Studies*
JTSA	*Journal of Theology for Southern Africa*
KJV	King James Version
m.	*Mishnah*
NAC	New American Commentary
NASB	New American Standard Bible
Neot	*Neotestamentica*
NET	New English Translation (Net Bible)
NESTTR	*Near East School of Theology Theological Review*
NIBC	New International Biblical Commentary
NIGTC	New International Greek Testament Commentary
NICNT	New International Commentary on the New Testament
NIDB	*New Interpreter's Dictionary of the Bible*
NIDNTT	*New International Dictionary of New Testament Theology*
NIV	New International Version
NIVAC	New International Version Application Commentary
NKJV	New King James Version
NLT	New Living Translation
NovT	*Novum Testamentum*
NRSV	New Revised Standard Version
NTL	New Testament Library
NTS	*New Testament Studies*
OMF	Overseas Missionary Fellowship
orig.	original
OUP	Oxford University Press
p.	*Palestinian Talmud*
Pap.	*Papyri*
par(s).	and parallel(s)
PEQ	*Palestine Exploration Quarterly*
Peregr.	*Peregrinus*, Lucian
Pesah.	*Pesahim*

PIB	Pontificio Instituto Biblico
PNTC	Pillar New Testament Commentary
PRS	*Perspectives in Religious Studies*
ReadingNT	Reading the New Testament
RB	*Revue biblique*
RelStud	*Religious Studies*
repr.	reprinted
rev.	revised
RevQ	*Revue de Qumran*
Sanh.	*Sanhedrin*
SAP	Sheffield Academic Press
SBET	*Scottish Bulletin of Evangelical Theology*
SBJT	*Southern Baptist Journal of Theology*
SBL	Society of Biblical Literature
SCJ	*Stone-Campbell Journal*
SCM	Student Christian Movement
SHBC	Smyth & Helwys Bible Commentary
SJT	*Scottish Journal of Theology*
Smyrn.	*Smyrnaeans,* Ignatius
SNTU	Studien zum Neuen Testament und seiner Umwelt
SP	Sacra Pagina
SPCK	Society for the Promotion of Christian Knowledge
SR	*Studies in Religion/Sciences Religieuses*
ST	*Studia Theologica*
s.v.	*sub verbum* (under the word)
SWJT	*Southwestern Journal of Theology*
t.	*Tosefta*
TDNT	*Theological Dictionary of the New Testament*
Them	*Themelios*
TJT	*Toronto Journal of Theology*
TNIV	Today's New International Version
TJ	*Trinity Journal*
TNTC	Tyndale New Testament Commentary
Trall.	*Trallians,* Ignatius
TS	*Theological Studies*
TU	*Texte und Untersuchungen*
TynBul	*Tyndale Bulletin*
USQR	*Union Seminary Quarterly Review*
War	*Jewish War,* Josephus
WBC	Word Biblical Commentary
WJKP	Westminster John Knox Press
WTJ	*Westminster Theological Journal*
WW	*Word and World*
ZNW	*Zeitschrift für die neutestamentliche Wissenschaft*

Acknowledgments

T WELVE YEARS AGO, I wrote the following: I need to thank many people who played a part in the production of this book. It was Dr. Douglas Moo's class on the Synoptic Gospels at Trinity Evangelical Divinity School in 1978 that first organized my thoughts on many of these topics. My Ph.D. mentor at the University of Aberdeen, Prof. I. Howard Marshall, helped clarify them even further. I am grateful to three years of undergraduate students at Palm Beach Atlantic College and nine years of graduate students at Denver Seminary who worked through this material in previous form, helped me to see additional questions I needed to address, and regularly reminded me when I was still not clear! I appreciate the invitation to teach a class combined of undergraduate and graduate students in 1996 as a visiting professor at the University of Denver, on the Life and Teaching of Jesus. That experience convinced me that much of the material in this book could be used and appreciated even in the less theological environment of a university religious studies department where I assigned a wider variety of readings.

I also thank Dr. David Dockery, who was the academic books editor at Broadman Press when this book was first conceived. He and Dr. Trent Butler, also of Broadman, encouraged me to pursue the type of textbook I envisaged. In more recent years Drs. John Landers and Steve Bond were very helpful in the processes of editing and marketing. On the other side of the Atlantic, Rev. David Kingdon and Mr. Frank Entwistle of InterVarsity Press were most supportive. Drs. David Garland, David Wenham, and William Klein read and commented on the entire manuscript and helped me improve it in numerous ways. A student, Beverly Durham, called numerous typographic errors and stylistic infelicities to my attention. As always, my wife Fran was my most thorough critic, as she too went over the whole work with a fine-tooth comb and made countless helpful suggestions.

Although this is my fifth singly-authored book, I have never yet dedicated one to my two girls. This was intentional; in the past both were not old enough to read and understand such a dedication. Now they can. So, to Elizabeth and Rachel, I say thank you. Thank you for playing so happily on your own and with each other so many times when I was supposed to be watching you but was also reading, writing, or typing this book. Thank you for loving Jesus with a childlike faith. My biggest prayer has been that as you grew up, your faith would grow too. I have also hoped that you would come to understand why I spent so much time working on this project. My life's greatest desire is that as many people as possible will come to know the Jesus of the Gospels, which is not always quite the same as the pictures of him we get in church or school. To God be all the glory!

Now, as I submit this second edition, I must add further acknowledgments: I could scarcely have imagined as many people using this book, particularly as a text-book, as I have learned has transpired over the last decade and a bit. I am very grate-ful that it has accomplished its intended purpose, and it is to help it continue to be of greatest value that I have produced this updated version. Now I have numerous addi-tional classes of students to thank for reading it and making suggestions for revision. I must also express appreciation to Drs. Ray Clendenen and Terry Wilder at B&H Publishing Group and Dr. Philip Duce at IVP in the United Kingdom as my recent and current editors for all their support and encouragement. My research assistants for the 2006–7 and 2007–8 school years, Scott Moore and Jonathan Waits, respec-tively, both provided invaluable assistance in reading, summarizing, and excerpting countless articles and sections of books, telling me which ones I needed to give more attention, what I could skip, and when I could rely on their material to get the gist of the authors' arguments. Jonathan, in particular, devoted the better part of his hours throughout the year to this project, without which it would not be appearing at all this promptly. Thanks so much, gentlemen!

It is only appropriate, likewise, to thank the faculty, administration, and trustees of Denver Seminary for granting me a sabbatical during the second half of 2008, during the first part of which I was able to finish the revision. The staff of our Carey S. Thomas Library continues to make this an enormously user-friendly environ-ment for research, as does the Ira J. Taylor Library at the Iliff School of Theology in Denver for materials we do not have. Tom Jacobs, our library's Collection Man-agement Librarian, managed to get an amazing number of things rapidly through interlibrary loan on those occasions when no local libraries had a given item, as did Kimberly Claire, our seminary bookstore manager until May 2008, and her staff, when I needed to order brand-new items not yet available in libraries. Erin Swan-strom, Administrative Assistant to our Academic Vice President, Dean and Interim Provost, graciously and capably turned the charts and diagrams into digital form, after the publishers were able to give me just an unformatted "text-only" copy of the first edition in digital form for my work on the revision.

It was mid-1996 when I first composed the dedication of this volume to our daughters, who were then nine and five. As I write these words, it is mid-2008, and they are twenty-one and seventeen. Elizabeth has just graduated this summer from the University of Roehampton, London, and become Mrs. Jonathan Little and a "lay student worker" for the St. Peter's Methodist Church in Canterbury, England. Rachel has just begun her freshman year at the University of Rochester in Rochester, New York. Both girls have far surpassed my dreams for them, both as followers of Jesus and as delightful young ladies, for which I am exceedingly grateful. Even as I continue to offer God all the glory, I am thrilled to continue to dedicate this book to Beth and Rachel!

INTRODUCTION

THIS BOOK IS designed to be a "one-stop shopping" textbook for courses on the Gospels. It has proved be of interest to thoughtful laypersons who desire to deepen their biblical roots, as well as to pastors and scholars looking for a current summary of the state of a wide swath of scholarship. But the book is written first of all with theological students in mind. It is the outgrowth of twenty-four years of my teaching on the topic, although my interest in the scholarly study of the Gospels goes all the way back to my first undergraduate course in religion. As I have studied on the Gospels first as an undergraduate and then as a graduate student, and as I have taught similar courses at both levels, I have discovered five topics that lecturers consistently want to introduce: (1) a brief history of the period between Old and New Testaments as a historical backdrop for studying Jesus and first-century Israel; (2) the critical methods that scholars use to study documents like Matthew, Mark, Luke, and John; (3) an "introduction proper" to each Gospel, that is, a discussion of who wrote it, when, where, to whom, with what kind of structure, under what circumstances, and with what distinctives; (4) a survey of the life of Christ, with comments on Jesus' primary teachings and actions; and (5) a synthesis of the major issues surrounding the historicity and theology of Jesus himself. When I was writing the introduction to the first edition of this book, I explained that I was unaware of any textbook that set out systematically to treat all five of these topics; hence, I had been assigning readings from multiple textbooks, never entirely compatible one with another.

This type of pedagogy, of course, has its place. Many instructors make the heart of a course their own lectures, with the assigned readings more supplementary or peripheral. Years ago I began teaching that way, too, but there are so many interesting and worthwhile topics to study in the Gospels that I quickly became frustrated with such a method. To avoid lecturing at dictation speed and to ward off students' frustrations with trying to take notes from my normal, rapid-fire conversational speech, I began to produce detailed, printed outlines of the major topics I wanted to cover. These eventually turned into a spiral-bound, photocopied notebook that students purchased at the start of the term and read in advance of each class. In this fashion, I could be much more selective about which topics I highlighted in class, I could provide supplementary "mini-lectures," and there was actually time for questions and discussion.

Nevertheless, I was not satisfied. Outlines communicate only so much, and I still had to clarify many of my cryptic entries in class. In addition, it is arguable that one of the major gaps in theological education today is helping students make connections from theory to application. For too long lecturers have simply left it up to their students to figure out how a given topic applies, if at all, to the real world of life and ministry. Connections that seem obvious to learned scholars do not necessarily come naturally to someone else's mind. With the growing maturity and diversity of typical student bodies, students themselves have much more to share from their own experiences than was once the norm. Yet, students must be taught to think theologically and analyze real-life problems from a biblical perspective, a rare feat in Christian circles that are dominated these days by a freewheeling pragmatism. When is there time, however, to do all this in the classroom?

As a result, I committed myself to writing out word for word everything I most wanted my students to know—in other words, to writing this book. Now I tell my classes that if they master nothing other than this one book, they still will have the heart of a very solid introduction to the four Gospels. To facilitate careful reading, I create weekly quizzes based on the review questions at the end of each chapter. (Italicized expressions highlight foreign words and important terms and concepts to further help the reader, as do numerous subtitles.) I still use some in-class time to highlight and emphasize the most important concepts in each section, but I have considerable time left for additional brief lectures, questions and answers, discussion, application, and case studies.

In fact, there are several ways the book can be used in conjunction with the classroom or lecture hall. I have pitched the level so that it may be read by upper-division college and introductory seminary students alike (in Great Britain, the rough equivalent respectively of first-degree university students in general and B.D. students more particularly). In the United States many colleges and seminaries offer quarter- or semester-long courses on only the Synoptic Gospels or the Life of Christ. Others cover all four Gospels. A few combine the Gospels and Acts. This book should be equally usable by teachers of all such courses. In some cases it will need to be supplemented by other readings; in some instances certain topics may be skipped. Although there is a logic to the sequence of sections and chapters, one need not assign the material in the order in which it appears. I have tried to make each chapter relatively self-contained, while at the same time employing an abundance of cross-references to material elsewhere in the book on the topic at hand. As a result, there is occasional overlap between discussions, but hopefully not so much as to distract someone reading sequentially through the work.

To attempt to cover so much material in a manageably-sized volume inevitably means that each discussion must be brief. Still, I have tried to get to the heart of what I think students need to know most about each topic. That, of course, also means that detailed defenses of the numerous positions I articulate are impossible.

I have tried not to overwhelm the reader with footnotes but have included enough (and more than in the first edition) so that interested students can pursue the most important and controversial topics further. The bibliographies at the end of each chapter also serve this objective and include works from a considerable diversity of points of view. With only rare exceptions, I limit myself to citing English language works although I have also read in some detail from Spanish-, French-, and German-language sources.

The perspective I adopt is broadly evangelical. This is not an approach I was taught in my initial formal theological education. It is a viewpoint to which I have come through my scholarly study of the Gospels, and it has been reinforced in numerous ways over the years. I do not write according to some prior doctrinal constraint imposed on me by my publisher or the institution at which I teach. Instead, I serve these communities because their views are compatible with my previously arrived-at perspectives. Much of that prior scholarly pilgrimage first found a published outlet in my book on the historical reliability of the Gospels, now thoroughly revised and updated, to which I refer readers for a further defense of positions adopted here.[1] A more thorough defense of my approach to John appears under separate cover.[2] I hope that teachers and students who do not always agree with me can concur that I have represented a broad cross section of scholarship in my survey and that this present textbook can be of use even among many who come to more conservative or more liberal conclusions at certain points.

In the last twelve years, several works have appeared that give readers more options for achieving something close to the five objectives I enumerated at the beginning of this introduction. I mention them briefly in ascending order of comprehensiveness. Clive Marsh's and Steve Moyise's second edition of *Jesus and the Gospels* treats (3) and (5) well, with bits and pieces of (2) and (4).[3] Charles B. Puskas' and David Crump's book succinctly introduces all but the survey of the life of Christ, with the distinction of having a more evangelical and a more liberal author teaming up as co-authors.[4] From a moderate Roman Catholic perspective, Frederick J. Murphy's *An Introduction to Jesus and the Gospels* treats in more detail almost the identical material as Puskas' and Crump's.[5] The single volume that comes closest to mine in all that it attempts to do is also the one I can recommend most highly, Mark L. Strauss's *Four Portraits, One Jesus: An Introduction to Jesus and the Gospels*, complete with glossy paper, colored pictures, and charts.[6] It is probably pitched at a slightly more elementary level than my book

---

[1] C. L. Blomberg, *The Historical Reliability of the Gospels,* rev. ed. (Nottingham: Apollos; Downers Grove: IVP, 2007).

[2] Idem., *The Historical Reliability of John's Gospel* (Leicester and Downers Grove: IVP, 2001).

[3] C. Marsh and S. Moyise, *Jesus and the Gospels,* 2nd ed. (London and New York: T&T Clark, 2006).

[4] C. B. Puskas and D. Crump, *An Introduction to the Gospels and Acts* (Grand Rapids and Cambridge: Eerdmans, 2008).

[5] F. J. Murphy, *An Introduction to Jesus and the Gospels* (Nashville: Abingdon, 2005).

[6] M. L. Strauss, *Four Portraits, One Jesus: An Introduction to Jesus and the Gospels* (Grand Rapids: Zondervan, 2007).

and contains almost no footnotes. For the reader willing to work through two volumes, Darrell Bock's excellent *Studying the Historical Jesus: A Guide to Sources and Methods* and *Jesus according to Scripture: Restoring the Portrait from the Gospels*[7] do everything I try to do, in even more detail, except to synthesize John and the Synoptics for the life of Christ section or to present a discrete segment on historical reliability. It would nevertheless appear that my volume may still fill a definable gap or niche in the literature.

To that end, this revised edition is about 15% longer than the original. There has been such a flurry of scholarly study and debate, even in just the last decade, particularly with respect to newer critical methods, the Gospel of John, the quest of the historical Jesus, issues concerning the canon and noncanonical Gospels, and the historical trustworthiness of the canonical material, that these are the areas where I have rewritten and/or supplemented the original text the most. I have reread every chapter, revised what seemed unclear or poorly worded, added small updates to most major sections, occasionally omitted something, noticeably improved the documentation in the footnotes, and thoroughly updated the bibliographies to reflect the best of the literature, current through the middle of 2008.

Who would have imagined twelve years ago the balkanization of the Bible-reading public into clumps of vociferous supporters of their favorite English translations, often accompanied by vitriolic rhetoric against other versions? That was then a distinction of the almost defunct King James Version only movement! Today, not only has that movement actually revived but it seems that far too many scholars, professors, pastors, and theological students, not to mention quite a few laypeople, rally in "groupie-like" fashion around one and only one of the NASB, NIV, NRSV, NKJV, NLT, TNIV, NET, HCSB, or ESV! Meanwhile, most of the people of the world continue at best to have only one reasonably accurate and readable translation of the Scriptures in their native tongues, while non-Christians in English-speaking countries too often assume that none of the translations is reliable or else we would not keep making new ones and quarrelling over existing ones! Surely, God grieves over the amount of energy and rancor that has been exercised creating and critiquing all of these versions, when every one of them is highly reliable and far more than adequate in communicating God's Word to readers of English. Still, each meets a definable need, either real or perceived, and I have been privileged to be a part of the translation process, at varying levels, of four of them (NLT, HCSB, ESV, TNIV). The best up-to-date primer on the strengths and weaknesses, distinctives and commonalities, of these and other important versions is now Gordon D. Fee's and Mark L. Strauss's *How to Choose a Translation for All Its Worth*.[8]

---

[7] D. Bock, *Studying the Historical Jesus: A Guide to Sources and Methods* and *Jesus according to Scripture: Restoring the Portrait from the Gospels* (Grand Rapids: Baker; Leicester: Apollos, 2002), for both volumes.

[8] G. D. Fee and M. L. Strauss, *How to Choose a Translation for All Its Worth* (Grand Rapids: Zondervan, 2007).

For those occasions in which I quoted an extended portion of a Bible verse (i.e., more than a single word or phrase), I thought seriously about providing my own translations or using a relatively even distribution of all of the above-mentioned versions so as to offend (or please) everyone (or no one) equally! Both approaches would have been too time-consuming, and the results would not have corresponded to anything with which readers could follow in any single edition of Scripture that they might access. I have chosen the TNIV as my default version, that is, when I do not otherwise indicate that I am using some different translation. In my estimation, it most often captures the best balance between readability, clarity, and twenty-first century English on the one hand and faithfulness and accuracy to the original languages of Scripture on the other. I have written in some detail on this elsewhere, so I will not repeat myself here.[9] Nevertheless, in deference to those who cannot accept a word like "person" substituting for the generic "man," or a gender-inclusive "he" being represented by a "they" or a "you," even when the context makes clear what the original connotation was, I have chosen alternate translations that avoid these phenomena when the TNIV utilizes them.[10]

Primarily for the sake of variety, that is, to avoid repeating the name "Jesus" over and over again, I have used "Christ" as an equivalent proper noun. Its original use as a title ("the Christ") is elucidated in chapter 19. In other cases, I vary terminology to let readers know I am aware of options, without rigidly confining myself to one form of speech: "intertestamental" or "Second Temple" period; Hebrew Bible, Torah, or Old Testament; heathen, pagan, Gentile, or Greco-Roman; and so on. In all these instances, I am not trying to upset or cater to anyone through my use of language or to further any agenda other than communicating as clearly, accurately, and interestingly as I can to the greatest number of English-language readers in our world today. If this continues to enable readers to understand the Jesus of the Gospels better, as it apparently has for many in its first edition, it will continue to serve its intended purpose.

---

[9] C. L. Blomberg, *"Today's New International Version*: The Untold Story of a Good Translation," in *Perspectives on the TNIV from Leading Scholars and Pastors* (Grand Rapids: Zondervan, 2004), 85–115; repr. in *BT* 56 (2005): 187–211. For additional detail, see esp. D. A. Carson, *The Inclusive Language Debate: A Plea for Realism* (Grand Rapids: Baker; Leicester: IVP, 1998).

[10] In other words, I have followed the TNIV only when it conforms to what have come to be known as the Colorado Springs Guidelines, itemized and defended in V. S. Poythress and W. A. Grudem, *The Gender-Neutral Bible Controversy: Muting the Masculinity of God's Words* (Nashville: Broadman & Holman, 2000). As it turns out, this still leaves the vast majority of my quotations completely acceptable in their TNIV form, a result one might not imagine from listening only to the critics!

Part One

HISTORICAL BACKGROUND FOR STUDYING THE GOSPELS

T HE UNDERSTANDING OF any religion depends heavily on the historical circumstances surrounding its birth. This is particularly true of Judaism and Christianity because of the uniquely historical nature of these religions. Centered on Scriptures that tell the sacred stories of God's involvement in space and time with distinctive communities of individuals called to be his people, the Judeo-Christian claims rise or fall with the truthfulness of these stories. For Christianity, the central story is about the life, death, and resurrection of Jesus the story that forms the topic of the four New Testament Gospels.

Because many courses on the life of Christ or the Gospels are the first in a series of classes surveying the entire New Testament, part 1 of this book includes some historical background relevant to the New Testament more generally (i.e., including Acts, the epistles, and Revelation). Still, its primary focus is to prepare students for an intensive study of Matthew, Mark, Luke, and John and the events they narrate. The three major chapter divisions—covering political, religious, and socioeconomic background—obviously overlap, especially when studying a world that knew nothing of the separation of church and state. Still, the divisions are a convenient way of arranging the major topics of historical background to prepare one for a sensitive and informed reading of the Gospels.

1

POLITICAL BACKGROUND

An Overview of the Intertestamental Period

F OR CENTURIES CHRISTIAN scholars have referred to the period from the last quarter of the fifth century BC to the first century AD as the *intertestamental period*.[1] One might just as naturally study this period as the culmination of or sequel to the Old Testament era. However, since surveys of the Old Testament have much more material to cover than studies of the New Testament, textbooks on the New Testament or the Gospels have usually been the place where an overview of these five centuries appears. Furthermore, any informed reading of the New Testament requires some familiarity with the events of this era.

The primary ancient source for the political developments in Israel during the centuries leading up to and including the life of Christ is Josephus's *Jewish Antiquities*, a twenty-volume work on the history of the Jewish people. For the decades immediately after Christ, Josephus's *Jewish War* is most useful. Josephus (AD 37–about 100) described himself as a one-time Pharisee and a military

---

[1] This is clearly a Christian term based on the belief that the New Testament is a second collection of revelations from God following the Hebrew Scriptures (the Christian Old Testament). In ecumenical circles, "the Second Temple era" is often preferred. This term refers to the period beginning with the rebuilding of the Jewish temple in the late sixth century BC and ending with its destruction in AD 70. The abbreviations BC (before Christ) and AD (*Anno Domini*—"in the year of our Lord") are often replaced with BCE (before the Common Era) and CE (the Common Era, i.e., when Judaism and Christianity coexisted).

general in the war against Rome (66–70), who subsequently became a loyal supporter of Rome and wrote voluminously under the patronage of the imperial court. Although clearly writing with pro-Roman biases, Josephus may be regarded as a relatively reliable historian; for some periods his works are all we have.[2]

Other information can be gleaned from the Old Testament *apocrypha* and *pseudepigrapha*. The apocrypha (from the Gk. word for "hidden") refers to a collection of fifteen short books or parts of books that have traditionally been accepted by Roman Catholics as part of the Old Testament canon or that appeared in ancient Greek translations of the Old Testament.[3] These include additions to older canonical works such as Daniel and Esther, books of wisdom literature similar to Proverbs (e.g., The Wisdom of Solomon and Ecclesiasticus [also known as ben Sira]), edifying novels (Tobit, Judith), and historical narratives (1 and 2 Maccabees). The pseudepigrapha (from the Gk. for "false ascriptions" [concerning authorship]) include more than sixty additional works.[4] Some of these were written in the names of very ancient Jewish heroes (e.g., Enoch, Moses, Levi, Abraham)—hence the name pseudepigrapha. The vast majority of these books were never accepted as inspired or canonical by any official segment of Judaism or Christianity.[5] The pseudepigrapha include apocalyptic literature, the last "testaments" of dying leaders, expansions of Old Testament narratives, wisdom and philosophical literature, psalms, prayers and odes, and various other miscellaneous works. Few of the apocrypha and pseudepigrapha even claim to be historical narratives, but their themes captured the interests of the Jews during the various time periods in which they were written. The most significant of these documents for reconstructing the history of intertestamental Israel are 1 and 2 Maccabees (from the apocrypha). These books narrate the events leading up to and including the Jewish revolt against Syria in the mid-second century BC, with 2 Maccabees usually viewed as a little less reliable than 1 Maccabees.

Many Jews came to believe that after Malachi, the last of the Old Testament prophets, prophecy ceased to exist in Israel and would arise again only in connec-

---

[2] An accessible edition of Josephus's writings for beginning students is *The Works of Josephus*, trans. W. Whiston (Peabody: Hendrickson, 1987). For a good overview of his life and work, see T. Rajak, *Josephus: The Historian and His Society*, rev. ed. (London: Duckworth, 2002). On his overall relevance for New Testament studies, see S. Mason, *Josephus and the New Testament* (Peabody: Hendrickson, 2003).

[3] A standard English translation and edition is *The New Oxford Annotated Apocrypha*, ed. B. M. Metzger and R. E. Murphy, rev. ed. (New York: Oxford, 1991). For good introductions, see D. A. deSilva, *Introducing the Apocrypha* (Grand Rapids: Baker, 2002); and D. J. Harrington, *Invitation to the Apocrypha* (Grand Rapids and Cambridge: Eerdmans, 1999).

[4] A standard collection in English translation, with commentary, is *The Old Testament Pseudepigrapha*, ed. J. H. Charlesworth, 2 vols. (Garden City: Doubleday, 1983–85). For an excellent introduction to the full range of primary, noncanonical Jewish literature relevant for New Testament backgrounds, see L. R. Helyer, *Exploring Jewish Literature of the Second Temple Period: A Guide for New Testament Students* (Downers Grove: IVP, 2002).

[5] Some branches of Eastern Orthodoxy at times have treated 1 Enoch as canonical.

tion with the events surrounding the arrival of the Messiah and his kingdom.[6] A reasonable date for the writing of Malachi is 433 BC,[7] and Josephus claimed that no Scriptures were written after the reign of Artaxerxes, who died in 424 (*Ag. Ap.* 1.8.40–41). So a survey of the intertestamental period begins where the Old Testament leaves off, with various repatriated Jews having returned from exile to Israel, rebuilding the temple, and seeking once again to serve their God in their land.

Why is this era important to study as background for the Gospels? Politically and socioeconomically, key developments occurred, an understanding of which is essential to a correct interpretation of the situation of the Jews in the time of Jesus. Religiously, Judaism was transformed into a set of beliefs and practices often quite different from Old Testament religion. For those inclined to see the hand of providence in history, numerous events occurred that prepared the way for the first-century world to be more receptive to the message of the gospel than in many other periods of history.

The Beginning of the Time between the Testaments: Jews Continue under Persian Rule (ca. 424–331 BC)

From the perspective of a secular historian, this is no point at which to begin a new era. Nothing earth-shattering happened with the death of Artaxerxes. Life continued much as it had during the time of Nehemiah, Haggai, and Malachi. The Persian rulers, with varying degrees of consistency, continued the policy inaugurated under Cyrus in 539 BC of allowing Jews in exile to return to their homeland, worship their God freely, and obey the laws of Moses. The Jews, of course, did not reestablish a kingship but began to look to future days when they could do so. An increased preoccupation with the Law was based on the convictions that their past exiles were punishment for disobedience and that God would grant them complete freedom when they achieved a substantial measure of obedience to his Word.

Three important new developments did take place, however, during the Persian period, which sowed the seeds for the transformation of Judaism by the first century. The first two of these were the rise of the *synagogue* and the beginning of the *oral Law*. In fact, no one knows for sure the origins of either institution; some would date one or both much earlier or later. It is reasonable to assume that the events of exile and return had a formative influence on both. Without access to a temple in which to gather or a divinely authorized place to offer sacrifices, Jews began to congregate in local places of worship. They drew on biblical texts such as 1 Sam 15:22 ("To obey is better than sacrifice") and substituted prayers of repentance and good works as the means of atonement for sin.[8] Because they sought

---

[6] This claim has been challenged, but see B. D. Sommer, "Did Prophecy Cease? Evaluating a Reevaluation," *JBL* 115 (1996): 31–47.

[7] P. A. Verhoef, *The Books of Haggai and Malachi* (Grand Rapids: Eerdmans, 1987), 160; for discussion of other options, see 156–59. Many critics, of course, date other OT books even later.

[8] Distinct buildings may not have been utilized for several more centuries, but "the origin of the 'synagogue' as a public assembly including torah-reading rituals is bound to the administrative structure of the land of Israel and goes back to the Persian period, more specifically to the reign of

to apply the *Torah* (Law) to every area of life, a body of oral tradition—interpretation and application—began to develop around the written Law of Moses to explain how to implement its commandments in new times and places.[9] Both the synagogue and the oral Law featured prominently in Jesus' interaction with Judaism centuries later.

The third development was the establishment of *Aramaic* as the main language for business and international relations throughout many parts of the Persian Empire, including Israel. A cognate language to biblical Hebrew, Aramaic became and remained the native tongue for everyday use among Jews in Palestine well into the first century. Indeed, by the time of Christ, many Jews were probably not fluent in Hebrew, as it had become a language largely limited to the reading of Scripture.[10]

Alexander the Great and the Hellenistic Period (331–167 BC)

The first major new era of Middle Eastern history after the end of the Old Testament period began with the defeat of the Persians by the Greeks. Winds of change were heralded by the defeat of Athens by Philip II of Macedon in 338 BC. This small kingdom in the north of what today is Greece had expansionist designs. The Greek historian-philosopher Isocrates challenged Philip with his famous declaration: "Once you have made the Persian subject to your rule, there is nothing left for you but to become a god."[11] Philip was assassinated two years later, however, and it fell to his son Alexander to strive for those goals.

Born in 356 BC, taught by Aristotle, and inspired by Achilles (the warrior in the *Iliad*), Alexander has been considered by many the greatest military ruler ever. In only thirteen years (336–323) he conquered and controlled virtually all of the former Persian Empire, plus some territories not previously under its control. His rule extended from Greece to India and from southern Russia to northern Africa.[12]

Artaxerxes I." So A. Runesson, *The Origins of the Synagogue: A Socio-Historical Study* (Stockholm: Almqvist & Wiksell, 2001), 479. For an overall history, see esp. B. Olsson and M. Zetterholm, eds., *The Ancient Synagogue from Its Origins until 200 C.E.* (Stockholm: Almqvist & Wiksell, 2003).

[9] For the diversity of ancient opinions concerning the development of the oral Torah, see B. D. Sommer, "Unity and Plurality in Jewish Canons: The Case of the Oral and Written Torahs," in *One Scripture or Many? Canon from Biblical, Theological, and Philosophical Perspectives*, ed. C. Helmer and C. Landmesser (Oxford and New York: OUP, 2004), 108–50.

[10] See further J. M. Watt, "The Current Landscape of Diglossia Studies: The Diglossic Continuum in First-Century Palestine," in *Diglossia and Other Topics in New Testament Linguistics*, ed. S. E. Porter (Sheffield: SAP, 2000), 18–36. For the view that Hebrew played a larger role in first-century Jewish life, at least within Israel, see S. Safrai, "Spoken and Literary Languages in the Time of Jesus," in *Jesus' Last Week: Jerusalem Studies in the Synoptic Gospels*, vol. 1, ed. R. S. Notley, M. Turnage, and B. Becker (Leiden and Boston: Brill, 2006), 225–44.

[11] Helmut Koester, *Introduction to the New Testament*, vol. 1, rev. ed. (Berlin and New York: de Gruyter, 1995), 8.

[12] For an excellent biography, see R. L. Fox, *Alexander the Great*, rev. ed. (Boston: Little, 2000). Cf. also N. G. L. Hammond, *The Genius of Alexander the Great* (Chapel Hill, NC: University of North Carolina Press, 1997).

Greek Rule under Alexander (331–323 BC)

Israel came under Greek rule in 331 BC as Alexander's armies swept eastward. Like most of the peoples conquered, the Jews were given the same relative freedoms of worship and government as under the Persians, so long as they remained loyal subjects of Greece. Alexander apparently hoped to unite the eastern and western parts of his empire and create a new hybrid of cultures, religions, and peoples, with all, however, permeated by *Hellenistic*[13] culture and influence. His turn-of-the-first-century biographer Plutarch, for example, claims that he founded as many as seventy new cities (*Alex.* 1), but most historians think this number is seriously exaggerated.

The voluntary dispersion of many of the Jews continued, as under Persia, since greater economic gain was to be had in many parts of the empire outside Israel. In fact, the largest Jewish community not in Palestine developed in one of Alexander's newly founded cities in Egypt, which he named for himself—Alexandria. This city became an important Christian center by the second century AD. Jews, under the influence particularly of the mid-first-century writer *Philo*,[14] as well as Christians, especially following the late-second-century theologian Origen, developed in Alexandria an allegorical form of exegesis that sought to harmonize the best of Greek philosophy with Jewish or Christian religion.

In Greece, Alexander and his armies had come from Greek cities with a history of democratic ideals. As he marched eastward, he encountered peoples used to acclaiming or even worshiping their rulers as gods and saviors, most notably the Egyptians with their Pharaohs. At first, Alexander was shocked by the inclination of his new subjects to grant him similar acclaim, but eventually, he accepted it and even came to demand it, to the horror and disgust of many of his own countrymen. Alexander's morals also decayed toward the end of his life, which ended prematurely just before his thirty-third birthday when, after a heavy bout of drinking, he caught a fever, possibly malaria, and died.

Numerous results of Alexander's conquests lasted well into the Roman period and the time of the rise of Christianity. First, Greek rule brought improved standards of living and administrative efficiency in an empire that came to be urban- rather than rural-centered. This shift facilitated mass communication; and news, including the gospel, could be spread rapidly by focusing on the major cities in each territory.

Second, Hellenization spread as the result of imperialism. Greek culture and influence could be found everywhere. For Jews, this provided significant enticements to disobey their Law. All the subjugated peoples were exposed to the breadth of Greek religion and philosophy. Major libraries (especially in Alexandria) and universities (especially in Tarsus) were founded. Jews divided among themselves as to whether or not it was acceptable to study, learn from, and incorporate into their lifestyles Hellenistic elements. Second Maccabees 4:10–17 describes some

---

[13] I.e., Greek—from *Hellas*, the Greek word for Greece.
[14] See *The Works of Philo*, trans. C. D. Yonge (Peabody: Hendrickson, 1993).

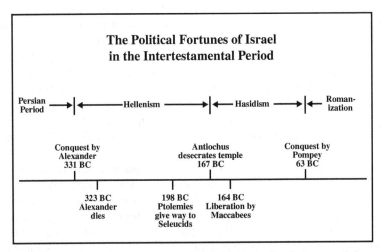

of the temptations of Hellenism in the late 170s BC: Greek forms of dress, with idolatrous associations attached to them; male athletic competition in the Greek gymnasia, often in the nude, contrary to Jewish scruples; and an interest in sports, with worship and sacrifice neglected! Other pressures on Jews to compromise their ways that began early under Hellenistic influence included attendance at or participation in the religiously explicit Greek theater and the availability and attractiveness of eating nonkosher food. The tensions of this era may perhaps be compared to the mutual pressure Western secularism and Islamic fundamentalism exert on people in various Arab countries today.

Thirdly, no doubt the most pervasive result of Alexander's conquests was the spread of the Greek language itself. Almost everyone who had to do business with the Greek soldiers and merchants who came to be located in every urban center had to learn to speak a little Greek. A simplified form of Attic (Athenian) Greek developed, now known simply as Hellenistic Greek. It was less flowery and semantically precise than its classical predecessors. The Greek of New Testament times became known as *koinē* (Gk. for "common") and reflected what Romans called the *lingua franca* (Lat. for "common language"). Thus even through the first century, many Jews in Palestine may well have been at least marginally trilingual, with some knowledge of *Hebrew* (probably limited in use to religious literature), *Aramaic* as their common vernacular, and *Greek* as the language of business, commerce, and relations with the military and political authorities.[15]

The extent of the spread of the Greek language is perhaps best illustrated by the need of diaspora Jews (i.e., outside Israel) to translate the Hebrew Bible

---

[15] It is regularly and rightly assumed that most of Jesus' words in the Gospels reflect the evangelists' translation and paraphrase of his original Aramaic into Greek. Still, we must not underestimate the possibility that on occasion the Gospels have preserved original Greek dialogues. See esp. S. E. Porter, *The Criteria for Authenticity in Historical-Jesus Research: Previous Discussion and New Proposals* (Sheffield: SAP, 2000), 126–80. More generally, cf. M. O. Wise, "Languages of Palestine," in *DJG*, 434–44.

into Greek as early as the mid-third century BC because of the disuse into which Hebrew was falling, even among the generally closed and tightly-knit Jewish communities. This translation of what we call the Old Testament became known in Roman times as the *Septuagint*, from the Latin word for "seventy." Traditions developed that seventy (or seventy-two) scholars were commissioned to produce this translation, and one late legend claimed that all worked independently to produce word-for-word identical copies! The latter claim is demonstrably false—the surviving manuscripts demonstrate the same complex history of formation and development of textual variants and traditions as do the Hebrew Bible and the Greek New Testament.

The importance of the Septuagint for New Testament studies, though, can scarcely be overestimated.[16] In a substantial majority of cases, the LXX (as it is customarily abbreviated) is often the version quoted in the New Testament, even when the Greek rendering varies from the Hebrew in some significant way. The Septuagint was clearly "the Bible" for most first-century diaspora Jews. An important area of scholarship that is only beginning to receive the attention it deserves involves the relationship among the different versions of the Septuagint and the ancient copies of the Hebrew Old Testament.[17] Until the discovery of the Dead Sea Scrolls, the oldest known Hebrew versions were copies of the *Masoretic* text (MT) from the ninth and tenth centuries after Christ, while portions of the Septuagint were half a millennium older. Now, however, we have copies and fragments from pre-Christian times of most Old Testament books in Hebrew. Occasionally, these older readings differ from the MT but support the LXX. So not every instance of a New Testament author seeming to differ significantly from the Old Testament involves his taking inappropriate liberties with the text; in some cases the LXX may well translate the underlying Hebrew more accurately than we first thought. But there are many other reasons for the distinctive uses of the Old Testament by New Testament writers, and much profitable study is yet to be undertaken in this field.[18]

Egyptian Rule under the Ptolemies (323–198 BC)[19]

When Alexander died he left no living heir to his kingdom, so a struggle for succession ensued among his generals. From 323–301 BC, the outcome of this

---

[16] The best introduction is K. H. Jobes and M. Silva, *Invitation to the Septuagint* (Grand Rapids: Baker; Carlisle: Paternoster, 2000). Cf. J. M. Dines and M. A.Knibb, *The Septuagint* (London and New York: T&T Clark, 2004).

[17] See esp. M. Hengel, *The Septuagint as Christian Scripture: Its Prehistory and the Problem of Its Canon* (London: T&T Clark, 2002; Grand Rapids: Baker, 2004).

[18] For an excellent introduction to OT textual criticism, see P. D. Wegner, *A Student's Guide to Textual Criticism of the Bible: Its History, Methods and Results* (Downers Grove: IVP, 2006), 163–203. For a more comprehensive treatment, see E. Tov, *Textual Criticism of the Hebrew Bible* (Minneapolis: Fortress; Assen: Van Gorcum, 2001). An outstanding resource for the use of the Hebrew Bible in the NT is now G. K. Beale and D. A. Carson, eds., *Commentary on the New Testament Use of the Old Testament* (Grand Rapids: Baker, 2007).

[19] For a selection of primary sources treating this and immediately subsequent periods, see M. Austin, *The Hellenistic World from Alexander to the Roman Conquest*, rev. ed. (Cambridge: CUP, 2006).

power struggle was uncertain; this time frame is known as the period of the *Dia-dochoi* (Gk. for "successors"). Initially, the empire was divided into four parts; then, into three. Finally, two dynasties controlling most of the land that Alexander had previously held were established by Seleucus and Ptolemy. The northern half, based in Syria, came under *Seleucid* control, and its rulers generally took the names either of Seleucus or Antiochus. The southern half, based in Egypt, was *Ptolemaic*, and its leaders consistently adopted the title of Ptolemy. Because Israel was precariously perched in the only stretch of fertile ground exactly between these two powers, it was consistently vulnerable to expansionist designs on the part of either.

From 311 BC on, Israel was securely in the hands of the Ptolemies. The Ptolemaic period seems to have been one of relative peace and freedom for the Jews, with a fairly good standard of living, but sources of information about this time are scarce. One source that has survived is the collection of Zenon papyri that describe the development in the first half of the third century BC of the institution of tax-farmers—local people, including Jews, co-opted into collecting taxes as go-betweens for the Hellenistic authorities. This practice continued into Roman and New Testament times, fueling the Jewish hatred for tax collectors that we see on the pages of the Gospels. During the second half of the third century, a rivalry also grew up between the households of two men named Onias and Tobias. The Oniads were high priestly families who objected to the growing Hellenism of Jewish life; the Tobiads were wealthy supporters of the Ptolemies and were more favorably disposed to Greek culture. This tension, too, continued for several centuries.[20]

The most famous and powerful ruler during this century was Ptolemy III (246–222 BC),[21] who promoted scientific investigation. Some of his astronomers even proposed that the earth was spherical, rather than flat, and computed its circumference with relative accuracy. But this information was not widely believed until the discoveries of Galileo in the early 1600s.

Syrian Rule under the Seleucids (198–167 BC)

In 198 BC, the Seleucid ruler Antiochus III conquered and occupied Israel, shifting the balance of power from south to north. For the next several decades, Jews were subject to Syria rather than Egypt. Antiochus III (who ruled from 222–187) and Seleucus IV (187–175) continued the Ptolemaic policy of limited freedom and self-government for Israel, but they also wished to keep on friendly terms with the growing power to their west—Rome. A peace treaty by Antiochus

---

[20] Cf. further B. Nogbri, "The Motivations of the Maccabees and Judean Rhetoric of Ancestral Tradition," in *Ancient Judaism in its Hellenistic Context*, ed. C. Bakhos (Leiden and Boston: Brill, 2005), 85–111.

[21] Or 221 BC. The dates given for many events in the ancient world often vary by a year or so in one direction or the other in different modern textbooks because of uncertainties in the calendars and other ancient forms of dating used. For the most part, this book will not note instances of these discrepancies but merely adopt widely held dates.

in 188 BC promised Rome substantial annual tribute, forcing the Seleucids to impose increasingly heavier taxation on their subjects.

Antiochus IV came to power in 175. He began significantly to alter the previously cordial relationship between the Seleucids and the Jews in Israel. At first his motives seemed strictly economic. He severely increased taxation to try to keep up with the payments to Rome. But he also began more actively to promote Hellenization, eventually to the extent of proclaiming himself a god—Antiochus *Epiphanes* (from the Gk. for "manifest"). The later historian Polybius commented that his detractors referred to him instead as *Epimanes*—a "madman" (*Histories* 26.1a)!

Relationships progressively deteriorated between Antiochus and the faithful Jews who objected to the growing Hellenism. These Jews were increasingly called the *Hasidim* (Hb. for "pious ones"). Conflict seemed inevitable when a man named Jason, the brother of the rightful heir to the high priesthood (Onias III), paid a large bribe to Antiochus to receive appointment to that office. The problem worsened when Menelaus, a Benjamite and thus not lawfully a priest at all, in turn outbid Jason and was installed as high priest shortly afterwards. After a military campaign by Antiochus in Egypt, a false rumor spread throughout Jerusalem that Antiochus had been killed, leading to public rejoicing and celebration. This prompted Antiochus, on his way home to Syria, to enter the temple sanctuary and carry off the equivalent of billions of dollars of sacred objects and treasury monies. He also allegedly massacred forty thousand Jews in one day.

After Antiochus's next Egyptian expedition, he again looted Jerusalem, set fire to parts of the city, and slaughtered many—all on a Sabbath, a time when the Jews would not resist. In addition he made virtually all of Judaism's distinctiveness illegal and transgressed its holiest laws by renaming the Jerusalem temple for Zeus Olympius, setting up a pagan altar there on which swine were sacrificed (the most unclean of animals in Jewish eyes), prohibiting circumcision and Sabbath observance, banning and burning copies of the Torah, and ordering sacrifices to pagan gods at various altars around the country.[22] Because Dan 11:1–30 predicted in detail the political events from the time of the Persian empire to Antiochus IV (though without mentioning him by name), many Jews understandably took verses 31–35—Daniel's famous "abomination of desolation"—to refer to Antiochus's desecration of the temple. First Maccabees 1:54 specifically relates this to the events on 15 Chislev (roughly December) in 167 BC when "they erected a desolating sacrilege upon the altar of burnt offering," although its specific nature is not described. Jesus later reapplied this imagery to the destruction of the temple

---

[22] For the entire period of Seleucid rule and the Maccabean uprising, see Dov Gera, *Judaea and Mediterranean Politics, 219 to 161 B.C.E.* (Leiden: Brill, 1998). *Contra* Gera's surprisingly positive assessment of Antiochus Epiphanes, see D. R. Schwartz, "Antiochus IV Epiphanes in Jerusalem," in *Historical Perspectives: From the Hasmoneans to bar Kokhba in Light of the Dead Sea Scrolls*, ed. D. Goodblatt, A. Pinnick and D. R. Schwartz (Leiden and Boston: Brill, 2001), 45–56. For an attempt to separate history from Maccabean redaction, see S. Weitzman, "Plotting Antiochus's Persecution." *JBL* 123 (2004): 219–34.

by Rome in AD 70 (Mark 13:14 pars.), and some interpreters take the imagery of Rev 11:2 to refer to a similar desolation at the end of human history just prior to Christ's return.

The Maccabean Revolt and the Hasmonean Dynasty (167–63 BC)

Needless to say, little further provocation was necessary to start a Jewish revolt. An aged priest, Mattathias, was ordered to sacrifice on one of the unlawful altars Antiochus had erected in a small town in northwest Judea called Modein. He refused, and when a fellow Jew came forward to obey the king's orders, Mattathias slew both his countryman and the soldier overseeing the sacrifice. Soon the priest and his five sons fled to the Judean hill country and organized a band of rebel Jews. They repeatedly surprised and defeated outposts of the much larger Syrian armies through the otherwise little-used tactics of guerrilla warfare, including nighttime attacks from their mountain hideouts and a willingness to defend themselves and fight on the Sabbath.

Mattathias died in 166 BC, but his son Judas, nicknamed *Maccabeus* (from the Gk. for "hammer[er]"), continued leading the attacks. The Syrian commander Lysias was unable to devote his whole attention to the Jewish insurgents because of internal divisions among the Seleucids and attacks from the Parthians to the northeast, so the Maccabees continued to win victories despite being outnumbered by as many as six to one (cf. 1 Macc 4:28–29). By 25 Chislev in 164 BC, Judas succeeded in regaining control of the temple precincts

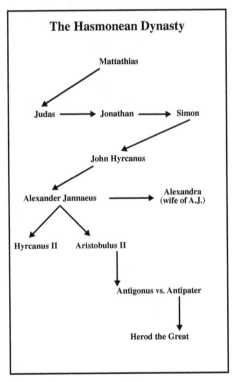

The Hasmonean Dynasty

and "purifying" the sanctuary. This crucial stage in the liberation of Israel from foreign rule is still celebrated today by Jews each December as *Hanukkah* (the Feast of "Dedication").[23] John 10:22 introduces one account of Jesus' teaching in the temple at precisely this festival.

Although Judas did not remove the Syrian forces from the Acra fortress in Jerusalem, a temporary peace was negotiated. Fortunately for the Jews, Antiochus

---

[23] Cf. further D. J. Harrington, *The Maccabean Revolt: Anatomy of a Biblical Revolution* (Wilmington, DE: Michael Glazier, 1988).

IV died in 164, and his successor, Antiochus V, was prepared to treat the Jews more favorably. Rome, too, sent a letter promising friendship (2 Macc 11:34–38). Still, as opportunity arose, Judas and his brothers continued to fight Syrian troops until the Seleucid presence was entirely removed from Israel in 142. This ushered in roughly eighty years of independence, still heralded as a golden age of Jewish nationalism. After Rome ended this period in 63 BC, Jews would never again live in Israel as a free, entirely self-governing people until the reestablishment of the nation after World War II.

The Maccabean revolt, like the events that led up to it, intensified Jew-Gentile hatred to a degree not typically found in Old Testament times. This enmity, with its accompanying Jewish nationalism, is an important phenomenon for understanding New Testament events. Consider, for example, Paul's speech to the Jerusalem crowd in Acts 22:3–21. Paul had almost been beaten to death because of the false rumor that he had brought Greeks into the temple, and had been rescued from the Jewish mob by the Roman soldiers who arrested him (21:27–29). When he spoke to the crowd in Aramaic, they quieted down and heard his defense (21:40–22:2). They could patiently listen to his claims about Jesus of Nazareth and to the story of his dramatic conversion. What they could not tolerate was his account of the Lord's commission: "Go; I will send you far away to the Gentiles" (22:21). With this "they raised their voices and shouted, 'Rid the earth of him! He's not fit to live!'" (v. 22).

The era of Jewish independence also reinstituted long dormant hopes of a restored kingship. Increasingly, certain strands of Judaism couched these in messianic language. When the Romans later overran Israel, the author of the pseudepigraphal Psalms of Solomon expressed this hope by echoing words from the canonical Psalms:

> Behold, O Lord, and raise up for them their king, the son of David,
> At the appointed time which, O God, you did choose,
> That he may reign over Israel, your servant.
> And gird him with strength, that he may shatter unrighteous rulers,
> And may cleanse Jerusalem from the Gentiles that trample her down in destruction.
> Wisely and righteously let him expel sinners from the inheritance,
> And destroy the sinner's pride as a potter's vessel,
> With a rod of iron may he break in pieces all their resources.
> Let him destroy the lawless Gentiles by the word of his mouth.
>
> (Ps. Sol. 17:21–24)[24]

---

[24] The translation is taken from R. P. Martin, *New Testament Foundations*, vol. 1 (Grand Rapids: Eerdmans, 1975), 110–11, who also provides a brief commentary on the larger passage in which these verses are embedded (109–14). For more on the ethos producing this kind of literature, see W. Horbury, *Jewish Messianism and the Cult of Christianity* (London: SCM, 1998). For a chronologically broader overview, cf. G. S. Oegema, *The Anointed and His People: Messianic Expectations from Maccabees to Bar Kochba* (Sheffield: SAP, 1998).

By the first century AD, these hopes reached a fever pitch in certain circles and spawned a variety of revolutionary movements.

Judas Maccabeus died around 160 BC and was succeeded by his brothers Jonathan (160–143) and Simon (143–34). While the Syrians still controlled part of Israel, they appointed Jonathan high priest, even though everyone recognized that he was not the legitimate successor to the office. The move was generally accepted as a stopgap measure in light of the extraordinary circumstances. When Jonathan died and Simon succeeded him as military and political leader, ridding the nation of the final vestiges of Syrian presence, "the Jews and their priests decided that Simon should be their leader and high priest forever, until a trustworthy prophet should arise" (1 Macc 14:41). What eventuated instead was a new hereditary succession of "priest-kings" that became known as the *Hasmonean* dynasty (after the name of Mattathias's great-grandfather).

After Simon died, Jewish rule finally passed to the next generation, to Simon's son John Hyrcanus (134–104 BC). Little by little the ideals of the original Maccabees were lost sight of as Hyrcanus devoted his reign primarily to territorial expansion and forced conversions, most notably of the Idumeans, living south of Judea, from whom Herod the Great would later emerge.[25] Hyrcanus also set the stage for the increased antagonism between Jews and Samaritans that carried over into New Testament times (John 4:9) as he destroyed a temple the Samaritans had built in their territory on Mount Gerizim. This alternate site for worship reflects the same theological debate mentioned by the Samaritan woman at the well in John 4:20. The Samaritans were the descendants of the foreigners who settled in Israel after the Assyrian invasion in 722 BC and with whom the Jews had often unlawfully intermarried. In New Testament times, they considered themselves believers in the God of Israel but limited their Scriptures to the Pentateuch, which existed in a slightly different version in their own dialect. They looked for a Messiah, called a *Taheb* (a "restorer"), who was arguably somewhat more of a teacher and a little less of a warrior-king than in the expectations of the Psalms of Solomon.[26]

The Hasidim, who had supported the Maccabean revolt on religious grounds, now reemerged to protest the corruption of the original ideals and the growing Hellenization, which even the Hasmoneans had begun to promote.[27] Probably it was this group from which the Pharisees emerged, calling the Jews back to faithful obedience to their Law. After an aborted one-year rule of Hyrcanus's son Aristobulus (103 BC), a second son, Alexander Jannaeus, began a lengthy reign (103–76 BC), in which he virtually obliterated the Maccabean ideals. On one occasion he

---

[25] Hyrcanus eventually controlled more territory even than Solomon had. See J. Sievers, *The Hasmoneans and Their Supporters from Mattathias to the Death of John Hyrcanus* (Atlanta: Scholars, 1990), 141–46.

[26] For more on the Samaritans, see I. Hjelm, *The Samaritans and Early Judaism: A Literary Analysis* (Sheffield: SAP, 2000); and R. T. Anderson and T. Giles, *The Keepers: An Introduction to the History and Culture of the Samaritans* (Peabody: Hendrickson, 2002).

[27] See further J. Geiger ("The Hasmoneans and Hellenistic Succession," *JJS* 53 [2002]: 1–17), who stresses how natural this would have seemed to the key power brokers and applies it specifically to their dynastic rule.

had more than eight hundred of the Pharisees who protested his policies crucified. Pro- and anti-Hellenization positions were thus solidified, creating a polarization that remained unresolved in New Testament times.

Jannaeus was determined that his wife Alexandra should succeed him. She ruled from 76–67 BC, was much more supportive of Jewish law, and was well liked. After her death a power struggle ensued between her sons Hyrcanus II and Aristobulus II. The former was the older son who had been supported by his mother, but the latter was the stronger and more ambitious. Both appealed for assistance from Rome, by now the strongest political power in the area. Rome, indeed, intervened; its general Pompey invaded Jerusalem in 63 BC, profaned the temple by entering the Holy of Holies, and put an end to the century of Jewish independence.

The Roman Period (63 BC through the Entire New Testament Era)

From at least 280 BC onwards, Rome had slowly been growing by deliberate expansionist policies. By 148 BC, for example, Macedon had fallen to the Romans. A subsequent near-century of civil war kept Rome from conquering far more territory more quickly, yet by the time of Pompey's invasion, Rome was already knocking on Israel's door. Egypt fell in 30 BC, and the Roman empire continued to grow well into the second century AD, by which time it embraced the largest geographical expanse ever unified by one political administration in antiquity, including major sections of what today are Britain, France, Spain, and Germany, as well as the former Persian and Hellenistic empires.

When Pompey entered Jerusalem, Aristobulus II decided to resist but was defeated. [28] Pompey recognized that Hyrcanus II would likely prove more loyal to Rome and so installed him as the high priest. An Idumean by the name of Antipater, the son of a man with the same name whom Jannaeus had made governor over Judea, was given the local political leadership. In general, Rome established "client-kings" at the provincial or regional levels. Antipater ruled from 63–43 BC. The Roman emperor during these years was Julius Caesar. Because of Antipater's crucial help for imperial troops in 47 BC in Alexandria, Julius reduced Israel's taxes, gave her permission to rebuild Jerusalem's walls and fortify other cities, and supplied Judaism with unique freedoms of religion. This was the origin of Judaism as a *religio licita* (Lat. for "legal religion"), which later exempted it from the requirement of sacrificing to those emperors who came to believe themselves to be gods.

From 42–40 BC, another power struggle ensued, this time between Herod, Antipater's son, and Antigonus, son of Aristobulus II and rightful heir to the Hasmonean throne. From 40–37 Antigonus gained the upper hand, but by 37 BC Herod had finally triumphed. He ruled as client-king over Israel for the next thirty-three

---

[28] See further E. Regev, "How Did the Temple Mount Fall to Pompey?" *JJS* 48 (1997): 276–89. Regev particularly examines the contradictory approaches to fighting on the Sabbath taken by different Jewish leaders, which was just one part of their overall disarray at the time.

years. The high priesthood remained a separate institution; its occupants were Roman appointees. This explains, for example, why the Gospels depict hearings of Christ before both Annas and his son-in-law Caiaphas (John 18:13). Although in Jewish law the high priesthood was for life, political fortunes under Rome were less secure. Annas had been appointed in AD 6 and deposed in 15. Caiaphas followed a short time later after three brief appointees and held his office until 37.

Herod is the second personality surveyed in this chapter to whom historians have given the title "Great." He ruled in Israel from 37–4 BC.[29] His reign was marked by massive building projects funded by heavy taxation in addition to his ample private means. The most astonishing of all was the temple in Jerusalem, rebuilt from ground up after the old remains were entirely razed. Although Herod's temple was completely destroyed by Roman armies in AD 70, the western retaining wall around the temple precincts was allowed to stand. It became known as the "wailing wall," where faithful Jews to this day go to pray. Other projects, the ruins of which are still visible, include fortresses at Herodion just south of Jerusalem and at Masada atop a huge natural outcrop of rock overlooking the Dead Sea, an amphitheater (now restored), and an aqueduct at Caesarea Maritima. Herod also rebuilt the capital city of Samaria and renamed it Sebaste (from the Gk. equivalent of "Augustus").

Before the start of Herod's reign, Julius Caesar had been assassinated (44 BC). Originally allies, Octavian, Caesar's nephew, and Mark Antony eventually vied for power. Octavian's defeat of Antony at Actium in 31 BC led to the suicide of both Antony and his wife Cleopatra. Taking the title of Augustus, Octavian reigned as the new emperor until AD 14.[30] Herod had originally been a staunch supporter of Antony, but he quickly convinced Augustus that he could prove equally loyal to him. Most historians credit Herod's success to his good relations with Rome. Indeed, he pursued an active policy of Hellenization and Romanization in Israel, but more subtly than some of his predecessors, all the while insisting that he was a genuine and obedient convert to Judaism. Though never well liked by the masses of Jews, he did gain a significant number of close followers who continued to support the dynasty of his descendants. They appear on two occasions in the Gospels and were known simply as Herodians (Mark 3:6; 12:13 par.).

Toward the end of his life, however, Herod became increasingly paranoid about potential coups and had several of his sons and his most beloved wife, Mariamne, executed to forestall what he feared were attempts to overthrow him. At one point, Augustus ironically remarked that he would rather be Herod's pig (which a Jew would not kill) than his son (whom Herod would kill). Although recorded in Latin, the remark probably preserves a play on words in Greek because of the similarity between *hus* (pig) and *huios* (son).[31] Thus, although there is no independent confirmation of the story in Matt 2:16 of Herod ordering the massacre of the

---

[29] For the explanation of the anomaly that Herod, ruler in Judea when Christ was born, died four years "before Christ," see below pp. 222–23

[30] For a recent biography, see P. Southern, *Augustus* (New York: Routledge, 1998).

[31] See Macrobius, *Saturnalia* 2.4.11.

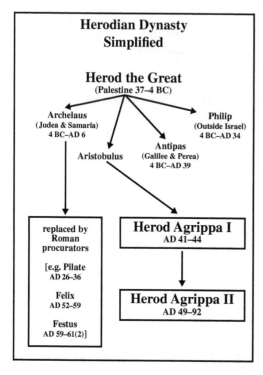

**Herodian Dynasty
Simplified**

Herod the Great
(Palestine 37–4 BC)

Archelaus
(Judea & Samaria)
4 BC–AD 6

Philip
(Outside Israel)
4 BC–AD 34

Antipas
(Galilee & Perea)
4 BC–AD 39

Aristobulus

replaced by
Roman
procurators

[e.g. Pilate
AD 26–36

Felix
AD 52–59

Festus
AD 59–61(2)]

Herod Agrippa I
AD 41–44

Herod Agrippa II
AD 49–92

young children of Bethlehem, the account is entirely in keeping with his character and actions at the end of his time in office.[32]

After changing his will several times in his dying days, Herod finally bequeathed his kingdom to three of his surviving sons: Archelaus, Antipas, and Philip. When Herod died, Archelaus instigated several oppressive measures against the Judeans that led the Jews to send an embassy to Rome to appeal the disposition of the will. Antipas and Philip eventually appeared as well, with Augustus deciding to give Judea (including Idumea) and Samaria to Archelaus. Antipas received Galilee and Perea; and Philip, the remaining provinces to the north and east of the Sea of Galilee (cf. Luke 3:1).

Jesus' parable of a nobleman who went to a distant land to receive a kingdom and was opposed by an embassy of citizens (Luke 19:11–27) may reflect these events. Archelaus's cruel treatment of the Jews continued, however, and subsequent appeals to Rome led to his banishment in AD 6. Little wonder that Matt 2:22–23 describes Jesus' family avoiding Judea and returning to Galilee after Archelaus replaced his father as ethnarch in the south.

Antipas's rule in Galilee was far more benign and included the rebuilding of Sepphoris and the construction of a new capital city on the shores of the Sea of Galilee named Tiberias in honor of the emperor who succeeded Augustus.[33] Since Sepphoris experienced a construction boom in the early twenties, just five miles or so from Nazareth, scholars wonder whether Joseph and Jesus may have plied some of their trade there, but the Gospels never mention either city. Perhaps Jesus, at least during his ministry, deliberately avoided these bastions of Hellenization and Romanization.[34] Antipas retained his "tetrarchy" until AD 39, when he too finally

---

[32] For details, see R. T. France, "Herod and the Children of Bethlehem," *NovT* 21 (1979): 98–120. On Herod more generally, see esp. P. Richardson, *Herod: King of the Jews and Friend of the Romans* (Columbia: University of South Carolina Press, 1996).

[33] An important major work that ranges widely over the entire Herodian family is H. W. Hoehner, *Herod Antipas* (Cambridge: CUP, 1972). Focusing more predominantly on Antipas, cf. M. H. Jensen, *Herod Antipas in Galilee* (Tübingen: Mohr Siebeck, 2006).

[34] Cf. further R. A. Batey, *Jesus and the Forgotten City: New Light on Sepphoris and the Urban World of Jesus* (Grand Rapids: Baker, 1991).

fell into Roman disfavor and was banished. Antipas is the Herod who appears at several points in Jesus' adult life on the pages of the Gospels (esp. Mark 6:14–29 pars.; Luke 13:31–33; 23:6–12).

After Archelaus's banishment from Judea, Rome began to appoint a series of procurators or prefects in the southern half of Israel—Roman governors sent to ensure a more direct link with and control by the empire. The most famous of these today, because of his appearance in Scripture, was Pontius Pilate (AD 26–36). Pilate succeeded in alienating the Jews more than all his predecessors. Josephus records three key incidents surrounding his governorship (*Ant.* 18.3.1–2; 18.4.1–2): installing military standards and shields in Jerusalem with imperial images that violated the second of the Ten Commandments; taking funds from the temple treasury to build an aqueduct; and putting down an uprising of Samaritans. The first incident ended peacefully after a nonviolent Jewish protest; the latter two, in mass bloodshed. While Luke 13:1–2 does not exactly match any of these incidents, it is in keeping with the spirit of Pilate that Josephus describes.

The picture of Pilate in the Gospels as in some ways more weak than cruel does not conflict with Josephus's portrait. If Christ's crucifixion is dated to AD 33, it would have occurred shortly after the demise in AD 31 of Sejanus, the praetorian prefect in Rome, whose previous actions unofficially branded him as anti-Semitic. Without imperial support, Pilate could not afford to be as repressive against the Jews as he once was. But even if the crucifixion took place in AD 30 (on the debate, see below, pp. 225–26). Pilate still would not have been in a position of great strength. Alienating the Jews too much could have led to deposition, as in the case of Archelaus. But Pilate does demonstrate strength in publicly acknowledging Jesus' innocence. At the same time, a Judean procurator had to take quite seriously any charge that he was "no friend of Caesar" (John 19:12). Being sent to govern the out-of-the-way and rebellious Judea was no great Roman honor, and one senses that such governors were regularly caught "between a rock and a hard place."[35]

After Antipas was banished from Galilee, all of Israel was temporarily reunited under Antipas's nephew, Herod Agrippa I (41–44). Agrippa, sympathetic to Judaism, was a friend and political appointee of the emperor Caligula (37–41) who had succeeded Tiberius (14–37). Herod Agrippa I is the Herod who appears throughout Acts 12, first martyring James the apostle, then imprisoning Peter, and finally being struck dead himself for his blasphemy. When Agrippa died, the emperor Claudius (41–54) returned Judea and Samaria to the hands of procurators. Acts mentions two of them in conjunction with the imprisonments of Paul: Felix (52–59) and Festus (59–61 or 62). Agrippa II, however, eventually succeeded his father as client-king in Galilee and ruled for nearly half a century (49–92), gradually regaining territory until he controlled about as much territory as Herod the Great originally held.[36]

---

[35] Cf. H. Bond, *Pontius Pilate in History and Interpretation* (Cambridge: CUP, 1998).

[36] On all the Herods, see N. Kokkinos, *The Herodian Dynasty: Origins, Role in Society, and Eclipse* (Sheffield: SAP, 1998).

Until the Roman emperor Nero (54–68) instigated a short-lived but intense persecution of Christians in Italy in 64–68, the period of Roman rule over Israel and, indeed, over the rest of the empire was primarily a positive one for the spread of Christianity. Seven major factors may be listed: First, Greek continued as the *lingua franca* of the empire. A politically unified realm preserved a linguistically unified people. No attempt was made to impose Latin on the masses outside Italy although some would have been used in military and trade relations. When one compares the dozen or more major languages spoken today in the same territory that Rome once occupied, one understands the boon to communication of having a common language. Second, the *pax Romana* (Roman peace) gave the heart of the empire freedom from warfare over an expanse of time and space previously unparalleled in Middle Eastern history. True, Rome continued to fight skirmishes with Parthia to its northeast and with Germany to the north, but these battles did not directly affect the daily life of most people in the lands depicted in the New Testament.

Third, a direct outgrowth of the first two points was the development of the most advanced transportation and communication systems of the ancient world, perhaps never again matched until the time of Reformation Europe in the 1500–1600s. "It has been estimated that the Roman government's mail service covered 75 km per day; messengers on horseback using relay stations, could cover as much as 100 km per day. Soldiers were expected to march 30 km daily."[37]

Fourth, a cosmopolitan spirit grew, particularly in the cities, which transcended national barriers. Old tribal distinctions and identities were breaking down, leaving people ripe for new religions or ideologies to fill the gaps. The gospel would meet many felt needs in this climate. Fifth but closely related was the elimination of many cross-cultural barriers to dialogue and the dissemination of new worldviews because of the cultural and political unification that was increasing.

Sixth, as long as Christianity was viewed as just another Jewish sect, it too received protection as a *religio licita*. Throughout the events of Acts, all of which were completed by about 62 (before Nero's persecution), Roman rulers consistently came to the rescue of Christians, particularly Paul. Only by the decade of the 60s was it clear to all that Christianity was significantly transcending its Jewish roots and becoming a major world religion, at which point it was no longer granted the legal status it previously enjoyed.

Finally, Rome implemented perhaps the most enlightened and advanced judicial processes of antiquity. It had its tyrants and despots to be sure, along with various breaches of conduct, but due process of law brought justice, at least for citizens, more consistently than in other ancient empires. Jesus, of course, was not a Roman citizen, but Paul was. One repeatedly reads of him receiving the legal benefits of his citizenship (esp. Acts 16:35–39; 22:23–29; 25:10–11).[38] Little

---

[37] Koester, *Introduction*, 314.

[38] Cf. further the important studies of H. W. Tajra, *The Trial of St. Paul* (Tübingen: Mohr, 1989); and B. Rapske, *The Book of Acts and Paul in Roman Custody* (Grand Rapids: Eerdmans; Carlisle: Paternoster, 1995).

wonder that many Christian historians have seen not only a theological but a historical application of Gal 4:4: "When the fullness of the time was come, God sent forth his Son" (KJV).

Already this overview of the intertestamental period has gone beyond the time of the life of Christ and even the events of the Book of Acts. It is worthwhile to continue briefly sketching major developments of Israel under Roman rule—first, because the logical terminus of this period does not come until at least the early second century and, second, because the *writing* of the Gospels and of the rest of the New Testament was probably not complete until at least the end of the first century.

Following the time of Felix and Festus in Judea, two particularly repressive and ruthless procurators were appointed who brought Israel to the brink of revolt: Albinus (62–64) and Gessius Florus (64–66). Taxation had steadily increased although Galilee to the north remained relatively prosperous. But many farmers had lost their fields to absentee landlords who held vast tracts of property and, in turn, hired their employees for irregular work at minimal wage, much like migrant workers today. Increasing indebtedness created foreclosures and, in extreme cases, jail sentences in debtors' prisons.

Despite Judaism's protection as a *religio licita*, not all had proceeded smoothly between Jews and Romans. In 41, Caligula tried to erect a statue of himself in the temple in Jerusalem. The fierceness of the protests[39] would almost certainly have led to a horrible massacre had word not reached Israel that Caligula had suddenly died. Under Claudius, in the late 40s, the empire experienced a famine that seems to have been most severe in Judea (cf. Acts 11:27–30; 2 Cor 8:1–9:15). In 49, Claudius expelled all Jews from Rome (many returned after his death in 54) because of frequent "disturbances," which the Roman historian Suetonius described as coming at the instigation of a man named Chrestus (*Claud.* 25.4). Most scholars believe that this is a garbled reference to *Christus* (Lat. for "Christ") and that conflicts between Christian and non-Christian Jews had provoked the riot. Then in 64, after the great fire of Rome, the emperor Nero looked for a scapegoat on whom to blame the destruction, particularly in view of rumors that he had started it. What resulted was the first state-sponsored persecution of Christians (Jewish or Gentile), now viewed as distinct from the historic Jewish community per se. But, for the most part, it was limited to Rome and its environs on the Italian peninsula.[40]

Meanwhile, tensions were building between Jews and Romans in Judea. In 61, the Greek residents of Caesarea erected a building partially walling in the local Jewish synagogue, and Nero replied to Jewish protests by revoking their status as legal equals to the Gentile inhabitants of the city. By 66 there was fighting in the streets. Gessius Florus ordered that the temple treasury be raided for political purposes. A combination of military, religious, and socioeconomic factors thus sparked the Jewish War with Rome, which lasted until AD 70. Nero's general

---

[39] On which, see N. H. Taylor, "Popular Opposition to Caligula in Jewish Palestine," *JSJ* 32 (2001): 54–70.

[40] For an assessment of Nero more generally, see E. Chamblin, *Nero* (Cambridge, MA: Harvard University Press, 2003).

Vespasian probably would have squelched the rebellion even faster were it not for Nero's suicide in 68 and the uncertainty of imperial succession. Eventually in 69, Vespasian himself became emperor—after the very short-lived tenures of Galba, Vitellius, and Otho—and left Titus, his commander, to complete the invasion of Israel and the recapture of Jerusalem. Titus destroyed the temple, burned various parts of the city, and took numerous prisoners of war back to Rome. The year 70 marked a decisive turning point in Jewish and Christian history. Never again were the Jews a credible political or economic force in Israel (until today), and if anyone still confused Jews and Christians, Christian refusal to join the Jewish revolt clearly separated the two religions from that point onward. Sporadic fighting continued at Zealot outposts until 73 or 74 when Rome besieged Masada, constructing a huge earthen ramp so as to storm the rocky stronghold, only to discover that virtually all of the 960 Jews defending it—men, women, and children—had committed mass suicide rather than surrender to the Romans. Or at least that is the way Josephus tells the story as part of his *Jewish War*, a detailed account of the exploits of those years.[41]

Casualties in Jerusalem were enormous, and the numbers of those deported sizable. D. A. Carson claims that "the savagery, slaughter, disease and famine (mothers eating their own children) were monstrous," and that "there have been greater numbers of deaths—six million in the Nazi death camps, mostly Jews, and an estimated twenty million under Stalin—but never so high a percentage of a great city's population so thoroughly and painfully exterminated and enslaved as during the Fall of Jerusalem."[42] This could partly explain Jesus' extravagant language in Matt 24:21: "For then there will be great distress, unequaled from the beginning of the world until now—and never to be equaled again" (but see also below, p. 404). The temple tax was now to be paid directly to Rome, and Roman troops were headquartered in Jerusalem.

While the war was still raging, one nonparticipating rabbi, Johanan ben Zakkai, requested and received permission to found a rabbinical school at the coastal town of Jamnia (Javneh). Following the war, Judaism as a religion largely survived thanks to the study and leadership provided from this academy. Jamnia is probably best known for its late first-century discussions about the biblical (i.e., Old Testament) canon and for its increasing dissociation from Christians. By the 80s or 90s, synagogue liturgies in various parts of the empire had added a nineteenth benediction, inserted as twelfth in the sequence, to those regularly recited. But this "blessing" was a euphemism for a curse—a curse on all heretics, with *Christian* Jews prominently included.[43] The Sanhedrin(s) (see below, p. 48) were

---

[41] For a thorough analysis of the war, see A. Berlin and J. A. Overman, ed., *The First Jewish Revolt: Archaeology, History, and Ideology* (New York: Routledge, 2002).

[42] D. A. Carson, "Matthew," in *Expositor's Bible Commentary*, ed. F. E. Gaebelein, vol. 8 (Grand Rapids: Zondervan, 1984), 501.

[43] The Hebrew expression was the *birkath ha-minim* ("a blessing [i.e., curse] on the heretics). Translated it read, "Let the Nazarenes and the heretics perish as in a moment, let them be blotted out of the book of the living and let them not be written with the righteous." Modern scholarship has often seen this as one decisive rejection by Judaism of Christianity by the end of the first century, but

replaced by the *beth din* ("house of judgment") as the new court of law for Jewish religious affairs. *Rabbinic* Judaism as a movement had begun, and the seeds were planted for a greater uniformity of belief and practice that did not exist in the days of the highly diverse sects of the pre-70 era or during the birth of Christianity.

A final Jewish revolt in Palestine took place in 132–35 under a man named Simeon, who was given the title *bar Kokhba* ("son of a star") and proclaimed the Messiah by Rabbi Akiba. This uprising was also decisively squelched.[44] Historians disagree over whether two edicts were the cause or the result of this rebellion: a ban on circumcision and plans to make Jerusalem a major center of pagan worship named Aeolia Capitolina. Economic conditions had also again deteriorated under the emperor Hadrian (117–38). At any rate, Jews were evicted from Jerusalem and forbidden to enter on pain of death, except for one day a year when they could lament their fate at the Wailing Wall. From this point on, Jewish Christianity also largely disappeared from view, although the factors behind its demise are complex and beyond the scope of this survey.

For Further Study

Introductory

Carter, Warren. *The Roman Empire and the New Testament: An Essential Guide*. Nashville: Abingdon, 2006.

Cassidy, Richard J. *Christians and Roman Rule in the New Testament: New Perspectives*. New York: Crossroad, 2001.

Cate, Robert L. *A History of the Bible Lands in the Interbiblical Period*. Nashville: Broadman, 1989.

Niswonger, Richard L. *New Testament History*. Grand Rapids: Zondervan, 1988.

Roetzel, Calvin J. *The World That Shaped the New Testament*. Rev. ed. Louisville: WJKP, 2002.

Rogers, Cleon L., Jr. *The Topical Josephus*. Grand Rapids: Zondervan, 1992.

Intermediate

Barnett, Paul. *Jesus and the Rise of Early Christianity: A History of New Testament Times*. Downers Grove: IVP, 1999.

Hayes, John H. and Sara R. Mandell. *The Jewish People in Classical Antiquity: From Alexander to Bar Kochba*. Louisville: WJKP, 1998.

Horsley, Richard A. *Scribes, Visionaries, and the Politics of Second Temple Judea*. Louisville and London: WJKP, 2007.

Jagersma, Henk. *A History of Israel from Alexander the Great to Bar Kochba*. London: SCM, 1985; Philadelphia: Fortress, 1986.

Murphy, Frederick J. *Early Judaism: The Exile to the Time of Jesus*. Peabody, MA: Hendrickson, 2002.

---

more recent studies increasingly agree that these developments took place more sporadically. For the latest in the ongoing discussion, see P. L. Mayo, "The Role of the *Birkath Haminim* in Early Jewish-Christian Relations: A Re-examination of the Evidence," *BBR* 16 (2006): 325–44.

[44] Cf. further W. Eck, "The Bar Kokhba Revolt: The Roman Point of View," *JRS* 89 (1999): 76–89.

Tomasino, Anthony J. *Judaism before Jesus: The Ideas and Events That Shaped the New Testament World.* Downers Grove and Leicester: IVP, 2003.

Witherington, Ben III. *New Testament History: A Narrative Account.* Grand Rapids: Baker, 2003.

Advanced

Collins, John J. and Gregory E. Stirling, eds. *Hellenism in the Land of Israel.* Notre Dame, IN: University of Notre Dame Press, 2001.

Feldman, Louis H. *Judaism and Hellenism Reconsidered.* Leiden and Boston: Brill, 2006.

Grabbe, Lester L. *Judaism from Cyrus to Hadrian.* 2 vols. Minneapolis: Fortress, 1992.

Hengel, Martin. *Judaism and Hellenism.* 2 vols. London: SCM; Philadelphia: Fortress, 1974.

Horsley, Richard A. *Galilee: History, Politics, People.* Rev. ed. Valley Forge: Trinity, 1995.

Sacchi, Paolo. *The History of the Second Temple Period.* Sheffield: SAP, 2000.

Smallwood, E. Mary. *The Jews under Roman Rule.* Leiden: Brill, 1981.

Bibliography

Mills, Watson E. *New Testament History and Background.* Lewiston, NY and Lampeter, Wales: Edwin Mellen, 2002. (Also covers the historical background material treated in chaps. 2 and 3.)

Questions for Review

1. What are the historical sources we have for reconstructing the intertestamental period? How reliable are they?

2. Why is this period of time important for understanding the New Testament? Consider both overall trends as well as developments unique to a particular portion of this history.

3. What are the major sections of time into which this period may be broken? What key dates and events occurred to mark the beginning and end of each section?

4. Who are the key historical figures who influenced the course of events for Israel? Consider both foreign rulers and internal, Jewish figures. How was each significant? Try to distinguish the most significant from the more peripheral individuals.

5. Be sure you can define any foreign or technical terms (particularly those in italics) in this chapter (and throughout the book).

2

RELIGIOUS BACKGROUND

Hellenistic and Jewish Religion

R ELIGION IN THE societies into which Christianity was born permeated almost every aspect of life. The ancient Mediterranean world
contained a cornucopia of religious options. We have already seen the
temptations that Jews faced to give in to various unlawful Greco-Roman practices.
Yet we have only scratched the surface when it comes to describing the bewildering diversity of belief systems and rituals that pervaded the Hellenistic world.
Judaism, too, was diverse, much more so before the fall of Jerusalem in AD 70
than afterwards. Intriguingly, almost every religious option of the first century has
its counterpart in today's world; only the names have changed. Careful readers
will want to look for such parallels as they proceed. Each has its strengths and its
weaknesses and a variety of similarities and differences with Christianity.

Hellenistic Religion

The Greco-Roman world in the age of Jesus Christ was in substantial religious flux. The first century has been seen as a time of "crisis of conscience." Old
worldviews and ideologies became increasingly outmoded. New cults abounded.
People were uprooted from their traditional homes and lands and encountered
conflicting truth claims as they resettled. Mixtures and combinations of beliefs
and behaviors created a pluralism often intolerant only of a narrow, exclusive

religion such as Judaism or Christianity.[1] We can sketch only the rough contours of the most prominent movements here.[2]

Traditional Mythology

The classic pantheon of Greek gods had reached its height in popularity during the fourth and fifth centuries BC—Zeus and Hera ("king" and "queen" on Mt. Olympus), Hermes (the messenger god), Apollo (the sun god), Poseidon (god of the sea), Aphrodite and Artemis (goddesses of love and fertility), and many, many more. After conquering Greece, Rome adopted most of the Greek gods and gave them Latin names: Jupiter and Juno (for Zeus and Hera), Mercury (for Hermes), Neptune (for Poseidon), and so on.[3] The origins of these gods and the mythological adventures surrounding them are debated. Probably they were the outgrowth of primitive animism or spiritism, in which objects and forces of nature were deified and worshiped. Later the gods were seen as distinct beings, described in very anthropomorphic (humanlike) categories, dwelling on the loftiest peak of the Greek mountains. They no doubt formed a primitive substitute for scientific understanding as people sought to explain both the regular and erratic behavior of heavenly bodies and the powers of nature. One had to know which god to whom to pray and sacrifice, and had to carry out the prescribed rituals in exactly the right ways in order to receive rain for crops, safety in sea travel, a large family, and so on.[4]

By the Christian era, however, belief in the traditional mythology was seriously declining. As scientific understanding developed, people realized, for example, that the sun was a fiery ball in the sky and not a god with a personality. The geographic limitations of the gods also hindered their staying power. The fact that Rome was able to overrun the land of the Greek gods demonstrated something of their impotence. Indeed, emperors from Alexander to Augustus regularly exceeded the accomplishments of the gods in their conquests. Urbanization, population mobility, the mingling of cultures, and the upheaval of stable, local traditions throughout the Roman world all led to the loss of appeal of the gods and goddesses of old. To be sure, Augustus attempted a renaissance of sorts of the traditional myths by building numerous temples to the gods in Rome and encouraging their use for worship, but this project was largely politically motivated. Stable traditions led to a stable, unified empire, and on several occasions Augustus hinted that

---

[1] R. MacMullen, *Paganism in the Roman Empire* (New Haven: Yale University Press, 1981), 2.

[2] Two excellent anthologies of primary sources for the study of Greco-Roman religions and philosophical writings are D. G. Rice and J. E. Stambaugh, *Sources for the Study of Greek Religion* (Missoula, MT: Scholars, 1980); and V. M. Warrior, *Roman Religion: A Sourcebook* (Newburyport, MA: R. Pullins & Co., 2002).

[3] For comparative lists of the most prominent gods and goddesses in the Greek and Roman pantheons, see E. Ferguson, *Backgrounds of Early Christianity* rev. ed. (Grand Rapids: Eerdmans, 2003), 154.

[4] For an excellent overview of beliefs and practices, see Hans-Josef Klauck, *The Religious Context of Early Christianity: A Guide to Greco-Roman Religions* (London: T&T Clark, 2000; Minneapolis: Fortress, 2003), 12–42.

his was the spirit (Lat. *genius*) that infused the powers or qualities the gods had traditionally represented.

The majority of first-century Greeks and Romans probably still gave lip service to the old mythology. For example, families poured out food and drink on their hearths or fireplaces (named after the Gk. goddess *Hestia*) as the sacred center of protection in each home. Nevertheless, there were only three prominent areas in which the myths still had substantial influence. First, they remained particularly tenacious in rural or insulated areas. Paul and Barnabas, for example, were mistaken for Zeus and Hermes at Lystra in Acts 14:12—a superstitious identification unlikely to have occurred in first-century Athens or Rome.[5] Second, the gods were consulted and believed to appear to people, particularly in their dreams, as they stayed overnight at healing shrines and received oracles of prophecy. The Asclepian shrines combined elements of medicine, recreation, and religion in a kind of ancient health spa.[6] Thousands of pilgrims consulted the oracle at Delphi, Greece, to seek guidance for planning political or religious events, while priests and priestesses at the Sibylline oracles claimed the ability to predict future events, particularly surrounding the end of the world. Third, seasonal and annual festivals and temple rituals still persisted,[7] often bringing great socioeconomic benefit to the local merchants or temple keepers. Two prominent New Testament examples surround the worship of Artemis in Ephesus (Acts 19:23–28) and the "sacred prostitution" practiced at the temple of Aphrodite in Corinth.[8]

Philosophies

Although today we think of philosophy as distinct from religion, it was not so in antiquity. All the major philosophers articulated worldviews about correct behavior as well as belief.[9] Indeed, the closest parallels in the Greco-Roman world to the Christian concept of conversion came when people became full-fledged adherents of a given philosophy.[10] Most of the major strands of Greco-Roman thought current in New Testament times were in some measure indebted to the fourth- and fifth-century BC philosophers Socrates and Plato, but the actual schools of thought they founded were no longer widespread. Platonism, however, bequeathed to the later empires a pervasive *dualism* between matter and spirit. Following Plato's famous allegory of the cave,[11] the material world was viewed as

---

[5] Cf. D. Béchard, "Paul among the Rustics: The Lystran Episode (Acts 14:8–20) and Lucan Apologetic," *CBQ* 63 (2001): 84–101.

[6] Still useful here is W. K. C. Guthrie, *The Greeks and Their Gods* (Boston: Beacon; London: Methuen, 1950), 247–53.

[7] These, rather than any weekly holidays (i.e., holy days), gave the Greco-Roman worker his or her needed periodic rest, which Jews accomplished through their Sabbath laws.

[8] On which, see further B. MacLachlan, "Sacred Prostitution and Aphrodite," *SR* 21 (1992): 145–62.

[9] For a good overview, see D. Sedley, ed., *The Cambridge Companion to Greek and Roman Philosophy* (Cambridge: CUP, 2003).

[10] Klauck, *Religious Context*, 334.

[11] *Republic*, VII. Plato compared life in this world to the perspective of that of a man chained facing the end of a cave, able to look only at the shadow of himself and of others on the back wall produced

a mere shadow of the unseen spiritual world of ideas. True reality was immaterial reality. Thus salvation was escape from the unreal world of matter to the real world of spirit by means of knowledge of the highest good or Supreme Mind. Sin was ignorance. Salvation produced a disembodied immortality of the soul, not a resurrection of the body. Plutarch (a "middle Platonist") tried, largely unsuccessfully, to reawaken interest in Plato's thought in the late first century AD. The thought of Socrates was, to a certain degree, preserved in the emphasis on rhetorical training of the movement known as the Sophists although at times, unfortunately, it valued style above substance. Paul probably combated some form of Sophistry in his epistles to the Corinthians, but this is less of a full-fledged religious worldview than the other philosophies.[12]

Other groups, however, do merit further consideration. For the most part, full-fledged devotees to the various philosophies were rare since wholehearted study often required an itinerant or peripatetic lifestyle. Only the economically elite, or those prepared to abandon normal occupations and beg for provisions, could afford this level of involvement. But the ideas of the major philosophies were far more widespread in their influence.

Stoicism. The original Stoic was Zeno, an early third-century BC philosopher who came to Athens and taught on outdoor porches (Gk. *stoa*). He was essentially a materialist, believing that all that exists is matter, except that he saw all matter infused with a "world-soul" that he called reason or *logos*. Stoicism was, therefore, also "pantheistic" (God is everything) or at least "panentheistic" (God is a part of everything).[13] The key to contentment in life was to realize what humans could control and what they could not. Where inexorable natural or moral law exists, one must simply accept it, do one's best to fit in, and remain in harmony with the cosmos. Zeno believed that in all apparent external evil, there was some greater good. One's goal, where possible, was to avoid all extremes of emotion or passion and to seek self-control, calmness, and stability in all circumstances. This goal was accomplished by focusing on reason and rationality. As the power of the mind was cultivated, one prepared oneself for death and unification with the Mind that fills the entire universe. Moral choices depended heavily on remaining true to one's conscience, and suicide became a noble option when there were no realistic alternatives to intense, long-term suffering. Stoicism seems to have been the most popular of the Greco-Roman philosophies.[14]

The most famous early first-century Stoic was Seneca, Nero's tutor as a boy and later adviser to the adult emperor early in his reign. The most famous late first-century Stoic was Epictetus, who taught that happiness was attainable only

---

by the light shining through the cave's mouth.

[12] For details, see B. W. Winter, *Philo and Paul among the Sophists,* rev. ed. (Grand Rapids and Cambridge: Eerdmans, 2002).

[13] D. Baltzly ("Stoic Pantheism," *Sophia* 42.2 [2003]: 3–33) combines these by speaking of how the Stoics thought a force (like heat) that filled and comprised all things could be conceived of as a personal power.

[14] Puskas and Crump, *Introduction to the Gospels and Acts,* 13.

by the conscious restriction of one's ambition. One must concentrate on cultivating inward virtues and distance oneself from the accumulation of external possessions. Paul encountered Stoics in Athens in Acts 17:18 and even quotes some of their own poets (Epimenides and Aratus in v. 28), stressing that God is immanent (cf. v. 27—"He is not far from any one of us"). But, against Stoicism, Paul balances God's presence with his transcendence; God is distinct from his creation (vv. 24–26). The description of the conflagration of the universe and its re-creation in 2 Pet 3:10 has reminded some commentators of the Stoic belief in the periodic destruction and rebirth of the cosmos, but this view seemed to have been abandoned by first-century Stoicism.[15]

Epicureanism. Epicurus also taught in Athens and founded his rival school of philosophy about the same time that Zeno was establishing Stoicism. If, from a Christian perspective, the "god" of Stoicism was too immanent, then the gods of Epicureanism were too transcendent. Epicurus, too, was a materialist, but he saw the whole universe as made up of tiny invisible particles (a view foreshadowing atomic science). He did not deny the existence of the traditional gods but saw them as of a similar substance as the world and so far removed from its affairs as to have no influence over it. Gods, thus, were unknowable, and death ended one's conscious existence.

The key to this life, therefore, was to maximize pleasure and minimize pain. This philosophy generated the famous slogan, "Eat, drink, and be merry, for tomorrow we die." But far from promoting hedonism, Epicurus was a somewhat sickly, retiring person who was seeking long-term peace of mind and happiness, not the immediate or wanton indulgence of bodily appetites. Epicureans placed a premium on cultivating friendship and enjoying cultural activities. Their philosophy clearly left the door open, however, to abuse and excess by those unprepared to delay gratification of bodily appetites for greater long-term pleasure. Paul encountered Epicureans in Athens in conjunction with the Stoics (Acts 17:18) and agreed with them, against the Stoics, that God is distinct from his creation. But he made it abundantly plain that God is also intimately involved with human affairs and one day will judge the whole world (vv. 24–31).[16]

Cynicism. Antisthenes (early fourth century BC) was probably the first philosopher to articulate Cynic thought,[17] but the name of the movement itself comes from one of his followers, Diogenes of Sinope. Diogenes was called a "dog" (Gk. *kuōn*—hence the term "cynic") by his detractors because of his vulgar, unkempt

---

[15] For a good analysis of the thought of this movement, see T. Brennan, *The Stoic Life: Emotions, Duties, Fate* (Oxford and New York: OUP, 2005).

[16] A plausible case has been made that the false teachers combated throughout 2 Peter were, in fact, Epicureans. See J. H. Neyrey, *2 Peter, Jude* (New York and London: Doubleday, 1993). But J. D. Charles (*Virtue amidst Vice: The Catalog of Virtues in 2 Peter 1* [Sheffield: SAP, 1997]) demonstrates how the evidence could also point in the direction of Stoicism!

[17] "Antisthenes' principal contribution to Cynicism lies in the distinction he established between nature and culture, giving greater importance to nature and downgrading culture or custom." See M.-O. Goulet-Cazé, "Religion and the Earlier Cynics," in *The Cynic Movement in Antiquity and Its Legacy*, ed. R. B. Branham and M.-O. Goulet-Cazé (Berkeley: University of California Press, 2000), 69.

lifestyle. He was known for deliberately violating social convention by using abusive language, wearing filthy clothing, and performing acts of sex or defecation in public. Cynicism as a movement was generally not so extreme. It evolved into a philosophy in which "the supreme virtue" was "a simple, unconventional life in rejection of the popular pursuits of comfort, affluence, and social prestige."[18] A later Cynic writer summed up his creed this way: "Take care of your soul, but take care of the body only to the degree that necessity requires" (Pseudo-Crates, *Ep.* 3). Cynics largely objected to wealth and relied on begging to survive, limiting their traveling possessions to a cloak, bag, and staff. The similarities between this aspect of their lifestyle and Jesus' teaching, especially his commands to the Twelve and the seventy in Mark 6:7–13 (and parallels) and Luke 10:1–8, respectively, have led some scholars to liken Jesus to a Cynic, but the differences outweigh the similarities.[19]

Skepticism. Founded by Pyrrho of Ellis (about 360–270 BC), skepticism sought to challenge "dogmatism"—the traditional claim that absolute truth could be known. A plausible case was made in certain circumstances for denying any absolute claims. Morality involved merely living according to the accepted norms of a given society. Skeptics did not absolutely deny God; that would have been inconsistent with their system. But they were the agnostics of the ancient world. Their resulting lifestyle was remarkably indifferent or apathetic to supporting any causes; it merely sought the suspension of judgment, the practice of peace and gentleness, and freedom from disturbance.[20]

Neo-Pythagoreanism. The first century saw a revival of interest in the teachings of the sixth-century BC mathematician and philosopher Pythagoras. Thus, Neo-Pythagoreans formed communal groups that devoted themselves to a combination of mathematical investigation, mysticism, numerology, vegetarianism, and a belief in reincarnation. They emphasized harmony, the resolution of opposites, and the discovery of the divine within oneself. A famous late first-century Neo-Pythagorean, Apollonius of Tyana, gained a considerable reputation as a miracle-worker. Some of the accounts of his miracles in the later, third-century biography of his life by Philostratus remarkably resemble Gospel narratives about Jesus, leading scholars to question whether one tradition influenced the other in any way. Usually, the conclusion is that they did not.[21] But Loveday Alexander has recently observed,

> There are obvious parallels between Apollonius and Jesus: "healings, exorcisms, doubting followers, ascension, mission" (Swain 1999:194). But Philostratus' Apollonius has everything the Jesus of the gospels lacks: noble birth, Attic purity

[18] R. H. Gundry, *A Survey of the New Testament*, 3rd ed. (Grand Rapids: Zondervan, 2003), 51.

[19] For the similarities, see F. G. Downing, *Christ and the Cynics* (Sheffield: JSOT, 1988). For the differences, stressing the independence of Jesus from true Cynicism, see H. D. Betz, "Jesus and the Cynics: Survey and Analysis of a Hypothesis," *JR* 74 (1994): 453–75.

[20] For a well laid out overview of *Stoics, Epicureans and Skeptics: An Introduction to Hellenistic Philosophy*, see the book so-entitled by R. W. Sharples (London and New York: Routledge, 1996).

[21] See E. Koskenniemi, "Apollonius of Tyana: A Typical ΘΕΙΟΣ ΑΝΗΡ?" *JBL* 117 (1998): 455–67. For a brief, readable, and convincing summary of what the true Apollonius was most probably like, see B. F. Harris, "Apollonius of Tyana: Fact and Fiction," *JRH* 5 (1969): 189–99.

of diction, rhetorical power, status as counsellor to the highest in the land, Socratic insouciance and divine power. It is not unreasonable to read Philostratus' *Life of Apollonius* as a deliberate attempt to out-narrate the gospels.[22]

Mystery Religions

Some historians have called this option the most characteristic type of religion during the Hellenistic period. With mythology on the wane and the philosophies largely reserved for the elite few, a major part of first-century Hellenistic life that increasingly filled the religious void for numbers of people involved the so-called mystery religions. This is a term for a wide variety of secret organizations or cults often largely unrelated to each other, but several common features can be observed. They sought to bring the initiate into communion with the god(s) or goddess(es) the cult worshiped. They often promised conscious, eternal life, in union with the gods, which so many other religious alternatives did not. They offered equality across the greatly stratified society that rigidly determined one's lot in so many other realms of life. At night in a forest, senator and slave could worship together as spiritual equals, even though by day the one might rule over the other. They also held out hope for transforming one's pilgrimage through life in a world beset with many seemingly arbitrary terrors, because their gods were not localized but had pioneered worldwide journeys themselves. Many of the people who would have been attracted to the mystery religions, therefore, would also have found Christianity appealing.

Some of the mystery cults arose out of ancient tribal and even fertility rituals. Some were indigenous to Greece; others were foreign imports, especially from Persia and Egypt. Several had periodic times of public pageantry, when the myths of their gods were reenacted. In addition, all had more regular, private meetings, with membership reserved for those who had gone through various initiatory rites. Sacramental meals, detailed rules for participation, and strong internal leadership characterized most mystery religions. A typical gathering involved a purification ceremony for members, mystical instruction, contemplation of sacred objects, the enactment of the divine story, and a crowning of new initiates.[23]

Ritual practices could vary dramatically, from the serene to the grotesque. The former category included meditations on an ear of corn or stalk of wheat in the cult of Demeter (a corn god), a quiet river bath as part of the cult of Isis (goddess of the Nile), or fellowship meals of bread and water in Mithraism (devotées of a bull-slayer). In the latter category were the Cybele cult's "blood baptism," in which the high priest stood in a pit beneath a wooden latticework, over which a bull was slaughtered so that the blood ran down and covered the face and garments of the priest.[24] Lower-level priests devoted to Atargatis castrated them-

---

[22] L. Alexander, "The Four among Pagans," in *The Written Gospel*, ed. M. Bockmuehl and D. A. Hagner (Cambridge: CUP, 2005), 237.

[23] J. B. Noss, *Man's Religions*, 6th ed. (New York and London: Macmillan, 1980), 49.

[24] For a vivid description of this ceremony, see the later Christian writer Prudentius, as quoted in J. B. Tyson, *The New Testament and Early Christianity*, rev. ed. (New York and London: Macmillan, 1984), 119.

selves, and the drunken orgies associated with the worship of Dionysus were well known and less a secret or mystery than many of the other cults' practices! One accurate generalization, harking all the way back to Aristotle, sounds remarkably contemporary: initiates into the mystery cults were "not to learn something, but to experience something."[25]

In post-New Testament times, Mithraism, originally from Persia, amalgamated with the Roman worship of *Sol Invictus* (the unconquerable sun), and a festival to Sol was celebrated every December 25. Christians took advantage of this "day off" to protest against Mithraism by worshiping the birth of Jesus instead. After the Roman empire became officially Christian in the fourth century, this date turned into the legal holiday we know today as Christmas. The celebration of the annual death and rebirth of the nature gods finds parallels and contrasts, too, with Christian teaching about the death and resurrection of Christ. But, prior to the second century, Mithras was merely a god who sprang from a rock and slew a bull as the groundwork for the creation of the human race. Only after the emergence of Christianity did Mithraism develop cult meals and the belief in the death and rebirth of its god.[26] Its male-only and militaristic nature, moreover, sharply distinguished it from Christian thought and practice in those days.[27]

Magic

Overlapping the mystery religions, but found in combination with many forms of belief and ritual, was the practice of magic.[28] Magic, as phenomenologists of religion use the term, has to do with the attempt to manipulate God or the gods into doing what a person wants by means of incantations, spells, formulas, or various ritual techniques. It is based on coercion rather than petition. Magic provided an alternative to the capricious behavior of the goddesses Fate and Fortune, who otherwise seemed so omnipotent. Often people wanted to make someone fall in love with them or to receive healing from illness or good weather for harvest. Hundreds of "magical papyri" with such spells and incantations have survived from centuries just after the New Testament era.[29] Many of them involve long lists of nonsense syllables or names of deities; occasionally, people tried to mix in Jewish or Christian names for God and Jesus into their lists. For example, the *Greek Magical Papyri* 12.270–307 includes the following invocation:

---

[25] Klauck, *Religious Context,* 87, citing Aristotle, *Frag. 15.*

[26] For the key primary literature, see H. D. Betz, *The "Mithras Liturgy": Text, Translation, and Commentary* (Tübingen: Mohr Siebeck, 2003).

[27] See further R. H. Nash, *The Gospel and the Greeks: Did the New Testament Borrow from Pagan Thought?* (Phillipsburg, NJ: P & R, 2003), 133–38; A. Tripolitis, *Religions of the Hellenistic-Roman Age* (Grand Rapids and Cambridge: Eerdmans, 2002), 47–59; and C. Calderón, "Los cultos de misterios y su influencia en el cristianismo," *Kairós* 40 (2007): 51–75. On the mystery religions more generally, cf. Ferguson, *Backgrounds,* 251–300.

[28] On the similarities between the two, see esp. M. W. Dickie, *Magic and Magicians in the Greco-Roman World* (London and New York: Routledge, 2001).

[29] The standard collection in English is H. D. Betz, ed., *The Greek Magical Papyri in Translation,* rev. ed. (Chicago and London: University of Chicago Press, 1992).

Greatest god, who exceeds all power, I call on you, IAO SABAOTH ADONAI
EILOEIN SEBOEIN TALLAM CHAUNAON . . . Abraham, Isaac, Jacob,
CHATHATHICH ZEUPEIN NEPHYGOR. . . . I have called on you, greatest god,
and through you on all things, that you may give divine and supreme strength to
this image and may make it effective and powerful against all [opponents] and
to be able to call back souls, move spirits, subject legal opponents, strengthen
friendships, produce all [sorts of] profits, bring dreams, give prophecies, cause
psychological passions and bodily sufferings and incapacitating illness, and
perfect all erotic philters.

In their most sinister forms, ancient magicians were akin to sorcerers, while magic
was similar to what we would today call the occult, including spells designed to
curse people.[30] Acts 19:19 describes a huge bonfire of magical scrolls at first-century Ephesus as a result of the preaching of the gospel. Horoscopes and stargazing
in hopes of divining the future also proved popular.

Gnosticism

Another increasingly prominent religious movement roughly coinciding with
the birth of Christianity was Gnosticism.[31] Based on the Platonic dualism of matter and spirit, Gnostics argued that the material world was inherently evil; only the
spirit world was potentially good. This led to one of two ethical systems. Some
engaged in hedonism, indulging their bodily appetites since they were irredeem-
able anyway. More commonly, Gnostics practiced asceticism and attempted to
deny themselves normal bodily satisfactions because the flesh was inherently corrupting. Both approaches may have been present in Corinth (cf. 1 Cor 6 and 7).

Salvation for the Gnostic thus involved the attempt of the soul to escape the
fetters of the body by recognizing and liberating the divine spark that dwells
within every person. This salvation became possible through *gnōsis* (Gk. for
"knowledge"), not of an intellectual nature but by a secret revelation known only
to members of a given Gnostic sect. The relevant knowledge usually involved
understanding one's divine origin, one's current state of slavery, and the redemptive possibilities of the future. One could then be said to have attained to the
resurrection already in this life; all that remained was for one to die and be fully
liberated from the material world. Second Thessalonians 2:2 may reflect such a
claim that Paul had to combat.

To articulate their theology, Gnostics developed an elaborate mythology. Each
sect had its own distinctive twists, but a composite account of generally common
features might read as follows: The original god of the universe is remote and

---

[30] For a good overview, see F. Graf, *Magic in the Ancient World* (Cambridge, MA and London: Harvard University Press, 1997). For more specialized studies, cf. M. Labahn and B. J. Lietaert Peerbolte,
eds., *A Kind of Magic: Understanding Magic in the New Testament and Its Religious Environment*
(London and New York: T&T Clark, 2007).

[31] Excellent introductions include R. Roukema, *Gnosis and Faith in Early Christianity* (London:
SCM; Harrisburg: Trinity, 1999); C. Markschies, *Gnosis: An Introduction* (London and New York:
T&T Clark, 2003); A. H. B. Logan, *The Gnostics: Identifying an Early Christian Cult* (London and
New York: T&T Clark, 2006); and Birger A. Pearson, *Ancient Gnosticism: Traditions and Literature*
(Minneapolis: Fortress, 2007).

largely unknowable. He did not directly create the heavens and the earth. Rather, from him came forth *aeons*—impersonal emanations usually described as abstract virtues or entities (e.g., love, light, truth, justice). Together with the remote god, these aeons formed the "fullness" (*plērōma*) of the godhead or deity—the same expression Paul applied to Christ in Col 2:9.[32] One of these aeons rebelled against God's designs by creating the material world; hence, matter is by nature evil. Another aeon thus had to be sent to redeem the world. This is usually *Sophia* (Gk. for "wisdom") although occasionally she is seen as the culprit rather than the savior. The ultimate goal of redemption is the restoration of all things to their pristine perfection.

Like the mystery cults, Gnosticism tended to be more charismatic and egalitarian than institutionalized forms of religion. As part of the process of freeing oneself from the constraints of the body, Gnostics sometimes promoted androgyny—a blurring of the distinctions between male and female—as the ideal form of human existence. All this, coupled with the personification of the divine Sophia as a woman, has led many modern feminist scholars to study ancient Gnosticism with great interest, and at times even to promote it.[33] The recent international popularity of *The Da Vinci Code* has caused many to believe numerous entirely fictitious claims made by novelist Dan Brown, both about Gnosticism and about Christian origins more generally.[34]

Information about Gnosticism became much more abundant just after World War II, with the discovery of the *Nag Hammadi Library* in Egypt—a collection of more than sixty mostly Gnostic documents, many of them in Coptic, generally dating from the mid-second to mid-fifth centuries AD. Some are complete editions of works that had previously been preserved only in Greek fragments; some had been known only through references in the early Church Fathers. Many were previously unknown to the modern world. These works include "Gospels" attributed to various disciples, including Mary, which usually comprise little more than lengthy discourses of the risen Jesus, supposedly given in private to different groups of his followers but articulating Gnostic thought. Other documents are more like epistles, treatises, or apocalypses.[35] Consistently in these works, the

---

[32] On Colossians as an excellent example of contextualizing the gospel to combat a distinctive kind of false teaching in a particular community, see D. Flemming, *Contextualization in the New Testament: Patterns for Theology and Mission* (Downers Grove: IVP, 2005), 214–33.

[33] See esp. E. Pagels, *The Gnostic Gospels* (New York: Random House, 1979); idem., *Beyond Belief: The Secret Gospel of Thomas* (New York: Random House, 2003); K. L. King, ed., *Images of the Feminine in Gnosticism* (Harrisburg: Trinity, 2000). Nevertheless, on balance, there are more texts in the Gnostic literature that denigrate the feminine as an inferior gender than those that exalt it.

[34] E.g., that the Gnostic Gospels claim that Jesus married Mary Magdalene; that they exalt her above the other apostles in recognition of women's leadership roles in the early church, which orthodoxy later suppressed; that some of these texts predate the canonical Gospels and are more reliable than they, and so on. For the true state of affairs, see esp. D. L. Bock, *Breaking the Da Vinci Code* (Nashville: Nelson, 2004); and B. Witherington III, *The Gospel Code: Novel Claims about Jesus, Mary Magdalene and Da Vinci* (Downers Grove: IVP, 2004).

[35] The standard English translation and edition is J. M. Robinson, ed., *The Nag Hammadi Library in English*, rev. ed. (Leiden: Brill, 1988; New York and London: HarperCollins, 1990).

Gnostic redeemer is equated with Jesus, even though little else resembling New Testament thought may survive.

Undoubtedly, the most significant find for studying the Gospels was the *Coptic Gospel of Thomas*. This document, falsely ascribed to the apostle Thomas, contains 114 separate sayings attributed to Jesus, largely without any narrative framework connecting them. Roughly one-third of the sayings are clearly Gnostic in outlook, between one-third and one-half are paralleled fairly closely in the canonical Gospels, and the rest are not demonstrably unorthodox but could lend themselves to Gnostic interpretations. Although there is no hard evidence for dating any of these sayings to earlier than the late second century, and although it seems likely that most of the paralleled sayings are revisions or distortions of canonical forms, some scholars have speculated that the Gospel of Thomas might consistently reflect an independent witness to the teachings of Jesus, older than the canonical Gospels.[36] More careful analysis renders this highly improbable, although it is possible that isolated sayings not previously known reflect authentic teachings of Christ (see also below, p. 435).[37] Nicholas Perrin argues that when one translates the Coptic Thomas back into Syriac and compares it with the late second-century Gospel harmony produced by Tatian known as the *Diatessaron*, one can account for the wording of Thomas' sayings as dependent on Tatian and on his sequence of texts as determined by catchwords linking each saying to the next (whereas only about half of the saying soffer such linkages in Greek or Coptic).[38] By its very nature, such a hypothesis is difficult to corroborate; a more common but still responsible conclusion suggests an early-to-mid-second-century date, while recognizing Thomas' largely parasitic use of the canonical Gospels or the traditions they contain.[39]

Indeed, larger questions of dating and chronology surround the origins of Gnosticism itself. Although it was popular a generation or two ago to assert that Christianity had borrowed its views of Jesus from a Gnostic "redeemer myth," it is now widely recognized that such mythology postdates the birth of Christian thought and more likely derived from earlier, more orthodox theology.[40] On the

---

[36] See esp. R. W. Funk, R. W. Hoover, and the Jesus Seminar, *The Four Gospels: The Search for the Authentic Words of Jesus* (New York: Macmillan, 1993). Cf. M. Meyer, *The Gospel of Thomas: The Hidden Sayings of Jesus* (San Francisco: HarperSanFrancisco, 1992); S. T. Patterson, *The Gospel of Thomas and Jesus* (Sonoma, CA: Polebridge, 1993).

[37] See esp. C. L. Blomberg, "Tradition and Redaction in the Parables of the Gospel of Thomas," in *Gospel Perspectives*, vol. 5, ed. D. Wenham (Sheffield: JSOT, 1985; Eugene, OR: Wipf & Stock, 2004), 177–205. Cf. R. Uro, *Seeking the Historical Context of the Gospel of Thomas* (London and New York: T&T Clark, 2003).

[38] N. Perrin, *Thomas and Tatian: The Relationship between the* Gospel of Thomas *and the* Diatessaron (Atlanta: SBL, 2002). See also his excellent introductory work, *Thomas, the Other Gospel* (Louisville and London: WJKP, 2007).

[39] H.-J. Klauck, *Apocryphal Gospels: An Introduction* (London and New York: T&T Clark, 2003), 108, 121–22.

[40] See esp. E. Yamauchi, *Pre-Christian Gnosticism: A Survey of the Proposed Evidences,* rev. ed. (Grand Rapids: Baker, 1983; Eugene, OR: Wipf and Stock, 2003). Irrespective of the dating, Gnosticism never taught that the Redeemer took on true human flesh as with the incarnation of Jesus.

other hand, non-Christian and even Jewish forms of Gnosticism (or forms that ulti-mately derived from Judaism)[41] do seem to predate or at least be contemporaneous with the composition of the New Testament. Clearly, several of the heresies Paul combats in his various epistles bear resemblance to later, more fully-developed Gnostic thought. Most scholars, therefore, use terms like "proto-Gnosticism" or "incipient Gnosticism" to speak of the various Gnostic-like ideas that developed throughout the first century. They then reserve "Gnosticism" proper for the schools of such second-century teachers as Basilides and Valentinus, and perhaps the late first-century Ephesian teacher Cerinthus, whose false teachings may have precipitated the writing of 1 John.[42]

The translation into English in 2006 of the Gnostic Gospel of Judas caused an international flurry of interest, both because it demonstrated the accuracy of the late-second-century Christian bishop of Lyons, Irenaeus, who had briefly described this heretical document, and because no portion of it had ever come to light before. Sensationalist claims were eventually replaced with more sober truth. There was no likelihood that this short account of portions of Jesus' last week contained any accurate historical information independent of the canoni-cal Gospels, especially when it claimed that Jesus promised that Judas would be rewarded in heaven for betraying him and thus making the atonement possible. Rather, the Gospel of Judas simply provided first-hand evidence of the lengths to which one Gnostic sect 150 years after Jesus' life went to invert the Gospels' accounts in calling good evil (e.g., the entire pre-Christian Jewish religion is vili-fied) and evil good![43]

Emperor Worship

Inasmuch as the new world rulers of the time of Christ seemed greater than the traditional gods themselves, it is not surprising that they should have eventu-ally been deified. By the middle of the first century, most Greeks and Romans gave some lip service to emperor worship, but those from the western parts of the empire, unused to taking such beliefs too seriously, probably viewed this as little more than an act of patriotism or an acknowledgment of the emperors' great powers (and occasionally virtue). Precedent for such practice could also be found in the deification of ancient Greek or Roman warriors (e.g., Hercules) or healers (e.g., Asclepius). In the eastern parts of the empire, where rulers had been deified for centuries, emperor worship was probably taken somewhat more seriously.

The first emperor to be deified was Julius Caesar, acclaimed after his death in 27 BC as a god by Augustus. This act, of course, legitimized Augustus as a "son of a god," but Augustus generally repudiated attempts, usually from the East, to

---

[41] On which, see esp. C. B. Smith II, *No Longer Jews: The Search for Gnostic Origins* (Peabody: Hendrickson, 2004).

[42] A good overview of the major Gnostic sects and teachers and their literature appears in J. Fin-egan, *Myth and Mystery: An Introduction to the Pagan Religions of the Biblical World* (Grand Rapids: Baker, 1989), 217–58.

[43] See further S. E. Porter and G. L. Heath, *The Lost Gospel of Judas: Separating Fact from Fiction* (Grand Rapids: Eerdmans, 2007).

worship him as a god during his lifetime (although recall our comments about his "genius" above, pp. 30–31). The precedent he established, however, was continued by Tiberius, who declared Augustus to be divine when he died in AD 14. Gaius Caligula (37–41) was the first emperor to seek acclamation as a god during his lifetime, and his increasingly bizarre behavior led some to think he had gone mad. The Roman Senate denied him deification at his death. Not until Nero (54–68) did an emperor seek to reinforce worship of himself—and then only toward the end of his reign and only sporadically and largely as part of the persecution of Christians in and around Rome (64–68). Domitian in the mid-90s finally sought to establish the practice on a more widespread scale although even then it was short-lived. Christian refusal to call the emperor "Lord and God" (*Dominus et Deus*) and to offer a pinch of incense in sacrifice to him must have struck the average Roman in somewhat the same way as the refusal by Jehovah's Witnesses to pledge allegiance to the flag strikes the average American today. But Christians saw in the sacrifice a blasphemous attribution to Caesar of the divine honors worthy of God alone, and thus, for the most part, they refused to participate. Jews, of course, were exempt because they were still under the protection of being a *religio licita*, at least until the events that precipitated the war with Rome in the late 60s.[44]

Judaism

The study of ancient Jewish thought is both easier and harder than the study of Hellenistic religion. It is easier because in most cases we have far more primary source material available. For that same reason, however, it is harder because mastering it all is virtually impossible for anyone who was not raised in those branches of orthodox Judaism that still require school children to study a huge amount of their ancient literature. In each case, one must try to filter information from the rabbinic material through the grids of its diverse historical contexts and theological biases.

Sources

In addition to the works of Josephus, the apocrypha, and the pseudepigrapha (on which, see above, pp. 8–9), the vast corpus of rabbinic literature sheds much light on ancient Judaism. Almost all of this material, as voluminous as several sets of major encyclopedias, originally circulated in oral form before being committed to writing. The written editions all postdate the first century, so one must exercise great care in trying to sift those traditions that are old enough to be relevant to a study of the New Testament or the life of Jesus from the majority of traditions that are considerably younger.[45]

---

[44] For a detailed overview of "divinized human beings" in the Greco-Roman world, see Klauck, *Religious Context*, 250–330. For a series of essays detailing the relevance of emperor worship for New Testament studies, see D. Horrell, ed., *The Imperial Cult and the New Testament* [= *JSNT* 27.3 (2005)], 251–373.

[45] No one has stressed this point more than the prolific Jewish scholar J. Neusner, who has gone through a number of phases in degrees of skepticism in his extraordinary career of writing literally

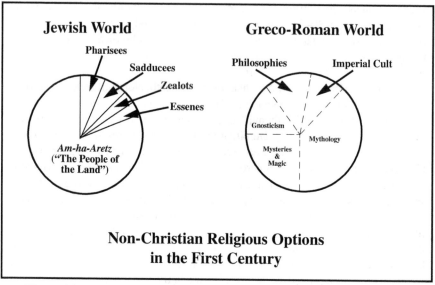

Jewish World

Pharisees

Sadducees

Zealots

Essenes

Am-ha-Aretz
("The People of
the Land")

Greco-Roman World

Philosophies   Imperial Cult

Gnosticism

Mythology

Mysteries
&
Magic

Non-Christian Religious Options
in the First Century

The oral laws that had been developing over the centuries (see above, p. 10) were first codified in the *Mishnah* (from the Hb. for "repetition"), a book slightly thicker than the Bible, by Rabbi Judah Ha-Nasi in about AD 200.[46] Its major divisions include *Zeraim* ("seeds"), *Moed* ("set feasts"), *Nashim* ("women"), *Nezikin* ("damages"), *Kodashim* ("hallowed things"), and *Tohoroth* ("cleannesses"). Sixty-three tractates or subdivisions reflect the Mishnah's preoccupation with minute legal matters. For example, the tractates of *Zeraim* deal with "gleanings," "produce not certainly tithed," "heave offerings," "fruit of young trees," and so on. Some of the tractates of *Nashim* treat "sisters-in-law," "marriage deeds," "vows," "suspected adulteresses," and "bills of divorce." Most all of the Mishnah's contents reflect the rulings by named and unnamed rabbis over legal disputes concerning these various topics. Legal material in the rabbinic literature is often called *halakah* (from the Hb. verb "to walk"). Supplementary tractates in subsequent years were added to the Mishnah and called *Tosefta* (from the Hb. for "addition" or "supplement"). An example of a halakah that preserved one of the many traditions about keeping a "kosher" table is found in the Mishnaic tractate *Hul.* 8.1: "No meat may be boiled with milk save meat of fish and

hundreds of books. As accessible as any is his *Judaism When Christianity Began: A Survey of Belief and Practice* (Louisville and London: WJKP, 2002). See also his *Rabbinic Literature and the New Testament: What We Cannot Show, We Do Not Know* (Valley Forge: Trinity, 1994). At the very least, one should require a given tradition to appear at least as far back as in a document from the Tannaitic period (the first three centuries of the Common Era) or attributed to a rabbi from that period, even if appearing in a later document. See now B. H. Young, *Meet the Rabbis: Rabbinic Thought and the Teachings of Jesus* (Peabody: Hendrickson, 2007), 109. Unfortunately, classic nineteenth-century works like A. Edersheim, *The Life and Times of Jesus the Messiah* (Peabody: Hendrickson, repr. 1993 [orig. 1883]) continue to be used uncritically as background for the NT, even though the rabbinic literature they mine spans a millennium or more of subsequent Jewish history.

[46] The standard English translation is by H. Danby (Oxford: OUP, 1933).

locusts. It is also forbidden to bring it to table together with cheese, save meat of fish and locusts. He who vows to abstain from meat is still free to partake of fish and locusts."

Not all of the oral tradition was halakhic, however. Much was *haggadah* ("story" or "narrative"), illustrating the various legal principles often by parables or anecdotes from the lives of famous rabbis. What is more, the oral tradition continued to develop in both halakhic and haggadic form even after the Mishnah was first compiled. Additional commentary on the topics of many of the tractates of the Mishnah and Tosefta was called *Gemara* (Hb. "completion"). This greatly expanded material was first codified in the fourth century AD. The encyclopedic results were called *Talmud* (Hb. "studying"). The first known edition of the Talmud came from Palestine, sometimes but probably falsely attributed to Jerusalem. Traditions and commentary continued to grow so that an even longer edition of the Talmud, the one that orthodox Judaism eventually came to treat as authoritative, was produced in Babylonia in the late fifth century, with further editing and additions made even beyond that date. An example of a Talmudic parable (haggadah), commenting on Eccl 9:8, appears in *b. Shabb.* 153a:

> Rabbi Johanan ben Zakkai said, "A parable. It is like a king who summoned his servants to a banquet without appointing a time. The wise ones adorned themselves and sat at the door of the palace; they said, 'Is anything lacking in a royal palace?' The fools went about their work, saying, 'Can there be a banquet without preparations?' Suddenly the king desired the presence of his servants. The wise entered adorned, while the fools entered soiled. The king rejoiced at the wise but was angry with the fools. He said, 'Those who adorned themselves for the banquet, let them sit, eat and drink. But those who did not adorn themselves for the banquet, let them stand and watch.'"

The parallels with Matt 22:10–13 and 25:1–13 are striking.

Rabbinic Judaism also produced detailed commentaries on a large number of the books of its Bible (the Christian Old Testament). These commentaries are known as *midrashim* (plural of *midrash*—Hb. for "searching out"). The oldest date perhaps as far back as the second century; others, from five hundred years or more later. These proceed sequentially through a book, but usually select only key verses for comment. Often the commentary involves the text only as a jumping off point to discuss numerous marginally related topics.[47] For example, in a midrash (*Genesis Rabbah*) on Gen 12:1 (Abraham's call to leave for Canaan), the commentary begins with a parable of a man fleeing a burning building, quotes Song 1:3 to compare Abraham to a tightly closed flask of myrrh opened to give fragrance at just the right time, allegorizes Song 8:8 to liken Abraham to one who

---

[47] The standard overview of Mishnah, Talmud, and Midrashim, complete with references to various modern translations and to studies of each work, is H. L. Strack and G. Stemberger, *Introduction to the Talmud and Midrash,* trans. and ed. M. Bockmuehl (Edinburgh: T&T Clark, 1991). See also J. Neusner, *Introduction to Rabbinic Literature* (New York: Doubleday, 1994); and C. E. Fonrobert and M. S. Jaffee, eds., *The Cambridge Companion to the Talmud and Rabbinic Literature* (Cambridge: CUP, 2007).

would unite the whole world, and continues by discussing Eccl 7:19, Jer 51:9, and so on.

Additionally, there are the *targums* (originally from an Akkadian word for "interpretation"). Already in pre-Christian times, the practice of reading the texts from the Hebrew Bible for the week, followed by an oral translation and paraphrase into Aramaic, had developed in the synagogues. Periodically, particularly in the most theologically significant portions of an Old Testament passage, the targumist inserted some of his own commentary in the form of an expanded narrative. Many of these targums on various biblical texts have survived, some from as far back as the first century.[48] A targum on Ps 45, for instance, adds words to make its interpretation explicitly messianic:

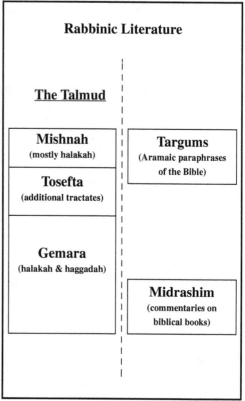

> Your beauty, O king Messiah, is better than that of the children of men; the spirit of prophecy has been placed upon your lips; this is why God has blessed you forever and ever. Gird your sword on your thigh like a valiant warrior so as to slay kings with princes; it is your honor and your prestige, and your prestige is great. Thus you shall succeed in riding upon the royal horses.

Predating the rabbinic literature (which by definition refers to documents written down after AD 70) is the entire library of the *Dead Sea Scrolls*. These range in age from nearly 200 BC to AD 70. In addition to all the ancient copies of biblical books preserved at Qumran on the shores of the Dead Sea (see above, p. 14), the caves containing the scrolls also yielded up dozens of books presumably produced by the Jewish community that lived there. Because it is generally agreed that most of these books reflect a distinctively Essene perspective (see below, pp. 52–54), they cannot be taken to be typical of all Second Temple Judaism. But there are remarkable parallels and contrasts with early Christian thought, and the Scrolls

---

[48] An excellent introduction with sample extracts from some of the most theologically interesting expansions of the Old Testament is P. Grelot, *What Are the Targums? Selected Texts* (Collegeville: Liturgical, 1992). An important reference work is S. Safrai, Z. Safrai, J. Schwarz, and P. J. Tomson, eds., *The Literature of the Sages*, vol. 2: *Midrash and Targum; Liturgy, Poetry, Mysticism; Contracts, Inscriptions, Ancient Science and the Languages of Rabbinic Literature* (Minneapolis: Fortress, 2006).

provide crucial background information on at least one important strand of Jewish belief and practice in Jesus' day.[49]

Finally, there is *Philo of Alexandria*. A voluminous writer, Philo was a Hellenistic Jew who wedded Jewish religion to Hellenistic philosophy. He wrote commentary on much of the Pentateuch as well as other philosophical and apologetic works, seeking to demonstrate by means of allegorical interpretation that Moses' teaching was compatible with, and indeed anticipated, the best of Greek thought. He is known for developing further Plato's dualism between earth and heaven (sometimes thought to lie behind Heb 8) and for his discourse on the *logos* or Word (also prominent in John 1:1–18).[50]

General Characteristics

Although pre-70 Judaism was far more diverse than the rabbinic movement that developed out of the ashes of the destruction of Jerusalem, one can still identify numerous consistent trends and developments with significant import for New Testament and Gospels studies.

1. Perhaps as a result of Persian influence, there was a noticeable increase in interest in *angelology and demonology*. Supernatural beings other than God are present but relatively rare in the Old Testament; they proliferate in intertestamental Jewish literature. Concepts of life after death, including the bodily resurrection of all people, either to everlasting life or to everlasting punishment (recall Dan 12:2), solidified as well.[51] Angels ministered to Jesus, too (Mark 1:13 pars.), exorcisms played a prominent role in his ministry (e.g., Mark 1:21–28; 3:20–30; 5:1–20 par.), and he frequently taught about heaven and hell (see esp. Matt 25:31–46).

2. A large quantity of poetry and wisdom literature emerged between the testaments—psalms, proverbs, and theodicies (reflections on the problem of evil). Building on the *personification of Wisdom* in Proverbs 8, much of this literature represented Wisdom (Hb. *hokhma*; Gk. *sophia*) as a quasi-divine emissary from God to humanity. Jesus, too, is portrayed as divine Wisdom in a variety of ways (see below, pp. 147, 187–88).[52] The combination of developments (1) and (2) meant that, while Judaism remained staunchly monotheistic, it became possible to talk about beings other than Yahweh himself (both angels and great human beings) in categories closely resembling deity.[53] After all, Dan 7:9, with its reference to

---

[49] A standard translation of the scrolls and their fragments is F. G. Martínez, ed., *The Dead Sea Scrolls Translated: The Qumran Texts in English* (Leiden: Brill, 1994). A Hebrew-English edition is also available. For an English translation of the distinctive forms of the OT found at Qumran, see M. Abegg, Jr., P. Flint, and E. Ulrich, *The Dead Sea Scrolls Bible* (San Francisco: HarperSanFrancisco, 1999). A comprehensive reference work is L. H. Schiffman and J. VanderKam, eds., *Encyclopedia of the Dead Sea Scrolls*, 2 vols. (Oxford: OUP, 2000).

[50] For an accessible primer, see K. Schenck, *A Brief Guide to Philo* (Louisville: WJKP, 2005).

[51] See further A. J. Tomasino, *Judaism before Jesus: The Ideas and Events That Shaped the New Testament World* (Downers Grove and Leicester: IVP, 2003), 73–102.

[52] For a complete outline of this development in Jewish thought, see B. Witherington III, *Jesus the Sage: The Pilgrimage of Wisdom* (Minneapolis: Fortress, 1994).

[53] See esp. L. T. Stuckenbruck and W. E. S. North, eds., *Early Jewish and Christian Monotheism* (London and New York: T&T Clark, 2004).

plural "thrones" in heaven where "the Ancient of Days took his seat," left the door open for much speculation about "two powers in heaven." The New Testament writers who directly equate Jesus with God go beyond any of these developments, but such trends may have made the transition somewhat easier for them.[54]

3. An increasingly *positive view of human nature* began to develop. Less was heard about the "original sin" of Adam and Eve that left all people in need of redemption, and more was said about each person's two impulses or natures (Hb. *yetser*)—one good and one bad. This emphasis, in turn, prepared the way for the emergence of "merit theology": the belief that one's good works and one's bad deeds would be weighed at the final judgment and whichever won out would determine one's eternal destiny. Other rabbis went even further and believed that the merits of the patriarchs, especially Abraham, could be imputed to later Jews. On the other hand, we must beware of claiming that this trend was overly influential. Since E. P. Sanders' groundbreaking work *Paul and Palestinian Judaism* was published in 1977,[55] scholars have recognized that one dominant framework of first-century Jewish thought was "covenantal nomism"—the Law was given to be obeyed as a response to the covenant God established with Moses (and before him, with Abraham). Just as Sinai came after the salvation experience of the Exodus, so obedience to the Law is the proper *response* to God's grace. In short, one does not obey the Law to get into God's covenant; one obeys it to *stay* in. Nevertheless, this position, too, can be overemphasized. One must be alert to the diversity within ancient Judaism so that one neither dismisses the accounts of Jesus' (or Paul's) disputes with certain Jews as historically improbable nor assumes that all Jews would have believed or acted the way those specific individuals and groups did.[56]

4. *Prayer and good works* came to be viewed as an adequate substitute for animal sacrifice. This was required if forgiveness of sins was to be obtained at all when the Jews were in exile or in the diaspora since access to the temple in Jerusalem became impossible. After the destruction of the temple in AD 70, this approach ensured Judaism's survival. Old Testament precedent was found in such passages as Hos 6:6 ("I desire mercy, not sacrifice") and Ps 51:16 ("You do not delight in sacrifice, or I would bring it"). Recall also 1 Sam 15:22 (above, p. 10). Even in pre-70 Israel, the primary context of worship for the average Israelite had already become weekly Sabbath synagogue service, along with the daily recitation of fixed prayers and confessions (particularly the *Shema*—Deut 6:4–6) and times of family devotions, rather than the seasonal pilgrimages to the temple that Scripture commanded.

---

[54] See esp. L. W. Hurtado, *One God, One Lord: Early Christian Devotion and Ancient Jewish Monotheism* (Philadelphia: Fortress, 1988; London: T&T Clark, 2003); and A. F. Segal, *Two Powers in Heaven: Early Rabbinic Reports about Christianity and Gnosticism,* rev. ed. (Leiden: Brill, 2002).

[55] E. P. Sanders, *Paul and Palestinian Judaism,* (London: SCM; Philadelphia: Fortress, 1977).

[56] The diversity of perspectives is perhaps best captured in D. A. Carson, P. T. O'Brien and M. F. Seifrid, eds., *Justification and Variegated Nomism,* vol. 1: *The Complexities of Second Temple Judaism* (Tübingen: Mohr Siebeck; Grand Rapids: Baker, 2001).

5. A massive interest in *apocalyptic* themes and literature developed. Instead of looking for the establishment of the kingdom of God on earth in all its fullness through ordinary, historical developments, more and more Jews came to believe that only supernatural intervention by God would usher in the messianic age. This belief easily led to a second: that it was the responsibility of a select group of Jews within the nation to prepare the way for the advent of that coming age by intense obedience to the Law. Both the Essenes at Qumran and the disciples of Jesus may be viewed as apocalyptic sects. In the latter case, though, the expectation is revised to allow for two messianic advents, and obedience to the Law is replaced by following Christ.[57]

6. *Synagogue worship* and study took on forms that became central in the development of the Christian church. The order of the Sabbath service was largely taken over by early Christian worshipers. Prayers and hymns opened and closed each service. In between came the reading of the Torah, Prophets, and Psalms (eventually in a fixed lectionary cycle), with the targum and homily (sermon) by one of the synagogue elders, based on the texts for the day. Assistants to the elders may have provided a model that later inspired the Christian office of deacon. The synagogue was also used for community gatherings of various kinds, most notably elementary education for boys from about ages five to twelve or thirteen. It is a myth that most first-century Jewish men were illiterate—an idea sometimes based on a mistranslation of Acts 4:13, which implies only that the first disciples were not formally apprenticed to a rabbi after reaching the age of thirteen.[58] Jews were also forbidden to use secular courts to solve their own civil disputes, so the synagogue leaders functioned as a local judiciary when necessary (cf. 1 Cor 6:1–11; Jas 2:1–13).

7. *Scribes* took on an increasingly more prominent role in society. Originally, they were mere copyists of Scripture, but their familiarity with its contents led them to become experts in and teachers of the Law. Indeed, the terms "lawyers" and "scribes" in the Gospels usually refer to the same group of individuals. They were found in any of the Jewish sects although most probably came from the Pharisees.[59] The two most famous scribes of the early first century were the Pharisees Hillel and Shammai, the former usually more liberal and the latter usually more conservative on various disputes about Torah. Jesus' teaching on divorce offers

---

[57] On apocalyptic backgrounds for the Gospels, see C. L. Holman, *Till Jesus Comes: Origins of Christian Apocalyptic Expectation* (Peabody: Hendrickson, 1996). N. T. Wright (*Jesus and the Victory of God* [London: SPCK; Minneapolis: Fortress, 1996], 202–20) argues vigorously that Jews were *not* looking to the end of the current world as we know it, merely to a new political arrangement within it. But see D. C. Allison, Jr., "Jesus and the Victory of Apocalyptic," in *Jesus and the Restoration of Israel*, ed. C. C. Newman (Downers Grove: IVP; Carlisle: Paternoster, 1999), 126–41.

[58] R. Riesner, *Jesus als Lehrer* (Tübingen: Mohr, 1981), 182–236. There is no comparable English-language presentation of this information. But cf. A. Millard, *Reading and Writing in the Time of Jesus* (Sheffield: SAP, 2000), esp. 154–84. Millard notes that the tradition that all adult men should be prepared to take a turn in reading from the Torah scroll in synagogue services would have made literacy among that subpopulation much higher than among the others of the day (157).

[59] See esp. C. Scham, *Jewish Scribes in the Second Temple Period* (Sheffield: SAP, 1998).

a good example of his response to one of these intra-Pharisaic debates (Matt 19:1–12). These scribes were the forerunners of the more formal post-70 office of rabbi. In Jesus' time, "rabbi" was still a more informal title for a "teacher," whether trained or untrained (cf. Matt 23:7–8; John 1:38, 49; 3:2, 26; 6:25).

8. The *Sanhedrin* played an increasingly prominent role in Jewish life, at least in Judea. This "supreme court" and legislative body wrapped into one, composed ideally of seventy-one members led by the high priest, included both Pharisees and Sadducees and perhaps other nonaligned elders of the people. Although over-all Pharisees seem to have out-numbered Sadducees in general and been more popular with the people, the distribution of court appointments usually led to a Sadducean majority on the San-

Major Annual Jewish Festivals		
Rosh Hashanah (New Year)	– – – –	1 Tishri (Sept. - Oct.)
Yom Kippur (Day of Atonement)	– – – –	10 Tishri (Sept. - Oct.)
Sukkoth (Tabernacles)	– – – –	15–22 Tishri (Sept. - Oct.)
Hanukkah (Dedication)	– – – –	25 Chislev (Nov. - Dec.)
Purim	– – – –	14 Adar (Feb. - Mar.)
Pesach (Passover & Unleavened Bread)	– – – –	14 Nisan 15–21 Nisan (Mar. - Apr.)
Pentecost	– – – –	6 Sivan (May - Jun.)

hedrin. After all, Rome appointed the high priests and wanted to ensure that the court remained loyal to the empire, and this loyalty came more easily for the Sad-ducees (see below, pp. 51–52). Otherwise, Rome largely permitted the Sanhedrin freedoms of self-government, while reserving the death penalty in at least certain cases for itself (cf. John 18:31).[60] Smaller sanhedrins (lower courts) also dotted the landscape, and it is not entirely certain if in Jesus' day there was one perma-nently appointed Great Sanhedrin, as later described in the Mishnah, or merely a variety of temporarily convened sanhedrins, including those directly under the high priest.

9. Judaism increasingly commended itself as *a religious option for the Gen-tile world*. Scholars dispute just how active Jews were at proselytizing (cf. Matt 23:15). Some believe this activity was largely limited to "following up" interested

---

[60] The evidence both inside and outside of Scripture on this last point is confusing and seem-ingly contradictory. One intriguing reference from the Palestinian Talmud (*p. Sanh.* 1.1 [cf. 7.2]), if accurate, would explain some of the discrepancies and coincide strikingly with the time of Jesus' crucifixion: "Forty years before the destruction of the temple the right to inflict the death penalty was taken away from Israel."

"God-fearers"—Gentiles who had already come to worship the God of Israel and obey much of his Law.[61] At any rate, monotheism was increasingly accepted in the Hellenistic world.

A good summary of the way in which first-century Judaism presented itself involves the three badges of national identity and the three symbols of that nationalism that permeated the corner of the world into which Christ was born.[62] Whatever else a Jewish man did or did not obey, three practices were virtually inviolable if he wanted to remain a member of the community in good standing— the dietary laws (keeping a "kosher" table), observing the Sabbath, and circumcision. Tellingly, Jesus challenged the first two of these head on (e.g., Mark 7:1–23 par. 2:23–3:6 par.), and Paul later spoke of the third as a matter of moral indifference (Gal 5:6)!

The three symbols that went along with these badges of national identity were temple, land, and Torah. The temple was the political, religious, and economic center of Israel, wielding enormous influence as home to hundreds of daily animal sacrifices and to thousands of seasonal pilgrims attending the annual festivals of Passover, Pentecost, New Year's (with the Day of Atonement) culminating in Tabernacles, and, of a much lesser scope, Hanukkah and Purim. The elaborate, ongoing ministry of as many as 20,000 priests and Levites taking their turns to serve in the temple and its precincts, with all the daily sacrifices and purity rituals that accompanied them, remained central in Jewish thinking.[63] Living in the land of Israel freed from foreign oppressors remained the dream of most, inasmuch as Scripture had promised the land to the Jews in perpetuity. But it was contingent on achieving adequate obedience to the Law; hence the third symbol, the Torah. All truth was contained in this book, if one knew how to find it; therefore, the Bible became the object of enormous amounts of study and exposition. Again, Jesus challenged the adequacy of all three of these institutions as they stood, seeing them instead as fulfilled in himself (cf., e.g., John 2:13–22; 4:19–24; Matt 5:17–48).

Individual Groups or Sects

The vast majority of Jews in Israel were not aligned with any special group. They were ordinary farmers and fishermen, craftsmen and merchants, trying to eke out a living. They no doubt believed in the God of Israel and tried to follow the primary laws of the Old Testament faithfully, offering sacrifices in the temple in Jerusalem for the forgiveness of sins when they were able to make the trip

---

[61] Thus S. McKnight, *A Light among the Gentiles: Jewish Missionary Activity in the Second Temple Period* (Minneapolis: Fortress, 1991). Defending the view that proselytization was far more widespread is L. H. Feldman, *Jew and Gentile in the Ancient World: Attitudes and Interactions from Alexander to Justinian* (Princeton: Princeton University Press, 1993).

[62] Cf. further N. T. Wright, *The New Testament and the People of God* (London: SPCK; Minneapolis: Fortress, 1992), 224–32.

[63] In some ways dwarfing the size and influence of the leadership sects discussed in the next section below. See O. Skarsaune, *In the Shadow of the Temple: Jewish Influences on Early Christianity* (Downers Grove: IVP, 2002), 101.

there. But they did not concern themselves with the numerous oral traditions and additional legislation that had grown up around the Bible. They probably longed for the redemption of Israel, and it was from this group of fairly faithful, rather ordinary, and at times impoverished Jews that Jesus found almost all of his first followers. Ancient Jewish sources refer to this group at times as the *'Am-ha-Aretz* ("the people of the land").[64]

The special groups probably comprised no more than five percent of the population in Jesus' day. These were the members of the four different parties or groups that played the most prominent roles among the leadership sects in first-century Jewish life: Pharisees, Sadducees, Essenes, and Zealots.[65]

Pharisees. According to Josephus, the Pharisees emerged at least as early as the reign of John Hyrcanus, opposing the combination of kingly and priestly power in the Hasmonean rulers. Their name probably means "separatists." They may well have grown out of the earlier *Hasidim* (see above, p. 19). From early on they were consistently opposed by the Sadducees, who had made their peace with the Hasmonean dynasty. The Pharisees were a generally popular and prominent group of laymen who sought to apply the Torah to every area of life.[66] Their primary domain was the synagogue, and their foremost concern was to create "a fence around the Torah," that is, to explain what various Mosaic laws meant and how they applied so that devout Israelites would know exactly how to obey God in any situation they might confront. Hence, they developed the so-called oral laws (the "traditions of the elders" in, e.g., Mark 7:5 and Matt 23:2), which were later codified in the Mishnah and which often brought them into conflict with Jesus.

The Pharisees' popularity continued into first-century times, except among the upper classes who feared them because of their ability to sway the masses. They remained staunchly anti-Roman but usually opposed violence as a means of ridding the land of its foreign oppressor. Instead, they sought to teach people to obey God's laws so that God himself would provide a savior in response to his people's obedience. Other distinctives that set them apart from the Sadducees in particular, at least according to Josephus, were their beliefs in an immortal soul, a bodily resurrection, future rewards and punishments according to one's works, the existence of angels and demons, and a combination of predestination and free will (or moral responsibility). Pharisees may have been the primary participants in a smaller group of first-century Jews known as the *haberim*, scrupulous lawkeepers

---

[64] On which, see esp. A. Oppenheimer, *The 'Am-ha-Aretz* (Leiden: Brill, 1977).

[65] See further A. I. Baumgarten, *The Flourishing of Jewish Sects in the Maccabean Era: An Interpretation* (Leiden: Brill, 1997; Atlanta: SBL, 2005).

[66] Modern scholars have frequently described them as applying the laws of temple and priestly purity to all of life, particularly in the areas of eating, tithing, Sabbath, and vows. See, e.g., J. Neusner, "Mr. Sanders' Pharisees and Mine," *SJT* 44 (1991): 73–95. For balanced mediations of the contemporary debate over the Pharisees between Neusner and E. P. Sanders (who sees them as less influential and distinct from other Jews than most scholars do), see D. R. de Lacey, "In Search of a Pharisee," *TynBul* 43 (1992): 353–72; and M. Hengel and R. Deines, "E. P. Sanders' 'Common Judaism,' Jesus, and the Pharisees," *JTS* 46 (1995): 1–70.

who were noted for communal fellowship and sharing meals together.[67] It was out of the Pharisaic movement more than any other single group that later Rabbinic Judaism emerged.

Christians, of course, know the Pharisees best as one group of Jewish leaders whom Jesus frequently denounced for hypocrisy and legalistic excess (see esp. Matt 23). But this is not the entire picture, even in the Gospels. Luke presents the Pharisees in a more favorable light on at least a few occasions (Luke 7:36; 11:37; 13:31), while John labels Nicodemus a Pharisee (John 3:1). As a member of the Sanhedrin (Mark 15:43), Joseph of Arimathea may well have been one too. Modern study of ancient Jewish sources has rightly stressed that the composite picture of Pharisaism is highly diverse.[68] It is simply not fair—and it smacks of anti-Semitism—to tar all the Pharisees with the same brush. In many ways Jesus was closer to the Pharisees than to any of the other Jewish sectarians; their quarrels were internecine or "family" disputes. Pharisees were the upstanding "conservative evangelical pastors" of their day, strongly convinced of the inerrancy of Scripture and its sufficiency for guidance in every area of life, if only it could be properly interpreted.[69] Yet it is precisely such an environment in which a healthy perspective on the Bible can easily give way to legalism. Even the Mishnah and Talmud, reflecting back from a later era on the diversity of types of Pharisees, admit more bad types than good.[70]

Sadducees. The Sadducees supported the Hasmoneans, as they reversed earlier policies of protesting the Hellenization of Israel. They were a small group composed almost entirely of the aristocracy and the well-to-do elite. Many were from priestly families; indeed, the name Sadducee probably comes from the priestly family of "Zadokites" (cf. 2 Sam 8:17). Evidence about them is scantier than for any of the other sects, but it suggests that in the years immediately before Christ's ministry, particularly under Caiaphas,[71] they had amassed great wealth in and around

---

[67] But the rabbinic sources contradict each other on this topic, so it is difficult to be sure. See T. Ames, "Fellowship, Pharisees and the Common People in Early Rabbinic Tradition," *SR* 34 (2005): 339–56.

[68] See esp. J. Neusner and B. D. Chilton, eds., *In Quest of the Historical Pharisees* (Waco: Baylor University Press, 2007).

[69] Although they exaggerate the similarities, cf. H. Falk, *Jesus the Pharisee: A New Look at the Jewishness of Jesus* (New York: Paulist, 1985; Eugene, OR: Wipf & Stock, 2003); and H. Maccoby, *Jesus the Pharisee* (London: SCM, 2003).

[70] Combining the accounts of *Sotah* 22b in both Palestinian and Babylonian Talmuds yields the following (somewhat tongue-in cheek?) description of seven types of Pharisees: the "shoulder" Pharisee who carries his religious duties upon his shoulder; the one who says, "Spare me a moment that I may perform a commandment;" the one who in his anxiety to avoid looking upon a woman dashes his face against the wall; the "pestle" Pharisee whose head is bowed like a pestle in a mortar; the Pharisee that constantly exclaims, "What is my duty that I may perform it?"; the Pharisee from love; and the Pharisee from fear. *Shabbat* 7:2 in the Mishnah gives a classic example of the kind of legalism into which the oral law at times could degenerate, with its list of thirty-nine prohibitions of various types of work on the Sabbath. But the possibility that these statements do not entirely reflect the condition of first-century Judaism must always be acknowledged.

[71] On whom, see also H. K. Bond, *Caiaphas: Friend of Rome and Judge of Jesus?* (Louisville and London: WJKP, 2004).

Jerusalem and had become particularly corrupt in their use of it in administering the temple. For example, the policy of introducing money changers into the temple precincts instead of housing them in the nearby Kidron Valley may have been a relatively recent innovation, against which Jesus protested (Mark 11:15–18 pars.).[72]

Sadducees rejected the oral law. Indeed, they held that although all of the Old Testament was God's word, only doctrine that could be demonstrated to be taught in the Pentateuch was binding. Hence they denied immortality, resurrection, angels, and demons. They strongly emphasized the freedom of the human will and living as God's people in this life. They did not protest Roman occupation of Israel, and they largely benefited from this stance by being able to administer and profit from the temple ritual.[73] Jesus repeatedly criticized the Sadducees without the balancing factors noted above in our discussion of the Pharisees. On one occasion, in response to their skepticism, he demonstrated the resurrection even from the books of Moses (Mark 12:18–27 pars., citing Exod 3:6). Because the Sadducees were so tied to the temple and its cult, they did not survive the fall of Jerusalem in AD 70.[74]

Essenes. Although Josephus describes this group alongside the Pharisees and Sadducees, they appear nowhere by name in the New Testament. Still, their presence on the shores of the Dead Sea near the Judean wilderness, in one quarter of Jerusalem, and in other major cities around the empire makes it probable that Jesus and his disciples interacted with them at times. The name Essene may come from the Aramaic *hasya*—pious or holy. Like the Pharisees, they may be descendants of the *Hasidim*. In fact, they reflect an even more radical protest against the Hellenization and Romanization of Israel than the Pharisees. Evidence from Qumran suggests the existence of a group at that site from mid-second century BC until just after the fall of Jerusalem.[75]

The Essenes were apocalyptically oriented. They were founded by an anonymous leader known from their literature as the "Teacher of Righteousness." They believed that Jerusalem and its temple had become hopelessly corrupt, especially under an individual called simply the "wicked priest" (probably Jonathan or Simon, brothers of Judas Maccabeus). They opposed those who taught Israel its Law as "seekers after smooth things" (probably the Pharisees). The present age had become so wicked that its end was surely at hand, but neither social action nor revolution could bring about the messianic age. Only withdrawal from society, intense devotion to the Law, and patient trust that God would intervene supernaturally with the armies of heaven to establish his kingdom could bring it. The Ess-

---

[72] Cf. M. Bockmuehl, *This Jesus: Martyr, Lord, Messiah* (Edinburgh: T&T Clark, 1994; Downers Grove: IVP, 1996), 109–12, and the literature there cited.

[73] For an excellent introduction to Pharisees and Sadducees, compared and contrasted with each other, and with brief reference to the Essenes, see G. Stemberger, *Jewish Contemporaries of Jesus: Pharisees, Sadducees, Essenes* (Minneapolis: Fortress, 1995).

[74] A small group of people who comprised the political supporters of the Herods were known as *Herodians*. Many, though not all, of them were Sadducees.

[75] For a chronological overview, see J. C. VanderKam, *The Dead Sea Scrolls Today* (Grand Rapids: Eerdmans; London: SPCK, 1994), 99–108.

enes placed strong emphasis on God's sovereignty and predestination. Needless to say, they saw themselves as the elect subgroup within Israel that would be present to fight for God when he began the "war between the sons of light and the sons of darkness"—described in detail in their document known as the War Scroll.[76]

Most Essenes lived in separate neighborhoods in the main cities. Qumran is the only completely monastic site of Essene life that we know about; therefore, it is precarious to generalize from the Dead Sea sect's literature to all Essenes. We know, for example, that elsewhere Essenes married and had children, whereas a vow of celibacy was required for Qumran initiates. Nevertheless, there were probably various parallels in urban Essenism to some of the other major characteristics of the Dead Sea sect: (1) a communal lifestyle, involving daily prayers, work, study, and ritual (including daily baths or baptisms to wash away the previous day's sins); (2) an extensive period of probation before being granted full-fledged membership (up to three years), followed by strict discipline and policies for excommunication of the recalcitrant; (3) a perception that they were fulfilling biblical prophecy, with (a) the Teacher of Righteousness as the prophet Moses predicted in Deut 18:18, (b) the entire sect as "a voice of one calling . . . in the wilderness" (Isa 40:3) and as inaugurating God's new covenant with his people (Jer 31:31–34), and (c) the events of their day as the fulfillment of numerous "end-time prophecies."[77] In addition, (4) the Qumran sectarians looked for the coming of two messiahs—one priestly and one kingly (since each had to come from different tribes). (5) They foreshadowed the messianic banquet of Isa 25:6 in the communal meals that they shared. (6) Significant interest in Melchizedek as a kind of archangel may provide some of the background for similar imagery in the Epistle to the Hebrews. (7) One entire scroll outlines a blueprint for a new temple but, short of its construction, the Essenes would not offer sacrifices. (8) The Copper Scroll refers to the burial of a vast hoard of wealth in the desert; if its account was true, the ability to rediscover the treasure has long since been lost.[78]

Of great fascination to contemporary readers are the various manuals of discipline and communal organization, hymns, prayers, psalms, liturgical texts, calendars, Old Testament commentaries, and apocalyptic literature that make up the Dead Sea Scrolls. Inaccurate but sensationalist claims have fueled this interest. The truth is that the vast majority of all the scrolls and their fragments have been translated. There is no conspiracy to hide information damaging to Christianity from

---

[76] On the interpretation of apocalyptic at Qumran, see C. A. Evans and P. W. Flint, eds., *Eschatology, Messianism, and the Dead Sea Scrolls* (Grand Rapids and Cambridge: Eerdmans, 1997).

[77] The various commentaries on the prophets repeatedly introduce their discussions with the term *pesher*, rendered in English as "this is that which [is fulfilled in . . .]." In other words, each prophecy is identified with some current event—the coming of the Romans, the apostasy of Israel, and so on. Referencing all quotations of the Old Testament at Qumran is D. L. Washburn, *A Catalog of Biblical Passages in the Dead Sea Scrolls* (Atlanta: SBL, 2002). Categorizing them according to introduction and commentary formulae is C. D. Elledge, "Exegetical Styles at Qumran: A Cumulative Index and Commentary," *RevQ* 21 (2003): 165–208.

[78] For these and related elements, see J. J. Collins and R. A. Kugler, eds., *Religion in the Dead Sea Scrolls* (Grand Rapids and Cambridge: Eerdmans, 2000).

the public. There are no Christian documents among the finds at Qumran and no references to Jesus or any Christian disciples anywhere in the literature.[79] A fragment of a text allegedly describing a slain Messiah is more probably to be translated as the Messiah slaying his enemies.[80] Interesting, recently translated fragments have emerged with apparent references to Messiah as Son of God, with beatitudes resembling some of Jesus' (including the equation of the "poor" with the Qumran community), and with language similar to Paul's expression "the works of the Law." None of this in any way threatens Christian faith or rewrites Christian origins; we are simply learning more and more about the diversity of the Jewish world into which Jesus emerged. Tantalizing parallels between Jesus and Qumran, and even more so between John the Baptist and Qumran (see below, p. 251), are balanced by an equally impressive list of differences.[81]

Zealots. Josephus refers to this group as the "fourth philosophy." They are the most loosely knit group of the four and probably should not be thought of as a formal party until the Jewish rebellion in the late 60s, but there were important precursors. In AD 6, Judas of Galilee led an uprising against a Roman census and registration of property under the Syrian governor Quirinius (cf. Acts 5:37). Throughout subsequent decades numerous self-appointed prophets and rebels emerged, some little more than bandits or terrorists, others commanding more of a following for a time. Acts 5:36 refers to one by the name of Theudas, and Acts 21:38 mentions an unnamed Egyptian who "led four thousand terrorists out into the wilderness some time ago." Josephus describes many more.

Simon the Canaanite is also called a "Zealot" in the Gospels (Luke 6:15; cf. Acts 1:13). The "thieves" on the crosses next to Jesus were called *lēstai* (Mark 15:27 pars.), perhaps better translated "insurrectionists." In the 50s and 60s, the *sicarii* ("dagger men") emerged, killing by stealth prominent local Jews who collaborated with Rome. An intriguing eccentric named Jesus ben Ananias made such a nuisance of himself for several years in the mid-60s, predicting first the destruction of the temple and ultimately his own demise, that he was flogged. He was later accidentally hit by a stone and killed (*J. War* 6.5.3). The story of the failure of the Jewish revolt against Rome is described briefly above (pp. 25–26). The Zealots had hoped they could repeat the Maccabean miracle and were convinced that God would honor military efforts to overthrow Rome, but they turned out

---

[79] Indeed, most all of the writings are in Hebrew, not Greek. One miniscule Greek fragment, with numerous holes in it, has been allegedly identified with a part of Mark 6:52–53, but it is in so bad a state of preservation that most scholars are not convinced that they can identify its contents at all. The most vigorous recent advocate of taking it as part of Mark was C. P. Thiede; see, e.g., his *Rekindling the Word: In Search of Gospel Truth* (Leominster: Gracewing; Valley Forge: Trinity, 1995), 37–57, 169–97. For a rebuttal, cf. G. Stanton, *Gospel Truth? New Light on Jesus and the Gospels* (London: HarperCollins; Valley Forge: Trinity, 1995), 20–32. For a good overview and refutation of sensationalist claims about Qumran more generally, cf. O. Betz and R. Riesner, *Jesus, Qumran and the Vatican* (London: SCM; New York: Crossroad, 1994).

[80] M. Bockmuehl, "A 'Slain Messiah' in 4Q Serekh Milhamah (4Q285)?" *TynBul* 43 (1992): 155–69.

[81] J. H. Charlesworth, "The Dead Sea Scrolls and the Historical Jesus," in *Jesus and the Dead Sea Scrolls*, ed. J. H. Charlesworth (New York and London: Doubleday, 1992), 1–74.

to be tragically mistaken. In striking contrast, Jesus' preaching was consistently nonviolent.[82]

By way of summary, one may think of first-century Judaism as a diverse collection of responses to the theological "contradiction" involved in living under foreign occupation in a land God had promised to give Israel forever. Pharisees sought to rectify the situation by internal reform; Sadducees benefited from the status quo and so rejected attempts to change the situation; Essenes saw no hope apart from complete withdrawal and a fresh start; and Zealots strove to overthrow the oppressors by military might. The average "person of the land" was too busy simply trying to survive to join any of these parties. But many of them no doubt looked for a messianic deliverer of some kind (cf. also below, pp. 476–77).

Conclusions

The first-century religious world offered a potpourri of possibilities for Greeks, Romans, and Jews alike. The Hellenistic options could be mixed together in various combinations (what is known as syncretism). A Roman equestrian, for example, might give lip service to emperor worship and the traditional myths at the appropriate times for doing so each year, study a little philosophy on the side, and participate in a mystery cult one night each week. Astrology, mixed with primitive astronomy, while not an entire religion or worldview, was often added onto whatever other religious beliefs and practices one followed. By Judeo-Christian standards, the general level of morality was abysmal. Religious ritual was generally divorced from ethical living. Far more prominent and accepted than even in our deteriorating Western world were the practices of homosexuality, heterosexual promiscuity, divorce, abortion, infanticide (especially of baby girls), slavery, and "sacred" prostitution.[83] The one well-known modern religious option that was extremely rare in the ancient world was pure atheism.[84]

Judaism's monotheism and morality stood out in sharp contrast, as did Christian life and thought as it emerged. But these religions, too, succumbed at times to syncretism, especially in their Gnostic varieties. In an age dominated by pluralism, when Greeks and Romans were willing to add anyone's god to their pantheon, the intolerance for polytheism by Jews and Christians was striking. To the extent that many Jews had come to believe that God would find his own

---

[82] The most balanced treatment of Jesus and the Zealot movement is M. Hengel, *The Zealots: Investigations into the Jewish Freedom Movement in the Period from Herod I until 70 A.D.*, rev. ed. (Edinburgh: T&T Clark, 1997). On the diversity of individuals and groups that fed this movement, see R. A. Horsley and J. Hanson, *Bandits, Prophets, and Messiahs* (Minneapolis: Winston, 1985; Harrisburg: Trinity, 1999). Cf. also W. Klassen, "Jesus and the Zealot Option," in *Wisdom of the Cross*, ed. S. M. Hauerwas, H. J. Huebner and C. K. Huebner (Grand Rapids: Eerdmans, 1999), 131–49.

[83] The famous quote from the ancient Greek Demosthenes still often applied to the first-century Roman empire: "Mistresses we keep for the sake of pleasure, concubines for the daily care of our persons, but wives to bear us legitimate children and to be faithful guardians of our households" (*Ag. Neaer*, 122).

[84] M. Goodman, *The Roman World 44 BC–AD 180* (London and New York: Routledge, 1997), 287.

ways of "saving" righteous Gentiles, early Christian insistence that Jesus was the only way (including for Jews!) seemed even more intransigent. The problems of pluralism and immorality that increasingly afflict our world today are not new; for appropriate responses to them, we need to turn again and again to the New Testament.

For Further Study

See the literature cited at the end of chapter 1. In addition, consult:

Introductory

ABD, s.v. "Cynics," "Epicureanism," "Gnosticism," "Mystery Religions," "Myth and Mythology (Greco-Roman)," "Pythagoreanism," "Roman Imperial Cult," and "Stoicism."

Cohn-Sherbok, Dan and John M. Court. *Religious Diversity in the Greco-Roman World: A Survey of Recent Scholarship.* Sheffield: SAP, 2001.

DJG, s.v. "Apocalyptic," "Dead Sea Scrolls," "Judaism," "Pharisee," "Scribes," "Revolutionary Movements," and "Sanhedrin."

Nash, Ronald H. *The Gospel and the Greeks: Did the New Testament Borrow from Pagan Thought?* Phillipsburg, NJ: P & R, 2003.

Tripolitis, Antonia. *Religions of the Hellenistic-Roman Age.* Grand Rapids and Cambridge: Eerdmans, 2002.

Intermediate

Cohen, Shaye J. D. *From the Maccabees to the Mishnah.* Rev. ed. Louisville: WJKP, 2006.

Ferguson, Everett. *Backgrounds of Early Christianity.* Rev. ed. Grand Rapids: Eerdmans, 1993.

Finegan, Jack. *Myth and Mystery: An Introduction to the Pagan Religions of the Biblical World.* Grand Rapids: Baker, 1989.

Klauck, Hans-Josef. *The Religious Context of Early Christianity: A Guide to Graeco-Roman Religions.* London: T&T Clark, 2000; Minneapolis: Fortress, 2003.

Nickelsburg, G. W. E. *Jewish Literature between the Bible and the Mishnah.* Philadelphia: Fortress, 1981.

Price, Simon. *Religions of the Ancient Greeks.* Cambridge: CUP, 1999.

Advanced

Grabbe, Lester. *Judaic Religion in the Second Temple Period.* London and New York: Routledge, 2000.

Safrai, Shemuel and M. Stern, eds. *The Jewish People in the First Century.* 2 vols. Assen: van Gorcum; Philadelphia: Fortress, 1974–76.

Saldarini, Anthony J. *Pharisees, Scribes and Sadducees in Palestinian Society: A Sociological Approach.* Grand Rapids and Cambridge: Eerdmans; Livonia, MI: Dove Publishers, repr. 2001.

Sanders, E. P. *Judaism: Practice and Belief, 63 BCE–66 CE.* London: SCM; Philadelphia: Trinity, 1992.

Schürer, Emil. *The History of the Jewish People in the Age of Jesus Christ*. 3 vols. Ed. and rev. Geza Vermes, Fergus Millar, Matthew Black. Edinburgh: T&T Clark, 1973–87.

Stemberger, Günter. *Jewish Contemporaries of Jesus: Pharisees, Sadducees, Essenes*. Minneapolis: Fortress, 1995.

Questions for Review

1. Give a brief synopsis of each of the major religious alternatives in both Hellenistic and Jewish religion of the first century. Who are the key characters involved?

2. From your own experience, identify some of the closest parallels to each of these alternatives in the contemporary religious world. How did (how does) authentic Christianity resemble and differ from each of these different options? How did they impact the rise of Christianity?

3. What is the Nag Hammadi Library? What are the Dead Sea Scrolls? What is the significance of both of these finds for our understanding of Christian origins?

4. What other general trends in intertestamental Judaism are important for understanding the birth of Christianity? What other sources do we have for identifying these trends?

3

SOCIOECONOMIC
BACKGROUND

Everyday Life in New Testament Times

Social and Economic History

U NTIL RECENTLY, HISTORIANS focused primarily, if not exclusively, on the deeds of the political or military leaders of a society. Historians of Christianity also scrutinized church leaders, but such scholars paid little attention to the everyday lives of ordinary people. Today there has been a renaissance of interest in such ordinary living. An overview of the social world of early first-century Palestine under Roman domination will help us read the Gospels better. We can visualize the events described and avoid importing anachronistic ideas of living conditions from our world back into a quite different time and place.

Geography
Israel was (and is) made up of four quite different kinds of terrain. (1) The fertile coastal plain contained port cities for seafaring and trade with the rest of the empire. Fruits and vegetables grew in abundance there. (2) The central hill country, which included farmable foothills as well as more rugged, rocky terrain pri-

marily producing timber, divided the country in two from north to south. The less rugged parts were home to shepherds and their flocks, vineyards (esp. for grapes and olives), orchards (esp. for fig trees), small terraced plots for other crops, and numerous small villages (Jerusalem being the much larger exception). (3) The valley of Jezreel in southern Galilee and the entire Jordan River valley formed the country's breadbasket where many grains, especially wheat, were grown, along with the other crops already noted. (4) In southern Judea and into Idumea, the great desert or wilderness area was used for little more than nomads and their various herds of sheep, goats, and camels.[1]

Most of the central ridge "mountains" varied in altitude from roughly 1,500–3,500 feet above sea level, although Mt. Hermon in the far northeast topped out at over 9,200 feet. In striking contrast, the Dead Sea is the lowest place above ground on earth at 1,296 feet below sea level. With roughly one hundred miles separating the two, it is still possible to go from below-freezing, snow-covered terrain to hot, dry desert land with 90°–100° F (or 32°–38° C) temperatures in a short span of time. Winter was the rainy season, and summer, the dry season, so that different crops were rotated through two harvests a year.[2]

In New Testament times, Jerusalem was the largest city in Israel. It was a city dominated by the temple and its precincts, occupying roughly one-quarter of the walled-in portion of the city, itself little more than one-half mile long on any given side. Other major edifices included Herod's Antonia Fortress, and an amphitheater and a horse-racing stadium he had constructed for Hellenistic entertainment.[3] Caesarea Maritimis was the next most important city, because of its role in the shipping trade and as home to the Roman prefect's headquarters. Sebaste (the Old Testament city of Samaria) was the center of population and administration in the province of Samaria, with Shechem being the next most important city. Sepphoris and Tiberias, the past and present capitals of Galilee, from the perspective of Jesus' adult ministry, were the two largest cities in Galilee.[4]

Population

Although many ancient censuses were taken, most of the records have been lost. Very rough estimates can be made based on what data do remain plus archaeolo-

---

[1] An excellent atlas, emphasizing the topography of biblical sites, is B. J. Beitzel, ed., *The Moody Atlas of Bible Lands* (Chicago: Moody, 1985). A fuller, state-of-the-art Bible atlas is now A. F. Rainey and R. S. Notley, eds., *Carta's New Century Handbook and Atlas of the Bible* (Jerusalem: Carta, 2007).

[2] An excellent introductory student's Bible atlas is H. T. Frank and R. S. Boraas, eds., *Atlas of the Bible Lands*, rev. ed. (Maplewood, NJ: Hammond, 2007). For vegetation and land cover, economy, mean annual rainfall, and mean temperatures, see pp. 7, 8, 10, and 11, respectively. See also M. A. E. Smith, ed., *Holman Book of Biblical Charts, Maps, and Reconstructions* (Nashville: B & H, 1993); and D. R. W. Wood, ed., *New Bible Atlas* (Leicester and Downers Grove: IVP, 1985).

[3] The authoritative study remains J. Jeremias, *Jerusalem in the Time of Jesus* (London: SCM; Philadelphia: Fortress, 1969). See also B. Pixner, *With Jesus in Jerusalem: His First and Last Days in Judea* (Rosh Pina, Israel: Corazin, 1996).

[4] For a more broadly based overview, see B. Pixner, *With Jesus through Galilee according to the Fifth Gospel* (Collegeville: Liturgical, 1996).

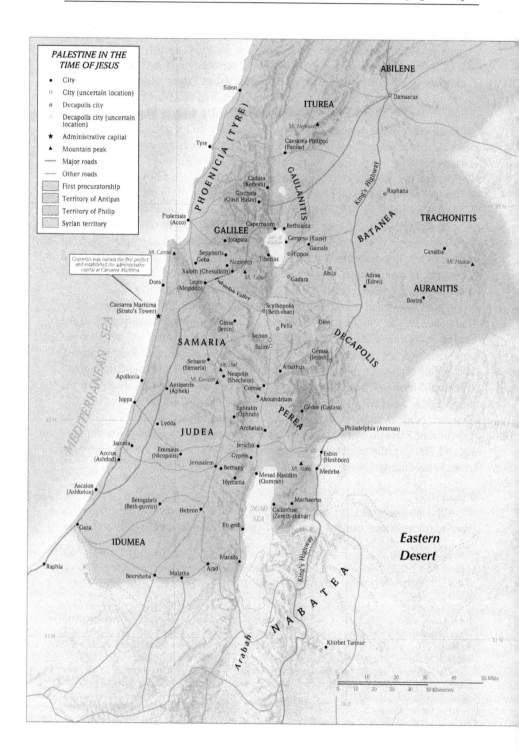

PALESTINE IN THE
TIME OF JESUS

- • City
- ○ City (uncertain location)
- ◎ Decapolis city
- ○ Decapolis city (uncertain location)
- ★ Administrative capital
- ▲ Mountain peak
- — Major roads
- — Other roads
- First procuratorship
- Territory of Antipas
- Territory of Philip
- Syrian territory

Coponius was named the first prefect
and established the administrative
capital at Caesarea Maritima

ABILENE

Sidon

ITUREA

Damascus

Mt. Hermon ▲

Tyre

Caesarea Philippi
(Panias)

PHOENICIA (TYRE)

GAULANITIS

King's Highway

Cadasa
(Kedesh)
Gischala
(Gush Halav)

Raphana

Ptolemais
(Acco)

Capernaum   Bethsaida

BATANEA   TRACHONITIS

GALILEE

Sea of
Galilee

Jotapata

Gergesa (Kursi)

Canatha

Mt. Carmel ▲

Sepphoris
Geba

Nazareth

Tiberias

Gamala
Hippos

Mt. Hauran ▲

Xaloth (Chesulloth)

Mt. Tabor

Abila

Adraa
(Edrei)

AURANITIS

Dora

Legio
(Megiddo)

Jezreel Valley

Gadara

Bostra

Caesarea Maritima
(Strato's Tower) ★

Scythopolis
(Beth-shan)

Ginae
(Jenin)

Dion

DECAPOLIS

MEDITERRANEAN SEA

Pella

SAMARIA

Aenon
Salim

Gerasa
(Jerash)

Sebaste
(Samaria)

Mt. Ebal ▲

Amathus

Apollonia

Mt. Gerizim ▲

Neapolis
(Shechem)

Antipatris
(Aphek)

Coreae

Joppa

Alexandrium

Ephraim
(Ophrah)

Gedor (Gadara)

PEREA

Lydda

JUDEA

Archelais

Philadelphia (Amman)

Jamnia

Emmaus
(Nicopolis)

Jericho

Azotus
(Ashdod)

Jerusalem

Cypros

Esbus
(Heshbon)

Bethany

Mt. Nebo ▲

Medeba

Ascalon
(Ashkelon)

Hyrcania

Mesad Hasidim
(Qumran)

Betogabris
(Beth-guvrin)

Hebron

DEAD
SEA

Machaerus

Callirrhoe
(Zereth-shahar)

Gaza

En-gedi

Eastern
Desert

IDUMEA

Masada

King's Highway

Raphia

Beersheba   Malatha

Arad

NABATEA

Arabah

Khirbet Tannur

0   10   20   30   40   50 Miles
0   10   20   30   40   50 Kilometers

gists' computations of the number of people that could have fit into various living spaces.[5] We know that cities were extremely crowded, with many people living in small homes right on top of each other. Even the countryside was often filled with many people working small plots of land. It has been estimated that the entire Roman empire contained 50 million inhabitants, of which 4 million were Jews. Perhaps about 700,000 Jews lived in Israel, with more than 3 million scattered throughout the diaspora. Alexandria and Antioch were Gentile cities with large Jewish populations.

Rome itself may have topped one million residents, with people constantly leaving the countryside and moving to the urban center of the empire in hopes of a better life. As many as one-third of the inhabitants were slaves, including numerous runaways. Alexandria may have had 750,000, and Antioch, 500,000 people. Athens and Tarsus were somewhat smaller but were important university towns. Ephesus, Philippi, Thessalonica, and Corinth were four other major cities, whose inhabitants possibly numbered more than 100,000. Jerusalem was somewhat smaller, with perhaps as few as 25,000 individuals within its walled-in portion, no more than 100,000 in the entire "metropolitan" area of three to four square miles, and perhaps considerably less.[6] The larger vicinity may have swelled to 200,000 or more, however, at festival times, particularly Passover, as Jews who could do so made pilgrimage to Jerusalem from throughout the empire. Most of them probably stayed in tents on the hilly country surrounding the city.

Although it is disputed, some argue that Galilee had as many or more Gentiles living in it as Jews—hence the name, "Galilee of the Gentiles" (cf. Matt 4:15).[7] Many lived in the two cities Herod Antipas (re-)built—Sepphoris and Tiberias. Yet the majority of Galilee was made up of as many as two hundred small villages, few as large as Capernaum, which had possibly one thousand inhabitants.[8] We must, therefore, avoid stereotyping Jesus and his disciples as roaming through largely uninhabited regions with large farms. Galilee was much more populated than we imagine it. Jew-Gentile tension, coupled with the fact that Jerusalem housed a large pro-Herodian priestly bureaucracy, could have led to strong rural-urban animosities. Yet, interestingly, except for the annual festival pilgrimages to Jerusalem, we have no record of Jesus ministering in any of the larger or pro-Roman cities. Sean Freyne plausibly suggests that this avoidance is "best explained as principled, based on Jesus' views of the values represented by these cities and his own call to minister to those who had become the victims of their elitist lifestyle."[9]

---

[5] See, e.g., J. L. Reed, *Archaeology and the Galilean Jesus: A Re-examination of the Evidence* (Harrisburg: Trinity, 2000), 62–97.

[6] Josephus gives substantially larger figures, but he is known to exaggerate with respect to numbers. Archaeologists' calculations of the population that could have fit in the various portions of Jerusalem, even given the high density of ancient cities, place more reliable upper limits on our numbers.

[7] E.g., Batey, *Jesus and the Forgotten City*. For the opposite view, see M. A. Chancey, *The Myth of a Gentile Galilee* (Cambridge: CUP, 2002). At least Galilee appears to have been more Hellenized than Judea.

[8] R. A. Horsley, *Galilee, History, Politics, People* (Valley Forge: Trinity, 1995), 193–94.

[9] S. Freyne, *Jesus, A Jewish Galilean* (London and New York: T&T Clark, 2004), 144.

Transportation and Communication

As previously noted, Rome had by far the best system of travel and communication in the ancient world, never again replicated until the seventeenth century or later. Main roads linked all major towns. Roman highways were paved with cobblestone and were wide enough for a pair of two-horse chariots to pass each other. Many people traveled in simpler ox-drawn carts, by donkey, or on foot. Most roads were simply dirt. A soldier or courier on horseback could average twenty-five to fifty miles a day, and double that in an emergency if fresh horses were available periodically. A wagon averaged seven to eight miles a day; on foot, people often traveled twenty. Nazareth to Jerusalem was thus about a three-day walk for someone in good health. The main roads were relatively safe, but the less well-traveled ones in desolate regions were favorite hideouts for thieves (cf. Luke 10:29–37).

Inns dotted the landscape, providing lodging for travelers, but many were notorious as hangouts for pirates and prostitutes. More reputable people preferred to stay in private homes with relatives, friends, or people who were recommended to them. Hospitality for traveling disciples was, therefore, highly prized in the early Christian world (cf. Matt 10:11–13; 3 John 5–8). Sea travel was popular, especially for trade, although it was always potentially dangerous. In winter, the high seas were generally impassable. Cargo boats measured up to 180 feet in length and could carry up to 1,200 tons of goods or 600 passengers and their provisions.[10] (Paul's prison boat carried 276 people—Acts 27:37.) A trip between Rome and Alexandria took as little as ten days going east or as long as three months traveling west, depending of course on wind and weather conditions.[11]

Boats also carried mail, as did overland couriers, but the most reliable form of delivery was through a personal acquaintance. Public news was often posted on notice boards in town squares or announced aloud by "heralds" at the marketplace or other public center of activity. The Greek word for herald (*keryx*) is related to the word that was frequently used for the early Christian proclamation (*kerygma*). Merchants traveling overland usually formed caravans with numerous carts and beasts of burden, both because of the quantity of merchandise and for the safety that numbers afforded.[12]

Municipal Facilities

Privacy was almost impossible in ancient cities, as crowded as they were. People deliberately spent most of their waking hours outside of or away from their houses. The Roman baths were a cross between a modern country club and a community recreation center. They included "hot tubs," exercise areas, libraries, and chapels. Similarly multifaceted were the Greek gymnasia—home to physical exercise for members and schooling for young boys. The town marketplace was

---

[10] A. C. Bouquet, *Everyday Life in New Testament Times* (London: Batsford, 1953; New York: Macmillan, 1977), 103.

[11] J. E. Stambaugh and D. L. Balch, *The New Testament in Its Social Environment* (Philadelphia: Westminster, 1986), 39.

[12] For more on "Travel and Trade," see the article so-entitled by B. M. Rapske in *DNTB*, 1245–50.

the center for trade and conversation. Excavations have revealed the rough ancient equivalent to our strip malls—stoa—laid out in a square with pillars supporting roofs extending out over various stores. Extensive night lighting has been uncovered in places too. Syrian Antioch, for example, had over two and one-half miles of oil-lit lamp poles.[13] The library at Alexandria housed over 500,000 volumes, but for the most part only the wealthy owned books privately.

Homes

The well-to-do, particularly in and around Rome, might own large multi-story, freestanding brick villas with inner atria where up to fifty people might gather. A large dozen-room house with three courts has been excavated in Capernaum, which some think may have been Peter's.[14] The upper room where the disciples met in Jerusalem would have formed part of one of the larger homes in that city. For the lucky few (i.e., the rich), Rome had constructed piping to provide hot and cold running water and sewage removal. In most parts of the empire, including Israel, among the vast majority who were not wealthy, houses were much smaller and amenities much plainer. Adobe and hewn stone were more common building materials. Most ordinary people lived in one-room, two-level dwellings with living quarters separated from and raised above the animal stalls. They were usually built with plain exteriors, one adjoining the next to form three sides of a rectangle with a shared inner courtyard. Tenement buildings in the larger cities were laid out like small multi-storied apartment complexes. Roofs of buildings were made of tile, thatch, or mud. In Palestine roofs were flat, and people socialized there and slept on them to cool off a little during hot weather.[15]

For all but the handful of rich, furniture was minimal: some kind of bedding, perhaps no more than mats on the ground; outdoor ovens for cooking; and a few chairs or benches. Indoors, a depressed area in the middle of a dirt floor could house a small, covered charcoal fire, which also heated the house during cool weather. Archaeologists have unearthed a wide variety of pottery, kitchen utensils, glassware among the wealthier homes, and other household tools. Lighting was by olive-oil lamps and torches. Ordinary folk availed themselves of chamber pots dumped outdoors into designated areas for refuse and runoff gutters placed in the middle of streets for sewage, leaving a generally foul-smelling and unsanitary environment. Local wells, cisterns for storing rainwater, and inter-city aqueducts provided most of the water supply. Every house, however modest, was usually equipped with a bolt and lock and shut up for the night. Windows were small, both for security and insulation purposes. The typical solitary aperture would have

---

[13] And equally elaborate paved roads, marble-lined streets, and other similar amenities. See Bouquet, *Everyday Life*, 27.

[14] E.g., V. C. Corbo, "Capernaum," in *ABD*, vol. 1, 866–69.

[15] See esp. P. Richardson, "Towards a Typology of Levantine/Palestinian Houses," *JSNT* 27 (2004): 47–68. Cf., for an earlier period, P. J. King and L. E. Stager, *Life in Biblical Israel* (Louisville and London: WJKP, 2001), 21–35. But styles changed so slowly that much of this book remains relevant for the first century as well.

made searching for a lost coin (Luke 15:8–10) difficult with a small candle or oil lamp.[16]

Meals and Daily Schedules

Farmers worked from sunup until sundown; craftsmen and artisans, almost as long. The well-to-do merchants worked much shorter hours, largely from early morning until just before noon and then perhaps for a short time again after a midday siesta.[17] Wealthier Romans enjoyed four meals a day and regularly ate meat and dairy products. Less well-to-do Jews were often limited to two meals. Bread formed the staple of their diet, supplemented by various fruits, nuts, and vegetables. Fish, especially near Galilee, were plentiful; most could afford to eat meat only on festivals and other special occasions. An invitation to a banquet thus gave ordinary folk a rare opportunity to eat food they might otherwise sample only at religious ceremonies (cf. Luke 14:12–14; 1 Cor 10:27–30). Wine was the basic drink and generally healthier than water or milk, but as much as three times as diluted as it is today.[18] Olive oil was a primary ingredient in cooking; honey, the main sweetener. Salt, sprinkled plentifully on meat, helped to preserve it in a world without refrigeration.

For most, the evening meal culminated a hard day's work, ended daylight hours, and offered a regular opportunity for more intimate socialization. People normally invited only good friends to join them in table fellowship. With little else to do after dark, they ate leisurely over as long as a two- to three-hour span of time and engaged in extensive conversation. For formal gatherings, one "reclined" at the table (cf. John 13:23). Cushions were provided alongside the benches on which the food was served, sometimes arranged into a square-cornered U-shaped configuration, on which one placed one's elbow and lay on one side, eating with the free hand. One's legs thus extended out perpendicular to the table. This explains, for example, how the disreputable woman at the house of Simon the Pharisee, coming in from the outside, had access to Jesus' feet to anoint them (Luke 7:38). It was also important to assume one's place at the table according to status (Luke 14:7–11). Some recent scholars have argued that the model of a Greco-Roman symposium—a lavish banquet followed by a time of wine-bibbing and other entertainment, ranging from philosophical discourse to sexual orgies— significantly influenced the Jewish world even in Israel.[19] But a careful analysis

---

[16] For these and many other customs, see E. M. Meyers, *Galilee through the Centuries: Confluence of Cultures* (Winona Lake: Eisenbrauns, 1999).

[17] For elaboration, see A. A. Bell, Jr., *A Guide to the New Testament World* (Scottdale, PA and Kitchener, ON: Herald, 1994), 200–2.

[18] Claims that ancient wine was unfermented or that Jesus and his disciples did not drink alcoholic beverages, however mild, are simply false. See, e.g., N. L. Geisler, "A Christian Perspective on Wine-Drinking," *BSac* 139 (1982): 46–56, who nevertheless argues for abstinence as an important strategic choice for Christians to make.

[19] See esp. D. E. Smith, *From Symposium to Eucharist: The Banquet in the Early Christian World* (Minneapolis: Fortress, 2003), 133–72. Cf. K. E. Corley, *Private Women, Public Meals: Social Conflict in the Synoptic Tradition* (Peabody: Hendrickson, 1993), 66–75.

shows this to be unlikely; the differences between Jewish banquets and Greco-Roman feasting noticeably outweigh the similarities.[20]

Clothing and Styles

The main garment for the average Jewish man was a linen or cotton "tunic" (Gk. *chitōn*), a loose-fitting, knee-length shirt, with a girdle or sash that could be tied around the waist while working or walking. In cooler weather a cloak (Gk. *himation*), sometimes of wool, was worn over the tunic (cf. Matt 5:40). Sandals or shoes, some form of head covering, and underwear rounded out a man's attire. For prayer, a Jewish man donned the distinctive shawls with fringes that were fingered, much like later Catholic rosary beads, along with the phylacteries—leather head and arm bands containing key Scriptures written in them. The Roman man wore the longer, distinctive toga—a form of dress forbidden to foreigners.

Women wore simpler but often more colorful robe-like garments. Many women probably draped a shawl over their hair in public, but not the full face veil we often think of. When they could afford it, Middle Eastern women also adorned themselves with large quantities of jewelry, perfume, and cosmetics. Jewish men were usually bearded, with longer hair than the average Roman. Women in both cultures usually had long hair, often worn in a bun, especially after getting married.[21]

Social Classes

The ancient Roman empire, like most traditional aristocratic empires in largely agrarian societies, concentrated more than half of the total wealth of all its subjects in the top 1 or 2 percent of its populace. This included the emperor and his court, other key political and military leaders, the landed aristocracy, and at times the most influential religious leaders. The bureaucracy necessary to serve these people, nationally and locally, swelled the ranks of the "rich" to perhaps 5 to 7 percent. A small "middle class"—people who earned enough to have modest savings and not live a merely day-to-day existence—comprised at most another 15 percent and included many priests and Pharisees in addition to the more fortunate merchants and traders, artisans and craftsmen, bankers and toll collectors. Up to 70 percent of the population were struggling farmers and fishermen or subsistence laborers working for others in fields or "factories." A denarius was a standard day's wage (cf. Matt 20:2) and enabled a laborer to buy food for himself and his family for the day with a little left over. Hired hands resembled modern migrant workers; their employment was seasonal. Any surplus they received had to be carefully saved. By any modern standards, these 70 percent lived in poverty. A bottom 10 percent, and sometimes more, made up the class of outcasts and

---

[20] C. L. Blomberg, *Contagious Holiness: Jesus' Meals with Sinners* (Leicester and Downers Grove: IVP, 2005), 65–96.

[21] On the veiling of women in the NT world, see esp. J. B. Hurley, *Man and Woman in Biblical Perspective* (Leicester: IVP; Grand Rapids: Zondervan, 1981), 254–71. Cf. also B. W. Winter, *After Paul Left Corinth: The Influence of Secular Ethics and Social Change* (Grand Rapids and Cambridge: Eerdmans, 2001), 121–41.

expendables. They were often below even the subsistence level, with starvation a real threat.[22]

Most of Jesus' disciples and other followers seem to have come from the poor majority. Still, if Joseph's carpentry shop benefited from the boom in the construction industry near Nazareth in Sepphoris, Jesus and his family might have moved up the ladder from the poor people they clearly were at his birth (see Luke 2:24; cf. Lev 12:8) into the lower end of the "middle class." Even relatively poor people often had at least one servant (cf. Luke 17:7–10), but the fact that Zebedee and sons had more than one (Mark 1:20) may single them out as slightly more prosperous. Whatever wealth their business gave them, however, Jesus' disciples left it behind for itinerant ministry with Christ. Jesus and his traveling troupe relied on the support that others offered, including considerable help from a strategic group of well-to-do women (Luke 8:1–3).[23]

A social class that cut across all the above economic distinctions was the class of slaves. Most ancient slaves were not the victims of racism but of conquest—prisoners of war, so to speak. Others were born slaves or sold themselves into slavery, to pay debts, for example. Unlike pre-Civil War America, the Roman world allowed slaves to own property, earn money, and often save enough to buy their own freedom. A slave in a wealthy household was sometimes more prosperous than most freedmen and exercised important responsibilities, including managing his master's estate and teaching his children. At the opposite end of the socioeconomic spectrum were large numbers of slaves who worked in appalling conditions in various mines throughout the empire.[24]

Economic Indebtedness and Its Relief

The first half of the first century offered increasing financial challenges to most Israelites, although Galilee remained relatively prosperous until the decade before the Jewish revolt. For many, however, taxation placed a heavy burden on all of one's earnings. The Jewish triple tithe—10 percent to priests and Levites, 10 percent for temple festivals, and 3 1/3 percent for the poor[25]—came on top of the sales taxes, customs, and annual tribute paid to the Roman government, much of which went to fund its vast military machine. Tax to Rome varied from about

---

[22] For a succinct summary of these social classes and how they functioned, see W. R. Herzog II, *Parables as Subversive Speech: Jesus as Pedagogue of the Oppressed* (Louisville: WJKP, 1994), 53–73.

[23] On the theme of the socioeconomic level of Jesus and his first followers, see further J. P. Meier, *A Marginal Jew: Rethinking the Historical Jesus*, vol. 1 (New York and London: Doubleday, 1991), 278–85.

[24] On slavery in the Roman empire, see K. Bradley, *Slavery and Society at Rome* (Cambridge: CUP, 1994); J. A. Glancy, *Slavery in Early Christianity* (Oxford and New York: OUP, 2002); and C. Hezser, *Jewish Slavery in Antiquity* (Oxford: OUP, 2005).

[25] On which, see F. E. Udoh, *To Caesar What Is Caesar's: Tribute, Taxes, and Imperial Administration in Early Roman Palestine (63 B.C.E.–70 C.E.)* (Providence: Brown University Press, 2005), 244–78. For application to the New Testament age, see esp. A. J. Köstenberger and D. A. Croteau. "Reconstructing a Biblical Model for Giving: A Discussion of Relevant Systematic Issues and New Testament Principles," *BBR* 16 (2006): 53–77.

three weeks' earnings per year to 30 percent of all one's income. The annual temple tax for Jerusalem amounted to a half-shekel—or two denarii (cf. Matt 17:24–27). No doubt, some Jews paid half or more of all their wages in tax of some form. The burden of unpayable taxes led to a lucrative business for loan sharks. Foreclosing on property followed inability to repay loans and led to people being sold into slavery or, worse, languishing in debtors' prisons.[26] Little wonder that the tax collectors, whether the chief Roman "publicans" or the more common Jewish middlemen (the "toll collectors"), were disliked!

In the more Hellenistic parts of the empire, the institution of patronage alleviated the needs of many seasonal laborers or other poor. Well-to-do aristocrats were expected to give generously to the needy through *patron-client* relationships, and the poor were expected to support their benefactors politically, give them public honor and acclaim, and perform various odd jobs for them.[27] No developed system of welfare existed in first-century Rome, save for the corn dole and some disaster relief after earthquakes or famines. The Jewish world had more developed systems for distributing food or money to the poor on a daily or weekly basis, but many people still "fell through the cracks."

Kinds of Work

Engaging in honest work was a high priority for Jewish men. Even rabbis had to be "bivocational" and earn their keep from some trade rather than from their religious activity. We have already spoken of the major crops raised by the farmers. Tilling the fields was done with ox-drawn plows; harvesting, by sickle; and sifting wheat from chaff, with a winnowing fork. Donkeys pulled huge millstones around and around in a circle to grind grain, winepresses turned grapes into pulp, and olive presses squeezed out the precious oil. Fishermen used dugoutlike canoes with large dragnets. All of these details crop up in the imagery used in the teachings of John the Baptist and Jesus throughout the Gospels.

Those engaged in more urban work or "industry" included cloth makers, potters, metal workers, the members of the building trades, basket weavers, and dyers. Villages and cities alike required bakers, butchers, and water sellers. A suspect industry among Jews was leather working since it involved the handling of pigskin. Luxury trades, often to help the rich in Rome grow richer, included gold- and silver-smithing, ivory carving, and dealing in ointments, spices, costly jewelry, silks, and expensive dyes.[28] Bankers increasingly practiced what today would be

---

[26] For more conservative estimates of the typical Jew's financial plight, see T. E. Schmidt, "Taxes," in *DJG*, 804–7. For less conservative ones, with information on indebtedness, see D. E. Oakman, *Jesus and the Economic Questions of His Day* (Lewiston: Mellen, 1986), 57–77. Exact records of amounts of Roman taxes are generally lacking; questions about how rigidly the Jewish taxes were enforced further complicate our ability to make precise calculations. Cf. also Udoh, *To Caesar What Is Caesar's*, 207–43.

[27] On patron-client relationships, see D. A. deSilva, *Honor, Patronage, Kinship and Purity: Unlocking New Testament Culture* (Downers Grove: IVP, 2000), 95–156.

[28] The lament of Revelation 18, with its long list of cargoes no longer available to greedy shoppers, mirrors the drain on the empire that first-century commerce created to supply the demands of

considered a very limited form of capitalism—using savings to give out loans, make modest investments, and grant interest to their customers. Moneychanging produced a profit as well—at times at extortionary levels. Quite commonly, inflation was nonexistent; people stored their metals in strongboxes at home so that exchanging products and services instead of hard currency sufficed for the purchase of goods.[29]

Teaching was "a humble, even despised occupation in classical antiquity because it meant running after customers asking for money and working long hours."[30] Not surprisingly, schoolteachers were often former slaves with no other trade to which to turn, and respect from both pupils and the public at large was low. The second-century satirist Juvenal calculated that "musicians and popular athletes earn more in a day than the teacher does in a year (*Sat.* 7.175–177, 240–243)."[31] Has much changed over the centuries? "University"-level education involved study with master philosophers; a rough Jewish equivalent involved would-be rabbis learning from older, established sages. Here, at least, the circumstances were not usually so desperate.[32]

Family

The family was the basic social unit in Israel in New Testament times. Children were a blessing from God and barrenness a curse, but children had no voice in the larger social world. Crucial to godly living was to know one's place within one's household and to function honorably in it. Men were the "breadwinners"; women worked hard in the domestic realm. It was expected that men would marry, and it was assumed something was wrong if they didn't. Later rabbis often quoted the saying, "He who has no wife dwells without good, without help, without joy, without blessing, and without atonement" (*Gen. Rab.* 17.2)! Throughout the empire, arranged marriages were still practiced; but, particularly under Roman influence, young men increasingly chose their own brides. Change in Israel took place much more slowly. Polygamy was extremely rare; few men could afford it![33]

Jewish men regularly married by eighteen, Romans by twenty-five, but Greeks often not until thirty. Girls of all three cultures, however, were usually wed soon after puberty, in their early to mid-teens. There is no reason to doubt, for example, that Mary was just such a teenage bride. The Jewish groom took his bride back to his father's house to live with the extended family, often in an additional room

the wealthy in Rome. See esp. J. N. Kraybill, *Imperial Cult and Commerce in John's Apocalypse* (Sheffield: SAP, 1996).

[29] For a detailed study of the coinage and monetization of that day, see R. Duncan-Jones, *Money and Government in the Roman Empire* (Cambridge: CUP, 1994).

[30] Ferguson, *Backgrounds of Early Christianity*, 109.

[31] Bell, *A Guide to the New Testament World*, 238.

[32] For rabbinic education, see esp. S. Byrskog, *Jesus the Only Teacher: Didactic Authority and Transmission in Ancient Israel, Ancient Judaism and the Matthean Community* (Stockholm: Almqvist & Wiksell, 1994), 136–96.

[33] Despite popular misconceptions, even in the OT, polygamy was almost exclusively limited to kings and other very wealthy aristocrats. See W. C. Kaiser, Jr., *Toward Old Testament Ethics* (Grand Rapids: Zondervan, 1983), 182–90.

built on. Extended families might include other relatives as well, along with any slaves the household might have. Divorces were common, though somewhat less so in the Jewish world than in Greece or Rome, but it was almost always only the man who had the right to initiate proceedings.[34]

Jewish boys were sent to school (usually in a synagogue) if one was available, from ages five to twelve or thirteen. Greek boys usually began school at age seven. Jews studied the Bible exclusively; Greeks concentrated on Homer and rhetoric. Rote memorization predominated in both cultures. At the beginning of adolescence, education usually ended and boys learned a trade, often their father's, though sometimes they worked as an apprentice to another man. Few girls had access to formal education; the one primary exception was among the well-to-do in Greco-Roman circles. Role relationships and differentiation remained very traditional throughout adulthood, with one important exception. Wealthier Roman women were in many cases given (or were taking) greater liberties to appear in public with or without their husbands, to participate in civic organizations and symposia, and at times to wear provocative dress and to indulge in the promiscuity that often accompanied mixed-gender public "parties."[35]

Entertainment and Leisure

For Jews, religious holidays provided a prominent opportunity for celebration. Sabbath was a joyous occasion as well as a day of rest. Festival worship was raucous by modern standards, though filled with times of reflection as well. For Greeks and Romans, who had no weekly days off, numerous annual holidays, temple rituals, and patriotic celebrations provided relief from daily routines. Throughout the ancient world, weddings and funerals often lasted up to a week, during which time whole villages rejoiced or mourned. In the Hellenistic world and among more Hellenized Jews, sporting events were popular, including the Olympic games, chariot races, and gladiatorial shows—initially limited to men killing wild beasts. Most major cities had large theaters where comedies and tragedies were frequently performed. These were off-limits to more traditional Jews because of the (pagan) religious themes and allusions, but all Jews enjoyed music[36]—especially singing and dancing—storytelling, and various forms of recreational "board games."

---

[34] Two excellent relevant anthologies are R. S. Hess and M. D. Carroll R., eds., *Family in the Bible: Exploring Customs, Culture, and Context* (Grand Rapids: Baker, 2003); and K. M. Campbell, ed., *Marriage and Family in the Biblical World* (Downers Grove: IVP, 2003).

[35] See esp. B. W. Winter, *Roman Wives, Roman Widows: The Appearance of New Women and the Pauline Communities* (Grand Rapids: Eerdmans, 2003). On women in the ancient Mediterranean world more generally, cf. S. Dixon, *Reading Roman Women: Sources, Genres and Real Life* (London: Duckworth, 2001); T. Ilan, *Jewish Women in Greco-Roman Palestine* (Peabody: Hendrickson, 1996); and E. Cantarella, *Pandora's Daughters: The Role and Status of Women in Greek and Roman Antiquity* (Baltimore and London: Johns Hopkins, 1987).

[36] On which, see W. J. Porter, "Music," in *DNTB*, 711–19.

Science and Medicine

Again, the Roman world was remarkably advanced for its day. Mention was made above of the discoveries of scientists under Ptolemy III (p. 15). Eratosthenes, the librarian at Alexandria during this period, also calculated relatively accurately the distance of the earth from the sun and conjectured the existence of the American continents. Botanists created detailed taxonomies of plants; geographers mapped the known world with considerable accuracy; and mathematicians such as Pythagoras and Archimedes had already developed many of the principles of modern geometry several centuries before Christ. Architects and engineers planned and erected state-of-the-art buildings. Physicians and dentists had all manner of sophisticated surgical instruments, but there was no anesthesia apart from strong drink or mild drugs. (Ancient sources describe a good physician as more or less immune to the screams of his patients!) Doctors were paid very poorly but were generally held in good repute. Druggists were far more suspect. All in all, there were still many chronically ill and disabled, for whom the medicine of the day could do nothing, and who often had to resort to begging.[37]

Cultural Anthropology and Sociology

A second major aspect of the socioeconomic background of any historical period is a recognition of the shared cultural values and the forms of interaction between social groups, networks, and institutions. We may consider each of these in turn.

Cultural Values

The cultural values of the ancient Mediterranean, as in many parts of the non-Western world today, were often quite different from those to which we are accustomed in North America or Europe.[38] To understand the significance of Jesus' ministry at numerous points, an awareness of these values proves crucial.[39]

Honor/Shame. Perhaps the most dominant of all the cultural values was the extent to which honor and shame permeated ancient society. It did not overly matter how much money one made or what trade a person practiced, but it mattered immensely if one acquitted himself or herself honorably in all things. Honor

---

[37] On the frequent ill health of most in the ancient Mediterranean world, see P. G. Bolt, "Life, Death, and the Afterlife in the Greco-Roman World," in *Life in the Face of Death: The Resurrection Message of the New Testament*, ed. R. N. Longenecker (Grand Rapids and Cambridge: Eerdmans, 1998), esp. 51–64.

[38] The following discussion is heavily indebted to B. J. Malina, *The New Testament World: Insights from Cultural Anthropology,* rev. ed. (Louisville: WJKP, 2001); and J. J. Pilch, *Introducing the Cultural Context of the New Testament* (New York: Paulist, 1991; Eugene, OR: Wipf & Stock, 2007).

[39] For general treatments of the sociology of the NT world, see esp. A. J. Blasi, J. Duhaime and P.-A. Turcotte, eds., *Handbook of Early Christianity: Social-Science Approaches* (Walnut Creek, CA: Altamira Press, 2002); D. G. Horrell, ed., *Social-Scientific Approaches to New Testament Interpretation* (Edinburgh: T&T Clark, 1999); and P. F. Esler, ed., *The First Christians in Their Social Worlds: Social-Scientific Approaches to New Testament Interpretation* (London and New York: Routledge, 1994).

was either ascribed or acquired. Repeatedly, the Jewish leaders challenged Jesus' honor by asking him questions designed to trap him (most notably, see Mark 11:27–12:34 pars.). Jesus not only avoided the traps but asked questions in reply that they could not answer (e.g., Mark 12:35–37 pars.). In so doing he acquired greater honor while they were shamed. The size of the following a teacher had also related directly to his honor in society's eyes. So when the multitudes stopped following Jesus because of the difficulty of his teaching, it is little wonder that he asked the disciples if they, too, were leaving (John 6:60–67). His honor was at stake. Herod's was, too, at the banquet during which he rashly promised up to half his kingdom to his stepdaughter. Mark, in his Gospel, nicely captures the dynamic when he explains why Herod acquiesced to the gruesome request for John the Baptist's head on a platter: "because of his oaths and his dinner guests" (6:26)![40]

Kinship Loyalties: Group vs. Individual Personality. The ancient Mediterranean personality was far more group-centered than we are with our rugged, Western individualism.[41] One owed responsibilities to one's extended family, neighborhood, trade guild or religious association, and other close acquaintances. Kinship groups preserved genealogies in many instances because they reminded one of particularly virtuous ancestors. The good name of a kinship group had to be upheld at almost any cost. Extended families worked together as single units of production, and sibling rivalry was to be squelched at its first signs. A friend was fiercely loyal in responding to any reasonable request with the understanding that reciprocal favors were then owed. The patriarch of the household determined its religious affiliation, with which all other members were to agree. In this context, Mark 3:31–35 and parallels prove highly countercultural—Jesus rejected conventional interpretations of Judaism and the authority of his biological family in favor of his own views and of his disciples as his closest "kin."[42] Conversely, by calling his disciples his "brother and sister and mother," he implied that they must be devoted to each other to the same degree that blood relatives normally were—a principle the Western church has rarely implemented. In the Majority World, "ethnic cleansing" and tribal genocide could be been greatly ameliorated if even just Christians would learn and act on the principle that loyalty to fellow believers, even of a different tribe or nationality, runs deeper than loyalty to one's kinship groups.[43]

Perception of Limited Good. In a world seventeen and eighteen centuries before the theoretical development of capitalism and socialism, respectively, most people assumed that, unless one was a member of the tiny percentage of well-to-do elite,

---

[40] See further D. A. deSilva, *The Hope of Glory: Honor Discourse and New Testament Interpretation* (Collegeville, MN: Liturgical, 1999). More briefly, cf. H. Moxnes, "Honor and Shame," *BTB* 23 (1993): 167–76. For detailed summaries of the elements of life affected by honor and shame, see V. H. Matthews and D. C. Benjamin, "Social Sciences and Biblical Studies," *Semeia* 68 (1994): 11–12.

[41] See esp. B. J. Malina, *Christian Origins and Cultural Anthropology: Practical Models for Biblical Interpretation* (Atlanta: John Knox, 1986).

[42] See also D. M. May, "Mark 3:20–35 from the Perspective of Shame/Honor," *BTB* 17 (1987): 83–87.

[43] On kinship values, cf. further deSilva, *Honor, Patronage, Kinship and Purity,* 157–239.

any significant increase in one's standard of living was at someone else's expense. In other words, there was a limited-sized "pie" of material resources to be divided up. Therefore, a farmer who had a sudden windfall of crops was expected to share with the needy, not to hoard it as the "rich fool" in the parable of Luke 12:13–21 did. Moreover, when fellow villagers or friends did give a person money or other material assistance, one was honor bound to repay them. People did not necessarily say "thank you" in the ancient world; they just returned the favor. In fact, thanking people could imply that one was not going to do anything more and hence would end the relationship of mutual give-and-take. Thus the Samaritan leper of Luke 17:11–19 who returns to give thanks to Jesus was perhaps not the man people would have expected Jesus to praise.[44] Christ, however, was trying to teach that God's grace is given without the possibility of repayment. Equally countercultural was Jesus' insistence that banquet-givers invite those who could not invite them in return (Luke 14:12–14). Paradoxically, God will reward such people in the life to come, but only when the motivation for their behavior is not that of wanting such a reward.[45]

Character Plus Performance. Unfortunately in today's corporate business environment, performance or productivity is often the "bottom line"—the only criterion for success. Yet, in most non-Western cultures one's character and integrity have been at least as important and usually more so. Good deeds were important to ancient Jews, and they were important to Jesus as well—but only to the extent that they disclosed one's true character. So, in the Sermon on the Mount, Christ taught that one's "fruit" reveals who a person is (Matt 7:15–20). It is not enough merely to hear his words; words must also be put into practice (7:21–27). On the other hand, performance without godly character is worthless; hence Jesus insisted that his disciples' righteousness exceed that of those scribes and Pharisees who typically opposed him (5:20).

Purity and Uncleanness. Because of all the ritual laws in the Old Testament, ancient Jews were constantly careful not to find themselves in a position of impurity or uncleanness and thus unable for a time to worship with God's people. Without any close modern equivalent, it is difficult for us to imagine living with these cultural values. A woman was more often unclean than a man, due to her monthly cycles. Various kinds of sicknesses, disabilities, or bodily discharges could render one more or less permanently unclean, so the social ostracism became a worse malady than the physical discomfort. When Jesus healed the woman who had suffered from a flow of blood "for twelve years" (Mark 5:25), we realize it was no physiological emergency. To have survived that long with so chronic a problem meant that, medically speaking, her symptoms were not life-threatening—she clearly could get "up and around." But because the woman was unclean for most

---

[44] B. J. Malina and R. L. Rohrbaugh, *Social-Science Commentary on the Synoptic Gospels* (Minneapolis: Fortress, 1992), 379.

[45] W. Braun shows how the elements of Luke 14:1–24 represent an "anti-symposium," challenging all of the elitist, exclusivist, competitive, and reciprocal values and customs of a typical Hellenistic symposium. See his *Feasting and Social Rhetoric in Luke 14* (Cambridge: CUP, 1995).

of that time, her healing was probably an even greater relief socially and culturally than physically.[46]

Another form of impurity resulted from a curse. One interesting belief widely held in ancient Mediterranean cultures was that certain people had the ability to cast spells on others merely with the power of a malignant stare—known as "the evil eye." In several places in the Gospels, the literal translation of the text makes reference to this belief. For example, in Matt 6:23 Jesus speaks of those whose eyes are evil, corrupting their entire selves. To avert the curse, one must seek to look at the world in wholesome ways, not coveting "mammon" (material goods), and then one's entire life will be pure (vv. 22, 24).[47]

The dietary laws, of course, were still in force during Jesus' ministry, as were the various handwashing rituals that went with them. Mark 7:1–20, not surprisingly, intertwines the two and comes to a climax with Jesus "declaring all foods clean" (7:19b). Those with whom one ate were also far more crucial than in our independent, modern Western world. One did not partake of table fellowship with someone who was ritually impure, lest one defile oneself in the process. But Jesus stands this on its head and argues, in essence, that it is holiness or wholeness (moral and ritual) that is more contagious that immorality. Declaring all foods clean implied that all people and peoples (from throughout the Gentile world) could now be thought of as ritually pure as well (cf. Acts 10:34–35).[48]

If Jews were no longer inherently more ritually pure than Gentiles, then this had implications for sacred geography, too. The degrees of purity within the temple precincts in Jerusalem—holy of holies, holy place, court of the Jews, court of the (Jewish) women, court of the Gentiles—continued descending as one moved further outward. Jerusalem was next most holy, then the land of Israel, and then Jewish communities in the diaspora. Fully Gentile territory remained the most profane or secular.[49] Christ's treatment of all individuals as equally pure, at least in ceremonial or ritual terms, cut through all these gradations of holiness. Illness, injury, or bodily deformity no longer requires one to separate oneself from the worshiping congregation. So too, for the Christian, there is no longer any uniquely *holy* land (cf. John 4:19–24), nor are church buildings or property somehow inherently more sacred than any other architecture or possessions.[50]

Present, Past, and Future. Modern Westerners are primarily future oriented. The present is of secondary importance, and the past matters least of all. In the ancient world the present was most important, then the past, and lastly the future (except for the handful of sufficiently wealthy people who could really plan ahead). In general, Jesus affirmed the value of living in the present—praying only

---

[46] Cf. J. J. Pilch, *Healing in the New Testament: Insights from Medical and Mediterranean Anthropology* (Minneapolis: Fortress, 2000), 66.

[47] Cf. J. H. Elliott, "The Evil Eye and the Sermon on the Mount: Contours of a Pervasive Belief in Social-Scientific Perspective," *BI* 2 (1994): 51–84.

[48] See further Blomberg, *Contagious Holiness*, 139–43.

[49] See further B. Chilton and C. A. Evans, *Jesus in Context: Temple, Purity, and Restoration* (Leiden: Brill, 1997).

[50] See further deSilva, *Honor, Patronage, Kinship and Purity*, 241–315.

for "daily bread" (Matt 6:11) and not worrying about tomorrow because of the sufficient troubles of today (v. 34). It is not wrong to plan ahead, but we had better leave room in our planning for God's will to overrule ours (cf. Jas 4:13–17).

Sociological Advocacy Models

Sociologists characteristically study the interrelationships among social groups. This aspect is the hardest one of a socioeconomic background study to apply to the ancient world because of the nature of the data that have survived. Often sociological studies of Scripture rely on applying theories or models that have proven true in societies other than those of Bible times because there is reason to believe the social dynamics would have been similar. But sometimes the theories have a bias against the supernatural or have outrun the evidence, or the supposedly analogous cultures are simply too far removed in time or geography from the first-century Roman empire to be helpful.[51] One thinks, for example, of attempts to explain early Christian response to the delay of Christ's return in terms analogous to twentieth-century South Sea Islander "cargo cults" (that looked for white-skinned deliverers to arrive in ships from across the Pacific as they had at some point in the past) or of explanations of Christ's miracles of healing or exorcism as merely the product of the power of suggestion—psychosomatic cures, as we might call them today.[52] Sometimes plausible cases can be made for competing explanations of ancient phenomena, depending on the branch of sociology utilized.[53]

A booming area of Gospels scholarship, however, looks for parallels between Jesus' contexts (and those of the movement he started) and the situations of minorities and marginalized people of various kinds in our world today. Typically, these kinds of studies eschew the older ideal of dispassionate, detached objectivity (as if that were even attainable) in favor of involved, advocacy movements. These involve various ethnic groups (e.g., African, Latin American, Asian, or African-American interpretations), national contexts (e.g., colonialism vs. postcolonialism), genders (esp. various feminist perspectives), and even sexual orientation (thus GLBT = gay/lesbian/bisexual/transgendered interpretations). These approaches can be further subdivided or combined (e.g. womanist [= African-

---

[51] See further M. R. Mulholland, Jr., "Sociological Criticism," in *Interpreting the New Testament: Essays on Methods and Issues*, ed. D. A. Black and D. S. Dockery (Nashville: Broadman & Holman, 2001), 170–86; E. M. Yamauchi, "Sociology, Scripture and the Supernatural," *JETS* 27 (1984): 169–92.

[52] Thus, e.g., J. G. Gager, *Kingdom and Community: The Social World of Early Christianity* (Englewood Cliffs, NJ: Prentice-Hall, 1975), 19–65; and J. D. Crossan, *The Historical Jesus: The Life of a Mediterranean Jewish Peasant* (San Francisco: HarperSanFrancisco, 1991), esp. 303–32.

[53] Thus structural functionalism leads G. Theissen in his *Sociology of Early Palestinian Christianity* (Philadelphia: Fortress [= *The First Followers of Jesus* (London: SCM)], 1978) to envision Jesus' apostles as a group of "wandering charismatics" supported by a second-tier of more settled disciples, while R. Horsley applies conflict theory in his *Sociology and the Jesus Movement*, rev. ed. (New York and London: Continuum, 1994) to describe Jesus' first followers as a nonviolent peasant revolt or prophetic protest against the corruption of society instead.

American feminist] or *mujerista* [= Hispanic feminist] approaches.[54] While any portion of Scripture can come under the scrutiny and interpretation of one or more of these approaches, Jesus' compassion for the outcasts of his day makes the Gospels a particularly significant part of the Bible for analysis and application by advocates within these various interpretive communities.

Ethnically- or Socioeconomically-Centered Liberation Emphases. Emerging initially out of post-Vatican II Roman Catholic circles in the late 1960s, particularly in Latin America, liberation theology often applied Marxist theories of economics to the Gospels. At one extreme, Jesus has been seen as promoting Communism. Christian thought has at times been said to be compatible with violent revolution. Jesus and his followers have been viewed as uniformly poor, and God is said to have a "preferential option" for the marginalized of society.[55] But, as we have noted above (p. 66), this overlooks the fact that the band of disciples, like the people to whom they ministered, probably encompassed a greater diversity of socioeconomic classes than just the poorest of their world.[56] Indeed, the whole vocabulary of "classes" in society, which we have also employed, is somewhat anachronistic. More crucial to whether one was in the mainstream or on the margins of society was whether or not one had honor, good relationships with friends or villagers (however economically poor one was), and ritual purity. Tax collectors, for example, often were well-off economically but were still considered outcasts in Jewish society because they collected tribute for the foreign oppressor (Rome). The average peasant (farmer or fisherman) was probably very poor, yet was aligned more with the "haves" than the "have-nots" of his community.[57]

Nevertheless, Jesus had an undeniably greater concern for the poor and the social outcasts of his world than many in the contemporary West do. His teaching, especially in the Sermon on the Mount (as we will see; pp. 292–93), affords no explicit precedent for *violent* resistance to evil. Yet most Western countries have revolutionary wars of various kinds in their histories which they often defend as just, due to circumstances considerably less severe than those of the most impoverished inhabitants of countries with the most totalitarian regimes or most dangerous police states in the twenty-first century. So we should probably try living for a prolonged period of time in such dire circumstances before we become too confident that all armed resistance movements violate Jesus' ethics!

---

[54] For overviews of a broad cross-section of these approaches, see esp. M. A. de la Torre, *Reading the Bible from the Margins* (Maryknoll: Orbis, 2002). For good anthologies of sample interpretations, see esp. R. S. Sugirtharajah, ed., *Voices from the Margin: Interpreting the Bible in the Third World*, rev. ed. (Maryknoll: Orbis, 2006); and F. F. Segovia and M. A. Tolbert, eds., *Reading from This Place*, 2 vols. (Minneapolis: Fortress, 1995).

[55] See esp. J. P. Miranda, *Communism in the Bible* (Maryknoll: Orbis, 1982).

[56] Evangelical critics, however, have too often stereotyped liberation theology along the lines of its most extreme practitioners. Far more balanced and exegetically nuanced, e.g., is J. L. Segundo, *The Historical Jesus of the Synoptics* (Maryknoll: Orbis, 1985).

[57] See further C. L. Blomberg, *Neither Poverty nor Riches: A Biblical Theology of Possessions* (Leicester: IVP, 1999; Downers Grove: IVP, 2001), esp. 105–9.

More immediately relevant for all interpreters of the Gospels is the need for us to read the texts through the eyes of those whose current situations of poverty or oppression put them in situations much more comparable to those of the original audiences of Jesus or the Gospel writers, who thus may capture their originally intended meaning more readily. How many well-to-do Christians have heard of Mark 14:7a ("the poor you will always have with you") but have no clue that the very next part of the verse reads "and you can help them any time you want"? Even fewer are aware that Jesus is alluding to Deut 15:11a ("There will always be poor people in the land"), which immediately *commands* God's people "to be openhearted toward those of your people who are poor and needy in your land." So they completely invert Jesus' meaning and think that he is relieving them from their need to help those poorer than themselves, especially fellow Christians, simply because we will never be able to eradicate *all* poverty in this age. More impoverished, oppressed or Majority World readers are more likely to recognize that one of the reasons there will always be poor among us is because there will always be corrupt oppressors who exploit them! Part of our responsibility to help them may actively involve resisting the corrupt regimes that exacerbate their plight.[58]

Cultural, Intercultural, and Postcolonial Interpretations. With the demise of numerous Marxist governments at the end of the 1980s and in the early 1990s, explicitly socialist forms of liberation theology declined in popularity. In their stead arose various other forms of critical analysis alternately referred to as cultural, intercultural, or postcolonial interpretation. Explicitly revolutionary movements have given way to approaches that simply (but significantly) highlight the important insights that minority or non-Western readers can bring to bear on and derive from the biblical texts.[59] In many cases, these challenge the exclusivism of traditional Christian claims. R. S. Sugirtharajah, for example, asserts that the greater global contest today is not among the major world religions but between "mammon and Satan on the one side, and Jesus, Buddha, Krishna, and Mohammed on the other." He then defines mammon as standing for "personal greed, avariciousness, accumulation, and selfishness," with Satan representing "structural and institutional violence."[60] While not corresponding directly to what Jesus meant by a person being unable to serve both God and mammon (Luke 16:13 par.), Sugirtharajah's approach certainly offers fresh food for thought for the average Westerner!

Less radically, George Soares-Prabhu compares the Great Commission of Matt 28:18–20 to a famous Buddhist scripture that commands monks to go into the world with the teaching of the *ehamma*—the good in the beginning, middle and

---

[58] Cf. ibid., 141–42.

[59] Good examples include D. S. Christopher, ed., *Text and Experience: Towards a Cultural Exegesis of the Bible* (Sheffield: SAP, 1995); R. S. Sugirtharajah, ed., *The Postcolonial Bible* (Sheffield: SAP, 1998); and H. De Wit, L. Jonker, M. Kool, and D. S. Schipani, eds., *Through the Eyes of Another: An Intercultural Reading of the Bible* (Elkhart, IN: Institute of Mennonite Studies, 2004).

[60] R. S. Sugirtharajah, *Asian Biblical Hermeneutics and Postcolonialism: Contesting the Interpretations* (Maryknoll: Orbis, 1998), 119.

end of everything—as "the Lord" does, based on the spiritual liberation the monk has experienced, as well as out of compassion for the world and for the happiness of many. By juxtaposing two partially parallel mandates, the differences also stand out more clearly. The person familiar with Buddhism will recognize more quickly than most others the distinctively Christ-centered focus of Jesus' commission as over against the human-centered emphasis of the Buddhist command.[61]

Entire one-volume Bible commentaries have begun to appear, employing intercultural foci. *The International Bible Commentary*, edited by William Farmer, has been co-published in English and Spanish and represents, as its subtitle announces, "a catholic and ecumenical commentary for the twenty-first century."[62] The *Global Bible Commentary* reflects a comparable mainline Protestant (and ecumenical) effort on a smaller scale.[63] A distinctively evangelical project is the *Africa Bible Commentary*.[64] A noteworthy feature of this volume is its inclusion of numerous African proverbs that make statements similar to those in various biblical texts. If anything, all three of these volumes can be criticized for not *more* consistently distinguishing themselves from typical Western commentary and/or standard critical approaches. Much better in this respect is *True to Our Native Land: An African American New Testament Commentary*, which draws on the wealth of American black literature, music, resistance efforts, and even art to illuminate and apply the biblical texts.[65]

Feminist Interpretations. Feminist scholarship may be seen as one branch of liberation theology, though, at least until quite recently, it has been dominated by the interests of North American or European women more than those of the Majority World. Some feminist analysis focuses primarily on reading the stories of Scripture through women's eyes. The Samaritan woman at the well, for example, then emerges as one whom Jesus treated with great dignity, as an unexpected heroine, especially in contrast to the great Jewish male teacher, Nicodemus, who merely became increasingly confused at Jesus' message (John 3–4).[66] Instead of assuming, as men typically do, that the Samaritan woman was a "loose" woman because she had had five husbands and was now living with a sixth man, we are alerted to the possibility that the men could have initiated the divorces for selfish reasons. Jewish women, as already noted, could rarely initiate divorce themselves. By this time possibly no man would dare marry her, thinking her to be a kind of *femme fatale* like the female protagonist in the intertestamental, apocryphal work of Tobit. Perhaps the best she could do for protection and sustenance in a patriarchal society was to accept a live-in lover. We cannot prove any of this, but it is

---

[61] G. M. Soares-Prabhu, "Two Mission Commands: An Interpretation of Matthew 28:16–20 in the Light of a Buddhist Text," *BI* 2 (1994): 264–82.

[62] (Collegeville: Liturgical, 1998).

[63] Ed. D. Patte (Nashville: Abingdon, 2004).

[64] Ed. T. Adeyemo (Grand Rapids: Zondervan; Nairobi: Word Alive, 2006).

[65] Ed. B. K. Blount (Minneapolis: Fortress, 2007).

[66] Cf. C. L. Blomberg, "The Globalization of Biblical Interpretation—A Test Case: John 3–4," *BBR* 5 (1995): 1–15.

no more improbable, historically and culturally, than the assumption that she was primarily to blame for every previous breakup.[67]

In other cases, as with liberation theology, feminism becomes more of an advocacy movement, arguing for the liberation of women based on Jesus' radically positive affirmation of them. Because Jesus encouraged Mary of Bethany to learn from him like any male disciple (Luke 10:38–42), it is natural to assume he wanted her later to teach and preach just as the Twelve did. Because Mary Magdalene reported what she heard and saw of the Risen Lord to the Twelve (John 20:17–18), she has come to be called "the apostle to the apostles" and surely not to be subordinated to them. Whether or not either of these texts implies this much, both of these interpretations remain consistent with evangelical views of Scripture. More radical are perspectives like those of Japanese feminist scholar Hisako Kinukawa, who believes that Mark's presentation of women's encounters with Jesus increasingly taught him to be less conventionally Jewish (i.e., chauvinistic) in his attitudes toward women.[68]

On the other hand, the most recent wave of more liberal feminist scholarship has increasingly agreed with traditional interpreters that one cannot derive full-fledged egalitarianism from the pages of the Gospels. Jesus stood out counterculturally from his context, but not to *that* extent. Such a step might have been almost unintelligible in the ancient Mediterranean world.[69] Jewish feminists conversely stress that Christian egalitarians have too often portrayed Jewish attitudes toward women at that time overly negatively or stereotypically, consciously or unconsciously to make Jesus stand out more strikingly in comparison. Liberating developments in the Jewish traditions of the day, even if comparatively minor ones, must not be overlooked.[70] Clearly feminist approaches to the Gospels, and to the rest of Scripture, span a large spectrum of approaches that must not be overly simplified, all bundled into one package, or summarily dismissed by those who do not identify themselves as supporters. Each proposal must be evaluated on its own merits.[71]

---

[67] See further A. Mathews, *A Woman Jesus Can Teach* (Grand Rapids: Discovery House, 1991), 24–26. G. R. O'Day and S. E. Hylen (*John* [Louisville: WJKP, 2006}, 53) suggest that the woman may have been "caught in a situation of levirate marriage (see Deut 25:5–10; Luke 20:27–33), in which the last male of the family has refused to marry her."

[68] H. Kinukawa, *Women and Jesus in Mark: A Japanese Feminist Perspective* (Maryknoll: Orbis, 1994).

[69] See esp. K. E. Corley, *Women and the Historical Jesus* (Santa Rosa, CA: Polebridge, 2002). Cf. J. H. Elliott, "Jesus Was Not an Egalitarian: A Critique of an Anachronistic and Idealist Theory," *BTB* 32 (2002): 75–91.

[70] As stressed, e.g., throughout R. S. Kraemer and M. R. D'Angelo, eds., *Women and Christian Origins* (Oxford and New York: OUP, 1999).

[71] To compare liberal and evangelical feminist perspectives on a given part of Scripture, see C. A. Newsom and S. H. Ringe, eds., *Women's Bible Commentary, Expanded Edition* (Louisville: WJKP, 1998); and C. C. Kroeger and M. J. Evans, eds., *The IVP Women's Bible Commentary* (Downers Grove: IVP, 2002), respectively.

Conclusion

Clearly a certain degree of social-scientific sophistication is necessary to evaluate these varied hypotheses and any new ones no doubt soon to emerge. The sociological and anthropological study of Scripture is flourishing with no signs of decline any time soon. Some theories are obviously reductionistic, that is, they do not allow for the supernatural or even for the uniqueness of every human agent. But many may be viewed simply as additional components of bettering our understanding of the historical background of the Bible and the nature of God acting in history. Sensitive readers of the Gospels will want to raise such questions as these: To what groups do various individuals in the text belong? What are the social dynamics of those groups? What are their goals? How might they be accomplished? What are the roles of power within the group and the means of attaining them? Are age groups or sex roles defined? What are the boundaries of acceptable behavior? Perhaps most important of all, to what extent does Jesus either affirm or critique the dominant patterns of social interaction in his world? And in moving to our day, how would he respond to our world? Where do we need to be countercultural to be faithful disciples? Which specific details of his teaching remain timelessly applicable, and which need to be applied differently today?[72]

For Further Study

Social and Economic History

Introductory

Bell, Albert A., Jr. *A Guide to the New Testament World*. Scottdale, PA and Waterloo, ON: Herald, 1994.

Bouquet, A. C. *Everyday Life in New Testament Times*. London: Batsford, 1953; New York: Macmillan, 1977.

Gower, Ralph. *The New Manners and Customs of Bible Times*. Rev. ed. Chicago: Moody, 2005.

Jenkins, Ian. *Greek and Roman Life*. London: British Museum Trustees; Cambridge, MA: Harvard University Press, 1986.

Porter, Stanley E., and Craig A. Evans, eds., *Dictionary of New Testament Background*. Downers Grove and Leicester: IVP, 2000.

Thompson, J. A. *Handbook of Life in Bible Times*. Leicester and Downers Grove: IVP, 1986.

Intermediate

Ferguson, Everett. *Backgrounds of Early Christianity*. Rev. ed. Grand Rapids: Eerdmans, 2003.

Freyne, Sean. *Jesus—A Jewish Galilean: A New Reading of the Jesus Story*. London and New York: T&T Clark, 2004.

---

[72] These and many similarly helpful questions are raised in H. C. Kee, *Knowing the Truth: A Sociological Approach to New Testament Interpretation* (Minneapolis: Fortress, 1989), 65–67.

Jeffers, James S. *The Greco-Roman World of the New Testament Era: Exploring the Background of Christianity.* Downers Grove: IVP, 1999.
Meeks, Wayne A. *The First Urban Christians.* Rev. ed. New Haven and London: Yale, 2003.
Stambaugh, John E., and David L. Balch. *The New Testament in Its Social Environment.* Philadelphia: Westminster, 1986.

Advanced

Freyne, Sean. *Galilee from Alexander the Great to Hadrian 323 BCE to 135 CE.* Rev. ed. Edinburgh: T&T Clark, 1998.
Hamel, Gildas. *Poverty and Charity in Roman Palestine, First Three Centuries CE.* Berkeley and Oxford: University of California Press, 1989.
Horsley, Richard A. *Archaeology, History, and Society in Galilee.* Valley Forge: Trinity, 1996.
Horsley, Richard A. *Galilee: History, Politics, People.* Valley Forge: Trinity, 1995.
Reed, Jonathan L. *Archaeology and the Galilean Jesus.* Harrisburg: Trinity, 2000.

Cultural Anthropology and Sociology

Introductory

Elliott, John H. *What Is Social-Scientific Criticism?* Minneapolis: Fortress, 1993.
Osiek, Carolyn. *What Are They Saying about the Social Setting of the New Testament?* Rev. ed. New York: Paulist, 1992.
Pilch, John J. *Introducing the Cultural Context of the New Testament.* New York: Paulist, 1991; Eugene, OR: Wipf & Stock, 2007.
Tidball, Derek. *An Introduction to the Sociology of the New Testament.* Exeter: Paternoster (= *The Social Context of the New Testament.* Grand Rapids: Zondervan), 1984.

Intermediate

DeSilva, David A. *Honor, Patronage, Kinship and Purity: Unlocking New Testament Culture.* Downers Grove: IVP, 2000.
Hanson, K. C. and Douglas L. Oakman. *Palestine in the Time of Jesus: Social Structures and Social Conflicts.* Minneapolis: Fortress, 1998.
Malina, Bruce J. *The New Testament World: Insights from Cultural Anthropology.* Rev. ed. Minneapolis: Fortress, 2001.
Malina, Bruce J. *Social-Science Commentary on the Gospel of John.* Minneapolis: Fortress, 1998.
Malina, Bruce J. and Richard L. Rohrbaugh. *Social-Science Commentary on the Synoptic Gospels.* Rev. ed. Minneapolis: Fortress, 2003.
Stegemann, Wolfgang, Bruce J. Malina, and Gerd Theissen. *The Social Setting of Jesus and the Gospels.* Minneapolis: Fortress, 2002.

Advanced

Kee, Howard C. *Christian Origins in Sociological Perspective.* Philadelphia: Westminster; London: SCM, 1980.

Lenski, Gerhard E. *Power and Privilege: A Theory of Social Stratification*. New York: McGraw-Hill, 1966.

Malina, Bruce J. *Christian Origins and Cultural Anthropology*. Atlanta: John Knox, 1986.

Oakman, Douglas E. *Jesus and the Economic Questions of His Day*. Lewiston: Mellen, 1986.

Rohrbaugh, Richard L., ed. *The Social Sciences and New Testament Interpretation*. Peabody: Hendrickson, 1996.

Bibliography

May, David M. *Social Scientific Criticism of the New Testament: A Bibliography*. Macon: Mercer, 1991.

Questions for Review

1. Choose several passages from the Gospels and discuss how your enhanced understanding of Jesus' social and cultural world illuminates the text. Consider, for example, the parable of the friend at midnight (Luke 11:5–8), Jesus' encounter with the Samaritan woman (John 4:1–42), or the story of the rich young ruler (Mark 10:17–31 pars.). Review each main subsection of the chapter and see how many applications you can find for each passage.

2. Can you think of any passages in the Gospels where you have previously visualized an anachronistic social or cultural setting? Discuss. Consider particularly how our modern, Western individualism distorts the group-centered mind-set of the biblical cultures.

3. What is the difference between asking questions of social and economic history and asking questions of cultural anthropology and sociology? What are the most significant contributions of each? What are some dangers inherent in the study of each, and especially in the latter?

4. Review each subsection of this chapter. Which details strike you as the most important for beginning theological students to be sure to master? Why?

Part Two

CRITICAL METHODS FOR STUDYING THE GOSPELS

T HUS FAR WE have surveyed background information relevant to the entire New Testament, though with primary attention to the Gospels. From here on our comments will be directed exclusively toward a better understanding of Matthew, Mark, Luke, and John.

Introduction to Critical Methodology

There are numerous "critical" (i.e., analytical) tools that scholars use to help them understand how these four Gospels came to be in the form we now know them. One major division among the methods distinguishes "lower criticism" from "higher criticism." *Lower criticism* is also known as textual criticism and is the science of sorting and comparing the existing manuscripts of an ancient document with a view to reconstructing the text of the original as accurately as possible. *Higher criticism* involves the various disciplines that seek to explain how that original document was composed—what sources the author used, how he put them together, under what circumstances he wrote, and so on.

Higher criticism can in turn be subdivided into two largely discrete disciplines: historical criticism and literary criticism. *Historical criticism* studies the prehistory of a text—all of the influences leading up to and including the final assembling of a finished product by the author or editor. *Literary criticism* analyzes the features of the text in the final form in which an author publishes it. In the case of the Gospels, there is also the interesting phenomenon that Matthew, Mark, and Luke are more similar to each other than different, whereas John's contents differ more. This means that many issues in the formation of Matthew, Mark, and Luke can and should be treated together, whereas the unique issues surrounding John's Gospel merit separate treatment.

The two chapters of part 2 thus treat the various branches of historical and literary criticism in turn. Issues common to the first three Gospels are also treated in these chapters, while topics unique to a particular Gospel are largely reserved for part 3. The rest of this introduction will make some brief remarks about the textual criticism of the Gospels; fuller treatments will have to be sought elsewhere.[1]

Textual Criticism

The existing texts of the Gospels are generally in as good a shape as any portion of the ancient copies of Scripture and in better shape than many parts. We, of course, have none of the autographs—the original documents themselves. But the oldest known fragment of any section of the New Testament that can be reliably dated is $\mathfrak{P}^{52}$, the John Rylands papyrus, containing portions of John 18:31–33, 37–38 from approximately A.D. 130—barely forty years after the original was first composed. Another two dozen papyri containing part or all of one or more of the Gospels date from the second, third, and fourth centuries and are housed in various museums and libraries around the world. The five oldest, most reliable, and most complete New Testaments date from the fourth and fifth centuries and all contain the Gospels quite well preserved.

Most modern English translations of the New Testament, particularly in "study Bibles," give footnotes (or marginal notes) listing the most significant alternate readings in the ancient manuscripts (called "textual variants") so that readers can know when part of a passage is in significant doubt. The modern editions of the Greek New Testament (UBS and Nestle-Aland) give a much fuller selection of these variants. In addition to numerous minor transmissional errors that can quickly be identified, there are a number of places in the Gospels in which a passage has been modified to make it more closely match parallel accounts in another Gospel (called "harmonistic variants"). Only rarely are entire Greek sentences in dispute. Three well-known examples that probably reflect later scribal additions are the doxology to the Lord's Prayer (Matt. 6:13b), Jesus' sweat in the garden of Gethsemane resembling great drops of blood (Luke 22:43-44), and the legend of the angel stirring up the water of the pool of Bethesda (John 5:3b–4). On the other hand, Luke 22:19b–20 is missing from some early texts but is probably original. The same may well be true of Jesus forgiving his enemies from the cross (Luke 23:34).

Only two lengthy passages in the entire New Testament are textually disputed; both of these come from the Gospels. The longer ending of Mark (16:9–20) is almost certainly not what Mark wrote. The two oldest and most reliable copies of the Gospel do not contain it (Codices *Sinaiticus* and *Vaticanus*). The style is quite different from the rest of Mark's Gospel, and some of the theology is potentially

---

[1] Most of which involve the textual criticism of the whole New Testament, inasmuch as the principles remain constant throughout. At the most introductory level, see David A. Black, *New Testament Textual Criticism: A Concise Guide* (Grand Rapids: Baker, 1994). The best elementary-to-intermediate level treatment is J. Harold Greenlee, *Introduction to New Testament Textual Criticism*, rev. ed. (Peabody: Hendrickson, 1995). For more comprehensive detail, see Kurt Aland and Barbara Aland, *The Text of the New Testament*, rev. ed. (Grand Rapids: Eerdmans; Leiden: Brill, 1989). For Gospels textual criticism specifically, cf. D. C. Parker, *An Introduction to the New Testament Manuscripts and Their Texts* (Cambridge: CUP, 2008), 311-47.

both heretical and fatal (see v. 18)! These verses themselves contain an inordinately large number of textual variants, and several manuscripts reveal still other alternate endings. Either the original ending of Mark was lost or the author deliberately ended abruptly with verse 8. Either way, early scribes tried to compensate for the abruptness by giving the Gospel a "proper" ending (see further below, pp. 414–15).[2]

John 7:53–8:11 is missing from even more of the oldest and most trustworthy texts. But whereas this story of the "woman caught in adultery" is again not at all likely to have been in the original Gospel of John,[3] a good case can be made that it preserves an account of something Jesus actually did. It fits Jesus' nature, teaching, and ministry, and may well have been handed down by word of mouth until some scribe copying the Gospel decided it was too good to leave out.[4] None of this should alarm the Christian reader; historically, the church's doctrine of Scripture has almost always stressed that it is only the contents of the *original* manuscripts that are authoritative, inspired, or inerrant. For whatever reason, God did not see fit to ensure that those documents were inerrantly preserved. Nevertheless, our ability to reconstruct what the originals looked like is exceedingly high. The contents of 97 to 99 percent of the text are certain beyond any reasonable doubt—far better than for any other documents of the same age. Furthermore, no doctrine of the Christian faith hangs on any disputed text.[5]

Two extremes thus need to be rejected. On the one hand, those who champion a "King James Bible Only" approach ignore the fact that thousands of manuscripts have come to light since its publication in 1611 in England. Moreover, the King James Version differed at various points from its earlier (unauthorized) English-language predecessors. There simply is no *Textus Receptus* (or "received [i.e., unaltered] text") in Greek or any other language that was copied without at least minor changes down through the centuries prior to the invention of the printing press. None of this makes the Bible inferior to, say, the Qur'an, which since at least its early years has been extremely carefully preserved.[6] God's providence

---

[2] For a plausible account of the origin of this longer ending of Mark, see James A. Kelhoffer, *Miracle and Mission: The Authentication of Missionaries and Their Message in the Longer Ending of Mark* (Tübingen: Mohr, 2000).

[3] The one point concerning this passage on which there is strong scholarly consensus. See Chris Keith, "Recent and Previous Research on the *Pericope Adulterae*: (John 7.53-8.11)," *CBR* 6 (2008): 377-404.

[4] See esp. Gary M. Burge, "A Specific Problem in the New Testament Text and Canon: The Woman Caught in Adultery (John 7:53-8:11)," *JETS* 27 (1984): 141-48. Even then there was not unanimous agreement as to where to locate the passage, with some manuscripts including it at the end of John, or in the middle of Luke or at the end of Luke!

[5] See further Daniel B. Wallace, "The Gospel According to Bart: A Review Article of *Misquoting Jesus* by Bart Ehrman," *JETS* 49 (2006): 327-49.

[6] John B. Noss (*Man's Religions*, 6th ed. [New York: Macmillan, 1980], 507, n. *) observes, "There is strong evidence that other collections [of Muhammad's teachings] were made that varied in containing more or less materials and to a certain extent in wording. A second and variant tradition says that the final canonical text resulted from the work of a committee appointed by the Caliph 'Uthmān and headed again by Muhammad's secretary. Four identical copies were made, and all previous texts were pronounced defective. The 'Uthmānic text met some resistance, but finally prevailed."

may be viewed as even greater when he preserves the exact amount of his original Scriptures necessary for an unerring guide to correct belief and behavior in the midst of all the vicissitudes of human scribal activity.[7]

On the other hand, we must avoid the misleading claims concerning the nature of textual corruption which regularly appear in Bart Ehrman's *Misquoting Jesus: The Story Behind Who Changed the Bible and Why*.[8] There is no reason to doubt the overwhelming probability, at least with the New Testament, and especially with the Gospels, that virtually every original reading of every line of text already appears within the wealth of text-forms already available to scholars. Discoveries of earlier, new manuscripts would be highly unlikely to demonstrate dramatic new readings, for the simple reason that the discoveries made during the last half-millennium of thousands of previously lost manuscripts spanning every decade from the second through the fifteenth centuries have not produced dramatic new readings. There is no slippery slope; there is no legitimate all-or-nothing form of reasoning on this debate. Doubts concerning a tiny number of texts do not translate into major questions on every page of Scripture.[9]

---

[7] See further D. A. Carson, *The King James Version Debate: A Plea for Realism* (Grand Rapids: Baker, 1979); and James R. White, *The King James Only Controversy: Can You Trust the Modern Translations?* (Minneapolis: Bethany, 2009).

[8] (San Francisco: HarperSanFrancisco, 2005).

[9] For a detailed, persuasive rebuttal of Ehrman, see Timothy P. Jones, *Misquoting Truth: A Guide to the Fallacies of Bart Ehrman's* Misquoting Jesus (Downers Grove: IVP, 2007).

4

HISTORICAL CRITICISM OF THE GOSPELS

THE UNIQUE FACT that we have four different accounts of the life of Jesus has generated interest throughout church history.[10] At the end of the second century, Irenaeus, bishop of Lyons in France, likened the presence of four Gospels to the existence of four winds or zones of the earth. He believed that theological distinctives accounted for the differences: John wrote of the divine Word of God; Luke, about Jesus' priestly role, Matthew, of his humanity; and Mark, of Christ as prophet (*Adv. Haer.* 3.11.8). Today, scholars agree that various theological distinctives characterize each Gospel but concur with Irenaeus only on his description of John.

A Survey of Views throughout History

During the first seventeen centuries of church history, the most common way of approaching the phenomenon of having four Gospels was that of producing a "harmony" of the four. In other words, a life of Christ was reconstructed with every text from each Gospel fitted into a possible place in one larger, composite

---

[10] Cf. the relevant material scattered throughout W. G. Kümmel, *The New Testament: The History of the Investigation of Its Problems* (Nashville: Abingdon, 1972; London: SCM; 1973); and S. Neill and T. Wright, *The Interpretation of the New Testament 1861–1986* (Oxford: OUP, 1988). At a more popular level, cf. R. A. Burridge, *Four Gospels, One Jesus: A Symbolic Reading* (London: SPCK; Grand Rapids: Eerdmans, 1994).

whole. The first known Christian harmony of the Gospels came from the late second-century Syrian, Tatian, and was called the *Diatessaron* (from the Gk. "through four"). Church greats for more than a millennium followed suit, though the details varied. Augustine and Calvin both wrote commentaries on a harmony of the Gospels as well.

Church Fathers generally assumed that Matthew, Mark, and Luke were written in that order, with Mark and Luke both knowing and using Matthew's Gospel, thus accounting for their similarities. It was often assumed that John, too, knew the other three but consciously chose to supplement them and not repeat much of the information already contained in the works of his predecessors.

The principles of the Enlightenment of the 1700s led to quite different approaches to Scripture. The Bible was studied by people, at first primarily in Germany, who were not necessarily believers or who bracketed their faith in order to leave the door open for historical conclusions quite at odds with traditional dogma. They studied the Bible like any other ancient document, not assuming in advance that everything in it was necessarily true, much less inspired.[11] With respect to the Gospels, the accounts of miracles came under close scrutiny. Late eighteenth-century and early nineteenth-century scholars such as Samuel Reimarus and H. E. G. Paulus developed *rationalist* or naturalistic interpretations of the miracle narratives: the feeding of the five thousand involved rich people in the crowds sharing their lunches after seeing the model of generosity by Jesus and the young man; Jesus only appeared to walk on the water—he was actually wading close to shore—and so on.[12]

In the 1830s, D. F. Strauss ushered in a new era in dealing with the Gospels. He rejected both the traditional attempts to harmonize them and the rationalist school of thought in favor of an understanding of Jesus' more spectacular deeds and claims as *myths*—pious but fictitious legends that couched theological beliefs about Jesus in narrative form.[13] In the middle of the nineteenth century, F. C. Baur built on the dialectical philosophy of G. W. F. Hegel (who also inspired Marx) and described the origins of Christianity in terms of "thesis-antithesis-synthesis."[14] Following the description of Paul's confrontation with Peter at Antioch (Gal 2:11–15), Baur divided all of the New Testament writings into three divisions: conservative Jewish Christianity (like Peter), liberal Law-free Gentile Christianity (like Paul), and later syntheses attempting to reconcile the two. As far as the Gospels were concerned, Matthew was the most Jewish (and thus most authentic); Luke,

[11] See esp. D. L. Dungan, *A History of the Synoptic Problem: The Canon, the Text, the Composition, and the Interpretation of the Gospels* (New York: Doubleday, 1999).

[12] See esp. H. S. Reimarus, *Fragments*, ed. C. H. Talbert (Philadelphia: Fortress, 1970; London: SCM, 1971 [Germ. orig. 1782]).

[13] D. F. Strauss, *The Life of Jesus, Critically Examined* (Philadelphia: Fortress, 1972; London: SCM, 1973 [Germ. orig. 1835]).

[14] See esp. H. Harris, *The Tübingen School* (Oxford: Clarendon, 1975).

the most Gentile or Pauline; and Mark, a second-century attempt to reconcile the two.[15]

Throughout the nineteenth century numerous scholars also composed "lives of Jesus." Believing that the Gospels were a blend of fact and fiction, they sought to strip away the later theological interpretations of the early church from the "historical Jesus." Tellingly, however, the "Jesuses" they produced all strikingly resembled whatever philosophy or ideology the given author himself propounded—whether revolutionary or pacifist, romantic or mystic. At the beginning of the twentieth century Albert Schweitzer, the theologian and musician who later became a famous missionary doctor to Africa, wrote a devastating exposé of how the authors of all these "lives" simply re-created Jesus in their own likenesses. Schweitzer's own understanding of Jesus, however, proved equally truncated: an apocalyptic prophet who believed the kingdom would come in all its fullness during his lifetime but who was sadly mistaken.[16]

Throughout the eighteenth and nineteenth centuries, scholars also became increasingly fascinated with the "Synoptic problem," as J. J. Griesbach first named it in the late 1700s. The Synoptic Gospels are Matthew, Mark, and Luke, so named because their similarities enable them to be set side by side in parallel columns in a *synopsis* (from the Gk. for "together look").[17] The Synoptic problem, then, is the question of their literary interrelationship. Griesbach broke from the tradition that had persisted since Augustine of seeing Mark and Luke each dependent on Matthew and argued that Mark was the last of the three Synoptic Gospels to be written, as an abridgment of Matthew and Luke. In the 1800s, particularly under the influence of C. H. Weisse and H. J. Holtzmann, a third explanation became dominant: Mark wrote first; then Matthew and Luke both used and expanded Mark's Gospel. It was also widely believed that Matthew and Luke had access to a second source, perhaps largely a compilation of sayings of Jesus, to account for most of the remaining material they shared which was not found in Mark.

The development of twentieth-century Gospels scholarship was characterized by successive interest in different critical tools, each building on its predecessor. For the first quarter of the century, *source criticism* predominated as further defense and elaboration of "Markan priority" flourished. The 1970s and 1980s saw a revival of interest in the Griesbach hypothesis, largely due to the tireless crusades of and international conferences organized by William R. Farmer.[18] In

---

[15] For a focused look at these and other key participants from the 1600s to the present, see R. A. Harrisville and W. Sundberg, *The Bible in Modern Culture: Baruch Spinoza to Brevard Childs*, rev. ed. (Grand Rapids and Cambridge: Eerdmans, 2002).

[16] A. Schweitzer, *The Quest of the Historical Jesus*, ed. J. Bowden (London: SCM, 2000; Minneapolis: Fortress, 2001 [Germ. orig. 1906]).

[17] The student will find the study of the Gospels (and an understanding of this chapter) greatly enhanced as he or she consults such a synopsis periodically. A standard English edition, using the RSV, is K. Aland, *Synopsis of the Four Gospels* (New York: United Bible Societies, 1982). A Greek-English edition is also available.

[18] Farmer's foundational work was *The Synoptic Problem* (New York and London: Macmillan, 1964; Macon: Mercer University Press, 1981). For his mature thought, cf. *The Gospel of Jesus: The*

the last twenty years, while still supporting Markan priority, Michael Goulder and Mark Goodacre have sparked some support for the view that Luke relied directly on Matthew as well as Mark.[19] Still, neither of these options has gained large amounts of support worldwide among New Testament scholars.

For the second quarter of the twentieth century, interest shifted to *form criticism*—an analysis of the period before the Gospels were written when stories and excerpts of Jesus' life and teachings circulated almost entirely by word of mouth. As its title suggests, form criticism also studied the distinctive interpretive principles that each kind of rhetorical or literary unit in the Gospels requires, along with the contexts within the early church in which the various forms of the Jesus-tradition were likely to have been preserved.

Not long after 1950, *redaction criticism* came to the fore. This discipline concentrates on the Gospel writers as redactors or editors. Redaction criticism sought to determine why they chose what they did to include or omit, how they arranged their material, and what distinctive theological emphases each wanted to stress. Since about 1975, interest has increasingly shifted to *literary criticism*—treating the Gospels as works of literature and analyzing their plots, themes, characterization, figures of speech, and so on.

During the last fifty years, the "quest of the historical Jesus" has reemerged too. After reaching an all-time low during the era of the prolific Rudolf Bultmann, who said that all we could know about Jesus was "*that* he lived and died,"[20] several of his students in the 1950s embarked on a "new quest" that admitted a fairly significant amount of Jesus' *teachings* as historical, at least in the Synoptic Gospels.[21] Since just before 1980, that quest has taken an even more conservative turn, buttressed primarily by a resurgence of interest in Jesus as a Jew. This so-called "third quest" for Jesus of Nazareth finds some historically accurate material in almost all major categories of Synoptic teachings and deeds of Jesus, although John is still seen as far more theological than historical.[22]

What do we make of this potpourri of perspectives that has emerged over the centuries, particularly in recent years? To begin with, we must admit that much of modern scholarship has adopted presuppositions that are not readily compatible with historic, Christian faith. Indeed, many proponents of "the historical-critical method" have defined it to include three quite skeptical principles of the nineteenth-

Pastoral Relevance of the Synoptic Problem (Louisville: WJKP, 1994).

[19] See esp. M. D. Goulder, *Luke: A New Paradigm*, 2 vols. (Sheffield: JSOT, 1989); and M. S. Goodacre, *Goulder and the Gospels: An Examination of a New Paradigm* (Sheffield: SAP, 1996).

[20] Harrisville and Sundberg, *The Bible in Modern Culture*, 235. When fleshing out this statement, however, Bultmann did affirm a small core of information about Jesus' ministry that could be accepted as historical. See his *magnum opus*, entitled *The History of the Synoptic Tradition*, rev. ed. (Oxford: Blackwell; New York: Harper & Row, 1968; Peabody: Hendrickson, 1994 [Germ. orig. 1921]).

[21] Beginning with E. Käsemann, "The Problem of the Historical Jesus," in *Essays on New Testament Themes* (London: SCM; Naperville, IL: Allenson, 1964 [Germ. orig. 1954], 15–47). In the U.S. the key impetus came from J. M. Robinson, *A New Quest of the Historical Jesus* (London: SCM; Naperville, IL: Allenson, 1959).

[22] For an overview, see B. Witherington III, *The Jesus Quest: The Third Search for the Jew of Nazareth*, rev. ed. (Downers Grove: IVP, 1997).

century philosopher Ernst Troeltsch: (1) "methodical doubt," whereby one is suspicious of any historical narrative unless strong corroborating evidence is found to support its claims; (2) the use of "analogy," so that events without precedent in history are inherently impossible; and (3) the principle of "correlation," which posits a closed continuum of natural causes and effects in the universe.[23] On the other hand, every one of the disciplines surveyed has relied on painstaking analysis of the actual data of the Gospels and has been used to varying degrees with profit by conservative scholars in ways that are compatible with orthodox faith.

The remainder of this chapter examines in more detail the three dominant methodologies of the period from about 1900 to 1975, all of which still are firmly entrenched in Gospel scholarship—source, form, and redaction criticism. *The order of our survey this time will correspond to the chronology of the events each method studies in the life of the early church*: first, form criticism with its focus on the period of oral tradition; next, source criticism with its analysis of the first written accounts about Jesus; finally, redaction criticism with its concentration on the role of the evangelists in producing the Gospels as we know them. A brief concluding section will scrutinize "canon criticism," which flows logically from redaction criticism. It is the study of the canonizing process and canonical form of all of the Gospels put together.

Luke, with the information he provides in his prologue (Luke 1:1–4), seems to have anticipated this threefold division of study of the formation of the Gospels.[24] He speaks of "the things that have been fulfilled among us" as being "handed down to us by those who from the first were eyewitnesses and servants of the word" (vv. 1b–2)—*the period of oral tradition*. He also states that "many [including at least Mark and Matthew?] have undertaken to draw up an account" of these things (v. 1a)—language in the Greek that most naturally refers to written narratives—*the oldest Gospels or Gospel sources*. But, having functioned as a careful historian (v. 3a), Luke likewise wanted to write his own distinctive account (v. 3b) in order to commend the truth of the Gospel (v. 4). This corresponds to the discipline of redaction criticism—*the stage of final redaction for theological purposes*.

If some readers wonder if all this "criticism" really is compatible with belief in the Gospels as inspired books, the answer is clearly yes. Of course, we must carefully examine any given practitioner's use of each method, for at times much "chaff" is mixed in with the "wheat." Nonetheless, the basic principles are not only sound, they are demanded if one believes in the accuracy of Luke's description of how he wrote. Given the similarities among Luke, Mark, and Matthew, and, to a lesser degree, John, it stands to reason that the other evangelists proceeded somewhat similarly. Gospel criticism is not inherently an alternative to belief in the inspiration of the texts, though it has been used that way by some radical critics. Rather, it is a study of the ordinary human means of writing that

---

[23] See further E. Krentz, *The Historical-Critical Method* (Philadelphia: Fortress, 1975; Eugene, OR: Wipf & Stock, 2002).

[24] R. H. Stein, *Studying the Synoptic Gospels: Origin and Interpretation,* rev. ed. (Grand Rapids: Baker, 2001), 44–45.

God's Spirit superintended so as to ensure that the final product was exactly what God wanted to communicate to his people (cf. 2 Pet 1:21).

Form Criticism of the Synoptic Gospels: The Period of Oral Tradition[25]

The Method

The rise of Gospel form criticism is associated primarily with three early twentieth-century German scholars: K. L. Schmidt, Martin Dibelius, and, above all, Rudolf Bultmann.[26] Analogous to work already being done in Old Testament studies, these scholars proposed three major stages to the analysis of the period of oral tradition behind the Gospels. First, they believed that the Gospels could be subdivided into discrete "pericopae" (self-contained passages) and analyzed according to the *form* (almost a "mini-genre") of each. Forms included parables, miracle stories, pronouncement stories (short controversial episodes climaxed by a key saying of Jesus), proverbs, wisdom sayings, "I-sayings," lengthier discourses, and so on.[27] Some of the labels also involved historical judgments: myths, legends, or utterances of early Christian prophets in the name of Jesus.

Second, form critics assigned each form to a *Sitz im Leben* ("situation in life") in the history of the early church. Pronouncement stories, it was believed, were widely used in popular preaching; miracle narratives, in apologetic interaction. Legends were supposedly created to glorify Jesus as a great hero. Parables were transmitted by popular storytellers, and so on.

Third, form criticism developed "laws" of the *transmission of tradition*. As bits and pieces of information about Jesus were passed along orally, it was claimed, stories tended to get longer, be embellished with additional unhistorical detail, be given explanatory clarifications and interpretations, have names supplied for previously unnamed characters, be given new contexts and new applications, and be grouped together with other individual teachings. It was the responsibility of the form critic, therefore, to try to strip away all these "secondary accretions" and find the historical kernel, if any, in each passage that represented what Jesus actually did or said.[28]

Several assumptions fueled the form-critical agenda. First, critics assumed that no one wrote down anything Jesus said while he was alive, and that the early Christians relied at first entirely on oral tradition. Second, oral tradition was

---

[25] Cf. further C. L. Blomberg, "Form Criticism," in *DJG*, 243–50; and D. L. Bock, "Form Criticism," in *Interpreting the New Testament*, eds. Black and Dockery, 106–27.

[26] K. L. Schmidt, *Der Rahmen der Geschichte Jesu* (Darmstadt: Wissenschaftliche Buchgesellschaft, 1969 [orig. 1919]); M. Dibelius, *From Tradition to Gospel* (New York: Scribner's Sons, 1965; London: James Clarke, 2000 [Germ. orig. 1919]); Bultmann, *The History of the Synoptic Tradition*.

[27] The most complete English-language analysis appears in J. L. Bailey and L. D. Vander Broek, *Literary Forms in the New Testament* (Louisville: WJKP, 1992). The most comprehensive treatment of all is K. Berger, *Formen und Gattungen im Neuen Testament* (Tübingen and Basel: Francke, 2005).

[28] The "laws" for the developing parable tradition formulated by J. Jeremias (*The Parables of Jesus*, 3rd ed. [London: SCM; Philadelphia: Westminster, 1972], 23–114) comprise a particularly influential and extensive example.

always viewed as composed of discrete units of material circulating independent-ly of each other. Third, the material that was preserved must have proved useful for some specific purpose in the life of the early church. Fourth, little biographi-cal, geographical, or chronological information about the events and teachings of Jesus' ministry was preserved; this all had to be "created" later. Fifth, analogies from the oral folklore of other countries—from as far away as Europe or Afri-ca—were used to reconstruct how the early Christian oral tradition would have developed. Sixth, it is unlikely that more than a handful of authentic Jesus texts survived this process unscathed. After all, who today, playing the child's game of telephone, expects a whispered message transmitted around a room of thirty or more people to come out the same at the end? One can hardly imagine numerous Jesus traditions passed around for a generation throughout the ancient Middle East to fare any better. Or so the critics claimed.[29]

Critique

Although form criticism developed primarily as a *historical* tool, one of its major strengths came as a by-prod-uct—its potential for *interpreta-tion*. In this sense, form criticism does for individual passages what literary criticism does for entire books (see chap. 5). It recognizes that the Gospels are not monolithic wholes but are composed of subunits of many different literary forms. Parables should not be interpreted in the same way as straightforward history; proverbs are not identi-cal to absolute truths; and pro-nouncement stories focus all attention on their climactic (and controversial) pronouncements. In several places the Synop-tic writers seem to have orga-nized their Gospels by grouping together stories of like form. Therefore an understanding of the different forms can help us recover the evangelists' outlines

Form Criticism	
Analysis of Form	INTERPRETATION
Sitz im Leben	HISTORY
Transmission of Tradition	

---

[29] See, e.g., B. D. Ehrman, *Jesus: Apocalyptic Prophet of the New Millennium* (Oxford and New York: OUP, 1999), 51–52.

and discover, for example, when not to assume that certain events are recorded in chronological order. In other words, the hermeneutical value of form criticism is enormous.[30]

As a historical tool, many tenets and assumptions of form criticism must be seriously questioned. There is nothing inherently improbable about each form being particularly useful for a given life-situation in the early church, but the actual data available to recover these are virtually nonexistent. The so-called tendencies of the tradition—to embellish and become increasingly "distinct"—find some support in how later apocryphal traditions dealt with the canonical Gospels. But *within* the canon, as one proceeds from Mark to Matthew and Luke, more often than not there is a tendency to abbreviate and streamline.[31] Many of the other assumptions about the lack of historical interest or care with which the tradition preserved details about Jesus' life and teaching are also questionable. Analogies from other continents and the development of oral folklore over a period of centuries are not as relevant as studies of first-century Jewish oral culture and what likely developed over only a few decades. In fact, a good case can be made that the oral tradition of Jesus' words and deeds was extremely conservative and painstaking in preserving historical truth accurately. We may list seven pieces of evidence:

1. *Memorization* was highly cultivated in first-century Jewish culture. As we have seen above (p. 69), it was the predominant method of elementary education for boys. The disciples of the prophets had memorized and passed on their founders' words. Venerated rabbis had at times committed the entire Bible (our "Old Testament") to memory. It would have been quite normal and expected for Jesus' disciples, revering their teacher, to commit to memory significant portions of his teaching and even brief narratives of his great works, and to have remembered those accounts accurately for a considerable span of time. As much as 80 percent of Jesus' teaching seems to have been cast in poetic form, which would have made its memorization that much easier. In addition, the technical language of receiving and passing on traditions in 1 Cor 11:2, 23, and 15:3 suggests that Paul recognized that he was delivering to the Corinthians fixed pieces of information he had been given by those who preceded him in Christ. Still, none of this would have precluded the disciples from paraphrasing, interpreting, and rearranging the material they had learned; that, too, was the convention of the day.[32] To varying degrees, prodigious feats of memorization, but with the "gist" of an episode rather than

---

[30] Cf. further W. W. Klein, C. L. Blomberg and R. L. Hubbard, Jr., *Introduction to Biblical Interpretation*, rev. ed. (Nashville: Nelson, 2004), 411–18.

[31] See esp. L. R. Keylock, "Bultmann's Law of Increasing Distinctness," in *Current Issues in Biblical and Patristic Interpretation*, ed. G. F. Hawthorne (Grand Rapids: Eerdmans, 1975), 193–210. R. Bauckham (*Jesus and the Eyewitnesses* [Grand Rapids and Cambridge: Eerdmans, 2006], 39–66) demonstrates the decreasing frequency of proper names in the tradition, at least until the fourth century.

[32] B. Gerhardsson, *Memory and Manuscript with Tradition and Transmission in Early Christianity*, 2 vols. bound in 1 (Grand Rapids: Eerdmans; Livonia, MI: Dove Booksellers, 1998); Riesner, *Jesus als Lehrer*; and S. Byrskog, *Story as History—History as Story: The Gospel Tradition in the Context of Ancient Oral History* (Boston and Leiden: Brill, 2002).

verbatim accuracy as the goal, characterized all of classical antiquity.[33] Moreover, with Birger Gerhardsson,

> If one compares the different versions of one and the same tradition in the Synoptic Gospels, one notes that the variations are seldom so general as to give us reason to speak of a fluid tradition which gradually became fixed. The alterations are not of the nature they would have been had originally elastic material been formulated in different ways. The tradition elements seem to have possessed a remarkably fixed wording. Variations generally take the form of additions, omissions, transpositions, or alterations of single details in a wording which otherwise is left unchanged.[34]

2. The continuing presence of *eyewitnesses* to the words and works of Christ, including hostile ones, throughout the entire period of the oral tradition, would have acted as a check to stories running wild or being created out of thin air.[35] Also, within the Christian community there would have been limits placed on the way the Gospel traditions were narrated. Traditional Middle Eastern villagers even today exercise considerable flexibility in orally transmitting cherished traditions, but the entire community knows the boundaries that cannot be transgressed and will correct a storyteller if he or she crosses over them.[36] Recent studies of "social memory" also demonstrate how checks and balances of various kinds help to streamline and somewhat standardize the ways communities, ancient and modern, corporately tell their own stories, with less variation than when individuals in a given group independently report on events.[37] Additionally, the center of apostolic leadership in Jerusalem with its various delegations and councils probably functioned as one of these key checks (cf. Acts 8, 10–11, 15).[38]

3. Although sacred traditions were handed down primarily by word of mouth, rabbis and their followers often took *private notes* of important material, which they consulted from time to time to refresh their memories. It would be unusual if Jesus' followers had not done the same.[39] One may also point to the prevalence of wax notebook tablets (cf. Luke 1:63) and to the concern among the Essenes at

---

[33] J. P. Small, "Artificial Memory and the Writing Habits of the Literate," *Helios* 22 (1995): 159–66. Cf. D. L. Bock, "The Words of Jesus in the Gospels: Live, Jive, or Memorex?" in *Jesus under Fire: Modern Scholarship Reinvents the Historical Jesus*, ed. M. J. Wilkins and J. P. Moreland (Grand Rapids: Zondervan, 1995), 73–99.

[34] B. Gerhardsson, *The Reliability of the Gospel Tradition* (Peabody: Hendrickson, 2001), 54.

[35] Bauckham (*Jesus and the Eyewitnesses*, 183–201) makes the plausible case that a number of the unnamed characters in the Gospels, particularly in Mark's passion narrative, in positions to pass on the accounts involving them, may have been kept anonymous in the tradition for their own protection.

[36] K. E. Bailey, "Informal Controlled Oral Tradition and the Synoptic Gospels," *AJT* 5 (1991): 34–54 (reprinted in *Them* 20 [1995]: 4–11); J. D. G. Dunn, "Altering the Default Setting: Re-envisaging the Early Transmission of the Jesus Tradition," *NTS* 49 (2003): 139–75.

[37] See esp. Bauckham, *Jesus and the Eyewitnesses*, 319–57. Cf. several of the articles in A. Kirk and T. Thatcher, eds., *Memory, Tradition, and Text: Uses of the Past in Early Christianity* (Atlanta: SBL, 2005).

[38] See esp. E. E. Ellis, *The Making of the New Testament Documents* (Leiden and Boston: Brill, 2002), 28–47.

[39] E. E. Ellis, "New Directions in Form Criticism," in *Jesus Christus in Historie und Theologie*, ed. G. Strecker (Tübingen: Mohr, 1975), 299–315; Millard, *Reading and Writing in the Time of Jesus*, 175–76, 202–4, 227–29.

Qumran to record in writing their Scriptural interpretations (unlike the Pharisees who kept written and oral laws more distinct). As a similar breakaway movement from more orthodox Judaism, Christianity probably had more in common with the Essenes than the Pharisees at this point.[40]

4. There was a *Sitz im Leben* already during the ministry of Jesus for his followers to have formulated *succinct summaries of his words and works*—the missions of the Twelve and the seventy—so that the first attempts to formulate the material that would later form part of the Gospels probably took place within months or weeks of the very events described. And early collections of his words would doubtless have been deemed most sacred.[41]

5. Despite all the flexibility in narration and apparent "contradictions" among the Gospels, these documents do not naturally read as though they included information created for the first time after Jesus' death and resurrection. If the early church felt free to "play fast and loose" with the Gospel tradition, why do there remain so many problem passages, the so-called *hard sayings* of Jesus? Why do we read that Jesus claimed not to know the time of his return (Mark 13:32 pars.)? Or what of the three passages that have misled some into thinking that he did claim to know—and predicted his return within the lifetime of his followers (Mark 9:1 pars.; Mark 13:30 pars.; Matt 10:23)? Conversely, if later Christian prophets spoke in the name of the risen Lord and had their teachings attributed to the earthly Jesus, why do we find *no sayings* of Christ in the Gospels to clear up major early church controversies—the dispute between Jews and Gentiles over whether or not to keep the Law, the role of circumcision in the Christian life, or a proper approach to speaking in tongues?[42] 1 Corinthians 7:10 and 12 testify to Paul's care not to create a word from the historical Jesus to solve sticky matters about divorce when he didn't have one.

6. Why, on the other hand, do we find *major emphases in the Gospels that are not stressed by the later church*? Perhaps the most striking of these is Jesus' characteristic reference to himself as "Son of Man." Our final chapter discusses the meaning of this title, but a point to be made here is that, except for one reference apiece in Acts and Revelation, this title never recurs throughout the rest of the New Testament even though it was Jesus' favorite. If distinctions between the pre-Easter and post-Easter Jesus were blurred, this omission would be inexplicable.[43]

---

[40] A. Millard, "Writing and the Gospels," *Qumran Chronicle* 5 (1995): 55–62.

[41] See esp. J. A. Baird, *Holy Word: The Paradigm of New Testament Formation* (London and New York: SAP, 2002).

[42] Against the view, more generally, that early Christian prophets created sayings of Jesus *de novo*, see D. Hill, *New Testament Prophecy* (London: Marshall, Morgan & Scott; Richmond: John Knox, 1979); and D. E. Aune, *Prophecy in Early Christianity and the Ancient Mediterranean World* (Grand Rapids: Eerdmans, 1983; Eugene, OR: Wipf & Stock, 2003). For a subsequent defense of that view, see M. E. Boring, *The Continuing Voice of Jesus: Christian Prophecy and the Gospel Tradition* (Louisville: WJKP, 1991); in turn countered by B. Witherington III, *Jesus the Seer: The Progress of Prophecy* (Peabody: Hendrickson, 1999), 293–328.

[43] For a more detailed list of similar contrasts, see E. E. Lemcio, *The Past of Jesus in the Gospels* (Cambridge: CUP, 1991).

7. It has sometimes been said that even if Jesus did not explicitly predict his return within one generation, his first followers were clearly looking for it (cf., e.g., 1 and 2 Thessalonians). What is more, people who think the world will soon end are not interested in writing literature, much less history. But the *massive production of literature at Qumran*, including the retelling of Old Testament history, despite the Essenes' belief that they were living very near to the end, belies this skepticism. Jews in general, moreover, had been wrestling from at least the eighth-century BC onwards with the tension between prophetic declarations that the Day of the Lord was at hand and the ongoing course of human history. Their most common solution was to cite Ps 90:4 that a day with the Lord is like one thousand years. So it is unlikely that a religion like Christianity which was birthed out of Judaism would have been unprepared to envision the possibility that human history might continue for a substantial period of time before Christ returned.[44]

Nevertheless, despite all these criticisms, the dominant presupposition of form criticism—that of an initial period of oral tradition for the Gospel material—is well founded. Mark and Luke in particular, as non-eyewitnesses of the events they narrated, would have depended on such tradition extensively. When we come to date the Gospels and their written sources, we will see that this period may have lasted only twenty to forty years rather than the forty to sixty years some posit (see chaps. 6–9), but any illumination of this first phase of Christian origins is to be welcomed. Then we must pass to the next phase—that of the first extensive written accounts of Jesus' life.

Source Criticism of the Synoptic Gospels

The Synoptic Problem[45]

From time to time in the history of the church, various people have suggested that there is no literary relationship among the Synoptic Gospels. They argue that the similarities can be explained because the Gospels describe the same events and because God inspired them.[46] The vast majority of careful students of the Gospels reject these conclusions, however. In addition to Luke's testimony (cited above, p. 91), four other features are not adequately accounted for by this approach. First, the parallelism between two Gospels is often *verbatim* for entire clauses or sentences and, even more commonly, identical except for an occasional substitution of a different word from the same root, a synonym, or a slight change in word order. Although statistics vary from textbook to textbook based on how exact the wording of two verses in two different Gospels must be for them to be labeled "parallel," a rough estimate of the amount of parallelism is as follows: Of the 661 verses in Mark, 500 recur in Matthew in parallel form and 350 recur in Luke. In

---

[44] See esp. R. Bauckham, "The Delay of the Parousia," *TynBul* 31 (1980): 3–36.

[45] For the points in this subsection, see esp. Stein, *Studying the Synoptic Gospels*, 29–152; and D. Guthrie, *New Testament Introduction*, rev. ed. (Leicester and Downers Grove: IVP, 1990), 136–208.

[46] So esp. E. Linnemann, *Is There a Synoptic Problem?* (Grand Rapids: Baker, 1992); and R. L. Thomas and F. D. Farnell, eds., *The Jesus Crisis: The Inroads of Historical Criticism into Evangelical Scholarship* (Grand Rapids: Kregel, 1998).

addition, there are another 235 verses common to Matthew and Luke that are not found in Mark.[47] This parallelism occurs not only with Jesus' teachings, where one might argue that the early church simply memorized them, but also with the narrative descriptions of what Christ did. Given the diversity of ways that two different authors can describe the same episode, such verbal parallelism virtually requires that one copied from the other or that both copied from a common source. A professor encountering a similar phenomenon on two students' term papers, even occasionally, would certainly agree!

Second, even with Jesus' sayings, it is noteworthy that this verbal parallelism occurs *in Greek*, that is, in translation of the Aramaic that Jesus originally spoke. Anyone who has studied a foreign language knows that there are often numerous ways to translate a given sentence or paragraph from one language to another. Repeated examples of identical translations suggest literary dependence of some kind, unless one posits the unlikely hypothesis that the first Jewish Christians circulated accounts of Jesus' teaching in fixed form in Greek translation.

Third, the agreement among the Synoptics extends to *parenthetical comments* or explanatory asides added by a particular author. For example, both Mark 13:14 and Matt 24:15 insert the remark, "let the reader understand," in the middle of their accounts of Jesus predicting the setting up of the "abomination that causes desolation" in the temple. Both Mark 2:10 and Matt 9:6 break off Jesus' words to the onlookers on the occasion of his healing the paralytic at exactly the same place: "But that you may know that the Son of Man has authority on earth to forgive sins . . ." (NIV). Both then go on to write, "he said to the paralytic," and continue with Jesus' words. These would be extraordinary coincidences if Matthew and Mark had no knowledge of each other or some common written document.

Fourth, the parallelism also involves the *order of episodes* that are not linked together chronologically. For example, Mark 2:1–3:6 combines a series of five controversy stories between Jesus and the Jewish leaders without ever indicating the sequence in which they took place. Yet, Matthew and Luke both preserve this exact sequence of episodes, although Matthew does insert intervening material (see Luke 5:17–6:11; Matt 9:1–17; 12:1–14). Or, on a smaller scale, Mark "sandwiches" the story of Peter's denial around his account of Jesus before the Sanhedrin (Mark 14:53–54, 55–65, 66–72). Matthew employs the identical stylistic device (Matt 26:57–58, 59–68, 69–75), an unlikely coincidence, particularly given the fact that Luke more conventionally rearranges the material into two discrete stories (Luke 22:54–62, 63–71).

If the overwhelming probability, then, is that the Synoptics are related at a literary level, what is the nature of that relationship? We will consider the most common and most probable answer to that question in three stages, in decreasing order of certainty: Markan priority, the Q-hypothesis, and additional sources distinct to Matthew and Luke.

---

[47] These statistics are taken from H. W. House, *Chronological and Background Charts of the New Testament,* rev. ed. (Grand Rapids: Zondervan, 2009), chart 9.

Markan Priority

Strengths. Numerous arguments of varying weights have cumulatively suggested to a majority of modern scholars that Mark was the first Gospel to be written and that Matthew and Luke both drew heavily on his work:[48]

1. At many points Mark's details are the most vivid, while Matthew and Luke omit what seem to be the touches of an eyewitness report: for example, "after sunset" in Mark 1:32 (cf. Matt 8:16), the "green" grass in Mark 6:39 (cf. Matt 14:19; Luke 9:14), or the "three hundred denarii" of Mark 14:5 (NKJV) (cf. Matt 26:9).[49]

2. Mark's grammar and style is often the roughest, whereas Matthew and Luke make it smoother. Mark has a fondness for asyndeton (leaving out conjunctions), parataxis (using just "and" when he does connect clauses), the historical present tense, redundancies, double negatives, and convoluted order of clauses.

3. Mark narrates potentially embarrassing or misleading details that the other evangelists omit or reword: for example, the apparent "error" (on which see below, p. 276, n. 26) in referring to Abiathar as high priest in 2:26 (cf. Matt 12:4; Luke 6:4); the statement that Jesus "could" work few miracles in Nazareth in 6:5 (cf. Matt 13:58; Luke 4:24); and Jesus' reply to the rich young ruler in 10:18: "Why do you call me good? . . . No one is good—except God alone" (cf. Matt 19:17).

4. Mark's is the shortest of the Gospels, yet within the passages he narrates, his is typically the fullest form. Of 92 passages that Mark and Luke have in common, Mark is longer 71 times. Of 104 he shares with Matthew, he is longer in 63.[50] It makes sense for Matthew and Luke to have abbreviated Mark's characteristically detailed accounts to make room for other information about Jesus they wanted to add; both Gospels occupy about the maximum length of material that could conveniently fit on an ancient scroll. If Mark were abridging Matthew and Luke, as Griesbach claimed, it would make little sense for him to lengthen those accounts that he did choose to include.

5. There is very little in Mark not reproduced in Matthew and Luke (less than 10 percent of his Gospel overall). Unless Mark were the first to write, why would he bother, with so little new or distinctive to say? Again, one answer has been to argue that he was trying to create a digest of the two, just as epitomizers often condensed long multi-volume histories in the ancient world into one manageably-sized volume. But careful analysis of Mark's style, format, and contents has

---

[48] Cf. esp. G. R. Osborne and M. C. Williams, "The Case for the Markan Priority View of Gospel Origins: The Two/Four Source View," in *Three Views on the Origins of the Synoptic Gospels*, ed. R. L. Thomas (Grand Rapids: Kregel, 2002), 19–96. More briefly, cf. S. McKnight, "Source Criticism," in *Interpreting the New Testament*, eds. Black and Dockery, 74–105; and C. A. Evans, "Sorting Out the Synoptic Problem: Why an Old Approach Is Still Best," in *Reading the Gospels Today*, ed. S. E. Porter (Grand Rapids and Cambridge: Eerdmans, 2004), 1–26.

[49] These examples are taken from Guthrie, *New Testament Introduction*, 151.

[50] C. L. Blomberg, "The Tradition History of the Parables Peculiar to Luke's Central Section" (Ph.D. diss., University of Aberdeen, 1982), 25–27.

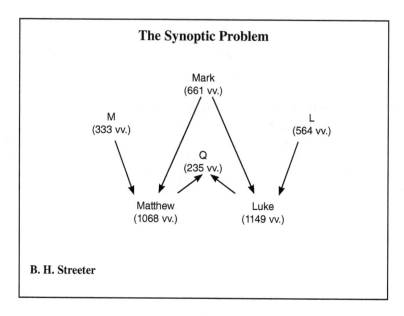

The Synoptic Problem

Mark
(661 vv.)

M
(333 vv.)

L
(564 vv.)

Q
(235 vv.)

Matthew
(1068 vv.)

Luke
(1149 vv.)

B. H. Streeter

shown that his work remains more unlike any known summary or digest from the ancient world than like one.[51]

6. Matthew and Luke only rarely deviate from Mark in sequence of passages or nature of wording in the same way at the same time, whereas Matthew and Mark frequently agree against Luke, and Luke and Mark frequently agree against Matthew. What this demonstrates is that Mark must be the "middle term" of the three, that is, he was either the first on which the other two drew, the last (abridging the first two, as with Griesbach), or the Gospel that drew on either Matthew or Luke and was in turn drawn on by the other one (as with Augustine's sequence of Matthew-Mark-Luke). "With the Augustinian hypothesis, we would have to think that Luke almost always chose to use Mark's wording rather than Matthew's; with the two-gospel hypothesis [Griesbach], we would have to assume that Mark almost never introduced any wording of his own. While possible, both procedures are less likely than the alternative."[52]

7. Mark contains the highest incidence of Aramaic words preserved in Greek transliteration: for example, *Boanerges* (3:17), *talitha koum* (5:41), *Corban* (7:11), *ephphatha* (7:34), and *Abba* (14:36).[53]

---

[51] See the detailed demonstration in R. A. Derrenbacker, Jr., *Ancient Compositional Practices and the Synoptic Problem* (Leuven: Leuven University Press and Peeters, 2005).

[52] D. A. Carson and D. J. Moo, *An Introduction to the New Testament,* rev. ed. (Grand Rapids: Zondervan, 2005), 97. For still less likely options, see the latter part of my survey of contemporary perspectives in C. L. Blomberg, "The Synoptic Problem: Where We Stand at the Start of a New Century," in *Rethinking the Synoptic Problem,* ed. D. A. Black and D. R. Beck (Grand Rapids: Baker, 2001), 17–40.

[53] These examples come from Stein, *Studying the Synoptic Gospels,* 59–63. For a wide-ranging study affirming a significant Aramaic substratum to the Gospel of Mark, see M. Casey, *Aramaic Sources of Mark's Gospel* (Cambridge: CUP, 1998).

8. There seems to be no other credible explanation for why Mark would have omitted all of the material common to Matthew and Luke if he had known about it since this includes much of Jesus' most beloved teaching (the Sermon on the Mount, numerous parables, instructions for establishing the church, etc.).

9. When one assumes that Matthew and Luke each redacted Mark, consistent patterns of theological emphasis emerge; on other theories, the patterns of editorial activity prove far less consistent.[54]

10. Applying the same principles that textual critics use to determine the oldest version of a given passage pays dividends as well in comparing parallel accounts between two Gospels. The kinds of changes that scribes regularly introduced to clarify, explain, or smooth out original readings more often than not resemble what Matthew and Luke would have done to Mark, if that is the correct way to explain their relationship.[55]

Weaknesses.[56] The most important arguments against Markan priority are:

1. Certain minor agreements of Matthew and Luke against Mark do exist. But these may be attributed to overlap between Mark and "Q" (see below), to natural changes in style or detail that writers might be expected to make independently of each other, or to reliance on other oral traditions.

2. A large chunk of Mark is missing from Luke (Mark 6:45–8:26), often called Luke's "Great Omission." But Luke probably had geographical reasons for leaving this out (see below, pp. 160–61).

3. The changes in the Gospel tradition are not as drastic if Mark wrote last rather than first. This may be true, but one dare not favor a view just because it is apologetically convenient. Our response to form criticism has demonstrated that there are plenty of other reasons for supporting the general trustworthiness of the Gospel tradition.

4. Markan priority is a hypothesis that was created primarily by modern, liberal scholars eager to find a miracle-free Jesus. This may well be true, but they did not succeed. Mark still has plenty of miracles, and the primary reasons for adopting Markan priority are independent of whatever motives may have prompted the exercise in the first place.

5. Strong patristic testimony supports Matthean priority. This is the one weighty objection to seeing Mark as having written first. Indeed, this external evidence fits certain internal evidence: Matthew's parallels to Mark do not as consistently seem

---

[54] See, e.g., the extraordinarily convoluted process of Luke's use of Matthew posited throughout A. J. McNicol, D. L. Dungan and D. B. Peabody, *Beyond the Q Impasse: Luke's Use of Matthew* (Valley Forge: Trinity, 1996); or the unremarkable observations on Mark's putative use of Matthew, hardly adding up to any significant patterns, in C. S. Mann, *Mark* (Garden City: Doubleday, 1986).

[55] See esp. M. C. Williams, *Two Gospels from One: A Comprehensive Text-Critical Analysis of the Synoptic Gospels* (Grand Rapids: Kregel, 2006). Cf. also H. W. Shin, *Textual Criticism and the Synoptic Problem in Historical Jesus Research: The Search for Valid Criteria* (Leuven: Leuven University Press and Peeters, 2004).

[56] The fullest critique remains H.-H. Stoldt, *The History and Criticism of the Marcan Hypothesis* (Macon: Mercer University Press; Edinburgh: T&T Clark, 1980).

to be later, editorial revisions as do Luke's. We will suggest in our introduction to Matthew that there is a way to harmonize this evidence with the arguments for Markan priority, and that Matthew may have composed his Gospel in stages, partly before reading Mark and partly afterwards.

The Q-Hypothesis

In the early 1800s, Friedrich Schleiermacher first created the symbol Q (from the German *Quelle*, meaning "source") to designate a hypothetical document on which Matthew and Luke drew. This would account for the material not found in Mark that they shared—almost exclusively sayings of Jesus. Although scholars have not accepted this hypothesis quite as strongly as they have Markan priority, it still finds a fair consensus of support.[57]

Strengths. Why not simply assume that Luke used Matthew or vice versa? The most important reasons include:

1. Although sufficient verbal parallelism occurs in places to suggest a literary relationship, the parallels are not as consistently close to each other as in the "triple tradition" (material found in all three Synoptics). This would be accounted for if both Matthew and Luke drew on a common source and redacted it independently of each other.

2. Sometimes Matthew seems to preserve the most literal account of Jesus' words; other times Luke does. Often, too, Matthew's style is more Semitic (most notably, in preserving Hebrew parallelism), whereas Luke's order seems more original. Who, for example, would have actually taken Matthew's long sermons (like the Sermon on the Mount) and scattered parallels to them throughout his Gospel the way Luke would have had to if he were directly dependent on Matthew?

3. The oldest testimony about the formation of Matthew, from the early second-century Christian writer Papias, as quoted by Eusebius in the early 300s (*Hist. eccl.* 3.39.16), says that "Matthew collected the oracles [of Jesus] in the Hebrew language [or "dialect"] and everyone translated [or "interpreted"] them as best he could." The Greek word for "oracles" (*logia*) most naturally means "sayings," not a full-fledged narrative Gospel, so perhaps Matthew himself was the author of something like "Q" before he (or a translator?) turned it into Greek.[58]

4. There is a general theological and stylistic homogeneity to a reconstructed Q. Recurring themes include teaching about wisdom, the more radical demands of itinerant ministry for the kingdom, the power and authority of Jesus, and a

---

[57] For a representative reconstruction of what Q could have looked like, complete with commentary on the resulting texts, see R. Valantasis, *The New Q: A Fresh Translation with Commentary* (London and New York: T&T Clark, 2005). For a full-blown technical analysis and commentary, cf. J. M. Robinson, P. Hoffmann and J. S. Kloppenborg, *The Critical Edition of Q* (Minneapolis: Fortress; Leuven: Peeters, 2000).

[58] This was the view Schleiermacher proposed. Although not widely held in recent times, comparatively recent defenders can still be found, most notably M. Black, "The Use of Rhetorical Terminology in Papias on Mark and Matthew," *JSNT* 37 (1989): 31–41; and D. A. Hagner, *Matthew 1–13* (Dallas: Word, 1994), xlvi.

lively hope for the end of the age to come soon. Form critics have even given Q a plausible *Sitz im Leben*—the wandering preachers who continued the tradition of Matthew 10 and Luke 9–10 (the sending of the Twelve and seventy) throughout Galilee after Jesus' death.[59]

Weaknesses.[60] Above all, Q has never been discovered; it is a purely hypothetical document. Still, the genre of a collection of Jesus' sayings is known to have existed, at least in heterodox Christian circles, with the Gospel of Thomas. The *Lives of the Eminent Philosophers* by Diogenes Laertius likewise compiles lengthy lists of key teachings of the subjects of its biographies. If the parallels between Matthew and Luke are not always close enough to suggest a written source, perhaps we should envision them relying on a common oral tradition instead. There is also little agreement on the exact delineation of Q's contents, its order, or its purpose. Some scholars prefer, therefore, to speak of a combination of shorter written and/or oral sources rather than one definite document.[61] Many scholars imagine that Q represents a complete Gospel of sorts so that by not including a passion narrative it reflects a community that did not believe in Christ's atoning death. Others rightly recognize the implausibility of such a community existing early in the history of the Jesus-movement and therefore reject the Q-hypothesis. But both of these approaches fail to observe that an epitome of someone's sayings by definition does not represent everything that others may have deemed of importance about that individual's life—and death.[62]

M, L, and Proto-Luke

The most prominent twentieth-century proponent of Markan priority and the Q-hypothesis was B. H. Streeter, an Englishman writing in the 1920s.[63] Streeter, however, went beyond the widely accepted "two-source hypothesis" to champion what came to be called the "four-source hypothesis." Streeter believed that, in addition to using Mark and Q, Matthew and Luke each had written sources of their own on which they drew; Streeter labeled these two additional sources "M" and "L" respectively. These supposed sources could account for much of the material unique to each of these two Gospels (333 verses in Matthew; 564 in Luke). Streeter also speculated that Luke wrote a first draft of his Gospel before seeing a copy of Mark ("proto-Luke") and then revised and expanded it consider-

---

[59] For good, representative, and recent treatments, see C. M. Tuckett, *Q and the History of Early Christianity* (Peabody: Hendrickson, 1996); and J. S. Kloppenborg Verbin, *Excavating Q: The History and Setting of the Sayings Gospel* (Edinburgh: T&T Clark, 2000).

[60] See esp. M. Goodacre, *The Case Against Q: Studies in Markan Priority and the Synoptic Problem* (Harrisburg: Trinity, 2002); and M. Goodacre and N. Perrin, eds., *Questioning Q: A Multidimensional Critique* (Downers Grove: IVP, 2004).

[61] It is also important to stress that scholarly study of Q has nothing to do with popular works of fiction, which from time to time have co-opted the symbol to refer to lost (or supposedly newly discovered!) documents, the contents of which contradict or radically supplement those of the canonical Gospels in some fashion (as, e.g., in D. Brown, *The Da Vinci Code* [New York and London: Doubleday, 2003], 256).

[62] D. Seeley, "Jesus' Death in Q," *NTS* 38 (1992): 222–34.

[63] See his classic work, *The Four Gospels: A Study of Origins* (London: Macmillan, 1924).

ably after reading Mark. This would account for the alternation of Markan and non-Markan material in Luke in large blocks (see below, p. 159) as well as the larger percentage of non-Markan, non-Q material in Luke than in Matthew. But this is the most tenuous of Streeter's proposals and does not currently command consensus acclaim.

As for M and L, some scholars have claimed to see a theological homogeneity in this material,[64] but often it corresponds merely to the redactional interests of Matthew and Luke. What is more, if Matthew was written by the apostle with that name, the material unique to his Gospel could simply reflect his personal reminiscences.[65] A plausible case can be made for Luke having relied on either a Semitic source or a Greek source written in a style very similar to that of the Septuagint for chapters 1–2: this information about the conceptions and births of John and Jesus is written in a much more Hebraic or Hebraic-sounding style than the rest of his Gospel.[66] It is also possible that a parable's source accounts for the large percentage of parables unique to Luke clustered in the central section of his Gospel (see below, p. 337). But beyond this, "M" and "L" remain highly speculative. The heavy reliance of ancient historians on numerous oral and written sources, alongside any eyewitness participation in events they may have had, leads us to assume that a comprehensive solution to the Synoptic problem may be quite complex and irrecoverable. Occam's razor[67] is decidedly unhelpful here!

To the beginning student, all this discussion of Gospel source criticism often seems irrelevant to their interests, but it is actually a crucial discipline in several respects. For those interested in the question of the historical reliability of these documents, it is important to understand as best as possible how they were formed. For example, if Q existed, it would probably be dated to the 40s or 50s. This puts us within ten to twenty years of the crucifixion and considerably shortens the period in which the Gospel traditions circulated exclusively by word of mouth. For those interested in the theological distinctives of the different evangelists, it is equally crucial to know who wrote first and who edited which document. Then one can separate tradition from redaction and have a better grasp of the unique emphases of each writer. That brings us naturally to phase three of the developing Gospel tradition: redaction criticism.

---

[64] See esp. S. H. Brooks, *Matthew's Community: The Evidence of His Special Sayings Material* (Sheffield: JSOT, 1987); K. Paffenroth, *The Story of Jesus according to L* (Sheffield: SAP, 1997).

[65] Nevertheless, evidence from the Church Fathers, esp. Ignatius, suggests that there may have been an "M," because a disproportionately large percentage of the quotations from Matthew come from the unparalleled portions of Matthew's Gospel.

[66] For a Semitic source, see S. C. Farris, *The Hymns of Luke's Infancy Narratives* (Sheffield: JSOT, 1985); for a Septuagintalized Greek source, see C.-W. Jung, *The Original Language of the Lukan Infancy Narrative* (London and New York: Continuum, 2004).

[67] The philosophical principle that in general the simpler argument is to be preferred to the more complex one.

Redaction Criticism: The Editorial Contributions
of the Synoptic Evangelists[68]

Again a trio of Germans is responsible for vaulting this discipline into promi-
nence: Günther Bornkamm on Matthew, Willi Marxsen on Mark, and Hans Conzelmann on Luke.[69] A good working definition of the method they pioneered
explains that redaction criticism "seeks to lay bare the theological perspectives
of a biblical writer by analyzing the editorial (redactional) and compositional
techniques and interpretations employed by him in shaping and framing the written and/or oral traditions at hand."[70] One may subdivide redaction criticism into
two complementary tasks: *reading horizontally* and *reading vertically.*[71] Reading
horizontally involves looking *across* a gospel synopsis to compare the differences
among parallels and to determine how later writers altered their sources. Reading vertically refers to looking *down* the given column of a synopsis (and hence
throughout the larger context of a specific Gospel) to see what themes and other
editorial distinctives repeatedly recur and whether or not they are paralleled in the
other Gospels. It also involves looking for editorial seams, summaries, introductions, and conclusions, and the outline or arrangement of material. All told, one
can get a good feel for a given writer's emphases through these procedures.

As with form criticism, redaction criticism has often been used by more radical
critics to deprecate the historical reliability of the Gospels. Some falsely assume
that what is told for theological purposes is less likely to be historical than is a
mere recitation of facts. Indeed, often the opposite is the case, as people pas-
sionately committed to a cause want the facts to be known. Post-holocaust Jews
insisted the story of the atrocities in Nazi Germany be told and retold so that
such horrors might never recur. They had a much greater vested interest in the
truth than those "revisionist" historians who argued that the holocaust had been
vastly exaggerated.[72] Redaction critics also often allege that what the Gospel writers added to their sources cannot be historical, ruling out the possibility of additional written or oral sources beyond Mark and Q, or in Matthew's case, personal
memory. Others exaggerate the extent to which minor stylistic variations reflect
theological motives. Some use a fairly atomistic form of analysis, counting word
frequencies to determine characteristic vocabulary and confidently pronouncing

---

[68] For excellent introductions, see D. A. Carson, "Redaction Criticism: On the Legitimacy and
Illegitimacy of a Literary Tool," in *Scripture and Truth,* ed. D. A. Carson and J. D. Woodbridge (Grand
Rapids: Zondervan; Leicester: IVP, 1983; Grand Rapids: Baker, 1992), 119–42; and G. R. Osborne,
"Redaction Criticism," in *Interpreting the New Testament,* eds. Black and Dockery, 128–49.

[69] G. Bornkamm, G. Barth, and H. J. Held, *Tradition and Interpretation in Matthew* (London:
SCM; Philadelphia: Westminster, 1963); W. Marxsen, *Mark the Evangelist* (Nashville: Abingdon,
1969); H. Conzelmann, *The Theology of St. Luke* (New York: Harper & Row, 1960; London: Faber &
Faber, 1961; Philadelphia: Fortress, 1982).

[70] R. N. Soulen and R. K. Soulen, *Handbook of Biblical Criticism,* rev. ed. (Louisville: WJKP,
2001), 158.

[71] Cf. G. D. Fee and D. Stuart, *How to Read the Bible for All Its Worth,* rev. ed. (Grand Rapids:
Zondervan, 2003), 135–40.

[72] Cf. Bauckham, *Jesus and the Eyewitnesses,* 499–505.

Two Kinds of Redaction Criticism

Matthew	Mark	Luke	John
Reading	Reading	Reading	Reading

READING HORIZONTALLY

| Vertically | Vertically | Vertically | Vertically |

on the traditional or redactional origin of almost every word or phrase in a passage. This, in fact, goes far beyond anything we can know for sure. With all the attention to diversity, one can lose sight of the substantial amount of agreement among the three Synoptics.

The value of redaction criticism stripped of these methodological improprieties and excesses, however, remains great, perhaps even more than that of source or form criticism. As an interpretive tool, it is equivalent to asking the question of each passage in the Gospels: "Why did the Gospel writer choose to include this in precisely the way he did?" Readers of the Gospels from the beginning of church history have recognized that the different writers had different theological emphases. The church's preoccupation with constructing harmonies of the life of Christ generally blurred these distinctions. Ironically, it is often those more conservative Christians, who insist most strongly on the inspiration and inerrancy of the very texts the evangelists penned, who pay least attention to the form in which those texts were inspired, opting instead to study an artificial, man-made synthesis of the four.

Surely, such harmonies have a legitimate place, and, indeed, our survey of the life of Christ below will make cautious use of them.[73] But we dare not lose sight of the fact that God inspired four Gospels, not one, and presumably for a reason! Every preacher choosing a text from the Gospels should, therefore, want to stress what the original author intended. For example, if one determines to preach on the feeding of the five thousand (a passage occurring in all four Gospels), the sermon should sound slightly different depending on which account one follows. The preacher must research that author's emphases and make the sermon correspond accordingly. Sadly, this is not often done. In our introductions to each of the four Gospels, how-

---

[73] Indeed, harmonization and redaction criticism can actually work hand in hand: the former demonstrating that passages are not contradictory; the latter explaining why they *do* differ in the ways they do. See C. L. Blomberg, "The Legitimacy and Limits of Harmonization," in *Hermeneutics, Authority, and Canon*, ed. D. A. Carson and J. D. Woodbridge (Grand Rapids: Zondervan, 1986; Eugene, OR: Wipf & Stock, 2005), 135–74.

ever, we shall highlight a variety of these distinctives and point out others at the
conclusions of most major sections of our survey of the life of Christ.

Canon Criticism and the Formation of the Canon

Canon Criticism

The work of two American scholars, Brevard Childs and James Sanders, in the
1970s through the 1990s, bequeathed yet one more brand of criticism to our array
of scholarly methods.[74] Disenchanted with the increasing sterility of source, form,
and redaction criticisms—especially in the hands of their more radical practitioners—Childs in particular argued in a series of impressive and lengthy works that
more attention should be paid to the final or canonical form of the text. At times,
this closely overlaps with redaction criticism and simply attempts to recover the
intention of the evangelists in "packaging" their Gospels as they did. In other
cases, however, canon criticism takes seriously the intentions of the early Christian communities in the fourth and fifth centuries as agreement was finalized on
exactly which books belonged in the New Testament and in which order.

Thus, for example, canon criticism looks beyond the diversity on which redaction criticism focuses to highlight the unity of themes between, say, Matthew's
and Luke's infancy narratives (chaps. 1–2 of each Gospel). Presumably, each
original audience had, at first, only its one Gospel so that highlighting this unity
goes beyond what can be ascribed to the evangelists' intentions. Again, canon
criticism may focus on a passage like the Sermon on the Mount and observe its
long history of interpretation in light of Paul's later teaching about the inability
to keep the Law. Although Jesus did not demonstrably mean for the Sermon to be
taken this way, canon criticism grants a certain legitimacy to using later texts to
interpret earlier ones, a kind of "halfway house" on the road to full-fledged systematic theology. In still other cases, canon criticism focuses on the significance
of the order of the books in the Bible (e.g., John's interrupting the original unity
of Luke-Acts because it, too, is a Gospel) or on the way different books' contributions to different themes balance each other out (Matthew and James on the need
for works of righteousness vs. Luke and Paul on salvation by grace). In the case of
Sanders, canon criticism focuses much more on the "intertextual" echoes between
Old and New Testaments.[75]

There is much in all this to be applauded. Any focus on the final form of a text
in its integrity is to be welcomed. But at the points where the results of canon criticism stand opposed to what would be derived from analyzing one biblical book
by itself in its original, historical setting, we must demur. If the locus of the inspiration or authority of Scripture is in what the first-century biblical writers themselves penned rather than in the fourth- or fifth-century Christian communities

---

[74] Most directly relevant to a study of the Gospels is B. S. Childs, *The New Testament as Canon*
(London: SCM, 1984; Philadelphia: Fortress, 1985), 57–209. More generally, cf. J. A. Sanders, *Torah
and Canon*, rev. ed. (Eugene, OR: Cascade, 2005).

[75] See also J. A. Sanders, *From Sacred Story to Sacred Text: Canon as Paradigm* (Philadelphia:
Fortress, 1987; Eugene, OR: Wipf & Stock, 2000).

that completed the canonizing process, then we must choose the meaning implied by the former over that attributed to the texts by the latter. Given this caveat, it is not clear that canon criticism offers anything very distinctive from certain forms of redaction or literary criticism. Scholarship as a whole seems to agree—the method has not widely caught on outside a handful of committed followers,[76] and it may not long outlive its vigorous advocacy by Childs and Sanders.

The Formation of the Canon

Although the topic of the development of the New Testament canon goes far beyond an introduction to the Gospels, it is one of those issues that often falls through the cracks in a curriculum and gets overlooked altogether. Other works will have to be consulted for details, but a few introductory remarks germane to Matthew, Mark, Luke, and John seem in order here. Already by the mid–second century there was wide agreement that there were four and only four narratives that accurately portrayed the life of Jesus. All the existing lists for the next three hundred years, until the various councils that finalized the New Testament canon once and for all (particularly in Carthage and Hippo at the end of the fourth century), agreed that Matthew, Mark, Luke, and John were the Gospels to be included, even though they occasionally disputed some of the epistles or the Apocalypse. To be sure, the Gnostic sects had their additional texts (see above, pp. 38–39), but we are not sure just how authoritatively they functioned even for those communities. No existing record ever suggests that any apocryphal Gospel was put forward for inclusion alongside the other four in any multi-volume collection of "Scripture."[77]

It is particularly misleading, therefore, to speak of lost Gospels or lost Christianities in ways that suggest that orthodoxy somehow suppressed viable Christian traditions or to claim that history is simply written by the winners.[78] The Gnostic and apocryphal Gospels are, to varying degrees, all parasitic on the canonical Gospels; indeed, they give tacit acknowledgment to the superior authority of those Gospels by trying to use New Testament characters or events to give credence to their perspectives. The occasional isolated monastery destroyed a few noncanonical documents, but such practices were scarcely widespread. The apostolic tradition prevailed in large part because later, competing options never commanded widespread credibility. The large number of Patristic works that interacted with heterodox theologies guaranteed that their viewpoints were never lost, and even the modern rediscoveries of long hidden texts have not unearthed any whose ide-

---

[76] In evangelical circles, see esp. the various works of R. W. Wall and E. C. Lemcio, several of which are collected in their anthology entitled *The New Testament as Canon: A Reader in Canonical Criticism* (Sheffield: JSOT, 1992).

[77] See the lists of books discussed, proposed and/or recommended to be excluded in L. M. McDonald and J. A. Sanders, eds., *The Canon Debate* (Peabody: Hendrickson, 2002), 591–97.

[78] As particularly with B. D. Ehrman, *Lost Scriptures: Books that Did Not Make It into the New Testament* (Oxford and New York: OUP, 2003); idem., *Lost Christianities: The Battles for Scripture and the Faiths We Never Knew* (Oxford and New York: OUP, 2003).

ologies or contents differ radically from the noncanonical literature that we have known about throughout all church history.[79]

The criteria used for including Matthew, Mark, Luke, and John, to the extent that we can recover them, are the same as for the rest of the New Testament: apostolicity (authorship by an apostle or a close associate of an apostle during the first century), orthodoxy (not contradicting the apostolic testimony that was handed down from earliest times), and relevance (widely used throughout the early church rather than being limited to one or a few small groups). The canonical sequence—Matthew, Mark, Luke, John—was no doubt developed partly because of the belief that they were written in that order. At least as important in putting Matthew first were the links between his work and the Old Testament: his was the most Jewish of the Gospels, containing the most quotations of the Old Testament and the greatest number of explicit comparisons and contrasts with it. The early church was not primarily intending to create a new canon of uniquely Christian books when it formed a "New Testament." Rather, by using that label, it affirmed its belief that the authority of these books equaled those of the Hebrew Bible, was to be understood as its fulfillment, and thus was now to be interpreted in light of what God had done in Christ.[80]

For Further Study

Because this chapter has surveyed several different disciplines, key bibliography for each individual discipline has already appeared in the footnotes. Here we will simply list several key works that treat most or all of the critical methods surveyed here. Several treat the literary methods discussed in chapter 5 as well. A distinctive of the volume by Green is that all writers illustrate the methods they discuss with reference to the same texts: Luke 3:1–20; John 4:1–42; 1 Cor 11:2–34; Jas 4:13–5:6; and Rev 5.

Introductory

Black, David A., and David S. Dockery, eds. *Interpreting the New Testament: Essays on Methods and Issues*. Rev. ed. Nashville: Broadman & Holman, 2001.

Blomberg, Craig. *The Historical Reliability of the Gospels*. Rev. ed. Leicester and Downers Grove: IVP, 2007.

Dockery, David S., Kenneth A. Mathews, and Robert B. Sloan, eds. *Foundations for Biblical Interpretation*. Nashville: Broadman & Holman, 1994.

Dunn, James D. G. *A New Perspective on Jesus: What the Quest for the Historical Jesus Missed*. Grand Rapids: Baker, 2005.

---

[79] See further D. L. Bock, *The Missing Gospels: Unearthing the Truth Behind Alternative Christianities* (Nashville: Nelson, 2006); J. E. Komoszewski, M. J. Sawyer, and D. B. Wallace, *Reinventing Jesus: What the Da Vinci Code and Other Novel Speculations Don't Tell You* (Grand Rapids: Kregel, 2006); and P. Jenkins, *Hidden Gospels: How the Search for Jesus Lost Its Way* (Oxford and New York: OUP, 2001).

[80] On the formation of the New Testament canon, see esp. F. F. Bruce, *The Canon of Scripture* (Leicester and Downers Grove: IVP, 1988); and B. M. Metzger, *The Canon of Scripture: Its Origin, Development, and Significance* (Oxford and New York: OUP, 1987).

McKnight, Scot. *Interpreting the Synoptic Gospels*. Grand Rapids: Baker, 1988.

Intermediate
Bock, Darrell L., and Buist M. Fanning, eds. *Interpreting the New Testament Text: Introduction to the Art and Science of Exegesis*. Wheaton: Crossway, 2006.
Green, Joel B., ed. *Hearing the New Testament: Strategies for Interpretation*. Grand Rapids: Eerdmans; Carlisle: Paternoster, 1995.
Marshall, I. Howard, ed. *New Testament Interpretation: Essays on Principles and Methods*. Exeter: Paternoster; Grand Rapids: Eerdmans, 1977; Eugene, OR: Wipf & Stock, 2006.
Porter, Stanley E., and David Tombs, eds. *Approaches to New Testament Study*. Sheffield: SAP, 1995.
Stein, Robert H. *Studying the Synoptic Gospels: Origin and Interpretation*. Grand Rapids: Baker, 2001. (Also includes discussion of form and redaction criticism.)

Advanced
Bultmann, Rudolf. *The History of the Synoptic Tradition*. Oxford: Blackwell; New York: Harper & Row, 1963 [Germ. orig. 1921].
France, R. T., and David Wenham, eds. *Gospel Perspectives*. Vols. 1–3. Sheffield: JSOT, 1980–1983.
Gerhardsson, Birger. *Memory and Manuscript with Tradition and Transmission in Early Christianity*. 2 vols. bound in 1. Grand Rapids: Eerdmans; Livonia, MI: Dove Booksellers, 1998.
Mournet, Terence C. *Oral Tradition and Literary Dependency: Variability and Stability in the Synoptic Tradition and Q*. Tübingen: Mohr Siebeck, 2005.
Piñero, Antonio and Jesús Peláez. *The Study of the New Testament: A Comprehensive Introduction*. Leiden: Deo, 2003.

Bibliography
McKnight, Scot and Matthew C. Williams. *The Synoptic Gospels: An Annotated Bibliography*. Grand Rapids: Baker, 2000.

Questions for Review

1. What are source, form, and redaction criticism? How does each method work? From an evangelical perspective, what are the strengths and weaknesses of each?

2. Specifically with regard to form criticism, what evidence must temper various theories of unbridled creativity among those who first handed down traditions about Jesus?

3. Why is Markan priority the most common solution to the Synoptic problem? Which arguments in its favor seem strongest? Which arguments against it seem strongest? What are the Q, M, and L hypotheses? What are their relative merits?

4. Why is it important to understand the literary interrelationship of the Gospels? Why is it necessary to postulate such a relationship at all?

5. What is canon criticism and how does it work? How was the canon of the New Testament formed in a nutshell, especially with respect to the Gospels?

5

LITERARY CRITICISM
OF THE GOSPELS

T HE TERM "LITERARY criticism" has been used to refer to just about any kind of analysis of a work of literature. Earlier in this century it was sometimes used synonymously with source criticism.[1] As we discussed in the previous chapter, from the late-1970s on, a number of scholars began calling for a paradigm shift in biblical studies away from detailed focus on the historical circumstances of an author and the historical processes involved in creating a text. Instead, the kind of literary criticism put forward as the primary model was an analysis of the text, as written, without reference to any information gleaned outside of the text concerning its formation or purposes. This shift was often linked to a shift in the hermeneutics of literature more generally, away from the conviction that meaning was determined by an author's intent. An intention, after all, is a mental process largely irrecoverable, especially when one is dealing with the texts of ancient authors from foreign cultures. Rather, meaning was said to reside in the texts themselves. Whatever an author may have desired, the only thing a reader could be expected to comprehend was the sense of the words that were actually written.[2]

---

[1] As documented in N. C. Habel, *Literary Criticism of the Old Testament* (Philadelphia: Fortress, 1971); and N. R. Petersen, *Literary Criticism for New Testament Critics* (Philadelphia: Fortress, 1978).

[2] See, classically, W. K. Wimsatt and M. C. Beardsley, "The Intentional Fallacy," in *The Verbal Icon*, ed. W. K. Wimsatt (Lexington: University of Kentucky Press, 1954), 2–18.

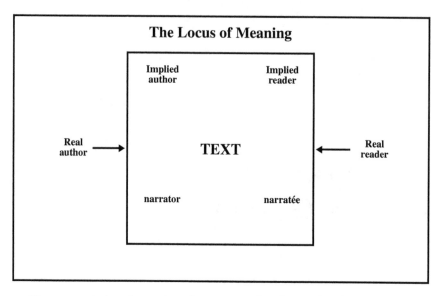

The more scholars focused on the process of understanding by the reader, the more a second phase in modern literary criticism emerged: reader-oriented theories of meaning. It became commonplace to argue that meaning did not reside in either authorial intention or texts themselves but in readers. At the more conservative end of this spectrum, meaning was said to emerge from the product of the interaction between text and reader. The text, as well as the "interpretive communities" to which readers belonged, put definite constraints on interpretation. At the more radical end of the spectrum, meaning was believed to be almost entirely "in the eye of the beholder." Cleverness and consistency in interpretation overshadowed truth or correspondence to any external world of realities.[3]

We will briefly survey two phases of modern literary criticism—*formalism-structuralism* and *poststructuralism*—and sample ways in which each has been applied to the Gospels. Then we will discuss another branch of analysis of the finished form of any literary product—*genre criticism*—to try to determine what genre of literature the Gospels are. This will clarify our hermeneutical expectations of these documents—for example, what kind of history and theology to look for in them. In turn, it will set the stage for our more detailed analysis of the four Gospels individually and the life of Christ himself.

---

[3] For an excellent, thorough overview of author-, text- and reader-centered periods of hermeneutical emphases, see S. E. Porter, "Literary Approaches to the New Testament: From Formalism to Deconstruction and Back," in *Approaches to New Testament Study*, ed. S. E. Porter and D. Tombs (Sheffield: SAP, 1995), 77–128.

Formalist-Structuralist Methods

The Bible as Literature/Narrative Criticism

Early in the twentieth century, secular literary criticism developed what became known as "formalism" or "new criticism." Emerging particularly out of a study of poetry, formalism dispensed with the gathering of information about authors' historical circumstances and what they might be trying to teach about the world in which they lived. Instead, it encouraged a meticulous analysis of the poems themselves as works of art with integrity of their own. Today, in biblical circles, the discipline of narrative criticism often reasonably approximates the designs of formalism more generally.[4] From one perspective, the development is not new. With the historic separation of church and state in America, English classes in public schools have long studied "The Bible as Literature." To avoid promoting religion through this exercise, teachers often focused primarily on such literary characteristics of biblical narratives as plot, characterization, symbolism, point of view, figures of speech, and so forth. Certainly, one does not have to deny either the historicity or the theological significance of the Scriptures to recognize that they are filled with many of the artistic devices of great works of literature.

An application of this analysis of the "surface features" of a text to the Gospels can, in fact, prove quite instructive. Major programmatic works were penned in the United States by Jack Kingsbury, David Rhoads and Donald Michie, Robert Tannehill, and Alan Culpepper.[5] Among evangelicals, Leland Ryken, long-time English professor at Wheaton College, was especially prolific.[6] Following these scholars' lead, one may concentrate, for example, on *plot* and note that the Gospels are not disinterested biographies selecting a representative sample of everything Jesus did in every major stage of his life. Rather, they highlight those events that created a growing conflict with the Jewish leaders and ultimately led to his death. Individual stories, like the parables, also contain plots. Some are "comic," that is, they have a "happy" ending—for example, the good Samaritan. But many are "tragic," ending on a note of judgment—for example, the parable of the talents or pounds.[7] Because the climax of a story usually comes near its end, how these stories culminate helps us determine which elements in them are stressed most.

---

[4] See esp. M. A. Powell, *What Is Narrative Criticism?* (Minneapolis: Fortress, 1990); and J. L. Resseguie, *Narrative Criticism of the New Testament: An Introduction* (Grand Rapids: Baker, 2005).

[5] J. D. Kingsbury, *Matthew as Story*, rev. ed. (Philadelphia: Fortress, 1988); D. M. Rhoads, J. Dewey, and D. M. Michie, *An Introduction to the Narrative of a Gospel*, rev. ed. (Minneapolis: Fortress, 1999); R. C. Tannehill, *The Narrative Unity of Luke-Acts: A Literary Interpretation*, 2 vols. (Philadelphia and Minneapolis: Fortress, 1986–90).

[6] See esp. L. Ryken, *Words of Life: A Literary Introduction to the New Testament* (Grand Rapids: Baker, 1987); L. Ryken and T. Longman III, eds., *A Complete Literary Guide to the Bible* (Grand Rapids: Zondervan, 1993); and L. Ryken, P. Ryken and J. Wilhoit, *Ryken's Bible Handbook* (Wheaton: Tyndale, 2005).

[7] See esp. D. O. Via, Jr., *The Parables: Their Literary and Existential Dimension* (Philadelphia: Fortress, 1967). For an application to an entire Gospel, see G. L. Parsenios, "'No Longer in the World' (John 17:11): The Transformation of the Tragic in the Fourth Gospel," *HTR* 98 (2005): 1–21.

Characterization distinguishes, among other things, between "flat" and "round" characters. In Matthew in particular, the Jewish leaders are mostly flat—one-dimensional—and in this case are portrayed in an unrelentingly negative light. However, the Jewish crowds, like the disciples, are more round or complex, sometimes siding with Jesus, sometimes opposing him, and on occasions simply remaining confused. Matthew sees more hope for them than for Jesus' opponents, who remain implacably antagonistic. In John, Nicodemus approached Jesus as though he were an exceptional, positive model from within the Jerusalem leadership (John 3:1). Yet his increasing bewilderment and diminishing role as a dialogue partner with Jesus suggests that, at that stage in his life at least, he just did not understand (vv. 2–15).[8] This characterization is reinforced by John's use of symbolism—Nicodemus came by night (v. 2), but those who turn to God through Jesus do not love the darkness but come into the light (vv. 19–21).[9] In Luke, Herod Antipas appears as a foil to both Jesus and John the Baptist and enhances recognition of both the similarities and the differences between the two (both speaking prophetically, but one preaching an austere message of judgment that threatens Herod, with the other calling for celebration in light of the kingdom's arrival which Herod thinks he can ignore).[10] Indeed, even characters from other contexts who reappear in a given gospel can be analyzed with respect to the themes that they highlight or introduce. For example, Stan Harstine studies references to the life of Moses in the Gospel of John as a key to the development of the plot with reference to the growing recognition of Jesus' identity. Moses functions as "a historical anchor, a witness, and an authoritative figure," all supporting the Fourth Gospel's perspective on Jesus as the divine Messiah.[11]

Indeed, John's Gospel uses a greater amount of *symbolism* and *double-entendre* (double-meanings) than the other three Gospels. In that conversation with Nicodemus, Jesus told him that to enter the kingdom of God a person must be born *anōthen*. This Greek word can mean "from above" or "again," and most commentators suspect that John implied both concepts when he chose this term to translate Jesus' original Aramaic words. Also in the early chapters of John, Jesus tells Mary at Cana, "My hour has not yet come" (John 2:4). In the immediate context, this statement appears to mean simply, "I'm not quite ready yet to work the miracle you've requested." The expression turns up again (e.g., John 7:6), until eventually Jesus' "hour" does come (12:23), and it becomes clear that "hour" refers preemi-

---

[8] F. P. Cotterell, "The Nicodemus Conversation: A Fresh Appraisal," *ExpTim* 96 (1985): 237–42.

[9] On this topic more generally, see D. M. Rhoads and K. Syreeni, eds., *Characterization in the Gospels: Reconceiving Narrative Criticism* (Sheffield: SAP, 1999). For a good Gospel-wide application, cf. P. L. Danove, *The Rhetoric of the Characterization of God, Jesus, and Jesus' Disciples in the Gospel of Mark* (London and New York: T&T Clark, 2005). For a thorough treatment of symbolism in John, see D. A. Lee, *Flesh and Glory: Symbol, Gender, and Theology in the Gospel of John* (New York: Crossroad, 2002).

[10] Cf. J. A. Darr, *Herod the Fox: Audience Criticism and Lukan Characterization* (Sheffield: SAP, 1998). For a related work, building on Darr's approach to characterization, see G. Yamasaki, *John the Baptist in Life and Death: Audience-Oriented Criticism of Matthew's Narrative* (Sheffield: SAP, 1998).

[11] S. Harstine, *Moses as a Character in the Fourth Gospel* (London and New York: SAP, 2002).

nently to the time of his death and resurrection. Probably, John saw a hint of this meaning already in the Cana narrative in chapter 2.[12] Deliberate Johannine ambiguity illustrates both characterization and symbolism. Not just Nicodemus but a large number of the minor characters in John can be alternately viewed as both faithful and fickle, understanding and confused. As Colleen Conway explains, even though John "presents us with a dualistic world in which the lines are sharply drawn, especially by the main character Jesus" (see further below, p. 193), "it is also a world populated with characters who are rarely so distinctly drawn. Their presence comments on the dualism of the Gospel, undercuts it, and subverts it. In the process, the notion of faith is also transformed. It becomes less stable, but no less productive."[13]

This last example of symbolism leads directly to another literary device—*foreshadowing.* Well-crafted stories often leave clues for readers to help them anticipate what will come later. Matt 2:1–12 describes surprising opposition to the birth of the Messiah by Herod and his Jewish supporters in Jerusalem and surprising acceptance, even worship, by the Magi—pagan astrologers! By the end of his Gospel, Matthew makes it clear that Jesus is a king for all peoples (28:16–20) and that "the kingdom of God will be taken away from you [the Jewish leadership] and given to a people [Jesus' followers from any ethnic background] who will produce its fruit" (21:43). In both Matthew and Mark, John the Baptist plays the role of a forerunner to Christ, not only in his ministry but also in his death (Mark 6:14–29 pars.). Matthew makes this point in a particularly striking way by juxtaposing the description of Jesus' rejection in Nazareth with John's arrest, imprisonment, and beheading (Matt 13:53–58; 14:3–12), even though John was arrested before the major events of Jesus' ministry (see 14:1–2; cf. Luke 3:19–20).[14]

The *point of view* of a narrator may be limited to what is known by a particular character in the story or it may reflect "omniscience"—the perspective of someone who understands all the events with the insights of everyone in the narrative. Appropriately, the Gospel narrators are omniscient, in this technical sense, although the more theological omniscience of God stands behind them too. We recognize that the evangelists claim to present God's perspective on the events they describe. What they put forward as positive models we are to imitate; what they criticize we are to reject. They accept a supernatural worldview, the possibility of miracles, the existence of angels and demons; and they want us to follow

---

[12] See further W. Carter, *John: Storyteller, Interpreter, Evangelist* (Peabody: Hendrickson, 2006), 107–28. There is now an entire series of books on the four Gospels that has adopted this format, all worthy of careful study: W. Carter, *Matthew: Storyteller, Interpreter, Evangelist* (Peabody: Hendrickson, 2004); F. J. Moloney, *Mark: Storyteller, Interpreter, Evangelist* (Peabody: Hendrickson, 2004); and M. C. Parsons, *Luke: Storyteller, Interpreter, Evangelist* (Peabody: Hendrickson, 2007).

[13] C. M. Conway, "Speaking through Ambiguity: Minor Characters in the Fourth Gospel," *BI* 10 (2002): 340.

[14] For a sketch of how Mark's rhetoric foreshadows Jesus' death at numerous points in his Gospel, see B. J. Incigneri, *The Gospel to the Romans: The Setting and Rhetoric of Mark's Gospel* (Leiden and Boston: Brill, 2003).

suit.[15] A key symbol can also produce a central point of view. Luke frames both his Gospel and Acts with ministry in and around the Jerusalem temple (Luke 1–2, 23; Acts 2–5, 21). Couple this with a probable outline of his two-volume work (see below, p. 162), and one realizes that Jesus' (or his disciples') ministering in the temple forms a key portion of the literary heart of Luke's narrative. However much Luke sketches the progress of the Gospel from Jerusalem to the "ends of the earth" (Acts 1:8), he is not rejecting the Jews.

Narrative time can play a significant role in indicating what is important to an author. Years may speed by in a matter of a few pages, whereas brief incidents may be narrated at great length. All four Gospels, though Mark and John in particular, are dominated by their passion narratives. That is to say, time slows down considerably as one approaches the death of Jesus. Literary criticism reinforces what we know theologically from the later New Testament writings: the most important aspects of Jesus' life were his death and resurrection.[16] Narrative time can build suspense within an individual story as well. Why did Jesus delay leaving for Bethany when told that Lazarus was gravely ill (John 11:6)? No doubt it was because he knew what no one else around him did, that he was going to raise Lazarus from the grave (vv. 38–44). Indeed, John offers a foreshadowing of that miracle with Jesus' cryptic remarks in v. 4: "This sickness will not end in death. No, it is for God's glory."[17]

We noted that formalism began primarily as a method of studying poetry, a form of literature that often seems to have "a life of its own" apart from original authorial intent. It is interesting that the written form of the majority of Jesus' teaching is at least semi-poetic. Various studies have profitably analyzed the Semitic parallelism in which it is often couched, along with numerous figures of speech—hyperbole (rhetorical exaggeration), irony or satire, simile and metaphor, paradox, and riddle. We dare not interpret literally a passage that employs one of these devices, lest we maim ourselves (cf. Matt 5:29–30) or take up arms when we are not supposed to (cf. Luke 22:49–51 with vv. 35–38)![18]

Narrative criticism in modern biblical studies also goes one step beyond older formalism and distinguishes among the *real author* of a text, the *implied author* (the image the text discloses of the author apart from external historical information), and the *narrator* (the personality in the text that actually tells the story).

---

[15] For a book-length treatment of point of view in an individual Gospel, see J. L. Resseguie, *The Strange Gospel: Narrative Design and Point of View in John* (Leiden: Brill, 2001). Less technically and more generally, cf. idem., *Narrative Criticism of the New Testament*, 167–96.

[16] M. Kähler's famous expression from a century ago remains germane here: Mark can virtually be thought of as a "passion narrative with an extended introduction" (*The So-Called Historical Jesus and the Historic, Biblical Christ* [Philadelphia: Fortress, 1964], 80 [Germ. orig. 1892]).

[17] For a full-length study of the topic of narrative time in one entire Gospel, see B. D. Schildgen, *Crisis and Continuity: Time in the Gospel of Mark* (Sheffield: SAP, 1998).

[18] For a good, brief introduction, see R. H. Stein, *The Method and Message of Jesus' Teaching*, rev. ed. (Louisville: WJKP, 1994), 7–32. For an excellent, in-depth look at one specific category, see T. Thatcher, *Jesus the Riddler: The Power of Ambiguity in the Gospels* (Louisville and London: WJKP, 2006). For a more technical study, cf. J. G. van der Watt, *Family of the King: Dynamics of Metaphor in the Gospel according to John* (Leiden and Boston: Brill, 2000).

So, too, one may distinguish among the *authorial readers* (whom the text was first intended to address), the *implied readers* (the image the text discloses of the intended audience apart from external historical information), and the *narratées* (the people to whom the story is told within the story line itself). For those who accept the traditional claims of authorship for the four Gospels, these distinctions seem less significant than they do for others. For example, in Luke's Gospel a good case can be made that while the narratée is merely Theophilus (Luke 1:3), the authorial readers are an entire Christian church (see below, p. 170). For John, the implied author would appear to be the "beloved disciple"—a character who also participates in the narrative and is described this way on five different occasions within the text. The narrator seems to be a person who can affirm that the beloved disciple's testimony is true (21:24). Whether the real author was identical to either one of these characters is a matter of ongoing scholarly debate (see below, pp. 197–200).

Reading the Gospels as literature can prove quite valuable. We recognize their artistic merit—their ability to affect our emotions as well as our intellects—as they captivate, encourage, and convict us. We are more sensitive to what is more central and what is more peripheral in individual stories. We understand how they function to create multiple levels of meaning—main themes, subordinate motifs, and allusive echoes to other well-known traditions, not least in the Old Testament. But we run across pitfalls as well. Much literary criticism assumes that the Gospels are not necessarily historical, or else it plays down their theological or religious content.[19] However, these assumptions are not inherent in the method; a well-crafted piece of historical writing also promotes certain ideological concerns in an artistic and aesthetically pleasing way. Indeed, it has been argued that the features of a text which an approach to the Bible as literature stresses are often those aspects of the reading process that come most naturally to first-time Bible readers not yet taught to treat Scripture atomistically (e.g., verse by verse). Especially when we recall that most people in biblical times would have first *heard* a given book read orally in the gathered community of God's people straight from start to finish, such elements as plot, characterization, repetition, style, and climax loom larger in importance than details that could be discerned only by multiple readings and cross references.[20]

Structuralism

In the 1970s and 1980s a much more esoteric branch of formalist analysis developed that did not scrutinize the obvious surface features of a text but sought to disclose primordial "deep structures" allegedly inherent in all narratives. In biblical scholarship, this method was closely associated with Daniel Patte and a school

---

[19] See esp. D. A. Templeton, *The New Testament as True Fiction: Literature, Literary Criticism, Aesthetics* (Sheffield: SAP, 1999).

[20] Cf. P. J. Achtemeier, "*Omne verbum sonat*: The New Testament and the Oral Environment of Late Western Antiquity," *JBL* 109 (1990): 3–27; and J. Dewey, "Oral Methods for Structuring Narrative in Mark," *Interpretation* 43 (1989): 32–44.

of his associates at Vanderbilt University.[21] Today, however, it is all but defunct. Short-lived interest can probably be attributed to two major factors: a highly technical vocabulary and methodology that were tedious to master, combined with little exegetical "payoff" not discernible through other methods. For example, "actantial analysis" sought to plot six major "actants" (characters or objects) that potentially formed the plot of every narrative, however otherwise complex it may have been: a "sender" tries to communicate an "object" to a "receiver" by means of a "subject," who may be aided by a "helper" or hindered by an "opponent."

One might thus reduce the parable of the rich man and Lazarus to its basic constituent elements: God wants to bring happiness and ultimately Paradise to the rich man by means of the man's proper response to Lazarus according to the commands of Moses and the prophets, but the man's reception of this good is thwarted by his own self-indulgence and luxurious living.[22] An advantage of such analysis is that it turns attention away from potentially distracting but peripheral details and debates (the nature of the afterlife, the reason for Lazarus' salvation, whether or not the closing verse of the parable hints at Jesus' resurrection, etc.). It is unclear that one would have to have developed this particular grid to recognize the main emphases of the story. Still other far more complex developments of structuralism go well beyond the scope of this brief introduction.[23]

Poststructuralist Methods

Deconstruction

The French philosopher Jacques Derrida was undoubtedly the most prominent figure behind this most avant-garde of modern literary developments. Deconstruction believes that all language is inherently unstable, that all attempts to communicate successfully are hindered by features in language that work against the understanding of meaning, and that any attempt to interpret a text discloses more about the condition of the interpreter than any inherent significance of the text itself. Deconstructionists, therefore, revel in deriving conflicting meanings from a given text and playing them off against each other.[24]

Parables have formed the most frequent part of the Gospels used for such deconstruction because the more cryptic forms of literature naturally lend themselves to "polyvalent" (multiple and diverse) readings. Dominic Crossan applied deconstruc-

---

[21] See esp. D. Patte, *What Is Structural Exegesis?* (Philadelphia: Fortress, 1976); and idem., *Structural Exegesis: From Theory to Practice* (Philadelphia: Fortress, 1978).

[22] P. Perkins, *Hearing the Parables of Jesus* (New York: Paulist, 1981), 69.

[23] A particularly concise and readable survey of the major methods that have been applied to the New Testament appears in R. F. Collins, *Introduction to the New Testament* (Garden City: Doubleday, 1983), 231–71.

[24] See esp. J. Culler, *On Deconstruction: Theory and Criticism After Structuralism*, rev. ed. (Ithaca: Cornell, 2007). More succinctly, cf. A. K. M. Adam, *Introduction to Postmodern Biblical Criticism* (Minneapolis: Fortress, 1995), 27–43. For detailed, technical applications to the Gospels, see S. D. Moore, *Poststructuralism and the New Testament: Derrida and Foucault at the Foot of the Cross* (Minneapolis: Fortress, 1994); and P. C. Counet, *John: A Postmodern Gospel: Introduction to Deconstructive Exegesis Applied to the Fourth Gospel* (Leiden and Boston: Brill, 2000).

tion to the parable of the hidden treasure (Matt 13:44) and concluded that its theme of abandoning everything for the sake of the kingdom ultimately meant abandoning the parable and then abandoning abandonment![25] Stephen Moore began with the wordplay (in English!) between the names "Mark" and "Luke" and "mark" as the stroke of a letter on a piece of paper and "look" meaning to see. He then proceeded to discuss Mark and Luke in association with a wide range of modern literature as two Gospels that stress written marks and the art of seeing, respectively.[26]

Of course, no deconstructionist consistently employs this method. The method is inherently unstable. Sooner or later, all communicators want to be understood for their actual intentions as expressed through spoken and printed words! Not surprisingly, interest in deconstruction, like structuralism before it, has clearly waned (dare we say deconstructed?), though not yet to the same degree.[27] One of the reasons for its slower dissolution is that in many circles it has "morphed" into more general *postmodern* criticism, which is a broader hermeneutical movement not as readily refutable. Indeed, to the extent that postmodernism refers to the importance of human communities in shaping our interpretive perspectives, to the rejection of the typically negative modernist evaluation of religion and spirituality, or to an emphasis on the aesthetic, the symbolic or ancient traditions, we can embrace postmodern approaches as an advance over modernism. But to the extent that they require affirming an ideological pluralism which forbids evaluating varying interpretations as better or worse than others, or insisting on the impossibility of even approximating objectivity in interpretation, or the non-existence of any moral absolutes, or asserting that language determines all thought and meaning, then we must reject it as inconsistent with both Christianity and human experience.[28]

Reader-Response Criticism

A second poststructuralist development in literary criticism will likely have a longer life. "Reader-response" (or "reader-centered" or "audience-centered" or "reader-oriented") criticism describes a loose collection of approaches that are united by the common feature of focusing on the act of reading (or listening) in interpretation.[29]

---

[25] J. D. Crossan, *Finding Is the First Act: Trove Folktales and Jesus' Treasure Parables* (Philadelphia: Fortress, 1979).

[26] S. D. Moore, *Mark and Luke in Poststructuralist Perspective* (New Haven and London: Yale University Press, 1992).

[27] Good critiques appear in S. Walker, "Challenging Deconstruction: A Look at Persons, Texts and Hermeneutics," *Churchman* 111 (1997): 239–48; and C. G. Bartholomew, "Babel and Derrida: Postmodernism, Language and Biblical Interpretations," *TynBul* 49 (1998): 305–28.

[28] Cf. further D. A. Carson, *The Gagging of God: Christianity Confronts Pluralism* (Grand Rapids: Zondervan, 1996); and D. R. Groothuis, *Truth Decay: Defending Christianity against the Challenges of Postmodernism* (Downers Grove and Leicester: IVP, 2000).

[29] Most credit S. E. Fish with providing the greatest impetus for this movement. See esp. his *Self-Consuming Artifacts,* rev. ed. (Berkeley: University of California Press, 1972; Pittsburgh: Duquesne University Press, 1998); and idem., *Is There a Text in This Class?* (Cambridge, MA and London: Harvard University Press, 1980). For wide-ranging applications to Matthew, with particular reference to chaps. 1–2, see M. A. Powell, *Chasing the Eastern Star: Adventures in Biblical Reader-Response Criticism* (Louisville: WJKP, 2001).

Some highlight how meaning changes during the reading process—the more that we understand about the development of a plot, the more the earlier details in that plot take on new significance. Others study the effects of reading a work for the second or third time, after one already knows the ending or acquires additional information about the events described in the text. For example, does John deliberately intend his audience to reflect back on Jesus' words about eating his flesh and drinking his blood (John 6:54) in light of their later reading of his Farewell Discourse (chaps. 13–17) and their knowledge of the Last Supper from Christian tradition? Is Mark's cryptic reference to a young man who fled naked from the Garden of Gethsemane (Mark 14:51–52) a kind of literary signature and self-reference? Do Mark and Matthew both want their readers to think about how ridiculous the disciples' question about how to feed the four thousand appears (Mark 8:4; Matt 15:33) after they have already experienced the feeding of the five thousand?[30]

Reader-response criticism has also helpfully stressed how much meaning readers really do create and import into texts, like it or not, based on their backgrounds, presuppositions, and, in Christian circles, theological traditions. Undoubtedly, we must admit that some of this is inevitable in a fallen world. Because of our limited perspectives, we may never fully grasp the full or fully correct meaning inherent in a text. In addition, reader-oriented theories of interpretation go a long way toward explaining why people in different cultures or communities hear various acts of communication differently or reach varying conclusions about what they think a text means. Yet, we dare not choose simply to celebrate the diverse meanings we create and stop trying to overcome the distorting effects of "eisegesis"— reading in meanings that are foreign to a text. Unless we acknowledge limits to the interpretive process, anything can be made to mean anything and successful communication becomes impossible. Such a conclusion is incompatible with the Christian conviction that God in Jesus and in his Word has spoken to humanity in ways that it can truly understand.[31] It is better to recognize that fixed meaning is present in an author's intentions disclosed through the symbols that remain in a written text, however partial our ability to recover that meaning may be. Only the significance or application of that unchanging meaning may vary from one individual to another.[32] In a "postmodernist" as well as poststructuralist age, in

---

[30] For a thorough survey of reader-response criticism applied to the Gospels, see S. D. Moore, *Literary Criticism and the Gospels* (New Haven and London: Yale University Press, 1989), 71–170. From an evangelical perspective, cf. J. L. Resseguie, "Reader-Response Criticism and the Synoptic Gospels," *JAAR* 52 (1984): 307–24.

[31] For these and other critiques, see P. R. Noble, "Hermeneutics and Post-Modernism: Can We Have a Radical Reader-Response Theory?" *RelStud* 30 (1994): 419–36; 31 (1995): 1–22.

[32] This approach is particularly associated with E. D. Hirsch, *Validity in Interpretation* (New Haven: Yale University Press, 1967). Hirsch has been rightly criticized at points, but the gist of his thesis can stand, esp. as nuanced, with the help of speech-act theory, by A. C. Thiselton, *New Horizons in Hermeneutics* (Grand Rapids: Zondervan, 1992); and K. J. Vanhoozer, *Is There a Meaning in This Text?* (Grand Rapids: Zondervan, 1998).

which belief in absolute truth is rapidly vanishing, we neglect these important distinctions at great cost.[33]

The Genre of the Gospels

What, then, is encoded in the texts of Matthew, Mark, Luke, and John to help us know how to interpret them on the "macro-scale"? Are they unadorned works of history or biography? Are they extended myths? historical fiction? In short, how do we assess the genre or literary form of an entire "gospel"?

When one compares the Gospels with modern biographies, vast differences emerge. Mark and John tell us nothing of Jesus' birth, childhood, or young adulthood. They devote almost half of their narratives to the events of the last few weeks of his life. Matthew and Luke add a few details from Christ's birth, while Luke narrates one event that occurred when Jesus was twelve, but nothing else appears before his adult ministry. In all four Gospels, to varying degrees, material is arranged topically as well as chronologically. The words of Jesus are paraphrased, abridged, explained, and recombined in a variety of ways. Little wonder that many modern scholars have looked for something other than "history" or "biography" to characterize the Gospels' genre.

Some of the suggestions that have been made involve "aretalogies"—Greco-Roman accounts of the life of a "divine man" that embellish or exaggerate the feats of a famous hero or warrior of the past. Others look to Jewish precedents and liken the Gospels to novels, perhaps at least partly historical. Still others use language of the theater and label the Gospels as "comedies" or "tragedies." Closely related is the identification of a Gospel as an "epic narrative." Some focus on the extensive use of the Old Testament (or the use by later Gospels of earlier ones as if they were sacred Scripture equivalent to the Old Testament) and identify individual Gospels as "midrash" (see above, pp. 43–44). One similar proposal thinks that Mark was a Christianized version of Homer's *Iliad* or *Odyssey*. The particularly cryptic character of parts of Mark has suggested to a few that the whole Gospel genre be considered a "parable" or an "apocalypse," while John's divergence from the Synoptics has led others to label his work a "drama."[34]

These and related suggestions capture certain dimensions of the Gospels, but none accounts for a majority of their features. An increasing number of scholars, therefore, recognize that the list of traits setting the Gospels apart from modern biographies does not distinguish them nearly so much from ancient Greco-Roman biographies or Greek and Jewish "historiography" (history-writing). Ancient writers were more highly selective, ideological, and artistic in narrating the great events of their day or the lives of key individuals. They arranged material thematically as well as chronologically. They included epitomes of key teachings of

---

[33] See further J. C. Poirier, "Some Detracting Considerations for Reader-Response Theory," *CBQ* 62 (2000): 250–63; and J. Barton, "Thinking about Reader-Response Criticism," *ExpTim* 113 (2002): 147–51.

[34] The preceding two paragraphs are an abbreviation of material covered in Blomberg, *The Historical Reliability of the Gospels*, 299–302; see also the literature there cited.

major rabbis and philosophers. They focused disproportionately on the last days of people's lives and on how they died, believing this to be one of the best indicators of their true character. There are unique features of the Gospels, to be sure, generally related to the unique events they narrate and the distinctive nature of the person of Jesus of Nazareth. But this makes them no less historical or biographical by the conventions of their day. Perhaps it is best, then, to refer to the Gospels as *theological biographies*.[35]

Loveday Alexander finds the closest parallels to the Gospels, with respect to their genre, in Philo's *Life of Moses* and in the anonymous Jewish work known as *The Lives of the Prophets*, both probably written in the first half of the first century. She concludes that this "suggests at the very least that biographical narrative provided a point of cultural contact between Greek and Jew, a flexible and readily comprehensible framework that could be moulded without difficulty to reflect the theology and cultural values of a particular ethical tradition."[36] At the same time, Martin Hengel has insisted that Mark himself may well have applied the name "Gospel" to his document and that, as the other Gospel writers (or their compilers) followed suit, they were not primarily affirming that they were writing works of the same genre nor even that they were composing conventional biographies according to the standards of the day. Rather, in keeping with the meaning of gospel (Gk., *euangelion*) as "good news," originally used for the message and ministry of Jesus, the label was designed "to bear witness in their works to the *one* saving message of Jesus Christ."[37]

In any event, what is important to conclude at the end of this two-chapter survey of modern methods of Gospel study is that there is a legitimate place for *historical, theological, and literary* study of Matthew, Mark, Luke, and John. Despite attempts of various scholars to pit one method against the other two, all three actually go hand in hand. Indeed, unless we approach the Gospels expecting to find historically reliable information, theologically motivated emphases, and delightful literary artistry, we shall overlook important dimensions of the texts and run the risk of misinterpreting them as well.

Application

The three Synoptic versions of the parable of the wicked tenants are printed on the facing page. Look for ways that each of the critical methods discussed in the last two chapters might apply to this passage. One sample application of each method is given by way of illustration:

1. *Source Criticism*. Mark 12:6 finds the landlord predicting that the tenants will respect his son, whereas Luke 20:13 reads, "perhaps they will respect him."

---

[35] Cf. esp. R. A. Burridge, *What Are the Gospels? A Comparison with Graeco-Roman Biography* (Cambridge: CUP, 1992).

[36] L. Alexander, "What Is a Gospel?" in *The Cambridge Companion to the Gospels*, ed. S. C. Barton (Cambridge: CUP, 2006), 28.

[37] M. Hengel, *The Four Gospels and the One Gospel of Jesus Christ* (London: SCM; Harrisburg: Trinity, 2000), 49.

The Wicked Servants

Matthew 21:33-46, TNIV

"Listen to another parable: There was a landowner who planted a vineyard. He put a wall around it, dug a winepress in it and built a watchtower. Then he rented the vineyard to some farmers and moved to another place. When the harvest time approached, he sent his servants to the tenants to collect his fruit. The tenants seized his servants; they beat one, killed another, and stoned a third. Then he sent other servants to them, more than the first time, and the tenants treated them the same way. Last of all, he sent his son to them. 'They will respect my son,' he said. But when the tenants saw the son, they said to each other, 'This is the heir. Come, let's kill him and take his inheritance.' So they took him and threw him out of the vineyard and killed him. Therefore, when the owner of the vineyard comes, what will he do to those tenants?"

"He will bring those wretches to a wretched end," they replied, "and he will rent the vineyard to other tenants, who will give him his share of the crop at harvest time."

Jesus said to them, "Have you never read in the Scriptures:

'The stone the builders rejected has become the cornerstone;

the Lord has done this, and it is marvelous in our eyes'?

Therefore I tell you that the kingdom of God will be taken away from you and given to a people who will produce its fruit. Anyone who falls on this stone will be broken to pieces, but anyone on whom it falls will be crushed."

When the chief priests and the Pharisees heard Jesus' parables, they knew he was talking about them. They looked for a way to arrest him, but they were afraid of the crowd because the people held that he was a prophet.

Mark 12:1-12, TNIV

Jesus then began to speak to them in parables: "A man planted a vineyard. He put a wall around it, dug a pit for the winepress and built a watchtower. Then he rented the vineyard to some farmers and moved to another place. At harvest time he sent a servant to the tenants to collect from them some of the fruit of the vineyard. But they seized him, beat him and sent him away empty-handed. Then he sent another servant to them; they struck this man on the head and treated him shamefully. He sent still another, and that one they killed. He sent many others; some of them they beat, others they killed. He had one left to send, a son, whom he loved. He sent him last of all, saying, 'They will respect my son.' But the tenants said to one another, 'This is the heir. Come, let's kill him, and the inheritance will be ours.' So they took him and killed him, and threw him out of the vineyard. What then will the owner of the vineyard do? He will come and kill those tenants and give the vineyard to others. Haven't you read this passage of Scripture:

'The stone the builders rejected has become the cornerstone;

the Lord has done this, and it is marvelous in our eyes'?"

Then the chief priests, the teachers of the law and the elders looked for a way to arrest him because they knew he had spoken the parable against them. But they were afraid of the crowd; so they left him and went away.

Luke 20:9-19, TNIV

He went on to tell the people this parable: "A man planted a vineyard, rented it to some farmers and went away for a long time. At harvest time he sent a servant to the tenants so they would give him some of the fruit of the vineyard. But the tenants beat him and sent him away empty-handed. He sent another servant, but that one also they beat and treated shamefully and sent away empty-handed. He sent still a third, and they wounded him and threw him out. Then the owner of the vineyard said, 'What shall I do? I will send my son, whom I love; perhaps they will respect him.' But when the tenants saw him, they talked the matter over. 'This is the heir,' they said. 'Let's kill him, and the inheritance will be ours.' So they threw him out of the vineyard and killed him. What then will the owner of the vineyard do to them? He will come and kill those tenants and give the vineyard to others." When the people heard this, they said, "God forbid!"

Jesus looked directly at them and asked, "Then what is the meaning of that which is written:

'The stone the builders rejected has become the cornerstone'?

Everyone who falls on that stone will be broken to pieces, but anyone on whom it falls will be crushed."

The teachers of the law and the chief priests looked for a way to arrest him immediately, because they knew he had spoken this parable against them. But they were afraid of the people.

Once the landlord is viewed as God, Mark's wording is subject to the misunder-standing that God did not know that his son would be rejected. Luke takes pains to clarify this. It is inconceivable that Mark would introduce this problem, but it makes perfect sense that Luke would try to alleviate it. Thus Mark seems clearly prior to Luke at this point.

2. *Form Criticism.* Only Luke clearly organizes the missions of the various ser-vants into an enumerated, threefold sequence. In Luke 20:10, the master sends one servant, in verse 11 another, and in verse 12 "a third." The mistreatments of each also build toward the climax of the sending of the son who is killed. This stylistic streamlining was characteristic of ancient oral tradition and was likely a product of the frequent repetition of this story during the period before it was written down.

3. *Redaction Criticism.* Only Matthew includes the verse in which Jesus declares that the kingdom will be taken away from the wicked tenants and given to a nation that will produce appropriate fruit (Matt 21:43). Once we recognize that Matthew understands the tenants as the Jewish leaders and the new nation as the church, we can see why he, in particular, would wish to include this part of the story. Of all the evangelists, we discover that Matthew was the most interested in highlighting the Jewishness of Jesus' message and the break that Christianity underwent from Judaism.

4. *Canon Criticism.* When Jesus first spoke this parable, some of his listeners might have had an inkling that he was referring to himself as the son and perhaps even predicting his violent death. But they would not have known that he would be crucified outside the city walls of Jerusalem. Many commentators, however, speculate that Matthew and Luke (unlike Mark) worded their descriptions of the tenants taking the son and casting him out of the vineyard before killing him as an allusion to the subsequent fate of Jesus (Matt 21:39; Luke 20:15). From a canoni-cal perspective, this could be justified as bringing out the significance of Jesus' original story in light of later developments.

5. *Narrative Criticism.* Formal literary analysis will observe that this is a tragic parable. The climax in all three versions comes with the judgment pronounced against the Jewish leaders, followed by the observation that they realized Jesus had told this parable against them. The central thrust of judgment that permeates the parable must not be lost in any exposition or application of it.

6. *Structuralism.* The three main characters or groups of characters in this par-able are the landlord, the wicked tenants, and the new tenants. Corresponding to a frequently recurring structure in Jesus' parables elsewhere, these characters stand, respectively, for God, his enemies, and his true people. Perhaps other details are to be allegorized, but even if so, they remain subordinate to these three foci. If Jesus meant the son to stand for himself, he has kept the son in a subservient role to the other main characters. This may actually argue for the passage's authenticity because later Christian reflection would probably have given the son a more prominent role.

7. *Poststructuralism.* The differences among Matt 21:40–41, Mark 12:9, and Luke 20:15b–16 are striking. Who asked the question about what the owner would

do? Who gave the answer? And what was the answer? Historically, it is unlikely that Jesus posed the question to a diverse crowd and received one answer from everyone as if from a choir replying in unison. He would have had to repeat the answer he endorsed. Ironically, this traditional kind of "harmonization" is actually given greater credence by reader- (or listener-) response approaches that remind us that different people will interpret the same story quite differently. So it is not surprising that some were ready to condemn the tenants, while others were appalled at their fate.

For Further Study

As in chapter 4, the following list includes only those works that cover a reasonably broad sweep of the issues raised in this chapter. Several of the works listed for further study at the end of chapter 4 also include various dimensions of literary criticism.

Introductory

Adam, A. K. M. *What Is Postmodern Biblical Criticism?* Minneapolis: Fortress, 1995.

Marguerat, Daniel, and Yvan Bourquin, *How to Read Bible Stories: An Introduction to Narrative Criticism.* London: SCM, 1999.

Powell, Mark A. *What Is Narrative Criticism?* Minneapolis: Fortress, 1990.

Resseguie, James L. *Narrative Criticism of the New Testament: An Introduction.* Grand Rapids: Baker, 2005.

Ryken, Leland. *Words of Life: A Literary Introduction to the New Testament.* Grand Rapids: Baker, 1987.

Intermediate

Alter, Robert, and Frank Kermode, eds. *The Literary Guide to the Bible.* Cambridge, MA: Harvard University Press, 1987.

McKnight, Edgar V. *Post-modern Use of the Bible: The Emergence of Reader-Oriented Criticism.* Nashville: Abingdon, 1988; Eugene, OR: Wipf & Stock, 2005.

Ryken, Leland, and Tremper Longman III, eds. *A Complete Literary Guide to the Bible.* Grand Rapids: Zondervan, 1993.

Ryken, Leland, James C. Wilhoit, and Tremper Longman III, eds., *Dictionary of Biblical Imagery.* Downers Grove and Leicester: IVP, 1998.

Vanhoozer, Kevin J. *Is There a Meaning in This Text?* Grand Rapids: Zondervan, 1998.

Advanced

Frye, Northrop. *The Great Code: The Bible and Literature.* New York: Harcourt, Brace, Jovanovich, 1982.

Malbon, Elizabeth S., and Edgar V. McKnight, eds. *The New Literary Criticism and the New Testament.* Sheffield: JSOT, 1994.

Moore, Stephen D. *Literary Criticism and the Gospels.* New Haven and London: Yale University Press, 1989.

Seeley, David. *Deconstructing the New Testament.* Leiden: Brill, 1994.

Thiselton, Anthony C. *New Horizons in Hermeneutics.* Grand Rapids: Zondervan, 1992.

Bibliography

Minor, Mark. *Literary-Critical Approaches to the Bible: A Bibliographical Supplement.* Westport, CT: Greenwood, 1996.

Powell, Mark A., et al. *The Bible and Modern Literary Criticism: A Critical Assessment and Annotated Bibliography.* Westport, CT: Greenwood, 1992.

Questions for Review

1. For each subdiscipline treated under the larger rubric of literary criticism, describe the heart of what the method does. Then assess some of its strengths and weaknesses.
2. Choose several passages from the Gospels and discuss how each of the various branches of literary criticism might illuminate the text. Consider, for example, the parable of the prodigal son (Luke 15:11–32), Jesus' conversation with Nicodemus (John 3:1—5), or the end of Mark's Gospel (Mark 16:1–8).
3. Can you think of passages in the Gospels where literary criticism helps us recognize what is (or is not) to be stressed theologically?
4. How might the genre of the Gospels be best described? Why is this option preferable to others that have been suggested? What difference does it make for interpretation?

Part Three

Introduction to the Four Gospels

BIBLICAL SCHOLARS OFTEN use the word "introduction" in a fairly narrow, technical way to refer to the study of the circumstances surrounding the formation of a particular portion of Scripture. Typically, discussions proceed from a determination of the author and his circumstances (date, place of writing, audience) to a discussion of the theology and structure of his work. In the case of the Gospels, strictly speaking, all four works are anonymous. That is to say, there is no chapter or verse that gives the name of the author in any instance. The headings on the existing manuscripts are not likely original. Four scribes probably would not have independently decided to entitle their documents, "The Gospel according to X." These titles were most likely added when the fourfold Gospel collection first began to circulate, at least by the early second century, to distinguish one document from another. Although we must take these early claims about authorship seriously, we dare not elevate them to the level of inspired Scripture. Even less certainty surrounds issues of date, destination, and place of origin.

In light of the above information, we will invert the typical sequence of discussing introductory topics in the following four-chapter section. Structure and theology will be discussed first based on the data that are observable in the texts themselves. Then we will see if that information helps us narrow down the options on the more speculative considerations of setting and author.

6

THE GOSPEL OF MARK

Structure

A NCIENT MIDDLE EASTERN writers were not as bound by logical, linear thinking as modern Western ones are. The Gospels, like most documents of their day, would have been written to be read aloud. Many listeners might never see or know how to read a written copy, so writing had to include repetition for emphasis and rhetorical markers that would make connections between sections clear.[1] The modern commentator always runs the risk, therefore, of imposing too much structure or symmetry when trying to outline these books. A second pitfall assumes that ancient historians or biographers were consistently concerned to write in chronological sequence; they were not. Many modern outlines of the Gospels simply divide the material according to an assumed historical or geographical progression of the life and ministry of Christ. There are too many places, however, where it is clear that an evangelist grouped materials together not for chronological reasons, but because they contain the same literary "form" or because they share a similar theme or topic. The words "then" and "now" in English versions often translate Greek words (*tote, nun*) which, like their English counterparts, can mean "therefore" or "so," rather than "later" or "at the same time." Many times successive stories in the Gospels are simply connected by Greek words for "and" (*kai* or *de*). A comparison of parallels in a synopsis shows

---

[1] With respect to Mark, see esp. R. A. Horsley, J. A. Draper, and J. M. Foley, eds., *Performing the Gospel: Orality, Memory, and Mark* (Minneapolis: Fortress, 2006).

how often events are narrated in a different order from one Gospel to the next. Therefore, we are safest in not assuming any chronological connection between individual passages unless the writer uses a term that unambiguously requires such a connection or unless some other cause-and-effect relationship demands it.

There is fairly widespread agreement concerning the general structure of Mark, but considerable disagreement as to exactly where specific sections begin or end.[2] This suggests that several passages may have been designed as transitions or "seams," bringing one stage of the narrative to a close and introducing a new stage. Still, we observe that Mark's Gospel falls into two main sections. Most of the first eight chapters use action-packed narratives to focus on the powerful ministry of Jesus, particularly as he gathers disciples and amazes crowds with his mighty deeds.[3] Following Peter's confession of Jesus as the Christ on the road to Caesarea Philippi (8:27–30), Jesus abruptly begins teaching about his coming suffering and death. From there on, all events move inexorably toward the cross. This disproportionate amount of attention to the last events of Jesus' life reflects the centrality of the crucifixion in early Christian thought. It also prompted Martin Kähler, a century ago, to give one of the more famous descriptions of the form of the Gospels as passion narratives with extended introductions (recall above, p. 116, n. 16).

The first half of Mark frequently groups a series of stories of like form (healings, controversies, parables, etc.), with a particular emphasis on Jesus' miracles. There are also two literary seams in which Mark has just described significant opposition to Jesus, appears to bring a section to a close, and then starts afresh with Jesus withdrawing from hostility and calling or commissioning his disciples for further service in a new location (3:7; 6:6b). In the second half of Mark, events proceed much more chronologically, with more emphasis on Jesus' teachings. But the narrative again seems to move to new scenes at two key points—with Jesus' triumphal entry into Jerusalem, and when the fateful Passover was approaching that would claim his life (11:1; 14:1). From 11:1 on, as noted above (p. 116), narrative time slows down considerably. Additional thematic groupings lead us to propose an outline that, following an introduction, divides each half of Mark's Gospel into three main sections with three main subsections apiece.[4]

---

[2] For a thorough survey of approaches, see K. W. Larsen, "The Structure of Mark's Gospel: Current Proposals," *CBR* 3 (2004): 140–60.

[3] This sense of action is enhanced by Mark's forty-two uses of "immediately" (Gk. *euthus*), at times virtually equivalent to little more than "the next important thing I want to tell you is . . ." The word appears only seven times in Matthew, once in Luke, and three times in John. Mark also delights in using the "historical present"—present tense verbs for past tense action—particularly with verbs introducing Jesus' speech, for the sake of emphasis and vividness. See, e.g., Mark 1:12, 21, 40; 2:5, etc.

[4] A few of the section headings are adopted or adapted from E. Schweizer, *The Good News according to Mark* (Richmond: John Knox, 1970; London: SPCK, 1971), 7–10. V. Taylor (*The Gospel according to St. Mark* [London: Macmillan, 1952], 107–11) is particularly helpful in stressing the smaller groupings according to form. In general agreement with the overall structure discerned here, with slight modification at points, are R. A. Culpepper, *Mark* (Macon, GA: Smyth & Helwys, 2007), 35–38; R. J. Kernaghan, *Mark* (Downers Grove and Nottingham: IVP, 2007) 24–25; W. L. Lane, *The Gospel according to Mark* (Grand Rapids: Eerdmans, 1974; London: Marshall, Morgan & Scott,

I. Introduction: The Beginning of the Gospel (1:1–13)
II. The Ministry of the Christ (1:14–8:30)
    A. The Authority of Jesus and the Blindness of the Pharisees (1:14–3:6)
        1. Introduction (1:14–20)
        2. Healing Miracles (1:21–45)
        3. Controversy Stories (2:1–3:6)
    B. The Parables and Signs of Jesus and the Blindness of the World (3:7–6:6a)
        1. Discipleship and Opposition (3:7–35)
        2. Parables (4:1–34)
        3. More Dramatic Miracles (4:35–6:6a)
    C. Jesus' Ministry to Gentiles and the Blindness of the Disciples (6:6b–8:30)
        1. More Mission, Opposition, and Miracles (6:6b–56)
        2. Clean and Unclean: Withdrawal from Israel (7:1–8:21)
        3. Physical and Spiritual Eyesight (8:22–30)
III. The Passion of the Christ (8:31–16:8)
    A. Predictions of Death and the Meaning of Discipleship (8:31–10:52)
        1. Cross and Resurrection Foreshadowed (8:31–9:29)
        2. On True Servanthood (9:30–50)
        3. Ministry in Judea in Light of the Cross (10:1–52)
    B. Jesus and the Temple (11:1–13:37)
        1. Entry and Judgment (11:1–25)[5]
        2. Teaching and Debate (11:27–12:44)
        3. Prediction of Destruction and Christ's Return (13:1–37)
    C. The Climax of Jesus' Life (14:1–16:8)
        1. Preparation for Suffering (14:1–72)
        2. Crucifixion (15:1–47)
        3. Resurrection (16:1–8)

The most commonly proposed alternative to this kind of structure is one that elevates a section approximating to III. A. to a main section of the Gospel, on Jesus' traveling to Jerusalem. This creates an overall outline of four main sections, with the final section, on the passion, then containing just two subdivisions.[6]

It has also been frequently observed that the main contours of this outline correspond to early Christian preaching as reflected in Acts. For example, in Acts 10:36–41 Peter describes the good news (cf. Mark 1:1) as God anointing Jesus through the Spirit (cf. 1:10). Jesus then begins his ministry in Galilee, doing good and healing many (cf. 1:16–8:26), moves on to Jerusalem (cf. chaps. 10–14), and

---

1975), 29–32; and F. J. Moloney, *The Gospel of Mark: A Commentary* (Peabody: Hendrickson, 2002), 21.

   [5] Verse 26 is not in the oldest and most reliable manuscripts. If it were to be accepted, it would go with vv. 1–25.

   [6] So, e.g., R. T. France, *The Gospel of Mark* (Grand Rapids: Eerdmans; Carlisle: Paternoster, 2002), vii–viii; and J. Marcus, *Mark 1–8* (New York and London: Doubleday, 2000), 62–64.

climaxes his career with his death and resurrection (cf. chaps. 15–16). It may well be that Mark's Gospel is the narrative expansion of a common outline used by many in the early church to tell the story about Jesus.[7]

Theology

Views of Jesus

What was Mark trying to do by sharply juxtaposing Christ's "successes" and his "failures"? Why does half of this Gospel focus on his mighty deeds and half on his suffering and death? Presumably, the answer to this question is crucial for unlocking Mark's theological perspectives on the person and work of Jesus. A common modern suggestion (associated esp. with Theodore Weeden) was that early attempts to tell the story of Jesus in Greek and Roman circles focused on portraying him as a "divine man" (Gk. *theios anēr*), akin to the semi-legendary heroes of Greco-Roman history who were deified upon their deaths. Mark, however, viewed this as a one-sided account of Jesus. While appropriating the emphasis on Jesus the wonder-worker, he then substantially qualified it by highlighting the ignominy of Christ's death.[8] More recently, Robert Gundry has stood this argument on its head, insisting that Mark was tempering a traditional emphasis on Jesus' suffering and death with a more triumphalist stress on his glory. Gundry finds a powerful Jesus even in chapters 9–16, inasmuch as he consistently predicts his suffering and fate, demonstrating that he is in control of his own destiny and not a victim of circumstance.[9]

Both approaches, however, seem too one-sided.[10] A writer wanting to play down a distorted emphasis in one direction would probably not devote a full half of his book to reinforcing that position. More likely Mark is trying to keep two essential truths in balance: Jesus' glory and the centrality of the cross, both in Jesus' life and in the lives of his disciples (see esp. 8:31–9:1). Analogously, Ralph Martin refers to Mark's Gospel as the one that best *balances an emphasis on Jesus' divinity with his humanity*.[11] Parallel to this is Mark's balance on authority

---

[7] This view is particularly associated with C. H. Dodd, *The Apostolic Preaching and Its Developments* (London: Hodder & Stoughton, 1936), 54–56.

[8] T. J. Weeden, *Mark—Traditions in Conflict* (Philadelphia: Fortress, 1971). B. Blackburn (*Theios Anēr and the Markan Miracle Traditions* [Tübingen: Mohr, 1991]) has demonstrated that there was no one, uniform "divine man" concept for early Christians even to consider appropriating. Another influential treatment that pits Mark against tradition is that of W. H. Kelber (*The Oral and the Written Gospel* [Philadelphia: Fortress, 1983; Bloomington, IN: Indiana University Press, 1997]), who finds Mark criticizing the *ecclesiastical* interests of the original apostles and substantially altering the course of the Gospel tradition by committing it to *writing*. For a rebuttal of Kelber, however, see D. N. Peterson, *The Origins of Mark: The Markan Community in Current Debate* (Leiden and Boston: Brill, 2000).

[9] R. H. Gundry, *Mark: A Commentary on His Apology for the Cross* (Grand Rapids: Eerdmans, 1993).

[10] As with both contributions to the more recent debate between J. F. Williams, "Is Mark's Gospel an Apology for the Cross?" *BBR* 12 (2002): 97–122; and R. H. Gundry, "A Rejoinder to Joel F. Williams's 'Is Mark's Gospel an Apology for the Cross?'" *BBR* 12 (2002): 123–39.

[11] R. P. Martin, *Mark: Evangelist and Theologian* (Exeter: Paternoster, 1972; Grand Rapids: Zondervan, 1973).

and servanthood throughout both "halves of his Gospel.[12] These approaches seem best, although if Mark was trying to achieve this balance by correcting a previous imbalance, the climactic role of Jesus' death and the amount of attention Mark devotes to it compared to the other Gospels suggest that Weeden is more on target than Gundry. But even with all the focus on Jesus' death, Mark's main point is to stress Jesus' defeat of death by means of the crucifixion of God's Son.[13]

Mark's distinctive christological titles line up with this balance between Jesus' divinity and humanity. Although not used often, *Son of God* (or just *Son*) occurs at strategic places in the Gospel to highlight Jesus' exalted role. "Son of God" forms part of Mark's "headline" to the Gospel (1:1)[14] and recurs again as part of the Roman centurion's climactic confession at the time of Jesus' death (15:39). In between, the heavenly voice refers to Jesus as "Son" at both his baptism and his transfiguration (1:11; 9:7). Elsewhere the title occurs only on the lips of demons, reflecting their supernatural knowledge of Jesus' identity (3:11; 5:7).[15] As God's beloved Son, Jesus functions in Mark as the one who has been sent by God, acts for God, speaks on behalf of God, and is vindicated by God.[16]

The other title Mark introduces in his opening verse is *Christ* (Gk. equivalent to Hb.,"Messiah"). This title is not common either; it does not recur until Peter's dramatic confession in 8:29 (and then six times thereafter). But all of chapters 1–8 seem to build toward that confession, only to have Peter's expectation subsequently redefined. What *is* prominent is a motif that has often been called the *messianic secret*. More so in Mark than in any other Gospel, Jesus frequently commands people not to tell anyone about his identity. In 8:30 he abruptly silences Peter without any of the praise or promises so well known from Matthew's version (Matt 16:17–19). Insight into parables is not to be given to "outsiders" (Mark 4:10–12), demonic confessions are rebuked (1:25, 34; 3:12), and spectacular miracles are to be reported to no one (1:44; 5:18–19, 43; etc.). William Wrede first promoted an influential view that Mark created this motif to justify his conviction that Jesus was the divine Christ and Son of God, when in fact Jesus himself had made no such claims. In other words, by creating both the claims and the "cover-up," Mark could account for why earlier stages of Christianity had not believed in Jesus as Messiah, and yet Mark himself could still promote the notion.[17]

---

[12] N. F. Santos, *Slave of All: The Paradox of Authority and Servanthood in the Gospel of Mark* (London and New York: SAP, 2003).

[13] Strikingly foreshadowed by all the supplicants in Mark's Gospel who approach Jesus under the shadow of possible death due to disease or demonic activity and yet are healed. See P. G. Bolt, *Jesus' Defeat of Death: Persuading Mark's Early Readers* (Cambridge: CUP, 2003).

[14] One important early manuscript (along with several later ones) lacks this title in 1:1, but the majority of early texts and the majority of texts overall contain it, so it is probably what Mark originally wrote.

[15] See esp. J. D. Kingsbury, *The Christology of Mark's Gospel* (Philadelphia: Fortress, 1983).

[16] C. D. Smith, "'This Is My Beloved Son: Listen to Him': Theology and Christology in the Gospel of Mark," *HBT* 24 (2002): 53–86.

[17] W. Wrede, *The Messianic Secret* (London: J. Clarke, 1971 [Germ. orig. 1901]).

It is far more probable that Jesus did indeed believe himself to be the Christ but was very cautious about accepting the title or allowing premature enthusiasm to overwhelm his mission because popular christological expectation did not leave room for a *suffering* Messiah (see further below, pp. 476–77). After the crucifixion and resurrection, Christ's more glorious nature could be described without as much fear of misunderstanding (9:9).[18] For Mark, however, 10:45 may be the most important verse in the Gospel in summarizing his emphasis on Jesus' road to the cross: "For even the Son of Man did not come to be served, but to serve, and to give his life as a ransom for many." The term "ransom" calls to mind the redemption of slaves in the marketplace and highlights the need for Jesus to die a substitutionary, atoning death. Jesus' words over the cup at the Last Supper point in the same direction: "This is my blood of the covenant, which is poured out for many" (14:24). As with the theology behind the sacrificial rituals in the Jewish and Greco-Roman temples, Mark is convinced that Jesus' death will make possible the forgiveness of humanity's sins.[19] Although Mark never uses the exact expression, the concept of *suffering servant* (as in Isa 52:13–53:12) perhaps best encapsulates this very human side of Jesus' nature and mission.[20] In short, the Gospel of Mark is about why Jesus died.[21]

Other Distinctive Themes

Disciples and Discipleship. At first glance, Mark's portrayal of the disciples is as surprising as the messianic secret motif. Often in dramatic contrast with their responses in the other Gospels, we read in Mark of their frequent failure and misunderstanding. They do not grasp Jesus' parables (4:11–13, 33–34), their hearts are hardened, they have little faith, they are perplexed after crucial miracles (4:40; 6:51–52; 8:4, 14–21), and they are unable to fulfill Christ's commission to exorcise (9:14–29). As already noted, Peter is rebuked immediately after his confession for failing to leave room in it for a suffering Messiah (8:33). The account of the disciples' spiritual blindness is contrasted with two miracle stories about the literally blind receiving their sight (cf. 8:22–26 and 10:46–52 in context). Ultimately, Peter denies Jesus; Judas betrays him; and all flee (chaps. 14–15). We can even describe Mark's whole Gospel as a parable, confounding those who look only on a material level rather than a spiritual one. Yet even while they fail to understand, Jesus' disciples remain those who responded to his initial call (1:16–20; 2:13–14; 3:13–19), are given truths that outsiders are not (4:14–20; 7:17–23),

---

[18] For an anthology of approaches to the Messianic secret, see C. Tuckett, ed., *The Messianic Secret* (London: SPCK; Philadelphia: Fortress, 1983). Most persuasive of these is that of J. D. G. Dunn, "The Messianic Secret in Mark," 116–31.

[19] Cf. A. Y. Collins, "The Signification of Mark 10:45 among Gentile Christians," *HTR* 90 (1997): 371–82.

[20] Cf. J. R. Edwards, "The Servant of the Lord and the Gospel of Mark," in *Biblical Interpretation on Early Christian Gospels*, vol. 1: *The Gospel of Mark*, ed. T. R. Hatina (London and New York: T&T Clark, 2006), 49–63.

[21] M. D. Hooker, *The Gospel according to Saint Mark* (London: A & C Black; Peabody: Hendrickson, 1991), 22.

and receive special privileges and promises about the future (14:28; 16:7). Thus their ultimate role seems ambivalent.[22]

At first glance, the women followers appear to fare better than the inner circle of the twelve men. They exemplify tenacious faith (5:28, 34; 7:29), sacrifice (12:41–44), and love (14:3–9). They stay at the cross, watch to see where Jesus is buried, and go to the tomb to tend to the corpse after the Sabbath has passed (chaps. 15–16).[23] But the most probable end of the Gospel relativizes these successes as the women respond to the angelic announcement of the resurrection with trembling and bewilderment, fleeing from the tomb and saying nothing to anyone because of their fear (16:8).[24] Ultimately, Mark shows the inability of all people, including would-be disciples, to respond properly to God in this present age, apart from God's acting on their behalf.[25]

Imminent Eschatology. As the first Gospel written, Mark still preserves a lively hope in Christ's near return, whereas later Gospels at times reflect a sense of delay.[26] The climactic promise that "He is going ahead of you into Galilee" (16:7), coupled with the emphasis on Christ's earlier ministry there, has led some to see Galilee as the place of revelation for Mark and the promised location of Christ's return that his followers are to anticipate.[27] It is also noteworthy that, although Mark has fewer teachings of Jesus than the other three Gospels, the one extensive "sermon" that he preserves is Christ's eschatological discourse (chap. 13).[28] One plausible analysis of Mark's narrative flow sees the entire Gospel building towards and foreshadowing the structure of this major sermon.[29] The intertwining of demonic and human opposition throughout the Gospel can be summed up with the label "cosmic apocalyptic eschatology."[30]

The Message about Jesus as Good News. Mark may well have been the first Christian to use the word "gospel" (Gk. *euangelion*, "good news") as a term for the story about Jesus rather than for the message Jesus himself brought (though cf. Rom 1:1–4 for a possible antecedent). That is the way the TNIV interprets Mark 1:1 (taking "of" to mean "about"), and in several places Mark adds the term

---

[22] Cf. esp. E. Best, *Following Jesus: Discipleship in the Gospel of Mark* (Sheffield: JSOT, 1981); idem., *Disciples and Discipleship: Studies in the Gospel according to Mark* (Edinburgh: T&T Clark, 1986); and D. W. Geyer, *Fear, Anomaly, and Uncertainty in the Gospel of Mark* (Lanham, MD and London: Scarecrow Press, 2000).

[23] Cf. esp. Kinukawa, *Women and Jesus in Mark.*

[24] A. T. Lincoln, "The Promise and the Failure: Mark 16:7, 8," *JBL* 108 (1989): 288–90; S. Miller, *Women in Mark's Gospel* (London and New York: T&T Clark, 2004), 197.

[25] J. Hanson, "The Disciples in Mark's Gospel: Beyond the Pastoral/Polemical Debate," *HBT* 20 (1998): 146.

[26] This has been exaggerated by those who misinterpret texts like 9:1 and 13:30 (and Matt 10:23) as Christ's "mistaken" belief that he would return within his disciples' lifetimes. Cf. also Schweitzer, *Quest of the Historical Jesus,* 315–54, 478–87.

[27] This view is particularly associated with Marxsen, *Mark the Evangelist.*

[28] Though this is tempered somewhat by the observation that references to Jesus as a teacher are frequent. V. K. Robbins latches on to this dimension of Mark in a one-sided but otherwise helpful study of *Jesus the Teacher: A Socio-Rhetorical Interpretation of Mark* (Philadelphia: Fortress, 1984).

[29] T. J. Geddert, *Watchwords: Mark 13 in Markan Eschatology* (Sheffield: JSOT, 1989).

[30] Marcus, *Mark 1–8,* 73.

"gospel" in this same sense into his narrative (e.g., 8:35; 10:29). The word occurs seven times in Mark, four times in Matthew, and never in Luke or John. Mark's literary product then naturally was given the identical label.[31]

Isaiah's New Exodus. By not beginning with any information about Jesus' birth or childhood, Mark is able to jump right into the account of John the Baptist as messianic forerunner. As he does, he cites Isa 40:3 concerning the one calling in the desert to prepare a way for the Lord (Mark 1:3), a prophetic reuse of the Exodus motif of entering the promised land from the desert applied to the time after Israel's exile into Assyria and Babylon. In an influential and widely acclaimed study, Rikk Watts has drawn attention to numerous parallels between Mark's Gospel and Isaiah's new exodus motif, which suggest Mark is patterning his account of Jesus' life and death after this model. Most centrally, God is delivering his exiled people from the power of the foreign empire and their idols, by means of a journey in which he leads his people from their exile to Jerusalem, culminating in their arrival in Israel's holy city where God is gloriously enthroned. But the context of Mal 3:1, joined with Isa 40:3 in Mark's opening Old Testament citation (Mark 1:2) reminds the reader as well of God's coming to his temple in judgment against those who reject him. This theme, too, plays itself out with increasingly ominous results as Mark's Gospel unfolds.[32]

Circumstances

What occasion in the life of the early church most probably elicited a Gospel with the structure and theological distinctives of Mark?[33] The bulk of the external evidence (the testimony of the early Church Fathers) that has been preserved associates Mark's Gospel with Rome or "the regions of Italy" (see the Anti-Marcionite Prologue to Mark, Irenaeus [*Adv. Haer.* 3.1.2], and Clement of Alexandria [quoted by Eusebius *Hist. eccl.* 6.14.6–7]—all near AD 200). Chrysostom, on the other hand, writing closer to AD 400, ascribes Mark's writing to Egypt.[34] Eusebius

---

[31] Cf. further Martin, *New Testament Foundations*, vol. 1, 23–27; Hengel, *Four Gospels*, 61–65.

[32] R. E. Watts, *Isaiah's New Exodus and Mark* (Tübingen: Mohr Siebeck, 1997). Cf. also L. Perkins, "Kingdom, Messianic Authority and the Re-constitution of God's People—Tracing the Function of Exodus Material in Mark's Narrative," in *Biblical Interpretation*, ed. Hatina, vol. 1, 100–15.

[33] To varying degrees the contributors to R. Bauckham, ed., *The Gospels for All Christians: Rethinking the Gospel Audiences* (Grand Rapids and Cambridge: Eerdmans, 1998) have challenged the notion of an original Christian congregation or collection of congregations to which each Gospel was initially intended. They have certainly succeeded in showing that modern Gospel critics have often read far too much about the readers' probable circumstances out of the varying details of the four Gospels, but they have not established the improbability of the earliest Christian testimony about the origins of the Gospels. See C. L. Blomberg, "The Gospels for Specific Communities *and* All Christians," in *The Audience of the Gospels: The Origin and Function of the Gospels in Early Christianity*, ed. E. W. Klink III (London and New York: T&T Clark, forthcoming).

[34] So apparently also does a document that has come to be called the "Secret Gospel of Mark." In 1958, M. Smith allegedly discovered in the Mar Saba monastery near Jerusalem an ancient letter apparently by Clement of Alexandria, which quoted twenty lines of Greek from a supposedly secret Gospel that Mark wrote in Alexandria after penning his original Gospel. The three excerpts quoted involve Jesus resurrecting a young man, teaching a young man at night who comes to him wearing

(*Hist. eccl.* 2.15–16) and Epiphanius (*Pan.* 6.10) harmonize these data by explaining that Mark went to Egypt after writing the Gospel in Rome.

The Roman origin of the Gospel is thus clearly the better attested and fits well with the internal evidence of Mark's narrative. The negative portrait of the disciples prior to the formation of the church, along with Mark's emphasis on the way of the cross as the precursor to glory, suggests a concern *to reassure a struggling community that it too could eventually cope and that victory comes only through suffering.* Given the Jewish Christians' expulsion from Rome in AD 49, growing tensions within the community and with the government after their return in the mid-50s, and the Neronic persecution from AD 64–68, *Roman Christians would have formed an audience much in need of such comfort and encouragement.* In other words Mark's concerns may have been first of all pastoral in nature.[35]

Other evidence that would fit Mark's writing to Roman Christians includes the various Latinisms he uses without explanation (e.g., *quadrans* for "penny" in 12:42 and *praetorium* for "palace" in 15:16), his frequent explanation of Jewish concepts and terms (e.g., ritual handwashing and *corban* in 7:3–4, 11), the apparent combination of mostly lower-class with a few more upper-class concerns, the mixed ethnicity of the people with whom Jesus interacts, his repeated dealings with people in houses (cf. the Roman house churches), and the like.[36] However, since these data could be harmonized with many different settings, we dare not put too much weight on them.

The external evidence concerning the date of the Gospel seems divided. According to Eusebius, Clement declared:

> When Peter had preached the word publicly in Rome and announced the gospel by the Spirit, those present, of whom there were many, besought Mark, since for a long time he had followed him and remembered what had been said, to

---

only a linen cloth, and refusing to receive three women who come to him in Jericho. Smith published his "findings" in *Clement of Alexandria and a Secret Gospel of Mark* (Cambridge, MA: Harvard University Press, 1973). Over the years a few scholars came to believe that this could have been a version of Mark earlier than our canonical Gospel, while a number suspected Smith of planting a forged document since all that anyone was ever able to produce of it outside the monastery were photographs, and it mysteriously disappeared after 1976. Most, however, assumed that it was a genuine reference to another apocryphal, Gnostic Gospel that shed no additional light on the historical Jesus. Recently, two major studies have significantly advanced the case for deeming it a forgery. See S. C. Carlson, *The Gospel Hoax: Morton Smith's Invention of Secret Mark* (Waco: Baylor University Press, 2005); and P. Jeffrey, *The Secret Gospel of Mark Unveiled: Imagined Rituals of Sex, Death, and Madness in a Biblical Forgery* (New Haven and London: Yale University Press, 2006). On the other hand, S. G. Brown (*Mark's Other Gospel: Rethinking Morton Smith's Controversial Discovery* [Waterloo, ON: Wilfrid Laurier, 2005]) argues that Mark himself wrote a second, more esoteric edition of his Gospel after the canonical one, from which Clement has quoted.

[35] See esp. Incigneri, *The Gospel to the Romans*; and H. N. Roskam, *The Purpose of the Gospel of Mark in Its Historical and Social Context* (Leiden and Boston: Brill, 2004), without necessarily accepting their conclusions concerning a post-70 date.

[36] For details, see C. C. Black, "Was Mark a Roman Gospel?" *ExpTim* 105 (1993): 36–40; cf. Culpepper, *Mark*, 26–29. For the most compelling alternative proposals, see J. Marcus, "The Jewish War and the *Sitz im Leben* of Mark," *JBL* 111 (1992): 441–62 (supporting a Palestinian or Syrian provenance); and P. J. J. Botha, "The Historical Setting of Mark's Gospel: Problems and Possibilities," *JSNT* 51 (1993): 27–55 (there is simply too little evidence to know).

record his words. Mark did this, and communicated the gospel to those who made request of him. When Peter knew of it, he neither actively prevented nor encouraged the undertaking. (*Hist. eccl.* 6.14.6–7)

Irenaeus, on the other hand, can be interpreted as believing that Peter had already died when Mark wrote, as he maintains that after Peter's and Paul's "departure" (Gk. *exodos*), "Mark the disciple and interpreter of Peter also transmitted to us what he had written about what Peter had preached" (*Adv. Haer.* 3.1.38–41). Peter's "departure" may, however, refer to his leaving Rome (or some other location) to travel somewhere else prior to his death. It is also important to observe that Irenaeus claims only that the *transmission* of the Gospel occurred after Peter's death, not necessarily its *composition*.[37] But if Mark wrote during Peter's lifetime, and if the early church tradition can be trusted that Peter was martyred under Nero before AD 68, then Mark must have composed his Gospel at some still earlier date (perhaps 64–65, when Nero's persecution was beginning).[38]

One piece of internal evidence often said to contradict a pre-70 date involves Jesus' prophecy of the destruction of the temple in Mark 13:14–23—an alleged creation by the evangelist after AD 70. Three factors make such a creation improbable: (1) These verses form a very muted reference to the destruction of the temple, if indeed that is what they refer to at all. "20-20 hindsight" would surely have made the allusion more explicit. (2) Jesus commanded his followers to flee to the Judean hill country, but what actually occurred during the Jewish war was Christian flight to Pella in the Transjordan. (3) Only an unwarranted antisupernaturalism would deny to Jesus the powers of predictive prophecy. Plus, given the volatile days in which Jesus lived, even an uninspired person might have successfully predicted such sacrilege![39]

A fair number of scholars across a variety of theological traditions thus dates Mark to the mid to late 60s during Neronic persecution in Rome.[40] But a complicating factor intrudes at this point: we have already given reason for believing that Luke wrote later than and in partial dependence on Mark (see above, pp. 99-101). When we come to the introduction to Luke (below, p. 171), we will see that a plausible case can be made for dating his Gospel to about AD 62. This, therefore, would require Mark to have been written earlier still, though perhaps by only a year or two. Paul reached Rome in about AD 60, and Peter may well have too. He was there at least by 63 or 64, with Mark (1 Pet 5:13), according to the most com-

---

[37] See esp. Gundry, *Mark*, 1042–43.

[38] As noted above (p. 54, n. 79), C. Thiede resurrected the argument of J. O'Callaghan (originally published as "¿Pápiros neotestamentarios en la cueva 7 de Qumrán?" *Bib* 53 [1972]: 91–100) that a fragment of Mark 6:52–53 is to be found at Qumran, which, if true, would virtually guarantee a pre-70 date because the Essene community there vanished after the Jewish War. But, also as noted above, this identification is highly improbable.

[39] See now the highly nuanced version of this dating by J. S. Kloppenborg ("*Evocatio deorum* and the Date of Mark," *JBL* 124 [2005]: 419–50), who thinks Jesus himself made the prediction but that Mark did not write it down in this form until after the destruction of the temple demonstrated that God himself had left the temple, as it were, making Israel now vulnerable to her enemies.

[40] See esp. M. Hengel, *Studies in the Gospel of Mark* (London: SCM; Philadelphia: Fortress, 1985), 1–30.

mon dating of Peter's first epistle (on the assumption that it is authentic). Since Peter's whereabouts throughout the 50s are almost entirely unknown, there is no reason that Peter and/or Mark could not have come sooner.[41] If Mark's Gospel stems from the late 50s or early 60s, then its qualification of a theology of glory with a theology of the cross would not be as direct an antidote to widespread persecution as if Mark were writing a few years later. But it might be an attempt to rebut triumphalist attitudes that were challenging and discouraging Christians in Rome, much like the views promoted by the Judaizers who were unsettling the Corinthians in about 56 (see 2 Cor 10–13).[42] On the other hand, Luke may have been written after AD 70 (see below, p. 171), in which case the Neronic persecution could be the best *Sitz im Leben* for Mark's Gospel. A date of *somewhere in the 60s* is probably our safest guess, without trying to narrow things down any more than that.[43]

Authorship

All of the traditions already cited, indeed all that have been preserved from antiquity, support *John Mark, companion of Peter and Paul, as author* (see Acts 12:12, 25; 13:5, 13; 15:37; Col 4:10; 2 Tim 4:11; Phlm 24; 1 Pet 5:13). Mark is best known for his falling out with Paul, but Paul's greetings in the epistles demonstrate that they were later reconciled. Presumably a Judean and Jewish Christian, Mark was the person whose mother's home was one of the meeting places for the early church in Jerusalem (Acts 12:12), so the family may have been relatively well off. Those in the early centuries who held to Mark as author included Irenaeus, Tertullian, Clement of Alexandria, Origen, Jerome, and the Muratorian canon. These sources also consistently associated the information in Mark's Gospel with Peter's preaching.[44] But the oldest and most important testimony, from very early in the second century and recorded by Eusebius in the early 300s, is

---

[41] On the other hand, J. Wenham's attempt to date Mark to the mid-40s (*Redating Matthew, Mark and Luke* [Leicester and Downers Grove: IVP, 1992], 146–72, 230–38]) depends on seeing Luke written in the mid-50s (on the basis of equating "the brother who is praised by all the churches for his service to the gospel" in 2 Cor 8:18 with Luke and the "service" being the writing of Luke's Gospel) and on Peter's departure to "another place" in Acts 12:17 being a reference to Rome. But Wenham's interpretation of the former passage is highly speculative, and his interpretation of the latter, while plausible, is based only on fairly late church tradition.

[42] E. E. Ellis ("The Date and Provenance of Mark's Gospel," in *The Four Gospels 1992*, ed. F. van Segbroeck, *et al.*, vol. 2 [Leuven: Leuven University Press and Peeters, 1992], 801–15) makes a plausible case for stages of composition, with Petrine or Markan input throughout, culminating in a final product composed in Caesarea in the mid-50s and delivered to Rome in the mid-60s. For a date at the beginning of the 60s, see Gundry, *Mark*, 1043. Interestingly, Gundry's hypothesis that Mark tempers a theology of the cross with a theology of glory could fit equally well into this time frame, a further reminder that Mark keeps the two themes in balance and that all dates must be tentative.

[43] Among recent evangelical commentators, Edwards, (*Mark*, 90) opts for "about" AD 65; B. Witherington III (*The Gospel of Mark: A Socio-Rhetorical Commentary* [Grand Rapids and Cambridge: Eerdmans, 2001], 31) insists on the late 60s; and France (*Mark*, 38) cautiously affirms the early 60s.

[44] For a full catalog of what we know historically about Mark, along with much later legendary material, see C. C. Black, *Mark: Images of an Apostolic Interpreter* (Columbia: University of South Carolina Press, 1994; Minneapolis: Fortress, 2001).

that of Papias. Papias himself cites an elder named John, presumably the apostle, as having taught that

> Mark became Peter's interpreter and wrote accurately all that he remembered, not indeed, in order, of the things said or done by the Lord. For he had not heard the Lord, nor had he followed him, but later on, as I said, followed Peter, who used to give teaching as necessity demanded but not making, as it were, an arrangement of the Lord's oracles, so that Mark did nothing wrong in writing down single points as he remembered them. For to one thing he gave attention, to leave out nothing of what he had heard and to make no false statements in them. (*Hist. eccl.* 3.39.15)

On the assumption that "in order" means in chronological order, this testimony also corroborates our observations about the frequently thematic nature of Mark's outline. It further fits our earlier conclusions about redaction criticism, namely, that the evangelists were deliberate and highly selective in what they chose to include, without thereby falsifying the material that was included.[45] Justin Martyr, a generation later in the mid-second century, uses the noun from the same root as the verb for "remembered" (*apomnēmoneuō*) in Papias' testimony to refer to Mark's Gospel as based on Peter's "remembrances" or "memoirs" (*apomnēmoneumata*) in *Dial.* 106.3.

Many contemporary scholars nevertheless dispute the reliability of these traditions for several reasons, especially including: (1) The author could not have been Jewish because of the Latinisms, a lack of Jewish coloring, the explanation of Hebrew terms and customs, and allegedly confused topography (cf. Mark 7:31, which has Jesus traveling to Galilee and the Decapolis, southeast of Tyre, by means of Sidon to the north). (2) The author could not have been Mark, the companion of Paul, because the Gospel shows no contact with Pauline theology. (3) The material could not have come from Peter because of the disparaging way the author treats the disciples, including Peter. (4) The material could not have come from any single, primary witness of the life of Christ because of the complex history of tradition that source, form, and redaction critics have demonstrated for the Gospel.[46]

In response, however, we must note: (1) The Gentile coloring of the Gospel is sufficient to demonstrate a primarily Gentile audience for whom the book was designed to be intelligible, but it cannot prove that its author was non-Jewish. Given the Hellenization of Palestine and the plentiful travels and ministry outside of Israel by the first generation of Christian leaders, it is extremely difficult to pontificate as to what Mark could or could not have written. Mark 7:31 reflects a circuitous

---

[45] On Papias' credibility, see esp. R. H. Gundry, *The Old Is Better: New Testament Essays in Support of Traditional Interpretations* (Tübingen: Mohr Siebeck, 2005), 49–73. Cf. also Bauckham, *Jesus and the Eyewitnesses*, 202–39.

[46] Although Mark is typically viewed as the first Gospel written, so that we have no written sources of his with which to compare his final edition, plausible suggestions have been made about pre-Markan units of tradition: a passion narrative, a collection of controversy stories, another of parables, cycles of miracles, and so on. For a summary of such probable "raw materials," see Marcus, *Mark 1–8*, 57–59. And detailed studies of Markan style confidently dissect numerous passages, dividing them into Markan and pre-Markan wording. Cf. esp. E. J. Pryke, *Redactional Style in the Marcan Gospel,* rev. ed. (Cambridge: CUP, 2005).

itinerary to be sure, but this would have been natural for an itinerant preacher.[47] (2) An emphasis on the cross is, in fact, one of Paul's theological centerpieces (cf., e.g., 1 Cor 2:2).[48] (3) It is arguable that no one but Peter could have authorized so negative a treatment of the disciples, given how quickly the early church began to exalt them, and Peter in particular. He may have wanted to be more modest or to combat an inflated view of himself. (4) Dependence on Peter in places does not rule out Mark's use of numerous other sources, oral and/or written, nor does it preclude his having edited source material and imposed his own stylistic imprint on each passage. (5) Given that Mark was not one of the Twelve but a relatively obscure character with a mixed record of ministry during his lifetime, it is unlikely that anyone unfamiliar with the true author of this Gospel but desiring to credit it to an authoritative witness would have selected Mark as his man. Little of interpretive significance depends on whether or not Mark was the author, but modern objections scarcely outweigh the unanimous testimony of the early church.

For Further Study

Commentaries

Introductory

Cole, R. Alan. *The Gospel according to Mark*. Rev. ed. TNTC. Leicester: IVP; Grand Rapids: Eerdmans, 1989.
Dowd, Sharyn. *Reading Mark*. Reading NT. Macon: Smyth & Helwys, 2000.
Garland, David. *Mark*. NIVAC. Grand Rapids: Zondervan, 1996.
Hurtado, Larry. *Mark*. NIBC. Peabody: Hendrickson, 1989.
Kernaghan, Ronald J. *Mark*. IVPNTC. Downers Grove and Nottingham: IVP, 2007.

Intermediate

Boring, M. Eugene. *Mark: A Commentary*. NTL. Louisville and London: WJKP, 2006.
Culpepper, R. Alan. *Mark*. SHBC. Macon, GA: Smyth & Helwys, 2007.
Edwards, James R. *The Gospel according to Mark*. PNTC. Grand Rapids: Eerdmans; Leicester: Apollos, 2002.
Hooker, Morna D. *The Gospel according to Saint Mark*. BNTC. London: A & C Black; Peabody: Hendrickson, 1991.
Lane, William L. *The Gospel according to Mark*. NICNT. Grand Rapids: Eerdmans, 1974; London: Marshall, Morgan & Scott, 1975.
Marcus, Joel. *Mark 1–8*. AB. New York and London: Doubleday, 2000.
Witherington, Ben III. *The Gospel of Mark: A Socio-Rhetorical Commentary*. Grand Rapids and Cambridge, 2001.

---

[47] A. Y. Collins (*Mark* [Minneapolis: Fortress, 2007], 9) correctly understands Mark's description of Jesus' route "as the deliberate construction of a wide-ranging journey in a great arc, approximately 270 degrees of a rough circle."

[48] Indeed, J. Marcus ("Mark—Interpreter of Paul," *NTS* 46 [2000]: 473–87) has stressed how similar Mark's and Paul's theologies of the crucifixion and atonement are.

Advanced

Collins, Adela Y. *Mark*. Hermeneia. Minneapolis: Fortress, 2007.

Evans, Craig A. *Mark 8:27–16:20*. WBC. Nashville: Nelson, 2001.

France, R. T. *The Gospel of Mark* NIGTC. Grand Rapids: Eerdmans; Carlisle: Paternoster, 2002.

Guelich, Robert A. *Mark 1–8:26*. WBC. Dallas: Word, 1989.

Stein, Robert H. *Mark*. BECNT. Grand Rapids: Baker, 2008.

Other Key Studies of Markan Introduction or Theology More Generally

Best, Ernest. *Mark: The Gospel as Story*. Edinburgh: T&T Clark, 1983.

Blount, Brian K. *Go Preach: Mark's Kingdom Message and the Black Church Today*. Maryknoll: Orbis, 1998.

Broadhead, Edwin K. *Naming Jesus: Titular Christology in the Gospel of Mark*. Sheffield: SAP, 1999.

Driggers, Ira B. *Following God through Mark: Theological Tension in the Second Gospel*. Louisville and London: WJKP, 2007.

Harrington, Daniel J. *What Are They Saying about Mark?* New York: Paulist, 2004.

Henderson, Suzanne W. *Christology and Discipleship in the Gospel of Mark*. Cambridge: CUP, 2006.

Hengel, Martin. *Studies in the Gospel of Mark*. London: SCM; Philadelphia: Fortress, 1985.

Kealy, Séan P. *Mark's Gospel: A History of Its Interpretation from the Beginning until 1979*. New York: Paulist, 1982.

Martin, Ralph P. *Mark: Evangelist and Theologian*. Exeter: Paternoster, 1972; Grand Rapids: Zondervan, 1973.

Stock, Augustine. *The Method and Message of Mark*. Wilmington: Glazier, 1989.

Telford, William R., ed. *The Interpretation of Mark*. London: SPCK; Philadelphia: Fortress, 1985.

Tolbert, Mary A. *Sowing the Gospel: Mark's World in Literary-Historical Perspective*. Minneapolis: Fortress, 1989.

Bibliography

Mills, Watson E. *The Gospel of Mark*. Lewiston and Lampeter: Mellen Biblical Press, 2002.

Questions for Review

1. What is a plausible overall outline for the Gospel of Mark? That is, how many main sections may it be divided into and by what criteria? What theology may be inferred from this structure?

2. According to typical evangelical reconstructions, who wrote this Gospel, when, where, to whom, and under what circumstances (to the extent that this information may be reasonably inferred)?

3. What are several of the major theological distinctives of this Gospel?

4. Take a passage from a Gospel synopsis that appears in all three Synoptics, and identify the probable theological emphases of Mark. Consider both the "horizontal" and the "vertical" dimensions of redaction criticism.

5. Given the emphases and probable circumstances of Mark's Gospel, in what settings in contemporary Christian living might it be even more acutely relevant than the other Gospels?

7

The Gospel of Matthew

Structure

M ATTHEW IS CONSIDERABLY longer than Mark. Whereas Mark begins with the ministry of John the Baptist and the adult Jesus, Matthew prefaces his narrative with two chapters about Jesus' ancestry, conception, and infancy (chaps. 1–2). Whereas Mark ends abruptly without a formal resurrection appearance, Matthew has a full chapter about Jesus' return from the grave and his final commissioning of the disciples (chap. 28). Whereas Mark has very few sections of extended teaching by Jesus, Matthew has five large blocks of discourse material ("sermons"). The first and last of these span three chapters; the middle three comprise one chapter apiece (chaps. 5–7; 10; 13; 18; 23–25). In the second, third, and fifth of these, Mark has much shorter blocks of corresponding teaching; in the first and fourth, he has virtually no parallels at all.

That Matthew intends these five major sermons of Jesus to be viewed as unified discourses punctuating his historical narrative is clear from the recurring refrains with which he concludes each of them: "When Jesus had finished saying these things . . ." (7:28; 11:1; 13:53; 19:1; and 26:1—which adds "all" before "these things"). Almost a century ago, B. W. Bacon popularized the view that these five sermons were the key to Matthew's structure and that Matthew was creating a new Law or Pentateuch of sorts, with the five sermons corresponding to the five books

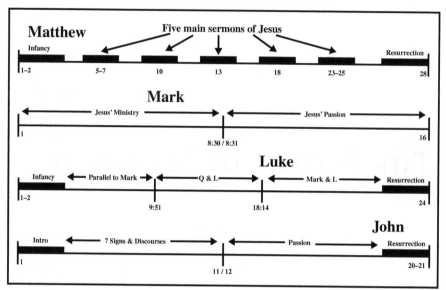

of Moses.[1] More recently, a second structural observation, promoted particularly by Jack Kingsbury, has been added to this. Twice, Matthew uses the identical formula, "From that time on Jesus began to . . ." (4:17; 16:21). Because the first appearance of this formula introduces the main phase of Jesus' adult ministry, beginning in Galilee, while the second corresponds to the pivot in Mark's Gospel that sets Christ on the road to the cross, it is probable that Matthew inserted these comments to divide his narrative into thirds: introduction, body, and extended conclusion or climax.[2] It is then common to find each of these subsections subdivided in terms of Matthew's alternating blocks of discourse and narrative.

One attractive way of outlining Matthew's Gospel is to see each pair of discourse-plus-narrative segments as highlighting a common theme. At the beginning of the "body" of the Gospel, Matthew stresses two main facets of Jesus' ministry—his preaching-teaching and his healing (4:23). The Sermon on the Mount clearly illustrates his authoritative teaching (cf. 7:29); chapters 8–9 go on to group together ten miracle stories (mostly healings) to demonstrate his authority in that realm too. Matthew 9:35 repeats the language of 4:23 very closely, confirming that chapters 5–9 belong together as a unified section. To this point in the narrative, Jesus has not experienced significant opposition, though the attitude expressed in 9:34 foreshadows what is to come. In his second sermon, however, Jesus calls and commissions the Twelve, preparing them to expect substantial

---

[1] B. W. Bacon, "The Five Books of Matthew against the Jews," *Expositor* 15 (1918): 56–66. See also the unpacking of this structure in his *Studies in Matthew* (New York: Henry Holt, 1930), 165–249.

[2] J. D. Kingsbury, *Matthew: Structure, Christology, Kingdom* (Philadelphia: Fortress, 1975). One of Kingsbury's students, D. R. Bauer, surveyed all the major structural options for Matthew's Gospel and refined his teacher's approach still further (*The Structure of Matthew's Gospel* [Sheffield: Almond, 1989]).

hostility (chap. 10). In the next two chapters of narrative, Jesus and his followers begin to experience that animosity (11:20–24; 12:1–14, 22–49).

Chapter 13 has long been seen as a turning point in Matthew's Gospel. Unlike Mark's chapter of parables (chap. 4), Matthew's divides evenly into one half addressed to the crowds in public and one half to the disciples in private (13:1–35; 13:36–52). Increasingly, Jesus is sifting his listeners into "outsiders" and "insiders." This progressive polarization is repeated in his subsequent ministry as his rejection among the Jews increasingly gives way to acceptance among the Gentiles and teachings that go beyond the bounds of Jewish convention or territory (13:53–14:36; 15:1–16:20). In the conclusion to the Gospel, the sequence of narrative and discourse is reversed. Matthew 16:21–17:27 finds Jesus repeatedly clarifying the implications of discipleship, and the sermon in chapter 18, delivered exclusively to the disciples, lays the foundation for the fledgling church. Matthew 19:1–25:46 is comprised of small and large blocks of teaching that increasingly warn about God's judgment on unbelief, particularly in Israel. The final chapters describing Jesus' passion, death, and resurrection balance the opening chapters of introduction. Putting this all together, we may propose an outline along the following lines:[3]

I. Introduction to Jesus' Ministry (1:1–4:16)
   A. Jesus' Origin (1:1–2:23)
   B. Jesus' Preparation for Ministry (3:1–4:16)
II. The Development of Jesus' Ministry (4:17–16:20)
   A. Jesus' Authority in Preaching and Healing (4:17–9:35)
      1. Introduction (4:17–25)
      2. Paradigmatic Preaching: The Sermon on the Mount (5:1–7:29)
      3. Paradigmatic Healing (8:1–9:35)
   B. Rising Opposition to Jesus' Mission (9:36–12:50)
      1. Opposition Predicted for the Disciples' Mission (9:36–10:42)
      2. Opposition Experienced in Jesus' Mission (11:1–12:50)
   C. Progressive Polarization of Response to Jesus (13:1–16:20)
      1. The Polarization Explained: Kingdom Parables (13:1–52)
      2. The Polarization Enacted: From Jew to Gentile (13:53–16:20)
III. The Climax of Jesus' Ministry (16:21–28:20)
   A. Focus on Coming Death and Resurrection (16:21–18:35)
      1. Implications for Discipleship: Correcting Misunderstandings (16:21–17:27)
      2. Implications for the Church: Humility and Forgiveness (18:1–35)

---

[3] See further C. L. Blomberg, *Matthew* (Nashville: Broadman, 1992). Cf. C. S. Keener, *A Commentary on the Gospel of Matthew* (Grand Rapids and Cambridge: Eerdmans, 1999), 37. One can also discern a broadly chiastic structure in the book, at least with the five discourses, reinforcing chap. 13 as the central, polarizing segment. Jesus' teaching in parables divides the crowds and sets the stage for the shift from Jesus' focus on those who are outsiders to his movement to his concern to teach and nurture those committed to him. See esp. P. F. Ellis, *Matthew: His Mind and His Message* (Collegeville: Liturgical, 1974).

    B.   The Road to Jerusalem: Impending Judgment on Israel (19:1–25:46)
        1.   True Discipleship vs. Harsher Condemnation for the Jewish Leaders
            (19:1–22:46)
        2.   Judgment on the Temple but also on the Nations (23:1–25:46)
    C.   Jesus' Ultimate Destiny (26:1–28:20)
        1.   Passion and Crucifixion (26:1–27:66)
        2.   Resurrection (28:1–20)

Theology

Views of Jesus

Teacher. Already, it is clear that one of Matthew's distinctive portraits, at least over against Mark, is that Jesus is the consummate Teacher. Most scholars have not accepted Bacon's proposal regarding the sermons as five books of new Law, but many have seen as prominent the theme of Jesus as a new Lawgiver, or as a new Moses more generally.[4] Like Moses, Jesus has miracles surrounding his infancy, causes turmoil among the rulers of the land, survives when babies his age are massacred, and retraces the journey of the Exodus to and from Egypt (chaps. 1–2). He remains in the wilderness forty days and forty nights in preparation for his ministry and then gives his programmatic teaching from a mountain (chaps. 4–5). Indeed, mountains remain significant places of revelation throughout the Gospel, both in the paralleled story of the transfiguration (17:1–9) and in the unparalleled finale of the Great Commission (28:16–20).[5] It must be stressed, however, that Jesus' teaching is considerably different from pure "Law" for Matthew; it is a higher-order "righteousness" (5:20), which brings rest rather than a burden (11:28–30). Put another way, with Jesus' moral demands comes a new empowerment for obedience not previously available.[6]

Son of David, King, and Royal Messiah. One of the most distinctive titles for Jesus in Matthew is "Son of David." It occurs nine times, eight of which are unparalleled in any other Gospel. Elsewhere the term appears in Luke four times and in Mark three times, but it is absent from all other New Testament documents. The title fits Matthew's Jewish orientation (see below) and the conventional expectation of a Messiah from the house of David who would exercise regal functions. Thus Herod and his followers in Jerusalem fear a literal king who will usurp their power (2:1–12), and Pilate wonders if Jesus is "king of the Jews" (27:11). Interestingly, whereas the people in power who should have been able to recognize a true Messiah cannot, the individuals who address Jesus as "Son of David" are consistently the powerless ones in need of healing (9:27; 15:22;

---

[4] See esp. D. C. Allison, Jr., *The New Moses: A Matthean Typology* (Minneapolis: Fortress, 1993).

[5] Cf. T. L. Donaldson, *Jesus on the Mountain* (Sheffield: SAP, 1985).

[6] The most thorough studies of Jesus as teacher in Matthew are Byrskog, *Jesus the Only Teacher*; and J. Y.-H. Yieh, *One Teacher: Jesus' Teaching Role in Matthew's Gospel Report* (Berlin and New York: de Gruyter, 2004). Both works highlight the uniquenesses of Jesus' role for Matthew and his communities, despite formal similarities to other influential Jewish or Greco-Roman teachers. Byrskog especially emphasizes the care with which Jesus' teaching would have been preserved.

20:30). Solomon, David's literal son, in Jewish tradition had come to be known as a miracle worker, while Isaiah's suffering servant was also said to heal people's diseases (Isa 53:4–6). Ezekiel 34:4 and 16 contrast the evil shepherds of exilic days with the coming messianic shepherd, including healing as a necessary part of the godly leader's ministry. Through any or all of these strands of thought, then, the messianic Son of David may well have been expected to be more of a healer than we have often realized.[7]

A Heightened Son of God? Mark 1:1 indicated that "Son of God" was an important title for Mark, but several scholars suggest that Matthew's use of the term even more closely approaches the full-fledged divinity that later creeds and confessions make explicit.[8] Again, key references frame Matthew's text (2:15; 26:63). The devil assumes Jesus to be God's Son at the temptation (4:3, 6). Only in Matthew do the disciples confess him as the Son of God after he walks on the water (14:33). Only in Matthew does Peter use this title as well as "Christ" in his climactic confession (16:16). In another framing device, Jesus is introduced as Immanuel (God with us) at his conception (1:23) and then promises his followers, "I am with you always," as part of the Gospel's closing words (28:20).[9]

Wisdom Incarnate? In 12:42 and 13:54, Jesus' wisdom is highlighted. In 11:19, John the Baptist and Jesus are said to vindicate God's wisdom. In 11:25–30, Jesus calls the lowly to himself and promises them rest, similar to the role of God's Wisdom personified in the intertestamental book of "wisdom literature" attributed to a Jesus, son of Sirach. These phenomena have suggested to some a distinctively Matthean concern to portray Jesus as God's Wisdom incarnate, building on the model of Proverbs 8–9.[10]

Lord. Perhaps the most important of Matthew's titles for Jesus is not one of his most distinctive. Numerous people call Jesus "Lord," and in many instances it need mean little more than "Master." But in several places the context suggests that Lord is the correct title for full-fledged disciples to use, particularly when they are in need of aid that only one who has divine power can supply (e.g., 8:2, 6,

---

[7] L. Novakovic, *Messiah, the Healer of the Sick: A Study of Jesus as the Son of David in the Gospel of Matthew* (Tübingen: Mohr Siebeck, 2005), 187. Cf. further K. Paffenroth, "Jesus as Anointed and Healing Son of David in the Gospel of Matthew," *Bib* 80 (1999): 547–54; and W. S. Baxter, "Healing and the 'Son of David': Matthew's Warrant," *NovT* 48 (2006): 36–50.

[8] Kingsbury, *Matthew*; idem., *Matthew as Story*; R. L. Mowery, "Son of God in Roman Imperial Titles and Matthew," *Bib* 83 (2002): 100–10.

[9] Indeed "God with us" can be seen as an integrating motif throughout Matthew. See D. D. Kupp, *Matthew's Emmanuel: Divine Presence and God's People in the First Gospel* (Cambridge: CUP, 1996).

[10] See esp. C. M. Deutsch, *Lady Wisdom, Jesus, and the Sages: Metaphor and Social Context in Matthew's Gospel* (Valley Forge, PA: Trinity, 1996). Tracing a "sapiential" or wisdom-centered emphasis throughout the entire Gospel is B. Witherington III, *Matthew* (Macon: Smyth & Helwys, 2006).

25; 9:28).[11] Then it would seem appropriate to speak of people "worshiping" the Lord even during his lifetime (cf. also 2:2, 8, 11; 14:33).[12]

Other Distinctive Themes

Particularism and Universalism in the Gospel Offer according to the Scriptures. One of the most striking distinctives, apparent already from the structure of Matthew's Gospel, is that Matthew is perhaps the most Jewish of all the Gospels, and yet at key places it also foreshadows the Gentile mission as clearly as any of the other three. Approximately twenty times Matthew cites a particular Scripture as fulfilled in the events of the life of Christ. Roughly half of these are unique to his Gospel. Five of them are found in the first two chapters as Matthew describes the events surrounding Christ's birth (see further below, pp. 233–34). The unparalleled quotations tend to follow the original Hebrew a bit more closely than the LXX, which is the version of choice for most of the paralleled citations.[13] Jesus' teaching can also be said to fulfill the whole of the Scriptures more generally (5:17–20). Although Jesus demands a greater "righteousness" than that of the Jewish leaders (v. 20),[14] the context of this claim (vv. 21–48) makes it clear that he is not just telling his followers to do a better job of keeping the Law. There are both continuities and discontinuities between the Old Testament and Jesus' teaching, but Christ's fulfillment of the Law, analogous to his fulfillment of Old Testament prophecies, suggests that he is the one to whom all of the Scriptures pointed and for whom they prepared. God's will can now be understood only by following Jesus and adhering to his teaching.[15] Or, in Schnackenburg's words, "Jesus proclaims a morality, made possible through God's boundless mercy, grounded in trust in his Father, and transcending legal prescriptions, that is directed to the love of God and reaches from love of siblings and love of neighbors all the way to love of enemies (5:43–48)."[16]

---

[11] Cf. further G. Bornkamm, "End-Expectation and Church in Matthew," in *Tradition and Interpretation in Matthew*, ed. Bornkamm, Barth and Held, 41–43.

[12] The verb that appears in these passages is *proskuneō*. It can mean to "fall down before" someone and/or to "worship" a person. The verb is a favorite of Matthew, appearing thirteen times compared to only twice in Mark and twice in Luke.

[13] On which, see esp. R. H. Gundry, *The Use of the Old Testament in St. Matthew's Gospel* (Leiden: Brill, 1967). The attempt by M. J. J. Menken (*Matthew's Bible: The Old Testament Text of the Evangelist* [Leuven and Dudley, MA: Leuven University Press and Peeters, 2004]) to attribute all of these divergent forms to variant editions of the LXX is unconvincing. For an up-to-date overview, see C. L. Blomberg, "Matthew," in *Commentary on the New Testament Use of the Old Testament*, ed. Carson and Beale, 1–109.

[14] "Righteousness," too, is a key theme for Matthew. See esp. B. Przybylski, *Righteousness in Matthew and His World of Thought* (Cambridge: CUP, 1980).

[15] R. Banks, "Matthew's Understanding of the Law," *JBL* 93 (1974): 226–42; D. J. Moo, "Jesus and the Authority of the Mosaic Law," *JSNT* 20 (1984): 3–49; R. Deines, "Not the Law but the Messiah: Law and Righteousness in the Gospel of Matthew—An Ongoing Debate," in *Built upon the Rock: Studies in the Gospel of Matthew*, ed. D. M. Gurtner and John Nolland (Grand Rapids and Cambridge: Eerdmans, 2008), 53–84.

[16] R. Schnackenburg, *The Gospel of Matthew* (Grand Rapids and Cambridge: Eerdmans, 2002), 10.

Three famous passages in Matthew have provoked much controversy as they all seem to limit Jesus' mission to only the Jews. He commands his followers to go nowhere among the Samaritans or Gentiles, seems to say that he will return before their ministry to the Jews is completed, and tells the Syrophoenician woman he was sent only to Israel (10:5–6, 23; 15:24). Matthew's Jewish flavor is further reinforced by his distinctive use of the term "kingdom of heaven," a typically Semitic circumlocution to avoid pronouncing the holy name of God.[17] This expression appears thirty-three times in Matthew but nowhere else in the New Testament, and parallel passages in Mark and Luke regularly have "kingdom of God" instead.

At the same time it is only in Matthew that Gentile Magi come and worship the Christ Child (2:1–12) or that a series of three parables is found predicting the demise of the current Jewish leadership (21:18–22:14). In the one parable of this cluster that also appears in Mark and Luke (the wicked tenants), Matthew alone includes Jesus' prediction that the kingdom would be "taken away from you and given to a people who will produce its fruit" (21:43). Only Matthew recounts Christ's "parable" of the sheep and the goats, with its emphasis on universal judgment of the world's peoples (25:31–46). Only Matthew includes Jesus' Great Commission, commanding the Twelve to make disciples of all people groups (Gk. *ethnē*, the same term used in chap. 25).

The best resolution of this apparent tension between Jewish particularism and multi-ethnic universalism sees Jesus' ministry unfolding in two stages. Before the cross and resurrection, Jews, as God's chosen people, were selected to hear Christ's message first. Inasmuch as many of them, particularly Israel's leadership, rejected the Gospel offer, Jesus' followers were to go out after his resurrection and proclaim his offer of salvation to everyone. Jesus' occasional contact with Gentiles during his lifetime foreshadowed this worldwide mission. Interestingly, Paul later recognized a priority of going to the Jews first, even during the church age, but he became the consummate apostle to the Gentiles (cf. his pattern of ministry throughout Acts; see e.g., 13:46; 18:6; 19:9). Romans 1:16 captures the sequence succinctly—the gospel "is the power of God for the salvation of everyone who believes: first for the Jew, then for the Gentile."[18] Like Paul, Matthew wishes to ground both stages very firmly in the Old Testament and Jewish expectation.

Discipleship and the Church. Although it has been overstated, there is nevertheless a perceptible difference between the fairly negative portrait of the disciples in Mark and a somewhat more positive picture of them in Matthew. In several key places where Mark emphasizes their lack of faith, Matthew focuses on the

---

[17] So almost all commentators. For a recent dissenting view, see R. Foster, "Why on Earth Use 'Kingdom of Heaven'? Matthew's Terminology Revisited," *NTS* 48 (2002): 487–99.

[18] Cf. A.-J. Levine, *The Social and Ethnic Dimensions of Matthean Social History* (Lewiston, ME: Edwin Mellen Press, 1988); Gene R. Smillie, "'Even the Dogs': Gentiles in the Gospel of Matthew," *JETS* 45 (2002): 73–97.

fledgling belief that they do have (e.g., Matt 8:26; 13:51; 14:33).[19] Matthew is also the only gospel ever to use the word "church" (Gk. *ekklēsia*)—three times in 16:18 and 18:17—or to include teaching about community discipline and forgiveness (18:15–35). Matthew's distinctive term for followers of Jesus is "little ones" (10:42; 18:6, 10, 14; 25:40), stressing their humble position before God. Matthew may reflect ongoing roles or even offices in the church to which he is writing with his distinctive references to wise men, prophets, and scribes (10:41; 13:52; 23:34). Matthew may further be concerned to oppose false teachers in his midst, who rely on their own "antinomian" (lawless) and "charismatic" claims to spiritual authority (cf. esp. 7:15–23).[20] Pentecostal scholar Blaine Charette concludes a study of the Spirit in this first Gospel with two areas in which he notes caution must be exercised—being wary of either devaluing the role of teaching or disconnecting the experience of the Spirit from Scriptural checks and balances.[21] Matthew would undoubtedly agree.

Conflict with Jewish Authorities. For a Gospel that is so thoroughly Jewish, it is surprising not only to discover Matthew's universalism but also to see how he portrays Jesus' encounters with the scribes, Pharisees, and Sadducees in so unrelentingly hostile a fashion. The woes of chapter 23 illustrate this in greatest detail, and 27:25 has been called by some the most anti-Semitic statement in the New Testament (as the crowds at Jesus' crucifixion cry out, "his blood is on us and on our children"). Matthew and Jesus refer to Jewish houses of worship as "their" synagogues (4:23; 9:35; 10:17; 12:9; 13:54), as if these men were not also Jewish. Matthew refers to the Sadducees in seven passages, always negatively, whereas they appear in all of the rest of the Gospels only twice. Yet, a text like 23:39 demonstrates that Matthew does not write off all Jews for all time. All Jesus' first followers remain Jewish, and missionary work must continue to include them and even give them priority (28:19, 10:23). Still, God's people are now being constituted as all those who follow Jesus in discipleship, not merely one chosen ethnic group.[22]

Circumstances

What situation in the life of the early church would give rise to such a bewildering combination of seemingly pro- and anti-Jewish positions? External evidence helps us to confirm our suspicion that Matthew wrote primarily to *Jewish Chris-*

---

[19] See, classically, Bornkamm, Barth and Held, *Tradition and Interpretation in Matthew*, 52–57. On discipleship more generally, see esp. M. J. Wilkins, *The Concept of Disciple in Matthew's Gospel: As Reflected in the Use of the Term Mathētēs* (Leiden: Brill, 1988). From a literary-critical perspective, cf. R. A. Edwards, *Matthew's Narrative Portrait of Disciples* (Harrisburg: Trinity, 1997).

[20] Particularly helpful on these topics is E. Schweizer, "Matthew's Church," in *The Interpretation of Matthew*, ed. G. N. Stanton (Edinburgh: T&T Clark, 1995), 149–77.

[21] B. Charette, *Restoring Presence: The Spirit in Matthew's Gospel* (Sheffield: SAP, 2000), 144–45.

[22] Cf. further D. A. Carson, "The Jewish Leaders in Matthew's Gospel: A Reappraisal," *JETS* 25 (1982): 161–74; J. Nolland, "Matthew and Anti-Semitism," in *Built upon the Rock*, ed. Gurtner and Nolland, 154–69.

tians. Most of the testimony states merely that Matthew wrote "to the Hebrews," although occasionally a place in Palestine is suggested (see Irenaeus, *Adv. Haer.* 3.1.1; Eusebius, *Hist. eccl.* 3.24.5–6; Jerome, *De virib. illustr.* 3). Modern scholars have often suggested Syria, especially its central city of Antioch,[23] which was up to one-seventh Jewish and a center of early Christian missionary effort (recall Acts 11:19–26, 13:1-3). Recently, a somewhat plausible case has been made for Sepphoris in Galilee.[24] At any rate, Jewish Christianity was always strongest in the eastern part of the empire.

More fruitful is discussion of the type of situation within Judaism that would have provoked this Gospel. Some have argued for a predominantly Gentile audience, and interpreted Matthew's Jewish emphasis as teaching Gentile Christians how to appropriate their Jewish heritage and Scriptures.[25] Others have remained content just to label the community "mixed." Most interpreters recognize Matthew's audience as a Jewish-Christian congregation or congregations *either on the verge of or just recovering from a substantial break from Judaism as a whole.* Graham Stanton helpfully suggests the concept of the church having broken from but still in vigorous debate with "the synagogue across the street."[26] Studies of "formative Judaism" point out how diverse Jewish thought and practice were before AD 70. After the destruction of the temple, however, only two primary branches emerged: rabbinic Judaism, carrying on to a certain degree the legacy of the Pharisees, and Christian Judaism, which would survive in large numbers only into the mid–second century. Needless to say, the tensions would have become quite high as each of these groups competed in the same communities to defend the claim that they alone were the true heirs to their religious heritage.[27] A situation like this very plausibly explains how Matthew could be so concerned to show Jesus as the fulfillment of all things Jewish and yet stress the rebellion of Israel's leaders, comparable in Matthew's mind to the hostility of the synagogue leadership in his day. Ulrich Luz explains succinctly: "The Gospel of Matthew is a response to the no of Israel's majority to Jesus. It is the attempt to come to terms with this no by

---

[23] Schnackenburg (*The Gospel of Matthew*, 5) goes so far as to declare, "All indications as to the place of Matthew's Gospel point to Antioch in Syria, at that time the third largest city in the Roman Empire (after Rome and Constantinople), a thriving trade center and a place of exchange between West and East."

[24] Esp. by A. M. Gale, *Redefining Ancient Borders: The Jewish Scribal Framework of Matthew's Gospel* (London and New York: T&T Clark, 2005).

[25] See esp. D. R. A. Hare's various works, although he has toned down how much he believes can be clearly inferred from the Gospel in his "How Jewish Is the Gospel of Matthew?" *CBQ* 61 (1999): 686–94.

[26] Several of his helpful studies on this topic are collected and augmented in G. N. Stanton, *A Gospel for a New People: Studies in Matthew,* rev. ed. (Edinburgh: T&T Clark, 1995).

[27] For three key writers who see Matthew's audience as still within Judaism, see J. A. Overman, *Matthew's Gospel and Formative Judaism: The Social World of the Matthean Community* (Minneapolis: Fortress, 1990); A. J. Saldarini, *Matthew's Christian-Jewish Community* (Chicago and London: University of Chicago Press, 1994); and D. C. Sim, *The Gospel of Matthew and Christian Judaism: The History and Social Setting of the Matthean Community* (Edinburgh: T&T Clark, 1998). These authors, however, fail to stress also the newness of Matthew's message as over against rabbinic Judaism. See D. A. Hagner, "Matthew: Apostate, Reformer, Revolutionary?" *NTS* 49 (2003): 193–209.

defining the community's position and to contribute to forming and preserving its identity in a situation of crisis and transition."[28] Paul Foster captures a probably correct balance by seeing Matthew as encouraging his largely Jewish Christian congregations actively to recruit more Gentile members.[29]

The common critical approach to Matthew has deduced from these observations that Matthew must have been written after AD 70. Some would insist that the Gospel must be dated to 85–100, after the so-called *birkath ha-minim* (see above, p. 26, n. 43).[30] The end of the first century seems to be the latest possible date because the Apostolic Fathers, beginning already at the turn of the century, were quoting Matthew on a regular basis. But, as we saw earlier, it is doubtful if one clear break ever occurred between Judaism and Christianity, and already in the events of Acts in the 40s and 50s, synagogues were expelling Paul and persecuting Jewish Christians who joined him. So it is not at all clear that Matthew must have been writing after 70.[31]

Scholars also frequently appeal to Matthew's versions of Jesus' predictions concerning the destruction of the temple. Matthew's Eschatological Discourse is little different from Mark's at this point (Matt 24:15–24; cf. Mark 13:14–23), but in the parable of the wedding banquet (Matt 22:1–14), only Matthew includes the details that the originally invited guests "seized his servants, mistreated them and killed them. The king was enraged. He sent his army and destroyed those murderers and burned their city" (22:6–7). This has struck many readers as a patently transparent reference to the Jewish rebellion against Rome, followed by the imperial burning and destruction of Jerusalem. For those who do not believe in the possibility of predictive prophecy, this passage ensures that Matthew was written after 70. Even for some who are not philosophically prejudiced in this way, the explicitness of detail convinces them that these words were written after the fact to make Jesus' original prophecy clearer. On the other hand, it is not true that most of Jerusalem was burned; it was primarily the temple that was set on fire. The imagery of a city's fiery destruction was frequently used in Jewish literature for warfare (cf., e.g., Judg 1:8, 1 Macc 5:28, Test. Jud. 5:1–5), so it need not be so specific a reference to the events of AD 70 at all.[32] In this event, its value for helping us date the Gospel disappears altogether.

One can become so eager to defend a pre-70 date, however, that one jumps on the bandwagon of inconclusive evidence. Carsten Thiede, for example, went against most of the scholarly world by dating the Magdalen papyrus of Matthew, known as

---

[28] U. Luz, *Matthew 1–7* (Minneapolis: Fortress, 2007), 55.

[29] P. Foster, *Community, Law and Mission in Matthew's Gospel* (Tübingen: Mohr Siebeck, 2004).

[30] E.g., H. W. Clarke, *The Gospel of Matthew and Its Readers: A Historical Introduction to the First Gospel* (Bloomington, IN: Indiana University Press, 2003), xxii–xxiii.

[31] Similarly, R. T. France, *The Gospel of Matthew* (Grand Rapids and Cambridge: Eerdmans, 2007), 15–19.

[32] Cf. J. A. T. Robinson, *Redating the New Testament* (London: SCM; Philadelphia: Westminster, 1976; Eugene, OR: Wipf & Stock, 2000), 19–21. J. Nolland (*The Gospel of Matthew* [Grand Rapids; Cambridge; Bletchley: Paternoster, 2005], 16) even declares "that the state of Mt. 24 excludes the possibility that Matthew wrote after A.D. 70."

𝔓[64] and housed in Oxford University, to the mid-first century. Yet a comparison of this manuscript with Gospel papyri housed in Barcelona and Paris makes it highly likely that all three documents formed a codex (book) from about AD 200.[33]

The external testimony of the early Fathers may prove more helpful at this point. Irenaeus (again in *Adv. Haer.* 3.1.1), endorsed by Eusebius (*Hist. eccl.* 5.8.2), believed that Matthew wrote "while Peter and Paul were preaching the gospel and founding the church in Rome," a reference that most naturally fits a date within the 60s. This could mesh with our conclusion concerning the Synoptic problem that Matthew relies in part on Mark (though Irenaeus himself thought Matthew wrote before Mark; see below). If Mark was written in the early to mid-60s and a copy soon fell into the hands of Matthew, he could have penned his Gospel shortly thereafter. Of course, those who find compelling internal evidence to place this Gospel after 70 will not imagine one early Church Father's testimony sufficient to challenge it.[34]

Various data within Matthew's Gospel might also support an earlier dating.[35] Why would only Matthew include references to the temple tax (17:24–27), offerings (5:23–24) and ritual (23:16–22), or to Sabbath-keeping in Judea (24:20) in an era (after 70) in which none of these was practiced any longer? Why would he stress Jesus' antagonism against the Sadducees in an age in which they had died out? One answer, of course, is that these things happened that way during Jesus' lifetime. But given the evangelists' consistent pattern of selecting episodes from Jesus' life that were theologically meaningful for their communities, one wonders if these data are not indirect pointers to a pre-70 date. The evidence is finely balanced, but we believe there is a slight weight in favor of opting for *a date in the 60s, sometime after the composition of Mark.*

Authorship

A generation or more ago, many critics believed "Matthew" was a Gentile writing for Gentiles. The dominant Jewish orientation of the Gospel coupled with the above survey of the probable circumstances of its composition, however, lead a majority today to conclude that the author was a Jewish Christian.[36] Tradition, of course, beginning with the superscription placed on early copies of this document, attributes the Gospel to *Matthew, also called Levi, a converted tax collector and one of Jesus' twelve apostles* (cf. Matt 10:3; 9:9–13; Mark 2:14–17). The most important early external evidence is again attributed to Papias, quoted by Eusebius (*Hist. eccl.*

---

[33] Cf. Thiede, *Rekindling the Word*, 20–32; with Stanton, *Gospel Truth?* 11–19.

[34] See, e.g., A. M. O'Leary, *Matthew's Judaization of Mark: Examined in the Context of the Use of Sources in Graeco-Roman Antiquity* (London and New York: T&T Clark, 2006), 102–7.

[35] See esp. R. H. Gundry, *Matthew: A Commentary on His Handbook for a Mixed Church under Persecution,* rev. ed. (Grand Rapids: Eerdmans, 1994), 599–609.

[36] For comprehensive detail of the options, and for advocates of the various positions on this issue and on the other introductory concerns surveyed in this chapter, see W. D. Davies and D. C. Allison, Jr., *A Critical and Exegetical Commentary on the Gospel according to Saint Matthew*, vol. 1 (Edinburgh: T&T Clark, 1988), 1–148.

3.39.16). There are several possible ways to translate different words in Papias' testimony, as reflected by the bracketed expressions in the following quote: "Matthew composed [compiled] his Gospel [sayings] in the Hebrew [Aramaic] language [dialect, style], and everyone translated [interpreted] as they were able."

This testimony allows for several variables: (1) Matthew could have functioned as a conservative editor or he could have composed material more creatively. (2) Matthew may have written what we know as his Gospel or he may have collected a group of Jesus' sayings together that formed the nucleus of a later full-fledged Gospel. (3) Matthew could have written in either Aramaic or Hebrew. (4) Others after Matthew might have translated his work into the Greek we now have, or Matthew might have translated the work himself with others later debating its interpretation.[37]

Perhaps the most significant of these variables is (2). The Greek word *logia* in Papias's remarks is a term that normally refers to "sayings" or "oracles" and is not naturally attached to an entire narrative Gospel. Some assume that Papias was referring to a whole Gospel because in his earlier testimony about Mark he had used the term there also. A careful reading of that text suggests that the logia refer back to Jesus' "oracles" (i.e., teachings) that Peter gave "as necessity demanded," even though Papias recognizes Mark wrote both about "the things said or done by the Lord."[38] We should then consider the possibility that what Matthew first wrote down in Hebrew was something along the lines of the reconstructed Q source. Indeed, although it goes beyond anything we can demonstrate, it has been plausibly suggested that this "first draft" of Matthew was what scholars call Q.[39] Then either Matthew himself or some other Greek-speaking Christian would have later incorporated into this first draft elements of Mark along with more distinctive traditions ("M") to create the Greek version of Matthew we now possess.[40]

The truthfulness of Papias's testimony, whatever the *logia* refer to, remains in doubt, however, so long as no ancient copy of any portion of Matthew *in Hebrew* is discovered. Yet the testimony of early Church Fathers that Matthew wrote something in Hebrew, often allegedly prior to Mark, is widespread and persistent (cf. esp. Irenaeus, *Adv. Haer.* 3.1.1; Eusebius, *Hist. eccl.* 5.10.3). In addition,

[37] Gundry, in the first edition of his commentary (entitled *Matthew: A Commentary on His Literary and Theological Art* [1982]) caused quite a stir in evangelical circles by arguing in detail that Papias refers to a Hebraic "style" of writing and that the style is one of "midrash," in which Matthew embellished his sources (Mark and Q) with fanciful, unhistorical, but theologically instructive detail, much like certain intertestamental sources treated Scripture. The full-blown theory was accepted by almost no subsequent writers, inside or outside evangelicalism, and was well-critiqued, whatever elements of truth it may contain here or there. Gundry, in turn, responded to his critics in the newer edition on pp. xi–xxx.

[38] See also M. Mosse, *The Three Gospels: New Testament History Introduced by the Synoptic Problem* (Milton Keynes and Colorado Springs: Paternoster, 2007), 119–20.

[39] T. W. Manson, *The Sayings of Jesus* (London: SCM, 1949; Grand Rapids: Eerdmans, 1979), 15–20; Black, "The Use of Rhetorical Terminology in Papias on Mark and Matthew," 31–41; Hagner, *Matthew 1–13*, xlvi.

[40] Witherington (*Matthew*, 5) suspects the special Matthean material goes back to Matthew but not the final edition of Matthew in the form in which we know it.

one fourteenth-century Hebrew manuscript of Matthew shows some evidence of being not just a translation of our canonical Greek text but reflecting certain independent renderings of an older Hebrew tradition. It is not inconceivable that it preserves a few traces of what Matthew originally wrote.[41]

It is also objected that Matthew does not read like a literal Greek translation from an underlying Hebrew text. But Matthew's "Q" passages regularly show signs of careful Semitic parallelism; Matthew is not without his Semitisms; and we need not argue that Matthew (or whoever) translated literally. Where we know that ancient sources have been translated from Hebrew into Greek (e.g., with some of Josephus's writings), there are also clear signs that the translator at times rendered his text freely and paraphrastically. What is more, as we have seen already in our discussion of Mark, it is difficult to claim that the Jewish Matthew, especially if he were a tax collector who needed to be literate and well conversant with the Gentiles for whom he worked, could not have produced a document based on prior Hebrew and Greek sources in reasonably good Greek style.

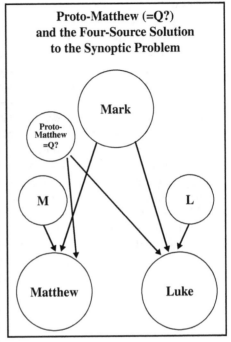

Proto-Matthew (=Q?) and the Four-Source Solution to the Synoptic Problem

There are other objections that critics raise to Matthew as author of this Gospel. The most important include (a) the anti-Jewishness already noted; (b) theological incompatibility with other Jewish-Christian sources; (c) the possibility that 13:52 is a self-reference to the author as a Christian "scribe," not a tax collector;[42] (d) the improbability of Matthew living beyond AD 85; and (e) the unlikelihood of an apostle borrowing from a non-apostolic author like Mark. Of these, only (e) proves at all significant.

Response to each of these charges includes: (1) If many scholars can agree that a Jew wrote this book in a situation of tension and polemic with non-Christian

---

[41] G. Howard, *The Gospel of Matthew according to a Primitive Hebrew Text* (Macon: Mercer University Press; Leuven: Peeters, 1987); idem., *The Hebrew Gospel of Matthew* (Macon: Mercer University Press, 1995). But, for a significant challenge to this view, see W. R. Petersen, "The *Vorlage* of Shem-Tob's Hebrew Matthew," *NTS* 44 (1998): 490–512.

[42] See esp. O. L. Cope, *Matthew: A Scribe Trained for the Kingdom of Heaven* (Washington: Catholic Biblical Association of America, 1976). L. M. Wills ("Scribal Methods in Matthew and *Mishnah Abot*," *CBQ* 63 [2001]: 241–57) stresses the stylistic similarities between Matthew and the "Sayings of the Fathers" tractate of the Mishnah, esp. with respect to their use of parallel couplets, to highlight Matthew's scribal origins.

Judaism, then Matthew, already once alienated from his contemporaries by his former profession, surely could have done so. (2) The Gospel of Matthew is actually quite compatible with the epistle of James, another probable early Jewish-Christian document, and not all Jewish Christianity was monolithic in its beliefs. (3) It is not at all clear that 13:52 is the author's self-reference but, even if it were, what would be more natural than a former tax collector to continue to use his writing skills and consider himself a Christian scribe? (4) We have already seen that Matthew's Gospel may be as early as the 60s but, if not, we do not have enough information, even in more legendary Christian writings, to surmise when Matthew died or how old he was at the time.

(5) The problem of Matthew's dependence on Mark is substantially eased by accepting the early traditions that Mark carried the authority of Peter's teaching with him (see above, pp. 136–37). Peter, James, and John formed the inner core of Christ's three closest followers. Put simply, Peter was present for certain events in Jesus' ministry when Matthew was not (cf., e.g., 17:1; 26:37). Even though Matthew did observe much that Mark described, it is surely conceivable that he would be curious to see how a Gospel based on Peter's preaching would look. Matthew scarcely depends on Mark slavishly and feels free to add much of his own material.[43]

Some commentators have noted that Matthew does seem to include more details in his story related to money matters (e.g., the story of the temple tax in 17:24–27 or parables like the unforgiving servant in 18:23–35). But it is not likely we can prove much from this. In short, there is no compelling reason to overturn the unanimous testimony of antiquity that Matthew/Levi was the author of the Gospel attributed to him. Even though Matthew was an apostle, he came from a disreputable background. No apocryphal works are attributed to him as they are to apostles like Peter, James, John, Thomas, Andrew or Bartholomew. He seems an unlikely candidate, even among the apostles, for later Christians to have selected in an attempt to give this Gospel greater authority, if indeed he were not the author. On the other hand, as with Mark, little of our ability to interpret the Gospel's historical context or exegetical detail hangs on this decision.[44]

For Further Study

Commentaries

Introductory

France, R. T. *The Gospel according to Matthew.* TNTC. Rev. ed. Leicester: IVP; Grand Rapids: Eerdmans, 1985.

---

[43] Cf. R. T. France, *Matthew: Evangelist and Teacher* (Exeter: Paternoster; Grand Rapids: Zondervan, 1989; Downers Grove: IVP, 1998), 74.

[44] Even as staunch a conservative as D. A. Carson ("Matthew," in *Expositor's Bible Commentary, Revised Edition,* vol. 9, ed. T. Longman III and D. E. Garland [Grand Rapids: Zondervan, forthcoming]) leaves the question of authorship open (and also notes that any date from 40–100 is possible).

Green, Michael. *The Message of Matthew*. BST. Leicester and Downers Grove: IVP, 2000.

Keener, Craig S. *Matthew*. IVPNTC. Downers Grove and Leicester: IVP, 1997.

Mounce, Robert H. Matthew. NIBC. Peabody: Hendrickson, 1991.

Ridderbos, H. N. *Matthew*. BSC. Grand Rapids: Zondervan, 1987.

Wilkins, Michael J. *Matthew*. NIVAC. Grand Rapids: Zondervan, 2004.

Intermediate

Allison, Dale C., Jr. *Matthew: A Shorter Commentary*. London and New York: T&T Clark, 2004.

Blomberg, Craig L. *Matthew*. NAC. Nashville: Broadman, 1992.

Carson, D. A. "Matthew." In *Expositor's Bible Commentary, Revised Edition*. Vol. 9. Ed. Tremper Longman III and David E. Garland. Grand Rapids: Zondervan, forthcoming.

France, R. T. *The Gospel of Matthew*. NIC. Grand Rapids and Cambridge: Eerdmans, 2007.

Garland, David E. *Reading Matthew*. ReadingNT. Rev. ed. Macon: Smyth & Helwys, 1999.

Keener, Craig S. *A Commentary on the Gospel of Matthew*. Grand Rapids and Cambridge: Eerdmans, 1999.

Morris, Leon. *The Gospel according to Matthew*. PNTC. Grand Rapids: Eerdmans; Leicester: IVP, 1992.

Witherington, Ben III. *Matthew*. SHBC. Macon: Smyth & Helwys, 2006.

Advanced

Davies, W. D., and Dale C. Allison, Jr. *A Critical and Exegetical Commentary on the Gospel according to Saint Matthew*. ICC. 3 vols. Rev. ed. Edinburgh: T&T Clark, 1988–97.

Gibbs, Jeffrey A. *Matthew 1:1–11:1*. CC. St. Louis: Concordia, 2006.

Gundry, Robert H. *Matthew: A Commentary on His Handbook for a Mixed Church under Persecution*. Rev. ed. Grand Rapids: Eerdmans, 1994.

Hagner, Donald A. *Matthew*. 2 vols. WBC. Dallas: Word, 1993–95.

Luz, Ulrich. *Matthew*. Hermeneia. 3 vols. Minneapolis: Fortress, 2001–7.

Nolland, John. *The Gospel of Matthew*. NIGTC. Grand Rapids: Eerdmans; Milton Keynes: Paternoster, 2005.

Turner, David L. *Matthew*. BECNT. Grand Rapids: Baker, 2008.

Other Key Studies of Matthean Introduction or Theology More Generally

Aune, David E., ed. *The Gospel of Matthew in Current Study*. Grand Rapids and Cambridge: Eerdmans, 2001.

Carter, Warren. *Matthew and Empire: Initial Explorations*. Harrisburg: Trinity, 2001.

France, R. T. *Matthew: Evangelist and Teacher*. Exeter: Paternoster; Grand Rapids: Zondervan, 1989; Downers Grove: IVP, 1998.

Gurtner, Daniel M. and John Nolland, eds. *Built upon the Rock: Studies in the Gospel of Matthew*. Grand Rapids and Cambridge: Eerdmans, 2008.

Luz, Ulrich. *The Theology of the Gospel of Matthew*. Cambridge: CUP, 1995.

Luz, Ulrich. *Studies in Matthew*. Grand Rapids and Cambridge: Eerdmans, 2005.

Neyrey, Jerome H. *Honor and Shame in the Gospel of Matthew*. Louisville and London: WJKP, 1998.

Overman, J. Andrew. *Matthew's Gospel and Formative Judaism: The Social World of the Matthean Community*. Minneapolis: Fortress, 1990.

Powell, Mark A. *God with Us: A Pastoral Theology of Matthew's Gospel*. Minneapolis: Fortress, 1995.

Saldarini, Anthony J. *Matthew's Christian-Jewish Community*. Chicago and London: University of Chicago Press, 1994.

Stanton, Graham N. *A Gospel for a New People: Studies in Matthew*. Edinburgh: T&T Clark, 1992; Louisville: WJKP, 1993.

Stanton, Graham N., ed. *The Interpretation of Matthew*. Rev. ed. Edinburgh: T&T Clark, 1995.

Stock, Augustine. *The Method and Message of Matthew*. Collegeville: Liturgical Press, 1994.

Bibliography

Mills, Watson E. *The Gospel of Matthew*. Rev. ed. Lewiston and Lampeter: Mellen Biblical Press, 2002.

Questions for Review

1. What is a plausible overall outline for the Gospel of Matthew? That is, how many main sections may it be divided into and by what criteria? What theology may be inferred from this structure?

2. According to typical evangelical reconstructions, who wrote this Gospel, when, where, to whom, and under what circumstances (to the extent that this information may be reasonably inferred)?

3. What are several of the major theological distinctives of this Gospel?

4. Take a passage from a Gospel synopsis that appears in all three Synoptics, and identify the probable theological emphases of Matthew. Consider both the "horizontal" and the "vertical" dimensions of redaction criticism.

5. Given the emphases and probable circumstances of Matthew's Gospel, in what settings in contemporary Christian living might it be even more acutely relevant than the other Gospels?

8

THE GOSPEL OF LUKE

Structure

T HE STRUCTURE OF Luke closely resembles parts of Mark's outline and parts of Matthew's. Where Luke narrates events contained in Mark, he follows Mark's sequence even more faithfully than Matthew does. Yet, like Matthew, Luke is about half as long as Mark, with significant material added from "Q" (material shared with Matthew but not found in Mark) and "L" (material unique to Luke). Like Matthew, too, Luke begins with two detailed chapters of the events surrounding Christ's birth and ends with a lengthy chapter highlighting resurrection appearances. Luke, however, is not characterized by the lengthy sermons of Matthew. As we noted in discussing Streeter's hypothesis about proto-Luke (above, p. 103), Luke alternates between large blocks of Markan and non-Markan material. Chapters 1–2 are wholly unparalleled in Mark. Luke 3:1–9:50, especially from 4:14 on, follows Mark's outline very closely for the bulk of Jesus' Galilean ministry, with occasional modifications. Luke 9:51–18:14 contains primarily teachings of Jesus from his itinerant ministry and includes almost exclusively Q and L material. From 18:15 on, Mark's outline is followed again but with more insertions of distinctively Lukan texts than in chaps. 4–9.

Whatever source-critical conclusions one draws from this, these major sections seem also to correspond to Luke's thematic structure. At first glance Luke seems to be the hardest Gospel to outline. A survey of commentators certainly reveals the least amount of agreement compared with treatments of Matthew, Mark, and

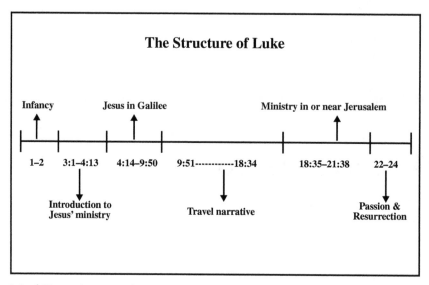

The Structure of Luke

Infancy   Jesus in Galilee   Ministry in or near Jerusalem

1–2   3:1–4:13   4:14–9:50   9:51------------18:34   18:35–21:38   22–24

Introduction to   Travel narrative   Passion &
Jesus' ministry   Resurrection

John.[1] Yet at the same time, we must always keep in mind when studying Luke that he wrote a sequel to his Gospel, the book of Acts. Although a full-fledged introduction to Acts lies beyond the scope of this text,[2] some observations are crucial for understanding Luke's Gospel.

One observation involves structure. It is widely agreed that Acts 1:8 presents a rough geographical outline for the events narrated in Luke's second volume: the gospel progresses from Jerusalem ever outward, through Judea and Samaria, eventually reaching "the ends of the earth." Thus Acts 1–7 describes the church in Jerusalem. After the stoning of Stephen, many believers move out, and Acts 8–12 narrates a variety of events explicitly in Judea, Samaria, and nearby areas. Then with the ministry of the newly converted Saul (Paul), the Gospel begins to travel throughout the known world (chaps. 13–28). Acts ends with Paul finally having reached Rome, the heart and capital of the Gentile world. Within one generation, an exclusively Jewish sect has become a major "worldwide" religion.[3]

---

[1] E.g., J. B. Green (*The Gospel of Luke* [Grand Rapids and Cambridge: Eerdmans, 1997]) follows the source-critical divisions noted above for the first half of his outline but then ends the central section at 19:48 and creates his final three sections topically—Jesus' teaching in the temple (chaps. 20–21), his suffering and death (chaps. 22–23) and his resurrection (chap. 24); J. Nolland (*Luke*, 3 vols. [Dallas: Word, 1989–93]) is content to divide the text into twenty-four sections without further grouping any of them together; while C. H. Talbert (*Reading Luke* [Macon: Smyth & Helwys, 2002]) finds four overarching sections after the prologue in 1:1–4—"Prophecies of Future Greatness" (1:5–4:15), "Anointed with the Holy Spirit" (4:16–9:50), "Guidance on the Way" (9:51–19:44), and "Martyrdom and Vindication" (19:45–24:53).

[2] But see C. L. Blomberg, *From Pentecost to Patmos: Acts to Revelation—An Introduction and Survey* (Nottingham: Apollos, 2007)(= *From Pentecost to Patmos: An Introduction to Acts through Revelation* [Nashville: B & H, 2007]), 9–23.

[3] Cf. further A. Fernando, *Acts* (Grand Rapids: Zondervan, 1998), 42–44; and I. H. Marshall, *The Acts of the Apostles: New Testament Guides* (Sheffield: JSOT Press, 1992), 13–30. Marshall also surveys the other major proposals for Acts' outline or structure.

This exact geographical sequence can be discerned in Luke's Gospel as well, only in reverse order. Interestingly, the sequence corresponds fairly closely to the source-critical divisions already noted, suggesting that the organization is deliberate. The opening chapters include a significant cluster of references to various Roman rulers and Roman appointees in power when the events surrounding Christ's life begin to unfold (1:5; 2:1; 3:1). As he does frequently in Acts, Luke situates his narrative within "empire history." As he follows Mark, Luke omits the entire section on Jesus' "withdrawal" from Galilee and adjoining material (Mark 6:45–8:26), leaving 3:1–9:50 narrating events almost exclusively from Jesus' Galilean ministry. We will discuss the significance of 9:51–18:14 more later (a section that probably extends at least to 18:31–34, which read like a conclusion and transition). Two interesting observations are that the only geographical references in this section place Jesus in or near Samaria (9:52; 17:11) and that immediately after this section he appears in Judea, en route to Jerusalem (18:35; 19:1, 11, 28, etc.). Christ, of course, is crucified and resurrected just outside the city walls of Jerusalem, but what is striking about the end of this Gospel is that Luke narrates none of Christ's later resurrection appearances in Galilee but several in or near Jerusalem. Luke 24 and Acts 1 also overlap in that each narrates the resurrection and the ascension of Christ.

All this strongly suggests that Luke was designing a two-volume, chiastically structured account of the life of Jesus and the growth of the early church.[4] There has been a huge flurry of recent interest, however, in the question of how much unity one should postulate between Luke and Acts, after scholars had become all but unanimous in their opinion that the two books were meant to be taken together.[5] But this specific structural observation has not played nearly the role in the discussion that it perhaps should have. The Gospel begins with the birth of Jesus in the context of Roman history and rule, then follows Jesus as he travels from Galilee, through Samaria and Judea to Jerusalem, zeroing in on the holy city of God's chosen people. In light of Israel's fateful decision on the whole to reject Jesus, the ministry of God's good news now progresses outward again via the same steps: from Jerusalem, to Judea and Samaria, and throughout the Gentile world, culminating with the preaching of the gospel by Paul extending as far as Rome. If one objects that "Galilee" and "the Gentile world" do not match, one has only to recall that, from late Old Testament days on, Galilee was often known as "Galilee of the Gentiles" (cf. Isa 9:1; Matt 4:15), and that in Jesus' day it was less

---

[4] K. Wolfe, "The Chiastic Structure of Luke-Acts and Some Implications for Worship," *SWJT* 12 (1980): 60–71; S. Greidanus, *The Modern Preacher and the Ancient Text: Interpreting and Preaching Biblical Literature* (Grand Rapids: Eerdmans; Leicester: IVP, 1988), 283; L. T. Johnson, *The Writings of the New Testament: An Interpretation*, 3rd ed. (Minneapolis: Fortress, 2002; London: SCM, 2003), 220.

[5] Triggered esp. by M. C. Parsons and R. I. Pervo, *Rethinking the Unity of Luke and Acts* (Minneapolis: Fortress, 1993). For a survey of the subsequent discussion, see esp. M. F. Bird, "The Unity of Luke-Acts in Recent Discussion," *JSNT* 29 (2007): 425–48. Cf. P. E. Spencer, "The Unity of Luke-Acts: A Four-Bolted Hermeneutical Hinge," *CBR* 5 (2007): 341–66. Spencer cogently re-defends the unity in genre, narrative, theology and reception history.

monolithically Jewish in population and culture than Judea.

One expects to find the most important part of a chiasm, or inverse parallelism, at its center, and one is not disappointed. The resurrection and ascension, twice narrated, form the heart of the Christian "kerygma" (proclamation) for Luke. Throughout the book of Acts, early Christian preachers announce not the crucifixion, as we might have expected from Mark, but the resurrection as the central feature that gives Jesus' life and death significance (e.g., Acts 2:24–36, 13:30–37, 17:18, 23:6).[6]

Trying to subdivide Luke's Gospel further, however, proves much more difficult. It seems likely that Luke grouped his material together in small thematic units, but beyond that there is no overarching pattern.[7] When we discuss Luke 9:51–18:34 in

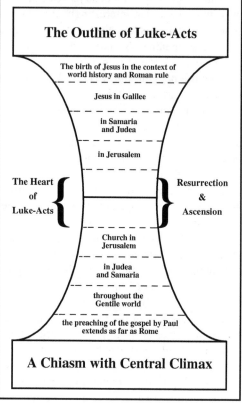

our survey of the life of Christ, we will comment on the possibility of a chiastically arranged parables source underlying this material, but for Luke's final outline it seems best simply to see each major division divided into numerous small units along the following lines:[8]

I. Introduction to Jesus' Ministry (1:1–4:13)
    A. Preface (1:1–4)
    B. Introduction to John the Baptist and Jesus (1:5–2:52)
    C. Preparation for Jesus' Ministry (3:1–4:13)
II. Ministry in and around Galilee (4:14–9:50)
    A. Preaching in Nazareth (4:14–30)

---

[6] Cf. esp. K. L. Anderson, *"But God Raised Him from the Dead": The Theology of Jesus' Resurrection in Luke-Acts* (Milton Keynes and Waynesboro, GA: Paternoster, 2006).

[7] For an important dissenting perspective, see D. S. McComiskey, *Lukan Theology in the Light of the Gospel's Literary Structure* (Milton Keynes and Waynesboro, GA: Paternoster, 2004). McComiskey finds four parallel segments with numerous corresponding subsections in 4:14–9:50, 9:51–13:21, 13:22–19:17, and 19:28–24:53.

[8] Particularly helpful in this task is I. H. Marshall, *The Gospel of Luke* (Exeter: Paternoster; Grand Rapids: Eerdmans, 1978), which I have followed at several points.

Theology

Views of Jesus[9]

Jesus' Humanity and Compassion for the Outcasts of Society. Although Luke preserves several of the key events that Mark and Matthew use to highlight Jesus' exalted nature, they do not dominate his narrative as much. None of the titles such as "Christ," "Son of God," or "Lord" is nearly as prominent. Rather, what strikes most readers of Luke's Gospel is how Jesus' humanity shines through, particularly in his association with and compassion for numerous categories of social outcasts. Four groups stand out in particular: (1) Samaritans and Gentiles; (2) tax collectors and sinners; (3) women; and (4) the poor.

---

[9] Cf. esp. R. F. O'Toole, *Luke's Presentation of Jesus: A Christology* (Rome: PIB, 2004).

1. Samaritans and Gentiles. Only Luke records the parable of the Good Samaritan (10:25–37) and the story of the ten lepers who were cleansed, with only the Samaritan leper returning to give thanks (17:11–19). Although Jesus does not leave Jewish territory in Luke, many commentators see foreshadowings of the later Gentile mission in such unique details as the sending out of the seventy (or seventy-two) in Luke 10:1–20, paralleling the numbers of nations in the world according to Genesis 10 (with the identical numerical variation between the MT and the LXX; cf. also 2:32 and 14:23). Certainly, by the time we reach Acts the Gentile mission becomes a dominant theme.[10]

2. Tax collectors and sinners. Readers who do not sense how unusual this combination of labels is, found in texts like 5:30, 7:34, and 15:1, have probably been in church too long! "Sinners" in this context refers to those who flagrantly violated the cultural and religious norms of Judaism. The parable of the prodigal son offers a classic example (15:11–32). Tax collectors are presented as another paradigm of the lawless—Jewish tollhouse keepers who collected customs and duties for the occupying Roman empire. They may not have been among the "down and out," but they were, in the minds of their contemporaries, at least "up and out." Not only does Luke use the phrase, "tax collectors and sinners," to characterize those who gathered around Jesus to hear him and were welcomed by him, but Luke alone tells two stories in which tax collectors were heroes—the parable of the Pharisee and the publican (18:9–14) and the conversion of Zaccheus (19:1–10).[11]

3. Women. Luke has far more women in his account than do the other Gospels. The birth narratives are told from the perspectives of Elizabeth and Mary (chaps. 1–2). The prophetess Anna appears alongside her male counterpart Simeon (2:25–38). Pairs of parables balance men's and women's characteristic roles—the mustard seed and leaven (13:18–21) and the lost sheep and lost coin (15:3–10). Both a woman and a man are healed of their crippling diseases on different Sabbaths (13:10–17; 14:1–6). Jesus affirms the notoriously sinful woman who anoints him with oil despite the complaints of his Pharisaic host (7:36–50). He praises Mary's devotion to his teaching, against the cultural norms of the day (10:38–42). Only Luke describes Jesus' itinerant ministry as being funded in part by the contributions of several well-to-do women who traveled with him (8:1–3).[12]

4. The Poor. Whereas Matthew's Jesus blesses the poor in spirit, Luke's blesses "you who are poor" (6:20). Jesus' programmatic manifesto in Nazareth, brought to the front of his Galilean ministry in Luke's outline, claims that he fulfills the mission of Isaiah's servant who was anointed by God "to proclaim good news to the poor" (Luke 4:18). The various teachings in 14:7–24 all demonstrate God's

---

[10] See esp. T. J. Lane, *Luke and the Gentile Mission: Gospel Anticipates Acts* (Frankfurt and New York: Peter Lang, 1996).

[11] Cf. D. A. Neale, *None but the Sinners: Religious Categories in the Gospel of Luke* (Sheffield: JSOT, 1991).

[12] Cf. esp. J. Kopas, "Jesus and Women: Luke's Gospel," *Theology Today* 43 (1986): 192–202. More recent feminist scholarship on Luke has often been less positive, complaining that Luke did not portray Jesus as a full-fledged egalitarian. But this is to impose an anachronistic criterion from today's world rather than judging Luke (and Jesus) in the light of first-century realities.

concern for the sick and dispossessed who are unable to help themselves or return favors. The parable of the rich man and Lazarus vindicates the poor beggar at the expense of his counterpart wallowing in luxury (16:19–31). Luke has become well-known as the Evangelist who most emphasizes Jesus' concern for the downtrodden and stigmatized.[13]

Savior. Perhaps the title that best sums up the themes of Jesus' humanity and compassion in Luke is "Savior." In 2:11 the angel announces, "Today in the town of David a Savior has been born to you; he is the Messiah, the Lord." Interestingly, "Savior" is the most distinctive title for Jesus in Luke. The Greek words for Savior and salvation (*sotēr; sotēria, sotērion*) occur eight times in Luke, nine times in Acts, and nowhere else in the Synoptic Gospels. Luke 19:10 arguably provides a one-verse summary of the entire Gospel: "For the Son of Man came to seek and to save what was lost." Interestingly, however, the title "Lord" features more prominently in Acts even than "Savior," as if Luke were trying to highlight different emphases in Jesus' ministry before the cross and resurrection than afterward.[14] I. H. Marshall, nevertheless, makes a compelling case for seeing "salvation" as the unifying theme for all of Luke's theology.[15]

Prophet. Unique to Luke is Jesus' revivification of the widow's son in Nain, a passage strikingly similar to Elisha's re-animation of the Shunammite woman's son (2 Kgs 4:8–37). Luke seems to recognize this similarity with his comment that the crowd responded by declaring, "A great prophet has appeared among us" (7:16). In another uniquely Lukan passage, Jesus apparently refers to himself as a prophet (13:33). Several scholars have seen the whole of Luke's central section (9:51–18:34) as paralleling topics found in a similar sequence in Deuteronomy,[16] or at least echoing themes characteristic of Deuteronomy's theology: (a) Jesus sent as God's messenger, (b) to warn a stiff-necked generation, (c) of its coming destruction, (d) only to be rejected.[17] Luke's use of the Old Testament is best summed up as a prophetic and christological use—all of the Scriptures point to Jesus and must be fulfilled by him (Luke 24:25, 44).[18]

Teacher of Parables. Twenty-eight of the forty passages most commonly classified as parables appear in Luke, fifteen of these found only in this Gospel. All

[13] Of the many excellent studies on this topic, see esp. W. E. Pilgrim, *Good News to the Poor: Wealth and Poverty in Luke-Acts* (Minneapolis: Augsburg, 1981); D. P. Seccombe, *Possessions and the Poor in Luke-Acts* (Linz, Austria: SNTU, 1982); and S. J. Roth, *The Blind, the Lame, and the Poor: Character Types in Luke-Acts* (Sheffield: SAP, 1997).

[14] C. F. D. Moule, "The Christology of Acts," in *Studies in Luke-Acts,* ed. L. E. Keck and J. L. Martyn (Nashville: Abingdon, 1966), 159–85.

[15] I. H. Marshall, *Luke: Historian and Theologian,* rev. ed. (Exeter: Paternoster; Grand Rapids: Zondervan, 1988; Downers Grove: IVP, 1998), esp. 77–102.

[16] E.g., J. Drury, *Tradition and Design in Luke's Gospel* (London: Darton, Longman & Todd; Atlanta: John Knox, 1976), 138–64.

[17] D. P. Moessner, *Lord of the Banquet: The Literary and Theological Significance of the Lukan Travel Narrative* (Minneapolis: Fortress, 1989). Cf. also J. S. Croatto, "Jesus, Prophet Like Elijah, and Prophet-Teacher Like Moses in Luke-Acts," *JBL* 124 (2005): 451–65.

[18] D. L. Bock, *Proclamation from Prophecy and Pattern: Lucan Old Testament Christology* (Sheffield: JSOT, 1987).

but one of these fifteen appear in the central section (9:51–18:34). For the most part, Luke's parables do not include Jesus' more enigmatic narratives, designed to weed outsiders from insiders (*à la* Mark 4 and Matt 13), but provide down-to-earth, simple, illustrative stories for Jewish peasant folk. Four of them have often been called example-stories because they seem to have a less symbolic nature than most: the good Samaritan (10:25–37), the rich fool (12:13–21), the rich man and Lazarus (16:19–31), and the Pharisee and the publican (18:9–14).[19]

The Resurrected and Exalted One, Benefactor. As already noted, when studying Acts, Christian preachers focus primarily on the resurrection and exaltation, not the crucifixion. This ties in with Luke's omission of the teaching about Christ's substitutionary atonement in Mark 10:45. Luke's parallel account, uniquely placed in the context of the Lord's Supper, focuses instead exclusively on the need for Christ's followers to imitate their master's servanthood. They must not expect reciprocity for the good deeds they perform (Luke 22:24–30). Instead of imitating the Hellenistic patrons (see above, p. 67), they can trust in Jesus as their ultimate benefactor who will pay them back in the ways the people they help cannot (cf. 14:12–14). At the same time as Luke's Gospel tones down Mark's emphasis on the cross, though, a passage like Acts 20:28 reminds us that Luke has not abandoned the doctrine of Christ's vicarious, sacrificial death altogether.[20]

Other Distinctive Themes

Stewardship of Material Possessions. Closely related to Jesus' concern for the poor in Luke is the emphasis on the need for Jesus' followers not to accumulate or hoard riches for themselves. Only Luke balances his beatitudes with woes—against those who are rich, well fed, laughing, and well spoken of (6:24–26). Only Luke includes the "hymns" of Mary and Zechariah, who speak of "the great reversal"—the powerful being rendered powerless and the lowly in Israel exalted (1:46–55, 67–79). Again, the parables of the rich fool and the rich man and Lazarus (chap. 16) carry pointed implications for those who spend all their riches simply improving their own lifestyles. The unjust steward is commended for using his wealth shrewdly; believers must do the same for kingdom purposes (16:1–13). Most Christians are not called to give up everything as the rich young ruler was (18:18–30); but Zaccheus voluntarily gives up half (19:1–10), and the faithful servants invest all they have for their master's work (19:11–27). Some liberation theologians have seized on Luke and exaggerated his teaching on stewardship to the point of arguing that it is impossible to be both rich and Christian. Nevertheless, Luke certainly knows nothing of rich Christians who are not generous in giving of their wealth to the needy (cf., e.g., 12:33; 14:33; and Acts 2:44–47)![21]

---

[19] For a book-length study, see J. T. Tucker, *Example Stories: Perspectives on Four Parables in the Gospel of Luke* (Sheffield: SAP, 1998).

[20] For a full, though perhaps overstated treatment, see P. Doble, *The Paradox of Salvation: Luke's Theology of the Cross* (Cambridge: CUP, 1996).

[21] For a thorough survey of perspectives, see T. E. Phillips, "Reading Recent Readings of Issues of Wealth and Poverty in Luke-Acts," *CBR* 1 (2003): 231–69. For a well-balanced book-length treatment, see K.-J. Kim, *Stewardship and Almsgiving in Luke's Theology* (Sheffield: SAP, 1998).

The Jewish People and Obedience to the Law. Throughout most of church history, commentators took it for granted that Luke was the Gospel with the greatest Gentile orientation. In comparatively recent scholarship, however, various writers have challenged this consensus.[22] They have pointed out that it is only Luke who at times has a moderately positive view of the Jewish leaders. For example, these authorities invite Jesus to their homes (7:36–50; 14:1–24) and warn him about Herod (13:31). We have already noted how the Gospel climaxes (and Acts begins) in the temple in Jerusalem, as though Luke acknowledges it as God's holy place. Most strikingly, Luke seems to go out of his way to describe how various individuals during Jesus' ministry and the life of the early church still obey the Jewish law (e.g., Luke 1:6, 59; 2:21–24), even as Christians (e.g., Acts 3:1; 18:18; 21:21–24). A whole spectrum of views has now emerged as to how Luke saw Jews and Gentiles related in Christ and as to whether or not part or all of the Mosaic Law was still incumbent on believers.[23] How the apostolic decree of Acts 15 is interpreted plays a crucial role in this debate. But a good case can still be made that while Luke is faithful to history by reporting how Jesus' first followers did not immediately break away from Judaism and its Torah, Luke's redactional emphases time and again point to a law-free Christianity as the desired goal to which God was ultimately guiding first-century events. Christ is the fulfillment of Judaism, not its preservation (see esp. Luke 24:44); the religion of God's people does not merely continue unchanged.[24]

Writing Christian History. The pioneering redaction critic of Luke was Hans Conzelmann.[25] Although virtually every one of his major tenets has been challenged, his views still remain influential. Conzelmann saw Luke as the first Christian historian, that is to say, the first Gospel writer to tell the story of Jesus as a part of the ongoing history of the world, or more precisely, of the history of God's dealings with his people. The latter has often been called "salvation history" (Germ. *Heilsgeschichte*). Clearly, Luke is the only one who wrote an Acts, a sequel to the Gospel, and at least to this extent Conzelmann's observation is on target. But "salvation history" for scholars has often meant inaccurate history in that Luke embellished his sources with unhistorical detail and at times fabricated sayings or events that were not what Jesus actually did or said. Other writers have therefore suggested terms such as "theological history" or "empire history" as less

---

[22] The pioneer in this movement was J. Jervell, *Luke and the People of God* (Minneapolis: Augsburg, 1972; Eugene, OR: Wipf & Stock, 2002).

[23] For surveys, see J. B. Tyson, ed., *Luke-Acts and the Jewish People: Eight Critical Perspectives* (Minneapolis: Augsburg, 1988); and idem., *Luke, Judaism, and the Scholars: Critical Approaches to Luke-Acts* (Columbia: University of South Carolina Press, 1999).

[24] C. L. Blomberg, "The Law in Luke-Acts," *JSNT* 22 (1984): 53–80; idem., "The Christian and the Law of Moses," in *Witness to the Gospel: The Theology of Acts*, ed. I. H. Marshall and D. Peterson (Grand Rapids and Cambridge: Eerdmans, 1998), 397–416.

[25] Conzelmann, *Theology of St. Luke*. Much more nuanced is D. Marguerat, *The First Christian Historian: Writing the "Acts of the Apostles"* (Cambridge: CUP, 2002). Despite the title, Marguerat does deal (much more briefly) with the Gospel of Luke as well as the Acts.

misleading.[26] Luke's details may well be accurate, at least by the historiographical standards of his day, but they were chosen because of their theological or spiritual significance in the context of the Roman empire.

Conzelmann became well known also for his interpretation of Luke as dividing history into three periods—the period of Israel, the time of Jesus, and the subsequent life of the early church. The German title of his work reflects this scheme—*Die Mitte der Zeit* ("The Middle of Time"). Whereas Mark and Matthew maintained the typical Jewish division of history into "this age" and "the age to come," while differing from conventional Judaism by seeing "the age to come" as having dawned with the ministry of Jesus, Luke separates the period of Jesus as a special, ideal age, distinct also from the life of the early church. For example, Conzelmann saw this period as a "Satan-free period," with the devil departing after Jesus' temptations (4:13) and not returning until just before the crucifixion. The book of Acts, on the other hand, reflected the era of *Frühkatholisizmus* ("early Catholicism"), in which the church was becoming increasingly institutionalized and less dependent on the Spirit than at first.

Closely tied in with all of this is the idea that Luke, of all the Gospel writers, most stresses the delay of the Parousia (Christ's return). Luke 12:35–38, 19:11, and 21:20–24 play down the possibility of an immediate return, while 12:20, 16:19–31, and 23:43 show that Christians need to reckon more with the possibility of their deaths before the Parousia. This too is part of the "early Catholic" trajectory of Luke.

Whatever one makes of all this, Conzelmann certainly described the church as it very quickly became and has often remained. It is more doubtful that it was so already in Luke's day and that Luke wanted to promote such a picture. While not stressing the immediacy of Christ's return, Luke does still retain a hope for its near arrival. Luke 17:20–21 and 22–37 nicely balance present and future eschatology, but the latter, lengthier passage certainly stresses the need to be ready for the end to happen at any time after Christ's death.[27] The parable of the minas/pounds (19:11–27) stresses the delay of the full arrival of the kingdom, but is immediately followed by the so-called triumphal entry, which stresses the kingdom's presence even if in unexpected guise.[28] The number of parallels that can be drawn between the ministries of Peter and Paul in Acts and Jesus in Luke belie the notion that Luke tries to paint a picture of the church era with significantly different strokes than the period of Jesus.[29] Nor is it clear that Satan was absent during most of Jesus' ministry (cf. 11:14–26; 22:31). But a key theme for Luke *is* "the demise of

---

[26] See, respectively, R. Maddox, *The Purpose of Luke-Acts* (Edinburgh: T&T Clark, 1982), 15–18; R. J. Cassidy, *Jesus, Politics, and Society: A Study of Luke's Gospel* (Maryknoll: Orbis, 1978), 1–19.

[27] See esp. J. T. Carroll, *Response to the End of History: Eschatology and Situation in Luke-Acts* (Atlanta: Scholars, 1988).

[28] L. Guy, "The Interplay of the Present and Future in the Kingdom of God (Luke 19:11–44)," *TynBul* 48 (1997): 199–37.

[29] For these and other parallelisms between Luke and Acts or within sections of Luke or Acts, see C. H. Talbert, *Literary Patterns, Theological Themes, and the Genre of Luke-Acts* (Missoula: Scholars, 1974).

the devil" (cf. 10:18–19).[30] Luke even describes certain miracles as if they were a kind of exorcism (cf., most notably, 8:24). All of Luke-Acts, to be sure, is pervaded by a progression of events that leaves no doubt that God, with a sovereign plan, is in charge.[31]

The Holy Spirit. The Spirit appears considerably more often in Luke than in Matthew or Mark. A characteristic expression of Luke's in both of his volumes is that someone is "filled with the Spirit," a recurring phenomenon that always leads to bold proclamation and service of the Gospel (e.g., Luke 1:15, 41; Acts 2:4; 4:31). Some interpreters, especially in the charismatic tradition, have found little difference in this portrait from the unpredictable comings and goings of the Spirit on God's people in Old Testament times and thus see his empowerment as a subsequent blessing after initial Christian existence.[32] But Luke, in agreement with the rest of the New Testament witness on the topic, also makes it clear that every Christian is "baptized" in the Spirit from conversion on (Luke 3:16; Acts 1:5, 11:16; cf. esp. 1 Cor 12:13). In other words, while believers are not always full of God's Spirit because they do not always fully yield themselves to him, the Spirit always lives and remains in them.[33] And despite the many mighty deeds of the Spirit through both Jesus and his followers, which Luke highlights throughout his two-part work, he also retains from his sources and adds in Acts numerous reminders that none of this exempts believers from suffering.[34] Indeed, by turning Jesus' fateful, final journey to Jerusalem into nine chapters rather than just one, and by highlighting in Acts Paul's similar final trip to the capital of Israel, Luke more than any other Gospel offers a paradigm for viewing the Christian life as a journey or pilgrimage, following in the way of Jesus.[35] More often than not, that way of discipleship includes suffering for his name's sake.[36]

Prayer, Joy, and Repentance/Conversion. The Holy Spirit empowers Jesus and his followers for many other kinds of ministries as well. One of these is prayer. Prayer is the focus of three parables unique to Luke (11:5–8; 18:1–8, 9–14) and features distinctively in critical moments in Christ's own life (e.g., 5:16; 6:12;

---

[30] S. R. Garrett, *The Demise of the Devil: Magic and the Demonic in Luke's Writings* (Minneapolis: Fortress, 1989).

[31] Cf. further J. T. Squires, *The Plan of God in Luke-Acts* (Cambridge: CUP, 1993).

[32] See esp. R. Menzies, *Empowered for Witness: The Spirit in Luke-Acts* (Sheffield: SAP, 1994).

[33] See esp. M. Turner, *Power from on High: The Spirit in Israel's Restoration and Witness in Luke-Acts* (Sheffield: SAP, 1996). For a thorough treatment that does justice to the proper emphases of both Menzies and Turner, see J. Hur, *A Dynamic Reading of the Holy Spirit in Luke-Acts* (Sheffield: SAP, 2001). For the reminder that the Spirit empowers Christians not only for bold proclamation of the Gospel but for works of social compassion and justice, too, see M. Wenk, *Community-Forming Power: The Socio-Ethical Role of the Spirit in Luke-Acts* (Sheffield: SAP, 2000).

[34] M. W. Mittelstadt, *The Spirit and Suffering in Luke-Acts: Implications for a Pentecostal Pneumatology* (London and New York: T&T Clark, 2004).

[35] See esp. P. C. Borgman, *The Way according to Luke: Hearing the Whole Story of Luke-Acts* (Grand Rapids and Cambridge: Eerdmans, 2006). Cf. also J. L. Resseguie, *Spiritual Landscape: Images of Spiritual Life in the Gospel of Luke* (Peabody: Hendrickson, 2004).

[36] S. Cunningham, *Through Many Tribulations: The Theology of Persecution in Luke-Acts* (Sheffield: SAP, 1998).

9:18, 28). Overall prayer features more often in Luke than in the other two Synoptics.[37] Another distinctive aspect of life in the Spirit in Luke is joy. The infancy narratives are filled with joyful poems or songs of praise, and the word "joy" itself is unusually common throughout the Gospel (e.g., 1:14; 2:10; 10:17; 15:7, 10). "Rejoice" and "praise" are also more frequent in Luke than in other Gospels. A key feature of the spiritual life over which to rejoice is God's wooing us back to himself. While repentance and conversion are central foci in all the Gospels, Luke, especially in Acts, seems to highlight these themes just a little more, too.[38]

Circumstances

The above survey clearly demonstrates a richness and diversity to Luke's theology that does not readily lead to a narrowly defined community or set of circumstances in which Luke must have been writing. The dominant concern about material possessions, furthered in Acts with its models of communal sharing (Acts 2:43–47; 4:32–37), suggests that Luke was addressing a Christian community at least somewhat more well-to-do than many, though not without poor people in its midst. *He would then be calling the better-off Christians to give generously and share with needier brothers and sisters in the Lord.*[39] Jesus' compassion for outcasts, coupled with the progress of the gospel from distinctively Jewish to predominantly Gentile contexts, also supports the traditional idea of Luke as *a Gentile writing to a mostly, if not exclusively, Gentile-Christian community.* Beyond this, details become hard to pin down. If the motif of the delay of the Parousia is not so prominent as to rule out a balancing concern for Christ's imminent return, then nothing about the date of the Gospel may be deduced from it. It has been fashionable to assume that Luke must be late because of this motif, written probably between 80 and 100,[40] but questions over the delay of Christ's return were surfacing already at the beginning of the 50s in Thessalonica (cf. the balance Paul tries to achieve between 1 and 2 Thessalonians). In the nineteenth century, the hypothesis associated with Ferdinand Baur and the so-called Tübingen school was popular. According to this view, Luke-Acts was a mid-second-century attempt to gloss over the severity of early Christian debate about the relationship of Law and Gospel.[41] This view has now been rightly abandoned.

The question of the fall of Jerusalem comes back to haunt commentators again in Luke. Luke 21:20–24 differs substantially from its parallels in Matthew

---

[37] See esp. S. F. Plymale, *The Prayer Texts of Luke-Acts* (New York and Frankfurt: Peter Lang, 1991).

[38] See, respectively, G. D. Nave, *The Role and Function of Repentance in Luke-Acts* (Atlanta: SBL, 2002); and F. Méndez-Moratalla, *The Paradigm of Conversion in Luke* (London and New York: T&T Clark, 2004).

[39] B. C. Frein ("Genre and Point of View in Luke's Gospel," *BTB* 38 [2008]: 11) speaks of a more "diverse, cosmopolitan" audience.

[40] F. Bovon (*Luke 1* [Minneapolis: Fortress, 2002], 9) declares that "it is fairly certain that [Luke] composed his two volumes between 80 and 90 CE."

[41] F. C. Baur, *The Church History of the First Three Centuries,* trans. from 3rd Germ. ed. Allan Menzies (London: Williams & Norgate, 1878), vol. 1, 77–82, 147–152.

and Mark and seems at first to require a post-70 date. The city would have been destroyed, so Luke could interpret for his readers what the "abomination that causes desolation" was—"Jerusalem surrounded by armies" and "trampled on by the Gentiles until the times of the Gentiles are fulfilled" (vv. 20, 24). This view does not require Luke to have invented these sayings after the fact. It fits our outline of Acts whereby ministry in Rome is the zenith of the progress of the gospel thus far and a fitting climax to the book, even if written some years after the events of its final chapter.[42]

On the other hand, many readers of Acts have puzzled over why Luke would emphasize Paul's arrest, imprisonment, and trials for eight chapters (Acts 21–28)—more than a quarter of his book—yet never give the outcome of Paul's appeal to Caesar or an account of his martyrdom, paralleling Jesus' fate. All this becomes even more perplexing inasmuch as a fair amount of early church tradition supports the claim that Paul was, indeed, released after his two years of house arrest in Rome, only to be rearrested and executed a few years later.[43] This state of affairs has convinced many conservative commentators that Acts must have been written immediately after the events it narrates so that Luke does not give the results of Paul's appeal because the emperor had not yet rendered his verdict. *This would require a date for Luke's Gospel of sometime before the book of Acts and no later than about AD 62* (the probable date of the end of Paul's house arrest in Rome).[44] Given that we must leave room for Luke to have received and utilized a copy of Mark's Gospel, it probably could not have been written more than a year or two before this date either.

Other factors make the decision between pre- and post-70 even more difficult. Is Paul's consistently positive view of Roman government throughout Acts a sign that Nero's pogrom has not yet started and that Christianity is still being treated as a *religio licita* (see above, p. 24)? Is Acts 20:25 a sign that Luke, in fact, does know that Paul has since been (re-) arrested, condemned, and martyred? Or is Paul's understanding that he would never again see the Ephesian elders one that changed later when he hoped to return to Ephesus (1 Tim 3:14; cf. 1:3—on the assumptions that the Pastoral Epistles are Pauline and stem from the years immediately after Paul's house arrest in Rome)? David Wenham has even created a meticulous reconstruction of what he believes is an original Eschatological Discourse, longer and more detailed than any of the Synoptic accounts, in which Luke 21:20 is not a reinterpretation of Mark 13:14 (or Matt 24:15) but stands before it as a part of what Jesus originally uttered: "When you see Jerusalem surrounded by armies and the abomination that causes desolation, which was spoken of by Daniel the

---

[42] Thus evangelical commentators like D. Williams (*Acts* [Peabody: Hendrickson, 1990], 13) and B. Witherington III (*The Acts of the Apostles: A Socio-Rhetorical Commentary* [Grand Rapids and Cambridge: Eerdmans, 1998], 62) defend exactly this position (AD 75 and "the early 80s," respectively).

[43] For details, see J. B. Polhill, *Paul and His Letters* (Nashville: Broadman & Holman, 1999), 393.

[44] The fullest defense of this position appears in C. Hemer, *The Book of Acts in the Setting of Hellenistic History*, ed. C. H. Gempf (Tübingen: Mohr, 1989), 365–410.

prophet standing in the holy place, let the reader understand . . ."[45] Darrell Bock argues that Luke's stress on the debate over Jew-Gentile relations fits more naturally in a pre-70 era,[46] but, as we saw with Matthew, this debate persisted, at least in the East, throughout the first century.

The external evidence helps us make little further progress. The only relevant datum is Irenaeus' testimony that Luke wrote after Matthew and Mark (*Adv. Haer.* 3.1.1). The Anti-Marcionite Prologue claims that Luke came from Syrian Antioch but wrote in Achaia. Plausible suggestions concerning Luke's audience have ranged from Rome to Philippi to Antioch, with little evidence for judging among them. In Acts, the first-person plural forms, presumably indicating Luke's presence with Paul, first appear during his time in Philippi (16:10), suggesting that Luke had either been living or ministering there before he joined the itinerant ministry of Paul and his co-workers. A slight presumption could thus favor a community or group of communities in Greece, especially if Luke also later ministered in the same area in which he wrote. If he wrote before the end of Paul's house arrest while still with him, then, of course, he would have been in Rome, but all this is highly speculative.

Internally, Luke addresses his Gospel to *Theophilus* (1:1—Gk. name meaning "lover of God"). But we know nothing about this individual except that Luke wanted to give him greater certainty about the truth of the faith. He could have already been a Christian or someone quite interested in Christianity (v. 4).[47] Given that Luke's prologue (1:1–4) closely resembles other Greco-Roman prefaces in which a patron's name is mentioned, Theophilus is most likely a well-to-do Greek who funded Luke's writing project.[48] By addressing him, Luke is not implying that he is the only or primary person for whom the book was written. The assumption from early in church history has been that Luke was writing to a Christian community, of which Theophilus may have been a part, just as much as all the other evangelists did. To claim with confidence more certainty regarding the circumstances of Luke's composition would go beyond the data.[49]

Why specifically did Luke write? In Luke 1:3–4 he explains, "With this in mind, since I myself have carefully investigated everything from the beginning, I too decided to write an orderly account for you, most excellent Theophilus, so

---

[45] D. Wenham, *The Rediscovery of Jesus' Eschatological Discourse* (Sheffield: JSOT Press, 1984; Eugene, OR: Wipf & Stock, 2003).

[46] D. L. Bock, *Luke 1:1–9:50* (Grand Rapids: Baker, 1994), 18.

[47] R. Garrison (*The Significance of Theophilus as Luke's Reader* [Lewiston and Lampeter: Edwin Mellen, 2004]) devotes an entire book to possible but non-demonstrable hypotheses built on these two options.

[48] Bovon, *Luke 1*, 22–23. For a detailed study of Luke's preface and its parallels, see L. Alexander, *The Preface to Luke's Gospel: Literary Convention and Social Context in Luke 1.1–4 and Acts 1.1* (Cambridge: CUP, 1993).

[49] The most comprehensive introduction of the last several decades, weighing all the various possibilities, remains J. A. Fitzmyer, *The Gospel according to Luke I–X* (Garden City: Doubleday, 1981), 35–62. Fitzmyer is even more thorough in his survey of Luke's distinctive theology (143–270), though here pride of place must go to F. Bovon, *Luke the Theologian: Fifty-five Years of Research (1950–2005)* (Waco: Baylor University Press, 2006).

that you may know the certainty of the things you have been taught." These verses suggest *historical, catechetical, apologetic,* and perhaps also *pastoral motives*
lay behind Luke's work. His concerns to situate events in light of empire history
and, in Acts, to portray the Roman government as not a threat to Christians (e.g.,
Acts 16:35–40; 18:12–17; 26:30–32) have suggested to many that Luke was trying to defend the church before Rome (or vice-versa).[50] The ambivalence with
which Luke treats the Jews (more positively than in the other Gospels but still
as Jesus' and the early church's primary opponents) also suggests some context
of Jew-Gentile tensions. We cannot say, as do some older commentators, that
the rupture between Luke's church and Judaism is long since past, but neither is
there enough evidence to demonstrate recent contentions that Luke's audience
and concerns are more Jewish than Gentile.[51] Walter Liefeld and David Pao may
have captured the correct balance when they conclude, given the possibility of
Luke himself being a God-fearer, that "while it is impossible to restrict Luke's
readership to the God-fearers, it is difficult to imagine his writing without at
least having them in mind."[52] Readers of almost every different walk of life have
found in Luke something to cherish; his is often considered the most universal
of all the Gospels. Perhaps that is the reason his purposes and circumstances
are so hard to pin down; he may have been deliberately trying to reach a wide
audience.

Authorship

Early church tradition is much more helpful here. The unanimous witness of
the Fathers is that *the writer named Luke was the Gentile disciple, Paul's "beloved
physician," so identified in Col 4:14, and Paul's companion for several portions
of his missionary journeys.* Proponents of this claim include the Muratorian canon, the Anti-Marcionite Prologue, Irenaeus, Clement of Alexandria, Origen, and
Tertullian. In favor of this claim are the so-called "we-passages" in Acts: four
sections in which the author uses the first-person plural to describe events during
Paul's ministry—Acts 16:10–17; 20:5–15; 21:1–18; 27:1–28:16. From Paul's letters we can learn of his main co-workers who accompanied him at various points
in his travels. Luke is the only one not otherwise mentioned in Acts who fits all
the data. Luke is nevertheless a relatively obscure figure. He was not among the
best known of Paul's companions, nor was he an apostle himself, so it seems
unlikely that anyone would have fictitiously attributed a Gospel to him. In the late
nineteenth century, William Hobart argued from the allegedly distinctive medical
language of Luke-Acts for a doctor as the author of this work,[53] but Henry Cad-

---

[50] See esp. P. W. Walaskay, *'And So We Came to Rome': The Political Perspective of St. Luke*
(Cambridge: CUP, 1983).

[51] As, e.g., in D. Juel, *Luke-Acts: The Promise of History* (Atlanta: John Knox, 1983).

[52] W. L. Liefeld and D. W. Pao, "Luke," in *The Expositor's Bible Commentary, Revised Edition,* ed.
T. Longman III and D. E. Garland, vol. 10 (Grand Rapids: Zondervan, 2007), 28.

[53] W. K. Hobart, *The Medical Language of St. Luke* (Whitefish, MT: Kessinger Publishing, repr.
2007 [orig. 1882]).

bury early in the twentieth century demonstrated that this vocabulary was just as frequent in non-medical writers.[54]

As with the other Gospels, many modern scholars dispute the traditional authorship claims. Those who hold to a very late date for Luke understandably find the theology and historical setting too late for a contemporary of Paul. Some argue that the "we-passages" reflect an eyewitness source that a later author used (a diary perhaps), preserving the original first-person language.[55] Others allege that such language is merely an artificial literary device, though the suggested parallels to this convention in other ancient literature have not proved convincing.[56] No doubt, the strongest argument against Lukan authorship has involved the alleged discrepancies between Luke's portrait of Paul in Acts and the picture of Paul that emerges from his firsthand comments in the undisputed epistles. Such a discussion would take us entirely outside the boundaries of Luke's Gospel and is, therefore, beyond the scope of this introduction. Suffice it to say that various scholars have quickly agreed that the differences in perspective demonstrate that Paul did not write Acts but fall short of proving that one of his followers, with independent interests and contexts, could not have done so.[57]

Given the resurgence of interest in Jewish concerns in Luke, it is not improbable to imagine that Luke was at one time a "God-fearer"—a Gentile who had already begun to worship the God of Israel and follow some or many of its laws.[58] But we cannot prove this. Attempts to equate him with a Jew[59] go well beyond the data and oppose the natural interpretation of Col 4:10–11, which seems clearly to distinguish Paul's Jewish supporters from the subsequent names listed in verses 12–14. As with our conclusions concerning Matthew and Mark, we find no compelling reason to reject the unanimous early church tradition but recognize that we can still find much interpretive common ground with those who choose other options.[60]

---

[54] H. J. Cadbury, *The Style and Literary Method of Luke: The Diction of Luke and Acts* (Whitefish, MT: Kessinger Publishing, repr. 2007 [orig. 1919]), 39–72.

[55] E.g., A. J. M. Wedderburn, "The 'We'-Passages in Acts: On the Horns of a Dilemma," *ZNW* 93 (2002): 78–98.

[56] Contrast V. K. Robbins, "By Land and by Sea: The We-Passages and Ancient Sea-Voyages," in *Perspectives on Luke-Acts,* ed. C. H. Talbert (Danville, VA: National Association of Baptist Professors of Religion, 1978), 215–42; with C. J. Hemer, "First Person Narrative in Acts 27–28," *TynBul* 36 (1985): 79–109.

[57] See further Blomberg, *From Pentecost to Patmos,* 11–12, and the literature there cited.

[58] E.g., J. Nolland, *Luke 1–9:20* (Dallas: Word, 1989), xxxii–xxxiii; Bovon, *Luke 1,* 8.

[59] As, e.g., throughout B. Shellard, *New Light on Luke: Its Purpose, Sources, and Literary Context* (London and New York: SAP, 2002).

[60] For a robust and detailed defense of Lukan authorship, see Hemer, *Acts,* 308–64.

For Further Study

Commentaries

Introductory

Bock, Darrell L. *Luke*. NIVAC. Grand Rapids: Zondervan, 1996.
Bock, Darrell L. *Luke*. IVPNTC. Downers Grove and Leicester: IVP, 1994.
Evans, Craig A. *Luke*. NIBC. Peabody: Hendrickson, 1990.
Lieu, Judith. *The Gospel of Luke*. EC. London: Epworth, 1997.
Tannehill, Robert C. *Luke*. ANTC. Nashville: Abingdon, 1996.

Intermediate

Evans, C. F. *Saint Luke*. London: SCM; Philadelphia: Trinity, 1990.
Green, Joel B. *The Gospel of Luke*. NIC. Rev. ed. Grand Rapids and Cambridge: Eerdmans, 1997.
Johnson, Luke T. *The Gospel of Luke*. SP. Collegeville: Liturgical, 1991.
Schweizer, Eduard. *The Good News according to Luke*. Atlanta: John Knox; London: SPCK, 1984.
Stein, Robert H. *Luke*. NAC. Nashville: Broadman, 1992.
Talbert, Charles H. *Reading Luke*. ReadingNT. Rev. ed. Macon: Smyth & Helwys, 2002.

Advanced

Bock, Darrell L. *Luke*. 2 vols. BECNT. Grand Rapids: Baker, 1994–96.
Bovon, François. *Luke 1*. Hermeneia. Minneapolis: Fortress, 2002.
Fitzmyer, Joseph A. *The Gospel according to Luke*. 2 vols. AB. Garden City: Doubleday, 1981–85.
Marshall, I. Howard. *The Gospel of Luke*. NIGTC. Exeter: Paternoster; Grand Rapids: Eerdmans, 1978.
Nolland, John. *Luke*. 3 vols. WBC. Dallas: Word, 1989–93.

Other Key Studies of Lukan Introduction or Theology More Generally

Bartholomew, Craig G., Joel B. Green and Anthony C. Thiselton, eds. *Reading Luke: Interpretation, Reflection, Formation*. Grand Rapids: Zondervan; Milton Keynes: Paternoster, 2005.
Bovon, François. *Luke the Theologian: Fifty-five Years of Research (1950–2005)*. Waco: Baylor University Press, 2006.
Buckwalter, H. Douglas. *The Character and Purpose of Luke's Christology*. Cambridge: CUP, 1996.
Conzelmann, Hans. *The Theology of St. Luke*. New York: Harper & Row, 1960; London: Faber & Faber, 1961; Minneapolis: Fortress, 1982.
Dollar, Harold E. *St. Luke's Missiology: A Cross-Cultural Challenge*. Pasadena: William Carey, 1996.
Esler, Philip F. *Community and Gospel in Luke-Acts: The Social and Political Motivations of Lucan Theology*. Cambridge: CUP, 1987.
Fitzmyer, Joseph A. *Luke the Theologian: Aspects of His Teaching*. New York: Paulist, 1989; Eugene, OR: Wipf & Stock, 2004.

Green, Joel B. *The Theology of the Gospel of Luke*. Cambridge: CUP, 1995.
Knight, Jonathan. *Luke's Gospel*. London and New York: Routledge, 1998.
Maddox, Robert. *The Purpose of Luke-Acts*. Edinburgh: T&T Clark, 1982.
Marshall, I. Howard. *Luke: Historian and Theologian*. Exeter: Paternoster; Grand Rapids:
    Zondervan, rev. 1988; Downers Grove: IVP, 1998.
O'Toole, Robert F. *Luke's Presentation of Jesus: A Christology*. Rome: BIP, 2004.
Powell, Mark A. *What Are They Saying about Luke?* New York: Paulist, 1991.
Shillington, George V. *An Introduction to the Study of Luke-Acts*. London and New York:
    T&T Clark, 2007.

Bibliography
Mills, Watson E. *The Gospel of Luke*. Rev. ed. Lewiston and Lampeter: Mellen, 2002.

Questions for Review

1. What is a plausible overall outline for the Gospel of Luke? That is, how many main sections may it be divided into and by what criteria? What theology may be inferred from this structure?
2. According to typical evangelical reconstructions, who wrote this Gospel, when, where, to whom, and under what circumstances (to the extent that this information may be reasonably inferred)?
3. What are several of the major theological distinctives of this Gospel?
4. Take a passage from a Gospel synopsis that appears in all three Synoptics, and identify the probable theological emphases of Luke. Consider both the "horizontal" and the "vertical" dimensions of redaction criticism.
5. Given the emphases and probable circumstances of Luke's Gospel, in what settings in contemporary Christian living might it be even more acutely relevant than the other Gospels?

9

THE GOSPEL OF JOHN

A NY READER WHO has worked carefully through Matthew, Mark, and Luke is immediately struck by how different a Gospel John is. Much that is central to all three Synoptics is entirely absent in John: Jesus' baptism, the calling of the Twelve, the exorcisms, the Transfiguration, the parables, and the institution of the Lord's Supper. John has numerous lengthy discourses of Jesus, but none of them matches any found in the Synoptics. Equally distinctive are the miracles of water turned into wine and the reawakening of Lazarus, an account of Jesus' early ministry in Judea and Galilee, his regular visits to Jerusalem, and the lengthy Farewell Discourse on the night before his crucifixion. As our survey of John's distinctive themes will demonstrate later in this chapter, there are equally prominent theological differences. There are also the same kind of apparent discrepancies with parallel passages in the Synoptics as periodically emerge among the Synoptics themselves. To top it all off, John's narrative demonstrates a uniform style, whether or not he is "quoting" Jesus, which differs considerably from the language of Christ that characterizes Matthew, Mark, and Luke.[1]

On the other hand, there is some overlap between John and the Synoptics: considerable attention to the ministry of John the Baptist, the feeding of the five thousand and walking on the water, Sabbath controversies with the Jews (particularly related to healing the lame and giving sight to the blind), Jesus' friendship

---

[1] For a helpful chart of a large number of these differences, categorized under seven headings, see P. N. Anderson, *The Fourth Gospel and the Quest for Jesus: Modern Foundations Reconsidered* (London and New York: T&T Clark, 2006), 98–99.

with Mary and Martha, and numerous events surrounding Jesus' passion. While the actual teachings of Jesus in John rarely repeat those of the Synoptics, the themes often dovetail closely: humility needed to enter the kingdom, an abundant harvest awaiting Christ's laborers, the dishonor a prophet receives in his home-land, judgment against unbelievers according to their works, the revelation of the Father through the Son to those the Father has granted him, Jesus as the Good Shepherd, true discipleship as servanthood, guidance through the Spirit for minis-try and proclamation, predicted future opposition for the disciples from the world, and authority to forgive or retain sins within the church.[2] Indeed, if one peruses a synopsis that includes Johannine parallels, almost every distinctive passage in John finds at least short conceptual counterparts in one or a handful of much shorter Synoptic sayings somewhere.[3]

Historicity

Can John be taken seriously as a historically trustworthy account of the life of Jesus in light of this combination of similarities and differences from the Syn-optics? Most modern scholars have thought not.[4] However the issue is not so clear-cut. We will look at a selection of the most famous "discrepancies" within specific passages as we survey the life of Christ in the next section of this book. But several general comments are in order here.[5] First, one of the reasons John seems so different is because *Matthew, Mark, and Luke are so similar* to each other. Actually, it is the latter observation that should at first glance be the more surprising and significant. It is precisely the similarities among the Synoptics that lead to conclusions about literary dependence. It is arguable, on the other hand, that John is largely independent of the Synoptics, at least in terms of direct literary borrowing (see below), and that this accounts for the diverse selection of details. Although clearly a hyperbole, John 21:25 nevertheless encapsulates an important truth: Jesus did so many things that, had four writers all written of him indepen-dently, their Gospels might all have produced books as different from each other as John is from the Synoptics.

---

[2] For these and other similarities and differences, complete with all the appropriate chapter and verse references, see Blomberg, *The Historical Reliability of the Gospels*, 197–203.

[3] Partially related is P. W. Ensor's observation ("Johannine Sayings of Jesus and the Question of Authenticity," in *Challenging Perspectives on the Gospel of John*, ed. J. Lierman [Tübingen: Mohr Sie-beck, 2006], 20) that "90% of Jesus' Johannine vocabulary either also occurs in his Synoptic speech, or, failing to occur there, also fails to occur in the Johannine literature outside dominical [Jesus'] speech (a fact which weighs against that vocabulary being particularly Johannine)."

[4] For an extreme, scathing perspective, see M. J. Casey, *Is John's Gospel True?* (London: Rout-ledge, 1996). For an irenic, centrist approach, cf. A. T. Lincoln, *Truth on Trial: The Lawsuit Motif in the Fourth Gospel* (Peabody: Hendrickson, 2000). For a rare anthology that includes all major perspec-tives, from evangelical to liberal, see P. N. Anderson, F. Just, and T. Thatcher, eds., *John, Jesus, and History*, vol. 1: *Critical Appraisals of Critical Views* (Atlanta: Scholars, 2007).

[5] For a detailed study of all these and related issues, see Blomberg, *The Historical Reliability of John's Gospel*. Cf. idem., "John and Jesus," in *The Face of New Testament Studies*, ed. S. McKnight and G. R. Osborne (Grand Rapids: Baker; Leicester: IVP, 2004), 209–26.

Second, even though the Fourth Gospel may be for the most part *literarily* independent of the Synoptics, it is hard to imagine its author being ignorant of the core kerygma that they share. He was almost certainly aware of the most common information widely reported about Jesus and could well have consciously chosen not to repeat most of it.[6] In a number of places, John refers to events from Jesus' life so briefly that one must assume he knew his audience would have previous knowledge about them, the kind on which the Synoptics wax eloquent (e.g., the imprisonment of John the Baptist (John 3:24), the trial before Caiaphas (18:24, 28a), and the reference to the "Twelve" (John 6:67–71). Conversely, we have seen a variety of theological and geographical motives for the outlines of the Synoptics. So it is conceivable that *Matthew, Mark, and Luke could have wanted to omit information* about Jesus (however precious it may seem to us) that did not fit their particular agendas (e.g., all of Jesus' visits to Jerusalem before his last Passover, which would account for their omission of the resurrection of Lazarus).

Third, a reverse kind of *interlocking* discloses numerous places where John explains something likely to have been puzzling to those familiar only with the Synoptic kerygma, suggesting closer points of contact between the two basic narratives than many acknowledge. For example, why did Jesus in Mark 14:49 refer to the numerous times he has taught in the temple courts without being arrested when in the Synoptics this final Passover of his adult ministry is the *only* time he has been portrayed teaching there? John's accounts of multiple trips to Jerusalem over roughly a three-year period supply the answer. Why does the Sanhedrin in the Synoptics have to pass Jesus over to Pilate rather than just executing him themselves under their own laws (Mark 15:1–3 pars.)? Only John answers the question: in most instances Rome had taken away their right to administer the death penalty (John 18:31). Numerous similar examples of this phenomenon could be cited.[7] Indeed, what John Robinson first called the "new look" on John way back in the late 1950s[8] has grown to such an extent that a significant minority of John's unique passages are now seen by most scholars as most likely being historically accurate, both because of details in the Synoptics they further illuminate and because they "cohere" with the generally accepted authentic core of the traditions about Jesus in Matthew, Mark and Luke.[9]

Fourth, at least some of the differences between John and the Synoptics can be explained on the basis of the *different audiences* within the Gospels' narratives. Only John chooses to record Jesus' "Farewell Discourse" (chaps. 13—17). The very intimate concerns Jesus shared with his disciples on his last night would understandably differ considerably from his more public teaching elsewhere. The

---

[6] An assumption now virtually proved by R. Bauckham, "John for Readers of Mark," in *The Gospels for All Christians*, ed. Bauckham, 147–71.

[7] See esp. L. Morris, *Studies in the Fourth Gospel* (Grand Rapids: Eerdmans, 1969), 40–63. Cf. D. A. Carson, *The Gospel according to John* (Grand Rapids: Eerdmans; Leicester: IVP, 1991), 52–55.

[8] J. A. T. Robinson, "The New Look on the Fourth Gospel," *TU* 73 (1959): 338–50. For Robinson, this culminated in his posthumously published work, *The Priority of John*, ed. J. F. Coakley (London: SCM, 1985; Oak Park, IL: Meyer-Stone, 1987).

[9] Nicely summarized in Anderson, *The Fourth Gospel and the Quest for Jesus,* 154–73.

same is true for Jesus' teaching in Jerusalem at festival times, which occupies much of John 5—11. Unique concerns and styles of speaking would naturally emerge when Jesus explained the significance of his ministry vis-à-vis the sacred institutions of Israel to its authorities in the midst of its holy city. All the more so would this be the case as John wrote to a community at the end of the first century with the unique, twin dangers of a hostile local Jewish leadership and emerging Gnosticism (see below, pp. 194–95). Numerous episodes or details from Christ's life would prove particularly important in this context that were not as crucial earlier in other settings.

Fifth, historical trustworthiness in the ancient world was not defined by the degrees of scientific precision or exact quotation that our modern society relishes. (And even we often accept as accurate a report of the "gist" of what someone has said.) We should freely admit that John wrote his entire Gospel in *his distinctive style*, paraphrasing, excerpting, and interpreting Jesus' words in his own language to bring out what he believed were their full and true significance. John's unique emphasis on the role of the Holy Spirit as an interpreter of Jesus' words no doubt explains much of the freedom he felt to do this (14:26; 15:26; 16:12–13).[10] Various scholars have plausibly seen the lengthier discourses in John, at least in part, as the product of several decades of early Christian reflection, preaching, and application of Jesus' authentic words to the needs of the emerging "Johannine community."[11] A disproportionate number of times these core teachings resemble Synoptic parables, one of the parts of the Synoptic tradition most widely acknowledged to go back to Jesus himself.[12] In other cases they involve what might be called "riddles"—similarly cryptic sayings.[13] Indeed, John's genre in places resembles Hellenistic "drama" more than straightforward historical reporting,[14] yet both genres may be effectively used to describe the story of someone's life and faithfully convey its significance.[15] Already in the late second century, Clement of Alexandria explained John's distinctives with these words: "Last of all John, perceiving that the bodily [or external] facts had been set forth in the [other] Gos-

---

[10] H. N. Ridderbos, *The Gospel of John: A Theological Commentary* (Grand Rapids and Cambridge: Eerdmans, 1997), 14–16.

[11] See esp. throughout B. Lindars, *The Gospel of John* (London: Oliphants: 1972; Grand Rapids: Eerdmans, 1981). At the core of each of these discourses is teaching that finds close conceptual parallels to shorter sayings in the Synoptics, and sometimes verbal parallels as well. On the other hand, Lindars' claim that every Johannine saying of Jesus introduced with *Amēn, amēn* ("Truly, truly") shows it to be an original saying of Jesus cannot always be sustained. See R. A. Culpepper, "The Origin of the 'Amen, Amen' Sayings in the Gospel of John," in *Jesus in Johannine Tradition*, ed. R. T. Fortna and T. Thatcher (Louisville and London: WJKP, 2001), 253–62.

[12] C. H. Dodd, *Historical Tradition in the Fourth Gospel* (Cambridge: CUP, 1963), 366–87. Cf. also E. Schweizer, "What about the Johannine 'Parables'?'" in *Exploring the Gospel of John*, ed. R. A. Culpepper and Clifton C. Black (Louisville: WJKP, 1996), 208–19.

[13] T. Thatcher, *The Riddles of Jesus in John: A Study in Tradition and Folklore* (Atlanta: SBL, 2000). Cf. also K. E. Dewey, "*Paroimiai* in the Gospel of John," *Semeia* 17 (1980): 81–99.

[14] See esp. J.-A. A. Brandt, *Dialogue and Drama: Elements of Greek Tragedy in the Fourth Gospel* (Peabody: Hendrickson, 2004).

[15] See esp. D. Tovey, *Narrative Art and Act in the Fourth Gospel* (Sheffield: SAP, 1997).

pels, at the instance of his disciples and the inspiration of the Spirit, composed a spiritual Gospel" (cited in Eusebius, *Hist. eccl.* 6.14.7).

Sixth, at the same time, there are some features of John's Gospel that actually make it *more like Greco-Roman historiography of the day* than the Synoptics. Richard Bauckham includes in this category the notably greater number of references to geography and topography, chronology, and reliance on eyewitness testimony; the far more plentiful narrative asides explaining potentially puzzling data to the work's readers; and the typically longer and more frequent discourses and dialogues.[16]

Seventh, although John writes in a fairly uniform style throughout his Gospel—even when Jesus is speaking—there are at least *145 words used only by Jesus* that appear nowhere in John's narrative sections.[17] And even when John's and Jesus' styles seem to merge, it is not impossible that John picked up some of his characteristic vocabulary from Jesus himself. A "Q"-passage that discloses many marks of authenticity (Matt 11:25–27; Luke 10:21–22) has often been called the "Johannine thunderbolt" in the middle of the Synoptic tradition because of its similarities to otherwise distinctively Johannine language. In these verses Jesus praises God for revealing himself not to the wise but to "little children" to whom he was pleased to make himself known. Matthew 11:27 concludes, "All things have been committed to me by my Father. No one knows the Son except the Father, and no one knows the Father except the Son and those to whom the Son chooses to reveal him."[18] To the extent that "Jesus the Sage" emerges as a dominant picture of Christ in both the Synoptics and John,[19] this text could account for a number of John's distinctive emphases—on Jesus as the one sent from God to reveal God's purposes to the world—and nevertheless still reflect historical tradition.

Eighth, as D. A. Carson has stressed, there are more than two dozen places in John where *misunderstandings occur that can be remedied only with the passage of time.* The most famous, no doubt, is the inability of Jesus' audience to understand his claim about the destruction and resurrection of the temple in 2:19. Only his disciples ever understood this claim, as referring to the temple of Jesus' body, and then only after his resurrection (2:22). The metaphorical significance of the entire Bread of Life discourse was largely lost on its audience (6:41–42, 52, 60), as much of his Farewell speech was even on his disciples (14:5, 8, 22; 16:17–18). Some who had apparently come to believe in him at the Feast of Tabernacles end up condemning him as he continues to challenge them with his heavenly origin and pre-existence (8:31–59). These and other similar examples demonstrate that John was not re-writing his Gospel solely from the perspective of insights attained by

---

[16] R. Bauckham, *The Testimony of the Beloved Disciple: Narrative, History, and Theology in the Gospel of John* (Grand Rapids: Baker, 2007), 93–112.

[17] H. R. Reynolds, *The Gospel of John*, vol. 1 (London and New York: Funk & Wagnalls, 1906), cxxiii–cxxv.

[18] On the pervasive influence of this passage in John, see J. W. Pryor, "The Great Thanksgiving and the Fourth Gospel," *BZ* 35 (1991): 157–79.

[19] As for B. Witherington, *Jesus the Sage: The Pilgrimage of Wisdom* (Minneapolis: Fortress, 1994); idem., *John's Wisdom: A Commentary on the Fourth Gospel* (Louisville: WJKP, 1995).

the time he wrote, but was remaining faithful to the understanding (or lack thereof) held by the various people in Jesus' audiences during his earthly ministry.[20]

Ninth, and closely related, *many of the details in John accurately fit pre-70 Judaism better than post-70 states of affairs* and are therefore not likely to have been made up at the end of the first century with no factual basis. With the destruction of the temple, all of the festival celebrations in Jerusalem that John stresses would have no longer been possible. Even more telling is the wide array of titles used of Jesus, especially early in John's Gospel, that sound particularly lofty from the vantage point of later Christian theologizing but which, in fact in Jesus' day were often mere synonyms for a Davidic, nationalistic, militaristic king. These include Son of Man, Son of God, King of Israel, Christ, and especially the prophet like Moses.[21]

Tenth, several of John's longer sermons unique to his Gospel show signs of *Jewish midrash*—the homiletical development of Old Testament texts—characteristic of the rabbis of the day but not of early Christian preaching (see esp. John 6:26–59[22]). Others contain core sections that clearly parallel the Synoptics but also demonstrate signs of careful construction and parallelism not easily susceptible to source-critical dissection. So the most reasonable assumption is that they were creations of Jesus in their current forms from the outset (see esp. the detailed *chiasms* in 5:19–30 and chaps. 14–16[23]). While admittedly this form of discourse differs in style from much of the Synoptic material, it is still easier to believe that it stems from the Jewish Jesus than from the Hellenistic milieu in which the Fourth Gospel was written (see p. 194).

Eleventh, John actually contains *more details of time and place* in the course of Jesus' ministry than do the Synoptics. It is only from John that we are able to determine that Jesus' ministry spanned approximately a three-year period. It is only John who preserves a careful chronological sequence of virtually all the details he narrates. Several studies have demonstrated how John's references to geography and topography prove remarkably accurate, particularly in and around Jerusalem. Archaeologists have identified and excavated the probable sites of such locations as the pools of Bethesda (5:2) and Siloam (9:11) and the "Stone Pavement" of Pilate's judgment seat (*Gabbatha*—19:13).[24] This accuracy of detail is

---

[20] See further D. A. Carson, "Understanding Misunderstandings in the Fourth Gospel," *TynBul* 33 (1982): 59–91.

[21] See esp. R. Bauckham, "Messianism according to the Gospel of John," in *Challenging Perspectives on the Gospel of John*, ed. Lierman, 34–68; repr. in *The Testimony of the Beloved Disciple*, 207–38.

[22] Cf. esp. P. Borgen, *Bread from Heaven: An Exegetical Study of the Concept of Manna in the Gospel of John and the Writings of Philo* (Leiden: Brill, 1965).

[23] Cf. esp. W. Brouwer, *The Literary Development of John 13–17: A Chiastic Reading* (Atlanta: Scholars, 2001).

[24] B. E. Schein, a pastor and tour leader in Israel for many years, was so impressed with this type of information that he wrote an entire commentary on the Gospel of John in travelogue form, an exercise which would have been almost entirely speculative if done with any of the Synoptics. See his *Following the Way: The Setting of John's Gospel* (Minneapolis: Augsburg, 1980). The most detailed accumulation of indirect evidence for John's reliability in matters of chronology, geography, and historical verisimilitude is Robinson, *The Priority of John*, 123–295.

all the more impressive since it appears incidentally. In other words, John does not seem to be trying to supply us with information that will enable us to reconstruct a detailed life of Christ. He is concerned to show Jesus as the fulfillment of the Jewish festivals (see below, p. 343), and so he stresses how Jesus went to Jerusalem at various feast times and narrates what he did there.

Twelfth, John is clearly *contextualizing the gospel* for an audience living under quite different circumstances than the communities to which Matthew, Mark, or Luke wrote. This would naturally affect both the style and contents of his writing. "Kingdom of God/heaven," so central to the Synoptics, appears a scant three times in John, but "eternal life" occurs seventeen times. Yet, Matt 19:16, 23–24 shows that the Synoptic Jesus understood the two expressions, at least in some contexts, as interchangeable.[25] The much more Greco-Roman audience of John's Gospel would have understood living forever much more readily than participating in the Jewish theocracy—the backdrop for God's kingly reign on earth. Contextualization could account for some of John's otherwise surprising omissions, too. Ancient rabbis told quite literally hundreds of parables that have been preserved in their literature, while there is not a single close parallel in all known Greco-Roman literature of antiquity (with Aesop's fables being the only even partially similar form).[26] Exorcisms took on magical characteristics in the Hellenistic world, absent from much of Judaism.[27] So the omission of these two forms of Jesus' teaching and miracle-working may likewise be explained by cultural differences.

Thirteenth, we must *avoid overestimating the differences*. It is often said, for example, that only John's Jesus actually claims to be divine. Yet Jesus' characteristic claims in John (the "I am" sayings) regularly invoke metaphorical language ("I am the gate," "I am the bread of life," etc.) that would not have been as transparent in its original setting as it is to us. John 8:25, 10:25, and 16:29 all remind us that the disciples did not think Jesus was speaking plainly to them until the last night of his life, and even then they misunderstood him![28] On the other hand, there are implicit claims scattered throughout the Synoptics that suggest there, too, that Jesus was indicating his oneness with God (see below, pp. 467–70).

Finally, in light of the central role of *such themes as "witness" and "truth"* (cf., e.g., 1:7–8, 19; 2:25; 3:11, 32–33; 5:31–40; 8:13–18; 15:26; 19:35, 21:24), it is difficult to imagine John dealing so creatively with the traditions he inherited as to actually distort them in ways that were truly unfaithful to the spirit of Jesus. Indeed, the entire Gospel outline is built around the theme of testimony, as we

---

[25] G. E. Ladd, *A Theology of the New Testament*, ed. D. A. Hagner, rev. ed. (Grand Rapids: Eerdmans, 1993), 290–95.

[26] See further H. K. McArthur and Robert M. Johnston, *They Also Taught in Parables: Rabbinic Parables from the First Centuries of the Christian Era* (Grand Rapids: Zondervan, 1990).

[27] E. Plumer, "The Absence of Exorcisms in the Fourth Gospel," *Bib* 78 (1997): 350–68.

[28] Even John 8:58 remains more indirect than if Jesus had walked up to someone and claimed explicitly, "I am God." Cf. J. F. McGrath, *John's Apologetic Christology: Legitimation and Development in Johannine Christology* (Cambridge: CUP, 2001), 103–16; and S. Motyer, *Your Father the Devil? A New Approach to John and the 'Jews'* (Carlisle: Paternoster, 1997), 209.

will see in our next section, as if John were a legal witness for the veracity of his narrative. Sometimes the religious meaning that people attach to certain historical events does not require their careful narration, but sometimes it does. If the Christian claim that God acted uniquely in Jesus of Nazareth in the ways John claims he did is to stand, then a narrative faithful to the events is a necessity. Even if it is still a minority viewpoint, what F. F. Bruce wrote a quarter century ago remains cogent:

> John presents the trial and execution of Jesus, as he presents everything else in his record, in such a way as to enforce his theological *Leitmotiv*: Jesus is the incarnate Word, in whom the glory of God is revealed. But the events which he presents in this way, and pre-eminently in the events of the passion, are real, historical events. It could not be otherwise, for the Word became flesh—the revelation became history.[29]

Structure

Like Mark, John falls into two "halves," one stressing Jesus' mighty deeds (chaps. 1–11) and one reflecting the events leading up to and including his death and resurrection (chaps. 12–21). The first eighteen verses reflect theologically on Jesus' pre-existence with God as the *logos* ("Word") who becomes incarnate, and thus this text functions as a prologue to the entire Gospel. Because 20:31 reads like a closing, many scholars have viewed chapter 21 as a later appendix added to a previous draft of the Gospel. More likely it is a deliberately designed conclusion to bring closure to certain issues raised in the opening chapter. For example, in chapter 1 we learn of the disciples' first calling (vv. 35–51); in chapter 21 we read of their reinstatement and further commissioning (vv. 15–23).[30] John 20:31 also makes the purpose of the Gospel clear: to promote belief in Jesus as the Christ (Messiah) and Son of God. This statement, coupled with the recurring theme of "witness" or "testimony" makes plausible an outline that understands all of John's information as witnessing to the truth of the Gospel so that people might believe it. A. E. Harvey has likened John's structure to the form of prophetic "lawsuit" (Hebrew, *ribh*) in the Old Testament, in which Scripture calls its readers to render a verdict on the evidence provided for them about God's dealings with his people (e.g., Ps 50; Isa 1:2–3; 3:13–15; Jer 2:4–13; Hos 4:1–3; Mic 6:1–5).[31]

Within the first half of the Gospel, chapters 2–11 are dominated by seven miracles (John calls them "signs") and seven major discourses of Jesus.[32] Several

---

[29] F. F. Bruce, "The Trial of Jesus in the Fourth Gospel," in *Gospel Perspectives*, vol. 1: *Studies of History and Tradition in the Four Gospels*, ed. R. T. France and David Wenham (Sheffield: JSOT Press, 1980; Eugene, OR: Wipf & Stock, 2003), 18. Cf. also G. M. Burge, "Situating John's Gospel in History," in *Jesus in Johannine Tradition*, ed. Fortna and Thatcher, 35–46; Ridderbos, *John*, 12–14.

[30] On the unity of chap. 21 with the rest of the Gospel, see P. S. Minear, "The Original Functions of John 21," *JBL* 102 (1983): 85–98. Cf. also the series of three articles by Franzmann and Klinger, Breck, and Ellis in *St. Vladimir's Theological Quarterly* 36 (1992): 7–15, 17–25, and 27–49.

[31] A. E. Harvey, *Jesus on Trial: A Study in the Fourth Gospel* (London: SPCK; Atlanta: John Knox, 1977).

[32] L. Morris (*The Gospel according to John*, rev. ed. [Grand Rapids: Eerdmans, 1995]) uses these as the organizing motifs for subdividing these chapters of John's Gospel, while interspersing other

pairs of signs and discourses are clearly related. For example, the feeding of the five thousand (6:1–15) leads into the Bread of Life Discourse (6:25–71). Healing the man born blind (9:1–41) illustrates Jesus' claim to be the Light of the World (7:1–8:59). But not all can be matched so neatly. More noteworthy are the structural indicators that suggest chaps. 2–4 and 5–10 are each to be taken as a unit. Chapters 2–4 begin and end with miracles in Cana, the only two explicitly enumerated "signs" of Jesus in this Gospel ("first," 2:11; "second" 4:54). All of the stories in these three chapters illustrate the newness of Jesus' ministry over against the old forms of Jewish religion. Chronologically, all of these events seem to precede Jesus' great Galilean ministry. Chapters 5–10 for the most part describe what Jesus did at festival times in Jerusalem, punctuating what we know from the Synoptics as a primary ministry in Galilee. Here John takes pains to stress Jesus as the fulfillment of the Jewish festivals—Passover, Tabernacles, and the "Dedication" (Hanukkah). Even the one main pair of events in this section not from Jesus' ministry in Jerusalem—the feeding of the five thousand and the walking on the water—is explicitly said to take place at Passover time. These events in turn lead to Jesus' sermon about the Bread of Life, which ties in closely with the symbolism of bread at Passover (chap. 6). Chapter 11 ties in with the rest of John's first main section by narrating Jesus' greatest miracle to date.

Chapters 12–21 also contain two major central portions. After the introduction in chap. 12 to the events that will culminate in Christ's death, chaps. 13–17 narrate what took place on the night of Jesus' betrayal and primarily comprise Jesus' Farewell Discourse to his disciples. Chapters 18–20 then recount the arrest, trials, crucifixion, and resurrection, containing the most extensive overlap with the Synoptics of any multiple-chapter section in John. Chapter 21 forms the conclusion. Putting this all together leads to a probable outline along the following lines:[33]

I. Introductory Testimony (1:1–51)
    A. Prologue (1:1–18)
    B. The Testimony of John and the First Disciples (1:19–51)
II. The Testimony of Signs and Discourses (2:1–11:57)

---

subdivisions as well. One could in fact outline all of John 2–11 in terms of these seven signs and discourses and material related to them: Sign 1: Water into Wine (2:1–11); Discourse 1: Born Again (2:12–3:36); Discourse 2: Living Water (4:1–42); Sign 2: The Official's Son (4:43–54); Sign 3: Healing the Paralytic (5:1–15); Discourse 3: Imitating the Father (5:16–47); Sign 4: Feeding the Five Thousand (6:1–15); Sign 5: Walking on the Water (6:16–24); Discourse 4: Bread of Life (6:25–71); Discourse 5: Light of the World (7:1–8:59); Sign 6: The Man Born Blind (9:1–41); Discourse 6: The Good Shepherd (10:1–21); Discourse 7: Oneness with the Father (10:22–42); Sign 7: Raising Lazarus (11:1–57).

[33] Cf. esp. G. L. Borchert, *John 1–11* (Nashville: Broadman & Holman, 1996); and idem., *John 12–21* (Nashville: Broadman & Holman, 2002). Because the death and resurrection of Lazarus (chap. 11) also foreshadows Jesus' own death and resurrection, a few commentators place the break between the two main halves of John after chap. 10. Because chap. 12 still contains key deeds and Jesus' reflection on them, many writers place the break after chap. 12. A compromise occasionally adopted is to set off chaps. 11–12 by themselves as a transitional section. The division after 11, however seems to be the best; 12:1 marks a clear shift in time and place. No more miracles ensue, and all events from here on lead inexorably to the cross.

A. Jesus and Jewish Institutions (2:1–4:54)
  1. Water into Wine—A New Joy (2:1–11)
  2. Temple Cleansing—A New Temple (2:12–25)
  3. Jesus, Nicodemus, and the Baptist—A New Birth (3:1–36)
  4. Jesus, the Samaritan Woman, and the Official's Son—A New Universalism (4:1–54)
B. Jesus and Jewish Festivals (5:1–10:42)
  1. Healing the Paralytic and Imitating the Father (5:1–47)
  2. The True Passover: The Bread of Life (6:1–71)
  3. The True Tabernacles: Living Water and Light of the World (7:1–9:41)
  4. The Good Shepherd and Oneness with the Father (10:1–42)
C. Jesus as the Resurrection and the Life (11:1–57)
III. The Testimony of Death and Resurrection (12:1–20:31)
A. Actions in Preparation for Death (12:1–50)
  1. Anointing in Bethany (12:1–11)
  2. Entry into Jerusalem (12:12–50)
B. Teaching in Preparation for Death (13:1–17:26)
  1. Servant Ministry vs. Betrayal (13:1–30)
  2. Farewell Discourse (13:31–16:33)
  3. High-Priestly Prayer (17:1–26)
C. Events Surrounding the Death Itself (18:1–20:31)
  1. Arrest, Trials, and Crucifixion (18:1–19:42)
  2. Resurrection (20:1–29)
  3. Purpose of the Gospel (20:30–31)
IV. Concluding Testimony (21:1–25)
A. The Reinstatement of the Disciples (21:1–23)
B. Epilogue (21:24–25)

Theology

Views of Jesus

Because John is otherwise so different from the Synoptics, it is significant that the two main titles used for Jesus in this Gospel's purpose statement (John 20:31) are identical to those used in Mark's headline verse (Mark 1:1)—the Christ and the Son of God. But "Son" for John is even more clearly identified with a heavenly figure than in the Synoptics. John 3:31–36 is a key Christological passage that sums up important Johannine themes: "The one who comes from above is above all. . . . For the one whom God has sent speaks the words of God, for God gives the Spirit without limit. The Father loves the Son and has placed everything in his hands. Whoever believes in the Son has eternal life, but whoever rejects the Son will not see life. . ."

Four other emphases are considerably distinctive within Johannine Christology:

Logos. Only John calls Jesus "the Word" (Gk. *logos*), particularly in his prologue (1:1–18). The background of this term has been endlessly debated—was
it Stoic, Philonic, Mandaean, Targumic, or something else? The expression was
widely used in a variety of ancient Hellenistic and Jewish sources. In Stoic pantheism it could refer to the animating life force or "world soul" that permeated all
the universe, while in the Hebrew Scriptures it could refer to God's spoken word.
In the targums the Aramaic equivalent *memra* was often substituted for names of
God, especially in Genesis 1. What all these and other uses have in common is
that the *logos* was a widely used term to refer to the way God or the gods revealed
themselves and communicated with humankind. John may well be exploiting this
diverse background to stress that Jesus is the way in which the true, living God
reveals himself and communicates with his people.[34] The revelation of true knowledge remains a key function of the Johannine Redeemer. John 1:14 is a crucial
verse in this context: "The Word became flesh and made his dwelling among us."
The *logos* is no mere vision or phantom; he became incarnate as a genuine human
being. Although John is better known for his emphasis on Christ's deity, the doctrine of the *logos* who became *sarx* ("flesh") is also an important reminder of his
full humanity, a theme which John also reinforces throughout his Gospel.[35]

Lamb of God. John is the only New Testament writer to call Jesus the "Lamb
of God" (John 1:29, 36; and twenty-seven times in Revelation). John the Baptist
links this expression with Jesus' role in taking away the sin of the world (1:29).
Undoubtedly, part of the background for the image is the sacrificial lamb of the
Jewish Passover. But the victorious, conquering Lamb of Revelation suggests that
John may also draw on the motif in intertestamental literature of a sheep or ram
who represents a messianic warrior and deliverer of God's people from their enemies (cf., e.g., *T. Jos.*19:8–9; *T. Benj.* 3).[36]

Wisdom and Agent. Even more so than in Matthew, numerous parallels emerge
between John's portrait of Jesus and personified "Wisdom" in Jewish sapiential
literature. In intertestamental works like the Wisdom of Solomon or the Wisdom
of Sirach, we find close parallels to the following emphases of John regarding
Jesus: coming into the world to enlighten those who had eyes to see (1:9), being
written of by Moses and the prophets (1:45; 5:46), being known by Abraham
(8:56), and having a glory that Isaiah saw (12:41). Wisdom, like Jesus, was also
said to come and go from heaven, supply God's people with bread to eat, and

---

[34] See esp. P. M. Phillips, *The Prologue of the Fourth Gospel: A Sequential Reading* (London and
New York: T&T Clark, 2006), 73–141. Phillips concludes, "Logos could be, for various readers, 'the
first principle', 'the Word of God', 'the Church's traditional teaching', 'divine reason', 'the second
God', 'the emanation from the Pleroma', 'Wisdom', 'Torah', 'the Memra of God'. . . . The author
of the Prologue could be making a claim that *logos* is a universal concept and so refers to them all"
(139).

[35] See esp. M. M. Thompson, *The Incarnate Word: Perspectives on Jesus in the Fourth Gospel*
(Peabody: Hendrickson, 1993).

[36] G. R. Beasley-Murray, *John,* rev. ed. (Nashville: Nelson, 1999), 24–25.

bring the dead to life. In addition, she regularly spoke in lengthy discourses.[37] Also prominent in John is the picture of Jesus as the one whom God, his heavenly Father, has sent (e.g., 3:17, 28, 34; 4:34; 5:23, 24, 30; etc.). This language draws on the Hebrew concept of the *shaliach*, a messenger or "sent one" who acts as an agent for his master. Often the agent acts on behalf of the master in ways that begin to blur the distinction between the two.[38]

God. The above three sections all prepare the reader for this fourth one. Although no text in John ever has Jesus explicitly declare, "I am God," John does make claims for Jesus that imply his deity. In the prologue, the *logos* was "with God" and "was God" (1:1). Seven times Jesus makes "I am" statements that describe his exalted nature and reflect wildly arrogant claims if, in fact, he is not in some sense divine. Thus he calls himself "the bread of life" (6:35), "the light of the world" (8:12; 9:5), "the gate for the sheep" (10:7), "the good shepherd" (10:11), "the resurrection and the life" (11:25), "the way and the truth and the life" (14:6), and "the true vine" (15:1). He claims to be one with the Father in a sense that the Jews interpret as blasphemy—too close an equation with God (10:30–33). After the resurrection, Thomas touches Christ's scars and cries out in worship, "My Lord and my God!" (20:28).[39]

One must be careful not to make either too little or too much of these claims. Many writers find all this "high" Christology so lofty as to be incompatible with the Synoptics.[40] Yet, Matthew and Luke describe Christ's virginal conception, and there are clear hints of Jesus' deity scattered around the Synoptics: Jesus claims to forgive sins with divine authority (Mark 2:5 pars.), accepts worship (Matt 14:33), and announces that people's final destiny before God will be based on their response to him (Mark 8:38; Luke 12:8–10). He applies further metaphors to himself that in the Old Testament are often reserved for Yahweh (Lord of the harvest, shepherd, sower, vineyard owner, bridegroom, rock, etc.).[41] A few critics, on the other hand, stress that none of the "I am" sayings in John reflects an unambiguously divine self-consciousness on Jesus' part, not susceptible to "subordina-

---

[37] For these and numerous other parallels, see Witherington, *John's Wisdom*, 18–27. For a detailed treatment of the cognitive and relational implications of this portrait for humans "saved" by this kind of Christ through the power of the Spirit, see C. Bennema, *The Power of Saving Wisdom: An Investigation of Spirit and Wisdom in Relation to the Soteriology of the Fourth Gospel* (Tübingen: Mohr Siebeck, 2002). Cf. also S. H. Ringe, *Wisdom's Friends: Community and Christology in the Fourth Gospel* (Louisville: WJKP, 1999).

[38] This would have been the key point disputed by non-Christian Jews. See esp. McGrath, *John's Apologetic Christology*, 77–78.

[39] For a detailed exegesis of John 1:1, 18; and 20:28 in the context of a thorough study of "God" as a Christological title, see M. J. Harris, *Jesus as God: The New Testament Use of* Theos *in Reference to Jesus* (Grand Rapids: Baker, 1992), 51–129.

[40] A good example, otherwise helpful in its understanding of John on his own terms, is J. D. G. Dunn, *Christology in the Making: A New Testament Inquiry into the Origins of the Doctrine of the Incarnation*, rev. ed. (London: SCM, 1989 [= Grand Rapids: Eerdmans, 1996]), 213–50.

[41] See further R. L. Reymond, *Jesus, Divine Messiah* (Phillipsburg, NJ: Presbyterian & Reformed, 1990), 94–126; P. B. Payne, "Jesus' Implicit Claim to Deity in His Parables," *TJ* 2 (1981): 3–23.

tionist" interpretations.[42] But their cumulative effect remains too powerful for us to content ourselves with a picture of Jesus as merely an emissary or spokesperson for God.

Other Distinctive Themes

Realized Eschatology. Whereas the Synoptics stress a future hope and the return of Christ, John defines eternal life and death as beginning now in this age, based on men's and women's responses to Jesus. John 3:18 is representative: "No one who believes in him will be judged; but whoever does not believe is judged already, because that person does not believe in the Name of God's only Son" (NJB). Or compare 5:24: "Anyone who hears My word and believes Him who sent Me has eternal life and will not come under judgment but has passed from death to life" (HCSB; cf. also 3:36; 9:39; 12:31). Yet this latter passage reminds us also that the future hope is not entirely absent from John, as it goes on immediately to describe the time of the coming resurrection of both the just and the unjust (5:25–29; cf. also 6:39–40; 12:25, 48; 14:3, 28). Whereas "kingdom" texts dominate the Synoptics, they are rare in John. But it is arguable that John uses "eternal life" with the same present and future dimensions as the kingdom to contextualize the Gospel as it moves out of a Jewish into a more Hellenistic context.[43]

Miracles as Signs and Their Relation to Faith. In the Synoptic Gospels, whenever someone asks for a "sign" (Gk. *sēmeion*), Jesus uniformly refuses to give one (e.g., Matt 12:38–39; 16:1–4 pars.). In John, however, "signs" function positively as reason to believe in Jesus (e.g., John 2:11; 4:53–54),[44] although John's Jesus never performs a miracle "on demand" merely to satisfy a skeptic either. There is a second set of texts in John that takes a more critical view of signs. In Cana, Jesus seems to speak with exasperation when he laments that "unless you people see signs and wonders . . . you will never believe" (4:48). Although Jesus praises Thomas's belief based on firsthand evidence, he goes on to add, "Blessed are those who have not seen and yet have believed" (20:29). Robert Kysar helpfully proposes that we understand three stages in John's concept of faith—an embryonic stage that is at least open to faith (which is required before God will grant any sign), preliminary faith based on signs, and a mature faith that no longer requires them.[45]

Incipient Trinitarianism and the Unity of Jesus' Followers in Love. Particularly in his private teaching to the disciples in the Farewell Discourse, Jesus comes as close as anywhere in the Gospels to the type of Trinitarian theology that would

---

[42] See esp. Robinson, *The Priority of John*, 34–97.

[43] The best known scholarly treatment of realized eschatology in John remains C. H. Dodd, *The Interpretation of the Fourth Gospel* (Cambridge: CUP, 1953), but it needs to be corrected occasionally by J. T. Carroll, "Present and Future in Fourth Gospel 'Eschatology'," *BTB* 19 (1989): 63–69.

[44] On which, see esp. W. H. Salier, *The Rhetorical Impact of the Semeia in the Gospel of John* (Tubingen: Mohr Siebeck, 2004).

[45] R. Kysar, *John, the Maverick Gospel*, rev. ed. (Louisville and London: WJKP, 2007), 95–102. Cf. C. S. Keener, *The Gospel of John: A Commentary*, vol. 1 (Peabody: Hendrickson, 2003), 272–79.

later issue from early Christian creeds and councils.[46] He insists that he is "in the Father" and "the Father is in" him (14:11); when he leaves, the Spirit will replace him as "another advocate" performing many of the identical roles he played (v. 16). Jesus' high-priestly prayer speaks of the Father's and Son's reciprocal glorification (17:1–5). Yet, Father, Son, and Spirit are not entirely interchangeable in function or status. John 14:28 preserves a classic "subordinationist" strain, with Jesus' declaration, "the Father is greater than I." John's characteristic language of the Father sending the Son or the Son doing only what the Father commands (see esp. 5:19–42) is never reversed. That is, the Son never sends the Father, and the Father never does what the Son commands. To use the language of later theological reflection, John preserves ontological equality within functional subordination among the members of the Godhead.[47]

Similar comparisons and contrasts emerge from a study of the key Johannine theme of the unity of all true disciples. John never confuses the creature with the creator or says that believers can become gods.[48] Jesus prays that all of his followers will experience a unity created by their relationship with God in Christ, so "that all of them may be one, Father, just as you are in me and I am in you" (17:21; cf. vv. 11, 23a). This unity is to produce a powerful evangelistic effect: "then the world will know that you sent me and have loved them even as you have loved me" (v. 23b). The spirit of Christian interpersonal relationships may be summed up by the one word "love" (see esp. 13:34 and 15:12), which fulfills the Law as it was embodied in Jesus (see esp. 1:17).[49] Even so, love throughout John's Gospel and his Epistles is consistently defined in terms of obedience and keeping God's commands, even to the point of sacrificing one's life for another as Christ did for us (see classically John 15:9–17). Even though the Greek word for covenant (*diathēkē*) does not appear in John, the whole portrait of the Christian's obligation in the Fourth Gospel may be conceived of as that of remaining faithful to the new covenant that now defines God's will for his people.[50]

The Election and Security of the Believer. John includes several distinctive texts that speak of God's (and Jesus') unique role in choosing, drawing, and preserving those who are his people. Most famous of these are probably 6:39 ("And this is the will of him who sent me, that I shall lose none of all those he has given me, but raise them up at the last day") and 10:29 ("My Father, who has given them to me, is greater than all; no one can snatch them out of my Father's hand"). The disciples did not choose Christ, but he chose them (15:16). Conversely, Judas's betrayal demon-

---

[46] For a thorough study, see A. J. Köstenberger and S. R. Swain, *Father, Son and Spirit: The Trinity and John's Gospel* (Nottingham: Apollos; Downers Grove: IVP, 2008).

[47] Cf. further C. Cowan, "The Father and Son in the Fourth Gospel: Johannine Subordination Revisited," *JETS* 49 (2006): 115–35.

[48] On the meaning of John 10:34 in context, see below, p. 350.

[49] Cf. G. C. A. Fernando, *The Relationship between Law and Love in the Gospel of John* (Frankfurt: Peter Lang, 2004).

[50] See esp. R. M. Chennattu, *Johannine Discipleship as a Covenant Relationship* (Peabody: Hendrickson, 2006).

strates that he was not elected to salvation; Christ protected all the Father gave him. The one who was lost was "the one doomed to destruction" (17:12).

Yet balancing this predestinarian emphasis is John's equally prominent use of the word "abide" (or "remain"; Gk. *menō*), particularly in chapter 15. Believers must abide in Christ, and then he will abide in them, so that they can bear much fruit (v. 4). Verse 2 offers a solemn warning that the Father "cuts off every branch in me that bears no fruit." John's own harmonization of these two seemingly contrary strands of thought in his theology is probably provided in 1 John 2:19, where he describes those who abandoned the church to follow false teachers: "They went out from us, but they did not really belong to us. For if they had belonged to us, they would have remained with us; but their going showed that none of them belonged to us."[51]

The Death of Christ as Exaltation/Glorification. It is sometimes argued that the death of Jesus in John is "docetic"—Christ is so in control of events that he only *seems* to be human (see, e.g., John 18:6; 19:11, 30). John 19:33–34 would surely preclude this; here John insists that the man Jesus truly died. Others argue that John has no theology of atonement, but 1:29 and 36 challenge this claim.[52] What is a genuine Johannine distinctive involves several references to Christ's crucifixion as exaltation or glorification. John appears to collapse the death, resurrection, and ascension of Christ all into one event, anticipating their final outcome. A key reference is 12:32—"But I, when I am lifted up from the earth, will draw all people to myself"—presumably anticipating both his physical crucifixion and spiritual exaltation. John 7:39; 12:16, 23; and 13:31 all anticipate Christ's "glorification" with similar double meanings. In particular, 12:23 reflects the culmination of a recurring motif throughout the Fourth Gospel. After repeatedly insisting that his "hour" had not yet come (2:4; 7:30; 8:20), now Jesus declares "the hour has come for the Son of Man to be glorified."

The Holy Spirit as Paraclete. The Holy Spirit is even more prominent in John than in Luke. Wholly unparalleled elsewhere is John's use of the term *paraklētos* in the Farewell Discourse to refer to the Spirit. The word does not have a precise English equivalent; in different contexts it can include such concepts as counselor, comforter, or advocate. Five discrete roles for the Paraclete emerge in John 14–16: helper (14:15–21), interpreter (14:25–31), witness (15:26–16:4), prosecutor (16:5–11), and revealer (16:12–16).[53] One plausible reconstruction of the Johannine church finds it as a "charismatic" holdout (putting Spirit-filled experi-

---

[51] On the balance between divine sovereignty and human responsibility, see D.A. Carson, *Divine Sovereignty and Human Responsibility in John: Biblical Perspectives in Tension* (London: Marshall, Morgan & Scott, 1981; Eugene, OR: Harvest House, 2002). On the commands to abide, in the contexts of promises of security, see C. D. Bass, " A Johannine Perspective of the Human Responsibility to Persevere in the Faith through the Use of Μένω and Other Related Motifs," *WTJ* 69 (2007): 305–25.

[52] Cf. J. Dennis, "Jesus' Death in John's Gospel: A Survey of Research from Bultmann to the Present with Special Reference to the Johannine Hyper-texts," *CBR* 4 (2006): 331–63.

[53] F. F. Bruce, *The Gospel of John* (Basingstoke: Pickering & Inglis; Grand Rapids: Eerdmans, 1983), 301–21.

ence at the forefront of the Christian life) against an increasingly institutionalized ecclesiastical world surrounding it.[54]

Anti-Sacramentalism. One of the puzzling features of John's narrative is that he gives more details surrounding the events of Christ's baptism and the institution of the Lord's Supper than do the Synoptics (1:19–34, chaps. 13–17), and yet he never actually describes either of these rituals. Many scholars have seen his teachings in 3:5 ("No one can enter the kingdom of God without being born of water and the Spirit") and 6:53 ("Unless you eat the flesh of the Son of Man and drink his blood, you have no life in you") as cryptic allusions to or foreshadowings of Christian baptism and the Lord's Supper. In context these make adequate sense as metaphorical references to the cleansing work of the Spirit in bringing new life and to identification with Christ in his suffering and death, respectively.[55] It is at least arguable that again John was trying to play down the role of these two rituals in an era that had already begun to value them too highly, viewing them perhaps as means of grace in and of themselves.[56]

Anti-Baptist Cult? John has also struck readers with the way he plays down John the Baptist's authority. Although in the Synoptics Jesus speaks of the Baptist figuratively as Elijah come again (Matt 11:14; cf. Luke 1:17), in the Fourth Gospel the Baptist explicitly denies that he is Elijah (John 1:21). He also denies that he is the Christ. The Fourth Gospel goes out of its way to stress that the Baptist recognized that he must decrease in importance while Jesus increased (3:30). Given the presence of a group of John the Baptist's followers in Ephesus in the mid-first century who had a very truncated understanding of the gospel (Acts 19:1–7) and given later testimony about second-century followers of John who elevated him to messianic status (Pseudo-Clementine *Recog.* 1.54, 60; cf. also the passing allusion in Justin, *Dial.* 80), it is at least plausible to suggest that John was trying to dampen any improper enthusiasm some in his church might have had for the Baptist when he was writing to Ephesus at the end of the first century (for place and date, see further below, p. 194).

Relationship to Judaism. Like Matthew, John has often been accused of being anti-Semitic (or, more precisely, anti-Jewish) because of his frequent use of "the Jews" as a seemingly blanket term for condemning all of Jesus' opponents. This expression occurs sixty-eight times in John and only sixteen times in all of the Synoptics. On the other hand, Jesus tells the Samaritan woman in 4:22 that "salvation is from the Jews."[57] A careful analysis of contexts shows that sometimes *Ioud-*

---

[54] G. M. Burge, *The Anointed Community: The Holy Spirit in the Johannine Tradition* (Grand Rapids: Eerdmans, 1987).

[55] Carson, *John*, 191–96 and 295–98; C. G. Kruse, *The Gospel according to John* (Leicester: IVP, 2003; Grand Rapids: Eerdmans, 2004), 48–49.

[56] See, cautiously, R. E. Brown, *An Introduction to the Gospel of John*, ed. F. J. Moloney (New York and London: Doubleday, 2003), 155. For a survey of approaches and a balanced assessment, cf. R. W. Paschal, Jr., "Sacramental Symbolism and Physical Imagery in the Gospel of John," *TynBul* 32 (1981): 151–76.

[57] For a detailed treatment of what appear to be both pro- and anti-Jewish sentiments in John, see R. Hakola, *Identity Matters: John, the Jews, and Jewishness* (Leiden and Boston: Brill, 2005).

aioi means merely Judeans (as opposed to Galileans), other times it is shorthand for the Jewish leaders, and frequently it refers to the general rejection of Jesus by the bulk (but not all) of the Jewish people. John recognizes as readily as the Synoptics that Jesus' first followers were all Jewish, so there is no universal indictment of an entire ethnic group here.[58] What John does stress, though, is how Jesus fulfills the purpose of all the major Jewish institutions and rituals, including the Scriptures themselves. Without ever using the explicit language of Jeremiah's new covenant prophecies (Jer 31:31–34), John has Jesus inaugurating everything that the new covenant anticipated.[59] The church is now the chosen people of God.

Dualisms. John certainly does like to paint pictures in very black-and-white colors. Pairs of opposites characterize various aspects of his theology: light vs. darkness, life vs. death, love vs. judgment, above vs. below, spirit vs. flesh, truth vs. falsehood, those who believe vs. the world. In reality there are many shades and nuances of perspective throughout humanity, but John points to the one central truth that ultimately all people will be judged by God and put into one of only two camps: those who have believed in Jesus and those who have not. Painting these stark contrasts makes sense in light of the "sectarian" context of John's community. When one is embattled by hostile forces both inside and outside the church, it is natural to warn against error with strong language, even as it is important, as John does, to stress love and unity. Another kind of dualism is not one of opposing but balancing theological concepts, but one of intended double meanings in passages that often led to misunderstandings that were corrected only after the resurrection (e.g., John 2:20–22; 3:5–15; 4:10–14; etc.).[60]

Circumstances

In the first half of the twentieth century, most scholarship assumed John to be very late and Hellenistic in origin. The assumption was common that its exalted Christology could have been the product only of a long, slow evolution away from a more primitive, Jewish understanding of Jesus that did not yet think of him as God. Today, however, particularly in light of the discovery of the Dead Sea Scrolls with their unrelenting dualism (e.g., "the sons of light vs. the sons of darkness")

---

[58] Robustly defending at length this rebuttal of charges of anti-Semitism in John is L. Kierspel, *The Jews and the World in the Fourth Gospel* (Tübingen: Mohr Siebeck, 2006).

[59] J. W. Pryor, *John, Evangelist of the Covenant People: The Narrative and Themes of the Fourth Gospel* (London: Darton, Longman & Todd; Downers Grove: IVP, 1992), esp. 157–80. Perhaps most significant of all is Jesus as the fulfillment of the temple itself, on which see esp. P. M. Hoskins, *Jesus as the Fulfillment of the Temple in the Gospel of John* (Milton Keynes and Waynesboro, GA: Paternoster, 2006).

[60] For a "paleofundamentalist manifesto for contemporary evangelicalism, especially its elites, in North America," see the book so subtitled by R. H. Gundry (*Jesus the Word according to John the Sectarian* [Grand Rapids and Cambridge: Eerdmans, 2002]). For a thorough study denying the sectarian nature of John's community but still stressing that according to his Gospel the Spirit alone, for those who abide in Christ, gives true understanding of the gospel message, see S. Hamid-Khani, *Revelation and Concealment of Christ: A Theological Inquiry into the Elusive Language of the Fourth Gospel* (Tübingen: Mohr Siebeck, 2000).

and the more thorough knowledge of the diversity of pre-70 Judaism, the Jewish-ness of John and even of his Christology is much more widely affirmed.[61] Timothy Ling has recently pointed to intriguing parallels between John's emphasis on Judea and locations that were centers of Essene activity (Jerusalem, Bethany) and his portrayal of the disciples as akin to the Essenes at Qumran, especially with their common purse (12:6). Ling suggests that John's community and John's under-standing of the community of Jesus and his followers reflect what social-scientists call virtuoso religion—the ability to establish distinctive and influential sects with-in mainstream religious structures rather than simply isolated from them.[62] Larry Hurtado's detailed demonstration of the widespread nature of first-century worship of Jesus makes John's high Christology seem noticeably less anomalous as well.[63]

Reasonably strong early church tradition, however, does date the Gospel to *the end of the first century, probably during the reign of Domitian (81–96), when John was a very old man ministering in Ephesus*. This picture results from combining the testimony of such writers as Irenaeus (*Adv. Haer.* 3.1.1, 3.3.4), Polycrates, Papias, Polycarp, and Clement, all quoted in Eusebius (*Hist. eccl.* 3.31.3, 3.39.4, 5.20.4–6, 6.14.7), Eusebius himself (3.24.7), and Jerome (*De virib. illustr.* 9).[64] Least secure of these details is the date. A few writers have argued for a pre-70 date, in part on the basis of present tense references to Jewish places destroyed in the war with Rome (e.g., John 5:2).[65] But this may simply reflect John's style. Other arguments tend to be from silences (such as no reference to the destruction of the temple), but these are of dubious worth in general (since a narrative about *Jesus* would not necessarily refer to events forty years after his death). Indeed, a good case can be made that the strong Johannine emphasis on Jesus as the fulfill-ment of the deepest meaning of the various Jewish rituals and festivals makes best sense if the temple has already been destroyed so that many Jewish laws can no longer be literally obeyed.[66] Recently, Edward Klink has challenged wholesale the notion of a Johannine community or the idea that the Gospel was written with Christians in any one locale particularly in mind.[67] But just as scholarship of the past half-century has usually overestimated how much the internal evidence of the Gospel enables us to flesh out a specific subsection of first-century Christianity

---

[61] See esp. Keener, *John*, vol. 1, 171–232. Cf. S. S. Smalley, *John: Evangelist and Interpreter*, rev. ed. (Downers Grove: IVP, 1998), esp. 14–43; Bauckham, *The Testimony of the Beloved Disciple*, 239–52; and J. Lierman, "The Mosaic Pattern of John's Christology," in *Challenging Perspectives on the Gospel of John*, ed. Lierman, 210–34.

[62] T. J. M. Ling, *The Judaean Poor and the Fourth Gospel* (Cambridge: CUP, 2006).

[63] L. W. Hurtado, *Lord Jesus Christ: Devotion to Jesus in Earliest Christianity* (Grand Rapids and Cambridge: Eerdmans, 2003).

[64] For the texts of the most important Patristic passages, see J. R. Michaels, *John* (Peabody: Hendrickson, 1989), 5–7. One ancient tradition has John banished by Nero before AD 70 (*Syriac History of John*), but it is of dubious historical worth.

[65] Most notably, Robinson, *Redating the New Testament*, 254–311.

[66] See esp. A. Köstenberger, "The Destruction of the Temple and the Composition of the Fourth Gospel," in *Challenging Perspectives on the Gospel of John*, ed. Lierman, 69–108.

[67] E. W. Klink III, *The Sheep of the Fold: The Audience and Origin of the Gospel of John* (Cambridge: CUP, 2007).

to which it was addressed, Klink overly minimizes the significance of the external evidence that would give Ephesus a pride of place in the readership of a text doubtless simultaneously intended to be spread further afield.[68]

A popular critical reconstruction of the Johannine community has described its development in two main stages (often with numerous, smaller phases identified as well). The first stage is a Jewish-Christian community perhaps in Palestine in the mid–first century, finding itself increasingly in tension with the Jewish authorities and eventually excommunicated from the synagogues (9:22; 12:42; 16:2). The second stage is a Christian community of a more mixed nature but predominantly Gentile, in Asia Minor in and around Ephesus, toward the end of the first century. Both Jewish and Hellenistic features in John's Gospel would then be adequately accounted for.[69]

On the other hand, it is not obvious why both of these strands of thought could not have been present simultaneously, given what we know about Ephesus at the end of the first century. Irenaeus and Eusebius both report on the presence of a heretical teacher named Cerinthus, clearly a docetist (believing only in Christ's deity and not his humanity) and probably a Gnostic, who ministered in Ephesus at the end of the first century (*Adv. Haer.* 3.2.1; *Hist. eccl.* 3.28.6, 3.31.3, 4.14.6). Revelation 2:9 and 3:9, however, refer to Jewish communities that were hostile to Christianity in two cities near Ephesus as "synagogues of Satan." Clearly, it was possible that *the church in Asia Minor had to combat both a growing Gnostic and an antagonistic Jewish presence.*[70]

Interestingly, the Johannine epistles seem to reflect a corrective or balancing emphasis to some of the Fourth Gospel's theological distinctives. Raymond Brown notes four in particular: (1) more of an emphasis on Jesus' humanity than on his deity; (2) the importance of keeping God's commandments vs. claims of sinlessness; (3) more future than present eschatology; (4) and an insistence that the community has already learned God's truth through his Spirit vs. the promise of being guided into further truth. All of these contrasts make sense against a backdrop of increasing Gnostic distortion of the Gospel. *It may well be that John*

---

[68] See Blomberg, "The Gospels for Specific Communities and All Christians." Both Klink and I interact heavily with the important article by M. M. Mitchell, "Patristic Counter-evidence to the Claim that 'Gospels Were Written for All Christians,'" *NTS* 51 (2005): 36–79. Klink (like others I cite) has successfully shown that one may not use the Patristic testimony as the *hermeneutical* key to interpreting any of the Gospels (*contra* Mitchell), but he has barely begun to interact with her presentation of the pervasiveness of testimony that limited the initial addressees to a particular place or type of early Christianity.

[69] The most nuanced articulation of this evolution, dividing itself into eight phases altogether, appears in J. Ashton, *Understanding the Fourth Gospel* (Oxford: Clarendon, 1991), 163–66. The most famous two-stage approach is that of J. L. Martyn (*History and Theology in the Fourth Gospel*, rev. ed. [Louisville and London: WJKP, 2003]), who argues that the references to excommunication in John refer to the events of John's day, not Jesus'. Successfully countering this view, despite its immense popularity, is T. Hägerland, "John's Gospel: A Two-Level Drama?" *JSNT* 25 (2003): 309–22.

[70] Similarly, Witherington, *John's Wisdom*, 27–29; D. M. Smith, *Johannine Christianity: Essays on Its Setting, Sources and Theology* (London and New York: T&T Clark, 1999; Columbia: University of South Carolina Press, 2001).

originally wrote as he did to contextualize the Good News about Jesus for a com-
munity beginning to be interested in or influenced by incipient Gnosticism, only
to find that the false teachers were picking up on those themes that orthodoxy and
Gnosticism had in common and emphasizing them at the expense of balancing
themes. The Johannine epistles, particularly 1 John, would then have been written
with slightly different emphases to try to correct the imbalance.[71]

A quite different reconstruction of the circumstances behind John's composition understands the Fourth Gospel as an evangelistic tract to unsaved Jews.[72] This
would certainly account for the emphasis on Jesus as the fulfillment of Jewish
institutions and festivals, but it is not as clear that a writer would use John's more
virulent polemic against Jesus' Jewish opponents if he were trying to win over
hostile opponents. Part of this argument also depends on translating John 20:31 as
". . . that you may believe that the Christ, the Son of God, is Jesus," that is, helping
people looking for a Messiah to recognize who he is. This translation is possible
but in this context not as probable.[73] There is a second issue surrounding this verse
as well. Slightly better textual evidence supports a reading of the verb "believe"
as a present rather than an aorist subjunctive, in which case the Church Fathers'
testimony is reinforced that John is writing first of all to those who already believe
in Jesus so that they might continue to believe in the face of this two-pronged
opposition.[74] Ben Witherington suggests a plausible compromise: John is writing
to Christians to help them, among other things, be more effective in evangelizing
non-Christian friends and relatives, with a special focus on Jews.[75]

A final issue involves the literary relationship of John and the Synoptics. As
noted already, commentators a century or more ago usually explained John's differences as due to the fact that John was writing last of all the four. He knew what
Matthew, Mark, and Luke had already written and for the most part felt no need
to repeat their information. In short, he went about supplementing their material.
Throughout much of the twentieth century, the pendulum swung dramatically to
the view that John was largely independent of the Synoptics.[76] There are relatively
few places in which John's wording is so close to that of the Synoptics, even

---

[71] R. E. Brown, *The Community of the Beloved Disciple* (New York: Paulist, 1979), 109–44. For
anti-docetic and anti-Gnostic tendencies present (though more muted) already in the Gospel of John,
see respectively U. Schnelle, *Antidocetic Christology in the Gospel of John* (Minneapolis: Fortress,
1992); and M. de Jonge, *Jesus, Stranger from Heaven and Son of God: Jesus Christ and the Christians
in Johannine Perspective*, ed. J. E. Steely (Missoula, MT: Scholars, 1977).

[72] See esp. D. A. Carson, "The Purpose of the Fourth Gospel: John 20:31 Reconsidered," *JBL* 106
(1987): 639–51; and idem., "Syntactical and Text-Critical Observations on John 20:30–31: One More
Round on the Purpose of the Fourth Gospel," *JBL* 124 (2005): 693–714.

[73] See J. V. Brownson, "John 20:31 and the Purpose of the Fourth Gospel," *Reformed Review* 48
(1995): 212–16.

[74] A. T. Lincoln, *The Gospel according to Saint John* (London and New York: Continuum; Peabody: Hendrickson, 2005), 504–7.

[75] Witherington, *John's Wisdom*, 2, 11, *et passim*. Likewise, A. Köstenberger, *John* (Grand Rapids:
Baker, 2004), 8.

[76] Usually credited with initiating this surge is P. Gardner-Smith, *St. John and the Synoptic Gospels*
(Cambridge: CUP, 1938).

where they run parallel, to prove literary borrowing. But if John is not dependent on the written form of the other three evangelists' compositions, then we can deduce nothing about the date of the Fourth Gospel on the grounds of literary borrowing. As noted above, though, a few writers have plausibly suggested a mediating approach: several sets of parallel texts suggest that John may well have known at least Mark but did not feel compelled to follow him closely (p. 179).[77] So any date from the 60s on is in theory possible. Older views that placed John well into the second century have been discarded, however, with the discovery of the John Rylands fragment—already at least one stage of copying removed from John's original and yet dating from around 125–140. *The traditional idea of a date in the 80s or 90s remains best.*[78]

Authorship and Sources

The internal evidence points to an individual whom five passages call "the disciple whom Jesus loved" (John 13:23; 19:26; 20:2; 21:7, 20) as the primary witness to the events of this Gospel (21:24). With the "new look on John" recovering an emphasis on the Jewish roots of the Fourth Gospel, most commentators today agree that the author himself could well have been Jewish, and even originally from Israel. "Disciple" for John does not necessarily mean one of the Twelve, however, and some have imagined the "beloved disciple" to be Lazarus (cf. 11:3),[79] Thomas,[80] or some other anonymous follower of Jesus.[81] It is more natural to think of one of Christ's inner circle, probably from the group of three that the Synoptics described as his closest followers (Mark 9:2; 14:33)—Peter, James, and John. The Fourth Gospel knows that Jesus had twelve apostles (John 6:67, 70, 71) but never names them all. It does, however, refer to Peter as separate from and paired with the beloved disciple on two occasions (20:2–9; 21:20–24). James, the son of Zebedee, was martyred too early to be this Gospel's author (AD 44; cf. Acts 12:1–2). That leaves only his brother, the apostle John. Interestingly, this John never appears by name in the Gospel, while the John that does appear is always the Baptist, without ever being called by that title. Unless John the apostle were known to be the author of this document, surely this omission of any further clarification as to which "John"

---

[77] See esp. Bauckham, "John for Readers of Mark;" Anderson, *The Fourth Gospel and the Quest for Jesus*, 101–24; and C. K. Barrett, *The Gospel according to St. John*, rev. ed. (London: SPCK; Philadelphia: Westminster, 1978), 42–54.

[78] So also Kruse, *John*, 30–32;

[79] See esp. V. Eller, *The Beloved Disciple: His Name, His Story, His Thought* (Grand Rapids: Eerdmans, 1987); cf. B. Witherington III, *What Have They Done with Jesus? Beyond Strange Theories and Bad History* (San Francisco: HarperSanFrancisco, 2006), 141–56.

[80] Note, e.g., how Peter and Thomas are paired in 21:1, and then Peter and the beloved disciple are compared and contrasted in vv. 7–23. The view is defended at length by J. H. Charlesworth, who also comprehensively surveys the other proposals and arguments concerning authorship, in *The Beloved Disciple: Whose Witness Validates the Gospel of John?* (Valley Forge: Trinity, 1995).

[81] See esp. Bauckham, *The Testimony of the Beloved Disciple*, 73–91.

was in view would be surprising. All this adds up to strong circumstantial evidence for equating the beloved disciple with the apostle John.[82]

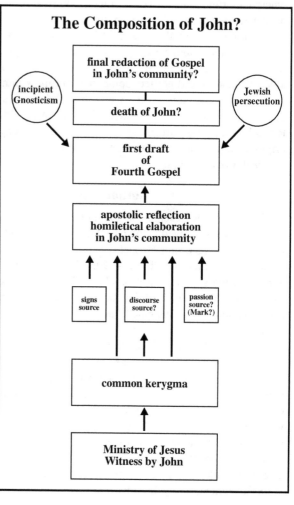

The external evidence generally concurs. Here, however, is the one Gospel for which early Church testimony is in one instance ambiguous. Papias (arguably the oldest surviving witness) declared: "If ever anyone came who had followed the presbyters, I inquired into the words of the presbyters, what Andrew or Peter or Philip or Thomas or James or John or Matthew, or any other of the Lord's disciples had said, and what Aristion and the presbyter John, the Lord's disciples, were saying" (cited in Eusebius, *Hist. eccl.* 3.39.4). It is not clear if Papias is referring to one or two different individuals named John here. Some, following Eusebius himself, believe he lists two different groups of Christians—first generation apostles and church leaders of Papias's day ("presbyter" can also be translated "elder"). If there were a presbyter John active in the early second century, one would not have to imagine the eighty- or ninety-year-old apostle still alive and capable of writing the Fourth Gospel at the end of the first century. Martin Hengel has redefended this interpretation in detail

---

[82] The detailed evidence for narrowing down the author of this Gospel to a Jew, from Israel, an eyewitness, an apostle, and then John is classically stated by B. F. Westcott, *The Gospel according to St. John* (London: John Murray, 1908; Eugene, OR: Harvest House, 2004), x–lii. Significantly expanding the evidence under each heading is Morris, *Studies in the Fourth Gospel*, 139–292. A thorough survey of arguments for and against the various proposed authors appears in Keener, *John*, vol. 1, 83–139.

and ascribed authorship of the Fourth Gospel to this John the presbyter (the same title given to the anonymous author of 2 and 3 John in the opening verses of those letters).[83] On the other hand, if the aged John were the only apostle still alive at the time to which Papias refers, it would explain John's inclusion in both lists: the first reference would link him with the other (now deceased) apostles; the second, with a fellow elder in the church of his day. This is the more common and more natural interpretation of Papias's testimony.[84]

Modern scholars, however, often reject Johannine authorship for several other reasons. For example, they claim that: (1) the Judean focus of the Gospel is inappropriate for someone of Galilean origin (cf. Mark 1:16–20), especially given this author's apparent connection with the high priest (John 18:15–16); (2) a "Son of Thunder" (Mark 3:17) would have been too volatile to pen this calm treatise; (3) John was illiterate (cf. Acts 4:13); (4) a Jew would not have used the phrase "the Jews" so critically; and (5) the apostle could not have called himself "beloved."

On the other hand, (1) John's focus on Judea and Jerusalem may be due to historical and theological reasons, and he could have accompanied Jesus on all his trips there. His closeness to Mary (John 19:26–27), who herself had priestly relatives (Luke 1:5, 36), could suggest that John also had friends or relations in high places.[85] (2) A simple nickname hardly determines someone's entire personality. (3) The view that John was illiterate is based on a mistranslation of Acts 4:13, which affirms only that John did not have formal rabbinic training. (4) We have already seen Matthew use equally pointed language in situations where Judaism staunchly rejected early Christianity. (5) This witness never calls himself the only disciple Jesus loved or the one he loved most, and his refusal to mention his name has even been seen as a mark of humility. More likely, the references to the beloved disciple could be redactional insertions by the final editors of the document John largely created. On the positive side, the simple but generally accurate *koinē* Greek used in all of the Johannine documents fits well with one who learned Greek as a second language. The only serious stumbling block to accepting Johannine authorship is the striking

---

[83] Hengel, *Johannine Question* (London: SCM; Philadelphia: Trinity, 1989). But Hengel's reconstruction of John the presbyter closely matches traditional reconstructions of John the apostle. Bauckham (*The Testimony of the Beloved Disciple*, 33–72), before defending the view that the Beloved Disciple is anonymous, also suggests that we should take seriously the possibility that a John the Elder, separate from the Apostle, authored the Fourth Gospel. But Bauckham's elder *was* the Beloved Disciple and eyewitness of Jesus' ministry, just separate from the Twelve, rather than a second generation disciple of the Apostle.

[84] See C. E. Hill, "What Papias Said about John (and Luke): A 'New' Papian Fragment," *JTS* 49 (1998): 582–629; Gundry, *The Old Is Better*, 52–55.

[85] R. A. Culpepper (*John, the Son of Zebedee* [Columbia: University of South Carolina Press, 1994], 62) believes that the story of Peter's denial requires the beloved disciple to be relatively unknown. Presumably, he means that this disciple, who accompanied Peter, if John the apostle, would have stood equally accused. But the accusers are only servants and bystanders. Perhaps they *did* know about John but were unsure of Peter, which is why they questioned him—more out of mockery than overt hostility. Charlesworth (*The Beloved Disciple*, 56) observes that Jerusalem depended on Galilean fishermen for their fish supply, so some of the more well-to-do fishermen would be the most likely to have access to the elite in Judea. As a family with more than one hired servant (Mark 1:20), Zebedee and his sons might have comprised just such a family.

difference in theology between him and the Synoptics. While we must not minimize the differences, they can certainly be exaggerated. Furthermore, one must not
underestimate the diversity that existed even within apostolic Christianity.

A related issue is that of Johannine source-criticism. Rudolf Bultmann's
ground-breaking commentary argued for three major sources behind the Fourth
Gospel: a signs source, discourse source, and passion source.[86] Supporting stylistic and literary evidence appears in a significant amount only for the first of
these.[87] There are intriguing "seams" in John's narrative where it appears that
material could have been reversed in sequence in some stage of editing or copying. The most noteworthy of these comes at John 14:31–15:1, in which Jesus
declares, "Come now; let us leave," and then continues for two more chapters with
his discourse. But it may well be that John did intend to portray Jesus as getting
up at that point and heading with his disciples from the Upper Room toward the
Garden of Gethsemane while continuing to teach.[88] Be that as it may, more recent
studies have stressed the stylistic and narrative unity of John's Gospel in its finished form.[89] As one writer put it (tongue-in-cheek), "If the author of the Fourth
Gospel used documentary sources, he wrote them all himself."[90]

Many commentators have taken a slightly different tack and tried to isolate
stages or levels of redaction within the Gospel. The prologue and final chapter
are regular candidates for "add-ons" to an original document. Various schemes
of two, three, and five stages of editing have proved popular,[91] but again the data
are too slippery to pin down any of these with confidence. The closing two verses
of the Gospel (21:24–25) support at least some minimal redactional activity, as
they distinguish the beloved disciple who recorded the events of the Gospel from
a group of people ("we") who "know that his testimony is true" and an "I" who
supposes that the whole world could not contain the books that could be written
about Jesus. The fact that 21:20–23 debunks a false rumor that had spread that the
beloved disciple would live until Christ's return makes the hypothesis attractive
that John had just died and a group of his followers or members of his church were
now editing his work for final publication.[92]

Such editing could have affected many parts of the Gospel, but we really
have no way of knowing for sure. Beyond this, theories of the composition of the

---

[86] R. Bultmann, *The Gospel of John* (Oxford: Blackwell; Philadelphia: Westminster, 1971 [Germ.
orig. 1941]).

[87] See esp. R. T. Fortna, *The Gospel of Signs: A Reconstruction of the Narrative Source Underlying the Fourth Gospel* (Cambridge: CUP, 1970); and idem., *The Fourth Gospel and Its Predecessor*
(Philadelphia: Fortress, 1988; London and New York: T&T Clark, 2004).

[88] Köstenberger, *John*, 445–46; Kruse, *John*, 313–14.

[89] See esp. A. Culpepper, *Anatomy of the Fourth Gospel: A Study in Literary Design* (Philadelphia:
Fortress, 1983); M. W. G. Stibbe, *John as Storyteller: Narrative Criticism and the Fourth Gospel*
(Cambridge: CUP, 1992).

[90] P. Parker, "Two Editions of John," *JBL* 75 (1956): 304.

[91] See, respectively, Martyn, *History and Theology*; R. Schnackenburg, *The Gospel according to St.
John*, vol. 1 (London: Burns & Oates; New York: Herder & Herder, 1968), 100–4; and R. E. Brown,
The Gospel according to John, vol. 1 (Garden City: Doubleday, 1966), xxxiv–xxxix.

[92] So, e.g., Beasley-Murray, *John*, 412; Kruse, *John*, 28–29.

Fourth Gospel tend merely to compound one speculative hypothesis with another. It seems safest to assume that at least a substantial core of the Gospel as we know it goes back to the apostle John, and any editing that may have occurred was done to put it into a form that enabled God's Spirit best to apply the truths of the Gospel to the Johannine community. The story of Jesus may have been contextualized, but it has not been distorted or falsified.

For Further Study

Commentaries

Introductory

Burge, G. M. *John*. NIVAC. Grand Rapids: Zondervan, 2000.

Kruse, Colin G. *The Gospel according to John*. Rev. ed. TNTC. Leicester: IVP, 2003; Grand Rapids: Eerdmans, 2004.

Michaels, J. Ramsey. *John*. NIBC. Peabody: Hendrickson, 1989.

Milne, Bruce. *The Message of John*. BST. Leicester and Downers Grove: IVP, 1993.

Whitacre, Rodney A. *John*. IVPNTC. Downers Grove and Leicester: IVP, 1999.

Intermediate

Beasley-Murray, George R. *John*. Rev. ed. WBC. Nashville: Nelson, 1999.

Borchert, Gerald L. *John*. 2 vols. NAC. Nashville: Broadman & Holman, 1996–2002.

Carson, D. A. *The Gospel according to John*. PNTC. Grand Rapids: Eerdmans; Leicester: IVP, 1991.

Lincoln, Andrew T. *The Gospel according to Saint John*. BNTC. London and New York: Continuum; Peabody: Hendrickson, 2005.

Moloney, Francis J. *The Gospel of John*. SP. Collegeville, MN: Liturgical, 1998.

Morris, Leon. *The Gospel according to John*. Rev. ed. NIC. Grand Rapids: Eerdmans, 1995.

Ridderbos, Herman N. *The Gospel of John: A Theological Commentary*. Grand Rapids: Eerdmans, 1997.

Witherington, Ben, III. *John's Wisdom: A Commentary on the Fourth Gospel*. Louisville: WJKP, 1995.

Advanced

Barrett, C. K. *The Gospel according to St. John*. Rev. ed. London: SPCK; Philadelphia: Westminster, 1978.

Brown, Raymond E. *The Gospel according to John*. 2 vols. AB. Garden City: Doubleday, 1966–70.

Keener, Craig S. *The Gospel of John: A Commentary*. 2 vols. Peabody: Hendrickson, 2003.

Köstenberger, Andreas. *John*. BECNT. Grand Rapids: Baker, 2004.

Schnackenburg, Rudolf. *The Gospel according to St. John*. 3 vols. London: Burns & Oates; New York: Herder and Herder; Seabury, 1968–82.

Other Key Studies of Johannine Introduction or Theology More Generally

Anderson, Paul N. *The Fourth Gospel and the Quest for Jesus: Modern Foundations Reconsidered.* London and New York: T&T Clark, 2006.

Anderson, Paul N., Felix Just, and Tom Thatcher, *John, Jesus, and History*, vol. 1: *Critical Appraisals of Critical Views*. Atlanta: SBL, 2007.

Ashton, John. *Understanding the Fourth Gospel.* Oxford: Clarendon, 1991.

Bauckham, Richard. *The Testimony of the Beloved Disciple: Narrative, History, and Theology in the Gospel of John.* Grand Rapids: Baker, 2007.

Bauckham, Richard, and Carl Mosser, eds. *The Gospel of John and Christian Theology.* Grand Rapids and Cambridge: Eerdmans, 2008.

Blomberg, Craig L. *The Historical Reliability of John's Gospel.* Leicester and Downers Grove: IVP, 2001.

Brown, Raymond E. *An Introduction to the Gospel of John.* Ed. Francis J. Moloney. New York and London: Doubleday, 2003.

Fortna, Robert T. and Tom Thatcher, eds. *Jesus in Johannine Tradition.* Louisville and London: WJKP, 2001.

Hengel, Martin. *The Johannine Question.* London: SCM; Philadelphia: Trinity, 1989.

Klink, Edward W. III. *The Sheep of the Fold: The Audience and Origin of the Gospel of John.* Cambridge: CUP, 2007.

Kysar, Robert. *John, the Maverick Gospel.* Rev. ed. Louisville and London: WJKP, 2007.

Kysar, Robert. *Voyages with John: Charting the Fourth Gospel.* Waco: Baylor University Press, 2006.

Lierman, John, ed. *Challenging Perspectives on the Gospel of John.* Tübingen: Mohr Siebeck, 2006.

Lozada, Francisco, Jr., and Tom Thatcher, eds. *New Currents through John: A Global Perspective.* Atlanta: SBL, 2006.

Martyn, J. Louis. *History and Theology in the Fourth Gospel.* 3rd ed. Louisville and London: WJKP, 2003.

Richey, Lance B. *Roman Imperial Ideology and the Gospel of John.* Washington: Catholic Biblical Association of America, 2007.

Robinson, John A. T. *The Priority of John.* London: SCM, 1985; Oak Park, Ill.: Meyer-Stone, 1987.

Smalley, Stephen. *John: Evangelist and Interpreter.* Rev. ed. Downers Grove: IVP, 1998.

Smith, D. Moody. *The Theology of the Gospel of John.* Cambridge: CUP, 1995.

Thatcher, Tom. *Why John Wrote a Gospel: Jesus-Memory-History.* Louisville and London: WJKP, 2006.

Thatcher, Tom, ed. *What We Have Heard from the Beginning: The Past, Present, and Future of Johannine Studies.* Waco: Baylor University Press, 2007.

Bibliography

Mills, Watson E. *The Gospel of John.* Lewiston and Lampeter: Mellen, 1995.

Questions for Review

1. What is a plausible overall outline for the Gospel of John? That is, how many main sections may it be divided into and by what criteria? What theology may be inferred from this structure?

2. According to typical evangelical reconstructions, who wrote this Gospel, when, where, to whom, and under what circumstances (to the extent that this information may be reasonably inferred)?

3. What are some of the unique issues surrounding the authorship of this Gospel that are not present with the Synoptics? What are some of the unique issues surrounding the source and redaction criticism of this Gospel?

4. What are several of the major theological distinctives of this Gospel?

5. In what ways is John more different from the Synoptics than they are from each other? Why might this be? Can its historicity be defended? If so, how? If not, why not?

6. Given the emphases and probable circumstances of John's Gospel, in what settings in contemporary Christian living might it be even more acutely relevant than the other Gospels?

Part Four

A SURVEY OF THE
LIFE OF CHRIST

I N THE MODERN era, conservative scholars have been preoccupied with fitting all of the details of the four Gospels together into a harmony of the life of Christ. Liberal scholars have been just as preoccupied with stressing the theological distinctives of each Gospel. Each of these approaches, when employed to the exclusion of the other, leads to a distorted understanding of the texts. Theology without harmonization discovers only distinctions and alleged contradictions without seeing how much the Gospels have in common and how they can be combined into a harmonious whole. Harmonization without appreciation for the theological distinctives of the Gospels trades the inspired form of the text for a humanly created one. It is our desire to keep both history and theology in their proper balance in this book.

Related to this balance are the results of the so-called "quest for the historical Jesus." What can we know about Jesus, from the Gospels or elsewhere, following strict historical method? The answers have varied widely from "virtually nothing" to "almost everything." It is our conviction that a fair-minded application of the standard criteria for assessing the historicity of any ancient document can lead to a substantial confidence in the reliability of the Gospel tradition, even though we lack the comparative data to authenticate more than the major themes and contours of that tradition.

The first chapter of part 4 will thus survey the various approaches to the historical Jesus that the last two centuries of scholarship have spawned, followed by a brief chronology of the life of Christ that provides the rationale for the subsequent divisions of Gospel material in the remaining chapters. These chapters will then read the Gospels themselves in a broad chronological sequence, to the extent that it is recoverable. We will watch for the most significant redactional emphases of each Gospel as highlighted previously in Part 3. We will assess the historicity of select details and comment on some of the most famous apparent "contradictions" within the texts. But we will focus primarily on the most important and interesting exegetical details. We do not have room for a full-fledged commentary on each episode from Jesus' life and ministry, but we can highlight main themes and patterns, and focus on particularly crucial or controversial texts. We will even try to debunk a few commonly held misinterpretations of passages and suggest occasional applications to contemporary Christian living.

10

THE HISTORICAL JESUS

THE QUESTS AND THE CHRONOLOGY

The Quests of the Historical Jesus

I T HAS BECOME common to speak of three quests or three phases of one modern quest of the historical Jesus. Inevitably, such historical review becomes schematized and oversimplifies continuities and discontinuities between different scholars and scholarly trends, but this is the way all history is written to one degree or another.[1]

The First Quest

In our survey of Gospel criticism (above, pp. 88), we spoke briefly of the late-eighteenth-through-end-of-nineteenth-century responses to the question of the miraculous. We may now review several of these schools of thought with respect to their portraits of Jesus more generally.[2] At least three main approaches predominated during this first quest of the historical Jesus. *Rationalists and mythologizers* alike determined that the Jesus of history was a mere man, shorn of any miracle-working abilities or "divine nature," even though they differed as to how

---

[1] Thus C. Marsh ("Quests of the Historical Jesus in New Historicist Perspective," *BI* 5 [1997]: 403–37) identifies nine separate quests, while M. F. Bird ("Is There Really a 'Third Quest' for the Historical Jesus?" *SBET* 24 [2006]: 195–214) wonders how helpful even three divisions prove to be.

[2] The story is told comprehensively in Schweitzer, *The Quest of the Historical Jesus*.

to explain the miracle stories in the Gospels. For Reimarus, Jesus was very much a Jew of his day, coming to fulfill the revolutionary sociopolitical hopes of his people. He thus waited in vain for the popular uprising he anticipated would help him overthrow Rome.[3] For Strauss, Jesus was a suffering Messiah who mistakenly believed that his death would spark the events that would bring about the literal, earthly Jewish kingdom of God.[4]

Romantics, most notably the French Catholic Ernest Renan, portrayed Jesus as the consummately gentle teacher of love, beauty, and joy who offered compelling moral precepts for his people. At a later stage in his life, however, Jesus abandoned this approach in favor of a miracle-working ministry, added an eschatological urgency to his message, and increasingly longed for martyrdom as an outgrowth of his messianic consciousness.[5] Nineteenth-century, *"old" liberals*, spearheaded by Adolf von Harnack, promoted a Jesus who fit in with their beliefs in social progress and moral evolution. Jesus was the great ethical teacher who stressed the fatherhood of God, the brotherhood of all humanity, the infinite value of a person's soul, and a higher righteousness by the way of love. For these liberals, the historical Jesus maintained this agenda consistently throughout his life.[6]

The first quest came to an end due to the combined writings of four key scholars. Martin Kähler's influential book discloses its theme in its title: *The So-Called Historical Jesus and the Historic, Biblical Christ (Die sogennante historische Jesus und die geschichtliche biblische Christus)*. In German, there are two quite distinct words for history: *Historie* (the actual chronicle of events) and *Geschichte* (the significance of those events). Kähler argued that the early Christian *kerygma* (faith-proclamation) was so intertwined with the actual life of Jesus that the two kinds of history were inseparable. Christians could believe in the significance of the story, even though it was largely impossible for historians to separate fact from significance. The second scholar, Johannes Weiss, still believing that the historical Jesus could be recovered, persuasively portrayed a consistently eschatological Jesus—one who preached the near arrival of the kingdom—in contrast to the social or ethical Jesuses of the previous "questers."[7] Third, William Wrede advanced his thesis about the messianic secret (see above, pp. 132–33). Whereas previous scholars had assumed that at least Mark, the earliest Gospel, provided a genuine window into Jesus' self-consciousness, Wrede challenged even this much, leaving only a handful of items in Mark that one could trust. Certainly, not enough remained to reconstruct a detailed description of the Jesus of history.

Fourth, and most important of all, Albert Schweitzer's detailed exposé of how nineteenth-century portrayals of Jesus regularly re-created him in the image of

---

[3] Reimarus, *Fragments*.

[4] Strauss, *Life of Jesus*.

[5] E. Renan, *The Life of Jesus* (Amherst, NY: Prometheus, 1991 [Fr. orig. 1862]).

[6] A. von Harnack, *What Is Christianity* (Philadelphia: Fortress; London: Ernest Benn, 1986 [Germ. orig. 1900]).

[7] J. Weiss, *Jesus' Proclamation of the Kingdom of God*, ed. R. H. Hiers (London: SCM, 1971; Chico, CA: Scholars, 1985 [Germ. orig. 1892]).

their authors led to widespread skepticism about the possibility of the undertaking. Schweitzer's own alternative, however, would remain extremely influential. As with Weiss, Schweitzer's Jesus was consistently eschatological, an apocalyptic Jew who became convinced God would supernaturally intervene to establish his kingdom on earth during his lifetime. Jesus sent out the twelve with this expectation (Matt 10:23), only to have it frustrated. The second stage in his ministry thus followed, as Jesus became convinced that he had to take upon himself the tribulations or messianic woes that many Jews believed had to precede the coming of a new age. This would be accomplished by his death, so he went to Jerusalem as a hidden Messiah, convinced he must become a martyr. Peter and Judas, each in their own ways, disclosed Jesus' messianic claims to the authorities so that he was crucified. That the kingdom did not immediately appear as he had envisioned implies that in one sense he died a failure.[8]

No Quest and the New Quest
The dominant figure in the history of biblical criticism and theology during the first half of the 1900s was Rudolf Bultmann. Bultmann combined and modified the major claims of Kähler and Schweitzer. He consistently set out to demonstrate that we could know virtually nothing about the historical Jesus because of the interweaving of history and faith throughout the Gospels. He agreed that some of what we could know resembled Schweitzer's portrait of a teacher with demanding ethical standards, but he believed that Jesus was looking for someone other than himself when he spoke of the coming Son of Man. Theologically, Bultmann viewed his historical agnosticism as a positive state of affairs because he thought any attempt to ground our faith in history would destroy the cardinal principle of Reformation Christianity—justification by *faith* alone. Building on Strauss, Bultmann developed a "demythologizing" agenda—trying to understand the theological truths that are left when one strips away the mythological husks in which the Gospel texts are wrapped. Following the existentialist philosopher Martin Heidegger, Bultmann saw the essence of Jesus' teaching as calling people to a moment-by-moment encounter with God—learning to live what he called "authentic existence" in the present, given the transience of life and the uncertainty of the future.[9]

Particularly due to Schweitzer's and Bultmann's influence, relatively few writers writing from the 1900s through the 1950s attempted to compose a life of Christ.[10] Then in 1953 at a reunion of Bultmann's students at the University of Marburg, Ernst Käsemann gave a paper entitled, "The Problem of the Historical Jesus." That paper launched what became known as the "new quest" for the Jesus of history. In it, he applied the dissimilarity criterion (see below, p. 219) that Bult-

---

[8] Schweitzer, *Quest of the Historical Jesus*, esp. 168–89.

[9] See esp. R. Bultmann, *Jesus and the Word* (New York: Scribner's, 1934; London: Collins, 1958). Cf. idem., *Jesus Christ and Mythology* (New York: Scribner's 1958; London: SCM, 1960).

[10] The contrast between periods, however, has often been exaggerated. See esp. Porter, *Criteria of Authenticity in Historical-Jesus Research*, 28–62. Porter, in fact, disputes how much we can or should distinguish separate quests altogether.

mann himself had developed, to argue that one could recover from the Gospels a significant historical core of information. This material showed Jesus to be an apocalyptic Jew who decisively challenged the religious authorities of his day and even the Torah itself.[11]

Two other scholars soon followed suit. James Robinson, an American, argued that an eschatological Jesus—indeed, the entire early Christian kerygma—demanded historical grounding. Robinson appealed to a newer understanding of history in which one does not have to engage in a rigid separation of fact from interpretation to determine a historical figure's intentions and commitments.[12] Back in Germany, Günther Bornkamm produced the first book-length treatment of Jesus to come out of the new quest. While still not accepting a messianic self-consciousness for Jesus, and while limiting his study primarily to the sayings material, thematically arranged, Bornkamm nevertheless believed that a large percentage of Jesus' teaching was authentic and disclosed his radically transcendent personality. The kingdom was both present and future. God as Father loved humanity but was calling people, through Jesus, to repent of sin.[13]

All of the initial "new questers" still shared, to varying degrees, Bultmann's commitment to existentialism, emphasizing how Jesus mediated God's divine presence to humanity with a directness that radically differed from the Judaism of his day. However, coming largely out of a Germany only a few years removed from the Nazi atrocities, the portraits of Judaism painted by the "new questers" were often caricatures that bordered on anti-Semitism.

The Third Quest

The 1960s and 1970s made it increasingly clear that the new quest would not advance beyond the old quest as far as its original proponents had thought. Again, historical Jesus research died down—until the early 1980s. Since then it has reemerged with great fervor. This so-called third quest[14] has several distinctives: (a) a rigorous examination and application of historical criteria to determine the authenticity of the various Gospel data; (b) a reclamation of Jesus the Jew, interpreting him clearly against the backdrop of the religious ideas and institutions of his day; and (c) a far more nuanced and detailed understanding of the diversity of early first-century Judaism.[15] Within the third quest, one may discern two broad "camps" or approaches.

---

[11] More conveniently accessible in Käsemann, "The Problem of the Historical Jesus," 15–47.

[12] Robinson, *New Quest of the Historical Jesus*. For his most recent book-length thoughts on the topic, see idem., *The Gospel of Jesus: In Search of the Original Good News* (San Francisco: Harper-SanFrancisco, 2005).

[13] G. Bornkamm, *Jesus of Nazareth* (London: Hodder & Stoughton; New York: Harper & Row, 1960).

[14] Initially so labeled by Neill and Wright, *The Interpretation of the New Testament 1961–1986*, 379.

[15] For a thorough survey, see B. Witherington III, *The Jesus Quest: The Third Search for the Jew of Nazareth,* rev. ed. (Downers Grove: IVP, 1997), from which some of the subtitles used in this section derive. Briefer and more selective in its coverage, but more current, is D. B. Gowler, *What Are They Saying about the Historical Jesus?* (New York: Paulist, 2007). More methodological in orientation and proceeding through major sections and themes of Jesus' ministry is M. J. McClymond, *Familiar Stranger: An Introduction to Jesus of Nazareth* (Grand Rapids and Cambridge: Eerdmans, 2004).

An Emphasis on the Deeds of Jesus. Quite unlike Bultmann and most of his disciples, many "third questers" focus more on the deeds of Jesus than on his sayings. They stress that one must adequately account for the indisputable fact of Jesus' crucifixion by Pontius Pilate and that his teachings alone were not a sufficient cause of his execution. They ask questions about his aims and beliefs more holistically. At least five main views of Jesus result from this approach, along with various combinations.

Jesus was an *eschatological prophet* according to E. P. Sanders, one of the pioneers in the third quest. Sanders restores Jesus to his rightful place as a first-century Jew convinced of the nearness of the end of the age. But Sanders plays down the Gospels' picture of Jesus in conflict with the Jewish leaders. He believes Jesus offered God's forgiveness to the wicked of his society, without making them first prove themselves by repenting. Sanders places great significance on the incident of the temple "cleansing," which he thinks is better understood as part of Jesus' expectation that the temple would be destroyed and rebuilt. In short, Jesus' agenda was one of restoring Israel to a right relationship with God.[16] Paula Fredriksen and Bart Ehrman have largely followed in Sanders' footsteps in seeing Jesus as an apocalypticist. They even revive Schweitzer's improbable view that Jesus expected the end of the world in his generation but was mistaken.[17] Dale Allison agrees with Sanders' basic portrait, without this idiosyncratic addition, but thinks that Jesus was somewhat more ascetic than is usually acknowledged.[18] Evangelical scholar Scot McKnight highlights Sanders' emphasis on restoring Israel but without jettisoning the authenticity of significant sections of the Gospels or denying the deity of Jesus as Sanders does.[19] Steve Bryan concurs, adding that Jesus modified Jewish understandings of Israel's "restoration" considerably more than any of these previous authors explicitly acknowledge.[20]

Jesus was a *charismatic holy man* in the view of Geza Vermes. This Jewish scholar has compared and contrasted Jesus with other influential religious leaders of his day who operated outside normal institutional channels, particularly Honi the Circle-Drawer and Hanina ben-Dosa. Both developed reputations for working miracles as a result of the effectiveness of their prayers—Honi for being able to make it rain and Hanina for a variety of healings and exorcisms.[21] From a

---

[16] E. P. Sanders, *Jesus and Judaism* (London: SCM; Philadelphia: Fortress, 1985); idem., *The Historical Figure of Judaism* (London and New York: Penguin, 1993).

[17] P. Fredriksen, *Jesus of Nazareth, King of the Jews: A Jewish Life and the Emergence of Christianity* (New York: Alfred Knopf, 2000); B. D. Ehrman, *Jesus: Apocalyptic Prophet of the New Millennium* (Oxford and New York: OUP, 1999).

[18] D. C. Allison, Jr., *Jesus of Nazareth: Millenarian Prophet* (Minneapolis: Fortress, 1998). See also B. J. Pitre, "Blessing the Barren and Warning the Fecund: Jesus' Message for Women Concerning Pregnancy and Childbirth," *JSNT* 81 (2001): 59–80.

[19] S. McKnight, *A New Vision for Israel: The Teachings of Jesus in National Context* (Grand Rapids and Cambridge: Eerdmans, 1999).

[20] S. Bryan, *Jesus and Israel's Traditions of Judgement and Restoration* (Cambridge: CUP, 2002).

[21] G. Vermes, a prolific author, first presented this portrait in *Jesus the Jew* (London: Collins, 1973; Philadelphia: Fortress, 1974; London: SCM, rev. 2001). His most recent book-length articulation is *The Authentic Gospel of Jesus* (London: Allen Lane, 2003; New York: Penguin, 2004).

liberal Christian perspective, Marcus Borg has developed a view of Jesus that sees him as a "Spirit-person," someone particularly in tune with the divine and able to be a conduit of God's Spirit to others.[22] From a more conservative Christian angle, Martin Hengel, too, accepts the label "charismatic" as the best description of Jesus.[23] Common to all of these writers is an emphasis on Jesus as a threat to the religious establishment because he did not accept the official spokesmen for Judaism as appropriate authorities, did not treat the Torah with adequate reverence from their perspective, and emphasized moral rather than ritual holiness.[24] David Catchpole has recently combined both of these first two categories in seeing Jesus as the final end-times prophet and the founder of charismatic, Spirit-filled community, but he stops just short of affirming Jesus' divinity.[25]

Other writers have portrayed Jesus as a *social reformer*. In varying ways Gerd Theissen and Richard Horsley have both stressed the impact they believe Jesus wanted to make on the Jewish society of his day. As an itinerant minister who spawned a following of wandering charismatics supported by local sympathizers in various villages (so Theissen),[26] Jesus was developing a renewal movement within Israel. Groups of disciples created countercultural communities based on the principle of loving even one's enemy. Yet they were still perceived as threats to the authorities due to their covert resistance to oppression (so Horsley).[27] William Herzog expands this tradition of reconstructing the historical Jesus to stress his role as a "pedagogue of the oppressed," who taught the peasants how to articulate and address various situations of oppression in which they found themselves.[28]

Pacifists, especially from the Anabaptist or Mennonite traditions, have often found an ally in Jesus, taking one additional step beyond what scholars in the last group propose. Thus they view him both as a non-violent revolutionary and a *proactive peacemaker*. A generation ago, André Trocmé explored Jesus' politics, his implied social ethic, and the significance of his proclamation of the arriv-

---

[22] See esp. M. J. Borg, *Jesus, a New Vision* (San Francisco: Harper & Row, 1987); idem., *Jesus: Uncovering the Life, Teachings, and Relevance of a Religious Revolutionary* (London and New York: HarperCollins, 2006).

[23] M. Hengel, *The Charismatic Leader and His Followers* (Edinburgh: T&T Clark, 1981; Eugene, OR: Wipf & Stock, 2005).

[24] Emphasizing Jesus' unique role in offering purity apart from the temple cult and the religious establishment is Bruce Chilton's sometimes outstanding, sometimes bizarre *Rabbi Jesus: An Intimate Biography* (New York and London: Doubleday, 2000). Various *Jewish* scholars' lives of Jesus often fall largely under this heading as well.

[25] D. Catchpole, *Jesus People: The Historical Jesus and the Beginnings of Community* (London: Darton, Longman & Todd; Grand Rapids; Baker, 2006).

[26] G. Theissen, *The Shadow of the Galilean: The Quest of the Historical Jesus in Narrative Form*, rev. ed. (London: SCM; Philadelphia: Fortress, 2007); G. Theissen and A. Merz, *The Historical Jesus: A Comprehensive Guide* (London: SCM; Minneapolis: Fortress, 1998).

[27] R. A. Horsley, *Jesus and the Spiral of Violence: Popular Jewish Resistance in Roman Palestine* (San Francisco: Harper & Row, 1987); idem., *Jesus and Empire: The Kingdom of God and the New World Disorder* (Minneapolis: Fortress, 2003).

[28] The expression comes from W. R. Herzog II, *Parables as Subversive Speech: Jesus as Pedagogue of the Oppressed* (Louisville: WJKP, 1994).

al of the biblical Jubilee.[29] American Mennonites like John Yoder and Thomas Yoder Neufeld believe that Jesus was as far from promoting a violent liberation movement like the Zealots as possible. But in creating the church as a counter-cultural community to model before the watching world the in-breaking kingdom of God, he established a mechanism for pointing out the failure of all other attempts to establish peace and justice and hence was implicitly subverting the established powers anyway.[30] The beatitudes and antitheses in the Sermon on the Mount explicitly highlight conflict resolution along with attitudes and behaviors that should minimize the amount of conflict one must face to begin with.[31] Irish Catholic scholar Sean Freyne falls somewhere in between this category and the last one with his study of how the culture and politics of Galilee shaped Jesus' agenda of "Jewish non-violent resistance with its critique of both religious and political imperialism."[32]

Still other scholars see in Jesus the *marginalized Messiah*. This perspective tends to accept the greatest amount of the Gospel data as authentic, of all the categories surveyed here. It recognizes that Jesus did claim to be the Jewish Messiah, however unconventional his concept of that role was. He was a teacher, a miracle worker, a prophet, and a gatherer of Israel, but it was ultimately his messianic claims and deeds that ran him afoul of the authorities. He who was committed to the marginalized of his society became marginalized himself and was executed. The moderate Roman Catholic scholar, John Meier, applies a rigorous critical methodology that Protestants, Catholics, Jews, and atheists can share in principle, in his still unfinished four-volume work, to come to these conclusions.[33] Anglican bishop of Durham, N. T. Wright, defends this perspective by means of a detailed mastery of Jewish backgrounds, as he argues that Jesus came announcing the end of the Jewish exile, spiritually speaking, and anticipating a messianic age in which God would dramatically improve *this* world, through his people, as the kingdom fully arrived.[34] Much more briefly, the works of Peter Stuhlmacher and Markus Bockmuehl support similar conclusions.[35] For Joseph Hellerman, the heart of

---

[29] A. Trocmé, *Jesus and the Nonviolent Revolution*, ed. C. E. Moore, rev. ed. (Maryknoll: Orbis, 2003 [orig. 1973]).

[30] See esp. J. H. Yoder, *The Politics of Jesus*, rev. ed. (Grand Rapids: Eerdmans; Carlisle: Paternoster, 1994).

[31] T. R. Yoder Neufeld, *Recovering Jesus: The Witness of the New Testament* (Grand Rapids: Brazos, 2007), esp. 205–20.

[32] S. Freyne, *Jesus, A Jewish Galilean: A New Reading of the Jesus Story* (London and New York: T&T Clark, 2004). A correct understanding of first-century Galilee itself has been a storm-center in much recent scholarship. For a survey of the diversity of opinions and how they bear on historical-Jesus research, see M. Rapinchuk, "The Galilee and Jesus in Recent Research," *CBR* 2 (2004): 197–222.

[33] J. P. Meier, *A Marginal Jew: Rethinking the Historical Jesus*, 4 vols. (New York and London: Doubleday, 1991–2009).

[34] See esp. N. T. Wright, *Jesus and the Victory of God* (London: SPCK; Minneapolis: Fortress, 1996). Cf. more briefly idem., *The Challenge of Jesus* (Downers Grove: IVP, 1999; London: SPCK, 2000).

[35] P. Stuhlmacher, *Jesus of Nazareth: Christ of Faith* (Peabody: Hendrickson, 1993); M. Bockmuehl, *This Jesus: Martyr, Lord, Messiah* (Edinburgh: T&T Clark, 1994; Downers Grove: IVP, 1996).

Jesus' mission was to fulfill in his person the deepest meaning of the distinctive badges of Jewish national righteousness, such as Sabbath, temple, dietary laws, ritual purity, and the like, but he understandably ran afoul of those who rejected these usually implicit and occasionally explicit claims.[36]

An Emphasis on the Sayings of Jesus. This second main category does not exclude the first; all of the "third questers" deal with both deeds and sayings, but most typically place more weight on one area or the other. Again, four main subcategories may be discerned. The first two focus on Jesus and Wisdom; the second two focus on Jesus the teacher of short, subversive sayings.

The most holistic of the four is the view that sees Jesus as the *incarnation of Divine Wisdom*, in continuity with the increasing development in Judaism of Wisdom as a personification for God (cf. Prov. 9; recall above, p. 45). Evangelical Methodist Ben Witherington surveys Jesus' relationships, deeds, and sayings, but he argues that the sayings are the most important. Supplementing prophetic and messianic categories, Witherington identifies Jesus above all as a sage, a divine emissary (Hb. *shaliach*; Gk. *apostolos*), and God's eschatological agent for revealing himself to humanity.[37] Jesus' teachings are often countercultural like those of Job and Ecclesiastes in the Old Testament. Of the views surveyed here, this one, along with the marginalized messiah view, most closely approximates historic Christian understanding of who Jesus was. The Jewish New Testament scholar David Flusser, whose writings regularly placed him tantalizingly close to orthodox Christian belief, likewise emphasized Jesus' wisdom and consciousness of representing God, even if he stopped just short of affirming actual incarnation.[38] Fully in sync with traditional convictions about the deity of Christ, yet writing from the perspective of a participant in historical Jesus research, is Pope Benedict XVI, who sees the organizing motif of Jesus' life as revealing the face of God and God's Wisdom to humanity, particularly in his teachings on faith, hope, and love.[39]

Elisabeth Schüssler Fiorenza has developed a wisdom perspective in portraying Jesus as a *sociopolitical liberator* and, more specifically, a feminist before his time. She has also vigorously argued for the importance of understanding Wisdom in the Gospels. But she stresses the feminine side of God, through the (feminine) Greek word for "wisdom" (*sophia*) that played an influential role in some Jew-

---

[36] J. H. Hellerman, *Jesus and the People of God: Reconfiguring Ethnic Identity* (Sheffield: Sheffield Phoenix, 2007).

[37] B. Witherington III, *The Christology of Jesus* (Minneapolis: Fortress, 1990); idem., *Jesus the Sage: The Pilgrimage of Wisdom* (Minneapolis: Fortress, 1994); and idem., *Jesus the Seer*. Harder to categorize because he nicely balances Jesus' teachings and actions but stressing Jesus as God's "final envoy" is M. de Jonge, *God's Final Envoy: Early Christology and Jesus' Own View of His Mission* (Grand Rapids and Cambridge: Eerdmans, 1998).

[38] Most recently, see D. Flusser with R. S. Notley, *The Sage from Galilee: Rediscovering Jesus' Genius*, rev. ed (Grand Rapids and Cambridge: Eerdmans, 2007). Flusser passed away in 2000, so this is a new edition of his *Jesus*, first published in Jerusalem by Magnes Press, 1997, edited by his premier Christian student and colleague.

[39] J. Ratzinger, *Jesus of Nazareth*, 2 vols. (New York and London: Doubleday, 2007).

ish and much Greek religious thought of the day. For Schüssler Fiorenza, Jesus himself is not divine Wisdom but rather "Sophia's prophet" and offspring. His teachings about and patterns of interacting with women, when separated from the later "repatriarchalizing" distortions of the early church, demonstrate him to be a true proponent of women's spiritual and social liberation in the best senses of those terms.[40] Esther Ng, however, has shown that, while Jesus certainly affirmed women in a way radically positive by the social norms of his world, he cannot be considered a full-fledged egalitarian, and subsequent New Testament Christianity still remained sufficiently liberating so as to counter Schüssler Fiorenza's charge that it degenerated from its earlier ideal form.[41] Liberation theology likewise saw in Jesus' teaching precedent for a preferential option for the poor and marginalized, often arguing that violent rebellion, if necessary, was justified to achieve its ends. But this view is exegetically quite difficult to sustain and is not nearly as popular today as it was before the collapse of Communism in a majority of the countries that once promoted it.[42]

John Dominic Crossan's influential and prolific literary output has portrayed Jesus as a *Cynic sage*. Crossan has applied virtually every modern critical method to the Gospels over the years to produce at times complementary, at times contradictory reflections on the historical Jesus.[43] He seems to have come to rest on a view of Jesus that finds him having more in common with itinerant Greek Cynic philosophers (on which, see above, pp. 33–34) than with any clearly Jewish categories of religious leader. Central to Crossan's reconstruction are Jesus' characteristic willingness to eat on equal terms with the outcasts of his day and his ability to work miracles (by psychosomatic powers of suggestion) that were phenomenologically indistinguishable from pagan "magic" (on which, see above, pp. 36–37). Little can be known of the events of his passion, but much can be recovered of his subversive teachings in parables and aphorisms (other short, pithy, and unconventional sayings). Promoting a radical egalitarianism, Jesus stirred up peasant hopes of a better life to a sufficient extent to threaten the Roman authori-

---

[40] E. Schüssler Fiorenza, *In Memory of Her: A Feminist Theological Reconstruction of Christian Origins*, rev. ed. (New York: Crossroad, 1994); idem., *Jesus: Miriam's Child, Sophia's Prophet: Critical Issues in Feminist Christology* (New York: Continuum, 1994). More recently, D. Soelle and L. Schottroff (*Jesus of Nazareth* [London: SPCK; Louisville: WJKP, 2002]) develop a similar perspective, concerned also to liberate Jesus from anti-Semitic portraits, including those they believe appear in the canonical Gospels.

[41] E. Y. L. Ng, *Reconstructing Christian Origins? The Feminist Theology of Elisabeth Schüssler Fiorenza: An Evaluation* (Carlisle and Waynesboro, GA: Paternoster, 2002). Cf. also Corley, *Women and the Historical Jesus*.

[42] One of the few comparatively well-grounded exegetical studies centered on the Gospels, was Segundo, *The Historical Jesus of the Synoptics*. Cf. also J. Sobrino, *Jesus the Liberator: A Historical-Theological Reading of Jesus of Nazareth* (Maryknoll: Orbis, 1993).

[43] One can trace his pilgrimage from narrative criticism (*The Parables: In Search of the Historical Jesus* [New York: Harper & Row, 1973]) to deconstruction (*Raid on the Articulate: Cosmic Eschatology in Jesus and Borges* [New York: Harper & Row, 1976]) to reader-response criticism (*Cliffs of Fall: Paradox and Polyvalence in the Parables of Jesus* [New York: Seabury, 1980]), all prior to his deployment of various forms of largely sociological analysis.

ties of his day, who are alone to blame for his execution. Unlike the other perspectives listed above, Crossan's relies heavily on the improbable assumptions that noncanonical documents (or their sources) can be dated to a period earlier than the canonical Gospels, and that in places they reflect a more historically reliable portrait of the life of Jesus.[44] The view that even Jesus' fairly low-key teachings and claims contained within them the potential to threaten and/or subvert identical imperial claims does, nevertheless, seem accurate. A flurry of studies over the last decade has supported this perspective, which N. T. Wright nicely summarizes with the aphorism that if Jesus is Lord, then Caesar is not![45] Among those who have studied the dynamics within the Roman empire and read the Gospels against this backdrop, no one has been more prolific than Warren Carter.[46]

The highly publicized Jesus Seminar has popularized Jesus as an *oriental guru*. During much of the 1980s and 1990s, a small group of mostly quite radical scholars, calling themselves the Jesus Seminar and co-chaired by Crossan and Borg, met periodically to vote on the probable authenticity of the various sayings and deeds of Jesus. In many ways their Jesus resembles that of Crossan, but only 18% of the Gospel sayings (including Coptic Thomas) and 16% of his deeds survive as closely resembling what Jesus actually said or did.[47] Among many of their wildly improbable methodological presuppositions are the notions that Jesus could never have spoken in more than very short, cryptic utterances, never spoke explicitly about himself, never talked about the future, never countenanced the possibility of final judgment, and never spoke any words that are not detachable from their contexts in the Gospels. Although the Seminar Fellows do not make the comparison themselves, the only conceivable analogy to their Jesus in the religious world of his day would be the stereotypic Eastern holy man with a reputation for speaking very little, save periodically to utter short profundities. The Seminar's mastermind, Robert Funk, worked this perspective up into a full-fledged narrative in which Jesus is a laconic sage and poet of the kingdom.[48] The Jesus Seminar's approach has been widely and severely critiqued, their claim to speak for a consensus of modern biblical critics is irresponsible, and in many ways they are a throwback to the methodology and conclusions of the "new quest" and even to

---

[44] See esp. Crossan, *Historical Jesus*; idem., *Jesus: A Revolutionary Biography* (San Francisco: HarperSanFrancisco, 1994). For a thoroughgoing critique, see P. R. Eddy, "Jesus as Diogenes: Reflections on the Cynic Jesus Thesis," *JBL* 115 (1996): 449–69. For a more moderate response, cf. D. Seeley, "Jesus and the Cynics Revisited," *JBL* 116 (1997): 704–12.

[45] E.g., T. Wright, *Romans for Everyone: Chapters 9–16* (London: SPCK; Louisville: WKJP, 2004), 33. Cf. idem., *Luke for Everyone*, rev. ed. (London: SPCK; Louisville: WKJP, 2004), 22–23.

[46] See esp. W. Carter, *Matthew and the Margins: A Sociopolitical and Religious Reading* (Sheffield: SAP; Maryknoll: Orbis, 2000); idem., *Matthew and Empire: Initial Explorations* (Harrisburg: Trinity, 2001).

[47] R. W. Funk, R. W. Hoover, and the Jesus Seminar, *The Five Gospels: The Search for the Authentic Words of Jesus* (New York: Macmillan, 1993); R. W. Funk and the Jesus Seminar, *The Acts of Jesus: The Search for the Authentic Deeds of Jesus* (San Francisco: HarperSanFrancisco, 1998).

[48] R. W. Funk, *Honest to Jesus: Jesus for a New Millennium* (San Francisco: HarperSanFrancisco, 1996).

Bultmann.[49] But, unlike most scholars, they deliberately courted the mass media to promote their views widely and, unfortunately, convinced many that they represented mainstream scholarship and cutting-edge "advances" in our knowledge of the historical Jesus.

Finally, we may speak of those who give pride of place to Jesus' role as *messianic herald of the kingdom*. The views of this group overlap considerably with those who identify Jesus as a marginalized Messiah, but one may detect a somewhat greater emphasis here on his sayings than on his deeds. James Dunn, stressing that ultimately all we have access to is Jesus the way he was remembered, gives priority to Jesus' announcement of the in-breaking reign of God, his good news for the poor, and his teachings on love and discipleship.[50] David Seccombe, a South African scholar, clearly delineates the link between Jesus as Messiah and inaugurator of God's reign: if the kingdom has arrived, it means that the king of that kingdom has come as well.[51] Here is where we find many evangelical participants in the quest for the historical Jesus landing,[52] but other more centrist scholars often paint reasonably similar portraits.[53] Certain elements of all of the previously presented portraits of Jesus may be combined with this one but not to the extent that Jesus' central concern to inaugurate the kingdom as the (countercultural) messianic king becomes blurred.

Assessment and Criteria of Authenticity

We could expand this chapter considerably if we also surveyed those minimalistic or idiosyncratic portraits of Jesus painted by scholars outside the guild of New Testament scholarship or by non-scholarly writers. Because of the pervasive influence of grass-roots developments throughout modern church history, especially in America, including anti-Christian attacks, the latter have often had more of an influence on public opinion than genuine peer-reviewed scholarship. Thus one recent, insightful survey of portraits of Jesus in the United States contains chapter headings that include not only "enlightened sage," "oriental Christ," and "rabbi" (similar to views we have already considered) but also "sweet savior," "manly redeemer," "superstar," "Mormon elder brother," and "black Moses."[54] What are

---

[49] Cf. esp. L. T. Johnson, *The Real Jesus: The Misguided Quest for the Historical Jesus and the Truth of the Traditional Gospels* (San Francisco: HarperSanFrancisco, 1996); with Wilkins and Moreland, eds., *Jesus under Fire*. More briefly, see C. L. Blomberg, "The Seventy-Four 'Scholars': Who Does the Jesus Seminar Really Speak For?" *Christian Research Journal* 17.2 (1994): 32–38.

[50] J. D. G. Dunn, *Jesus Remembered* (Grand Rapids and Cambridge: Eerdmans, 2003).

[51] D. P. Seccombe, *The King of God's Kingdom: A Solution to the Puzzle of Jesus* (Carlisle and Waynesboro, GA: Paternoster, 2002).

[52] E.g., E. P. Meadors, *Jesus the Messianic Herald of Salvation* (Tübingen: Mohr Siebeck, 1995; Peabody: Hendrickson, 1997); D. W. Kennard, *Messiah Jesus: Christology in His Day and Ours* (New York: Peter Lang, 2008).

[53] E.g., L. E. Keck, *Who Is Jesus? History in Perfect Tense* (Columbia: University of South Carolina Press, 2000; Minneapolis: Fortress, 2001); J. Gnilka, *Jesus of Nazareth: Message and History* (Peabody: Hendrickson, 1997).

[54] S. Prothero, *American Jesus: How the Son of God Became a National Icon* (New York: Farrar, Strauss and Giroux, 2003).

we to make of this almost bewildering variety of "Jesuses"? It would be easy to despair of employing historical methodology to come up with any probable conclusions and/or to argue that the whole enterprise is ideologically misguided.[55] In fact, after certain eccentric portraits are bracketed, we find a surprising amount of agreement with respect to both historical method and the results of its application. Craig Evans summarizes five main gains of the third quest: (a) understanding the ethnically, religiously, and socially Jewish contexts of the historical Jesus; (b) recognizing Jesus' aims and mission; (c) approximating Jesus' self-understanding; (d) accounting for the specific nature of his death; and (e) interpreting the miracle stories, especially the resurrection.[56]

One of the main reasons certain scholars still disagree as to how much of the Gospel portraits can be corroborated by historical research has to do with initial presuppositions. An antisupernaturalist worldview will clearly rule out much *a priori*. A second important issue involves the "burden of proof." Does one assume a saying or deed of Jesus to be authentic unless contradictions or inconsistencies with other data emerge? Or does one assume all the data to be inauthentic unless good reasons can be marshaled for accepting them? The former approach is the standard one in the investigation of other ancient historical documents, but the latter approach, unfortunately, is the one more often applied to the Gospels.[57]

Why this apparent double standard? The most common answer is because the Gospels are not straightforward accounts of history or biography; they are the products of faith communities that could easily have biased their reporting—intentionally or unintentionally—in order to glorify their founder, Jesus. But at least two replies to this argument need to be stressed. First, an ideological bias can actually create a greater concern to tell the story "straight." For example, as noted above (p. 105), it has often been the Jewish historians of the holocaust during World War II who have proved the most accurate, precisely because they wanted to do all they could to ensure that such horrors never again occur. Fledgling Christianity would have needed to tell the story straight because it experienced sufficient opposition to its unique claims that Jesus was God's Messiah, bodily raised from the dead, and worthy of the same titles previously reserved for Yahweh, God of Israel, himself. This opposition came at times from Jewish leaders and other eyewitnesses of Jesus' ministry, who could have successfully discredited Christian claims, were they in any

---

[55] Ironically, this is a view maintained by many fundamentalists (e.g., Thomas and Farnell, eds., *The Jesus Crisis*), despite its roots in the Enlightenment's divorce of faith from history. For convincing defenses of the need for conservative scholars to remain involved in the historical Jesus quests, see M. F. Bird, "Shouldn't Evangelicals Participate in the 'Third Quest for the Historical Jesus'?" *Them* 29 (2004): 5–14; and M. W. Pahl, "Is Jesus Lost? Evangelicals and the Search for the Historical Jesus," *Them* 31 (2006): 6–19.

[56] See esp. C. A. Evans, "Assessing Progress in the Third Quest of the Historical Jesus," *JSHJ* 4 (2006): 35–54.

[57] See S. C. Goetz and C. L. Blomberg, "The Burden of Proof," *JSNT* 13 (1981): 39–63.

substantial way false to history.[58] Second, in antiquity, all history writing was ideologically biased. No one ever thought of recording information merely for information's sake, as we sometimes do. Instead, the attitude was one of asking, if history didn't teach certain lessons or morals, why preserve it? Yet our history textbooks are filled with "facts" about the ancient world far less well attested than the Gospel data.[59]

On the other hand, even for those who insist that we begin from a position of methodical doubt, various standard "criteria of authenticity" have been developed that can go a long way toward enhancing our confidence in the reliability of the Gospel record.[60] Four stand out in particular:

1. The *dissimilarity* criterion looks for information about Jesus in which he noticeably diverges both from the conventional Judaism of his day and from the major emphases of the early church (including the redactional emphases of a given evangelist)—as with his use of parables, the kingdom of God, or the "Son of Man" title. Potentially awkward or embarrassing information about Jesus also falls into this category. Such material would not likely have been invented by any Christian, Jew or Gentile. This criterion cannot be used to determine what is characteristic of Jesus, merely what is distinctive, but it can yield a "critically assured minimum" of historical information. Unfortunately, material that does not pass this criterion has often been labeled unhistorical. This, of course, would require Jesus to have been totally different from every Jew of his day and misunderstood by every one of his followers, a hypothesis which is patently absurd.[61]

2. The criterion of *multiple attestation* takes several forms. That which appears in more than one Gospel, more than one Gospel source, or more than one literary form stands a better chance of being authentic than that which is singly attested. This, in broad strokes, lends an inherent plausibility to most of the main contours of Jesus' ministry—for example, conflicts with the Jewish leaders, healings and exorcisms, and the events leading up to and including his passion. Again, it is unfortunate that some use this criterion negatively to exclude singly attested material. Material that cannot be corroborated may still be historical; we may simply have fewer ways of knowing with as high a degree of confidence.

3. The criterion of *Palestinian environment* or *Semitic language* reminds us that in many ways Jesus was thoroughly a person of his times. Despite the fact that the

---

[58] Cf. further P. W. Barnett, *Jesus and the Logic of History* (Leicester: Apollos, 1997; Downers Grove: IVP, 2001).

[59] See esp. A. N. Sherwin-White, *Roman Society and Roman Law in the New Testament* (Oxford: OUP, 1963; Eugene, OR: Wipf & Stock, 2004). Cf. P. Merkley, "The Gospels as Historical Testimony," *EQ* 58 (1986): esp. 328–36.

[60] For a full history of their development and use, complete with strengths and weaknesses, see Porter, *Criteria of Authenticity in Historical-Jesus Research*, 63–102. For an example of the extent to which they can be positively applied in the recovery of the Jesus of history, see already R. Latourelle, *Finding Jesus through the Gospels: History and Hermeneutics* (New York: Alba House, 1979).

[61] So esp. A. E. Harvey, *Jesus and the Constraints of History* (London: Duckworth; Philadelphia: Westminster, 1982). For a thorough critique of the criterion, see G. Theissen and D. Winter, *The Quest for the Plausible Jesus: The Question of Criteria* (Louisville and London: WJKP, 2002), 1–171.

Gospels were written in Greek in an age when the church was primarily Hellenistic in culture, features unique to Palestinian culture or environment are preserved (details of village life, agriculture, etc.). Language that reads like a fairly literal translation of a distinctively Semitic idiom frequently appears—for example, "the poor" (from Hb. *anawim*) meaning those afflicted with both spiritual and material poverty. When these kinds of phenomena occur, we may suspect that we are in touch with tradition at least as old as early Palestinian Jewish Christianity, perhaps dating back to Jesus himself. Again, a negative use of this criterion is not as valid. Distinctive Greek idioms may reflect an evangelist's paraphrase, and occasionally Jesus himself probably spoke in Greek. Non-Palestinian cultural elements may reflect a Gospel writer's desire to "contextualize" his message without falsifying the gist of the account—as when Luke replaces Mark's Palestinian thatched roof with Greco-Roman tiling (cf. Mark 2:4 with Luke 5:19). On occasion, Jesus may well have conversed directly in Greek with some non-Jewish (or even Hellenistic Jewish) conversation partner.[62]

4. Finally, the criterion of *coherence* identifies details that do not pass the above criteria in and of themselves but fit in very much with the distinctive style, form, or content of those teachings and actions of Jesus that do pass the criteria (cf., e.g., our argument below that the "nature miracles" fit in closely with Jesus' parables and other teachings about the kingdom of God—p. 311).

Secondary criteria, less conclusive but at times suggestive, include the *tendencies of the developing tradition* (what shows signs of being a later development of an earlier form, or vice versa), *necessary explanation* (what must have happened to account for a later historical fact—e.g., the crucifixion or the rise of Easter faith), and vividness as a pointer to an eyewitness report of a given account. But for almost every alleged tendency of the tradition, an opposite one can be found,[63] and the latter two criteria are highly subjective.

A promising advance in the last decade has appeared in the writings of a trio of German scholars, Gerd Theissen, Annette Merz, and Dagmar Winter and, independently, from N. T. Wright. The Germans call it the criterion of historical plausibility (*die Plausibilitätskriterium*),[64] while Wright dubs it the criterion of *double similarity and double dissimilarity*.[65] In this four-part criterion, sayings or deeds of Jesus from the Gospels (or parts thereof) that demonstrate not only significant discontinuity from previous Judaism and subsequent Christianity but also enough continuity with both movements as to be credible in their setting, rather than anachronistic, may be accepted as authentic. The criterion is not used negatively to exclude material, only positively to argue for what, on sheer historical grounds, most likely may

---

[62] See esp. Porter, *Criteria of Authenticity in Historical-Jesus Research*, 126–80.

[63] As demonstrated in detail by E. P. Sanders, *The Tendencies of the Synoptic Tradition* (Cambridge: CUP, 1969).

[64] Theissen and Merz, *Historical Jesus*, 115–18; Theissen and Winter, *Quest for the Plausible Jesus*, 172–225.

[65] Wright, *Jesus and the Victory of God*, 131–33.

be attributed to the historical Jesus. Despite acknowledged subjectivity in application, this criterion appears to mark a significant advance in the discussion.[66]

By now the student who believes in the inspiration of the Bible may be asking, "Where is the Holy Spirit in all of this discussion?" or "Don't we simply accept the trustworthiness of the Gospels on faith?" The answer to the first question is clearly that the Spirit's inspiration has *not* explicitly been taken into account by those who have engaged in the quest for the historical Jesus, liberal or conservative. *By definition* the quest involves ascertaining what can be known on purely historical grounds—what results believer and unbeliever alike can affirm. In response to the second question, it is undoubtedly true that the believer will affirm by faith more than what history can demonstrate, but there is much to be said for arguing that such faith *builds* on the evidence that does exist, rather than flying in its face.[67] In Part Five we will return to some of these reflections and synthesize our findings, as well as advance further arguments for the trustworthiness of the Gospel tradition.

The Chronology of the Life of Christ

Dating the details of the life of Jesus is at times an uncertain proposition. The dates of some events in the ancient world are well established, some are reasonable approximations, while others are educated guesses at best. What we call the first century included the years 754–854 for the Romans (reckoning from the supposed date of the founding of Rome) and 3760–3860 for the Jews (counting from the supposed date of the creation of the world). But ancient historians did not use these numbers nearly so much as they referred to the "nth" year of a certain king's reign. Here ambiguities crop up. Some writers reckon from the exact date of a king's accession to the throne; others, from the first full calendar year of his reign. Some use "exclusive reckoning" (e.g., the second through fifth years would total three years); others, "inclusive reckoning" (with second through fifth equaling four years by counting "two, three, four, and five"). What is more, Jewish and Roman calendars started at different times of the year. So a comparison of the standard textbooks on biblical chronology will regularly yield a variation of a year in one direction or another for many dates. The encyclopedia articles listed in the bibliography at the end of this chapter present the primary references from the ancient writers on which we base our information.[68] For the sake of simplifying matters and not overwhelming the introductory student, our discussion here will not list all that data.

---

[66] *Contra* Porter, *Criteria for Authenticity in Historical-Jesus Research*, 121–22. Porter does not interact with Wright, only the Germans, nor does he discuss the gains made in the major works on the historical Jesus by any of these authors as they employ this criterion.

[67] See esp. throughout P. R. Eddy and G. A. Boyd, *The Jesus Legend: A Case for the Historical Reliability of the Synoptic Jesus Tradition* (Grand Rapids: Baker, 2007). Cf. also Stanton, *Gospel Truth?*

[68] Cf. also M. Wojciechowski, "The Basic Chronology of the Life of Jesus," *Qumran Chronicle* 5 (1995): 74–83.

The Birth of Christ

Paradoxical as it sounds, the date of Christ's birth was probably somewhere between *6–4 BC*. Our division of the calendar into BC (before Christ) and AD (*anno domini* = in the year of the Lord) is, of course, a Christian invention. It began to catch on as early as the ninth and tenth centuries but was not formally adopted in Europe until the era of Pope Gregory XIII in the late 1500s. The oldest recorded attempt to fix a date for the birth of Jesus was made in the early sixth century by Dionysus Exiguus, who failed to take the evidence of Josephus into account. The date we call AD 1 eventually became so well entrenched that changing the calendar proved impossible. According to Josephus's information about the death of Herod the Great and the start of the reigns of his sons, Herod must have died in what we now know as 4 BC. Because, shortly before his death, he had the babies in Bethlehem slaughtered "who were two years old and under, in accordance with the time he had learned from the Magi" (Matt 2:16), it may be that Christ had been born up to two years earlier. Attempts to link the star of Bethlehem (2:2, 9–10) with an unusual conjunction of planets (7 and 6 BC) or the appearance of a comet or supernova (5 BC) have produced more precise suggestions, but if this "star" was a fully supernatural phenomenon, then it cannot be used to further our quest of a date for Jesus' birth.[69]

The statement in Luke 2:2 that Jesus was born when Quirinius was governor of Syria, complicates matters. The only governorship of Quirinius we know about for sure began in AD 6. Yet the Greek word for "governor" is a very general one that can refer to many leadership roles, and there is some evidence to suggest that Quirinius may have held administrative duties under earlier rulers. It is also possible that we should translate this verse as "this was the census that took place *before* Quirinius was governor of Syria," though this solution is perhaps less likely. References to Roman censuses in Egypt every fourteen years could suggest more widespread registration on a similar schedule. Fourteen years before AD 6 would be either 9 or 8 BC, depending on the kind of counting, inclusive or exclusive, employed. If a census were ordered in Rome at this time (Augustus himself refers to one that he ordered in 8 BC, but it is unknown how widespread it was), compliance as far east as Israel could easily still be occurring by 7–6 BC.[70] Thus, however sketchy, the data that do remain largely converge around a credible period of a couple of years for the birth of Christ.

The day of Jesus' birth is even more uncertain. At least by the third century, Christians in the Western part of the Roman empire began to celebrate "Christmas" on December 25, a holiday for worshiping *Sol Invictus* ("the unconquerable sun"—see above, p. 36); in the East, on January 6. Both dates also coincided at times, in the ancient calendars, with the winter solstice. So it is doubtful if these dates reflect any information about the actual day on which Jesus was born,

---

[69] M. Kidger (*The Star of Bethlehem: An Astronomer's View* [Princeton and Chichester: Princeton University Press, 1999]) surveys the full range of options.

[70] Cf. further Bock, *Luke 1:1–9:50*, 903–9; Blomberg, *Historical Reliability*, 248–49, and the literature there cited.

just times that were already Roman holidays on which Christians could celebrate their festivals with comparative impunity. Some historians point to the fact that shepherds would have watched their flocks *at night* (Luke 2:8) primarily in the springtime when most lambs were born, so perhaps Jesus was born in the spring. Still, we have no way of being sure.

Beginning of Christ's Ministry

A number of pieces of data must be assembled and interpreted to try to arrive at a starting point for Christ's adult ministry.

(1) According to Luke 3:1, John the Baptist was preaching in the fifteenth year of Tiberius Caesar. Tiberius' rule began in AD 14, suggesting a date of either 28 or 29 for the ministry of John. But in 12, Augustus gave Tiberius joint rule in the Eastern provinces, so it is possible, though probably less likely, that Luke calculated from this date, which would yield the year 26 or 27 for John's preaching.

(2) In Luke 3:23, Jesus is said to be "about thirty years old when he began his ministry." This is clearly a rough estimate that would fit any of the above dates, though it is closer to the exact mark if we accept the earlier date.

(3) In John 8:57, Jesus' opponents comment that he is not yet fifty, but this is clearly a round number to stress how few years have elapsed in his life compared to the time since Abraham.[71]

(4) In John 2:20, "the Jews" protest to Jesus that "it has taken forty-six years to build this temple, and you are going to raise it in three days?" According to Josephus, rebuilding of the temple began in Herod's eighteenth year, which, counting from 37 BC, would give a date of 20 or 19 BC for the beginning of the project.[72] Adding on forty-six more years (and remembering that there was no year "zero") would then yield either AD 27 or 28 for the first Passover of Christ's ministry.

(5) The choice of date for the outset of Christ's ministry is also affected by the number of years one assigns to that ministry and by the date one comes up with for the crucifixion (see below). But for now *27 or 28 seems to be the most probable date for the beginning of John's and Jesus' ministries.* How long John

---

[71] Beasley-Murray (*John*, 139) suspects it may allude to one possible date for ending the prime working years of a man's life, by analogy with Num 4:2–3, 29; 8:24–25.

[72] The Greek for "build" is aorist, leading H. W. Hoehner (*Chronological Aspects of the Life of Christ* [Grand Rapids: Zondervan, 1977], 40–43) to argue that it cannot refer to the still incomplete temple precincts as a whole but must refer to the more limited and completed work of building the inner sanctuary. But this took only a year and a half, and the aorist "was built" is even less likely to mean "has been standing for [46 years]." In fact, Hoehner's interpretation of the aorist is too narrow. It frequently appears in Scripture with an ingressive or consummative sense (referring to the beginning or end of a process) without any necessary implications about that process's continuation or completion. See D. B. Wallace, *Greek Grammar beyond the Basics: An Exegetical Syntax of the New Testament* (Grand Rapids: Zondervan, 1996), 558–61. Wallace still opts for a crucifixion date of AD 33 because he dates the completion of the sanctuary to 18–17 BC, adds 46 by exclusive reckoning, and obtains a starting date for Jesus' ministry of AD 29, requiring closer to a four-year ministry. But even if one starts counting from the completion of the sanctuary a year later than typically, one may still add 46 by inclusive reckoning, arrive at AD 28, and obtain the chronology adopted here, with closer to a two-year ministry.

ministered before Jesus was baptized we do not know. Most scholars allow for at least a few months; some for up to a year.

The Length of Christ's Ministry

Down through the centuries various Christians have proposed a one-, two-, three-, or four-year ministry for Christ. The most common of these proposals has been a three-year ministry, give or take a few months. The relevant data come primarily from John since the Synoptics mention only one Passover. (1) John explicitly mentions three Passovers (John 2:13; 6:4; and 12:1). (2) John 5:1 refers to an unnamed feast of the Jews. Some manuscripts call this "the feast" (rather than "a feast"). "The" central feast for the Jews would have been Tabernacles, but for Christian Jews (such as John) it would have been Passover. If this feast were a Passover, another year must be added to John's chronology.[73] (3) It is difficult to decide if the account of Jesus' cleansing the temple at Passover in John 2:13–25 is a separate event from the temple cleansing during the last week of his life (see Mark 11:12–19 pars.) or if John has moved this account forward as a kind of headline for Jesus' entire ministry.[74] If the latter, then we might deduct a year, although Jesus could have still been in Jerusalem for a Passover early in his ministry without having cleansed the temple. (4) In the Synoptics there are two hints of the passing of springtimes. In Mark 2:23–28 and parallels, Jesus and his disciples pick and eat grain from the fields that would have ripened at spring harvest time. At the feeding of the five thousand, Mark comments on the "green" grass (6:39), a phenomenon unusual in the wilderness (v. 32) except right after the winter rains. *All of this makes a ministry of two to three years, and possibly even a little longer, quite probable.*

For those who see a roughly three-year period, it is common to divide it into three stages: a "year" of obscurity (embracing all of the events prior to Jesus' great Galilean ministry); a "year" of popularity (up until the aftermath of the feeding of the five thousand, when many of Jesus' more loosely associated followers abandoned him, as in John 6:66); and a "year" of rejection (from after the feeding of the five thousand until his death).[75] These, of course, are broad generalizations that do not characterize every detail of each of these periods, and the first two phases cannot be dated to a set number of months. Each may have been more or less than a year. Still, the labels create a helpful schematic for painting the ministry of Christ in broad strokes.

---

[73] A few have tried to add still another year on the basis of John 4:35 in which Jesus refers to the fields being ripe for harvest, suggesting to some that John is speaking in January or February before the spring harvest. But this fits well with the feast of John 5:1 as being either the spring Passover of the fall Tabernacles of that same calendar year, since Israel had two growing seasons. Plus, it is not certain that Jesus intends to make any statement about time of year at all; he is more likely applying a common proverb to the harvest of ripe souls awaiting evangelists.

[74] For arguments for and against, see Blomberg, *Historical Reliability of the Gospels*, 216–19.

[75] See, e.g., Gundry, *Survey of the New Testament*, 111–16.

The Crucifixion of Christ

We know that Christ died during the reigns of the prefect Pilate (AD 26–36), the high priest Caiaphas (AD 18–36), and the tetrarch Antipas (4 BC–AD 37). It would seem that he was crucified on a Friday (the day before the Sabbath, as in Mark 15:42 par.) and the day after the evening on which the initial Passover meal was celebrated (Mark 14:12, 14, 16 pars.).[76] But John seems to indicate Christ being crucified on the day of the Passover celebration, before the initial meal was eaten (John 13:1; 18:28; 19:14, 31). So, was Passover, following the Jewish custom of counting a day from sundown to sundown, from Thursday night to Friday night or from Friday night to Saturday night?[77] Because we know that Passover was celebrated on the 15th day of the month Nisan and calculated from the appearance of the new moon, we can use astronomical data to determine the years this date fell on a Friday or Saturday.[78] But weather conditions always made it doubtful whether the first sliver of a new moon would be sighted on the first or second day of a new month. As it turns out, a case can be made for Passover having fallen on either Friday or Saturday in AD 30 or 33, although it is more difficult to date the festival in 33 on a Friday.

Choosing between these dates is extremely difficult. If one equates the cosmic disruptions in Mark 15:33 and Acts 2:19–20 with a lunar eclipse, then the year must be 33.[79] Yet if the darkness is a wholly supernatural phenomenon, then this information is of no help. If the earliest plausible date for the beginning of Christ's ministry is 28, and if it could be as late as 29, and if one is convinced that he had about a four-year ministry, then it is natural again to opt for 33. But with all the uncertainties noted above, it is not at all impossible that Jesus' ministry lasted only two years or a little more and that the bulk of it occurred during 28–30.

---

[76] Some have argued for a Wednesday crucifixion on the grounds that in Matt 12:40, Jesus predicts that he will be in the "heart of the earth" for "three days and three nights," thus requiring three full days before Resurrection Sunday. But this interpretation fails to recognize the standard Jewish idiom of using "a day and a night" to refer to any portion of a twenty-four-hour period of time. See Gundry, *Matthew*, 244, for references.

[77] Numerous suggestions have been made: (1) Jesus followed an Essene or Galilean calendar that differed from others (unlikely because of the confusion that would have been caused in Jerusalem by different groups of Jews celebrating the various parts of the week-long festival on different days). (2) Jesus and the Twelve celebrated by themselves a day early because he knew he was to die (possible, but without any corroborating evidence, and cf. Mark 14:12). (3) The Synoptics are right and John is wrong; John wants to bring out the theology of Jesus as Passover Lamb by this unhistorical modification (plausible, but elsewhere John seems to bring out the theological significance of Jesus at the various festivals without such falsification of the data). (4) John is right and the Synoptics are wrong (this fits John's concern for chronology but the Synoptic change then seems unmotivated). (5) Both John and the Synoptics actually agree that Jesus ate the Passover meal Thursday night and was crucified on Friday (this seems best; John 13:1–2 does not refer to the Passover meal per se; 18:28 can refer to the *chagigah* lunchtime meal on the day after the initial sacrifice of the lambs; and 19:14, 31 probably refer to the day of preparation for the Sabbath in Passover week (cf. Mark 15:42). For details, cf. Blomberg, *Historical Reliability*, 221–25.

[78] See the exhaustive compilation of data in Herman H. Goldstine, *New and Full Moons: 1001 B.C. to A.D. 1651* (Philadelphia: American Philosophical Society, 1973).

[79] See esp. C. G. Humphreys' and D. G. Waddington's influential article ("Dating the Crucifixion," *Nature* 306 [1983]: 743–46).

If Sejanus' demise (AD 31) put Pilate in a more awkward position, which would account for his behavior at Jesus' trial (see above, p. 23), then once more 33 emerges as the winner. Still, none of this can be demonstrated very conclusively. Also relevant is the dating of the events in the book of Acts and the life of Paul. It is somewhat easier to fit all of those details into a period beginning with AD 30; things are a much tighter squeeze if one waits until 33. Among commentators who take the Gospel data seriously enough to reconstruct any kind of a chronology, *30 thus emerges as the more common favorite.*[80] Fortunately, little of great exegetical significance rests on these exact dates.

Further Details of the Life of Christ

From the other festivals men-

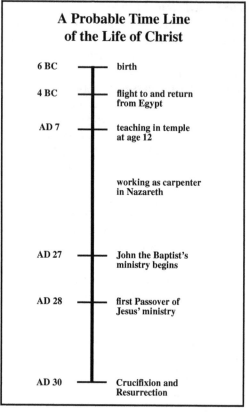

A Probable Time Line of the Life of Christ

6 BC	birth
4 BC	flight to and return from Egypt
AD 7	teaching in temple at age 12
	working as carpenter in Nazareth
AD 27	John the Baptist's ministry begins
AD 28	first Passover of Jesus' ministry
AD 30	Crucifixion and Resurrection

tioned in the Gospel of John, we may fill in the details of Jesus' trips to Jerusalem. As for the outset of his ministry, it is customary to assume that all of John 1:19–4:42 preceded the Galilean ministry narrated by the Synoptics because the healing of the nobleman's son in Cana (4:43–54) closely resembles the healing of the centurion's servant near the outset of Jesus' ministry in Galilee (Matt 8:5–13 par.). The preceding events of John 2:13–4:42, which all take place further south, would then have occurred before Christ begins in earnest in Galilee. If John 5:1 refers to Tabernacles, then it would have punctuated the Galilean ministry since chapter 6 proceeds with the feeding of the five thousand and the walking on the water back north. Jesus' climactic journey to Jerusalem in the Synoptics (beginning in Luke 9:51; Mark 10:1 par.) does not seem to allow for any return to Galilee, so it presumably takes place after his penultimate trip to Jerusalem in John 7:1–10:21. After his ministry in Jerusalem at Hanukkah (John 10:22–39), Jesus

---

[80] After a thorough analysis of the options and considering both the pre- and post-crucifixion data, R. Riesner (*Paul's Early Period: Chronology, Mission Strategy, Theology* [Grand Rapids and Cambridge: Eerdmans, 1998]) concludes, "the fourteenth of Nisan (7 April of the year AD 30) is, apparently in the opinion of the majority of contemporary scholars as well, far and away the most likely date of the crucifixion of Jesus."

seems to remain in the southern part of Israel until his fateful entry into Jerusalem a week before his death (10:40–11:57). All of this, admittedly, is very tentative; nevertheless it may be helpful to lay out these conclusions in chart form (see next page):[81]

Date	Event
late 27?	Appearance of John the Baptist
early 28	Baptism of Jesus
	Early events of John 1–2
spring 28	Passover of John 2:13
spring-fall 28	Rest of events of John 3–4
	Ministry in Galilee as in Synoptics
fall 28	Tabernacles (?) of John 5:1
until spring 29	More ministry in Galilee as in Synoptics
spring 29	Passover time feeding of five thousand (John 6:4 pars.)
until fall 29	End of ministry in Galilee, withdrawal and return
fall (Oct.) 29	Tabernacles (John 7:1–10:21) and return to Galilee
Nov–Dec. 29	"Perean ministry"—Jesus' final trip to Jerusalem
late Dec. 29	Hanukkah in Jerusalem (John 10:22)
winter–spring 30	Ministry in and around Judea and Jerusalem
Apr. 2–6, 30	"Triumphal entry," "passion week"
Apr. 7–9	Crucifixion and resurrection

Beyond this, it is difficult to construct an exact account of when and where every detail in Christ's life belongs. In making this observation we must avoid two commonly held but extreme views that prove unwarranted. One is the claim that the reconstruction of a complete harmony of Christ's life, fitting every episode of the four Gospels into a single, connected, coherent narrative, is impossible. It has often been done, and the sequence of events from one scholar's harmony to the next is in many respects strikingly similar. Irreconcilable contradictions in sequence occur only when one reads in chronological order where it is not explicitly affirmed (see above, pp. 128–29) or assumes that all passages remotely similar to each other represent true parallels.[82]

---

[81] Cf. esp. Robinson, *Priority of John*, 157.

[82] This, too, requires nuancing. It is absurd to assume something happened twice, just to reconcile apparent contradictions among the Gospels, when parallel texts clearly locate the event at the same time and place in Jesus' ministry (e.g., two resurrections of Jairus' daughter or two celebrations of the Last Supper). On the other hand, it is gratuitous to assume that every "Q"-saying was uttered in one and only one context, even though Luke and Matthew consistently differ on where they place many of these teachings of Jesus (e.g., the Lord's Prayer or the parable of the lost sheep). For an attempt to bring some methodological control to this enterprise for one important sample of Jesus' teachings (the parables), see C. L. Blomberg, "When Is a Parallel Really a Parallel? A Test Case: The Lucan Parables," *WTJ* 46 (1984): 78–103.

Stages of Jesus' Ministry in the Gospels

On the other hand, it is precisely the frequent topical grouping and thematic rearrangement of details from one Gospel to the next that makes the opposite conclusion—that there is one and only one way to fit all of the data together—equally unwarranted. Numerous different harmonies have been created that do not agree in every detail, and we simply lack sufficient data in many instances to decide which the most plausible chronology is. For example, which events in Christ's great Galilean ministry took place before the Sermon on the Mount and which ones took place after? In Luke 6:12–16, Jesus calls all Twelve of his disciples just before preaching his great sermon. This has suggested to many that all of the events in Mark 1:1–3:19—that is, up through the calling of the Twelve—should also precede the Sermon. But a number of these events appear in Matthew after the Sermon (see esp. chaps. 8, 11, and 12). Once we realize that both Mark and Matthew are grouping thematically at this point, the chronological question could be decided either way. We simply do not know.

Our outline of the life of Christ for the rest of Part Four will proceed chronologically when we have sufficient information for doing so and thematically when we do not. We will generally follow Mark's outline for these thematic groupings—Jesus' healings, controversy stories, parables, and miracles—while inserting other examples of the same forms from the other Gospels. We will use discrete sections to treat Matthew's, Luke's, and John's material that is unparalleled in Mark, noting thematic patterns there as well. For those who want one plausible harmony of the sequence of events in Christ's life that goes into more detail than the broad chronological outline given above, many synopses are available. The standard scholarly synopsis of all four Gospels is that of Aland (see below, p. 230), to which the student is encouraged to refer throughout our discussions in the chapters to come. The following is a slight modification of Aland's sequence, complete with section references, which reflects one plausible outline of the major stages of Christ's career. Within each major portion listed, the details again proceed by a combination of chronological and thematic factors, the exact nature of which is at times irrecoverable.[83]

Birth and Childhood (§2–5, 7–12)
Preparation for Ministry (§13–16, 18, 20)
Beginning of Jesus' Public Ministry (§21–29)
Early Galilean Ministry (§30–32, 34–41, 49)
Sermon on the Mount (§50–83)
Later Galilean Ministry, Including Trip to Jerusalem (§84–86, 89–150)
Withdrawal from Galilee (§151–63)
Return Home (§164–73)
Further Ministry in Jerusalem (§238–50)
"Perean" Ministry (§174–237)
Final Judean Ministry (§251–68)
Final Ministry in Jerusalem (§269–304)
The Passion (§305, 307–51)
The Resurrection (§352–57, 366–67, 364–65)

For Further Study

The Quest for the Historical Jesus

Overviews

Bock, Darrell L. *Studying the Historical Jesus: A Guide to Sources and Methods.* Grand Rapids: Baker, 2002.

Bockmuehl, Markus, ed. *The Cambridge Companion to Jesus.* Cambridge: CUP, 2001.

Charlesworth, James H. *The Historical Jesus: An Essential Guide.* Nashville: Abingdon, 2008.

Chilton, Bruce D., and Craig A. Evans, eds. *Studying the Historical Jesus: Evaluations of the State of Current Research.* Leiden: Brill, 1994.

Evans, C. Stephen. *The Historical Christ and the Jesus of Faith: The Incarnational Narrative as History.* Oxford: Clarendon, 1996.

Gowler, David B. *What Are They Saying about The Historical Jesus?* New York: Paulist, 2007.

Hagner, Donald A. *The Jewish Reclamation of Jesus.* Grand Rapids: Zondervan, 1984; Eugene, OR: Wipf & Stock, 1997.

Harrisville, Roy A., and Walter Sundberg. *The Bible in Modern Culture: Baruch Spinoza to Brevard Childs.* Grand Rapids and Cambridge: Eerdmans, 2002.

Marshall, I. Howard. *I Believe in the Historical Jesus.* London: Hodder & Stoughton; Grand Rapids: Eerdmans, 1977; Vancouver: Regent, 2001.

---

[83] Going well beyond what the evidence can demonstrate, e.g., are theories that divide Jesus' Galilean and/or Perean ministries into three separate "tours."

Neill, Stephen C., and Tom Wright. *The Interpretation of the New Testament 1861–1986.* Oxford: OUP, 1988.

Schweitzer, Albert. *The Quest of the Historical Jesus: First Complete Edition.* Ed. John Bowden. London: SCM, 2000; Minneapolis: Fortress, 2001 (Germ. orig. 1906).

Wilkins, Michael J., and J. P. Moreland, eds. *Jesus under Fire: Modern Scholarship Reinvents the Historical Jesus.* Grand Rapids: Zondervan, 1995.

Witherington, Ben, III. *The Jesus Quest: The Third Search for the Jew of Nazareth.* Rev. ed. Downers Grove: IVP, 1997.

Anthologies

Dunn, James D. G., and Scot McKnight, eds. *The Historical Jesus in Recent Research.* Winona Lake, IN: Eisenbrauns, 2005.

Levine, Amy-Jill, Dale C. Allison, Jr., and J. Dominic Crossan, eds. *The Historical Jesus in Context.* Princeton: Princeton University Press, 2006.

The Chronology of the Life of Christ

Chronology

Caird, G. B. "The Chronology of the New Testament." S.v. "Life of Jesus." In *IDB*, 1: 599–603.

Donfried, Karl P. "Chronology: New Testament." S.v. "Chronology of the Life of Jesus." In *ABD*, 1: 1012–16.

Downs, David J. "Chronology of the NT." S.v. "Chronology of the Life of Jesus." *NIDB*, 1: 633–34.

Finegan, Jack. "Chronology of the New Testament." S.v. "Chronology of the Life of Jesus." In *ISBE*. 1: 686–89.

Hoehner, Harold W. *Chronological Aspects of the Life of Christ.* Grand Rapids: Zondervan, 1977.

Vardaman, Jerry, and Edwin M. Yamauchi, eds. *Chronos, Kairos, Christos.* Winona Lake, IN.: Eisenbrauns, 1989.

Life of Christ

Bock, Darrell L. *Jesus according to Scripture: Restoring the Portrait from the Gospels.* Grand Rapids: Baker, 2002.

Drane, John. *Son of Man: A New Life of Christ.* Alresford: Hunt & Thorpe; Grand Rapids: Eerdmans, 1993.

Guthrie, Donald. *Jesus the Messiah.* Rev. ed. Grand Rapids: Zondervan; London: Pickering & Inglis, 1982.

Moore, Mark E. *The Chronological Life of Christ.* Joplin, MO: College Press, 2007.

Stein, Robert H. *Jesus the Messiah: A Survey of the Life of Christ.* Downers Grove: IVP, 1996.

Harmonies and Synopses

Aland, Kurt. *Synopsis of the Four Gospels: English Edition.* New York and London: United Bible Societies, 1982.

Knight, George W. *A Simplified Harmony of the Gospels.* Nashville: Broadman & Holman, 2001.

Pentecost, J. Dwight. *A Harmony of the Words and Works of Jesus Christ*. Grand Rapids: Zondervan, 1981.

Thomas, Robert L., and Stanley N. Gundry, eds. *The NIV Harmony of the Gospels*. San Francisco: Harper, 1988.

Throckmorton, Burton H., Jr. *Gospel Parallels: A Synopsis of the First Three Gospels*. Rev. ed. Nashville: Thomas Nelson, 1992.

Bibliographies

Evans, Craig A. *Jesus*. IBR Bibliographies #5. Grand Rapids: Baker, 1992.

Evans, Craig A. *Life of Jesus Research: An Annotated Bibliography*. Leiden: Brill, 1996.

Kissinger, Warren S. *The Lives of Jesus: A History and Bibliography*. New York and London: Garland, 1985.

Questions for Review

1. What are the three quests of the historical Jesus? How are they similar to or different from each other?
2. What are the major scholarly options for understanding the historical Jesus? Which one seems most probable to you and why?
3. Explain the criteria of authenticity, both in general and criterion by criterion.
4. To what extent can we confidently reconstruct a chronology of the life of Christ? To what extent can we not? What are the relatively fixed dates and how do we arrive at them?

11

THE BIRTH AND CHILDHOOD OF JESUS

The Gospel of Mark begins with Jesus already grown up. Matthew and Luke, however, each devote two chapters to describing the events surrounding his birth. John's prologue is much more theological, developing the concepts of Jesus' pre-existence and incarnation. We will begin by looking at Matthew and Luke because, even though they differ considerably on the events they narrate, these two Gospels do actually provide information about the beginning of Jesus' life. Because there is almost no verbal parallelism between Matthew 1–2 and Luke 1–2, the two evangelists are probably relying on their distinctive sources or traditions at this point. The reasons for each including what they did will become clear as we survey each "infancy narrative." Still we should not lose sight of the fact that there is considerable agreement on the main details: The engaged couple Mary and Joseph are the parents, yet Jesus was conceived while Mary was still a virgin, by the power of the Holy Spirit, in the time of Herod. Both parents were godly. An angel makes the announcement of the coming birth and names the child in advance. The birth occurs in Bethlehem, but the family eventually settles in Nazareth. Jesus' Davidic heritage and messianic role are stressed in each.[1] Beyond this, Matthew and Luke largely go their separate ways.

---

[1] Cf. further Fitzmyer, *Luke I–IX*, 307.

Matthew's Infancy Narrative (Matt 1–2)

The Genealogy of Jesus (1:1–17) [Aland §1, 6]

Matthew stresses the theological significance of Jesus right from the outset. Jesus is the Jewish Messiah—the Christ—and the descendant of King David. He is also the descendant of Abraham, the father of the Jewish nation (v. 1). Yet Abraham's offspring were promised to be a blessing to all nations (Gen 12:2–3), and this universalist strain is foreshadowed in Matthew's genealogy as well. Unexpectedly, five women's names are included—Tamar, Rahab, Ruth, Uriah's wife (Bathsheba), and Mary. All but Mary had Gentile connections of some kind, and all including Mary had a cloud of suspicion surrounding their sexual behavior, whether or not it was warranted.[2] If the Messiah can be born from this kind of ancestry, he can be a deliverer for all kinds of people, even disreputable ones.

Even though the Old Testament mentions several additional ancestors, Matthew arranges his names into three groups of fourteen, with David as the fourteenth. In Hebrew the *gematria* (the sum of the numerical equivalents of the consonants in a word) for David was 14 (D+V+D = 4+6+4). Given the popularity of various creative uses of gematria in ancient Judaism, Matthew may well have employed this device to stylize his genealogy and stress Jesus as Son of David. The verb "to beget" (NIV "was the father of") can mean "to be one's ancestor," so there was no problem in leaving names out. The word "whom" in verse 16 is feminine, making it clear that Matthew is claiming that only Mary was Jesus' biological parent.

Events Surrounding Jesus' Birth (1:18–2:23) [Aland §7, 8, 10, 11]

Everything else Matthew includes in chapters 1–2 has to do with one of five Old Testament texts he finds fulfilled in the time of Jesus' infancy. From these passages we learn about the "who" and the "where" of Christ's birth: chapter 1 portrays Jesus as the Christ, the Son of David, and Immanuel; chapter 2 describes the significance of Jesus in Bethlehem, Egypt, and Nazareth.[3] As elsewhere with the Gospels' use of the Old Testament,[4] some of these prophecies are fairly literal, straightforward predictions that have now come to pass. For example, 2:6 notes

---

[2] J. Schaberg (*The Illegitimacy of Jesus: A Feminist Theological Interpretation of the Infancy Narratives*, rev. ed. [Sheffield: SAP, 1995]) goes beyond the evidence in arguing for Jesus as a literal bastard. But *suspicions* of illegitimate births or sexual relations did shroud each of these five women; see C. L. Blomberg, "The Liberation of Illegitimacy: Women and Rulers in Matthew 1–2," *BTB* 21 (1991): 145–50. Jesus may well have lived much of his life under the shadow of the charge that he was a bastard and experienced the accompanying stigma that a culture of honor and shame unleashed on those so accused. See esp. S. McKnight, "Jesus as *Mamzer* ('Illegitimate Son')," in *Who Do My Opponents Say I Am? An Investigation of the Accusations Against the Historical Jesus*, ed. S. McKnight and J. B. Modica (London and New York: T&T Clark, 2008).

[3] Krister Stendahl, "Quis et Unde? An Analysis of Matthew 1–2," in *Judentum, Urchristentum, Kirche*, ed. W. Eltester (Berlin: Töpelman, 1960), 94–105.

[4] On which, see the individual articles on each Gospel in Beale and Carson, eds., *Commentary on the New Testament use of the Old Testament*. On this passage in particular, see esp. T. L. Howard, "The Use of Hosea 11:1 in Matthew 2:15: An Alternative Solution," *BSac* 143 (1986): 314–28, who speaks of "analogical correspondence" between the two passages. Cf. also D. G. McCartney and P. Enns, "Matthew and Hosea: A Response to John Sailhamer," *WTJ* 63 (2001): 97–105.

that the Messiah must be born in Bethlehem (Mic 5:2). Choosing his birthplace is not part of the Messiah's "job description" that Jesus could have set out to accomplish, so this kind of fulfillment has considerable apologetic value.

On the other hand, some fulfillments are clearly typological. Typology here means "the recognition of a correspondence between New and Old Testament events, based on a conviction of the unchanging character of the principles of God's working, and a consequent understanding and description of the New Testament event in terms of the Old Testament model."[5] Matthew's use in 2:15 of Hos 11:1, for example, involves a text that is not prophetic in its original context but a past tense reference to God having called Israel out of Egypt. Still, Christians saw a divinely intended coincidence in the fact that Jesus, like the Israelites, had to flee and return from Egypt as part of God's process of inaugurating a covenant with his people. In general, they believed that redemptive history followed patterns that repeated themselves, often on ever grander scales, demonstrating the same God at work in each instance.[6] (The Gk. and Hb. verbs for "fulfill" in these contexts carry the sense of "fill full."[7]) This logic, too, has considerable apologetic force, even if it differs from straightforward prediction and fulfillment.

In still other cases there may be a combination of literal and typological fulfillments. The famous Isa 7:14 prophecy of a virginal conception (Matt 1:23) is forward-looking, but the fact that the son was to be born in Ahaz's day (Isa 7:15–16) implies at least a provisional fulfillment in Isaiah's lifetime. Probably "virgin" (Hb. *'almah*) meant simply "a young woman of marriageable age," and the promised son was Maher-Shalal-Hash-Baz (8:3). Yet in the larger context of Isaiah 7–9, the son to be born who will be called Immanuel ("God with us," as in 7:14; 8:8) is also identified as "Mighty God" (9:6). The Septuagint later translated Isa 7:14 with a Greek word (*parthenos*) that more strictly referred to a woman who had never had sex. Doubtless, Matthew felt justified in concluding that Isaiah's prophecy was not exhausted in Ahaz's day, and that the true, ultimate intent of the prediction was to point to Jesus.[8] In fact, the semantic range of "fulfill" that could include the concepts of "completing" or "filling full" allowed for multiple fulfillments of prophecy of varying kinds.[9] We will now make additional exegetical comments on each of the five passages of Matt 1:18–2:23 in turn.

The Conception of Jesus (1:18–25). Betrothal was a binding contract, but the marriage was not consummated until after the wedding, often a year or more

---

[5] R. T. France, *The Gospel according to Matthew* (Leicester: IVP; Grand Rapids: Eerdmans, 1985), 40.

[6] For a detailed study of typology, see L. Goppelt, *Typos: The Typological Interpretation of the Old Testament in the New* (Grand Rapids: Eerdmans, 1982; Eugene, OR: Wipf & Stock, 2002).

[7] J. R. D. Kirk, "Conceptualising Fulfillment in Matthew," *TynBul* 59 (2008): 77–98.

[8] For an explanation of these and related concepts and an excellent survey of interpretive options, see J. T. Willis, *Isaiah* (Austin: Sweet, 1980), 158–68. Cf. also J. M. Hamilton, Jr., "'The Virgin Will Conceive': Typological Fulfillment in Matthew 1:18–23," in *Built upon the Rock*, ed. Gurtner and Nolland, 228–47.

[9] M. J. Wilkins, *Matthew* (Grand Rapids: Zondervan, 2004), 78. See further C. L. Blomberg, "Interpreting Old Testament Prophetic Literature in Matthew: Double Fulfillment," *TJ* 23 (2002): 17–33.

later. Young Jewish women frequently married in their early teens to men several years older than them. We have no reason to suspect Mary and Joseph were any different. The perspective throughout this passage is primarily Joseph's, suggesting that it may first have been related by him. Joseph's "righteousness," however, reflects a key theme of Matthew and may be the evangelist's additional emphasis. It does not mean Joseph was sinless, merely godly. His righteousness may be observed both in his intentions to obey the oral Torah that required divorce in the case of sexual unfaithfulness and in his desire to spare Mary the worst of public humiliation.[10] The name of the child, "Jesus," is a Greek translation of the Hebrew, "Joshua," which means "Yahweh saves" or "Yahweh is salvation." That the newborn child will save *his* people from their sins reminds us that salvation remains for the Jew first and then also for the Gentiles (recall above, p. 149).[11]

Birth in Bethlehem and Visit of the Magi (2:1–12). Despite popular Christmas cards and carols, Matthew never says that the Magi were wise men or kings and that there were three of them (although they do bring three gifts fit for royalty)! *Magoi* were astrologers, probably from Persia, who combined a primitive science of stargazing with attempts to understand the signs of the times and of the future. By Jewish standards, their religion and occupation would have made them appear foolish.[12] Here is another hint at the universal impact of the Gospel and a striking contrast with the reaction of Herod and the Jerusalemites (dominated by priestly and government families). The people who were least expected to worship the Christ-child come to do so, while those who should have been awaiting him are threatened by his arrival.[13] The star has often been explained as a comet, a conjunction of planets, or a meteor (recall above, p. 222), but none of these rationalistic attempts to explain the seemingly supernatural succeed in accounting for the element of timing and location. Matthew makes one change in verse 6 to the text of Micah by adding "by no means." Although this seems to negate the original meaning of the prophecy, one must understand Matthew's point to be that although Bethlehem *was* small and of little significance as a town in and of itself, the birth of the Christ child *now* gave it great importance.[14] Mary and Joseph have apparently settled into a home there (v. 11), but they will soon be told to flee.

Flight to Egypt (2:13–15). In modern terms, this passage portrays Jesus and his family as refugees.[15] It is sometimes argued that Luke leaves no room in his narra-

---

[10] On the "normal" rabbinic-era divorce, see D. Instone-Brewer, *Divorce and Remarriage in the Bible: The Social and Literary Context* (Grand Rapids and Cambridge: Eerdmans, 2002), 114–17.

[11] Cf. also B. Repschinski, "'For He Will Save His People from Their Sins' (Matthew 1:21): A Christology for Christian Jews," *CBQ* 68 (2006): 248–67.

[12] M. A. Powell, "The Magi as Wise Men: Re-examining a Basic Supposition," *NTS* 46 (2000): 8.

[13] Cf. R. A. Horsley, *The Liberation of Christmas: The Infancy Narratives in Social Context* (New York: Crossroad, 1989; Eugene, OR: Wipf & Stock, 2006), 39–60.

[14] Carson ("Matthew," 88) calls it a "merely formal" contradiction.

[15] Keener, *Matthew*, 109. Cf. A. E. Martínez, "Jesus, the Immigrant Child: A Diasporic Reading of Matthew 2:1–23," *Apuntes* 23 (2006): 84–114.

tive for this journey, but we do not know how much time is implied by Luke 2:39. Anywhere from a few months to a couple of years might well have elapsed.[16]

Massacre of the Innocents (2:16–18). The same kind of typology seems to be involved here as with Matthew's use of Hos 11:1. Jeremiah 31:15 refers to women at the time of the exile bemoaning the loss of their children, but is already alluding back to Rachel as the personification of the mothers of Israel. Just as her children, Joseph and Benjamin, were threatened with "being no more" in Egypt, so, too, these later women cried when their sons departed, some in exile and some in death. Now Matthew reapplies the motif one more time to the mothers in Bethlehem whose babies were slaughtered by Herod's troops.[17] We must not exaggerate the numbers involved; in a town this small there may have been no more than about twenty children two years old or younger.[18] Verse 16 suggests that the Magi may have arrived as late as two years after Jesus' birth; they certainly do not belong in manger scenes next to the shepherds!

Return to Nazareth (2:19–23). There is no Old Testament passage that contains the statement, "He will be called a Nazarene" (v. 23). But this is also the only "quotation" Matthew introduces with a plural reference to prophets. Presumably, then, he is summarizing a key theme of various prophecies without actually citing any one of them. But which theme is in view? The two most common suggestions have involved (1) a play on words on the Hebrew *nezer* (branch)—referring to Jesus' regal, messianic role as the "branch" of Jesse (i.e., from David's line; cf. Isa 11:1)—and (2) taking Nazareth as proverbial for a "backwater" or "hick" town (cf. John 1:46) and referring to the theme of the Messiah's obscurity (see esp. Isa 52:14; 53:2–9).[19] In conjunction with (1), Num 24:17–19 may also be in Matthew's mind, with its reference to Israel's coming star and scepter who would rule the nation, interpreted messianically in many Jewish circles. Then all of Matthew 2 can be seen as framed by two specific allusions to this passage, with the star that the Magi saw providing the opening reference.[20]

Matthew, then, is clearly writing not merely as a historian but as a theologian with apologetic motives to show Jesus as the true fulfillment of Old Testament hopes for a perfect, Davidic king. This has implications for contemporary Christian apologetics too. It is sometimes observed that there are dozens of fulfillments of prophecy in the Gospels and that the odds of all these coalescing around one

---

[16] Cf. Nolland, *Matthew*, 122: "these are not serious problems to harmonisation in the kind of literature where sequencing and time links are frequently part of narrative technique rather than reflecting a concern with historical detail."

[17] Or in the words of Witherington (*Matthew*, 70–71), "Rachel wept from her grave for the exiles and now is weeping again from the grave."

[18] On these and other main aspects of this passage, see esp. France, "Herod and the Children of Bethlehem."

[19] A third option, that Jesus is being likened to a Nazirite (like Samson), proves less likely, both because of the improbable orthographic changes required and because Jesus' ministry scarcely resembled the asceticism of Nazirites.

[20] D. Instone-Brewer, "Balaam-Laban as the Key to the Old Testament Quotations in Matthew 2," in *Built upon the Rock*, ed. Gurtner and Nolland, 207–27.

individual are microscopically small.[21] The problem is that only a handful of the Old Testament texts "fulfilled" in the Gospels are of the straightforward predictive variety. Yet once we enter into the ancient Jewish mind-set, there is still great apologetic value in the broader concepts of fulfillment found on the pages of the New Testament. When key events heralding the salvation of God's people recur in strikingly similar patterns, surely, that, too, is testimony to the fact that all is not merely happening by chance.

Conclusion

To sum up, Matthew's infancy narrative stresses three key themes. First, *Jesus is the hope of Israel*, its long-awaited Messiah, and the fulfillment of the Old Testament. Second, *through him blessings will be extended to the Gentiles* and to others who are now ostracized. Third, *Jesus is the legitimate king and ruler*, not Herod, not the priests in Jerusalem, nor any other earthly authorities. Today, too, Jesus' Lordship implicitly challenges all merely human leaders' pretensions to ultimate power.[22]

Luke's Infancy Narrative (Luke 1–2)

The Preface (1:1–4) [Aland §1]

We have already alluded to the function of this paragraph in helping to identify the purposes and circumstances of Luke's writing (above, p. 172). Composed in highly elegant literary Greek, it follows the form of preface found in numerous other historical and biographical works of the day.[23] It describes the formation of the Gospel tradition in the three stages analyzed by form, source, and redaction criticism (see above, p. 91). It justifies study of Luke as both a historian and theologian and suggests that he aimed at a level of trustworthiness in both spheres. That he writes an "orderly account" (v. 3) implies deliberate structure, though not necessarily chronological or "consecutive order" (*contra* the NASB).[24]

The Birth Stories (1:5–2:52) [Aland §2–5, 7–9, 11–12]

Abruptly, with 1:5, Luke adopts a very Semitic form of Greek writing. From chapter 3 on, he uses standard *koinē*, though with a bit more literary artistry than the other evangelists, but not as elegantly as the preface or as Hebraic in style as the rest of these two chapters. This style has often raised the question of whether Luke might have been translating material written in Hebrew or Aramaic here. Given that much of this information had to have come from the closest relatives

---

[21] See, e.g., J. McDowell, *The New Evidence That Demands a Verdict,* rev. ed. (Nashville: Nelson, 1999), 164–92.

[22] Cf. S. Hauerwas, *Matthew* (Grand Rapids: Brazos, 2006), 38; Carter, *Matthew and the Margins,* 42–43.

[23] Alexander (*Preface to Luke's Gospel*) finds the closest parallels in scientific treatises, only one step removed from the most literate and classical of Greek styles.

[24] Green, *Luke,* 44.

of Jesus, the suggestion is not improbable.[25] Indeed, Luke 1–2 reflect the perspectives of Elizabeth and Mary more than the male characters, leading one to speculate about Luke having interviewed someone like Mary herself.

Whereas Matthew structures his infancy narrative around Old Testament "prophecies," Luke organizes his to provide an overview of God's plan of salvation and to highlight the similarities and differences between John the Baptist and Jesus. First, the birth of John is foretold (1:5–25); then the birth of Jesus is predicted (1:26–38). The two mothers, Elizabeth and Mary, next come together, showing how the stories of their two sons intersect (1:39–56). Then the birth and growth of John are narrated (1:57–80), followed by the birth and growth of Jesus

The Infancy Stories of Jesus

Matthew	Luke
conceived of a virgin (1:18–25)	birth of John the Baptist predicted (1:5–25)
born in Bethlehem (2:1–12)	birth of Jesus predicted (1:26–38)
out of Egypt (2:13–15)	the two mothers visit (1:39–56)
	birth of John the Baptist (1:57–80)
wailing in Ramah (2:16–18)	birth of Jesus (2:1–40)
called a Nazarene (2:19–23)	Jesus in the temple at age 12 (2:41–52)

(2:1–52). Numerous parallels make it clear that Luke is drawing attention to the similarities between John and Jesus as heralds of a new age: born to godly, Jewish parents,[26] who experienced miraculous conceptions involving the Holy Spirit and outward "signs"; angelic promises of the coming prophetic and redemptive significance of the children; impact first for Israel but then beyond, offering deliverance in both spiritual and socioeconomic realms; initial fear and disbelief on the part of the parents followed by acceptance and praise to God; and details of the circumcision, naming, and subsequent growth of the children.

On the other hand, it is also clear that Luke wants to portray Jesus as greater than John. The miracle of a virginal conception is greater than that of merely opening a once-barren womb. John will be the forerunner who will point others

---

[25] The most sophisticated attempt to defend this suggestion is S. C. Farris, "On Discerning Semitic Sources in Luke 1–2," in *Gospel Perspectives*, vol. 2, ed. R. T. France and D. Wenham (Sheffield: JSOT, 1981; Eugene, OR: Wipf & Stock, 2003), 201–37, which overlaps in part with his more wide-ranging study, *Hymns of Luke's Infancy Narratives*. Challenging Farris's conclusions and opting for Luke consciously employing Septuagintal style in these chapters is Jung, *Original Language of the Lukan Infancy Narrative*.

[26] As with the statement about Joseph being righteous in Matt 1:19, "blameless" in Luke 1:6 does not mean sinless, just generally upright and law-abiding.

to Jesus. Only Jesus is called "Savior," "Christ," and "Lord" (2:11). Indeed, the sheer amount of space devoted to the birth and growth of Jesus far outstrips that allotted to John.[27]

The Birth of John Foretold (1:5–25). John was born to a priestly family of impeccable credentials. With approximately eighteen thousand priests in first-century Israel, the opportunity that Zechariah received to minister in the Holy Place in the temple was a once-in-a-lifetime experience. The angel's announcement identified the child to be born as special. Teetotaling was uncommon in the Old Testament; for someone permanently to be filled with the Spirit "even before he is born" (lit., "from his mother's womb;" a more accurate rendering than NIV's "from birth" in v. 15) was unprecedented. Both of these features reinforce more explicit imagery that links John with a prophetic role of calling people to repentance and preparing the way of the Lord, like Elijah of old (v. 17; cf. further below, p. 251). Zechariah is struck dumb for not believing the angel, presumably on the grounds that a devout student of Scripture such as himself would have been very familiar with the stories of God opening the wombs of women like Sarah, Rachel, and Hannah.[28] But his faith will return, and he will later praise God. Elizabeth, on the other hand, rejoices and immediately credits God with taking away the social stigma that barrenness created in ancient Judaism (v. 25).

The Birth of Jesus Foretold (1:26–38). Mary, too, has an angel come and promise her a miraculous conception (cf. also 3:23). Gabriel addresses her as "highly favored" (Gk. *kecharitōmenē*, lit. "having been given grace" or "having been treated graciously" in v. 28). The later Latin mistranslation of this verb by the expression "full of grace" (*gratia plena*) led to the traditional Roman Catholic conception of Mary as somehow uniquely meritorious or deserving of this honor. In fact, the original language strongly suggests it was God who simply took the initiative to bestow grace.[29] The child Mary would bear was to be "the Son of the Most High," which in this context is a Davidic, regal, messianic title (cf. v. 32a with vv. 32b–33). Protestants as well as Catholics have been embarrassed by Mary's seeming disbelief in response (v. 34). But instead of trying to exonerate her as initially less skeptical than Zechariah, we should recognize that she was being promised something entirely unprecedented in Jewish history. Verse 38, at any rate, concludes with her humble acceptance of Gabriel's explanation.[30]

---

[27] For more on the similarities and differences between John and Jesus in this context, see Nolland, *Luke 1–9:20*, 40–41.

[28] Bovon (*Luke 1*, 51) determines that Zechariah's question in v. 18 "is an expression of culpable unbelief (v. 20)," whereas "Mary's words, "How will this happen?" (v. 34), express questioning belief and are therefore legitimate (v. 38).

[29] As is now widely recognized even by Roman Catholic scholars. See, e.g., R. E. Brown, *The Birth of the Messiah,* rev. ed. (New York and London: Doubleday, 1993), 325–27; Fitzmyer, *Luke I–IX,* 345–46.

[30] For a detailed Protestant survey of Mary in the New Testament and the apocrypha, addressing a cross-section of historical, theological, and literary questions, see B. R. Gaventa, *Mary: Glimpses of the Mother of Jesus,* rev. ed. (Minneapolis: Fortress, 1999). At a more popular level, cf. esp. S. McKnight, *The Real Mary: Why Evangelical Christians Can Embrace the Mother of Jesus* (Brewster, MA: Paraclete, 2007).

Mary Visits Elizabeth (1:39–56). When Mary arrives at the home of her "relative" (cf. v. 36), the older woman, Elizabeth, repeats the angel's blessing (vv. 41–45). Here is the first of Luke's numerous references to someone who boldly proclaims God's word as being "filled with the Holy Spirit." *In utero*, John "leaps" for joy, showing that he, too, is empowered by the Spirit (v. 41). Mary is "blessed" by God and called the "mother of my Lord" (though never the "mother of God"). She responds with a poetic outburst of praise, often referred to as a "hymn," that repeatedly echoes Hannah's psalm in 1 Sam 2:1–10. It may well be a composition she had carefully crafted soon after Gabriel visited her. The hymn is the first of several in Luke's infancy narratives. Together they point to the Christ Child as the coming salvation of Israel but also as "a light for revelation to the Gentiles" (2:32; cf. 1:54–55). They combine spiritual and socioeconomic dimensions of that salvation, promising to remove the oppressive powerful and rich from their thrones (1:52–53).[31] Mary once more refers to being called blessed, but only because of the great things God has done for her (vv. 48–49). Her "song" (vv. 46–55) has been called the *Magnificat*, after the first word in its Latin translation ("magnifies," or, as in the NIV, "glorifies" in v. 46). With the other hymns of Luke 1–2, it occupies a treasured place in the history of the church's liturgy.

The Birth and Growth of John (1:57–80). Events transpire joyfully as predicted, and Zechariah's and Elizabeth's child is born. To everyone's surprise, they choose not to name him after his father, or any other relative, but call him John ("The Lord is gracious"). Zechariah is released from his muteness and is also filled with the Spirit, praising God in hymnic form for bringing his promised salvation. His song (vv. 68–79) has been called the *Benedictus* (Lat. for "blessed"; NIV "praise," in v. 68).[32] It, too, combines promise of physical rescue from Israel's enemies with spiritual restoration (forgiveness of sins) and hints at an extension of these blessings beyond the boundaries of Israel. The covenant with Abraham is being fulfilled, including the blessing of all nations, and it will benefit those "living in darkness" (v. 79), a term not naturally limited to Jewish people.[33] John will be a prophet of God to point the way (v. 76). Verse 80 summarizes John's growth to maturity in one clause and then alludes to his departure to the wilderness, where we will meet him again, baptizing (see below, p. 250).

The Birth and Growth of Jesus (2:1–52). The birth of Jesus took place six months after John came into the world (cf. 1:26), probably in around 6 BC (see above, pp. 222–23).[34] The details about the census registration serve to stress Joseph's link with David and the appropriate "pedigree" for the Messiah. Here is the famous "Christmas story" that has generated so many idyllic manger scenes.

---

[31] Strikingly absent, however, is any hint of violence, in contrast to stories of "blessed" women of Israel's past like Jael and Judith. See B. E. Wilson, "Pugnacious Precursors and the Bearer of Peace: Jael, Judith and Mary in Luke 1:42," *CBQ* 68 (2006): 436–56.

[32] Here is the climax of Luke's material about John. See R. J. Dillon, "The Benedictus in Micro- and Macrocontext," *CBQ* 68 (2006): 458.

[33] On the exalted Christology implied here, see S. Gathercole, "The Heavenly *Anatolē* (Luke 1:78–9)," *JTS* 56 (2005): 471–88.

[34] See also M. D. Smith, "Of Jesus and Quirinius," *CBQ* 62 (2000): 278–93.

We ought to read the text again, with a reliable translation, more carefully! The manger is a feed-trough, and the delivery takes place among animals. The word in verse 7, traditionally translated "inn" (*kataluma*), elsewhere in the New Testament means "guest room" (Luke 22:11; Mark 14:14). Joseph and Mary would have no doubt made arrangements to stay with family or friends in a town overcrowded by the registration, but so would have many others. In a small Palestinian home of one or two rooms, the milking cow and perhaps a few other animals often stayed in a corner on ground level, separated from the raised portion of the rest of the house by the manger.[35] "Mary and Joseph, then, would have been the guests of family or friends, but their home would have been so overcrowded that the baby was placed in a feeding trough."[36] One apocryphal tradition even speaks of Jesus being born in a cave (*Protevangelium of James* 18–19).

The announcement to shepherds furthers the humble, even humiliating circumstances of the Messiah's birth. Shepherds were often despised in the first century for their nomadic lifestyle and reputation for theft. For their part, Mary and Joseph were poor enough that they would offer the sacrifices for those unable to afford sheep (see v. 24; cf. Lev 12:8). It was to such lowly people and not to the emperor or his court that God sent still more angels to proclaim, "Today in the town of David a Savior has been born to you; he is the Messiah, the Lord" (v. 11).[37] As noted earlier, Savior is the most distinctive title in Luke; Lord, the most characteristic in Acts (see above, p. 165). Verse 14 (the *Gloria in Excelsis*—Lat. for "glory in the highest") has also been much misunderstood. The best textual evidence supports not "on earth peace, good will toward men" (KJV) but "on earth peace to men of good will," with the concept behind "men of good will" being "people he [God] favors" (HCSB).[38] Just a few verses later, Mary will be promised that her son's ministry will cause grief as well as joy in Israel (vv. 34–35). Jesus will later proclaim that for some he came not to bring peace but division (Luke 12:51–53 par.).

Jesus' family proceeds to raise the child as a Law-abiding Jewish boy. In taking him to the temple for various rituals, they meet the aged prophet Simeon who was promised he would live to see the Messiah born. He can now die in peace, after he "sings" the final Spirit-led hymn of Luke's infancy narratives (the *Nunc Dimittis*—"Now dismiss . . ."—vv. 29–32). Here appears the most explicit reference to the Messiah's ministry extending to the Gentiles (v. 32, alluding to Isa 42:6 or 49:6). Simeon's testimony is matched by that of the elderly prophetess,

---

[35] See esp. K. E. Bailey, *Jesus through Middle Eastern Eyes: Cultural Studies in the Gospels* (Downers Grove: IVP, 2007), 35–37.

[36] Green, *Luke*, 129.

[37] Thus combining elements of Davidic Messiahship and divine Lordship in the rescue of God's people. Cf. further M. L. Strauss, *The Davidic Messiah in Luke-Acts: The Promise and Its Fulfillment in Lukan Christology* (Sheffield: SAP, 1995), 113–17.

[38] This expression ("men of [God's] good pleasure") finds a particularly close parallel in one of the more fragmentary Dead Sea Scrolls. See A. Wolters, "Anthropoi Eudokias (Luke 2:14) and 'NSY RSWN (4Q416)," *JBL* 113 (1994): 291–92.

Anna. Luke is fond of pairing male and female characters in parallel roles.[39] But verses 22–40 break the parallelism between Jesus and John and reinforce the point that the ministry of Jesus will be far greater.

The final part of this section sums up Jesus' growth (vv. 41–52). The only incident Scripture records about Christ between his infancy and his adult ministry is this story of his astounding the Jewish leaders with his answers to questions in the temple at age twelve. The occasion could have been the forerunner to the later *bar mitzvah* ("son of the commandment") ceremony, in which boys, usually at age thirteen, read and expounded the Law for themselves and "came of age," religiously speaking.[40] Jesus also hints at his special relationship with God, by referring to the temple as "my Father's house" (v. 49).[41] But the later apocryphal literature goes much further and turns the child Jesus into a prodigy—fashioning sparrows out of clay and causing them to fly away, miraculously stretching lumber in Joseph's carpenter's shop to help him balance a bed, and withering up a belligerent playmate to the horror of his parents (Infancy Gospel of Thomas 2, 13, 3).[42] The historical truth is that we do not have a shred of solid evidence to determine what else Jesus did before age thirty, except that he no doubt worked diligently as Joseph's apprentice and then as partner. In fact, although Jesus amazes the authorities when he is twelve, nothing miraculous is described here. He is never said to be teaching his teachers, as popular conception has so often imagined. Luke seems intent at the climax of the passage precisely to stress Jesus' full *humanity*. He complied with his parents' wishes, went home with them as an obedient child (v. 51), and grew in the ways all normal children do—intellectually, physically, spiritually, and socially (v. 52).[43]

The Genealogy of Jesus (3:23–28) [Aland §6, 19]

Unlike Matthew, Luke records Jesus' genealogy from Jesus' day back through history and goes well beyond Abraham, all the way to Adam, who is then called "son of God." Luke is the Gospel most stressing Jesus' humanity and universal significance. But Jesus is also Son of God in a unique sense as Luke seems to indicate by placing his genealogy between Jesus' baptism and temptation, two occasions in which Jesus demonstrated that sonship (3:22; 4:3). The names of ancestors closest in time to Jesus diverge considerably from Matthew's list, and not merely because each list is selective. The two most common attempts to harmonize these data have suggested that either (a) Luke gives Mary's genealogy (v. 23b hints that Jesus was not the biological son of Joseph), while Matthew gives Joseph's ancestry; or, perhaps more likely, (b) Luke gives Jesus' human ances-

---

[39] B. Thurston, "Who Was Anna? Luke 2:36–38," *PRS* 28 (2001): 48. The entire article (47–55) is a good study of this prophetess.

[40] Or the year before such a ceremony. Liefeld and Pao ("Luke," 85) observe that "it was considered helpful for a boy to attend the Jerusalem festivals for a year or two before becoming a son of the covenant so that he would realize what his new relationship involved."

[41] Literally, "the things of my Father." Cf. the KJV's "about my Father's business."

[42] See esp. the Infancy Gospel of Thomas (not to be confused with the Coptic Gnostic Gospel by the same name, discussed above, p. 39).

[43] C. H. Talbert, *Reading Luke,* rev. ed. (Macon: Smyth & Helwys, 2002), 40.

try through Joseph, while Matthew gives Jesus' legal and royal ancestry through Joseph (the lines diverging when certain men left no biological heirs).[44]

Conclusion

In short, Luke's opening chapters present many of the same themes as Matthew's, albeit by way of an almost entirely different selection of stories. *Jesus is the Davidic Messiah coming as the consolation of Israel, but he is also "a light to enlighten the Gentiles." He will be both Savior and Lord, bringing spiritual and socioeconomic liberty*, with special compassion for women, the poor, and other social outcasts, inverting the world's standards and beliefs. As the Gospel of Luke and the Book of Acts unfold, however, it will be clear that, unlike Matthew, Luke's greatest interests involve universal, Gentile themes. Jesus is clearly "the man for all people."

Historicity and Theology of the Virginal Conception and the Birth of Christ

Historicity

What are modern readers to make of the amazing stories of Christ's virginal conception? How historically reliable are these birth narratives more generally, permeated as they are with miraculous dreams, angels, and a traveling star? Of course, if one rules out the supernatural *a priori*, there is much here that will have to be dismissed or radically reinterpreted. For those open to a God who occasionally intervenes miraculously into his universe, however, several arguments favor the trustworthiness of this material.

First, the lack of straightforward correspondence between many of the details of Christ's birth and the Old Testament texts matched with them argues powerfully for the evangelists not having invented these data as pious legends or "midrashic" embellishments of their sources. Had they felt free to invent parts of their stories, they could easily have made them match the Old Testament texts more closely. As it stands, the events of the first century are the non-negotiables; the Gospel writers "mine" the Old Testament looking for parallels.[45]

Second, as already noted, Luke's preface most closely mirrors those of other relatively trustworthy historical works, while the abrupt shift into a more Semitic Greek for chapters 1–2 suggests the use of early Jewish sources, perhaps stemming from Mary herself. Matthew's emphasis on Joseph's perspective might then suggest traditions ultimately coming from his side of the "holy family."

---

[44] For details of what are actually four different variants of this latter proposal, see Bock, *Luke 1:1–9:50*, 920–23.

[45] Cf. further R. T. France, "Scripture, Tradition, and History in the Infancy Narratives of Matthew," in *Gospel Perspectives*, vol. 2, ed. France and Wenham, 239–66. *Contra* esp. significant portions of Brown, *Birth of the Messiah*; Gundry, *Matthew*; and E. D. Freed, *The Stories of Jesus' Birth: A Critical Introduction*; all of whom find Matthew (and, perhaps to a lesser degree, Luke) creatively inventing material in numerous places. G. Vermes (*The Nativity: History and Legend* [London: Penguin; New York: Doubleday, 2006]) finds little more than the birth of Jesus to Mary and Joseph in the latter years of Herod's reign to be historical.

Third, although it is often observed that no other ancient sources record Herod's "massacre of the innocents," this event may have been on such a small scale and so politically insignificant as not to merit attention. Then again, a passing reference in a section of the pseudepigraphal *Testament of Moses* that includes after-the-fact "prophecies" about Herod may actually allude to the slaughter (6:4—"He will kill both old and young, showing mercy to none"). The problems with Luke's census have also cast doubt on his trustworthiness, but we have already commented on some possible resolutions of those problems (above, pp. 222–23).

Fourth, and most important, it is unlikely that early Christians would ever have invented the narratives of the virginal conception itself. Its nature is barely described (contrast the later apocryphal *Protevangelium of James*, which describes Mary's unbroken hymen—even after Jesus' birth [19.3–20.1])! Mary is told only that the Holy Spirit would "overshadow" her (Luke 1:35), and she apparently believes from this point on (vv. 38, 45). Luke's narrative shows remarkable tact and restraint compared to various Greco-Roman myths of "virgin births"—Alexander's mother being surrounded by a sacred python so that her husband Philip could not approach her on the night of their son's conception, or the gods appearing in human form to copulate with mortal women in crass, anthropomorphic fashion.[46] Narrators creating pious legends usually go into much more detail than Luke does here. It is also important not to underestimate the scientific knowledge of the ancient world. People then knew that a human man and woman were needed to produce children, so it will not do to attribute the origin of the Gospel stories to pre-scientific gullibility. The idea of a virginal conception obviously created a scandal in some circles (cf. John 8:41); consistent post-New Testament polemic alleged that Jesus was an illegitimate child (e.g., Origen, *Ag. Cels.* 1:32).[47] Finally, nothing is made of this doctrine elsewhere in the New Testament, save for possible hints in Gal 4:4 and Mark 6:3. All of these observations make it highly unlikely that the church would have included these accounts unless there were strong historical reasons for doing so.[48]

Theology

The virginal conception neither proves the incarnation nor is demanded by it.[49] Nevertheless, it is a very fitting way to reinforce the Christian conviction that Jesus

---

[46] For these and other parallels, see the discussion in J. G. Machen, *The Virgin Birth of Christ* (New York: Harper & Row, 1930; London: James Clarke, 1987), whose overall argument remains one of the strongest in defense of the historicity of this event. Davies and Allison (*Matthew*, vol. 1, 214-16) briefly survey both Jewish and Hellenistic "parallels," concluding that none of them accounts for the stories we find in Matthew and Luke.

[47] J. P. Sweeney's survey ("Modern and Ancient Controversies over the Virgin Birth of Jesus," *BSac* 160 [2003]: 142–58) stresses these points.

[48] See further G. Loobuy, "The History of the Virginal Conception: A Study in Argumentation," *EJT* 13 (2004): 91–101.

[49] On this point, and on the historicity and theology of the virginal conception more generally, see esp. C. E. B. Cranfield, "Some Reflections on the Subject of the Virgin Birth," *SJT* 41 (1988): 177–89; H. D. Buckwalter, "The Virgin Birth of Jesus Christ: A Union of Theology and History," *EJ* 13 (1995): 3–14.

is both fully God (divine paternity) and fully man (human maternity). He is thus able to be both an adequate substitute and an adequate representative for us in his "cross-work." In Luke, the emphasis is on Jesus as God's absolute gift, reminding us of salvation by grace. In Matthew, the emphasis is on Jesus as Immanuel, God in solidarity with us. Given how little the New Testament and even the Gospels make of this doctrine, it probably does not deserve to rank among the top five fundamentals of the faith.[50] Yet it remains a cherished truth not to be glibly denied or explained away.

John's Prologue (John 1:1–18) [Aland §1]

Background and Form

John's Gospel begins entirely differently than the other three. In modern scholarship this prologue has often been viewed as a classic example of late Hellenistic thought because of its high Christology: equating Jesus with the *logos* (see above, p. 187) and the *logos* with God. The language about "light" shining "in the darkness" (v. 4), about understanding, recognition, and knowledge (vv. 5, 10, 18), along with the expression "fullness" (Gk. *plērōma* in v. 16), suggested to many that these verses more resembled later Gnostic thought than earliest Christian orthodoxy. Other alleged parallels have been identified in Mandaism, Stoicism, and Philo.

Within the last generation, however, it has been increasingly recognized that all of these features are explicable within a thoroughly Jewish milieu. The Aramaic targums often substitute the word *memra* ("word") for God's name, especially in the opening chapters of Genesis. In other words, God created by his word. The Dead Sea Scrolls have revealed numerous dualisms, most notably the description of the War between the Sons of Light and the Sons of Darkness. Also, John's use of "fullness" appears in the context of contrasting grace and Law. There may be a proto-Gnostic environment in which John is trying to contextualize the Gospel, but in so doing he is opposing Gnostic thought with fundamentally Jewish categories. More climactic and significant in the prologue even than the declaration of the Word being God is verse 14—"The Word became flesh and made his dwelling among us"—a fully human incarnation against all docetic denials. At this point, John goes beyond any concept Judaism had developed as well.[51]

As we have seen previously, John is most likely addressing a diverse audience influenced by many backgrounds, including both Jewish and Gnostic (p. 195). He uses language well known in a variety of religious contexts but invests it with Christian content. He thus dramatically points out that Jesus is the one to whom all general revelation was pointing and whom all human religions were ultimately seeking ("the true light that gives light to everyone" in v. 9).[52]

---

[50] As in "fundamentalism," stemming from A. C. Dixon and L. Meyer, eds., *The Fundamentals*, 12 vols. (Chicago: Testimony Publishing, 1910–1915).

[51] Cf. esp. D. Boyarin, "The Gospel of the Memra: Jewish Binitarianism and the Prologue to John," *HTR* 94 (2001): 243–84.

[52] Cf. F. J. Moloney, *The Gospel of John* (Collegeville: Liturgical, 1998), 42: "its use would have been familiar to a multiplicity of readers and listeners. In the end the Johannine use of *logos* is determined by the universal truth that a word is essentially about communication."

The prologue is poetic in form, but there is little agreement on the number and nature of its stanzas. Some have postulated a pre-Johannine form, but this, too, is largely speculation.[53] In any event, the prologue as it stands is thoroughly Johannine, introducing the key themes and characters of his narrative.

Exegetical Remarks

Verses 1–18 seem to form a chiasmus of at least seven parts. Verses 1–5 and 16–18 both focus on the nature of the Word, verses 6–8 and verse 15 both focus on John the Baptist's testimony to the Word, and verses 9–11 and 14 both focus on the incarnation of the Word. Verses 12–13 then comprise the climactic center, highlighting the positive reception of the Word.[54]

The Nature of the Word (vv. 1–5, 16–18). In conscious allusion to Gen 1:1,[55] John begins by proclaiming the *logos* as preexistent with God from before creation (vv. 1a, 2). Not only that, but "the Word was God" (v. 1b). Though not identical to God the Father, the *logos* fully shared in his divinity. The ancient Arian heresy (still reflected in certain modern sects like the Jehovah's Witnesses) stressed the fact that "God" in the Greek lacks the definite article. Supporters of Arius in the fourth century translated verse 1b as, "the Word was a god," making Christ the first created being, however exalted he may have been. This translation overlooks the grammatical principle that in a vast majority of cases in a sentence of the form "x is y" (two nouns joined by a form of the verb "to be"), if the author wants to distinguish one of the nouns as the subject of the sentence, then only that noun is given the article.[56] In other words, the form of this sentence ensures that we take "the Word" as the subject, rather than translating "God was the Word." No further theological corollaries may be drawn from the grammar.

The Word was also God's agent for all of creation (v. 3). Not only does this allude to God speaking all things into existence in Genesis 1, but it also picks up the theme of God's Wisdom personified as springing forth before all creation and remaining active throughout the entire process (Prov 8:22–31). In him is spiritual, eternal life, which the *logos* has revealed to all humanity (vv. 4–5a). Nevertheless many continue

---

[53] For a survey of options and a presentation of a reasonably promising hypothesis, see E. L. Miller, *Salvation History in the Prologue of John* (Leiden: Brill, 1988). On the likelihood of the prologue in its current form being composed to introduce the major themes of the Gospel, perhaps even after the writing of the rest of the Gospel, see *idem*, "'In the Beginning': A Christological Transparency," *NTS* 45 (1999): 587–92.

[54] With slight modification and elaboration, R. A. Culpepper, "The Pivot of John's Prologue," *NTS* 27 (1980): 1–31; J. Staley, "The Structure of John's Prologue," *CBQ* 48 (1986): 241–64; S. Voorwinde, "John's Prologue: Beyond Some Impasses of Twentieth-Century Scholarship," *WTJ* 64 (2002): 15–44.

[55] Indeed, the Christology of the entire prologue may well have developed from the Genesis creation account and subsequent Jewish traditions elaborating its theology. See M. Endo, *Creation and Christology: A Study on the Johannine Prologue in the Light of Early Jewish Creation Accounts* (Tübingen: Mohr Siebeck, 2002).

[56] This rule is often called Colwell's rule, after the detailed examination of it by Greek grammarian E. C. Colwell, in "A Definite Rule for the Use of the Article in the Greek New Testament," *JBL* 52 (1933): 12–21. Its precise formulation is that "definite predicate nouns usually lack the article." In the NT, Colwell determined that this held true 87% of the time.

The Johannine Prologue
(John 1:1–18)

The Logos and God
(vv. 1–5) creation
humanity

The witness of John
the Baptist (vv. 6–8)

Response to the
Logos: Negative
(vv. 9–11)

The Logos and humanity
(vv. 16–18) re-creation
God

The witness of John
the Baptist (v. 15)

Response to the
Logos: Positive
(v. 14)

Benefits of Belief
(vv. 12–13)

to reject him, but evil will not triumph (v. 5b). The verb at the end of verse 5 is better translated "overcome" than "understand" (TNIV margin). The Word has revealed himself as the ultimate disclosure of the invisible God, a God of grace and blessing, who has moved beyond the Law (vv. 16–18). Not that grace and truth were absent from the Old Testament period, but they characterize the New Testament age even more. Verse 16 reads literally, "We have all received from his fullness, even grace instead of grace." One level of grace supersedes the previous one.[57]

The Testimony to the Word (vv. 6–8, 15). The primary role of John the Baptist in the Fourth Gospel is to testify about Jesus. John the apostle goes out of his way to stress that the Baptist is not the Messiah but merely a witness to him. As suggested above, this was probably in response to a sect or group of people in Ephesus claiming more for John than they should have (see p. 192).[58] This prologue thus alternates between Jesus and John, reminiscent of the structure of Luke 1–2, but for a quite different reason.

The Incarnation of the Word (vv. 9–11, 14). The *logos* came both to fallen humanity in general ("the world" in vv. 9–10) and to Jews in particular ("his own" in v. 11), but he was rejected by a majority of people in both categories. This coming is described as the Word being made flesh and dwelling among us (v. 14). The Greek verb "dwelt" comes from the same root as "tabernacle" (*skēnē*) and was used in the LXX because it contained the three identical consonants as the Hebrew for God's *shekinah* glory. The incarnation thus harks back to the days of the Israelites "tenting" in the wilderness and following God's presence, which dwelt among them as a cloud by day and pillar of fire by night. Yet, the glory of

---

[57] R. B. Edwards, "χάριν ἀντὶ χάριτος (John 1:16): Grace and the Law in the Johannine Prologue," *JSNT* 32 (1988): 3–15.
[58] Cf. also Keener, *John*, vol. 1, 388–91; Lincoln, *John*, 101.

God revealed in Jesus is the glory of the unique Son, the "One and Only" (a more accurate translation than "Only Begotten"[59]).

The Reception of the Word (vv. 12–13). Today it is commonplace to speak of "receiving" Jesus into one's life. This language is relatively rare in the New Testament (though cf. John 13:20 and Col 2:6), but it is important nonetheless. Reception is defined as "belief in his name," which implies trust in his power or authority. Those who trust in Jesus acknowledge him as their master and become God's spiritual children, with a new authority or status (NIV "right") themselves. As the center of the chiasm, verses 12–13 create the climax of the prologue, which "by way of *inclusio* epitomizes the very purpose for which the Gospel was written: for people to 'believe' and have life 'in his name' (cf. 20:31)."[60]

Conclusion

Here then is one of the most important and extensive teaching passages of "high Christology" in all of the New Testament—clearly delineating the preexistence and deity of Jesus. Here are the seeds of later Nicene creedal doctrine, finalized in AD 325.[61] Yet John's prologue is equally insistent on Christ's genuine humanity, against any Gnostic docetism. In context, John starts from a point of agreement with his opponents (Christ's deity) and tries to move them on to the point on which they disagree (his humanity). Today, the historic Christian faith usually finds itself combating those who deny Christ's deity, the opposite error. But how many professing Christians really believe in Christ's full humanity? The number of people who have fallen into pronounced or prolonged sin and who then protest that Jesus could not possibly relate to them or forgive them suggests that docetism is not far from any of us.

For Further Study

Matthew 1–2 and Luke 1–2

Alexander, Loveday. *The Preface to Luke's Gospel: Literary Convention and Social Context in Luke 1.1–4 and Acts 1.1.* Cambridge: CUP, 1993.

Brooke, George J., ed. *The Birth of Jesus: Biblical and Theological Reflections.* Edinburgh: T&T Clark, 2000.

Brown, Raymond E. *The Birth of the Messiah.* Rev. ed. New York and London: Doubleday, 1993.

Brown, Raymond E. *The Virginal Conception and Bodily Resurrection of Jesus.* New York: Paulist, 1973.

Farris, Stephen C. *The Hymns of Luke's Infancy Narratives.* Sheffield: JSOT, 1985.

Freed, Edwin D. *The Stories of Jesus' Birth: A Critical Introduction.* Sheffield: SAP, 2001.

---

[59] See, e.g., Keener, *John*, vol. 1, 412–16; Kruse, *John*, 70–71.

[60] Köstenberger, *John*, 38.

[61] Lincoln, *John*, 98. Cf. also W. S. Kurz, "The Johannine Word as Revealing the Father: A Christian Credal Actualization," *PRS* 28 (2001): 67–84.

Horsley, Richard A. *The Liberation of Christmas: The Infancy Narratives in Social Context.* New York: Crossroad, 1989; Eugene, OR: Wipf & Stock, 2006.

Jung, Chang-Wook. *The Original Language of the Lukan Infancy Narrative.* London and New York: T&T Clark, 2004.

Machen, J. Gresham. *The Virgin Birth of Christ.* New York: Harper & Row, 1930; London: James Clarke, 1987.

Vermes, Geza. *The Nativity: History and Legend.* London: Penguin; New York: Doubleday, 2006.

John 1:1–18

Endo, Masanobu. *Creation and Christology: A Study on the Johannine Prologue in the Light of Early Jewish Creation Accounts.* Tübingen: Mohr Siebeck, 2002.

Evans, Craig A. *Word and Glory: On the Exegetical and Theological Background of John's Prologue.* Sheffield: JSOT, 1993.

Harris, Elizabeth. *Prologue and Gospel: The Theology of the Fourth Evangelist.* Sheffield: SAP, 1994.

Miller, Ed L. *Salvation History in the Prologue of John.* Leiden: Brill, 1988.

Phillips, Peter M. *The Prologue of the Fourth Gospel: A Sequential Reading.* London and New York: T&T Clark, 2006.

Questions for Review

1. What are several of the major structural features that characterize Matthew's and Luke's birth narratives? John's prologue?
2. What is the distinctive theology that each of these three writers wishes to communicate in the opening portions of his Gospel?
3. What kinds of uses of the Old Testament appear in Matthew 1–2? What is the relevance to Christian living of these various kinds of uses?
4. How do the birth narratives of Matthew and Luke differ from common conceptions of Christmas in the culture today? In the church?

12

THE BEGINNINGS OF
JESUS' MINISTRY

The Ministry of John the Baptist

We next encounter Jesus as an adult. All four Gospels agree that he began his public ministry soon after the rise of John the Baptist's movement. There are many questions we would love to answer about what Jesus and John were doing previously and why John seemed to have so little prior knowledge of his carpenter relative. We have already commented on Jesus' probable socioeconomic standing, education, and work in his father's trade. John's priestly lineage may have left him slightly better off. Beyond this, the reliable sources are simply silent. We may perhaps infer that nothing during this period unusually distinguished Jesus or John.

Background

Traditionally, John has been viewed as a lone figure without recent precedent in the Jewish world of his day. Indeed, just as many Jews believed that prophecy had ceased since the time of Malachi, Christians have regularly seen John's ministry as the resumption of that prophecy. But the discoveries of the Dead Sea Scrolls at Qumran have led to widespread questioning of this traditional view. Soon after the discoveries, exaggerated claims were made: John (or even Jesus) was an Essene and had lived with the Dead Sea sect. Occasionally, these claims are revived, but an increasing consensus adopts a mediating position. John (more so than Jesus) may well have met the Essenes in Qumran or elsewhere, and his message has significant features in common with them. Ultimately, however, the differences between the two movements outweigh the similarities.[1]

What are those points of comparison and contrast? Similarities include (1) the location of John's primary ministry, at least according to the Synoptics, in the Judean wilderness between Jerusalem and the Dead Sea; (2) belief in the fulfillment of Isa 40:3 in each of the two movements (Mark 1:3 pars.; 1QS 8:12–14); (3) an ascetic lifestyle emphasizing repentance and purification from sin; (4) immersion in water as a central ritual to symbolize this purification (at Qumran the residents took daily ritual baths for this purpose); and (5) prophecy about baptism in spirit or fire with reference to coming salvation and judgment (Matt 3:11 par.; 1QH 3:29–36; 4:21).[2]

On the other hand, John's ministry was by no means limited to these places and practices. If we accept evidence from the Fourth Gospel, he ministered up and down the Jordan valley. Bethany beyond the Jordan (John 1:28) may well refer to Batanea in the northeast,[3] and Aenon near Salim (3:23) was probably in Samaria.[4] Although, like many of the Essenes, John had a priestly background, the role he adopted much more closely resembled that of a prophet, specifically a prophet like Elijah. He wore the identical prophetic garb (cf. Mark 1:6a with 2 Kgs 1:8) and preached a similar message of imminent judgment for those who failed to repent. As the forerunner, preparing the way of the Lord, John fit in well with the prophecies in Mal 3:1 and 4:5–6 about Elijah returning before the Day of the Lord. When John denied that he was Elijah in John 1:21 he probably meant only that he was not the literal Elijah returned from heaven whom some Jews awaited.[5] After all, Luke 1:17 insists that John will come "in the spirit and power of Elijah," while in Mark 9:13 and parallels, Jesus declares that Elijah has already come "and they have done to him everything they wished."[6]

---

[1] See esp. J. E. Taylor, *The Immerser: John the Baptist within Second Temple Judaism* (Grand Rapids and Cambridge: Eerdmans, 1998), 15–48. Cf. C. M. Pate, *Communities of the Last Days: The Dead Sea Scrolls, the New Testament and the Story of Israel* (Downers Grove: IVP, 2000), 81–82, 141–42.

[2] W. S. LaSor, *The Dead Sea Scrolls and the New Testament* (Grand Rapids: Eerdmans, 1972), 142–53. Cf. also VanderKam, *Dead Sea Scrolls Today*, 168–70.

[3] See esp. R. Riesner, "Bethany beyond the Jordan (John 1:28): Topography, Theology and History in the Fourth Gospel," *TynBul* 38 (1987): 29–63. On the other hand, M. Piccirillo ("The Sanctuaries of the Baptism on the East Bank of the Jordan River," in *Jesus and Archaeology*, ed. J. H. Charlesworth [Grand Rapids and Cambridge: Eerdmans, 2006], 433–43) believes that either Bethabara or Wadi al Kharrar, just east of the Jordan across from Judea, is a more probable location.

[4] J. Murphy-O'Connor ("John the Baptist and Jesus: History and Hypotheses," *NTS* 36 [1990]: 359–74) makes a plausible case for John's having gone to Galilee as well, under the conviction that his message was intended for all Israel. This would account for how he got in trouble with Antipas, tetrarch of Galilee and Perea.

[5] M. de Jonge ("Jewish Expectations about the 'Messiah' according to the Fourth Gospel," *NTS* 19 [1972–73]: 246–70) notes also that many Jews believed in a "hidden Messiah" who would not know who he was or have any power until Elijah came and revealed him. John may well have wanted to deny this notion too.

[6] See further M. Ohler, "The Expectation of Elijah and the Presence of the Kingdom of God," *JBL* 118 (1999): 461–76.

Even John's asceticism (e.g., the desert diet of Mark 1:6b[7]) finds parallels out-side Qumran. In particular, Josephus describes a Jewish holy man named Bannus, who led an austere desert life reminiscent of John's (*Life*, 2:11). Other popular prophetic resistance movements also began in the wilderness, though unlike most of them, John's was nonviolent.[8] By adding to this a purification ritual in the Jordan River, John may have envisioned himself as preparing a cleansed people to reoccupy the land of Israel, as it were, just as the original Israelite inhabitants of the Promised Land, after their years of wilderness wanderings, were newly consecrated before crossing over the Jordan on dry ground.[9]

Message (Mark 1:2–6 pars.; Luke 3:7–18 par.; John 1:19–51) [Aland §13–16, 21]

Mark: The Key Summary. Mark 1:4 reflects the Synoptic Gospels' epitome of what John was all about: "preaching a baptism of repentance for the forgiveness of sins." Although there are uncertainties about how early the practice began, it is possible that Jews were already familiar with the concept of baptism as the initiatory rite they required of proselytes to their religion.[10] As already noted, the Essenes in Qumran practiced daily ritual bathing. The size of baptismal pools excavated demonstrates that these were most likely immersions. John, however, was unique in calling upon all Jews to be baptized as a once-for-all action signifying their repentance from sin. "Repentance" in Greek (*metanoia*) referred to a change of mind, but the corresponding term in the Hebrew Bible (*shuv*) indicated a dramatic change of action as well. The genitive case in the expression "baptism of repentance" is probably either subjective ("baptism produced by repentance") or descriptive ("baptism characterized by repentance").

"For the forgiveness of sins" may be a misleading translation. It is unlikely that John taught that the ritual of baptism itself produced forgiveness. Interesting corroboration of this comes from Josephus, who described John's ministry in the context of a later defeat of Antipas' army:

> But to some of the Jews the destruction of Herod's army seemed to be divine vengeance, and certainly a just vengeance, for his treatment of John, surnamed the Baptist. For Herod had put him to death, though he was a good man and had exhorted the Jews to lead righteous lives, to practice justice towards their fellows and piety towards God, and so doing to join in baptism. In his view this was a necessary preliminary if baptism was to be acceptable to God. They must not employ it to gain pardon for whatever sins they committed, but as a consecration of the body implying that the soul was already thoroughly cleansed by right behaviour. (*Ant.* 18:5.2)

---

[7] On which, see esp. J. A. Kelhoffer, "'Locusts and Wild Honey' (Mk 1:6c and Mt 3:4c): The *Status Quaestionis* Concerning the Diet of John the Baptist," *CBR* 2 (2003): 104–27.

[8] On the nature of John's prophetic ministry, see esp. R. L. Webb, *John the Baptizer and Prophet: A Sociohistorical Study* (Sheffield: JSOT, 1991; Eugene, OR: Wipf & Stock, 2006).

[9] Cf. C. Brown, "What Was John the Baptist Doing?" *BBR* 7 (1997): 37–49.

[10] Arguing strongly for this is Keener, *John*, vol. 1, 446–47.

The Greek preposition *eis* ("for") can also be translated "directed towards" or "with reference to," and it is probably one of these looser senses in which baptism is for the forgiveness of sins.[11] In any event, John's message would have proven shockingly radical as he called the complacent in Israel to recognize that their ancestry was not adequate to keep them in God's favor.

John's ministry was not an end in itself, however. He also predicted a "coming one" (possibly a messianic title based on Ps 118:26 and possibly the Tg. Isa 5:26–27[12]), whose status would make John seem like a menial slave in comparison (Mark 1:7). John baptized merely in water; the one who was coming would baptize with the Spirit. The Greek expression alternately translated as the baptism "in," "with," or "by" the Spirit occurs seven times in the New Testament, six of them citing this statement of John (Mark 1:8; Matt 3:11; Luke 3:16; John 1:33; Acts 1:5; 11:16). In light of Acts 1–2, the expression is at least a reference to the outpouring of God's Spirit on Jesus' followers at Pentecost, initiating the "church age." The seventh reference comes in 1 Cor 12:13, in which Paul declares all the Corinthian believers, including many who were quite immature, to have been baptized in the Spirit. This, therefore, must coincide with their conversion experience. There is no biblical warrant for employing this phrase to refer to any subsequent work of the Spirit or so-called "second blessing." Luke has a term for later empowerings, when he refers to people repeatedly being "filled" with the Spirit (see above, p. 169).[13]

The Distinctives in Q. Matthew and Luke go on to add a paragraph in which John warns the Jewish leaders who have come to observe his baptism. They are a group of "vipers"—poisonous stakes that killed their mothers during birth![14] Nothing less than a thoroughgoing change of lifestyle will suffice; they must "produce fruit in keeping with repentance" (Matt 3:8). Otherwise, judgment will be imminent: "The ax is already at the root of the trees" (v. 10). Judgment is also depicted by the metaphor of the threshing floor, as the farmer sifts the wheat from the chaff (v. 12). Matthew and Luke each agree that John predicted Jesus' baptism would be not only with the Spirit but also with fire (v. 11). The Spirit's coming is like a refiner's fire, purifying that which can withstand the heat and burning the rest, disclosing its worthlessness.[15]

---

[11] See esp. M. J. Harris, "Appendix," *NIDNTT*, vol. 3, 1208. Alternately, we may take "of repentance" to be the key qualifier of "baptism" and retain the translation "for" for *eis*. Thus, "without repentance, baptism effectuates nothing." Thus, T. R. Schreiner and S. D. Wright, *Believer's Baptism: Sign of the New Covenant in Christ* (Nashville: B & H, 2006), 306.

[12] G. D. Kirchhevel, "He That Cometh in Mark 1:7 and Matthew 24:30," *BBR* 4 (1994): 105–11. Cf. M. E. Boring, *Mark: A Commentary* (Louisville and London: WJKP, 2006), 41.

[13] Cf. further J. D. G. Dunn, *Baptism in the Holy Spirit: A Re-Examination of the New Testament Teaching on the Gift of the Spirit in Relation to Pentecostalism Today* (London: SCM; Philadelphia: Westminster, 1970); C. S. Keener, *Crucial Questions about the Holy Spirit* (Grand Rapids: Baker, 1996), 17–78.

[14] C. S. Keener, "'Brood of Vipers' (Matthew 3.7; 12.34; 23.33)," *JSNT* 28 (2005): 3–11.

[15] Cf. further C. L. Blomberg, "Baptism of Fire," in *Evangelical Dictionary of Biblical Theology*, ed. W. A. Elwell (Grand Rapids: Baker; Carlisle: Paternoster, 1996), 49. See also much of A. W. D. Hui, "John the Baptist and Spirit-Baptism." *EQ* 71 (1999): 99–115. C. Bennema ("Spirit-Baptism in

Luke's Unique Additions. Luke 3:10–14 adds still one more paragraph about John's ethical instructions and radical demands. As is characteristic of Luke, he ties his story in with "empire history" (vv. 1–2). He also includes a longer quote from Isaiah 40 in verses 4–6. By extending the reference, it culminates with the prophecy that "all people will see God's salvation" (v. 6). As we have already seen, Luke stresses God's universal offer of salvation in Jesus.[16]

Johannine Distinctives. Although there are significant points of overlap between the treatments of John the Baptist in the Fourth Gospel and in the Synoptics (see esp. John 1:23, 26–27, 30, 32), the distinctives are more pronounced. Above all, John is a witness to Jesus.[17] The Fourth Gospel emphasizes who the Baptist is not (vv. 20–21), possibly to counter a Baptist-worshiping sect (see above, p. 192). The writer has John testify that Jesus is the "Lamb of God"—Passover sacrifice, apocalyptic warrior, and suffering servant all wrapped up into one (vv. 29, 36).[18] He omits any explicit reference to Jesus' baptism but develops at length the accounts of Jesus' calling of his earliest disciples. One of the first two is Andrew; the other is unnamed. Both transfer their allegiance from John to Jesus (vv. 35–40). Andrew in turn calls Peter. Jesus "finds" Philip (v. 43), who then brings his friend Nathanael (arguably the same person as the Synoptics' Bartholomew). There is no mention of any full-time commitment to itinerant discipleship here; that apparently still awaits the more formal commissioning scenes in Galilee (see below, p. 272).

Perhaps the most noteworthy distinctive of these early verses in John is the remarkable collection of titles with which people address Jesus. He is not only the Lamb of God, but Rabbi (v. 38), Messiah (v. 41), Son of God (v. 34), and King of Israel (v. 49). In verse 45 he is the one written about in the Law and Prophets. Could so many people during their first encounters with Jesus have come to such exalted impressions of him? They had heard the Baptist's testimony for some time, and Jesus no doubt had a very "charismatic" personality. But at this stage, none of these titles needs to mean more than that people were hoping that Jesus was the long-awaited Messiah. As developing events will demonstrate, these fledgling disciples probably still had a very nationalistic conception of that Messiah—one who would come to overthrow Rome and its oppressive armies.[19]

The most enigmatic part of John 1 may be verses 47–51. Jesus calls Nathanael "an Israelite in whom there is no deceit"—a play on the two names for the patriarch Jacob/Israel, since "Jacob" meant "deceiver" (v. 47). In reply to Nathanael's surprised question about how Jesus knew him, Christ explains, "I saw you . . . under the fig tree" (v. 48). It has been pointed out that a seat under a fig tree was often a

---

the Fourth Gospel: A Messianic Reading of John 1,33," *Biblica* 84 [2003]: 35–60) argues that for John, even "baptism in the Spirit" by itself connotes this twofold immersion of people by Jesus' revelatory Spirit, which they then choose either to accept or to reject.

[16] On Lucan emphases, cf. further C. M. Murphy, *John the Baptist: Prophet of Purity for a New Age* (Collegeville: Liturgical, 2003), 81–83.

[17] See, e.g., Ridderbos, *John*, 62.

[18] For a full survey of options, see C. W. Skinner, "Another Look at the 'Lamb of God'," *BSac* 161 (2004): 89–104.

[19] Cf. Köstenberger, *John*, 71–72, 83–84; Moloney, *John*, 56.

place of prayer, but perhaps more significant are those passages that speak about the coming age of blessing when every Israelite will sit in peace under his own fig tree (e.g., 1 Kgs 4:25; Mic 4:4, 1 Macc 14:12), at least one of which appears in a seemingly messianic context (Zech 3:10).[20] Jesus also promises greater wonders than mere insight into Nathanael's character—"You shall see heaven open, and the angels of God ascending and descending on the Son of Man" (v. 51). This clearly alludes to Jacob's dream about the ladder to heaven (Gen 28:10–12). But how does the order "ascending and descending" apply to Jesus? Perhaps it is a cryptic foreshadowing of the cross and resurrection—angels accompanying Jesus to bear his body to heaven, in keeping with typical Jewish belief, and returning to announce his resurrection (as in Matt 28:2 par.).[21]

Additional Events in John's Life

Further Testimony to the Christ (John 3:22–36) [Aland §28–29]. For some unspecified period of time, John's and Jesus' ministries overlapped. Both baptized and made disciples (3:22–23), though apparently Jesus let his followers do most of his baptizing for him (4:2). As time went by, Jesus' ministry began to eclipse John's, but John deferred to him with great magnanimity: "He must become greater; I must become less" (3:30). John was still just a witness, a best man for the bridegroom (v. 29).[22]

Imprisonment (Mark 6:17–20 pars.) [Aland §144]. Eventually, John found himself in trouble with Antipas because he had boldly criticized him for marrying his brother Philip's ex-wife Herodias in violation of Lev 18:16. Josephus does not identify the brother of Antipas referred to here as Philip the tetrarch but as another Herod (*Ant.* 18.5.1). He also states that John was imprisoned in Machaerus (18.5.2), a fortress in Perea. Josephus' portrait is also more unrelentingly negative toward Antipas than Mark's. But it is conceivable that these details can be harmonized.[23] Mark's depiction of Antipas makes him a "rounder" character (recall the categories of narrative criticism above, p. 113) than Matthew's, but both accounts agree on Herodias as John's most consistent and dangerous opponent.[24] Luke describes John's imprisonment much more briefly and much earlier

[20] Köstenberger, *John*, 83; Kruse, *John*, 87.

[21] Cf. Bruce, *John*, 62–63. C. Rowland ("John 1.51, Jewish Apocalyptic and Targumic Tradition," *NTS* 30 [1984]: 498–507) notes that the Targum on Genesis describes the angels going from earth to heaven to invite their companions to come and see the pious man whose features are fixed on God's glorious throne. This would fit Jesus well too.

[22] In a culture of honor and shame, to defer willingly to another whose honor was increasing at one's own expense, was counterculturally gracious indeed. See J. H. Neyrey and R. L. Rohrbaugh, "'He Must Increase, I Must Decrease' (John 3:30): A Cultural and Social Interpretation," *CBQ* 63 (2001): 464–83.

[23] Hoehner, *Herod Antipas*, 124–49. There is reason to believe that there was a Herod Philip distinct from Philip the tetrarch. See also P. V. Harrison, "Competing Accounts of the Baptist's Demise," *Faith and Mission* 24 (2007): 26–42.

[24] For an excellent analysis, see D. M. Hoffeditz and G. E. Yates, "Femme Fatale Redux: Intertextual Connection to the Elijah/Jezebel Narratives in Mark 6:14–29," *BBR* 15 (2005): 199–221.

in his narrative than do the other Gospels (Luke 3:19–20), probably to deal with all his material on John the Baptist in a tidy, thematic unit.

John's Doubts and Jesus' Reassurance (Matt 11:2–19 par.) [Aland §106–107]. From prison, John sends messengers to Jesus to ask him if he really is the "coming one" (vv. 2–3). Despite John's earlier testimony and association with Christ, the question is entirely understandable. Prison was not part of John's expected plan for the unfolding of redemption. His apocalyptic message of judgment did not seem to be coming to fruition, while Jesus was becoming known much more for his compassion for his enemies. Jesus does not answer John's question directly but tells him to consider the significance of his miracles[25] and concern for the poor (vv. 4–6)—an allusion to his Nazareth manifesto (Luke 4:16–19), which in turn echoed the servant passage of Isa 61:1–2 (see further, below, p. 271). In so doing, Jesus not only tacitly acknowledges his messianic ministry but redirects John's attention to its true nature.

As John's disciples return to report to their master, Jesus continues to talk to the crowds about John. He affirms John's ministry with the highest of praise. Verses 7–8 covertly compare him with Antipas, who minted coins with reed insignia and lived in pampered regal luxury.[26] But it is John, not any king, who is the greatest mortal who has lived thus far (v. 11a). Still, John will not live to see the kingdom fully inaugurated with Christ's death and resurrection, and thus every subsequent believer has an advantage on which he misses out (v. 11b). John is the greatest of the Old Testament age prophets and the fulfillment of prophecies about the coming of Elijah (vv. 13–14). But a greater power is now present that causes violent people to attack it, as Herod has already done by imprisoning John (v. 12).[27]

Jesus concludes his address to the crowds with a short parable that laments ironically how neither John's harsh message of judgment nor Jesus' carefree association with "sinners" has met with the approval of the Jewish leadership. Yet he promises that God's wisdom, represented by both of these emissaries, will be vindicated (vv. 16–19). It is those who *do* God's works, flowing from their commitment to him, not just those who *claim* to be his spokespersons, who will be demonstrated to be righteous.[28] This little parable reminds us in a nutshell how

---

[25] A viewpoint strikingly paralleled in 4Q521 from Qumran. For details, see H. Kvalbein, "The Wonders of the End-Time: Metaphoric Language in 4Q521 and the Interpretation of Matthew 11.5 par.," *JSP* 18 (1998): 87–110.

[26] G. Theissen, *The Gospels in Context: Social and Political History in the Synoptic Tradition* (Edinburgh: T&T Clark, 1992), 26–42.

[27] Matthew 11:12b is notoriously difficult to translate, but the NIV rendering does not seem as likely as the TNIV (and most other translations): "the kingdom of heaven has been subjected to violence, and violent people have been raiding it." See G. Schrenk, "βιάζομαι, βιαστής," *TDNT*, vol. 1, 609–14.

[28] Cf. C. Shantz, "Wisdom Is As Wisdom Does: The Use of Folk Proverbs in Q 7:31–35," *TJT* 17 (2001): 258: "In effect, [the parable] tells them that it is all well and good to judge the actions of John and Jesus, but as long as they remain sitting on their agora, as it were, they do nothing to prove the value of their wisdom. It is by action that they will demonstrate their virtue, not by their judgments against those whose missions were expressed in either asceticism or at an open table."

similar John and Jesus were in some respects and how different they were in others.[29]

John's Death (Mark 6:14–16, 21–29 pars.) [Aland §143–144]. The Gospels suggest that Herodias, even more than Herod, is the individual who wants to get rid of John. She gets her chance at a royal party when her daughter's dancing lures Herod into making a rash vow. Drink and sexual innuendoes, though not explicitly mentioned here, were common enough in the Herodian household and may have contributed. Antipas is more concerned not to go back on his word in public than to see justice carried out, so he agrees to John's execution by beheading. As John pointed the way forward to Jesus as Messiah in his lifetime, so his execution prefigured Jesus' own death at Roman hands.[30]

Historicity

Given the early Christian concern to play down the role of John the Baptist and to exalt Jesus, just about everything that places John in a positive light is likely to be historical: the considerable early impact of his ministry, numerically and geographically; the fact that Jesus' first disciples came from John's followers; the possibility that Jesus himself first followed John for a while; and Jesus' praise of John as the greatest of all who had previously lived. The strong contrast between John's austere message and Jesus' joyful ministry (Matt 11:16–19 par.) must also reflect authentic tradition; Christians would not likely have portrayed Jesus' precursor as so different from Christ himself. John's ministry of baptism further satisfies the "double similarity and dissimilarity" criterion (recall p. 220) in differing from the kinds of baptism practiced by both Judaism and the early church. On the other hand, the strong line of continuity from Judaism through Jesus to Paul and the early church on the need for repentance for the forgiveness of sins in view of the in-breaking kingdom makes it difficult to imagine John teaching anything different. That John uses no well-established titles for Jesus as Messiah (despite the suggestiveness of "coming one" and "lamb of God") likewise speaks for his veracity here. His death at the hands of Antipas is corroborated by Josephus.[31]

The Baptism of Jesus (Mark 1:9–11 pars.) [Aland §18]

Just as the Gospels often group material thematically, we have kept all the story of John the Baptist together except for the accounts of his baptism of Jesus. We now return to pick up this incident and then follow the course of Jesus' ministry as it subsequently unfolds. Here is the key commissioning of Christ for his public years of itinerant preaching, teaching, and healing.

---

[29] Despite the one-sided title, a good source for both continuities and discontinuities is D. C. Allison, Jr., "The Continuity between John and Jesus," *JSHJ* 1 (2003): 6–27.

[30] C. L. Blomberg, *Interpreting the Parables* (Downers Grove and Leicester: IVP, 1990), 208–10.

[31] Cf. esp. J. P. Meier, *A Marginal Jew: Rethinking the Historical Jesus*, vol. 2 (New York and London: Doubleday, 1994), 19–233.

Its Purpose

Matthew and John reflect the most self-consciously on the purpose of Jesus' baptism. If it was related to repentance for the forgiveness of sins, did Jesus think he had sinned? Matthew insists not, inserting the unparalleled verse that John tried to prevent Jesus from going through with the ceremony (Matt 3:14). Instead, Jesus replied that it was proper to do so "to fulfill all righteousness" (v. 15). Given Matthew's characteristic use of "fulfill" to mean "complete everything to which God's Word has pointed" (recall above, p. 233), he presumably understands Jesus' words as a way of identifying with John's baptism and putting his stamp of approval on it.[32] No doubt that is why Matthew summarizes John's and Jesus' ministries with the identical words: "Repent, for the kingdom of heaven has come near" (3:2; 4:17). To the extent, however, that repentance in ancient Israel involved a corporate confession of the nation's sins, Jesus could participate.[33] In short, he does all that God requires. John's testimony in the Fourth Gospel to Jesus as the Lamb, apparently uttered at this very time (John 1:29), points him out also as the one who would perform God's will in atoning for the sins of humanity.

Accompanying Signs

All four Gospels refer to a dove, but all use a simile to clarify that the Spirit's descent on Jesus was "like" a dove (Matt 3:16; Mark 1:10; Luke 3:22; John 1:32). We do not know what was literally visible, but something reminded the onlookers of a dove. Doves in the ancient world could symbolize peace, love, and even divinity itself, but the most obvious reference would be to the activity of God's Spirit in creation, just as Gen 1:2 spoke of him "brooding" or "hovering" over the waters.[34] Jesus now begins a work of re-creation. The voice from heaven also suggests the resumption of divine revelation after the centuries of its cessation.

Its Message

God declares Jesus his beloved Son with whom he is well pleased (Mark 1:11 pars.). Most commentators find allusions in this declaration to Ps 2:7 and Isa 42:1. The former is part of a royal psalm; the latter falls in one of the servant passages of Isaiah. Both "son" and "servant" seem to have been understood in a messianic sense by important segments of pre-Christian Judaism (see 4QFlor. 10–14 and Tg. Isa. 42:1, respectively). Therefore it would appear that God is forthrightly declaring Jesus to be both kingly Messiah and suffering servant.[35] There is also

---

[32] Cf. Nolland, *Matthew*, 152.

[33] Cf. Boring, *Mark*, 40.

[34] One of the smaller Dead Sea Scroll fragments, known as "A Messianic Vision," seems to confirm this conclusion, with its line, "over the poor will His Spirit hover and the faithful will he support with his strength." This is the first unambiguous ancient Jewish allusion to Gen 1:2 in a messianic context and suggests that the dove at Jesus' baptism refers to Jesus as the bringer of a new creation. See D. C. Allison, Jr., "The Baptism of Jesus and a New Dead Sea Scroll," *BAR* 18.2 (1992): 58–60; cf. Collins, *Mark*, 148.

[35] Wright, *Jesus and the Victory of God*, 536–37.

an incipient Trinitarianism in this baptism: God speaks and the Spirit descends on the man Jesus.

Its Historicity

Because of the theological problems created by Jesus accepting John's baptism that symbolized repentance of sin, it is inconceivable that the early church would have created this story. In view of the messianic overtones of the account, it is likely that Jesus' baptism would have spawned widespread eschatological fervor, however misguided. Thus the credibility of the rash of exalted titles applied to Jesus in the latter half of John 1 is also enhanced.[36]

The Temptation of Jesus (Mark 1:12–13; Matt 4:1–11 par.) [Aland §20]

So far in the Gospels God has disclosed Jesus' identity from heaven, but will Christ be faithful to his role as his ministry unfolds? One might expect Jesus' baptism to launch him instantly into fame and prosperity. Instead, God allows the devil to test him to see what kind of Messiah he really will be. Mark stresses that the temptations come immediately after the baptism. Many Christians have faced some of their greatest struggles soon after their conversion or some act of recommitment rather than before it. We ought not to be quite as surprised as we sometimes are when this pattern continues to recur.[37]

Background and Sources

Only Matthew and Luke narrate the temptation in any detail. Mark records merely that it happened, who was involved, where, and for how long.[38] Interestingly, however, he alone adds that Christ was with the wild beasts. Mark agrees with Matthew that angels served him. Probably both comments are meant to stress Jesus' triumph over temptation and sovereignty over creation.[39] The presence of beasts adds to the danger and even to the demonic threat of the desert (cf. *T. Naph.* 8:4; Luke 11:24). The forty-day period of Jesus' testing calls to mind Moses' period of preparation for forty days and nights before receiving the Law (Deut 9:9) as well as the Israelites' wanderings in the wilderness for forty years. Jesus is a new and better Moses and will succeed where Israel as a whole had failed.[40]

---

[36] See esp. R. Bauckham, "Messianism according to the Gospel of John," in *Challenging Perspectives on the Gospel of John*, ed. Lierman, 34–68.

[37] Wilkins, *Matthew*, 168, who sums up the principle for a believer's proper response as, "Resist the devil in the power of the Spirit through the guidance of the Word to accomplish the will of God."

[38] On the other hand, it can be argued that Mark sees Jesus' temptation as continuing throughout his ministry; see S. R. Garrett, *The Temptations of Jesus in Mark's Gospel* (Grand Rapids and Cambridge: Eerdmans, 1998).

[39] J. B. Gibson, "Jesus' Wilderness Temptation according to Mark," *JSNT* 53 (1994): 3–34. Culpepper (*Mark*, 39) sees the vanquishing of demonic forces as a theme integrating all of Mark 1.

[40] Cf. France, *Matthew*, 128: "The story of the testing in the wilderness is thus an elaborate typological presentation of Jesus as himself the true Israel, the 'Son of God' through whom God's redemptive purpose for his people is now at last to reach its fulfillment.'"

Agency and Sequence

Mark stresses that the temptations came immediately after the baptism. There is an important balance in the description in all three Synoptics between God's Spirit initiating the sequence of events and the devil as the direct agent of temptation. A pair of crucial truths is encapsulated here: God is always sovereign and allows no temptation except that which furthers his broader purposes. Yet he never directly tempts anyone (cf. Jas 1:13) and is wholly dissociated from evil.[41] Matthew and Luke both agree that Jesus was tempted by Satan in three particularly acute ways: to turn stones into bread, to be supernaturally rescued from death after jumping off the temple portico, and to receive all the world's kingdoms in return for worshiping Satan. Luke, however, has the last of these two in reverse order, probably because of the climactic importance of the temple for him. But here is one of those classic cases in which a Gospel writer connects his episodes merely with "ands" or "buts," so that chronological sequence should not be inferred.

Their Nature and Christ's Resistance

There are fascinating parallels between the three temptations of Christ, the three temptations in the Garden of Eden (Gen 3:6), and the three kinds of temptation 1 John 2:16 lists to summarize "everything in the world."

Jesus' temptations	Adam & Eve's temptations	1 John 2:16
turn stones into bread	tree was good for food	lust of the flesh
see all kingdoms	pleasing to the eye	lust of the eyes
save life spectacularly	desirable for gaining wisdom	pride of life

Whether or not any of these parallels was intentional, together they point out that Jesus did experience representative temptations of all kinds; therefore, the writer of Hebrews could declare that Christ was "tempted in every way, just as we are— yet was without sin" (Heb 4:15 NIV).[42]

In the immediate context of Matthew and Luke, it is significant that the devil recognizes Jesus' sonship. "If you are the Son of God" in Matt 4:3 should probably be translated, "Since you are the Son of God."[43] The devil knows full well who Jesus is, but he tries to seduce him into being the wrong kind of Son—a triumphant, regal Messiah who foregoes the road to the cross and is unfaithful to his

---

[41] Cf. France, *Matthew*, 126. For an example of how this plays out in Satan's offering Jesus all the kingdoms of the world, see D. Rudman, "Authority and Right of Disposal in Luke 4.6," *NTS* 50 (2004): 77–86.

[42] So also Wilkins, *Matthew*, 168. H. J. M. Nouwen (*In the Name of Jesus: Reflections on Christian Leadership* [New York: Crossroad, 1993]) sees these three temptations as paradigms of ones all Christian leaders face: the desire to be relevant at the expense of prayer; popular at the expense of ministry; leading at the expense of being led.

[43] The Greek is a first-class conditional clause, which does not introduce any doubt into the condition. It is assumed to be true, at least for the sake of argument. According to J. Boyer's count ("First-Class Conditions: What Do They Mean?" *GTJ* 2 [1981]: 76–77), only in 37% of the New Testament uses of this grammatical form is the condition actually true, but this is one of the clearer examples of such an instance.

Father's will. The primary weapon Christ uses to defeat the devil is Scripture. In each case, he refutes the tempter by quoting Deuteronomy (8:3; 6:16; 6:13). In the second case, the devil quotes Scripture, too (Ps 91:11–12), but misapplies it.

Christ's temptations may well have been to a certain degree subjective or visionary, though no less real or diabolical. The text gives no locale for the "Mount of Temptation," though tourists are regularly shown one overlooking Jericho! In fact, there is no mountain on earth from which one can literally see all the kingdoms of the world. Nor would it have been possible for Jesus to do arduous mountain climbing or even temple climbing after a forty-day period without food, unless he drew on the very supernatural power for helping himself that the devil was enticing him to employ.[44] Christ's refusal to succumb to the tempter's snares points out at one and the same time his sinlessness and peccability. Many liberal theologians have denied the former; many conservative ones, the latter. Yet without the possibility of sinning, his temptation could hardly be said to have been like ours; without the reality of his not sinning, his atonement could scarcely have been vicarious or substitutionary.[45]

Historicity

As with Jesus' baptism, it is hard to imagine any early Christian inventing this story. Here Jesus is at his most vulnerable, reflecting the weakness of his humanity, in contrast with Satan who is depicted as having the power to offer real alternatives to Christ's God-ordained mission. If Christ thought it important to have disciples close enough to him in Gethsemane to hear his prayers there (before they fell asleep!), he would presumably have told his followers about these temptations in the wilderness as well.

From Cana to Cana (John 2–4)

John 1:19–4:42 has often been called Christ's early Judean ministry since he seems to be based near John the Baptist and near Jerusalem. Yet, chapters 1 and 3 give no precise location for Jesus' ministry of baptizing, and two of the events in chapters 2 and 4 take place in Galilee and Samaria, respectively. As noted above (p. 224), this has also been called his year of obscurity. But a year passes by only if 2:13 is a transposition of the account of his final Passover and if 5:1 also refers to a Passover. Either way, this is a period of obscurity only in contrast to the huge crowds that throng around Jesus during his great Galilean ministry to come. We will do more justice to John's intentions in these chapters if we resist the temptation to try to locate every detail chronologically and focus on what he wants to teach us about Christ through these episodes. The overall outline of John suggests

---

[44] R. H. Mounce, *Matthew* (Peabody: Hendrickson, 1991), 31; Wilkins, *Matthew*, 160 n. 15. Liefeld and Pao ("Luke," 101) observe that "in an instant" in Luke 4:5 "probably shows that this part of the temptation involved a vision."

[45] Cf. M. J. Erickson, *Christian Theology,* rev. ed. (Grand Rapids: Baker, 1998), 736: "while he could have sinned, it was certain that he would not. There were genuine struggles and temptations, but the outcome [at least to God] was always certain."

that these three chapters form one discrete subsection, bracketed by the two references to signs done in Cana as an "inclusio" (a framing device of repetition to mark the beginning and end of a literary unit).[46]

The First Miracle: Water into Wine at the Cana Wedding (2:1–12) [Aland §22–23]

Early in his career, Jesus is invited to a wedding during which the wine runs out. Inability to provide for the festivities would have caused the host of the multi-day party acute social embarrassment and shame.[47] Drinking wine in moderation, particularly with meals, was commonplace in the ancient Jewish world. At times it was healthier than the water that was available (cf. above, p. 186). Various Scriptures and intertestamental works considered wine a gift of gladness and rejoicing from God (see esp. Sir 31:27–28; cf. Ps 104:15; Judg 9:13). It was considerably more diluted than our modern wines but still could cause drunkenness if someone overindulged (cf. the caricature of Jesus in Luke 7:34 as a "glutton and a drunkard" because of his willingness to join in such merriment).

Mary, too, has been invited to this wedding, and she turns to her son for help in this time of need (v. 3). Jesus' cryptic reply that his hour has not yet come (v. 4), if taken at face value, would imply that he is not prepared to help just now. In light of similar statements throughout John, however, it suggests that the climactic hour of his self-revelation still lies in the future. The original idiom of Jesus' reply involves no disrespect, meaning something like "what do you want from me?"[48] but stresses his acquiescence to God's sovereign timing. Mary is not rebuffed and trusts that Jesus can still help in some way. In fact, he does work a miracle to help out his host, but it occurs unobtrusively, even secretly, convincing only those with eyes of faith.

The remaining details in the passage suggest that more is involved than merely compensating for an awkward social *faux pas*. In an otherwise sparse narrative, the detail of verse 6 stands out. Why bother noting that the water jars were used for Jewish rites of purification? Given, too, that wedding banquets in Jewish literature often symbolized the messianic age, many commentators have seen a symbolic level of meaning here: Jesus is bringing the wine of the new age, a joy that transcends and replaces the old "water" of Jewish ritual. This interpretation is made probable by the fact that in the Synoptics he will tell a parable about not putting new wine in old wineskins to make a very similar point (Mark 2:22 pars.). Verse 10 here reinforces this: Jesus has saved the best wine for last.[49] John adds one of

---

[46] Cf. Carson, *John*, 104.

[47] R. H. Williams, "The Mother of Jesus at Cana: A Social-Science Interpretation of John 2:1–12," *CBQ* 59 (1997): 679–92.

[48] J. N. Rhodes, "'What Do You Want from Me?' (John 2.4)," *BT* 52 (2001): 445–57. The NIV translation of v. 4a ("Dear woman, why do you involve me?") is better than many. The Greek reads literally, "What [is it] to me and to you, woman?"—idiomatic language that is easily misunderstood in English.

[49] See further C. L. Blomberg, "The Miracles as Parables," in *Gospel Perspectives*, vol. 6, ed. D. Wenham and C. Blomberg (Sheffield: JSOT, 1986; Eugene, OR: Wipf & Stock, 2003), 333–37. Cf.

his favorite themes—that this "sign" revealed Jesus' glory and helped to produce faith (v. 11, though recall our balancing comments above, p. 188).

Clearing the Temple in Jerusalem (2:13–25) [Aland §24–26]

Most commentators see this as a chronologically relocated passage whereby John highlights the significance of Christ's coming death and resurrection early on in his Gospel as a kind of headline for what is to come.[50] On the other hand, there are hints in both John and the Synoptics that something like this account may indeed have happened early in Christ's ministry. Most notable are the references to the forty-six years of building the temple (John 2:20), which dates this event to about AD 28 (see above, pp. 223–24), and the garbled accusation at Christ's trial that he would destroy the temple and build another "not made by man" (Mark 14:58 par. NIV). This accusation becomes intelligible if Jesus had spoken the words of John 2:19 two or three years earlier and if his claims had become distorted during the time that had since elapsed.[51] Moreover, Jesus' "failure" to produce the kind of sign requested in verse 18 to justify his authority in making the mess in the temple that he did would normally have publicly shamed a person sufficiently that no further punishment would have been necessary. A later similar action would have shown Jesus to be literally "shameless" in the authorities' eyes and thus too uncontrollable without arrest and conviction.[52]

More significant for John is what this temple incident symbolized. It probably should be called a temple clearing rather than a cleansing. To be sure, Jesus rued that his Father's house had been turned into a marketplace (v. 16), but buying and selling animals was necessary if sacrifices were to continue. It is likely, then, that John sees a more radical implication in Jesus' words: the temple and its entire sacrificial system are about to be replaced.[53] Verse 19 corroborates this understanding, as Jesus speaks of substituting his resurrected body for the temple, a prediction that is not understood until after it has been fulfilled (vv. 20–22). John notes that the disciples later saw a fulfillment of Ps 69:9 as well (v. 17). When God's people have been zealous for true worship, they have often been persecuted. John closes the story with another reference to the positive value of signs, but he adds a cautionary note that belief based merely on signs may often prove fickle (vv. 23–25).

Kruse, *John*, 91–96; Ridderbos, *John*, 107.

[50] E.g., J. R. Michaels (*John* [Peabody: Hendrickson, 1989], 50) argues that each of the two main sections of John begins with a chronologically dislocated but programmatically emphasized episode—the temple cleansing in 2:13–25 and the anointing of Jesus at Bethany in 12:1–10. Cf. L. J. Kreitzer, "The Temple Incident of John 2:13–25: A Preview of What Is to Come," in *Understanding, Studying and Reading: New Testament Essays in Honour of John Ashton*, ed. C. Rowland and C. H. T. Fletcher-Louis (Sheffield: SAP, 1998), 93–101.

[51] Cf. esp. Robinson, *Priority of John*, 125–31; Köstenberger, *John*, 106.

[52] E. R. Richards, "An Honor/Shame Argument for Two Temple Clearings," *TJ* 29 (2008): 19–43.

[53] See esp. K. A. Mathews, "John, Jesus and the Essenes: Trouble at the Temple," *CTR* 3 (1988): 101–26. Cf. K. J. Wenell, *Jesus and Land: Sacred and Social Space in Second Temple Judaism* (London and New York: T&T Clark, 2007), 52–60; Hellerman, *Jesus and the People of God*, 167–88.

Jesus and Nicodemus: The Gospel in a Nutshell (3:1–21) [Aland §27]

An example of superficial interest in Jesus without true understanding follows. Nicodemus, a leading Pharisee, comes to Jesus praising him as a heaven-sent teacher because of his signs. As the conversation continues, Nicodemus' ignorance simply becomes more pronounced.[54] Here is the context for Jesus' famous declaration that a would-be disciple must be "born again" (v. 3). The Greek can also be translated "born from above" (*anōthen*), and the double meaning may well be intentional.[55] Verse 5 further defines this new birth as "born of water and the Spirit." There are at least four main interpretations of this clause: (a) a reference to Christian baptism as described in Acts and the rest of the New Testament (but historically this will not begin until after Pentecost, and John elsewhere plays down allusions to the baptism and the Lord's Supper—see above, p. 192); (b) a reference to John's baptism as a sign of repentance (but would this leave Nicodemus so incredulous?); (c) a reference to physical birth plus spiritual birth (cf. v. 6; but the use of "water" as a metaphor for physical birth was relatively rare in antiquity); and (d) a reference to the spiritual cleansing predicted in Ezek 36:25–27 that would characterize messianic times. Option (d) seems most likely, though perhaps in combination with some form of (a) or (b).[56] This new birth is the result of the Spirit's sovereign, unpredictable activity, just like the wind (v. 8). The Greek *pneuma* can mean both wind and S/spirit. Jesus' ministry blows Nicodemus away by not fitting conventional Pharisaic expectations (v. 9).

Verses 10–21 elaborate further. The last use of the first person ("I" or "we") comes in verse 12, and verse 15 rounds out a paragraph, so it is possible that verses 16–21 are John's own commentary on the dialogue just narrated. In verses 10–15 Jesus observes that the principles he has enunciated should be simple to understand compared with more esoteric matters that have no earthly analogies (vv. 10–13), but the key to understanding Jesus is accepting him as the Son of Man who must be crucified and exalted (vv. 14–15). John (or Jesus) then stresses that there are ultimately only two options available to people: those who believe in the Son will have eternal life; those who reject him will be condemned. Verse 16, of course, is one of the most precious promises in the entire Bible and is often

---

[54] See Cotterell, "The Nicodemus Conversation," for a helpful discourse analysis of this passage, highlighting how Nicodemus' contributions to the conversation become increasingly shorter, while Jesus increasingly points out this Pharisee's lack of understanding. Nicodemus will reappear in two slightly more positive contexts in John (7:45–52; 19:38–42), but nowhere are we told that he ever became a full-fledged disciple. Later apocryphal traditions made this claim, but it seems better to follow J. M. Bassler ("Mixed Signals: Nicodemus in the Fourth Gospel," *JBL* 108 [1989]: 635–46) in observing that, within John, Nicodemus always remains a sufficiently ambivalent character as to represent those who are (just) outside the kingdom.

[55] There is also a striking parallel with Matt 18:3, leading several commentators to speculate that the Synoptic saying was the historical kernel on which this Johannine narrative, a homiletical elaboration of the Johannine community, was built. See esp. Lindars, *John*, 48, 150–51.

[56] For a thorough survey of options and a defense of (d), see L. L. Belleville, "'Born of Water and Spirit': John 3:5," *TJ* 2 (1981): 125–41. G. R. Beasley-Murray ("John 3:3, 5: Baptism, Spirit and the Kingdom," *ExpTim* 97 [1986]: 167–70) ably defends the combination hypothesis. See also Lincoln, *John*, 150.

memorized.[57] But verses 17–21 prove equally crucial, stressing also the dark side of Jesus' message. All of God's condemnation remains fair, however, because those who live in "darkness" have chosen rebellion over living in the "light" (vv. 19–20).

John 3:22–36 repeats and reinforces the themes of the Nicodemus dialogue, only now the conversation continues between John the Baptist and his disciples. There is the same ambiguity here as to when the Baptist's words end and when the apostle's begin. Arguably, the break comes between verses 30 and 31. (For further comments, see above, p. 114)

Jesus and the Woman at the Well in Samaria (4:1–42) [Aland §30–31]

Again, the fourth evangelist narrates a lengthy dialogue between Jesus and an "outsider," but the contrasts between this episode and the story of Jesus and Nicodemus could hardly be more striking. He was powerful since he was male, a Jew, probably well off, a religious leader, and a model of piety and wisdom. She was powerless since she was female, a Samaritan, probably poor, unlikely to have had access to any religious education, and an outcast because of her marital history. Yet, she is the individual who responds positively to Jesus' claims and winds up being a witness to bring many of her townspeople to the Lord.[58]

Verses 1–9 find Jesus, surprisingly, taking the initiative to talk to this unnamed woman at the well. In so doing, he crosses over three social boundaries that made such conversation surprising—their differences in gender and in religious/ethnic background, along with the taboo against associating with one who carried the stigma of sexual immorality.[59] The narrative overall has often been used as a model of *how* to do evangelism, and certain relevant principles may be derived from it.[60] Far more central to John's purpose is his concern to present a paradigm of *whom* to evangelize. The gospel breaks down all humanly-erected boundaries that categorize certain people as second-class citizens.

In verses 10–15 Jesus turns the conversation to spiritual matters, referring to his ability to offer the woman "living water." At first she does not grasp the metaphor. "Living water" could simply mean "flowing water" (as opposed to the well water), which was preferred in Jewish purification rites. Once she understands that Jesus means something more than this, she wants an inexhaustible supply. Before responding to her request, Jesus shifts the topic to make the woman con-

---

[57] For its precise translation and connection to the context, see R. H. Gundry and R. W. Howell, "The Sense and Syntax of John 3:14–17 with Special Reference to the Use of ΟΥΤΩΣ. . .ΩΣΤΕ in John 3:16," *NovT* 41 (1999): 24–39.

[58] For elaboration of these contrasts and outcomes, see C. L. Blomberg, "The Globalization of Biblical Interpretation: A Test Case—John 3–4," *BBR* 3 (1995): 1–15. For a good survey of approaches to interpretation, see D. S. Dockery, "Reading John 4:1–45: Some Diverse Hermeneutical Perspectives," *CTR* 3 (1988): 127–40.

[59] Which may or may not have been deserved (recall above, 77–78). See also J. N. Day, *The Woman at the Well: Interpretation of John 4:42 in Retrospect and Prospect* (Boston and Leiden: Brill, 2002).

[60] For a recent example, better than most, because it *does* pick up on the central dimensions of gender, religion, and ethnicity, see E. J. Wyckoff, "Jesus in Samaria (John 4:4–42): A Model for Cross-Cultural Ministry," *BTB* 35 (2005): 89–98.

front her marital situation (vv. 16–19). While he displays a remarkable openness to the "sinners" of his society, he also calls all of them to repent. Here his reference is more subtle. Nevertheless, it makes a lasting impression on the woman, who will later insist, with some exaggeration, that she met a man who told her everything she ever did (vv. 29, 39). The setting of Jacob's well (v. 6) and the comparison between Jesus and Jacob (v. 12) again suggest a contrast with Judaism. The old water of the Torah, even in its Samaritan form, must give way to Jesus' new, living water.

It is unclear if verses 20–24 are a red herring on the woman's part to distract attention from the problem. They are certainly an integral part of the conversation for John, who is stressing how Jesus replaces all "holy space." Already the dispute between Jews and Samaritans concerning whether to worship on Mt. Zion (Jerusalem) or Mt. Gerizim in Samaria (all based on a debate over the interpretation of Deut 12:5) is moot. God's people may now worship him anywhere they want, "in spirit and in truth" (v. 24).[61]

Verses 25–26 bring the conversation to its climax. Jesus reveals himself clearly to this woman as the Messiah. Ironically, he is more direct with her than with any of his Jewish contemporaries, at least early in his ministry. This may well be because the Samaritan expectation of a Messiah (*Taheb,* meaning "converter" or "redeemer") was in some respects less nationalistic or militaristic than much Jewish expectation, and thus less susceptible to misinterpretation.[62] The aftermath of Jesus' conversation occupies verses 27–42. The woman and many of her townspeople come to believe. "Savior of the world" (v. 42) invests Jesus with the authority claimed by the Roman emperors and may hint at Samaritan animosity to imperial oppression.[63] Jesus encourages his followers to recognize that the fields are "ripe for harvest" (v. 35). The disciples, too, at first fail to grasp his figurative intent (v. 33). But he elaborates, and this passage has become a key text for evangelistic and missionary work in all ages. Verses 37–38 articulate key principles: some sow while others reap, but there is always urgent work to be done regardless of the immediate results.

The details of the miracle of 4:43–54 will be discussed in conjunction with its Synoptic parallels (below, pp. 278–79). We have come full circle to Cana again and are ready to proceed to Jesus' great Galilean ministry.

Historicity

The similarity of the water-into-wine miracle to Jesus' parable of the wineskins speaks for its authenticity. So also does the potentially embarrassing light

[61] On this theme, see esp. W. D. Davies, *The Gospel and the Land: Early Christianity and Jewish Territorial Doctrine* (Berkeley: University of California Press, 1974). Cf. Wenell, *Jesus and Land*; Hellerman, *Jesus and the People of God*, 188–202.

[62] Brown (*The Gospel according to John*, vol. 1, 172–73) points out that the Samaritans were looking more for a teacher and lawgiver. Cf. also R. A. Whitacre, *John* (Downers Grove and Leicester: IVP, 1999), 107.

[63] R J. Cassidy, *John's Gospel in New Perspective* (Maryknoll: Orbis, 1992), 34–35. Cf. Kruse, *John*, 142.

in which it paints the relationship between Jesus and Mary, along with the possible misunderstanding created by having the Lord produce so much wine for merrymaking! The cleansing of the temple has parallels with Synoptic tradition, and we have already commented on the possible relationships with the similar incident there (above, p. 263). The dialogue with Nicodemus is not unlike various Synoptic stories that pit Jesus against the Jewish leaders, and his key claim in John 3:3 ("No one can see the kingdom of God without being born again") closely resembles Matt 18:3 ("Unless you change and become like little children, you will never enter the kingdom of heaven"). More than one wealthy Jewish leader named Nicodemus in the powerful Gurion family is attested in rabbinic traditions

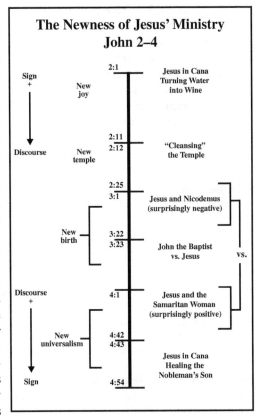

The Newness of Jesus' Ministry
John 2–4

from about this time period.[64] John 3:29 contains the nucleus of a small parable about a bridegroom that could easily have generated the dialogue that surrounds it. The encounter with the Samaritan woman places Jesus in numerous potentially compromising positions and ties in perfectly with the Synoptics' emphasis on his role as a "friend of tax collectors and sinners." John 4:35–38 is closely reminiscent of Matt 9:37–38.[65] Finally, the healing of the nobleman's son is so similar to the miracle involving the centurion's servant in Q (Matt 8:5–13; Luke 7:1–10) that some take them to be variants of the same event. All these considerations support a general trustworthiness of these episodes, even if John narrates them in his own distinctive style and for his unique purposes.[66]

Theology

John 2–4 is a very carefully structured unity. It begins and ends with miracles in Cana. In between appear two central discourses that contrast dramatically with each other—Jesus' dialogues with Nicodemus and the Samaritan woman. The

---

[64] Bauckham, *Testimony of the Beloved Disciple*, 137–72.
[65] See esp. P. W. Ensor, "The Authenticity of John 4.35," *EQ* 72 (2000): 13–21.
[66] Cf. further Blomberg, *Historical Reliability of John's Gospel*, 85–104.

main points of the four main parts of this section all stress the newness of Jesus' ministry. The new age he is ushering in brings a new joy (2:1–12), a new worship and temple (2:13–25), a new birth (3:1–36), and a new universal offer of salvation even to the most outcast of society (4:1–54).[67] Overall, "the main themes of this narrative might be summed up alliteratively as wedding, water, worship and witness."[68] We begin to understand a little better the contrast John intended in 1:16–17 between the grace of the period of the Law and the greater grace and truth that came through Jesus Christ.

For Further Study

John the Baptist

Kazmierski, Carl R. *John the Baptist: Prophet and Evangelist.* Collegeville: Liturgical, 1996.

Meier, John P. *A Marginal Jew: Rethinking the Historical Jesus.* Vol. 2. New York and London: Doubleday, 1994.

Murphy, Catherine M. *John the Baptist: Prophet of Purity for a New Age.* Collegeville: Liturgical, 2003.

Taylor, Joan E. *The Immerser: John the Baptist within Second Temple Judaism.* Grand Rapids and Cambridge: Eerdmans, 1997.

Webb, Robert L. *John the Baptizer and Prophet: A Sociohistorical Study.* Sheffield: JSOT, 1991; Eugene, OR: Wipf & Stock, 2006.

Wink, Walter. *John the Baptist in the Gospel Tradition.* Cambridge: CUP, 1968.

Jesus' Baptism and Temptation

Garrett, Susan R. *The Temptations of Jesus in Mark's Gospel.* Grand Rapids and Cambridge: Eerdmans, 1998.

Gerhardsson, Birger. *The Testing of God's Son (Matt. 4:1–11 & par.): An Analysis of an Early Christian Midrash.* Lund: Gleerup, 1966.

Gibson, Jeffrey B. *The Temptations of Jesus in Early Christianity.* Sheffield: SAP, 1995; London and New York: T&T Clark, 2004.

McDonnell, Kilian. *The Baptism of Jesus in the Jordan: The Trinitarian and Cosmic Order of Salvation.* Collegeville: Liturgical, 1996.

John 2–4

Aus, Roger. *Water into Wine and the Beheading of John the Baptist.* Atlanta: Scholars, 1988.

Day, Janeth N. *The Woman at the Well: Interpretation of John 4:1–42 in Retrospect and Prospect.* Boston and Leiden: Brill, 2002.

Julian, Paul. *Jesus and Nicodemus: A Literary and Narrative Exegesis of Jn. 2,23–3,36.* Frankfurt and New York: Peter Lang, 2000.

---

[67] This last theme continues in the account of the healing of the nobleman's son in 4:43–54, inasmuch as the man is most likely a Gentile. See A. H. Mead, "The βασιλικός, in John 4.46–53," *JSNT* 23 (1985): 69–72.

[68] Lincoln, *John*, 182. One might want to add wine, whip, word, and woman!

Okure, Teresa. *The Johannine Approach to Mission: Contextual Study of John 4:1–42.* Tübingen: Mohr Siebeck, 1988.

Questions for Review

1. What are the most important issues of historical background and exegetical or interpretive commentary worth highlighting in order to understand each of the following: (1) the ministry and message of John the Baptist; (2) the baptism of Jesus by John; (3) the temptations of Jesus?
2. What do all the episodes of John 2–4 have in common? What is the main point of each? How can we tell?
3. Compare and contrast Jesus' encounters with Nicodemus and with the Samaritan woman. What is John's purpose in juxtaposing these two episodes as he does? What are the lessons of each individually?

13

JESUS' GALILEAN MINISTRY—EARLIER STAGES

The period of Jesus' greatest visibility and popularity now ensues. As we have previously noted, all of the Synoptic Gospels group material thematically at places, so it is impossible to be sure what took place in exactly what order. We will mostly follow Mark's outline for his first three chapters to trace the kinds of events that were typical of the earlier part of Jesus' great Galilean ministry. Then we will pause to look in more depth at the Sermon that encapsulates the heart of what he was trying to teach throughout this region.

Healings, Controversies, Discipleship and Opposition

The Theme of Jesus' Ministry (Mark 1:14–15 pars.) [Aland §32–33]

After John is imprisoned, Jesus emerges on center stage of Galilean religious life. Mark summarizes his message in language reminiscent of John's. People must repent and believe the good news he is preaching. God's kingdom is arriving. The "kingdom" of God is a concept that is best understood as God's "kingship." It refers primarily to God's rule or reign rather than to a geographical realm. It is a power more than a place.[1] After a century or more of debate, there is widespread agreement among contemporary scholars that from the standpoint of Jesus' min-

---

[1] For an excellent survey of scholarship, see B. D. Chilton, "The Kingdom of God in Recent Discussion," in *Studying the Historical Jesus*, ed. B. Chilton and C. A. Evans (Leiden: Brill, 1994), 255–80. Although language of God's kingship is relatively rare in the Old Testament, it is more common in

istry this kingly power is both present and future.[2] The verb translated "has come near" (*ēngiken*) in Mark 1:15 has been the subject of detailed scrutiny. Is the kingdom just very close, or has it in some sense actually arrived? Despite a few demurrals, the latter seems most likely.[3] Jesus' ministry is inaugurating a new era in human history (see further, below, pp. 448–52).

Characteristically, Matthew expands his discussion of Jesus' setting up his ministry in Galilee by pointing out how it fulfills prophecy (Matt 4:13–17). He also phrases the summary of Jesus' teaching so it exactly matches that of John the Baptist (v. 17; cf. 3:2). For the most part, however, Matthew avoids using the expression "kingdom of God," substituting instead "kingdom of heaven." This expression occurs thirty-three times in Matthew's Gospel and nowhere else in the New Testament. The numerous occasions on which these expressions appear interchangeably in otherwise parallel passages (including within Matthew himself—see, e.g., 19:23–24) make it clear they are synonyms. It seems that Matthew is following Jewish scruples and using a "circumlocution" or euphemism for the divine name to avoid treating something holy in an overly familiar way.[4]

Luke does not begin his account of Jesus in Galilee with a one-line epitome of his teaching but rather narrates the story of Jesus' preaching in his hometown of Nazareth. Luke 4:14–15 confirms what the parallels in Matthew and Mark suggest—that this incident actually happened quite aways into the Galilean ministry (cf. Mark 6:6b–13 par.). Yet, Luke places it early, as a programmatic "headline" for this section of his Gospel, to make it clear what Jesus was all about and to foreshadow the opposition that would later intensify (vv. 16–30). As was the custom, a distinguished guest is invited to read from the biblical scroll one of the passages designated for a given Sabbath and then to expound it. Jesus reads a text that includes one of Isaiah's servant prophecies (Isa 61:1–2) and then stuns his audience by declaring it to be fulfilled in him at that very moment. Here appear several of Luke's favorite themes: empowerment by the Spirit, reversal of fortune for the socioeconomically disadvantaged, and holistic healing of body and spirit. In essence, Jesus is announcing the arrival of the Jubilee year, when all debts

---

the Jewish targums and refers to God acting "in strength." It was not that he was not previously king, but his sovereignty is now being demonstrated in a new, clearer, and even more powerful fashion.

[2] For a history of developments over the last century, see W. Willis, ed., *The Kingdom of God in 20th Century Interpretation* (Peabody: Hendrickson, 1987). A minority dissents from this consensus and tries to eliminate the future apocalyptic element from Jesus' teaching in favor of a timeless or "permanent eschatology." On this view Jesus subverts conventional categories of this world's teaching much as in an older form of existentialism. See esp. Funk, Hoover, and the Jesus Seminar, *Five Gospels.* Cf. also Funk, *Honest to Jesus.*

[3] G. R. Beasley-Murray, *Jesus and the Kingdom of God* (Exeter: Paternoster; Grand Rapids: Eerdmans, 1986), 72–73; B. Chilton, *Pure Kingdom: Jesus' Vision of God* (Grand Rapids: Eerdmans, London: SPCK, 1996), 60–66.

[4] See, e.g., M. A. Beavis, *Jesus and Utopia: Looking for the Kingdom of God in the Roman World* (Minneapolis: Fortress, 2006), 72. J. T. Pennington ("The Kingdom of Heaven in the Gospel of Matthew," *SBJT* 12 [2008] 44–52), however, believes "kingdom of heaven" adds the dimension of God's will coming to be done "on earth, as it is in heaven" (i.e., as in the Lord's Prayer).

are forgiven (cf. Lev 25:8–55).[5] Interestingly, Luke's quotation of the Old Testament ends just before Isaiah's words continue with "and the day of vengeance of our God" (Isa 61:2b), probably because Jesus understood he would be coming twice—now to save and only later to judge. The audience marvels at his "gracious words" (v. 22), but he keeps on speaking and directs attention to Gentiles whom God favored over his chosen people in Old Testament times. This turns their wonder into outrage and leads to a spontaneous attempt to kill Jesus, which seems to be miraculously thwarted.[6]

Gathering Disciples (Mark 1:16–20 pars.) [Aland §34, 41]

All three Synoptics agree that Jesus called several of his disciples very early in his Galilean ministry. The four specifically named here are Peter, Andrew, James, and John. Levi/Matthew will appear shortly. In light of the previous association of at least some of these individuals with Jesus in Judea (John 1:35–51), we must not overestimate how instantaneous their decisions were to leave family and occupation and join Jesus' itinerant ministry.[7] That they did leave was nevertheless a radical move, given the cultural responsibility to submit to parents and fulfill family obligations. Jesus' behavior stood typical rabbinic practice on its head. Instead of sifting among "applicants," Jesus took the initiative to command people to follow him.[8] And, unlike the prophets who pointed people to God, Jesus pointed people to himself.

Luke includes in this context an account of a miraculous fish-catch (Luke 5:1–11). Jesus uses this object lesson to explain that now his followers will be fishing for people (Luke 5:10; cf. Mark 1:17; Matt 4:19). "The call to discipleship means also a call to ministry."[9] We as well see something of a balance between intentional mission and allowing for the Spirit to act in a sovereign, unpredictable fashion.[10] Although Peter will obey, he fears one who is so holy and impulsively but tellingly blurts out, "Go away from me, Lord; I am a sinful man" (Luke 5:8).

---

[5] See esp. R. B. Sloan, *The Favorable Year of Our Lord: A Study of Jubilary Theology in the Gospel of Luke* (Austin: Schola, 1977).

[6] On this whole passage, cf. esp. W. W. Klein, "The Sermon of Nazareth (Luke 4:14–22)," in *Christian Freedom: Essays in Honor of Vernon C. Grounds*, ed. K. W. M. Wozniak and S. J. Grenz (Lanham, MD: University Press of America, 1986), 153–72. See also M. Prior, *Jesus the Liberator: Nazareth Liberation Theology (Luke 4.1–30)* (Sheffield: SAP, 1995).

[7] Cf. S. O. Abogunrin, "The Three Variant Accounts of Peter's Call: A Critical and Theological Examination of the Texts," *NTS* 31 (1985): 587–602; T. A. Wayment, "Jesus' Early Ministry in Judea and Jerusalem," in *The Life and Teachings of Jesus Christ: From Bethlehem through the Sermon on the Mount*, ed. R. N. Holzapfel and T. A. Wayment (Salt Lake City: Deseret, 2005), 208.

[8] D. L. Bock, *Jesus according to Scripture: Restoring the Portrait from the Gospels* (Grand Rapids: Baker; Leicester: Apollos, 2002), 99. Boring (*Mark*, 60) adds that "there is no parallel to such an unmotivated call story in ancient literature."

[9] Hooker, *Mark*, 60.

[10] On which, see the two-volume *opus magnum* of E. J. Schnabel, *Early Christian Mission* (Downers Grove and Leicester: IVP, 2004).

A Series of Exorcisms and Other Healings (Mark 1:21–45 pars.)
[Aland §35–40, 42, 50]

Mark 1:21–34 has been described as a typical day in the life of Jesus the healer. Capernaum is now Jesus' "home base" (cf. also Matt 4:12–16). Mark groups together representative examples of Jesus' healings, including exorcisms, throughout the rest of this chapter. What stands out in each instance is Christ's authority over the powers of Satan and sickness. Numerous reports of other Jewish and Greco-Roman healers or exorcists have been preserved from the ancient world, but Jesus distinguishes himself from all of them by the directness of his approach. He invokes no lengthy list of deities, recites no formulaic incantations, and uses no magical paraphernalia to cast his spells. A simple word of rebuke is all it takes.[11]

One of the striking features of the Gospels' exorcisms is the regular recognition by the demons of Christ's true identity (cf. Mark 1:24 par.). In fact, early on in the Synoptics, only the demons grasp Jesus' full identity. Surprisingly to us, Jesus always rebukes these proclamations, but, in fact, this is spiritual warfare at work. One of the keys to gaining supernatural power over an opponent is to invoke his name (cf. Jesus' own strategy in Mark 5:9). "The recognition-formula is not a confession, but a defensive attempt to gain control of Jesus . . . [in hopes that] the use of the precise name of an individual or spirit would secure mastery over him."[12] But, in every instance, the demons' ploys fail, and Jesus casts them out. Interestingly, Mark notes that the synagogue worshipers call the exorcism a "new teaching" (1:27), linking Jesus' command to the demon with his more formal exposition for the worshipers.[13] Matthew, too, summarizes Jesus' early ministry as demonstrating unique authority in both preaching/teaching and healing (Matt 4:23–25).

Although exorcisms and healings are often linked in the Gospels, they are also distinguished from one another (Mark 1:32–34).[14] Mark 1:29–39 relates further examples of each, while verses 40–45 proceed to recount in more detail the healing of a particular leper. This passage illustrates several themes: (a) Jesus' divine power; (b) his compassion for the sick (and/or outrage at the sickness and its effects[15]); (c) his willingness to be considered ritually defiled by touching the man; (d) the miracle as a proof to the people—not merely of the leper's health but

---

[11] The two definitive works on the topic are G. H. Twelftree, *Jesus the Exorcist: A Contribution to the Study of the Historical Jesus* (Tübingen: Mohr; Peabody: Hendrickson, 1993); and idem., *In the Name of Jesus: Exorcism among Early Christians* (Grand Rapids: Baker, 2007).

[12] Lane, *Mark,* 74.

[13] France (*Mark*, 106) recognizes that "the congregation thus discern an integration in the different aspects of Jesus' ministry, in which authoritative teaching and authority over demons cohere into a single ἐξουσία [authority], which is unprecedented."

[14] *Contra* the claim that the ancients could not tell the difference, and so attributed various physiological maladies to demon possession when we know better. On the widespread recognition of the distinction in antiquity, see E. Yamauchi, "Magic or Miracle? Diseases, Demons, and Exorcisms," in *Gospel Perspectives*, vol. 6, 89–183.

[15] A somewhat weakly attested variant substitutes "enraged" for "had compassion" in v. 41. But the former is a less common trait attributed to Jesus and not as likely to be added by later scribes, so

also of who Jesus was;[16] and (e) testimony by deed rather than word. On the "messianic secret" motif that appears in verse 44 (see above, p. 132).

A Collection of Pronouncement Stories (Mark 2:1–3:6 pars.) [Aland §43–47]

Mark next groups together a series of five stories, all of which fall into the category that form critics call "pronouncement stories" (see above, p. 92). They are also sometimes called conflict or controversy stories. In ancient Greek, they would have fallen under the larger category of anecdote, or *chreia*, from a word meaning "useful."[17] In each case the climax of the account is a radical pronouncement by Jesus that challenges Jewish tradition and leads to conflict with the authorities. Mark will balance these five controversies early in his Gospel with five more at its climax (Mark 11:27–12:37). The five here arguably form a chiasm: two that include controversial healings (Mark 2:1–12, 3:1–6); two that involve debates about food—when to harvest it and with whom to eat it (2:13–17, 23–28); and a central climactic pair of metaphors about the joy and newness of the kingdom (2:18–20, 21–22).[18]

The Healing of the Paralytic[19] (2:1–12 pars.). Although this account begins as yet another example of the healing miracles that chapter 1 highlighted, the real focus quickly turns to Jesus' claim to be able to forgive sins (v. 5). Jesus may have been playing off the conventional Jewish belief that sickness was often a punishment for sin, but he arrogates to himself divine authority in pronouncing the man forgiven. To the Jewish leaders, this borders on blasphemy. How can he back up his claim? It is always easier to say that someone is spiritually whole than to declare that person to be physically well because the latter is more quickly disproven; therefore, Jesus performs the harder task to corroborate the easier (vv. 9–12).[20]

The Call of Levi/Matthew (2:13–17 pars.). Here Jesus' crucial and controversial pronouncement likens his role to a physician's—calling not the spiritually healthy but the sick. His words, "I have not come to call the righteous, but sinners"

---

it may in fact be original. Cf. TNIV: "Jesus was indignant." It also fits in with Jesus' "strong warning" in v. 43.

[16] "As a testimony to them" (v. 44) should perhaps be translated "as a testimony *against* them." Cf. Mark 6:11 and 13:9, and see France, *Mark*, 120.

[17] Defined by M. C. Moeser (*The Anecdote in Mark, the Classical World and the Rabbis* [London and New York: SAP, 2002], 20–21) as "a brief narrative, either oral or written, describing an incident, including its setting, which involves one or more persons and which focuses on an action, saying, or dialogue; the function of an anecdote is to entertain, instruct, relate an historical incident, characterize a person, or authoritatively legitimate a specific opinion, a specific practice, or a broader view of reality."

[18] J. Dewey, *Markan Public Debate* (Chico: Scholars, 1980); Boring, *Mark*, 73. For the parallel material in Matthew 11–12, a less obvious chiastic structure has been discerned by D. Boerman, "The Chiastic Structure of Matthew 11–12," *CTJ* 40 (2005): 313–25.

[19] The term should not be construed in a modern, technical sense. The man obviously could not walk. Perhaps "cripple" in modern English covers the semantic range of the Greek *paralutikos* better. See D. N. Peterson, "Translating παραλυτικός in Mark 2:1–12: A Proposal," *BBR* 16 (2006): 261–72.

[20] Nolland, *Matthew*, 381.

A Chiasmus
of Pronouncement Stories
Mark 2:1–3:6

A 2:1–12	A' 3:1–6
Healing the	Healing
paralytic	on Sabbath

B 2:13–17	B' 2:23–28
Call of Levi/	Plucking grain
Eating with	on Sabbath
sinners	

C 2:18–22
Saying on fasting
and on old vs. new

(v. 17), are ambiguous on two counts. (1) Who are the sinners? Probably not just the *Am haaretz*, because Jesus himself is one of them, and the Pharisees could hardly object to his associating with his own kind. More likely these tax collectors epitomize the more notorious wayward in Jewish society because of their treachery in working for Rome. Not only does Jesus eat with such people, against all social taboos, but he accepts them as his followers without first requiring them to pass through a probationary period of penance.[21] (2) Who are the righteous? Presumably, the Jewish leaders. Is Jesus then speaking ironically? Perhaps, though it may be at this stage that Jesus is merely accepting their self-designation at face value for the sake of argument.[22] Matthew again adds a quotation of Scripture (Matt 9:13; cf. Hos 6:6), which does not depict an absolute dichotomy (mercy rather than sacrifice) but a statement of relative priorities (mercy much more than sacrifices; cf. Ps 51:16–19). Luke distinctively adds one of his characteristic references to "repentance" (Luke 5:32).

The Question of Fasting (Mark 2:18–22 pars.). Again Jesus seems indirectly to link himself with God. He rejects the Pharisaic traditions of fasting twice weekly because it is time to celebrate a wedding feast, a common Jewish image for the messianic banquet. The bridegroom, an Old Testament metaphor for Yahweh (e.g., Isa. 61:10; 62:5; Jer 2:2, 32), is here. But Jesus seems to be referring to himself! One day, though, he will be taken away (a veiled reference to the crucifixion?). Then fasting, as part of mourning, will be appropriate.[23] As the metaphors of the wine and wineskins demonstrate, a joyful new age has arrived demanding new ways and not just a patched-up Mosaic covenant. Matthew has sometimes been taken as disagreeing with this; he adds, "both [covenants?] are preserved" (Matt 9:17). However, in context, "both" more naturally refers to both the new wine and the new wineskins.[24] Luke adds a cryptic comment as well: "No one after drinking old wine wants the new, for he says, 'The old is better.'" (Luke 5:39 NIV). But this

---

[21] On which, see esp. Sanders, *Jesus and Judaism*, 174–211. Cf. Blomberg, *Contagious Holiness*.

[22] Cf. France, *The Gospel according to Matthew: An Introduction and Commentary*, 168: "*Righteous* is not entirely ironical: in their sense of the word they *were* 'righteous' (*cf.* Phil. 3:6), but it is precisely the adequacy of such righteousness that Jesus constantly calls in question."

[23] Whether that "day" extends on throughout the Christian age is uncertain. Christian fasting appears only twice in the rest of the New Testament, both in contexts of seeking God's guidance for crucial ecclesiastical decisions (Acts 13:2–3; 14:23). Gundry (*Mark*, 133) comments, "Thus the statement does not point to an ongoing practice of fasting in the church, but centers on the person of Jesus."

[24] Hagner, *Matthew 1–13*, 244.

should probably be taken as an ironic lament over those who are rejecting Jesus' "new wine."[25]

Sabbath Controversies (Mark 2:23–3:6 pars.). The final two pronouncement stories in this sequence challenge traditional Jewish understandings of the Sabbath. It is not clear that Jesus breaks any laws of Scripture, though he clearly violates the oral Torah. Reaping and threshing were two of the thirty-nine definitions of work forbidden on the Sabbath in the Mishnah (*Shab.* 7:2). The Mishnah also forbade the healing on the Sabbath of an individual whose life was not in danger (*Yoma* 8:6). Jesus not only cuts through all this casuistry, he claims to be "Lord of the Sabbath" (Mark 2:28), the one who can decide how the Sabbath laws now apply. The precedent to which he appeals—David eating the sacred showbread (1 Sam 21:1–6[26])—involves a case of breaking not just the oral but also the written Law. In Matthew's account, Jesus adds a statement that "one greater than the temple is here" (Matt 12:6). In the case of the man with the shriveled hand, all three Gospels agree that Jesus believed it was right to "do good" on the Sabbath (Mark 3:4 pars.), and this could include a lot of what even the Old Testament called "work." So it would seem that Jesus was suggesting very far-reaching changes in how his followers were to observe the fourth commandment.[27] Matthew adds a pointed comparison between the Jews' willingness to rescue a sheep in danger, and their objecting to his healing a man (cf. Luke 13:10–17; 14:1–6). Little wonder that, with Mark 3:6 and parallels, we reach a mini-climax of opposition to Christ early in his ministry.[28]

The Formal Call of the Twelve (Mark 3:7–19/Luke 6:12–19) [Aland §48–49]

Following a transitional summary statement about Jesus' ministry thus far (Mark 3:7–12), Mark proceeds to narrate the formal call of the twelve men who would become Christ's closest followers (vv. 13–19). In Luke, the parallel statements immediately precede Christ's Sermon on the Plain. So, to the extent that we can identify a place to locate this sermon chronologically, it should probably be inserted here. But Mark betrays no knowledge of the sermon, and his thematic

---

[25] Pao and Liefeld, "Luke," 127.

[26] On the famous contradiction between Abiathar in Mark 2:26 and Ahimelech in the 1 Samuel account, see J. W. Wenham, "Mark 2.26," *JTS* 1 (1950): 156. Mark may be referring to the larger section of the scroll identified by the name of "Abiathar"; the identical Greek construction (*epi* with the genitive) is used similarly in Mark 12:26.

[27] For the major options throughout church history in interpreting and applying the OT Sabbath commands for the New Testament age, see *Perspectives on the Sabbath*, ed. C. Donato (Nashville: B & H, forthcoming). For the approach adopted here, see esp. D. A. Carson, ed., *From Sabbath to Lord's Day* (Grand Rapids: Zondervan, 1982). France (*Mark*, 144) observes, "While few could object in theory to the notion that the Sabbath exists to benefit people (after all, it is repeatedly declared to be a day of joy) and is a time for 'doing good', to make such broad principles the basis for the decision on what is and is not permissible is to threaten to overturn the whole halakhic process."

[28] For a fascinating study of "From Opposition to Hostility: Changing Reactions During Jesus' Ministry," see the essay so entitled by J. C. Lane in *The Life and Teachings of Jesus Christ,* vol. 2: *From the Transfiguration through the Triumphal Entry*, ed. R. N. Holzapfel and T. A. Wayment (Salt Lake City: Deseret, 2006), 125–51.

A Brief Sketch of Jesus' Twelve Disciples

Simon *(Simōn)* from Heb. for "hearing." Called **Peter** *(Petros)* or **Cephas** *(Kephas)*, meaning "rock" in Greek and Aramaic, respectively. Leader and frequent spokesman for the Twelve. Married and resided in Capernaum. Denied Jesus three times but was restored to fellowship (John 21). First leader of Jerusalem church following Pentecost in fulfillment of promises of Matt. 16:16–19. Both 1 and 2 Peter are attributed to him. Tradition claims that he was martyred under Nero in the 60s and crucified upside down.

Andrew *(Andreas)* from Gk. for "manliness." Brother of Peter; both were originally fishermen from Bethsaida and previously disciples of John the Baptist. He appears incidentally in Mark 13:3, John 6:8, and 12:22.

James *(Iakōbos)* from Heb. name "Jacob" (see Gen. 25:26 for its meaning). Another Galilean fisherman. Son of Zebedee, a relatively prosperous fisherman. One of the "Sons of Thunder" (Mark 3:17), possibly explaining his apparent vindictiveness in Luke 9:52–54 and selfishness in Mark 10:35–40. Mother was Salome; he was thus possibly Jesus' cousin. Executed by Herod Agrippa I not later than A.D. 44 (Acts 12:2). Probably therefore not the James who wrote the letter of James nor the leader of the Apostolic Council (Acts 15).

John *(Iōannēs)* from Heb. "the Lord is gracious." Brother of James. With James and Peter, part of the inner circle of three. Special relationship to Mary indicated in John 19:25–27. Peter's "right-hand man" throughout Acts. To him are attributed the Fourth Gospel, three epistles, and Revelation, the last of these while in exile on Patmos. Traditionally viewed as the "beloved disciple" of John 13:23–26; 19:25–27; 20:2–10; and 21:2, 20–23. Tradition also says he ministered in his old age to the church in Ephesus and was the only one of the Twelve not to die a martyr's death for his faith (though a minority tradition disputes this).

Philip *(Philippos)* from Gk. "horse lover." With Simon and Andrew, one of Jesus' first disciples (cf. John 1). From Bethsaida. Appears briefly in John 6:5–7; 12:21–22; and 14:8–9. Not to be confused with Philip the deacon in Acts 6 and 8.

Bartholomew *(Bartholomais)* from Heb. "son of Talmai." Traditionally viewed as same person as Nathanael *(Nathanaēl)*, from Heb. "God has given"—Philip's companion in John 1—since always paired with Philip in Synoptic lists, and since Bartholomew not a given name but a patronymic.

Matthew *(Maththaios)* from same Heb. phrase as Nathanael. Called **Levi** in parallel passages, after the son of Jacob by that name. A converted tax collector. Traditionally identified as author of Gospel that bears his name. Jesus risked scandal in reaching out to him and his friends. Son of Alphaeus. Later legends describe his travel to Ethiopia and martyrdom there.

Thomas *(Thōmas)* from Heb. "twin." Became famous for doubting the resurrection of Jesus until he personally saw and touched him (John 20:24–29). But also revealed a fierce loyalty to Jesus, irrespective of the cost (John 11:16). Possibly reliable tradition associates him with the later evangelization of India.

James the less *(Iakōbos ho mikros)*. Alternately translated "James the younger." Son of (another?) Alphaeus or Cleopas. His mother, another Mary, was among the women at Jesus' tomb. Little else known.

Judas *(Ioudas)* from Heb. "Judah" ("praise"). Son of a Jacob (James). Also called Thaddaeus and, in some textual variants, Lebbaeus. Only recorded words appear in John 14:22. Little else known.

Simon the Zealot (or Caananite, from the Heb. for "Zealot"). Converted from the sect of Jewish revolutionaries that later rebelled against Rome and was defeated in A.D. 70.

Judas Iscariot *(Iskariōth)*. Infamous for betraying Jesus. Treasurer for the Twelve and a thief. Iscariot is usually interpreted as from Heb. for "man of Kerioth." Other options include a derivation from the word *sicarii* ("assassins")—a radical wing of the Zealot movement—or from "false one." Ended his life by hanging himself and falling from the rope so as to "burst his bowels asunder" (cf. Matt. 27 with Acts 1).

groupings make it convenient for us to continue following his narrative until the end of chapter 3 before discussing the Sermon. Matthew does not list the names of the Twelve until Jesus' later missionary discourse (Matt 10), but there he makes it clear that they had already been gathered together for some time (v. 1). The number twelve is theologically significant. Just as twelve tribes of Israel constituted God's people at the institution of the Mosaic covenant, so now twelve disciples will form the foundation for God's people at the beginning of the new covenant. Here, all those who follow Jesus are the true, renewed, or restored Israel.[29] The chart on page   gives a very brief synopsis of what we know about each of the Twelve. Much additional legendary material exists, but it is often very difficult to sift out the small portion that may be based on historical fact.[30] The chart summarizes the most important items that we *can* know, primarily from the Gospels.

The Healing of the Centurion's Servant (Matt 8:5–13; Luke 7:1–10; John 4:43–54?) [Aland §85]

One additional healing/pronouncement story occurs in Jesus' early Galilean ministry, apparently just after the Sermon on the Mount/Plain. It is not found in Mark, but it is natural to treat it here along with other episodes of like form from the same period in Christ's ministry. In both Matthew and Luke, Jesus heals from a distance the sick slave of a centurion from Capernaum. In Matthew, the man himself seems to come to request the healing, while in Luke he sends Jewish emissaries to plead on his behalf. The "contradiction" is more apparent than real since ancient convention permitted one to speak of a person acting through his agents.[31] Matthew's polemic against the Jewish leaders gave him reason to employ this convention (see above, p. 150, and cf. Matt 8:11–12, verses unique to Matthew's account). Luke is more willing to portray the Jews in a positive light, but primarily these spokesmen function to testify to the worthiness of this good Gentile. Thus Luke's account more clearly prefigures the coming Christian mission to the Gentiles.[32] Indeed, this passage preserves striking parallels to the conversion of a later Gentile centurion, Cornelius (Acts 10). Both versions agree, however, that Jesus' authority is now demonstrated ever more greatly. He does not even have to be physically present with people in order to heal them.

---

[29] See esp. throughout Wright, *Jesus and the Victory of God*; and Dunn, *Jesus Remembered*. Witherington (esp. throughout *Christology of Jesus*) prefers to talk of a "freed Israel."

[30] For an accessible summary of these legends and/or extra-biblical historical information, see C. B. Ruffin, *The Twelve: The Lives of the Apostles after Calvary,* rev. ed. (Huntingdon, IN: Our Sunday Visitor, 1984). More technically, cf. E. Hennecke, *New Testament Apocrypha*, ed. W. Schneemelcher, vol. 2 (London: Lutterworth; Philadelphia: Westminster, 1965), 35–74. Curiously, most of this information has been omitted or drastically abbreviated in the revised version (Cambridge: James Clarke; Louisville: WJKP, 1992).

[31] Cf. our modern convention of reading in a newspaper, "The President announced today that. . ." when, in fact, the report was written by a speech writer and read by his press secretary. Cf. also Bock, *Luke 1:1–9:50*, 632.

[32] On the debated issue of the Gentile mission, see esp. M. F. Bird, "Who Comes from the East and West? Luke 13:28–29/Matt. 8:11–12 and the Historical Jesus," *NTS* 52 (2006): 441–57. Cf. Bovon, *Luke 1*, 265.

In Matthew, this healing comes as the second in a series of three episodes in which Jesus cures those who were socially ostracized by orthodox Jews: a leper, the centurion, and a woman (Matt 8:1–4, 5–13, 14–15). With his predilection for quoting the Old Testament, Matthew sees in all this a fulfillment of Isa 53:4: "He took up our infirmities and bore our diseases" (8:16–17). In the modern charismatic debate, this quotation has often been used to try to resolve the question of whether or not there is physical healing in the atonement. In context, it probably does not address this issue at all, but points out Jesus' concern to abolish categories of *ritual* uncleanness.[33]

As noted earlier, John includes a very similar story about a royal official's son whom Jesus heals at a distance from a life-threatening fever (John 4:43–54). The language is vague enough at several points that this could be a variant of the story that Matthew and Luke record. John's *basilikos* could be a Gentile military officer. Matthew's *pais* could be a son as well as a servant although Luke uses *doulos*, which normally just means a slave.[34] But we do not have enough information to be sure. The two events may also be entirely separate.[35] We must resist the temptation to think that we have anything like an exhaustive account of Jesus' ministry. The types of things the Gospels narrate are no doubt representative selections of many other similar incidents. John's point in narrating this particular story is to stress again that miraculous signs can and should produce faith, but that one should not have to depend on them (cf. vv. 53 with 48, taking the latter as a cry of exasperation and noting that the man has to go away believing without seeing—v. 50; recall also above, p. 189).[36]

Jesus' Family, Critics, and True Followers (Mark 3:20–35 pars.) [Aland §116–121]

The final segment of Mark 1–3 contrasts Jesus' disciples with his opponents. Here is the first of several places where Mark employs a sandwich-like (ABA) structure to compare and contrast two events. By breaking up one narrative into two parts and putting the second one in between, Mark invites the reader to view the two as closely linked in some way.[37] Here the reactions of Jesus' family and relatives (3:20–21, 31–35) are sandwiched around the attacks by the Jewish leaders (vv. 22–30). We realize that even Jesus' biological kin do not understand him, although their hostility is a little less vicious than that of the Pharisees and scribes (cf. "He is out of his mind" in v. 21 with "He has an evil spirit" in v. 30). By way of contrast, his disciples, whether or not biologically related, form his true family as they do God's will (vv. 33–35). In a culture that valued family commitments above all other social obligations, Jesus' call did, indeed, prove radical and

---

[33] D. E. Garland, *Reading Matthew*, rev. ed. (Macon: Smyth & Helwys, 1999), 107.

[34] For a detailed list of proposals of harmonizing all of the seemingly discrepant details on this theory, see E. F. Siegman, "St. John's Use of Synoptic Material," *CBQ* 30 (1968): 182–98.

[35] E.g., Carson, *John*, 234; Ridderbos, *John*, 174–75.

[36] Cf., e.g., Whitacre, *John*, 115–16.

[37] T. Shepherd, *Markan Sandwich Stories: Narration, Definition, Function* (Berrien Springs, MI: Andrews University Press, 1993).

inflammatory.[38] Tragically, now as then, the greatest opposition to that call often comes from inside those circles of people who think they are actually being loyal to God but are perverting a living relationship with Jesus into a legalistic list of dos and don'ts far beyond the comparatively few biblical absolutes.[39]

The scribes' slander (v. 22) remained a common Jewish explanation of who Jesus was, well into later centuries. The Talmud would insist that "Jesus the Nazarene practiced magic and led Israel astray" (*b. Sanh.* 43a, 107b). No record exists of ancient Jews attempting to deny Christ's miracle-working activity; they merely ascribed his power to the devil rather than to God.[40] Jesus' reply to his original critics was twofold. First, their charge was self-contradictory. Satan does not work to destroy his own efforts; it is the Messiah who comes to bind Satan (vv. 23–27). Second, their charge was self-condemning. It was widely acknowledged that there were other Jewish exorcists with God-given powers;[41] would the Pharisees want to accuse all of them of being diabolically inspired (Matt 12:27/Luke 11:19)? Indeed, such charges border on committing an unforgivable sin—"blasphemy against the Holy Spirit" (Mark 3:28–30).

This intriguing expression has caused needless consternation for countless Christians over the centuries. Could a true believer ever commit such a sin? It is important to keep this reference in context. Jesus' critics here are not his disciples but his most malicious, implacable opponents who would later nail him to the cross. In context, blasphemy against the Holy Spirit means the persistent equation of Christ's power with the demonic by those who refuse to believe him. All other sins—based on more ambiguous evidence—are forgivable (v. 28).[42] There is no evidence anywhere in Scripture that an individual who genuinely desires to repent

---

[38] See esp. S. C. Barton, *Discipleship and Family Ties in Mark and Matthew* (Cambridge: CUP, 1994), 67–96. Cf. D. M. May, "Mark 3:20–35 from the Perspective of Shame/Honor," *BTB* 17 (1987): 83–87; and C. L. Westfall, "Family in the Gospels and Acts," in *Family in the Bible*, ed. Hess and Carroll R., 125–47.

[39] Cf. Wilkins, *Matthew*, 379: "It's a well-known phenomenon of Christian experience that when we are doing a good work for the Lord, we can expect opposition. But it's most heartbreaking when we find that the opposition comes from within. Israel was often Israel's worst enemy." The same has been true of the church.

[40] For a book-length study of *Jesus in the Talmud*, see the volume so entitled by P. Schäfer (Princeton and Oxford: Princeton University Press, 2007). On this particular charge in its Gospel contexts, see D. D. Sheets, "Jesus as Demon-Possessed," in *Who Do My Opponents Say I Am?* ed. McKnight and Modica, 27–49.

[41] Cf. further Harvey, *Jesus and the Constraints of History*, 98–119. On the other hand, R. Shirock ("Whose Exorcists Are They? The Referents of οἱ υἱοὶ ὑμῶν at Matthew 12.27/Luke 11.19," *JSNT* 46 [1992]: 41–52]) makes a strong case that "your sons" refer to Jesus' disciples who will later judge Israel (Matt 19:28 par.).

[42] Notice the imperfect tense in v. 22 (lit., "they kept on saying"). Mark speaks of blasphemies "of men" being forgiven; Matthew and Luke, of blasphemies "against the Son of man." The latter probably reflects the ambiguous nature of this title (see below, pp. 470–73). Rejecting Christ when the evidence is less than crystal clear is always reversible as long as one lives. But without such a reversal, such rejection inevitably leads to spiritual death. With R. A. Guelich, *Mark 1–8:26* (Dallas: Word, 1989), 185: "One commits the 'unpardonable sin,' therefore, by rejecting God's redemptive overture for humanity in Jesus Christ." But v. 28 "assures whoever seeks God's forgiveness that God's comprehensive amnesty includes all sins committed against others as well as against God."

and turn back to God is denied the opportunity. Indeed, the very consternation that causes some believers to wonder if they have committed the unforgivable sin by definition demonstrates that they have not.[43] But some professing Christians who attribute views and behaviors with which they disagree to demonic origin far too glibly had best beware. Blasphemy against the Spirit might well apply to "the horrible practice of saying this person or that person is of the devil, when one is in no position to spiritually evaluate where that person is." Again, "there is a propensity among some Christians to readily demonize the powerful people they do not understand, especially politicians, foreigners, people of other religions, and the like. It is interesting that while Jesus was often critical about the hypocrisies and misdeeds of others, he never resorted to *ad hominen* attacks, attacking a person as a person. He stuck to the facts."[44]

Matthew and Luke go on to include in this context additional important teachings of Jesus. If he casts out demons not by Beelzebub but by God's Spirit, then this is a further sign of the presence of God's kingdom. Matthew 12:28/Luke 11:20 is one of the clearest passages in the Gospels to support "realized eschatology"— the arrival of the kingdom, at least in part, with the person and work of Christ.[45] Matthew 12:38–42/Luke 11:29–32 explains part of the reason the Jewish leaders misunderstand. They are looking for unequivocal signs susceptible to no misinterpretation. God never grants anything that conclusive; he refuses to coerce faith. The sign of the death and resurrection of Christ (analogous to the experience of the prophet Jonah[46]) should be adequate.[47] Finally, it is not enough to expel evil; one must replace it with a positive good. Otherwise a greater number of demons may return (Matt 12:43–45/Luke 11:24–26).

Historicity

That Jesus came announcing a partly present, partly future kingdom as the centerpiece of his message is widely acknowledged to be at the heart of what we can know about the historical Jesus. The "kingdom of God" is not an expression found in the Old Testament, but the concept of God as king is pervasive. After the Gospels, Christian writers preferred other expressions such as "eternal life" or "salvation" for their summaries of Jesus' proclamation. Jesus' inauspicious begin-

---

[43] Cf. L. Hurtado, *Mark* (Peabody: Hendrickson, 1989), 66: "A person doing such a thing would have no concern about Christ's forgiveness for it. So, the very anxiety lest one may have done something that cuts one off from Christ's forgiveness is, ironically, evidence that one believes Christ to be sent from God, and thus proof that one cannot have committed the sin warned against here."

[44] Witherington, *Matthew*, 255.

[45] On the existing connection in some Jewish thought between exorcism and the arrival of God's reign, see C. A. Evans, "Inaugurating the Kingdom of God and Defeating the Kingdom of Satan," *BBR* 15 (2005): 49–75.

[46] On which, see esp. D. Rudman, "The Sign of Jonah," *ExpTim* 115 (2004): 325–28.

[47] Unlike Mark, the Q material has Jesus saying that no sign will be given "except the sign of Jonah"—Christ's death and resurrection—corresponding to Jonah's time in and out of the great fish (Matt 12:39–40; Luke 11:29–30; cf. also Matt. 16:4). But this is not a material contradiction with Mark because this kind of "sign" was precisely not the kind of sign requested. See further J. Gibson, "Jesus' Refusal to Produce a 'Sign' (Mk 8.11–13)," *JSNT* 38 (1990): 37–66.

ning in Nazareth is scarcely flattering—able to work few miracles and having to escape from the mob's death threats—and would not likely have been invented. His appeal to Isa 61:1 grounds his claims in the Jewish Scriptures, but his declaration to have fulfilled them was unparalleled. Yet later pious fiction would probably have placed more explicit titular claims on Jesus' lips.

Gathering disciples matches other Jewish testimony about Jesus' ministry (e.g., *b. Sanh.* 43a). But, as noted, unlike conventional rabbis, he called his followers rather than "receiving applicants." The number twelve, tying in with the twelve tribes of Israel, also grounds Jesus' behavior in the Judaism of his day, but it was not a number Christians felt had to be preserved after their initial replacement of Judas by Matthias (Acts 1:20–26). The inclusion of Judas, the arch-traitor, virtually guarantees the accuracy of the list; no one playing fast and loose with history would have kept such a villain among the inner core of Jesus' followers.[48]

As already noticed, Jesus' exorcisms are attested to by non-Christian Jewish sources, yet they differ from others of his day by their simplicity and directness (see above, p. 273). Jesus does not even pray to his Father first, as his contemporary Hanina ben Dosa was known to do. The apostles, on the other hand, exorcise *in Jesus' name* (e.g., Luke 10:17; Acts 16:18). The Gospels' exorcisms appear in multiple sources, including both Mark and Q, and multiple forms, including summary statements (e.g., Luke 8:1–3), other healings (e.g., Mark 9:14–29 pars.), and parables (Mark 3:27 pars.). The fact that the demons engage in spiritual warfare with Jesus and are not always instantly vanquished also speaks against Christian creation. The criterion of coherence, moreover, comes into play as the exorcisms are a key sign of the arrival of God's kingdom (Matt 12:28 par.).[49]

That Jesus performed physical healings is also widely conceded, again as an important attestation of the kingdom's inauguration and of Jesus' identity (see esp. Matt 11:4–6 par.), although debate remains over whether they were genuinely supernatural events or psychosomatic cures by the power of suggestion. Again, there is the distinctive directness by which a simple command effected a cure. There are three passages that involved the characteristic ancient use of spittle or mud (Mark 7:33; 8:23; John 9:6), and in one of these a two-stage healing potentially makes Jesus' powers appear deficient (Mark 8:23), so it, too, is not likely to have been fabricated. Several of the healings involve Jesus seemingly going out of his way to cause controversy—risking defilement by touching lepers, healing non-emergency maladies on the Sabbath, and favoring the outcasts as recipients of his miracle-working ministry (women, Samaritans, Gentiles, etc). These features, too, set him off from his contemporaries and were not widely imitated by his followers. It was holiness, not uncleanness, that Jesus believed was "contagious"—a difficult idea for most religions to accept, much less practice.[50]

---

[48] Dunn, *Jesus Remembered*, 510.

[49] Meier, *A Marginal Jew*, vol. 2, 648–77.

[50] See esp. M. Borg, *Conflict, Holiness, and Politics in the Teaching of Jesus* (New York and Toronto: Mellen, 1984); cf. Blomberg, *Contagious Holiness*; idem., "Jesus, Sinners and Table Fellowship," *BBR* 19 (2009): 35–62.

The closest "parallels" in antiquity come from Philostratus' *Life of Apollonius* (on whom, see above, pp. 34–35), but these seem to be too late to have influenced Gospel accounts of Jesus. Further support for the authenticity of Jesus' healing miracles comes from their appearance in multiple sources and forms, including later Christian testimony in Acts 10:38 and Heb 2:4, and from the brief remarks of the Jewish historian Josephus in *Ant.* 18:63–64.[51]

Jesus' pronouncement stories offer a further example of material that passes the "dissimilarity test." All the debates are thoroughly conceivable within an early Jewish milieu, but in each case Jesus takes a radical perspective—claiming authority to forgive sins, dispensing with traditions about when to fast and with whom to feast, and challenging the prevailing Sabbath laws and the traditional ways of honoring one's biological family. Yet the Christology in the story of the healing of the paralytic is only implicit; no title save "Son of Man" is used. The early church quickly reverted to more conservative practices concerning eating and not eating, Sabbath restrictions, and "family values," so again this material would not likely have been invented and neither would have charges of blasphemy against Christ!

Conclusion and Theological Distinctives

Despite the differences in where they place these various events, Matthew, Mark, and Luke all demonstrate widespread agreement about the types of things Jesus did early in his Galilean ministry: he called men and women to repent, gathered disciples, exorcised and healed, challenged conventional Jewish wisdom with the radical newness of the gospel, created a new family out of those who would follow him, and engendered considerable hostility among at least a handful of his nation's leaders. All of this demonstrated a new and vibrant presence of God's reign.

In addition, each evangelist has distinctive emphases of his own. Mark stresses the messianic secret, Jesus' authority, and the radical newness of Jesus' ministry, and he places initial hostility with the Jewish leaders early in his narrative. Matthew heightens the focus on who Jesus is and on the requirements of discipleship, particularly by grouping key miracles of healing and related teachings into a two-chapter unit (Matt 8–9). Together, this section combines with the sermon of chapters 5–7 to disclose Jesus' authority in both preaching/teaching and healing. The conflict stories are postponed until chapter 12 as Matthew portrays a more linear development of official Jewish hostility to Jesus. As throughout his Gospel, he also adds several examples of how various events have fulfilled Old Testament prophecy. Luke is less unrelentingly negative in his portrait of the Jewish leaders,

---

[51] See esp. G. H. Twelftree, *Jesus the Miracle Worker: A Historical and Theological Study* (Downers Grove: IVP, 1999). While skeptical of the authenticity of a handful of passages and a handful of details in other passages he believes to be largely historical, Meier (*A Marginal Jew*, vol. 2, 630) nevertheless makes this highly significant generalization: "Viewed globally, the tradition of Jesus' miracles is more firmly supported by the criteria of historicity than are a number of other well-known and often readily accepted traditions about his life and ministry. . . . Put dramatically but with not too much exaggeration: if the miracle traditions from Jesus' public ministry were to be rejected *in toto* as unhistorical, so should every other Gospel tradition about him"!

stresses Christ's compassion for outcasts, and highlights his calls for repentance. Otherwise he follows Mark's sequence more closely than Matthew does.

The Sermon on the Mount

As we noted above (pp. 276–78), not too far along into his Galilean ministry, Jesus went up into the hill country to pray and formally call twelve of his followers (Mark 3:13–19; Luke 6:12–16). Matthew reserves a list of the Twelve for a later stage in his narrative but knows that a small group of Jesus' followers were recognized as his "disciples" earlier on (Matt 5:1). On this occasion, he taught those disciples, along with larger crowds thronging about the periphery, what has become his most famous sermon. It is the quintessential teaching of Jesus. In view of Matthew's theological emphases overall (above, pp. 146–47) and the setting in the mountains of this specific sermon, one may speak of Jesus promulgating a new Law or of interpreting Torah for his community.[52] But one must not minimize the radical nature of this interpretation, as he established his ethic on an internalized righteousness that cannot be adequately fulfilled merely by an assessable performance of a collection of laws, no matter how detailed.[53]

Matthew and Luke each include versions of the address (Matt 5–7; Luke 6:20–49), though Matthew's is considerably longer. Each begins with beatitudes; moves on to teachings about love, especially for one's enemies; and ends with illustrations about the need to respond correctly to Jesus, including the parable of the wise and foolish builders. Luke has Jesus teaching on a level place (Luke 6:17), leading some to call Luke's version the Sermon on the Plain, and even to postulate that Jesus spoke two different addresses. But Luke knows that Jesus has been in the mountains (v. 12), and he would have stood on some small plateau in order to teach large crowds, so there is no necessary contradiction between the two Gospels, and no need to imagine two entirely separate discourses.[54]

The standard, critical view of the relationship between Matthew's and Luke's sermons is that each writer has drawn a variety of teachings from Q to create the appearance of the one, unified discourse that now exists. Luke may have preserved an original core sermon from Q relatively intact, but Matthew has augmented it greatly. This idea is not inherently implausible or objectionable; something like it was suggested by Calvin centuries before the rise of modern biblical scholarship.[55] It is no less plausible that Jesus spoke a discourse much longer than either Matthew or Luke has preserved and that each has excerpted from that original.[56]

---

[52] J. A. Draper, "The Genesis and Narrative Thrust of the Paraenesis in the Sermon on the Mount," *JSNT* 75 (1999): 25–48.

[53] K. E. Brower, "Jesus and the Lustful Eye: Glancing at Matthew 5:28," *EQ* 76 (2004): 291–309.

[54] See esp. Bock, *Luke 1:1–9:50*, 931–44.

[55] J. Calvin, *A Harmony of the Gospels: Matthew, Mark, and Luke*, ed. D. W. Torrance and T. F. Torrance, vol. 1 (Edinburgh: St. Andrew; Grand Rapids: Eerdmans, 1972 [Lat. orig. 1555]), 168.

[56] Cf. G. A. Kennedy, *New Testament Interpretation through Rhetorical Criticism* (Chapel Hill: University of North Carolina Press, 1984), 67–69. Given that most of the places in which Luke has sermonic material not found in Mark, Luke is merely extending a series of teachings that are partially

Given the complexity and uncertainty of Synoptic source criticism, it is even conceivable that the origins of the canonical accounts combine something of both of these approaches.

History of Interpretation

The Sermon on the Mount has been a favorite of Christians over the centuries, and there have been a multitude of approaches to interpreting it; one survey counts no less than thirty-six![57] This should come as no surprise, given the strenuous demands of Jesus' message, not least his summary that we are to be "perfect" as our "heavenly Father is perfect" (Matt 5:48). We can probably simplify matters, however, and itemize eight major schools of thought that have dominated the history of Christian exegesis of the sermon.

Traditional Catholic. Medieval Catholicism solved the problem of the difficulty of Jesus' teachings by postulating two tiers of Christians. They argued that these more strenuous commands for righteousness need be implemented literally only by those in certain clerical or monastic orders. But the Sermon is addressed to all of Christ's disciples and to larger crowds, without any hint of such a division in its original setting.

Lutheran. Martin Luther read the Sermon much like he understood Paul's view of the Law. The Sermon was Law, not Gospel, meant to drive us to our knees in repentance for our inability to keep God's moral standards. By pointing out our need of grace and a Savior, it brings us back to Christ in contrition. But, again, the Sermon is not addressed first of all to those wanting to learn how to enter the kingdom but to those who had already expressed allegiance to Christ in some form.

Anabaptist. Many of the radical Reformers applied the Sermon's ethics in an extremely literal fashion to promote full-fledged pacifism in both personal and civil arenas. The later Russian Christian writer Leo Tolstoy promoted a similar perspective. But we will see that the historical background for Jesus' teaching is the environment of village life in Palestine under Roman occupation. Varying circumstances may require different practices. Further, Jesus is addressing his followers with standards for how they should live in community. It is not obvious that all his principles are directly transferrable to the state or government.

Old Liberal and Postmillennial. In the nineteenth century, there was great optimism about the possibility of Christianizing the earth—by both missionary work and the application of Christian principles to the laws of countries. Many believed that the fullness of the kingdom would be ushered in prior to Christ's return through the efforts of Christians empowered by the Spirit. Then the ethics of the Sermon could be widely implemented. The numerous wars and genocides

---

paralleled in Matthew, this hypothesis gains in probability. Cf. Ellis, *Making of the New Testament*, 177, n. 206.

[57] C. Bauman, *The Sermon on the Mount: The Modern Quest for Its Meaning* (Macon: Mercer University Press, 1985). For the history of interpretation, see esp. W. S. Kissinger, *The Sermon on the Mount: A History of Interpretation and Bibliography* (Metuchen, NJ: Scarecrow, 1975); and cf. J. P. Greenman, T. Larsen, S. R. Spencer, *Reading the Sermon on the Mount through the Centuries* (Grand Rapids: Brazos, 2007).

of the twentieth century have largely dispelled this optimism, though postmillennialism has made a comeback in certain pockets of Christianity today, especially as a response to the widespread success of the gospel in parts of the majority world. A secular equivalent whose heyday has now passed is Marxism.

Interim Ethic. At the turn of the century, Albert Schweitzer promoted his view that Christ thought the end would come within his lifetime (recall above, p. 89). This gave his ethic a greater urgency than it now has, since we realize that world history may continue for centuries. The texts that Schweitzer took as implying Christ mistakenly thought that the end was immediate (Mark 9:1 pars.; Mark 13:30 pars.; Matt 10:23), however, probably do not imply that at all.[58]

Existentialist. Particularly through the writings of Rudolf Bultmann (recall above, 90), a major twentieth-century movement reinterpreted Jesus' kingdom ethics in terms of personal transformation that occurs when one embraces "authentic existence." This approach usually rejects finding any absolute ethics in the Sermon, but views them instead as a profound challenge to personal decision making in light of the consciousness of human finitude and divine encounter. Contemporary postmodern interpretations bear a striking resemblance to mid-twentieth-century existentialist ones, even if in slightly different garb. We will see that there are places in the Sermon that dare not be absolutized, but existentialists did not develop a sufficiently convincing hermeneutic by which the entire Sermon could be "demythologized," nor has postmodernism any more successfully deconstructed it. More often than not, their thoroughgoing relativistic presuppositions are incompatible with historic Christianity (recall above, pp. 118–19).

Classic Dispensationalist. An older dispensationalist view often taught that the Sermon was part of Jesus' kingdom offer to the Jews. Had they accepted it, people would have lived by the ethics Jesus taught. Because they rejected it, the kingdom has been entirely postponed until the millennium, at which point the seemingly impossible ideals of the Sermon will be realized. But it is hard to maintain that these commands are only for a "golden age" of human morality, since they include provisions for responding to evil, persecution, hatred, and rejection. Not surprisingly, this view has been largely abandoned by "progressive dispensationalists" in the current theological scene.[59]

Kingdom Theology. A widespread consensus of scholarship today thus opts for an eighth view, given particular currency by the numerous writings of George Ladd.[60] If the kingdom has been inaugurated (partially present now but only ful-

---

[58] See Blomberg, *Historical Reliability of the Gospels*, 64–65. See also below, pp. 324, 332–33, and 369.

[59] A label especially associated with the movement spearheaded by C. A. Blaising and D. L. Bock, and reflected in their *Progressive Dispensationalism* (Wheaton: Victor, 1993).

[60] See esp. G. E. Ladd, *The Presence of the Future: The Eschatology of Biblical Realism* (Grand Rapids: Eerdmans, 1974; London: SPCK, 1980); and idem., *A Theology of the New Testament*, rev. and ed. D. A. Hagner (Grand Rapids: Cambridge, 1993). Cf. also G. H. Stassen and D. P. Gushee, *Kingdom Ethics: Following Jesus in Contemporary Contexts* (Downers Grove: IVP, 2003). For an important, brief statement of the perspective with direct reference to the Sermon on the Mount, see R. A. Guelich, "The Matthean Beatitudes: 'Entrance Requirements' or Eschatological Blessings?" *JBL* 95 (1976):

ly to be realized after Christ's return—see above, p. 271), then it seems best to assume that Jesus' ethics are also meant for believers now. We must admit that they are only partially realizable in the present age, even though they remain the ideal for which we all should strive, as we yield ourselves to the Spirit. This is not a "works-righteousness" by which we become Christ's disciples, but a "fruit befitting repentance" whereby we demonstrate our continuing allegiance to him.

There is no doubt an element of truth in every one of the perspectives surveyed, but we believe this last one has most completely captured the correct approach. What is more, while Jesus' ethics clearly apply to individual lives, and while Christians ought to use all legal means in whatever societies they find themselves to promote their ethics in the public arena, Jesus' sermon is not addressed, first of all, either to the individual or to the state but to the *community* of his followers. As the church of Jesus Christ, corporately, in local communities, learns increasingly to follow his ethics, his will is implemented on earth, and men and women are drawn to the faith.[61]

Contents and Exegesis of Matthew 5–7

Matthew's Sermon on the Mount is carefully structured, with a pattern of grouping Jesus' teachings into units of three or multiples of three items. The nine beatitudes plus the salt and light sayings form the introduction (5:3–16). The thesis paragraph follows: Jesus demands a "greater righteousness" (5:17–20). Six illustrations of this ensue, contrasting the Law with his ethic (5:21–48). Three examples of not parading one's piety come next (6:1–18). Then appear three teachings about wealth and worry (6:19–34), with three sections on how to treat others proceeding (7:1–12), including the Golden Rule as the climax of the body of the Sermon (v. 12). The conclusion of Jesus' classic message uses three illustrations to focus on the only two options open by way of response: acceptance or rejection (7:13–27).[62] Interestingly, there are parallels to almost every saying of Jesus in the Sermon elsewhere in Jewish writing, but the cumulative effect of Jesus' teachings and the context of the arrival of the kingdom into which they are set makes them stand out as noticeably different (cf. 7:28–29).[63]

The Beatitudes (5:3–12) [Aland §51]. Jesus opens his Sermon with "kingdom blessings" (vv. 3, 10). The Greek word *makarios* means blessed, fortunate, or to be congratulated.[64] The tenses of the verbs are mostly future, but the first and eighth beatitudes give present tense blessings—"theirs is the kingdom." So we are

---

415–34. For incisive, practical application to personal discipleship, see W. W. Klein, *Become What You Are: Spiritual Formation according to the Sermon on the Mount* (Tyrone, GA and Milton Keynes: Authentic Media, 2006).

[61] See esp. D. Fleer and D. Bland, eds., *Preaching the Sermon on the Mount: The World It Imagines* (St. Louis: Chalice, 2007).

[62] This outline is heavily indebted to D. C. Allison, Jr., "The Structure of the Sermon on the Mount," *JBL* 106 (1987): 423–45. Cf. also Hagner, *Matthew 1–13*, 84.

[63] S. Sandmel, *Judaism and Christian Beginnings* (Oxford: OUP, 1978), 357.

[64] France, *Matthew*, 161, notes that "the Australian idiom 'Good on yer' is perhaps as close as any to the sense." The closest American equivalent to this might be "Good for you!"

reminded of the partially present realization of these blessings, coupled with their full manifestation in the age to come.

The first kind of person to be considered blessed is "the poor in spirit" (v. 3). Luke's parallel refers merely to the "poor" (Luke 6:20). Many have viewed this as an outright contradiction between the Gospels. But the probable Hebrew behind the Greek word for poor (*ptōchoi*) is *anawim*, which increasingly in the latter part of the Old Testament came to be used for the materially oppressed or impoverished within Israel who recognized that God was their only hope or refuge (as, e.g., in Isa 61:1). Although Luke is more interested in the social dimension (see above, pp. 166–67), he recognizes a spiritual side to the oppression as well (6:22–23). So it is best to understand both

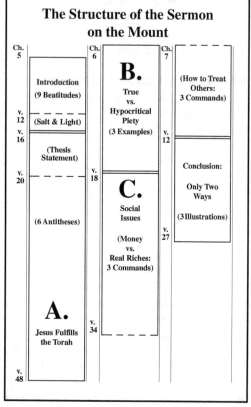

The Structure of the Sermon on the Mount

evangelists' beatitudes as congratulating "those who because of sustained economic privation and social distress have confidence only in God."[65]

This two-pronged focus then runs right through the rest of the beatitudes. Those who mourn may be repenting of sin or lamenting the lack of implementation of God's righteous standards on earth. The meek can be the spiritually humble or the physically oppressed. The righteousness for which we must hunger and thirst is both spiritual and social, and so on.[66] The composite portrait of a follower of Jesus is a stark inversion of what the Greco-Roman world considered admirable.

---

[65] Carson, "Matthew," 131. Cf. also F. D. Bruner (*Matthew, A Commentary: The Christbook*, rev. ed. [Grand Rapids: Eerdmans, 2004], 159): "If we say that 'blessed are the poor in spirit' means 'blessed are the rich, too, if they act humbly,' we have spiritualized the text away. On the other hand, if we say 'blessed are the poor' means 'poor people are happy people,' we have secularized the text. . . . Jesus incorporated both Matthew's spirituality and Luke's sociality, getting the best of each."

[66] For a detailed exposition balancing the social and spiritual dimensions of these texts, see M. H. Crosby, *Spirituality of the Beatitudes: Matthew's Vision for the Church in an Unjust World*, rev. ed. (Maryknoll: Orbis, 2005).

To borrow a term from contemporary Hispanic culture, blessed are all those who are not "macho"![67]

Metaphors of Salt and Light (5:13–16) [Aland §52–53]. Values as countercultural as those expressed in the beatitudes might suggest to some that Jesus was promoting monasticism. Verses 13–16 dispel that notion. Jesus' disciples must remain effective change agents within the world. Of all the images salt evoked in ancient society, most relevant to this context is its role in arresting corruption and decay.[68] Light, in a world without electricity, was all the more valuable a commodity for illuminating one's way and giving guidance.

Jesus and the Law (5:17–48) [Aland §54–59]. The combination of Jesus' countercultural beatitudes and his commands to model those values within society could easily have led his listeners to question whether he was overthrowing the Law of Moses. Verses 17–20 introduce the body of the Sermon and answer this question in a nutshell. Jesus has not come to abolish the Old Testament, but neither is he preserving all things unchanged. In "fulfilling" the Law, he is bringing to completion all that to which it pointed (v. 18b—"until everything is accomplished"). The later New Testament church would come to the conclusion that major aspects of the Law no longer needed to be literally practiced—for example, the sacrifices, dietary laws, temple festivals, circumcision, and so on. In later eras, Christian theologians would speak of retaining the moral law but not literally preserving the ceremonial/ritual or civic/civil laws. These latter kinds of laws are obeyed by Christians when they turn to Jesus, the once-for-all sacrifice for human sin, and love their neighbor as themselves in fashions appropriate to the settings they find themselves in. In short, every Old Testament commandment must today be filtered through a grid of fulfillment in Christ to see how its application may have changed.[69]

Two popular but opposing views that the text does not support must be avoided here. One is that all Old Testament teaching not explicitly rescinded in the New Testament is still in force. By this logic, however, newlyweds should still be free from military service or other civil duties for their first year of marriage (Deut 24:5), and men would still need to have forelocks and avoid jagged beard edges (Lev 19:27). The other is that all Old Testament teaching not explicitly reaffirmed in the New Testament is to be jettisoned. By this logic, divination and sorcery would now be acceptable (*contra* Lev 19:26) as would transvestism (*contra* Deut 22:5). Instead, the historical background and purpose of each of the Old Testament's 613 laws must be determined, as best as possible. Each must then be

---

[67] Here is the core of truth to the approach of D. Willard, *The Divine Conspiracy: Rediscovering Our Hidden Life in God* (San Francisco: HarperSanFrancisco, 1998), 100. Willard argues that each beatitude refers to people who in the world's estimation are nobodies. But to allege that Jesus is blessing "spiritual zeros" or "those without a wisp of 'religion,'" i.e., otherwise negative qualities, appears to invert Jesus' intended meaning almost entirely.

[68] Ridderbos, *Matthew*, 94. Cf. Mounce, *Matthew*, 42; D. K. Ogden and A. C. Skinner, *The Four Gospels: Verse by Verse* (Salt Lake City: Deseret, 2006), 182.

[69] Hagner, *Matthew 1–13*, 106. Cf. further Klein, Blomberg and Hubbard, *Introduction to Biblical Interpretation*, 344–50.

related to a category of law that the New Testament does discuss. Finally, in light of the New Testament treatment of each particular legal category, a corresponding application for the church age must be ascertained.[70] If the poor have no access to fields and their crops, laws of gleaning (e.g., Lev 19:9–10) will afford them no help, but low-cost, neighborhood stores that still avoid completely free handouts may prove an effective substitute. If tattoos form part of pagan worship services today, they remain as forbidden as in the ancient Near East (as in Lev 19:28). But if they display a Christian message or symbol on an appropriate part of the body, they may well glorify God! Kingdom standards actually demand a greater righteousness than that practiced by the Jewish leaders (Matt 5:20), which involves fewer pat answers to complex questions and more, internalized, Spirit-led, case-by-case applications. But Jesus also promises to supply precisely this greater spiritual empowerment needed for such tasks (cf. +1:28–30).[71]

Matthew 5:21–48 are known as the six "antitheses." They provide illustrations of Jesus' relationship to various laws by contrasting traditional Jewish interpretations with Jesus' understanding of their significance. Three of the antitheses seem to intensify and internalize the Law's demands (vv. 21–26, 27–30, 43–47), but the other three seem to revoke certain portions of the Torah (vv. 31–32, 33–37, 38–42). The unifying feature of all six is that Jesus shows himself to be the Law's sovereign interpreter, explaining how it applies in the new age he is inaugurating.[72] It is also possible to divide five of the six antitheses (excepting vv. 31–32) not just into two parts but into three: the old prohibitions in the Law that are no longer adequate; Jesus' new set of prohibitions; and positive practices or "transforming initiatives" to implement the principles behind the prohibitions.[73]

First, Jesus condemns not only murder but hatred and abusive language. One must thus take positive steps to be reconciled with one's adversary (vv. 21–26). Second, not only is adultery sinful but so is lust.[74] Disciples must take drastic

---

[70] Cf. esp. C. J. H. Wright, *An Eye for an Eye: The Place of Old Testament Ethics Today* (Downers Grove [=*Living as the People of God* (Leicester)]: IVP, 1983); idem., *God's People in God's Land: Family, Land, and Property in the Old Testament* (Grand Rapids: Eerdmans; Exeter: Paternoster, 1990); idem., *Walking in the Ways of the Lord: The Ethical Authority of the Old Testament* (Leicester: Apollos, 1995).

[71] Cf. T. G. Long, *Matthew* (Louisville: WJKP, 1997), 54: "Jesus is not calling his hearers to determine how righteous the scribes and Pharisees are and then to do them one better. . . . No, the followers of Jesus are called to a different *kind* of righteousness that seeks to be ever expressive of the merciful, forgiving, reconciling will of God that lies at the center of the law."

[72] For a survey of the various interpretations of this matter, which comes to the same conclusions, see esp. Moo, "Jesus and the Authority of the Mosaic Law."

[73] For the detailed exegesis, see G. H. Stassen, "The Fourteen Triads of the Sermon on the Mount (Matthew 5:21–7:12)," *JBL* 122 (2003): 267–308. For a full-orbed interpretation of the sermon from this perspective, see idem., *Living the Sermon on the Mount: A Practical Hope for Grace and Deliverance* (San Francisco: Josey-Bass, 2006).

[74] But it is important to stress that "looking . . . in order to desire her" is "specifically of wanting (and planning?) sexual relations." "The focus is thus not (as some tender adolescent consciences have read it) on sexual attraction as such, but on the desire for (and perhaps the planning of) an illicit sexual liaison" (France, *Matthew*, 204).

Matthew 5:33–48
Oaths, Retaliation, and Loving One's Enemies

Jesus' Command	Counterexamples	Historical Background	Church Application
don't swear (take oaths) (v. 34)	Paul uses God's name to assure truth of his claims (Gal. 1:20; 2 Cor. 1:23)	Pharisees got off hook if they swore by something other than God	be so trustworthy and straight-forward that your word can be taken at face value
don't resist evil (v. 39)	exorcisms (Gospels, Acts) spiritual warfare (Eph. 6)	"resist" was legal term; thus don't take to court	believers shouldn't sue other believers (1 Cor. 6)
turn the other cheek (v. 39)	Jesus withdraws from hostility (Matt. 12:15; 14:13)	backhand slap was a typical Jewish insult	allow an insult without retaliation (Rom. 12:14)
give your cloak (v. 40)	those who have nothing to give away (Matt. 10)	collateral in legal proceedings was clothing	be more generous by doing more than just what you are asked/required to do
go the extra mile (v. 41)	the need for rest (Mk. 6:31)	helping Roman soldiers carry equipment on forced marches (conscription)	same as above
give to the one who asks to borrow (v. 42)	don't give pearls to swine (Matt. 7:6)	reluctance to give loans when near to Jubilee	choose wisely how you give but then don't begrudge lack of repayment
love your enemies (v. 44)	hate sin (Rev. 2:6; Jude 23) resist the devil (1 Peter 5:9)	no personal vengeance; leave justice to the law	use due process to air grievances; seek the best interest of those you don't like

action to remove themselves from situations that would nurture it (vv. 27–30).[75] Third, Jesus takes a more stringent stand on divorce (for details here, see below, pp. 357–58). Fourth, he condemns oath-taking and commands his followers to be people of unswerving integrity (vv. 33–37). Fifth, he abolishes the *lex talionis* (the Mosaic "law of retaliation") in favor of doing good to one's opponents (vv. 38–42).[76] Finally, he commends loving one's enemy (vv. 43–47). No Old Testament text ever says to hate them, but, given God's commands to exterminate some of them, it was undoubtedly a natural inference for many! The culmination of all of this is the command to be perfect (v. 48). The word here (Gk. *teleios*) is perhaps better translated "mature" or "complete."[77] The Lukan parallel employs synecdoche (a part for the whole) to highlight one key component of this maturity— showing mercy (Luke 6:36).

Throughout Matt 5:33–42, we find a series of commands, all of which are "contradicted" elsewhere in the New Testament. This is a tip-off that these are not to be absolutized but to be understood in their historical context.[78] Jesus does not abolish all oaths (cf. Gal 1:20; 2 Cor 1:23) but condemns the Pharisaic casuistry that permitted oaths in the name of certain sacred objects to be less binding than oaths that directly invoked God's name. Jesus clearly resists evil with his exorcisms, but *anthistēmi* ("resist," v. 39) often meant to resist in a legal context or to resist with violence.[79] "Turning the other cheek" is not a call to allow oneself or one's loved ones bodily injury. The backhanded slap across the cheek was a characteristic Jewish insult to one's "inferior." Jesus calls us to allow insults without feeling compelled to trade them (cf. Rom 12:14).[80] Giving one's cloak was an action of offering collateral in a law court; going the extra mile meant being conscripted by Roman soldiers to carry their equipment. Jesus tells his listeners to give freely to the one who asks to borrow from them (v. 42; cf. Luke 6:30, 34) because lenders were more reluctant to give loans just before the Jubilee year when all debts were to be forgiven. Jesus' ethics remain radical, but they must be implemented intelligently. The examples in these verses take the form of "focal

---

[75] Verses 29–30 form an excellent example of hyperbole or rhetorical exaggeration. They cannot be intended literally because a blind or maimed person can still lust! Cf. the helpful comments of J. R. W. Stott, *The Message of the Sermon on the Mount* (Leicester and Downers Grove: IVP, 1978), 89.

[76] On which, see esp. J. F. Davis, *Lex Talionis in Early Judaism and the Exhortation of Jesus in Matthew 5.38–42* (London and New York: T&T Clark, 2005).

[77] D. C. Allison, Jr., *The Sermon on the Mount: Inspiring the Moral Imagination* (New York: Crossroad, 1999), 105. Cf. Keener, *Matthew*, 215. Or, with Nolland (*Matthew*, 271), "whole" or "entire"— "wholeheartedness" before God and "lack of compromise with pagan practices."

[78] Particularly helpful here is R. A. Horsley, "Ethics and Exegesis: 'Love Your Enemy' and the Doctrine of Non-Violence," *JAAR* 54 (1986): 3–31. Cf. D. L. Turner, *Matthew* (Grand Rapids: Baker, 2008), 174–75.

[79] Provocatively developing an entire social ethic from the latter position is W. Wink, *Jesus and Nonviolence: A Third Way* (Minneapolis: Fortress, 2003).

[80] Cf. Keener, *Matthew*, 197.

instances"—extreme commands that attract our attention to a key ethical theme that must be variously applied as circumstances change.[81]

The final antithesis, on enemy love, is arguably the single most distinctive portion of Jesus' entire ethic. This observation dovetails with Jesus' words that if we do not obey him on this count, we are no better than the pagans (v. 47). With his reference to perfection following immediately (v. 48), he may also be hinting that loving one's enemies is the clearest mark of Christian maturity. Romans 12:17–21 echoes these words in a context that also gives the state the right to wield the sword (13:4), so it is not obvious that a full-blown doctrine of pacifism can be derived from the Sermon, but, on a personal level, revenge is clearly excluded. The three-part pattern of the "antitheses," concluding with transforming initiatives or positive antidotes to the problems presented, reinforces the beatitude on peacemaking and highlights the need for God's people, whatever their views on war, to support proactive measures to reduce conflict and promote reconciliation in local, national, and international contexts.[82]

Religious Hypocrisy (6:1–18) [Aland §60–63]. Having stressed in the antitheses that righteousness is not merely external, Jesus now goes on to address the right motives for outward acts of piety. Three examples—almsgiving, prayer, and fasting—all illustrate the same principle: good deeds are not to be done for human praise (6:1). In 5:16 the disciples were told to perform their good deeds in public but so that others might praise the Father. In the context of the second of the three illustrations, Jesus adds what has come to be known as the Lord's Prayer (6:9–13), though it might better have been entitled the Model Prayer or the Disciples' Prayer, since it is one prayer Jesus never prayed nor could have ("forgive us our trespasses").[83]

The prayer is carefully structured. The first half focuses on God's desires; the second half, on human needs. The first half also balances God's intimacy with his sovereignty. Jesus' distinctive use of Abba (the Aramaic near equivalent of "daddy") for Father (Mark 14:36) probably lies behind the opening clause of the Lord's Prayer. But God is also the heavenly Father whose reign must advance and whose will must be accomplished. The second half of the prayer balances the believer's material needs (daily bread; cf. esp. Prov 30:7–9[84]) with his or her spiritual needs (forgiveness of sin and protection from evil). "Lead us not into temptation" is a misleading translation since God tempts no one (Jas 1:13). Probably the sense is "do not let us succumb to temptation."[85] The traditional ending

---

[81] R. C. Tannehill, "The 'Focal Instance' as a Form of New Testament Speech: A Study of Matthew 5:39b–42," *JBL* 50 (1970): 372–85.

[82] See esp. G H. Stassen, *Just Peacemaking: Transforming Initiatives for Justice and Peace* (Louisville: WJKP, 1992); idem., *Just Peacemaking: Ten Practices for Abolishing War,* rev. ed. (Cleveland: Pilgrim, 2004).

[83] Although he could have confessed the corporate sins of Israel.

[84] On the possible background of these verses for other parts of the Lord's Prayer as well, see R. W. Byargeon, "Echoes of Wisdom in the Lord's Prayer (Matt 6:9–13)," *JETS* 41 (1998): 353–65.

[85] Davies and Allison, *Matthew,* vol. 1, 612–13; Witherington, *Matthew,* 147. J. A. Fitzmyer ("And Lead Us Not into Temptation," *Bib* 84 [2003]: 261) concludes that God may well let us remain in

("for yours is the kingdom") is not in the oldest and most reliable manuscripts and is probably the pious addition of a later scribe who wanted to give the prayer a "proper" conclusion. It may be based on 1 Chr 29:11–13.

Matthew 6:7–8 encourages the disciples to use this prayer to distinguish themselves from the heathen, not just to repeat it thoughtlessly like a magical formula. Ironically, some in the history of the church have done just that, while others have overreacted by refusing ever to pray it! It remains a superb model, but it can become meaningless if used mechanically. The concepts, not the exact wording, are what matter the most.[86]

Wealth and Worry (6:19–34) [Aland §64–67]. The rationale for the sequence of the next two sections of the Sermon is less clear. One influential approach has seen them as unpacking the petitions of the second half of the Lord's Prayer, but the parallels are not consistently close. More likely, the transition is that even when a person's behavior and attitudes are correct, the greater righteousness demanded of disciples is not present unless God rather than money is served. Verses 19–21 command us not to accumulate too many possessions—a sure sign that our treasure is on earth and not in heaven. Verses 22–24 stress how decision making in this arena affects all of life. One either serves material possessions ("mammon") or God. Verses 25–34 repeatedly command us not to worry about material needs; God will take care of us. Here is where it is crucial to understand the community focus of the Sermon. Taken as an individual promise, verse 33 is patently false; committed believers have frequently starved to death. To the extent that God's people as a whole (the verbs are second person plural commands) seek God's righteous standards, they will by definition share their surplus with the needy in their midst. Luke's parallel to this verse (Luke 12:31) confirms this interpretation, as it is embedded in a context that commands believers to sell their possessions and give to the poor (v. 33).[87]

How to Treat Others (7:1–12) [Aland §68–71]. The final triad in the body of the Sermon groups together commands about social behavior. Disciples must not be judgmental or censorious (vv. 1–5a), but they must make discerning judgments about the behavior of others (vv. 5b–6).[88] They must pray boldly and persistently

---

places where we might experience temptation, but we, not he, are always to blame if we give in to temptation.

[86] For an excellent, detailed treatment of the prayer overall, see J. M. Lochmann, *The Lord's Prayer* (Grand Rapids: Eerdmans, 1990). Much more briefly, cf. N. T. Wright, *The Lord and His Prayer* (London: SPCK, 1996; Grand Rapids: Eerdmans, 1997); and G. O'Collins, *The Lord's Prayer* (New York: Paulist, 2007).

[87] Cf. R. A. Guelich, *The Sermon on the Mount: A Foundation for Understanding* (Waco: Word, 1982), 373: "Part of the presence of the Kingdom is indeed material blessings. Therefore, we can hardly live under God's reign, receive his blessings, and not use them to help alleviate the evil of hunger and need elsewhere." On vv. 19–34 more generally, see also C. L. Blomberg, "On Wealth and Worry: Matthew 6:19–34—Meaning and Significance," *CTR* 6 (1992): 73–89.

[88] Verse 1 forbids judgmentalism, not analysis and assessment, as the rest of the paragraph makes clear. Cf. Witherington (*Matthew*, 154): "it makes no sense whatsoever in light of the other discourses of Jesus in this Gospel, particularly the critiques of the Pharisees and other religious leaders, to see this as some sort of call never to criticize anyone or anything. . . . The issue here has to do with unfair

for their needs and expect God to answer them (vv. 7–11). Still, Jesus presupposes that we remember the clause from the Lord's Prayer, "your will be done" (6:10).[89] Moreover, God gives only good gifts (7:11), and unfortunately our perspective on what is truly good is often quite warped. Finally, Christ brings the body of the Sermon to a close with an epitome that captures the heart of his ethic: the so-called Golden Rule (v. 12). It is often pointed out that many other Jewish teachers, along with a few from other religions, taught much the same thing, but most of them phrased it negatively—in essence, "Don't treat others the way you wouldn't want to be treated." Jesus is the only person to state the principle in this emphatically positive form.[90] Taking the initiative in doing good is always more challenging than simply avoiding evil.

Conclusion: Only Two Ways (7:13–27) [Aland §72–75]. Jesus' vintage Sermon concludes with three illustrations that all make the same point. Ultimately, there are only two options: to be for Jesus or against him. He hopes we will all hear, obey, and follow. The narrow vs. the wide gate (vv. 13–14) reminds would-be disciples that the road may be fraught with difficulty. The good vs. the bad tree (vv. 15–20) calls on disciples to demonstrate their genuineness by producing proper fruit. As noted above (p. 149), Matthew may have been combating false teachers in his own midst. Clearly, some of those who prove false are nevertheless involved in ministry—preaching, exorcising, or performing miracles. Verses 21–23 make it clear that they have been masquerading, as Jesus declares, "I never knew you" (v. 23). Finally, the wise vs. the foolish builder calls on us to establish a secure foundation by not only hearing but also obeying Jesus' teaching. Many have admired the ethics of the Sermon on the Mount without accepting Jesus' personal claims on their lives (in this century, most notably Mohandas Gandhi), but Christ does not consider that option acceptable.[91]

The Crowd's Reaction (7:28–29) [Aland §76]. Jesus' words elicit amazement because of their unique authority. It is not that the Jewish leaders did not have immense power, but their teaching always had to be grounded in Scripture or in the teaching of previous rabbis. In this sermon, Jesus cites no one to corroborate his views, and he quotes Scripture only to reinterpret it dramatically. Such brashness borders on lunacy unless it reflects a divine mandate.[92]

---

critiques, uncharitable evaluations, and also, as the metaphorical illustration makes clear, judging others by a different standard than one uses to judge oneself."

[89] And the principle of corporate responsibility discussed above in the context of 6:33. See esp. J. Murphy-O'Connor, "The Prayer of Petition (Matthew 7:7–11 and par.)," *RB* 110 (2003): 399–416.

[90] For a list of the twelve most commonly cited parallels, see Bock, *Luke 1:1–9:50*, 596–97. Most well known of all is Hillel's so-called "Silver Rule" (clearly not a Jewish designation!): "What is hateful to you, do not do to your neighbor; that is the whole Torah, while the rest is commentary" (*b. Shab.* 31a).

[91] Cf. Hauerwas, *Matthew*, 92: Jesus "does not want our admiration. What he has taught, what he is, requires nothing else than our lives."

[92] Cf. Carson, "Matthew," 196. For more detail on most of the points noted under the Sermon thus far, see C. L. Blomberg, "The Most Often Abused Verses in the Sermon on the Mount," *SWJT* 46 (2004): 1–17, and the literature there cited.

The Sermon on the Plain (Luke 6:20–49) [Aland §78–83]

Almost all of the teaching in Luke's abbreviated sermon has appeared in Matthew's longer version or is parallel in form to what does appear (extra beatitudes, contrasting woes, etc.). Luke's account is equally carefully structured and divides naturally into three parts: (1) introductory blessings and warnings (vv. 20–26); (2) central teachings about loving one's enemies (vv. 27–36); and (3) three concluding illustrations of an appropriate response to Jesus—rejecting judgmentalism, bearing good fruit, and building wisely (vv. 37–49). Luke, as a Gentile writing to Gentile Christians, understandably omits all of Matthew's material contrasting Jesus' teaching with the Law and challenging the behavior of the Jewish leaders. What remains, however, focuses all the more pointedly on that most distinctive aspect of Jesus' ethic—enemy love.[93] Plus, as noted above, Luke has considerably more interest in the socioeconomic plight of people in this life.

Historicity

Just about every major theme in Jesus' great sermon passes the "dissimilarity" test. The "ethical perfectionism" outlined here goes beyond that which any religious tradition could be expected to follow—or invent! Jesus blesses the poor, while many in Judaism saw the rich as blessed. The beatitude form was common in Judaism, but Jesus' exaltation of the humiliated was uncommon in any ancient religion. The sayings about disciples as salt and light fit Jesus' characteristic use of metaphor. His transcendence of the Law—fulfilling yet not abolishing it—walks a tightrope rarely maneuvered successfully in Judaism or Christianity.[94] The hyperboles of the antitheses create strenuous commands indeed; yet we have seen that their meanings are clarified once one recognizes the distinctive background of a Palestinian village setting. Non-retaliation and enemy love are among the least paralleled teachings, even in Judaism. The Lord's Prayer echoes Jewish sentiment in almost every clause, yet it creates a distinct package with its "Abba"-intimacy and kingdom theology. Jesus' words on stewardship and judgmentalism are also too demanding for later Christians to have readily created them. The Golden Rule finds numerous parallels, but, as noted, most of them are phrased negatively. The concluding "two ways" section follows an established Jewish form of writing but with a distinct christological focus. Little wonder the crowds marveled at Jesus' unique authority!

---

[93] On which, see esp. C. A. Smith, ed., *At the Cross at the Crossroads: Loving Our Enemies in the 21st Century* (Manila: OMF Literature, 2007).

[94] To be sure, a typical "tradition history" of the Sermon has postulated conflicting tendencies represented here and throughout: a radical Jesus toned down and "re-Judaized" by early Jewish Christianity. See esp. H. D. Betz, *Essays on the Sermon on the Mount* (Philadelphia: Fortress, 1985); idem., *The Sermon on the Mount* (Minneapolis: Fortress, 1995). But Matthew as redactor did not find these tendencies contradictory or he would have eliminated at least one of them. So there is no reason not to ascribe the balance to Jesus himself, given the resulting double similarity and double dissimilarity.

For Further Study

Healings, Controversies, Discipleship, and Opposition

Beasley-Murray, G. R. *Jesus and the Kingdom of God.* Exeter: Paternoster; Grand Rapids: Eerdmans, 1986.

Beavis, Mary Ann. *Jesus and Utopia: Looking for the Kingdom of God in the Roman World.* Minneapolis: Fortress, 2006.

Carson, D. A. *When Jesus Confronts the World: An Exposition of Matthew 8–10.* Grand Rapids: Baker, 1987; Rev. ed. Carlisle: Paternoster, Rev. ed., 1995.

Chilton, Bruce D. *Pure Kingdom: Jesus' Vision of God.* Grand Rapids: Eerdmans; London: SPCK, 1996.

Dewey, Joanna. *Markan Public Debate.* Chico: Scholars, 1980.

Hess, Richard S., and M. Daniel Carroll R., eds. *Family in the Bible: Exploring Customs, Culture, and Context.* Grand Rapids: Baker, 2003.

Hultgren, Arland J. *Jesus and His Adversaries: The Form and Function of the Conflict Stories in the Synoptic Tradition.* Minneapolis: Augsburg, 1979.

Kuthirakkattel, Scaria. *The Beginning of Jesus' Ministry according to Mark's Gospel (1,14–3,6).* Rome: BIP, 1990.

Longenecker, Richard N., ed. *Patterns of Discipleship in the New Testament.* Grand Rapids and Cambridge: Eerdmans, 1996.

Moeser, Marion C. *The Anecdote in Mark, the Classical World and the Rabbis.* London and New York: SAP, 2002.

Twelftree, Graham H. *Jesus the Exorcist: A Contribution to the Study of the Historical Jesus.* Tübingen: Mohr; Peabody: Hendrickson, 1993.

The Sermon on the Mount/Plain

Introductory

Carson, D. A. *The Sermon on the Mount: An Evangelical Exposition of Matthew 5–7.* Grand Rapids: Baker, 1978; Rev. ed. Carlisle: Paternoster, 2001.

Carter, Warren. *What Are They Saying about Matthew's Sermon on the Mount?* New York: Paulist, 1994.

Klein, William W. *Become What You Are: Spiritual Formation According to the Sermon on the Mount.* Tyrone, GA and Milton Keynes: Authentic Media, 2006.

Fleer, David, and Dave Bland, eds., *Preaching the Sermon on the Mount: The World It Imagines.* St. Louis: Chalice, 2007.

Stassen, Glen H. *Living the Sermon on the Mount: A Practical Hope for Grace and Deliverance.* San Francisco: Josey-Bass, 2006.

Stott, John R. W. *The Message of the Sermon on the Mount.* BST. Leicester and Downers Grove: IVP, 1978.

Intermediate

Allison, Dale C., Jr. *The Sermon on the Mount: Inspiring the Moral Imagination.* New York: Crossroad, 1999.

Guelich, Robert A. *The Sermon on the Mount: A Foundation for Understanding.* Waco: Word, 1982.

Lapide, Pinchas. *The Sermon on the Mount: Utopia or Program for Action?* Maryknoll: Orbis, 1986.

Strecker, Georg. *The Sermon on the Mount: An Exegetical Commentary*. Nashville: Abingdon, 1988; Rev. ed. Edinburgh: T&T Clark, 1999.

Talbert, Charles H. *Reading the Sermon on the Mount: Character Formation and Decision Making in Matthew 5–7*. Grand Rapids: Baker, 2006.

Topel, L. John. *Children of a Compassionate God: A Theological Exegesis of Luke 6:20–49*. Collegeville: Liturgical, 2001.

Advanced

Betz, Hans Dieter. *The Sermon on the Mount*. Hermeneia. Minneapolis: Fortress, 1995.

Betz, Hans Dieter. *Essays on the Sermon on the Mount*. Philadelphia: Fortress, 1985.

Davies, W. D. *The Setting of the Sermon on the Mount*. Cambridge: CUP, 1964.

Patte, Daniel, *Discipleship according to the Sermon on the Mount: Four Legitimate Readings, Four Plausible Views of Discipleship, and Their Relative Values*. Valley Forge: Trinity, 1996.

Bibliography

Kissinger, Warren S. *The Sermon on the Mount: A History of Interpretation and Bibliography*. Metuchen, NJ: Scarecrow, 1975.

Questions for Review

1. According to Mark, what kinds of activity occupied the earlier stages of Jesus' Galilean ministry? How does he summarize the heart of Jesus' message?

2. What does the "kingdom of God" mean?

3. What are we to learn about Jesus through his exorcisms of demon-possessed people? from other miracles of healing?

4. What is a pronouncement story? What else is it called? How does understanding this form help us in interpreting the stories in Mark 2:1–3:6 and elsewhere?

5. Why did Jesus call a special group of twelve disciples? What was unique about their calling?

6. What is the preferred approach to interpreting the Sermon on the Mount adopted in this book? Why is this one preferred? What difference does it make?

7. Identify several of the exegetical highlights of the Sermon. What issues would you most want to explain to the type of people among whom you typically live and work if you were teaching a series of studies on this Sermon? What would you stress and why?

8. What relationship between Jesus and the Law is disclosed in 5:17–20 and the following antitheses (vv. 21–42)? How are we most probably to understand the seemingly impossible demands of the second half of these (vv. 33–42)?

14

Jesus' Galilean Ministry—Later Stages

The Synoptic Gospels all continue to arrange their material topically, and so will we. Mark resumes his narrative with a group of Jesus' parables (4:1–34) followed by a series of some of his more spectacular miracles (4:35–6:6; 6:30–56). The sending of the Twelve (6:7–13) will be discussed later (below, pp. 331–33) and the death of John the Baptist (6:14–29) has already been treated (above, p. 257). In 7:1–9:50, Jesus withdraws from Galilee, both in spirit (by offering his most scathing critique of the Jewish traditions thus far) and in reality (by traveling to the north and to the east). Only brief periods of return to Galilee intervene before he begins his climactic journey to Jerusalem. This chapter thus falls naturally into three parts: Jesus' parables, his miracles, and his withdrawal from Galilee. The last of these sections will also treat his final days of ministry in Galilee before he embarks on the road to the cross.

Parables

Interpretive Method
A parable is a brief metaphorical narrative. The Greek *parabolē* comes from two words that mean "to throw alongside," alluding to the symbolic or analogi-

cal nature of a parable.[1] It is a story with two levels of meaning. *Parabolē*, like its Hebrew equivalent, *māshāl*, could refer to a wide variety of forms, including proverbs, allegories, prophetic discourses, and enigmatic sayings. Throughout most of the history of the church, Christians treated the parables of Jesus as detailed allegories. The most famous example was Augustine's treatment of the Good Samaritan (Luke 10:30–35) as a story about Adam who left the heavenly city and was attacked by Satan. The Law and the Prophets were unable to save him, but Christ, the Samaritan, did rescue him, taking him to the church for safekeeping until he should return. Such interpretation, however, entirely neglects the point of the story as an answer to the question of the lawyer, "Who is my neighbor?" (vv. 25–29, 36–37).[2]

At the end of the nineteenth century, Adolf Jülicher produced a voluminous work sounding the death knell to this type of interpretation.[3] Pointing out the inconsistencies and absurdities of the competing allegorical interpretations of virtually every parable of Jesus, Jülicher argued that each parable made only one main point and that details within the parables were not to be allegorized. They are merely lifelike reflections of first-century Palestine used in service of the overall point of a story. Thus the good Samaritan is simply an example of compassionate behavior for the needy that we should imitate (v. 37). Most twentieth-century interpretation has followed Jülicher and has stressed that the purpose of Jesus' parables is to illustrate truths about God's kingdom. Thus a lot of ink has been spilled over the question of whether the parables demonstrate God's kingly reign to be primarily future, primarily present, or some of each. The last of these options reflects the consensus that has emerged, particularly through the influential work of Joachim Jeremias.[4]

The most recent phase of research has stressed literary and structural analyses of the parables along with relevant sociological background. Jesus' stories are no mere illustrations but "weapons of warfare." They draw people into a seemingly innocuous story only to confront them with the demands of discipleship in ways that subvert conventional religious tradition and expectation.[5] Not every detail in a parable is lifelike. A Samaritan as hero would surely have shocked and even repulsed Jesus' Jewish audiences, but that is exactly the point: even one's mortal enemy is one's neighbor.

A minority view that has remained (and steadily grown) ever since Jülicher now challenges his two main points head-on: Jesus' parables may not be the

[1] See esp. J. W. Sider, *Interpreting the Parables: A Hermeneutical Guide to Their Meaning* (Grand Rapids: Zondervan, 1995).

[2] For a representative cross-section of such interpretations, see S. L. Wailes, *Medieval Allegories of Jesus' Parables: An Introduction* (Berkeley: University of California Press, 1987).

[3] A. Jülicher, *Die Gleichnisreden Jesu*, 2 vols. (Freiburg: Mohr, 1899). One of the oddities of modern scholarship is that this enormously influential work has never been translated into English.

[4] Jeremias, *Parables of Jesus*.

[5] See esp. B. B. Scott, *Hear Then the Parable: A Commentary on the Parables of Jesus* (Minneapolis: Fortress, 1989); cf. idem., *Re-imagine the World: An Introduction to the Parables of Jesus* (Sonoma, CA: Polebridge, 2001).

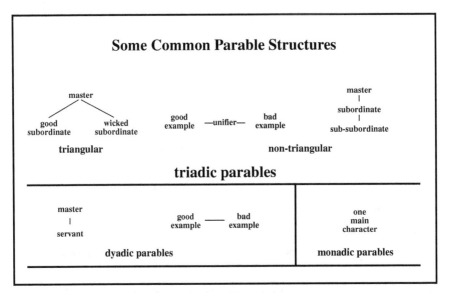

detailed allegories that the church often made them, but they do have a limited number of allegorical elements.[6] It is also not as obvious as Jülicher claimed that they teach only one central truth. If one focuses on the Samaritan, one finds a model of compassion. If one adopts the perspective of the man in the ditch, one learns that even one's enemy can be neighborly. But both of these points could have been made without ever introducing the priest and Levite. Presumably, at least a third lesson is present: religious duty (or whatever other motive may have been in these clerics' minds when they passed by the wounded man) is no excuse for lovelessness.[7]

I have elsewhere argued that a valuable working hypothesis for interpreting the parables may be to look for one main point associated with each main character or group of characters in the parables. More often than not, this approach leads to three main points associated, in turn, with a master figure and two contrasting subordinates. This approach seems to fit best with the way ancient rabbinic parables were interpreted, and it corresponds reasonably well to the way many literary narratives in various cultures communicate truth. The parables are generally lifelike, but usually, in at least one glaring instance in each text, something very unrealistic

---

[6] See now the compendious treatment by K. R. Snodgrass, *Stories with Intent: A Comprehensive Guide to the Parables of Jesus* (Grand Rapids and Cambridge: Eerdmans, 2008). Cf. esp. A. J. Hultgren, *The Parables of Jesus: A Commentary* (Grand Rapids and Cambridge: Eerdmans, 2000). Nuancing this approach to argue that key parables of Jesus are synecdoche (the part standing for the whole) or metonymy (one thing standing for something larger to which it is closely related) are, respectively, S. I. Wright, *Tales Jesus Told: An Introduction to the Narrative Parables of Jesus* (Carlisle: Paternoster, 2002); and R. Etchells, *A Reading of the Parables of Jesus* (London: Darton, Longman & Todd, 1998).

[7] Cf. K. E. Bailey, *Through Peasant Eyes: More Lucan Parables* (Grand Rapids: Eerdmans, 1980), 48; R. W. Funk, *Parables and Presence* (Philadelphia: Fortress, 1982), 29–34.

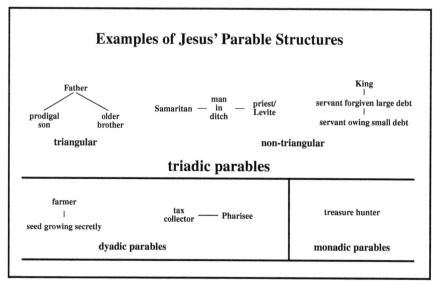

Examples of Jesus' Parable Structures

triangular — Father (prodigal son / older brother)

non-triangular — Samaritan — man in ditch — priest/Levite; King | servant forgiven large debt | servant owing small debt

triadic parables

dyadic parables — farmer | seed growing secretly; tax collector —— Pharisee

monadic parables — treasure hunter

provides a clue to the spiritual or metaphorical level of truth that Jesus intended to convey. The proper antidote to excessive allegorization is not to exclude allegory from parables altogether but to insist that any claim about a certain detail standing for something else in a given passage must fit with what an early first-century Jewish audience could have grasped. Jewish parables contain numerous "stock metaphors," with kings for God, harvests for judgment, servants for God's people, and so on. But labeling the "inn" in the parable of the Good Samaritan as the church is clearly anachronistic because the church did not yet exist.[8]

The contexts in which the Gospel parables occur support the mediating perspective advocated here. In two instances the evangelists themselves attribute to Jesus a relatively detailed allegorical interpretation of a given parable—for the sower (Mark 4:13–20 pars.) and for the wheat and weeds (Matt 13:37–43). The critical consensus since Jülicher has had to argue that these were the unhistorical creations of the early church that had already misunderstood Jesus. But with almost every parable, some brief introductory or concluding remarks by either Jesus or the evangelist narrating the story imply that main characters in the passage carry allegorical freight. For example, the prodigal son clearly stands for tax collectors and "sinners," with the Pharisees and scribes as the older brother (Luke 15:1–2).[9] Or in the parable of the children in the marketplace, the playmates proposing the different games probably stand for Jesus and John, while their recalci-

---

[8] See further Blomberg, *Interpreting the Parables*; idem., *Preaching the Parables: From Responsible Interpretation to Powerful Proclamation* (Grand Rapids: Baker, 2004). An excellent resource for sampling a large number of the oldest and most similar Jewish parables is H. K. McArthur and R. M. Johnston, *They Also Taught in Parables: Rabbinic Parables from the First Centuries of the Christian Era* (Grand Rapids: Zondervan, 1990).

[9] Cf. K. E. Bailey, *Finding the Lost: Cultural Keys to Luke 15* (St. Louis: Concordia, 1992), 109–93; and idem., *Jacob and the Prodigal: How Jesus Retold Israel's Story* (Downers Grove: IVP, 2003).

trant friends represent Jesus' and John's contemporaries who rejected them (Matt 11:16–19).[10]

Of course, many critics will jettison all of these contextual indicators as inauthentic. But if Jesus' earliest interpreters all uniformly misunderstood him, then it is rather presumptuous for us to claim to know better what Jesus originally meant. Better to utilize the contexts of the Gospels or else admit sheer ignorance![11] But if we follow the interpretations of the text, it is virtually impossible to limit a given parable to one single meaning. For example, is Luke 18:1–8 about persistent prayer (so v.1) or about God's eagerness to vindicate his elect (so vv. 6–8)? Those committed to the one-point rule of interpretation have debated endlessly which of these two truths is more central, but if the passage can make one point per character, the stalemate is resolved. The judge is a foil to teach about the character of God; the widow, about the proper response of his people.[12]

The majority of Mark's parables appear in chapter 4 of his Gospel. Matthew has additional parables in his parallel chapter 13. Luke's parallel section in chapter 8 is more abbreviated. Other parables in Matthew are primarily clustered towards the end of Jesus' life; others in Luke, in his distinctive central section. We will make selected comments about those passages later but focus primarily on Mark 4 and parallel material here.

The Parables of Mark 4, Matthew 13, and Luke 8

The Sower (Mark 4:1–9, 13–20) [Aland §122, 124]. Mark presents his first parable of Jesus as a "parable about parables" (cf. v. 13). Understanding it will open the door to understanding the rest of Jesus' stories, indeed the rest of his teaching more generally.[13] Here is another reason we must admit at least a limited amount of allegory in Jesus' parables, since this is one of those two passages in which Jesus himself gives a more detailed allegorical explanation (vv. 13–20). But the allegory is natural. Jewish literature provides ample precedent for viewing the seed as God's word (most notably 4 Ezra 9:30–33). Once this is established, then all the other details fall into place.[14]

The story is about the various ways God's word is received. At first glance there seem to be five main "characters" or foci—the sower and four different kinds of soil sown with seed. It seems clear from the principle of "end-stress" and from the nature of farming that the first three kinds of soil belong together as illustrations of inadequate response. The only harvest a farmer cares about is that

---

[10] E.g. Fitzmyer, *Luke I–IX*, 678–79. Cf. H. C. Kee, "Jesus: A Glutton and a Drunkard," *NTS* 42 (1996): 374–93.

[11] B. Gerhardsson, "If We Do Not Cut the Parables Out of Their Frames," *NTS* 37 (1991): 321–35.

[12] F. Stern, *A Rabbi Looks at Jesus' Parables* (Lanham, MD and Oxford: Rowman & Littlefield, 2006), 204–7.

[13] M. A. Tolbert, *Sowing the Gospel: Mark's World in Literary-Historical Perspective* (Minneapolis: Fortress, 1989).

[14] See esp. P. B. Payne, "The Authenticity of the Parable of the Sower and Its Interpretation," in *Gospel Perspectives*, vol. 1, 163–207.

which produces mature fruit. So, too, the only true disciples in this story are those who endure and yield an abundant harvest. Simon Kistemaker concisely captures the three main points associated with the sower, the bad soil, and the good soil, along with the three subpoints related to each of the three kinds of bad soil: "The Word of God is proclaimed and causes a division among those who hear; God's people receive the Word, understand it, and obediently fulfill it. Others fail to listen because of a hardened heart, a basic superficiality, or a vested interest in riches and possessions."[15] All of these responses are illustrated within the Gospels. Despite the widespread rejection of Jesus, his followers are assured that God's kingdom will advance. A hundredfold yield for an ancient harvest was unusual and points to the surprisingly large growth of God's reign.[16]

Jesus' Rationale for Speaking in Parables (Mark 4:10–12, 21–25, 33–34 pars.) [Aland §123, 125, 130]. In between the parable of the sower and its explanation, Jesus' disciples ask him why he uses this form of teaching. Jesus' reply has perplexed many. He seems to be saying that parables conceal truth rather than reveal it (vv. 11b–12). Yet even Jesus' enemies elsewhere catch on to his meaning in his parables (Mark 12:12 pars.). An adequate answer to this dilemma requires several considerations: (1) True, spiritual understanding in the Bible is never merely cognitive but also volitional. That is, unless one acts on Jesus' teaching by becoming an obedient disciple, one has not truly understood his message. (2) Jesus is using a shrewd rhetorical device. Parables, once they drive home their lessons, either attract or repel. Those who are not prepared to accept Jesus often become even more hostile against him (again cf. Mark 12:12 pars.), but others are convicted and repent. (3) Jesus is quoting Isa 6:9–10 from a context in which the prophet was told to pronounce judgment on an already rebellious nation. Yet the end of the chapter (6:13) promises that a godly remnant will reemerge. God never so exercises his judgment in this life as to prevent anyone who wants to move from becoming "outsider" to "insider" from doing so.[17]

In short, Jesus is revealing secrets not previously understood about God's plans for his people (vv. 11a, 21–23). For those already out of touch with God, his enigmatic yet forceful way of revealing these secrets in parables, to illustrate the coming kingdom of God, will further repel and repulse (cf. vv. 24–25). For those open to Jesus' claims, greater understanding and discipleship will result (cf. v. 33). Still, God is sovereign and is portrayed as choosing some people for treatment different from others. Douglas McComiskey explains this as Jesus "declar-

---

[15] S. Kistemaker, *The Parables: Understanding the Stories Jesus Told,* rev. ed. (Grand Rapids: Baker, 2002), 40.

[16] This point has been disputed, but see esp. R. K. McIver, "One Hundred-Fold Yield—Miraculous or Mundane? Matthew 13.8,23; Mark 4.8,20; Luke 8.8," *NTS* 40 (1994): 606–8. Cf. Marcus, *Mark 1–8,* 292–93.

[17] See Lane, *Mark,* 159: "The citation of Isa. 6:9f. does not mean that 'those outside' are denied the possibility of belief. It indicates that they are excluded from the opportunity of being further instructed in the secret of the Kingdom as long as unbelief continues." Cf. R. J. Kagarise, "Divine Sovereignty, Human Responsibility, and Jesus' Parables: The Structure and Meaning of Matthew 13:10–17," *EJ* 19 (2001): 29–41; France, *Mark,* 193–201.

ing that most Jews are still *corporately* in exile. Jesus divides his audience into two groups: disciples of Jesus, who as a group are restored from exile (at the very least the spiritual component) and are in the kingdom, and the crowd, who as a group (spiritually mixed) are still fundamentally characterized by corporate exile."[18] As for the "mystery" of the kingdom, this is best defined as the fact that God's reign is present but not with irresistible power, as so many expected or wanted.[19]

The Seed Growing Secretly (Mark 4:26—29) [Aland §126]. This parable contains only two foci—a farmer and his seed. From the farmer's perspective, the harvest is always uncertain, dependent on the vagaries of nature. From the perspective of this particular seed, a good crop is guaranteed, thanks to the sovereignty of God. Cranfield captures both of these concepts in his summary of the parable's meaning: "As seedtime is followed in due time by harvest, so will the present hiddenness and ambiguousness of the kingdom of God be succeeded by its glorious manifestation."[20] Or, with France, "despite appearances to the contrary, [the kingdom of God] is growing, and the harvest will come. It will come in God's time and in God's way, not by human effort or in accordance with human logic."[21]

The Mustard Seed and Leaven (Mark 4:30–32 pars.; Matt 13:33 par.) [Aland §128–129]. These short, twin parables arguably do make only one main point, though it may be expressed as the contrast between two foci—great endings out of small beginnings. The mustard seed was proverbial for its smallness and usually grew big enough to be considered only a medium-sized bush. This one becomes "the largest of all [lit.] vegetables" (Mark 4:32), so that Matthew and Luke can call it a "tree" (Matt 13:32; Luke 13:19). Luke also contextualizes the story for a Greek audience by specifying the "field" (Matt 13:31) or "ground" (Mark 4:31) as part of a "garden" (Luke 13:19). The illustration clearly surprises the audience with the size of the plant. So, too, God's kingdom will have a surprisingly large size and effect, considering its inauspicious start with Jesus' "ragtag" band of followers. The reference to the birds of the air nesting in its branches may allude to Ezek 17:23 or Dan 4:12, in which the birds stand for Gentiles. God's reign extends so widely that even non-Jewish people are included.[22]

A few commentators interpret the parable of the leaven differently, with the yeast as a symbol for corrupting influence within the church. Although leaven is often a symbol of corruption in the Bible, most notably in the context of using only unleavened bread for Passover, it is not always so used (cf. esp. Lev 23:17). The immediate context here makes a negative interpretation highly unlikely. Jesus frequently pairs parables that make the same basic point (e.g., Luke 14:28–32;

---

[18] D. S. McComiskey, "Exile and the Purpose of Jesus' Parables (Mark 4:10–13; Matt. 13:10–17; Luke 8:9–10)," *JETS* 51 (2008): 84–85 (italics his).

[19] See G. E. Ladd, *The Gospel of the Kingdom: Scriptural Studies in the Kingdom of God* (Exeter: Paternoster, 1959; Grand Rapids: Eerdmans, 2000), 56. Or as Marcus (*Mark 1–8*) phrases it, "God's new age is arriving, *despite all evidence to the contrary*" (italics his).

[20] C. E. B. Cranfield, *The Gospel according to St. Mark,* rev. ed. (Cambridge: CUP, 1977), 168.

[21] France, *Mark,* 215.

[22] Cf. Hultgren, *Parables of Jesus,* 396. Cf. Collins, *Mark,* 255–56.

15:3–10; Matt 13:44–46), and the Gospel writers frequently pair examples of balancing concerns for men and women (esp. Luke; see above, p. 164), Similar patterns are probably present in these two passages.[23]

The Wheat and Weeds and the Dragnet (Matt 13:24–30, 36–43, 47–50) [Aland §127, 131, 133]. The wheat and weeds is the second parable for which Jesus offers a detailed, allegorical interpretation (vv. 37–43). Again, the story line is one any first-century Jew could have readily grasped: God and Satan as opponents, each trying to thwart the other's schemes. The three main foci are the farmer, the wheat, and the weeds. The parable can be divided into three episodes, corresponding to which of these three holds, for a time, the upper hand. In the beginning, the weeds seem to have won (vv. 24–28a). Evil at times seems to have thwarted God's purposes in the world. Then it turns out that the wheat survives after all (vv. 28b–30a). God's kingdom will advance despite the seeming indistinguishability of his people from his enemies.[24] Finally, Judgment Day will sort all things out properly (v. 30b). The wicked will be destroyed, and the righteous will enjoy God's presence forever.

The parable of the dragnet (vv. 47–50) has the same triangular structure—fishers, good fish, and bad fish—but without the focus on the period of time preceding judgment. There is also perhaps a hint of the Gentile mission here: the fishers catch "all kinds" of fish (v. 47). The Greek word translated "kind" (*genos*) often refers to a "tribe" of people and is somewhat unusual when used with fish.[25]

The Treasure and the Pearl (Matt 13:44–46) [Aland §132]. As with the twin parables of the mustard seed and leaven, these short illustrations arguably make only one main point, though it can be expressed in at least two different ways: the inestimable value of the kingdom or the need to sacrifice all in order to obtain it. In the first parable, the man stumbles across the treasure; in the second, he is searching for costly pearls. Whether seeking or stumbling, people who find out about God's kingly reign should do whatever it takes to submit to it.[26]

The Scribe Trained for the Kingdom of Heaven (Matt 13:51–52) [Aland §134]. As the conclusion to Matthew's "sermon" in parables, Jesus compares the under-

---

[23] Hultgren, *Parables of Jesus*, 405–6. Cf. John Nolland, *Luke 9:21–18:34* (Dallas: Word, 1993), 727–30.

[24] Augustine's famous interpretation of this feature as justification for a mixed church of believers and unbelievers is unjustified. Jesus explicitly declares that "the field is the world" (v. 38). The confusion results from mistakenly equating God's kingdom (v. 41) with the church. God's kingly reign is exercised in the entire world, not just among his people, even if at times in different ways in each sphere. Cf. Turner, *Matthew*, 352.

[25] See esp. J. D. M. Derrett, "'ΗΣΑΝ ΓΑΡ 'ΑΛΙΕΙΣ (Mk. 1.16): Jesus's Fishermen and the Parable of the Net," *NovT* 22 (1980): 125–31.

[26] So almost all commentators. Occasionally, the suggestion is made that the treasure hunter and pearl fisherman stand for Christ who purchased our atonement. But a parallel rabbinic parable urges the children of Israel to purchase the Promised Land based on the analogy of a merchant buying a treasure in a far-away land, without implying any literal financial transaction or that Israel merits the purchase in any way. See *Mekilta* (a midrash on Exodus), tractate *Beshallach* 2.142ff. Cf. esp. B. H. Young, *The Parables: Jewish Tradition and Christian Interpretation* (Peabody: Hendrickson, 1998), 206–10.

standing disciple to a householder who brings out of his storehouse things old and new. As we discussed under Matt 5:17–20, Jesus' kingdom teaching has points of both continuity and discontinuity with the Jewish Law and the Old Testament age. Discerning followers will identify both.[27]

The Ministries of Various Women (Luke 7:36–8:3) [Aland §114–115]

The only other parable in all the Gospels not naturally treated in a later section of our book is the short story of the two debtors in Luke 7:41–43. In context, Jesus has been invited to dine with Simon the Pharisee. While at the banquet he becomes the subject of lavish attention by a disreputable woman (a prostitute?) who has come in off the street (vv. 36–38).[28] Aware of Simon's displeasure, he tells the story of two debtors, one forgiven a small debt and one forgiven a much larger debt. The answer to the parable's closing question as to who will be more grateful is obvious, but Jesus is intending to compare the woman with the debtor forgiven more and proceeds to declare her sins forgiven (v. 47).

The subsequent rationale, "for she loved much" (NIV) was used by traditional Catholic thought to justify a kind of works-righteousness. It is now widely agreed that Jesus is claiming that the woman's love demonstrated her prior forgiveness (cf. TNIV: "as her great love has shown"). Grammatically, "for" (or "because") modifies "I tell you," not "her many sins have been forgiven."[29] In other words, Jesus can *declare* that her sins are forgiven because of this public demonstration of the fact. As in Mark 2:17, Jesus does not question the Jewish leader's estimation of himself as someone in need of less forgiveness. The parable is open-ended and offers Simon continued fellowship as well, though not without challenging his lack of hospitality. The final word of the passage overall is an announcement of the woman's salvation (v. 50). The refrain, "Your faith has saved you," recurs in three other Gospel contexts (Mark 5:34 pars.; Mark 10:52 par.; Luke 17:19). In each of these other passages, Jesus has physically healed someone but seems to be pointing out that the individual has also become right with God. A similarly holistic understanding of salvation may be implied in Luke 7:50, although we have no explicit mention of the woman having been previously healed by Christ of any physical affliction.[30]

Luke nevertheless immediately proceeds to describe several women whom Jesus has healed, who in turn provide out of their material resources support for

[27] For application of this parable to the theme of excellence in theological education, see D. A. deSilva, "Scribes Trained for the Kingdom," *AshTJ* 29 (1997): 1–6.

[28] On the full range of options for who this woman described literally as "a sinner in the city" might be, with special attention to the contexts in which a woman's hair was unbound—not all of them sexually suggestive—see C. H. Cosgrove, "A Woman's Unbound Hair in the Greco-Roman World, with Special Reference to the Story of the 'Sinful Woman' in Luke 7:36–50," *JBL* 124 (2005): 675–92.

[29] J. J. Kilgallen, "Faith and Forgiveness: Luke 7,36–50," *RB* 112 (2005): 372–84. Cf. Fitzmyer, *Luke I–IX*, 691–92; and Green, *Luke*, 313–14.

[30] See further C. L. Blomberg, "'Your Faith Has Made You Whole': The Evangelical Liberation Theology of Jesus," in *Jesus of Nazareth: Lord and Christ*, ed. J. B. Green and M. Turner (Carlisle: Paternoster; Grand Rapids: Eerdmans, 1994), 75–93.

Jesus and his itinerant troupe. Indeed, they, too, go on the road with Jesus (Luke 8:1–3). Most notable among these is Mary Magdalene, who, contrary to popular lore, is not equated with the notorious woman of 7:36–50.[31] At least one of these women (Cuza's wife) would have been quite well-to-do; perhaps they all were. Although these women are apparently not as privileged as Christ's twelve closest (male) disciples, that they would travel with him would have proved scandalous enough in the ancient world. In view of Luke 10:38–42, he probably taught them and treated them as equal to any of the male members of the larger group of crowds and followers that regularly attached themselves to him.[32]

Historicity

It is widely agreed that the parables form the very core of the authentic teachings of Jesus. They reflect his distinctive and characteristic manner of illustrating the kingdom of God. Rabbinic Judaism has bequeathed to us over two thousand parables, but almost all are used in service of the exegesis of a text of Scripture, the one thing Jesus almost never does with his parables. Christ uses many of the same stock characters as the rabbis did—kings and masters for God; servants and sons for God's people; banquets and harvests for the final judgment; and so on.[33] His stories regularly depend on standard features of Palestinian peasant life, but almost always with a surprising twist somewhere in each passage. Purely at the level of aesthetics, many literary critics would consider Jesus' parables unrivaled. Of course, the parables have also been the subject of many hypotheses about the developing tendencies of the tradition, but these have often relied on assuming that pairs of very different parables (e.g., the wedding feast in Matt 22:1–10 and the great banquet in Luke 14:16–24) were necessarily variations of one original. The undeniably allegorical elements and interpretations have regularly been rejected, too, but if our argument for the existence of limited allegory in the parables is valid then these objections dissipate.[34]

Theological Distinctives

As elsewhere, the Synoptists' theological distinctives shine through in their unique treatments and arrangements of Jesus' parables. Mark highlights the disciples' lack of understanding and the obfuscatory role of the parables. He also sees a correct understanding of the parables as a key for discerning the meaning of his

---

[31] Nor is she ever said to be married, either in the Bible or in any other ancient historical source, to Jesus or anyone else. This is the stuff of popular fiction, from medieval times to the present.

[32] On several of these women, esp. Joanna, see further R. Bauckham, *Gospel Women: Studies of the Named Women in the Gospels* (Grand Rapids and Cambridge: Eerdmans, 2002). On Mary Magdalene, see esp. E. de Boer, *Mary Magdalene—Beyond the Myth* (London: SCM; Harrisburg: Trinity, 1997).

[33] See further D. Stern, *Parable in Midrash: Narrative and Exegesis in Rabbinic Literature* (Cambridge, MA: Harvard University Press, 1994).

[34] Cf. further P. B. Payne, "The Authenticity of the Parables of Jesus," in *Gospel Perspectives*, vol. 2, 329–44. On the so-called tendencies of the tradition, cf. esp. Jeremias' claims (*Parables of Jesus*, 23–114) with my critique (Blomberg, *Interpreting the Parables*, 79–94).

Gospel more generally.[35] Matthew has the largest grouping of parables in any one chapter of the Gospels at the exact literary center or pivot of his narrative. Chapter 13 forms the turning point at which Jesus increasingly focuses on his disciples and on people outside of Israel because of his homeland's growing rejection of him. This chapter is thus a key transition from Jesus' self-disclosure to Israel, and, as regularly in Matthew, a fulfillment of the Old Testament appears (Matt 13:35; cf. Ps 78:2).[36] Luke places the sower into a context of three passages that all deal with how to hear and obey the word of God correctly (Luke 8:4–21; cf. esp. vv. 11, 18, 21).[37] And the parable of the two debtors is embedded in a context that illustrates several of Luke's favorite themes, most notably Jesus' compassion for women and the moral outcasts of society and his holistic healing of body and spirit.

Miracles

Background Considerations

As with the parables, a number of broader issues must be raised before we can proceed immediately to interpreting the miracle stories in Mark 4–6 and elsewhere. Can people in today's scientific world believe in miracles? If there are examples of extraordinary phenomena that science cannot explain, how can we decide what is truly supernatural? How may we distinguish a genuine miracle from a hoax or a legend? Given that miracle stories proliferated in the ancient world, is it not more likely that the Gospel writers were simply portraying Jesus as yet another divine wonder-worker, deifying their heroes as so many Greeks and Romans had done? Might they have even borrowed from other myths in their composition of the Gospel accounts?

Detailed answers to these and related questions lie largely outside of our scope in this book, but they have appeared elsewhere.[38] Here we can simply sketch some directions in which the interested student might proceed. One's overall worldview and presuppositions loom large in this kind of discussion. If one believes in a supernatural God who rules the universe, miracles are a natural (though not necessary) corollary of such theism. If one believes in a closed universe where every event is determined by a mechanistic system of cause and

---

[35] See, e.g., K. R. Snodgrass, "A Hermeneutic of Hearing Informed by the Parables with Special Reference to Mark 4," *BBR* 14 (2004): 59–79.

[36] Even the parables discourse itself breaks into halves—first Jesus addresses "outsiders," then exclusively "insiders" (13:1–35, 36–52). For the probably chiastic structure of 13:1–52, see D. Wenham, "The Structure of Matthew XIII," *NTS* 25 (1979): 517–18. For an excellent treatment of this discourse more generally, see A. O. Ewherido, *Matthew's Gospel and Judaism in the Late First Century C.E.: The Evidence from Matthew's Chapter on Parables (Matthew 13:1–52)* (New York and Bern: Peter Lang, 2006). Cf. also W. Carter and J. P. Heil, *Matthew's Parables: Audience-Oriented Perspectives* (Washington, DC: Catholic Biblical Association of America, 1998), 36–95.

[37] Talbert, *Luke*, 97.

[38] See, e.g., C. Brown, *Miracles and the Critical Mind* (Exeter: Paternoster; Grand Rapids: Eerdmans, 1984); and R. D. Geivett and G. R. Habermas, *In Defense of Miracles: A Comprehensive Case for God's Actions in History* (Downers Grove: IVP, 1997). More briefly, cf. Blomberg, *Historical Reliability of the Gospels*, 104–36.

effect, the Gospel miracles will be incredible. In a post-Einstein, post-Heisenberg age, fewer and fewer philosophers of science are making such sweeping pronouncements.[39] The intelligent design movement, in which structures of "irreducible complexity" point to a Creator behind numerous biochemical features of the universe—most notably blood clotting, cilia, the human immune system, material transportation within cells, and the synthesis of nucleotides (the building blocks of DNA)—has commanded the support of an ever-increasing number of scientists, and not just Christian ones.[40] Almost every doctor who has been in practice for some length of time can testify to having treated patients who have been inexplicably healed of serious ailments shortly after times of intense prayer on their behalf. Other well-documented "paranormal" events show how little science really can make absolute pronouncements after all.[41] Indeed, many New Testament scholars today are prepared to grant that Jesus performed genuine healings, even if they do not accept every detail that the Gospels record about those healings.[42]

More difficult, however, are the so-called "nature miracles" that tend to be clustered in Mark 4:35–6:56. Can we really believe in Jesus stilling a storm, multiplying the loaves and fishes, walking on the water, or raising the dead? What about all the similar legends from antiquity associated with other religious figures that no one takes seriously as historical fact? Yet, upon closer inspection, the differences between these Gospel miracles and their apparent parallels in other religious literature outweigh the similarities, especially if one limits oneself to *pre-Christian* parallels. Jesus never works a miracle solely to benefit himself. He shows no interest in the merely spectacular and, indeed, regularly refuses to give a sign to satisfy skeptics. He does not first pray to God, mutter some religious incantation, or utilize magical objects. The way in which the miracle occurs is often left altogether unstated.[43]

---

[39] See, e.g., R. C. Koons, "Science and Theism: Concord, Not Conflict," in *The Rationality of Theism*, ed. P. Copan and P. K. Moser (London and New York: Routledge, 2003), 72–90; R. J. Berry, "Divine Action: Expected and Unexpected," *Zygon* 37 (2002): 717–27.

[40] See esp. M. J. Behe, *Darwin's Black Box: The Biochemical Challenge to Evolution*, rev. ed. (New York and London: Free Press, 2006). Cf. W. A. Dembski, *The Design Inference: Eliminating Chance through Small Probabilities* (Cambridge and New York: CUP, 1998); and idem., *Signs of Intelligence: Understanding Intelligent Design* (Grand Rapids: Brazos, 2001).

[41] See, e.g., the remarkable collections of apparently true stories of non-religious "miracles" in G. Ashe, *Miracle* (London: Routledge & Kegan Paul, 1978); and J. Houston, *Reported Miracles: A Critique of Hume* (Cambridge: CUP, 1994).

[42] Four works that all have passage-by-passage analyses of the credibility of the various Gospel miracles and that find most of them in most parts historically credible are H. van der Loos, *The Miracles of Jesus* (Leiden: Brill, 1965); L. Sabourin, *The Divine Miracles Discussed and Defended* (Rome: Catholic Book Agency, 1977); R. Latourelle, *The Miracles of Jesus and the Theology of Miracle* (New York: Paulist, 1988); and G. H. Twelftree, *Jesus the Miracle-worker.*

[43] For more on the key differences between the canonical accounts of Jesus' miracles and other miracle stories from the ancient Mediterranean world, see E. Eve, *The Jewish Context of Jesus' Miracles* (London and New York: SAP, 2002); and Blackburn, *Theios Anēr and the Markan Miracle Traditions.* Cf. also Klauck, *Apocryphal Gospels*, 223.

Instead, each of the more unusual "nature miracles" coheres closely with Jesus' teaching about the kingdom of God, teaching that is widely accepted as authentic. Indeed, it is interesting how themes from Jesus' parables, regularly cited as among the most indisputably authentic parts of the Gospels, closely match the points of his nature miracles. We have already seen the similarity between his turning water into wine and his parable of the wineskins (see above, p. 262). We will later highlight the remarkable correspondence between the miracle of withering the fig tree and Jesus' parable on the same topic (see below, pp. 367–68). In this section we will note how the miracles of Mark 4–6 all draw people's attention to Jesus and make them confront the question of his identity. They are enacted "object lessons" about the nature and arrival of the kingdom of God. In this light, we should perhaps think twice before automatically dismissing them as impossible.[44]

The Miracles of Mark 4:35–6:56 pars. and Related Passages

In the following passages we see Jesus' power and authority over disaster, demons, disease, and death.

Stilling the Storm (Mark 4:35–41 pars.) [Aland §136]. Countless generations of Christians have applied this passage as if it were a promise that Jesus would "still the storms of this life." In context, all three Synoptists agree that it had a very different purpose: to make people address the question, "Who is this? Even the wind and the waves obey him" (Mark 4:41 pars.). All of the details of the story highlight Jesus' sovereign authority and calm in the midst of chaos. In the Old Testament, it is Yahweh who alone has the power to still the raging tempests of the sea (cf. Jonah 1–2; Ps 104:7; 107:23–32). At Qumran, the fragment 4Q521 promises that the heavens and earth will obey God's Messiah. The gospel writers contrast Jesus' power with the disciples' lack of faith. Mark puts it pointedly: Even after the storms have calmed (unlike Matt 8:26), Jesus rebukes his followers: "Why are you so afraid? Do you still have no faith?" (Mark 4:40).[45] The miracle is meant to instill greater faith in Jesus as the Son of God. Jesus does not always still the storms of life, but he does promise to preserve spiritually those who believe in him in the midst of those storms.[46]

Exorcising the Gerasene[47] Demoniac (Mark 5:1–20 pars.) [Aland §137]. We have seen Jesus exorcise before, but now he faces a case of multiple demons in a man whom Mark, in particular, goes out of his way to describe as unusually sav-

---

[44] Cf. further C. L. Blomberg, "The Miracles as Parables," in *Gospel Perspectives*, vol. 6, 327–59.

[45] G. Bornkamm ("Stilling of the Storm in Matthew," in *Tradition and Interpretation in Matthew*, ed. Bornkamm, Barth and Held, 52–57) has made famous the argument that Matthew wants to portray the disciples in a considerably more positive light by limiting Jesus' rebuke to *before* the miracle and by stressing that they have "a little faith." We must grant that there are shades of emphases, but it is hard to see Matt 8:26 as a compliment under any circumstances!

[46] Garland, *Matthew*, 160.

[47] The best textual evidence has Mark and Luke reading "Gerasene," while Matthew has "Gadarene." Some textual variants in each Gospel opt for "Gergesene." While the cities of Gadara and Gerasa were a considerable distance from the eastern shores of Galilee, Khersa (modern-day Kursi) was close by. It is conceivable that either or both of the spellings in Greek, Gerasa and Gergesa, could have resulted from trying to transliterate Khersa, and it is probable that by Gadara Matthew means

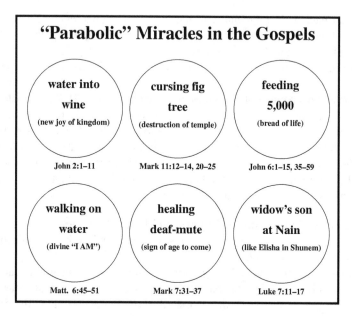

"Parabolic" Miracles in the Gospels

water into wine
(new joy of kingdom)

John 2:1–11

cursing fig tree
(destruction of temple)

Mark 11:12–14, 20–25

feeding 5,000
(bread of life)

John 6:1–15, 35–59

walking on water
(divine "I AM")

Matt. 6:45–51

healing deaf-mute
(sign of age to come)

Mark 7:31–37

widow's son at Nain
(like Elisha in Shunem)

Luke 7:11–17

age and afflicted. Jesus' power to deal with this situation, therefore, magnifies his divine authority all the more. As in Mark 1:24, the demons' knowledge of Christ reflects spiritual warfare, which Christ combats by eliciting their name, "Legion" (v. 9). Their banishment into the pigs reflects the fact that Christ's first coming was not the time of the complete and final judgment of the demonic realm (cf. Matt 8:29). They are still allowed to destroy life, but in this instance not human life. No self-respecting Jew would have bemoaned the loss of these pigs by the (Gentile?) farmers; they knew God's law against eating the pork for which the pigs were presumably being raised.[48] As with the stilling of the storm, one of the purposes of the miracle is to instill faith (Mark 5:19–20), though as with the miraculous fish catch, some of those who come immediately into the presence of one so powerful and holy plead with him to leave (v. 17).[49]

Many people today doubt the reality of demons or demon possession. Christians who have worked with those caught up in the occult can testify to too many strikingly similar incidents that still take place for such skepticism to prove con-

---

simply the larger region of Gadara, of which Khersa was a part, not the city with the same name. Cf. Cranfield, *Mark*, 176; and Witherington, *Mark*, 180.

[48] Gundry, *Mark*, 262: "Because of their revulsion against pigs, a Jewish audience would find humorous satisfaction in the drowning of the herd as well as in the self-banishment of the unclean spirits." So, too, Marcus, *Mark 1–8*, 352.

[49] Kernaghan (*Mark*, 105) suggests that the townspeople were frightened because it became clear that local evil could no longer be safely contained in the demon-possessed man, but they were not willing to turn to Jesus as the sole source of protection against that evil that could now destroy pigs helter-skelter.

vincing.[50] Others attribute more to direct demonic activity than is warranted. In Scripture, demon possession is regularly reserved for incidents involving several of the following phenomena observed in Mark 5:1–20 and parallels: "(1) a disregard for personal dignity (nakedness), (2) social isolation, (3) retreat to the simplest kind of shelter, (4) demons' recognition of Jesus' deity, (5) demonic control of speech, (6) shouting, and (7) extraordinary strength."[51] It is sometimes argued that Christians cannot be demon-possessed, only oppressed. However these are not terms that actually appear in Scripture, and, indeed, the expression often translated "demon possession" is merely the one Greek word *daimonizō* (literally, "to demonize"), which leaves unspecified the extent of the devil's power in such an individual. It is certainly true, though, that Scripture gives no grounds for the notion that a person, Christian or otherwise, can be influenced by the devil in the seven ways just noted apart from voluntarily yielding oneself to evil influences (cf. 1 John 4:4).

Raising Jairus' Daughter and Healing the Hemorrhaging Woman (Mark 5:21–43 pars.) [Aland §138]. As one of his trademarks, Mark sandwiches together two related stories here. They also belong together chronologically. Jesus is summoned to heal a synagogue ruler's daughter who is at the point of death. Before he can respond, he must also deal with a woman who has had an intermittent flow of blood for twelve years.[52] Both episodes involve Jesus risking defilement by touching the ritually impure. Yet the ministry and message of Jesus bring good news and cleanness for all the socially ostracized. In the case of the hemorrhaging woman, her ritual impurity might have been a more severe problem than even the physical malady, given its chronic (but obviously not life-threatening) condition.[53] In the case of Jairus' daughter, Jesus' power is disclosed via the greatest miracle he has worked to date—raising the dead. In both instances, Jesus indicates that the

---

[50] See, e.g., M. S. Peck, *Glimpses of the Devil: A Psychiatrist's Personal Accounts of Possession, Exorcism, and Redemption* (New York and London: Free Press, 2005); A. B. Finlay, *Demons: The Devil, Possession and Exorcism* (London: Blandford; New York: Sterling, 1999); and several of the chapters in A. N. S. Lane, ed., *The Unseen World: Christian Reflections on Angels, Demons and the Heavenly Realm* (Carlisle: Paternoster; Grand Rapids: Baker, 1996). For a global perspective, cf. A. S. Moreau, T. Adeyemo, D. G. Burnett, B. L. Myers and H. Yung, eds., *Deliver Us from Evil: An Uneasy Frontier in Christian Mission* (Monrovia: CA: MARC, 2002).

[51] Liefeld and Pao, "Luke," 163.

[52] Matthew breaks up Mark's sandwich and narrates each story in its own right (Matt 9:18–26). This relieves him of the necessity of having to tell of the arrival first of Jairus and then later of messengers who inform him that his daughter has died. As a result, he seems to contradict Mark and Luke as to when the girl passed away. But this kind of literary convention was common in antiquity and would not have been viewed as an "error." Moreover, time of death in the ancient world was notoriously imprecise. Cf. further R. H. Stein, *Difficult Passages in the Gospels* (Grand Rapids: Baker, 1984), 33–34. For a slightly different angle on essentially the same solution, see Witherington, *Mark*, 186 and n. 64.

[53] See esp. M. J. Selvidge, *Woman, Cult and Miracle Recital: A Redaction Critical Investigation on Mark 5:24–34* (Lewisburg, PA: Bucknell University Press; London: Associated Presses, 1990). For the view that concern for the woman's physical healing proved foremost for Jesus, see S. Haber, "A Woman's Touch: Feminist Encounters with the Hemorrhaging Woman in Mark 5:24–34," *JSNT* 26 (2003): 171–92.

faith of those seeking the miracles is an operative principle in helping to produce what they desire (Mark 5:34, 36). Thus a miracle can be designed to produce or strengthen faith (as above) or it can be worked in response to faith (as here).

Raising the Son of the Widow in Nain (Luke 7:11–17) [Aland §86]. At some point in his later Galilean ministry, Jesus also performed a second "revivification."[54] It occurs only in Luke's Gospel but is best treated in this survey of nature miracles. It contains striking parallels to the story of Elisha raising the Shunammite widow's son (2 Kgs 4:18–37), not least of which is the "coincidence" of Nain occupying approximately the same site as Old Testament Shunem (cf. also a similar miracle by Elijah in 1 Kgs 17:17–24). Did the crowd recognize these parallels when it responded by calling Jesus "a great prophet" (Luke 7:16)? It seems likely that at least Luke intends to call attention to the similarities. A later parallel of sorts attributed to Jesus' near contemporary Apollonius of Tyana has suggested to some that Luke sees Christ as fulfilling both Jewish and pagan hopes. But a mid–first-century date for Luke's writings would rule out his awareness of the Apollonius stories (recall above, pp. 34–35).

Healing the Blind Men and the Dumb Demoniac (Matt 9:27–34) [Aland §96–97]. As in Luke's, Matthew's accounts of Jesus' miracles during his Galilean ministry largely duplicate Mark's. But Matthew also adds a couple of brief passages unique to his Gospel. They run closely parallel to the kind of miracle that Jesus will perform again later (cf. Matt 12:22–24; Mark 7:31–37; 10:46–52), so we will reserve comments for those occasions.

Rejection in Nazareth (Mark 6:1–6 pars.) [Aland §139]. As noted above, this is probably the same incident that Luke amplifies and places earlier in his outline (Luke 4:16–30; cf. above, p. 271). The distinctive of Mark's more chronological placement is to highlight that after working so many great deeds elsewhere, Jesus could do few miracles in his hometown because of their lack of faith (vv. 5–6). Matthew rewords Mark's account slightly to make it clear that it was not that Christ was impotent, but that he chose to respond differently because of the Nazarenes' skepticism (Matt 13:58).[55] This passage also contains the sole references in the Gospels to Jesus as a carpenter and son of a carpenter (Mark 6:3; Matt 13:55). It is unique in naming Jesus' brothers and referring to his sisters.[56]

---

[54] The word "resurrection" is perhaps best reserved for what happened to Jesus and will one day happen to all believers—a reawakening to life that will never again end. M. J. Harris uses "revivification" and "reanimation" for a return to life that presumably again later ended in death, in his excellent survey of this category of miracles, "'The Dead Are Restored to Life': Miracles of Revivification in the Gospels," in *Gospel Perspectives*, vol. 6, 295–326.

[55] Witherington (*Mark*, 200) insightfully observes: "The problem with hometown folks is that they know both too much and too little about a person. What they know has to do with their memories of what a person was like while growing up and becoming an adult. Once one has left town and gone elsewhere, they know little about what is or is not true about the person over that period of time."

[56] Contemporary Catholic commentators increasingly recognize that the older Roman view that the Greek words for "brothers" and "sisters" here are to be translated as "cousins" rested on dogma rather than exegesis. The two major options for how Joseph and Mary had these other children are that they were born of normal sexual relations *after* Jesus' birth or, probably less likely, that they were Joseph's children by a *former* marriage. See esp. Meier, *A Marginal Jew*, vol. 1, 324–32.

Feeding the Five Thousand (Mark 6:30–44, 53–56 pars.) [Aland §145–146, 148–149]. Here Jesus' motive is neither to instill nor to respond to faith but merely to exhibit compassion (Mark 6:34). However it is not primarily his compassion for the crowd's hunger, but "because they were like sheep without a shepherd," an allusion to Ezekiel 34 (esp. v. 5), in which the prophet laments how Israel languished without adequate leadership. This chapter reverberates with messianic overtones as God predicts a coming day when his people will experience proper shepherding. The feeding of the five thousand also harks back to the time of Moses when God first provided bread in the wilderness. In view of Deut 18:18, many Jews came to expect that the Messiah would reenact this miracle on a grander scale (for further Old Testament parallels, cf. Ps 132:15; 1 Kgs 17:9–16; and 2 Kgs 4:42–44).[57] As with the previous passages, this "gift-miracle"[58] is also fundamentally Christocentric—pointing out Jesus as the Messiah.

John's account brings out this Christology most explicitly as he narrates Jesus' subsequent discourse in the Capernaum synagogue (John 6:25–59) and its aftermath (vv. 60–71). Here Jesus identifies himself as the Bread of Life (vv. 35, 48). He is responding to a request to repeat Moses' miracle (vv. 30–31). What more did they want after the previous feeding? Or is this a different crowd who had not been present on that occasion? In Jesus, God is giving his people true, spiritual bread from heaven (vv. 32–33, 41–42, 50–51).[59] The messianic implications of the feeding miracle were not lost on the crowd present then, but they misinterpreted what kind of Messiah Jesus was, as they were hoping for an earthly king (v. 15).

Five additional themes emerge from Jesus' discourse: (1) Instead of doing works to please God, Jesus insists that the solitary work needed is to have faith in him (vv. 28–29).[60] (2) Whether or not the questioners in verses 30–31 had seen or heard of the feeding of the five thousand, John's literary juxtaposition of miracle and sermon reinforces his theme that faith based on signs may often prove inadequate. If the feeding miracle can't convince, probably nothing will. (3) Jesus preserves his true followers; he will lose none of those the Father has given him (vv. 37–40). Yet God's drawing power in giving people to Christ does not come "by the savage constraint of a rapist, but by the wonderful wooing of a lover" (v. 44).[61] He knows that Judas was never truly his but is destined to betray him (vv. 64, 70–71). (4) One must eat Christ's flesh and drink his blood (vv. 51–58). These words are often seen as a foreshadowing of the Eucharist, but nothing in John's immediate context would indicate that Jesus' audience could have understood them thus, and the words of the Last Supper consistently relate the bread

---

[57] Cf. Marcus, *Mark 1–8*, 404–21.

[58] The term comes from Gerd Theissen, *The Miracle Stories of the Early Christian Tradition* (Edinburgh: T&T Clark; Philadelphia: Fortress, 1983), 103–6. Theissen offers perhaps the best form-critical subdivision of the miracle stories available.

[59] On this theme, and on the structure and significance of the sermon more generally, see P. Borgen, *Bread from Heaven* (Leiden: Brill, 1965).

[60] For detailed elaboration, see P. W. Ensor, *Jesus and His Works: The Johannine Sayings in Historical Perspective* (Tübingen, Mohr, 1996).

[61] Carson, *John*, 293.

to Christ's body, not to his flesh. Further, on this interpretation, verses 51, 53–54, and 56–58 would seem to demand that the Eucharist itself imparted salvation, a doubtful interpretation in view of verse 63 (in which Christ's "words" give life). The learned Jew would recall that God's Wisdom, too, called out to people to eat of her and her food (Sir 24:19–21; Prov 9:5). More likely, consuming Christ's flesh and blood are graphic metaphors for people being associated so closely with Jesus that they also suffer and die for him if necessary.[62] (5) The larger crowd of disciples falls away, leaving only the Twelve (v. 66). In a Johannine equivalent of sorts to Peter's confession on the road to Caesarea Philippi (Mark 8:27–30 pars.), Peter speaks for the Twelve, confessing Jesus alone as the "Holy One of God" whose words impart "eternal life" (vv. 68–69).[63]

Walking on the Water (Mark 6:45–52 pars.) [Aland §147]. Immediately after his feeding miracle, Jesus sends the disciples on ahead of him to cross back over the lake to Galilee.[64] After a severe storm stalls their progress, he appears to them walking on the lake. Although the storm ceases and the boat reaches its destination, once again the primary point behind the miracle is not one of physical rescue. Rather Christ is revealing the transcendent dimension of his nature. "It is I" (Gk., *egō eimi*) in Mark 6:50 echoes the identical words of Exod 3:14, with its divine name, "I AM." So, too, the verb "pass by" (v. 48) is the same as used in the LXX of Exod 33:19 and 34:6 for God "passing by" (i.e., revealing himself to) Moses. Job 9:8 and Ps 77:19 provide further Old Testament background for Yahweh as the one who treads upon the sea. Christ is here disclosing his divine nature.[65]

Unique to Matthew is the episode of Peter's attempt to imitate his Lord (Matt 14:28–31). Indeed, Matthew has five distinctive insertions involving Peter in chapters 14–18 (cf. also 15:15; 16:17–19; 17:24–27; and 18:21). None is very flattering; Matthew is arguably trying to combat an overly exalted view of Peter that was beginning to creep into certain circles already in his day.[66] As noted above (p. 149), Matthew ends his version of the miracle far more positively than Mark

---

[62] C. K. Barrett (*Church, Ministry, and Sacraments in the New Testament* [Exeter: Paternoster; Grand Rapids: Eerdmans, 1985], 74–75) believes that John wrote when the Eucharist was in danger of becoming a mechanical rite believed to secure salvation in and of itself, and so he dissociated these traditions from any overtly Eucharistic context to make it clear that faith in Christ alone was salvific. As in John 3:5, with "born of water," however, John's readers may be meant to see a secondary, sacramental allusion. Cf. esp. D. Gibson, "Eating Is Believing? On Midrash and the Mixing of Metaphors in John 6," *Them* 27 (2002): 5–15; Witherington, *Mark*, 219.

[63] See further P. N. Anderson, *The Christology of the Fourth Gospel: Its Unity and Disunity in the Light of John 6* (Tübingen: Mohr, 1996).

[64] A contradiction has been alleged between Mark 6:45 ("to Bethsaida") and John 6:17 ("to Capernaum"), but if the disciples were setting out from due east of the Sea of Galilee, both cities would be to the northwest, with the former as possibly a stopping point en route to the latter. The storm, as it turns out, blows them far enough south so that they actually land at Gennesaret (Mark 6:53), more directly to the east.

[65] Cf. further J. P. Heil, *Jesus Walking on the Sea: Meaning and Gospel Functions of Matt. 14:22–23, Mark 6:45–52 and John 6:15b–21* (Rome: BIP, 1981); and Patrick J. Madden, *Jesus' Walking on the Sea: An Investigation of the Origin of the Narrative Account* (Berlin and New York: de Gruyter, 1997).

[66] A. Stock, "Is Matthew's Presentation of Peter Ironic?" *BTB* 17 (1987): 64–69.

does, but confession of Jesus as Son of God (14:33) will recur with serious mis-understanding in 16:16–23, showing that "hardened hearts" could still have been present even in this context (Mark 6:52). Mark links this lack of understanding to the feeding of the five thousand. Had the disciples fully captured the christologi-cal implications there, they would have better caught the point of Jesus' walking on the water as well.[67] Mark 6:53–56 generalizes about Jesus' miracle-working activity and brings this subsection of his Gospel to an end.

Additional Distinctive Material in Matthew and Luke (Matt 11:20–30 par.) *[Aland §108–110].* Understanding and properly responding to Christ's ministry of miracles is no trivial pursuit. Jesus here berates cities in which his ministry was prominent for their failure to repent, and he notes that it will be more tolerable for God's archenemies in Old Testament times (Tyre, Sidon, Sodom, and Gomorrah) than for these towns (vv. 20–24). On the other hand, those who are responding are the "babes" of this world—those who do not pride themselves in their religious or intellectual credentials (vv. 25–27). As we see consistently in Scripture, these verses balance a predestinarian motif with a clear indication of human free will ("No one knows the Father except . . . those to whom the Son chooses to reveal him" and "Come to me, all you who are weary and burdened" in vv. 27–28). Together these two passages (vv. 20–24, 25–30) stress that God demands much of those to whom much is given, but his yoke (in contrast to those Jews taking upon themselves the "yoke of the Torah"?) is easy and his burden light (vv. 28–30). With the greater demand comes a greater empowerment.[68]

Historicity

We have already noted the distinctive problems posed by the nature miracles and tried to reply briefly to certain philosophical, scientific, and historical objec-tions to their credibility. We have stressed their coherence with Jesus' central theme of the kingdom of God. They are not primarily miracles of rainmaking as with Jesus' contemporary, Honi the Circle-Drawer. They are not myths of fertility as with the cyclical births and resurrections of Greco-Roman religion. They show great restraint in detail compared to the later Christian apocrypha. Their closest parallels are found in the Elijah/Elisha material of 1 and 2 Kings; Old Testament background should enhance the case for their authenticity. As with the physi-cal healings and exorcisms, these miracle stories appear in multiple sources and forms, some of them arguably pre-Markan.[69] And they bear the signs of realism in a Palestinian milieu, down to minute detail. For example, in Galilee, women mourners walked in front of a bier rather than behind it as in Judea. Thus it was natural for Jesus to address the widow of Nain before approaching the casket

---

[67] S. W. Henderson, "'Concerning the Loaves': Comprehending Incomprehension in Mark 6.45–52," *JSNT* 83 (2001): 3–26. She stresses that the disciples also failed to grasp "their own active partici-pation in the inbreaking, eschatological kingdom that Jesus inaugurates" (26).

[68] On 11:25–30, see esp. C. Deutsch, *Hidden Wisdom and the Easy Yoke* (Sheffield: JSOT, 1987).

[69] See esp. P. J. Achtemeier, "Toward the Isolation of Pre-Markan Miracle Catenae," *JBL* 89 (1970): 265–91. Cf. Marcus, *Mark 1–8*, 371–72.

(Luke 7:13–14).[70] But would Luke have likely "got this right" if he were inventing the story, given that Judean customs were in general better known? These miracles also include Aramaic words transliterated into Greek (e.g., *Talitha koum* in Mark 5:41) and embarrassing details (such as Christ's question "Who touched my clothes?" in Mark 5:30). The original Christological significance is usually somewhat blurred by later theological overlays (eucharistic motifs at the feeding of the five thousand, questions about faith and discipleship in the two miracles on the storm-tossed sea, etc.). All in all, unless one simply rules out such phenomena *a priori*, a substantial case for their historicity can be marshaled.

Theology and Conclusion

As with other portions of the life of Christ, each evangelist has his own distinct theological emphases surrounding Jesus' miracles. Mark contrasts the miracle-working Messiah with the suffering Messiah by his relegation of almost all of his miracles to the first half of his Gospel (chaps. 1–8). Matthew consistently abbreviates or omits peripheral details from Mark to streamline his accounts and focus the Christological issues more clearly. Luke has been said to have a slightly more "magical" view of Jesus' miracles (e.g., Luke 8:44–46) and to stress the conquest of Satan's power and domain (e.g., 10:18–20; cf. also 8:35 with 39; 13:11–12).[71] John, as we have seen, links miracles with discourses as signs to encourage faith, but as faith matures, signs may well prove less necessary.

The purposes of Jesus' miracle-working ministry have been described as "evidential, evangelistic, empathetic, and eschatological."[72] There is no predictable relationship between miracles and faith. Sometimes faith helps to produce a miracle; sometimes a miracle is meant to instill faith where it is absent. Challenging Jewish tradition, breaking down social barriers, and demonstrating compassion for the suffering are all important subordinate themes. But the primary focus is Christological—to demonstrate that Jesus is the divine Messiah and that the kingdom of God is now breaking into human history with new force (cf. Matt 11:2–6 par.; Luke 11:20 par.). Miracles by definition are exceptional events; we should never expect or demand them of God. We cannot predict when he, in his sovereignty, may work one, though there is some slight evidence from history and human experience that they may be more prevalent whenever God's reign is forcefully advancing into an area largely enslaved by the powers of darkness.

Withdrawal from Galilee and Return

After the bulk of his Galilean ministry, Jesus withdraws from his homeland and spends a fair amount of time in provinces to the north and east. Even after his return to Galilee, the Synoptics still describe his repeated departures. It is also during this time that he elicits Simon Peter's dramatic confession that Jesus is

---

[70] Harris, "Revivification," 298–99.

[71] J. M. Hull, *Hellenistic Magic and the Synoptic Tradition* (London: SCM, 1974), 87–115.

[72] D. J. Moo, "Synoptic Gospels" course notes, Trinity Evangelical Divinity School, Deerfield, IL: Fall Quarter, 1978.

the Christ. Still, Peter does not understand that the Christ must suffer, so Jesus increasingly turns to address this topic. This shift in focus is regularly perceived as a major pivot in the life of Christ, as he moves into his third main period of ministry. This period of "rejection" (recall above, p. 225) will culminate in his final journey to Jerusalem and the fate that awaits him there. For the remainder of this chapter we will survey these developments under two main headings: Jesus' withdrawal from Galilee, followed by Peter's confession and its aftermath.

Withdrawal

For this section of Christ's life we are dependent solely on Matthew and Mark. Mark 7:1–8:26 has no corresponding parallels in Luke. This section of Mark forms the bulk of what source critics call Luke's "Great Omission" because Luke does not want to digress from his geographically oriented outline that traces Christ's ministry from Galilee, through Samaria and Judea, to Jerusalem (recall above, p. 162).

Preparation for Ministry outside Israel: On Defilement (Mark 7:1–23 par.) *[Aland §150]*. Immediately before Jesus literally departs from Jewish territory, we read of an episode that depicts him breaking from Jewish theology as dramatically as at any point thus far.[73] Jewish leaders from Jerusalem have come to Galilee and criticize Jesus for allowing his disciples to violate the ceremonial cleanliness laws of handwashing (vv. 1–5). These were part of the oral but not the written Torah. Jesus replies first by criticizing the hypocrisy of another portion of the Pharisees' traditions, the laws of *corban* (vv. 6–13). Although there is some uncertainty over the details, the basic practice seems to have been one of dedicating donated monies to God for use in the temple after one's death. Meanwhile a person could still gain income from the funds, but no one else was allowed to benefit from them, even if they were in dire need.[74]

Having dissociated himself from the oral laws more generally, Jesus returns to the specific issue of handwashing to declare that it is not food and drink (which go into the body) but evil thoughts, speech, and behavior (which come out of the body) that truly defile (vv. 14–23). The principle enunciated here had the potential of abolishing the entire ritual law of the Old Testament. By Mark's day, the evangelist could add the parenthetical explanation that Jesus' words overturned all the dietary laws (v. 19b).[75] Of course, if all foods are clean, then ritual handwashing is unnecessary and the major barrier to fellowship with the Gentiles is lifted. It is unlikely that the sweeping implications of all this were understood on the spot. Peter later had to experience a threefold vision from God declaring unclean

---

[73] Now two of the three "badges of national righteousness" (see above, p. 49) have been directly challenged—Sabbath keeping and the dietary laws. Guelich (*Mark 1:8–26*, 362), following Gnilka, remarks, "A spiritual break precedes a geographical break in Jesus' ministry with Israel." Cf. also Keener, *Matthew*, 414.

[74] Witherington (*Mark*, 226) remarks, "It is truly hard to imagine a more strongly worded way of enforcing the obligations of children to their parents, especially of dependent parents."

[75] Cf. C. Stetler, "Purity of Heart in Jesus' Teaching: Mark 7:14–23 par. as an Expression of Jesus' Basileia Ethics," *JTS* 55 (2004): 467–502.

food clean, followed by his encounter with the Gentile Cornelius who repented in response to Peter's preaching, before the church understood on a widespread basis (Acts 10:1–11:18).[76] Matthew characteristically heightens the polemic with his reference to the Jewish leaders as blind guides (Matt 15:14).

Exorcising the Syrophoenician Woman's Daughter (Mark 7:24–30 par.) [Aland §151]. Jesus now withdraws from Galilee. At first, his theology seems as nationalist or exclusivist as the Jewish leaders' approaches. A Gentile woman requests healing for her daughter, but Jesus replies that he "was sent only to the lost sheep of Israel" (Matt 15:24). This verse appears only in Matthew's Gospel and fits his Jewish particularism. In fact, Jesus calls the woman and her daughter "dogs," the standard Jewish epithet used to insult Gentiles (Mark 7:27 par.)! Nevertheless, the woman offers a clever retort, is praised for her faith, and receives the healing she requested. What is going on here? At least three observations may help us reply: (1) Jesus is following the consistent biblical pattern of going to the Jew first and then to the Greek (cf. Rom 1:16 with Mark's "first" in v. 27 here). The time for wholesale Gentile ministry will not come until after his resurrection. (2) The diminutive form *kunarion* has suggested to some that Jesus is more affectionate in referring to the woman's child as a household pet—a "little puppy." More probably, he is being deliberately blunt, knowing the woman's faith and wanting to draw it out for the sake of those around him as she demonstrates her tenacity.[77] (3) Galileans resented the Syrian provincial leadership that often doled out governmental funds so that Jews received only the "crumbs." Jesus may be seeing how the woman will respond if he suggests the tables be turned for a change.[78]

Healing the Deaf-Mute in the Decapolis (Mark 7:31–37 par.) [Aland §151–52]. Jesus remains in Gentile territory for this next miracle. It is unique in that the recipient of the healing is a person who "could hardly talk" (v. 32). The word used here (*mogilalos*) is found elsewhere in the Greek Bible only in the LXX of Isa 35:6, where such a person is said to be able to "shout for joy" when the messianic age arrives. This is also one of three passages in which Jesus uses spit or saliva as part of the healing process (Mark 7:23, 8:33; John 9:6). This practice has parallels

---

[76] Cf. D. L. Bock, *Acts* (Grand Rapids: Baker, 2007), 389–90. Bock notes, too, that the apostolic decree does not imply that the dietary laws remain in force for Jewish Christians. *Contra* D. J. Rudolph, "Jesus and the Food Laws: A Reassessment of Mark 7:19b," *EQ* 74 (2002): 291–311. Cf. also C. L. Blomberg, "The Christian and the Law of Moses," in *Witness to the Gospel*, ed. Marshall and Peterson, 397–416.

[77] "In Mark, the focus is on the aptness of the woman's verbal reply. She has passed the honor challenge and is rewarded for her good answer. Thus the scene needs to be seen as Jesus testing a foreigner, not as Jesus merely reflecting the parochialisms of his day" (Witherington, *Mark*, 251).

[78] For these and other approaches, see G. S. Jackson (*"Have Mercy on Me": The Story of the Canaanite Woman in Matthew 15.21–28* [London and New York: SAP, 2002]), who then goes on to propose the quite different view that the account for Matthew functions as a paradigm for how the "worst" of outsiders may take on Jewish-Christian identities and become part of his community. This approach requires the unlikely view that the story functioned in almost diametrically opposite fashions in Matthew and Mark. For a provocative feminist-liberationist approach, cf. L. A. Guardiola-Sáenz, "Borderless Women and Borderless Texts: A Cultural Reading of Matthew 15:21–28," *Semeia* 78 (1997): 69–81.

in primitive medicine and magic. It may be Jesus' way of contextualizing his ministry for a Hellenistic audience in order to communicate to them that he is about to heal a person, even if more supernatural forces are also at work.[79]

Feeding the Four Thousand and Follow-Up Conversations (Mark 8:1–21 pars.) [Aland §153–155]. The geographical sequence suggests that Jesus is still outside Galilee because after the feeding miracle he crosses the lake and lands at Magadan (probably another name for Magdala) on the west bank (Matt 15:39).[80] The miracle is remarkably similar to the feeding of the five thousand, but this time Jesus' compassion reflects a serious hunger problem among the crowds (Mark 8:2–3). Nevertheless, the abundant provision of food again points to Jesus as the Messiah (cf. above, p. 315). As this episode forms part of Jesus' withdrawal from Galilee, it is attractive to suggest that Jesus is repeating for a mixed or predominantly Gentile audience the type of miracle he previously worked for a more Jewish crowd. Previously, they had collected twelve baskets of leftovers (the number of the tribes of Israel); this time they pick up seven (a number of completeness, standing for all of humanity). Even the Greek words for "basket" in the two passages differ (*kophinos* and *spuris*), corresponding, respectively, to characteristic Jewish and Hellenistic bags or sacks. Jesus will be the Bread of Life for both Jews and Gentiles.[81] The disciples' obtuseness seems total (v. 4), given their presence at the earlier feeding miracle, but Matt 15:33 may suggest that this time they felt the onus was on them to imitate Jesus ("Where could *we* get enough bread?")[82]

Two dialogues follow immediately on the heels of the miracle (Mark 8:1–10). Back in Galilee, certain Pharisees request a sign from heaven (vv. 11–13). Coming just after the feeding miracle, the request is highly ironic. Clearly, they were looking for a sign that could be interpreted in no other way than that God was at work, but what kind of miracle would ever meet this criterion for a die-hard skeptic (cf. Luke 16:31)? Jesus refuses their request. Even were such a sign possible, God does not work miracles "on demand," particularly when they are demanded by his critics. "In the Synoptic Gospels the demand for 'signs' is itself a sign of attempting to gain by empirical means what can only be gained by faith and trust."[83]

Second, Jesus again crosses the lake with his disciples (vv. 14–21). In verse 15, they misunderstand his warning about figurative leaven (the corrupting influ-

---

[79] Collins (*Mark*, 372–73) prints partially parallel Greco-Roman texts in some detail.

[80] The parallel in Mark 8:10 refers to the otherwise unattested "Dalmanutha." But Magdala may be a variant of the name *Migdal Nunya* ("fish tower"), referring to a village just outside of Tiberias. Removing the first syllable from these two words would then yield *Dalnunya*, a form that could easily give rise in translation to Dalmanutha.

[81] On these parallels and on other examples of Jesus repeating in Gentile territory what he has done at home, see E. K. Wefald, "The Separate Gentile Mission in Mark," *JSNT* 60 (1995): 3–26. Cf. France, *Matthew*, 600.

[82] Cf. Nolland, *Matthew*, 643.

[83] Edwards, *Mark*, 236–37.

ence of the Jewish leaders[84]) as a rebuke for not bringing enough literal bread. Jesus reminds them of the two feeding miracles to try to get them thinking at the metaphorical level again. He who provided so abundantly can surely meet their physical needs, but they need to recognize who Jesus is and not misunderstand as the Jewish leaders have. One may also hear overtones about Jew-Gentile unity here. Just as Jesus provided bread for both groups, so one loaf (v. 14) will be adequate for everyone's needs as they again head across into pagan territory.[85]

Healing the Blind Man in Bethsaida (Mark 8:22–26) [Aland §156]. As Jesus ministers near the boundary of Jewish and Gentile territory, we read about the only "two-stage" healing in the Gospels. As with the use of saliva, we may be meant to recognize God's sovereignty in healing people with whatever methods he chooses.[86] Given the disciples' spiritual blindness in the preceding passage, it is difficult not to see also a deliberately metaphorical meaning in the story. Like this blind man, the disciples begin with only partial sight and require further illumination (see esp. 8:18). This will come in the very next passage, with Peter's confession, but subsequent events will demonstrate that only after the resurrection will the disciples really understand as they should.

Peter's Confession and Its Aftermath

The Pivot of Jesus' Ministry (Mark 8:27–9:1 pars.) [Aland §158–60]. Once again Jesus is traveling outside of Galilee, this time in the vicinity of Caesarea Philippi. It may not be coincidental that here an ancient center of worship of the Hellenistic god Pan thrived. The city Paneas had also been renamed in honor of the emperor and Herod Philip. Where more appropriate to determine if Jesus' followers understood his true, divine identity? In short compass and in sharp juxtaposition to each other, Peter expresses the high and low points of the disciples' christological understanding. Matthew's account here is by far the fullest (Matt 16:13–28).

On the one hand, Peter confesses that Jesus is "the Christ, the Son of the living God" (v. 16). In context, this is a substantial improvement on the popular belief that Jesus was merely one of the prophets (v. 14). It is a divinely revealed insight (v. 17). It elicits Jesus' promise that he will build his church "on this rock" (v. 18). Extensive medieval debates have made it difficult to read this text as Jesus originally intended it. Roman Catholicism at the time of the Reformation used this pas-

---

[84] For incisive contemporary application, esp. for pastoral and theological students, see R. C. Newman, "Breadmaking with Jesus," *JETS* 40 (1997): 1–11. We, too, must avoid the errors of both Pharisees and Sadducees, positioning ourselves in between conservative and liberal extremes, withdrawal from and assimilation to society, dogmatism and skepticism, legalism and antinomianism (7–8).

[85] So esp. N. A. Beck, "Reclaiming a Biblical Text: The Mark 8:14–21 Discussion about Bread in the Boat," *CBQ* 43 (1981): 49–56.

[86] J. K. Howard ("Men as Trees, Walking: Mark 8.22–26," *SJT* 37 [1984]: 163–70) observes that this is the closest miracle of Jesus to an actual medical healing, particularly if the blindness was not congenital, the man had severe cataracts, the saliva washed away dried secretions, and the pressure of Jesus' fingers on the man's eyes was able first to dislodge and then to relodge the lens in the proper position.

sage to support the authoritative ministry of each successive bishop of Rome (i.e., pope) in an unbroken chain of apostolic succession from the days of Peter onward. Luther, in turn, argued that the rock was Christ. Various scholars and theologians before and since have adopted a mediating position, that it was Peter's confession of Jesus as the Christ that was the "rock" on which the church would be built.[87]

In the original setting, however, it makes little sense to take the rock as anything but Peter himself. Why else make a play on words using Peter's name ("You are 'a rock' [Gk. *Petros*] and on this rock [*petra*]. . .")?[88] Peter has just told Jesus who he is; now Jesus tells Peter who he is. What is more, soon Jesus will call Peter a different kind of rock ("a stumbling stone"—v. 23), which contrasts all the more poignantly with this conversation if he has here directly called Peter a foundational stone. Recognizing Peter as the rock in no way commits us to any doctrines about the papacy or apostolic succession. There is nothing of these Roman traditions in this context, and indeed Matt 18:18 will apply the identical authority granted to Peter in 16:19 to the entire community of disciples. Peter is foundational in that he was the leader of the early church in Jerusalem and a key figure in opening the door to Samaritan and Gentile missions in Acts 8 and 10.[89] The church he led in its infancy will never succumb to the powers of death ("gates of Hades"). That door-opening ministry of offering forgiveness to all who repent is described in verse 19 as receiving "the keys of the kingdom." Thus God in heaven and Christians on earth mutually agree on who or what is "bound" or "loosed" (cf. John 20:23).[90]

On the other hand, although Peter seems to grasp something of Jesus' unique relationship with God, he is still not prepared for a suffering Messiah who refuses to overthrow Rome or promote Jewish nationalism. That is why Jesus must silence him for the time being (Mark 8:30 pars.) and proceed to instruct his followers about his own upcoming death (8:31–9:1 pars.). Here appears the first of three key "passion predictions," as the period of Jesus' rejection begins (8:31–32; 9:30–32; 10:32–34). How quickly Peter turns from "hero" to "culprit"! He "rebukes" Jesus for his predictions (8:32), and Jesus has to "return the favor" (v. 33). In replying, "Get behind me, Satan!" he is not saying Peter was possessed by demons, but he is very seriously stressing that Peter is reflecting the same perspective as the devil, who wanted to keep Christ from the road to the cross. Jesus goes on to teach the

---

[87] For a full discussion of options, historically and today, see C. C. Caragounis, *Peter and the Rock* (Berlin and New York: de Gruyter, 1990).

[88] The inflectional ending of *petra* is feminine and so had to be altered to -*os* to form a masculine proper name. In Aramaic *kepha* would have been used for both forms.

[89] Cf. further France, *Matthew*, 622–23.

[90] A grammatical debate about whether the future perfect passive periphrastic constructions should be translated "will be bound/loosed" or "will have been bound/loosed" is probably best resolved with the mediating sense of "will be in a state of boundedness/loosedness." Jesus is not saying that heaven ratifies Christians' decisions or vice-versa, merely that they are in accord when Christians are properly exercising their ministries. See S. E. Porter, "Vague Verbs, Periphrastics, and Matt. 16:19," *FN* 1 (1988): 155–73. Very similar but substituting "process" for "state" is D. Ekem, "Another Look at the Translation of Matthew 16.19," *BT* 55 (2004): 119–24.

Twelve about the necessary self-renunciation that true discipleship requires (vv. 34–38). This may lead to the shame attached to a criminal's execution by crucifixion (v. 34) or involve denial of the goods or status of this world (vv. 35–37), but it will result in a heavenly glory that far more than compensates (v. 38).[91] Only one who was in some sense divine himself could legitimately make the claims of this last verse.

Mark 9:1 and parallels is one of the most enigmatic sayings in the Gospels, but given the passage that immediately follows, it probably has something to do with the Transfiguration.[92] While Christ's second coming, and with it the full manifestation of the kingdom in all its power, was yet a long way off, a few of Jesus' followers would see glimpses of his transcendent glory within just a few days. Those glimpses and their aftermath are described in the next section.

The Transfiguration and Its Sequel (Mark 9:2–29 pars.) [Aland §161–163]. While for Jesus and his followers, suffering and death must precede permanent glory, both are allowed to experience foretastes in this life. For believers, those foreshadowings often provide the necessary sustenance for perseverance during the difficult times, along with the reminder of the command from the heavenly voice to listen to and follow Jesus.[93] His transfiguration contains numerous parallels to the experience of Moses on Mt. Sinai at the time of the receiving of the Law and is doubtless intended to reflect a theology of Jesus as a new Moses, inaugurator of a new covenant, and prophet par excellence: Luke, in particular, highlights these connections. (1) Jesus is on a mountain.[94] (2) He hears a heavenly voice, giving the same message as at his baptism, echoing prophecies of sonship and servanthood. (3) There is an enveloping cloud and an appearance of God's glory. (4) Talk centers on Jesus' "exodus" (Luke 9:31—NIV "departure"). (5) Peter proposes to build "booths" as in the wilderness wanderings.[95] (6) Moses and Elijah, messianic precursors and recipients of mountaintop theophanies, appear with Jesus. (7) The disciples must listen to Jesus (v. 7), in fulfillment of Deut 18:15–18. (8) All this occurs "after six days" (Mark 9:2; cf. Exod 24:16).[96]

---

[91] Hooker (*Mark*, 208) captures it succinctly: "The cost is comprehensive, but so is the reward."

[92] See esp. Cranfield, *Mark*, 285–88. Cf. France, *Matthew*, 641; Witherington, *Mark*, 261–62; and C. A. Evans, *Mark 8:27–16:20* (Nashville: Nelson, 2001), 29. Other suggestions for the kingdom of God coming in power have included the resurrection, Pentecost, the establishment of the church, the destruction of Jerusalem in AD 70, and the mistaken belief that Christ would return within the lifetime of some of his hearers.

[93] See esp. J. P. Heil, *The Transfiguration of Jesus: Narrative Meaning and Function of Mark 9:2–8, Matt 17:1–8 and Luke 9:28–36* (Rome: PIB, 2000).

[94] The mountain is unnamed. Tradition identifies it as Mt. Tabor in central Galilee. But this "mountain" is only 1900 ft. high, and a fortress topped it in Jesus' day. Modern scholars have often suggested Mt. Hermon (9200 ft. and northeast of Galilee), but it may have been too distant and rugged. Liefeld and Pao ("Luke," 181–82) prefer Mt. Meron, the highest mountain within Israel at nearly 4000 ft., just northwest of the sea of Galilee.

[95] Or do these three "tents" (*skēnē*) allude to the "tabernacle" as a kind of way of veiling God's glory, as argued by R. E. Otto, "The Fear Motivation in Peter's Offer to Build τρεῖς σκηνάς," *WTJ* 59 (1997): 101–12?

[96] Luke's "about eight days" (v. 28) loses this allusion but does not contradict Matthew and Mark because both expressions were standard references to a week's time.

Again, the disciples fail to grasp what is happening. Peter wants to prolong the mountaintop experience (Mark 9:5), but this is not the time or place to dwell on glory.[97] As they descend, they ask about Elijah (vv. 11–13 par.). His coming as forerunner to restore all things does not seem to leave room for the Messiah's suffering and death (Mal 4:5–6). If John the Baptist has fulfilled prophecy and yet been executed, how can the Christ expect anything less?[98] In the valley beneath, the nine disciples who did not accompany Jesus up the mountain have been unable to fulfill their prior commissioning (Mark 6:7 pars.), as they have failed to cast out a demon from an epileptic boy (Mark 9:14–29 pars.). Again, the contrast between Jesus' majesty and the disciples' failure proves striking. Jesus performs the exorcism but castigates his followers for acting like the "unbelieving generation" that is more overtly rejecting him. Their problem was a lack of prayer (v. 29; some late manuscripts add "and fasting"), that is, a failure to trust utterly in God. Matthew goes on at this point to add Jesus' promise about the power of even a little faith (Matt 17:20–21), but these words must always be balanced with his prior command to leave room for God's will to overrule ours in all our prayers (6:10).

Further Teachings on Discipleship (Mark 9:30–50 pars.) [Aland §164, 166–168]. As with his first passion prediction, Jesus' second meets with a lack of understanding and with distress (vv. 31–32 pars.). So Mark appends a collection of Jesus' teachings, the parallels to which are somewhat more scattered in Matthew and Luke. All focus on the lowliness, service, and life of peace required by a faithful pilgrim on the road to the cross.[99] Jesus' disciples are arguing about greatness (v. 33–34), so he explains that they must (a) have a child- or servant-like attitude (vv. 35–37); (b) recognize as legitimate anyone ministering under Jesus' authority, whether or not in their regular circle (vv. 38–41);[100] (c) avoid the possibility of scandal—for others and themselves—in light of coming judgment (vv. 42–49); and (d) live at peace among themselves and with others (v. 50).

Discussion about the Temple Tax (Matt 17:24–27) [Aland §165]. At this point, Matthew alone includes a curious little story about a dispute over paying the annual half-shekel tax for the upkeep of the Jerusalem temple. Jesus makes two main points. First, he and his followers as "children of the kingdom" should be exempt. This fits his consistent rejection of Jewish civil and ritual law; believers are now free from these Old Testament requirements. Second, however, he refuses to cause unnecessary offense and so encourages a voluntary contribution. The method of

---

[97] Indeed, the fleeting nature of the glory may well be intended to counter a triumphalist interpretation even of the Transfiguration account itself, to say nothing of the whole Gospel, at least with respect to what believers can expect in this life. See T. W. Martin, "What Makes Glory Glorious? Reading Luke's Account of the Transfiguration over against Triumphalism," *JSNT* 29 (206): 3–26.

[98] Cf. C. L. Blomberg, "Elijah, Election, and the Use of Malachi in the New Testament," *CTR* 2 (1987): 100–8.

[99] H. Fledderman, "The Discipleship Discourse (Mark 9:33–50)," *CBQ* 43 (1981): 57–75.

[100] Luke 11:23 (par. Matt. 12:30) states the converse of this text ("He who is not with me is against me"), but this claim is equally appropriate in its context: all non-Christians, however benign, are ultimately against Christ. But all true Christians, whether or not they are in *our* "elite" circles, are ultimately on our side.

payment—catching a fish with a coin in its mouth—ensures that no hardship for anyone is created in the process![101]

Historicity

The authenticity of several of the themes and literary forms in Mark 7–9 and parallels (e.g., miracle stories or conflicts with the Jewish leaders) has already been discussed in previous sections. In addition, we may note the following arguments for the historicity of various passages discussed here: (1) Jesus' implicit challenge to the kosher laws satisfies the double similarity and dissimilarity criterion; it was a key issue in Israel and for the first generation of Jesus followers, but Jesus differed radically from the rest of Judaism but was not immediately followed by most in early Christianity.[102] Indeed, Rom 14:14 may preserve an allusion to this very teaching of Christ. (2) Jesus' "insulting" behavior toward the Syrophoenician woman passes the test of "embarrassment," but it is understandable in a Jewish milieu, and his cryptic repartée is characteristic. The form and contents of the passage closely parallel those of the healing of the Capernaum centurion's son (Matt 8:5–13 par.). (3) *Ephphatha* in Mark 7:34 preserves a rare Aramaic word in the Gospels, and the two healings of blind men (Mark 7:31–37 par. and 8:22–26) describe a kind of miracle unparalleled in ancient Judaism or the early church. (4) Mark 8:11–13, 14–21 and parallels cohere with Jesus' classic unwillingness to respond to his opponents on their terms. He evades their trap and then issues a characteristically metaphorical warning.

The interchange between Peter and Jesus on the road to Caesarea Philippi raises broader historical questions. It has often been disputed whether or not Jesus even intended to found a church. That is, did he imagine his followers living long enough to establish an ongoing fellowship, and did he ever imagine it turning into the highly developed and organized institution that it became? The answer to the latter question may well be "no," but he probably did envisage a community of his followers that would outlive him and carry on his mission for a considerable time.[103] In Judaism, a Messiah implied a messianic community, a new or renewed Israel. The Greek word for "church" (*ekklēsia*) translates the Hebrew *qāhāl*, which is the standard Old Testament term for the "assembly" of God's people. The nature of Jesus' ethical teaching on taxes, divorce, nonretaliation, enemy love, stewardship of wealth, and so on clearly presupposes some signifi-

---

[101] W. Carter ("Paying the Tax to Rome as Subversion Praxis: Matthew 17.24–27," *JSNT* 76 [1999]: 3–31) applies similar logic to the *fiscus Judaicus* after AD 70—i.e., when the temple tax was now paid to Rome instead. R. Bauckham ("The Coin in the Fish's Mouth," in *Gospel Perspectives*, vol. 6, 219–52) argues that Christ and the disciples are virtually penniless at this point in their ministry. A half-shekel equaled two drachma or denarii and, hence, two days' minimum wage.

[102] T. R. Hatina ("Did Jesus Quote Isaiah 29:13 against the Pharisees? An Unpopular Appraisal," *BBR* 16 [2006]: 79–84) shows that Isa 29:13 was used already in pre-Christian Judaism (as in Mark 7:5–7 par.) to denounce the "traditions of the elders," while J. G. Crossley ("Halakah and Mark 7:4: '. . . and Beds'," *JSNT* 25 [2003]: 443–47) demonstrates the authenticity of the ritual washing practices debated.

[103] Cf. esp. Meier, *A Marginal Jew: Rethinking the Historical Jesus*, vol. 3 (New York and London: Doubleday, 2001), 125–97.

cant interval during which his disciples would have to confront all of the problems of ordinary living. Even the portions of this passage unique to Matthew contain numerous Semitisms that could be a literal translation of Jesus' exact wording: "Son of the living God," the beatitude form ("Blessed are you"), *bar-Jonah* ("son of Jonah"[104]), "flesh and blood" (as an idiom for mortal humanity), the play on Peter's name Cephas ("rock"), the "gates" of Hades (i.e., the power of death), and the imagery of binding and loosing. So whether or not Matthew is actually prior to Mark at this point or is simply supplementing his standard sources, he is likely relying on historical tradition.[105]

Jesus' subsequent calls to radical discipleship (Mark 8:34–38; 9:33–50 pars.) are among the "hard sayings" not readily invented. Peter's rebuke of Christ and Jesus' response (8:32–33 pars.) are so unflattering that they, too, are likely historical. Jesus' threefold prediction of his passion and resurrection (Mark 8:31; 9:31; 10:33–34 pars.) is more disputed. But even apart from supernatural knowledge, awareness of the precedent of the Maccabean martyrs and of the general tenor of Jewish-Roman relationships in the first century would surely have suggested to Jesus that he was on a collision course with the authorities of his day. Only in Matt 20:19 is death by crucifixion ever actually mentioned; "prophecies" after the fact would surely have been more explicit. If Jesus anticipated martyrdom, then he presumably expected vindication by God as well. Except among the Sadducees, resurrection was the standard Jewish hope for the age to come, but there was no expectation of a crucified and resurrected Messiah, so again Jesus' predictions fit what is both conceivable and yet distinctive in a Jewish milieu.[106] Finally, Mark 9:1 is a potentially embarrassing verse that nevertheless presupposes something like the transfiguration narrative that follows to make any sense of it. Second Peter 1:16–18 claims to provide independent, eyewitness attestation of this event.[107]

Theological Distinctives

Again, each of the Synoptists puts his own distinctive stamp on this material. *Mark* 8:27–30 clearly forms the hinge that separates the two halves of Mark's Gospel, transitioning from Christ the glorious miracle-worker to Jesus the suffering servant (recall, above, pp. 129–30). To highlight the disciples' lack of understanding, Mark creates a twofold sequence of feeding miracles, sea crossings, conflicts with the Pharisees, conversations about bread, healings, and confessions

---

[104] Or more probably "son of John" (NLT) *contra* the NIV and most translations. *Bariōna* could be the contracted form of *bar Johanan*, and John 1:42 and 21:15 both refer to Simon as son of John.

[105] Cf. further G. Lohfink, *Jesus and Community: The Social Dimension of Christian Faith* (Philadelphia: Fortress, 1984; London: SPCK, 1985); L. Goppelt, *Theology of the New Testament*, vol. 1 (Grand Rapids: Eerdmans; London: SPCK, 1981), 207–22; and B. F. Meyer, *The Aims of Jesus* (London: SCM, 1979), 185–97.

[106] For a thorough defense of the historicity of the passion predictions, see H. F. Bayer, *Jesus' Predictions of Vindication and Resurrection* (Tübingen: Mohr, 1986). Cf. C. A. Evans, "Did Jesus Predict His Death and Resurrection?" in *Resurrection*, ed. S. E. Porter, M. A. Hayes and D. Tombs (Sheffield: SAP, 1999), 82–97.

[107] On both the historicity and meaning of the Transfiguration, see further S. N. Williams, "The Transfiguration of Jesus Christ," *Them* 28 (2002): 13–25; 28 (2003): 16–27.

of faith (6:31–7:37; 8:1–30).[108] *Matthew* also makes Peter's confession a pivotal point (16:13–20; see above, pp. 144–45) but groups the material leading up to this hinge into parallel cycles of ministry among Jews and Gentiles. Jesus is the Bread of Life for both groups (14:13–36; 15:1–16:12).[109] *Luke* creates his turning point a little further in his narrative (at Luke 9:51, on which see below, pp. 335–36). As already noted, Luke omits all of Jesus' withdrawal from Galilee for geographical/ theological purposes but groups material parallel to Mark in Luke 9:1–50 to form a preview of Jesus' journey to Jerusalem. Here he highlights themes of Christology, especially viewing Jesus as the eschatological prophet, and discipleship.[110]

For Further Study

Parables

Introductory

Gowler, David B. *What Are They Saying about the Parables?* Mahwah, NJ: Paulist, 2000.
Kistemaker, Simon. *The Parables: Understanding the Stories Jesus Told.* Rev. ed. Grand Rapids: Baker, 2002.
Sider, John W. *Interpreting the Parables: A Hermeneutical Guide to Their Meaning.* Grand Rapids: Zondervan, 1995.
Stein, Robert H. *An Introduction to the Parables of Jesus.* Philadelphia: Westminster, 1981.
Wenham, David. *The Parables of Jesus: Pictures of Revolution.* London: Hodder & Stoughton; Downers Grove: IVP, 1989.
Wright, Stephen I. *Tales Jesus Told: An Introduction to the Narrative Parables of Jesus.* Carlisle: Paternoster, 2002.

Intermediate

Bailey, Kenneth E. *Poet and Peasant* and *Through Peasant Eyes.* 2 vols. Grand Rapids: Eerdmans, 1983.
Blomberg, Craig L. *Interpreting the Parables.* Downers Grove and Leicester: IVP, 1990.
Dodd, C. H. *The Parables of the Kingdom.* London: Nisbet, 1935; New York: Scribner's, 1936.
Donahue, John R. *The Gospel in Parable: Metaphor, Narrative and Theology in the Synoptic Gospels.* Philadelphia: Fortress, 1988.
Etchells, Ruth. *A Reading of the Parables of Jesus.* London: Darton, Longman & Todd, 1998.
Hedrick, Charles W. *Many Things in Parables: Jesus and His Modern Critics.* Louisville: WJKP, 2004.

---

[108] Lane, *Mark,* 269.

[109] Cf. C. L. Blomberg, *Matthew* (Nashville: Broadman, 1992), 210.

[110] On which, see D. P. Moessner, "Luke 9:1–50: Luke's Preview of the Journey of the Prophet Like Moses from Deuteronomy," *JBL* 102 (1983): 575–605; and Robert F. O'Toole, "Luke's Message in Luke 9:1–50," *CBQ* 49 (1987): 74–89.

Herzog, William R., II. *Parables as Subversive Speech: Jesus as Pedagogue of the Oppressed.* Louisville: WJKP, 1994.

Jeremias, Joachim. *The Parables of Jesus.* 3rd ed. London: SCM; Philadelphia: Westminster, 1972.

Longenecker, Richard N., ed. *The Challenge of Jesus' Parables.* Grand Rapids and Cambridge: Eerdmans, 2002.

Young, Brad H. *The Parables of Jesus: Jewish Tradition and Christian Interpretation.* Peabody: Hendrickson, 1998.

Advanced

Hultgren, Arland J. *The Parables of Jesus: A Commentary.* Grand Rapids and Cambridge: Eerdmans, 2000.

Scott, Bernard B. *Hear Then the Parable: A Commentary on the Parables of Jesus.* Minneapolis: Fortress, 1989.

Schottroff, Luise. *The Parables of Jesus.* Minneapolis: Fortress, 2006.

Snodgrass, Klyne R. *Stories with Intent: A Comprehensive Guide to the Parables of Jesus.* Grand Rapids and Cambridge: Eerdmans, 2008.

Bibliography

Kissinger, Warren S. *The Parables of Jesus: A History of Interpretation and Bibliography.* Metuchen, NJ: Scarecrow, 1979.

Miracles

Introductory

Deere, Jack S. *Surprised by the Power of the Spirit.* Grand Rapids: Zondervan, 1993.

John, Jeffrey. *The Meaning in the Miracles.* Norwich: Canterbury, 2001; Grand Rapids: Eerdmans, 2004.

Kistemaker, Simon. *The Miracles: Exploring the Mystery of Jesus' Divine Works.* Grand Rapids: Baker, 2006.

Smedes, Lewis B., ed. *Ministry and the Miraculous.* Pasadena: Fuller Theological Seminary, 1987.

Intermediate

Brown, Colin. *Miracles and the Critical Mind.* Grand Rapids: Eerdmans; Exeter: Paternoster, 1984.

Geivett, R. Douglas, and Gary R. Habermas. *In Defense of Miracles: A Comprehensive Case for God's Actions in History.* Downers Grove: IVP, 1997.

Latourelle, René. *The Miracles of Jesus and the Theology of Miracle.* New York: Paulist, 1988.

Twelftree, Graham H. *Jesus the Miracle-worker: A Historical and Theological Study.* Downers Grove: IVP, 1999.

Advanced

Eve, Eric. *The Jewish Context of Jesus' Miracles.* London and New York: SAP, 2002.

Kee, Howard C. *Miracle in the Early Christian World*. New Haven and London: Yale University Press, 1983.

Meier, John P. *A Marginal Jew: Rethinking the Historical Jesus*, vol. 2. New York and London: Doubleday, 1994.

Theissen, Gerd. *The Miracle Stories of the Early Christian Tradition*. Edinburgh: T&T Clark; Philadelphia: Fortress, 1983.

van der Loos, Hendrik. *The Miracles of Jesus*. Leiden: Brill, 1965.

Wenham, David, and Craig Blomberg, eds. *Gospel Perspectives*. Vol. 6, *The Miracles of Jesus*. Sheffield: JSOT, 1986; Eugene, OR: Wipf & Stock, 2003.

Withdrawal from Galilee

Bayer, Hans F. *Jesus' Predictions of Vindication and Resurrection: The Provenance, Meaning, and Correlation of the Synoptic Predictions*. Tübingen: Mohr, 1986.

Booth, Roger P. *Jesus and the Laws of Purity: Tradition History and Legal History in Mark 7*. Sheffield: JSOT, 1986.

Caragounis, Chrys C. *Peter and the Rock*. Berlin and New York: de Gruyter, 1990.

Fowler, Robert M. *Loaves and Fishes: The Function of the Feeding Stories in the Gospel of Mark*. Chico: Scholars, 1981.

Heil, John P. *The Transfiguration of Jesus: Narrative Meaning and Function of Mark 9:2–8, Matt 17:1–8 and Luke 9:28–36*. Rome: PIB, 2000.

Meier, John P. *A Marginal Jew: Rethinking the Historical Jesus*, vol. 3. New York and London: Doubleday, 2001.

Questions for Review

1. What principles should we most keep in mind in interpreting parables? Choose a specific parable and illustrate.
2. Explain Mark 4:10–12.
3. What principles should we most keep in mind in interpreting Jesus' miracles, and particularly his "nature miracles"? Choose a specific miracle and illustrate.
4. Discuss the relationship in the Gospels between miracles and faith.
5. What is the main point of Jesus' "withdrawal from Galilee"? Illustrate from several texts.
6. What is the main point of Peter's "confession"? How does he still not understand?

15

ADDITIONAL TEACHINGS OF JESUS IN MATTHEW, LUKE, AND JOHN

W E HAVE GENERALLY been following Mark's outline for the Galilean ministry of Christ. At logical points we have inserted related material from the other Gospels. Now it is time to go back and pick up the pieces we have skipped, before moving to the climactic days of Jesus' life in and around Jerusalem. In Matthew, this includes two major sermons (chaps. 10 and 18), arguably though not necessarily collections of Jesus' teachings from several different contexts. In Luke, this involves all of the unparalleled parts of his large central section (9:51–18:34), most of which are teachings, many of them in parables. In John, we must consider the intermediate visits of Christ to Jerusalem and the controversies with the Jewish leaders in which he became embroiled there (most of chaps. 5–11).

Matthew 10 and 18

The Missionary Discourse (Matt 9:36–10:42) [Aland §98–105]

Context (Matt 9:36–10:4). At some point, roughly midway through his Galilean ministry, Jesus commissioned his disciples to begin replicating his work of preaching, teaching, and healing. The potential harvest was great, but the laborers needed to be multiplied (9:35–38). It is at this point that Matthew gives the names of the Twelve (10:1–4), although they have actually been chosen earlier (cf. above, pp. 276–78). The sermon, as Matthew presents it, falls into two main sections: instructions for ministry during Jesus' lifetime (vv. 5–16), followed by a look ahead to coming persecution and circumstances after his death and resurrection (vv. 17–42). Only the latter section contains instructions that are necessarily generalizable to later generations of disciples.[1]

Message (10:5–42). In the short run, the disciples must restrict themselves to Jewish territory (vv. 5–6) and travel light, dependent on the hospitality of those among whom they minister (vv. 7–16). The apparent harshness of these baggage restrictions and short visits stems from the urgency of getting the message out, not from the limited scope of the mission.[2] As explained above (p. 149), Jesus insists that the Jewish people hear the gospel first, but he will later command the disciples to go to all ethnic groups with their message (28:18–20). In fact, even before his death, he will rescind some of these specific instructions about provisions for the journey (Luke 22:35–38), but the basic task of proclaiming the gospel and healing people clearly continues on into the Book of Acts.

Verses 17–42 divide into three main parts. First, Jesus describes the prospect of future hostility (vv. 17–25). It is inevitable because of the disciples' attachment to Christ (vv. 24–25), but the Spirit will protect and guide them through it all (vv. 17–23). Indeed, he will give them an opportunity for witness (v. 18). There is a fine balance between being on one's guard (v. 17) and yet not worrying (v. 19). The promise of the Spirit giving us words to speak when unexpected persecution catches us by surprise (vv. 19–20) hardly warrants lack of preparedness for normal preaching and teaching ministry.[3] The hostility promised in vv. 21–23 must not be due to our tactlessness but to the inherent offense of the heart of the gospel. Here appears one of the more puzzling verses in Matthew's Gospel, as Jesus promises the disciples that they will not have finished going through the cities of Israel "before the Son of Man comes" (v. 23b). Had this prediction come in verses 5–16, we might imagine it to be a reference simply to the short-term mission of the disciples, but in this context of future hostility, that interpretation does not fit well. More likely, Jesus is predicting the perennially incomplete nature of the

---

[1] Wilkins, *Matthew*, 391–92. For a helpful literary analysis of the sermon, see D. J. Weaver, *Matthew's Missionary Discourse: A Literary-Critical Analysis* (Sheffield: JSOT, 1990). For a more wide-ranging exegesis, see E. C. Park, *The Mission Discourse in Matthew's Interpretation* (Tübingen: Mohr, 1995).

[2] A classic apparent contradiction among Gospel parallels involves whether or not Jesus forbade a staff and shoes altogether or only prohibited the disciples from taking extra ones. For a survey of the various commonly proposed solutions, see B. M. Ahern, "Staff or No Staff," *CBQ* 5 (1943): 332–37. For a more recent source-critical explanation, see Blomberg, *Historical Reliability of the Gospels*, 187–88. Matthew's account may be a conflation of the sending of seventy (-two), described in Luke 10, with that of the Twelve, described in Mark 6, in which the commands varied slightly.

[3] "To take this assurance as an excuse for lazy preachers, insisting that all Christian utterance must be spontaneous and unprepared, is to take it seriously out of context" (France, *Matthew*, 392)!

Jewish mission and perhaps also hinting at its ongoing priority.[4] In context, verses 24–25 do not teach that students cannot outstrip their teachers in competence, but that they cannot escape the persecution that the master endured.

Second, the proper reaction to hostility is to fear God, not people (vv. 26–31). Physical death is far less ultimate than eternal punishment. Third, as at the end of the Sermon on the Mount, there are essentially only two options: either to acknowledge Jesus or to reject him (vv. 32–42). Those who want to remain faithful may wind up alienating their families, but God must take a higher priority (vv. 34–37).[5] The Christian life may lead even to martyrdom, but the compensation will far outweigh the loss (vv. 38–39).[6] Eventually, everyone will be judged on the basis of their reception of Christian witnesses (vv. 40–42), so the seemingly high cost is more than worth it. "Receiving Jesus' representatives with even a cup of cold water (10:42; Mk 9:41) probably refers to accepting into one's home the missionaries who have abandoned their own homes and security to bring Christ's message (10:11; cf. also 25:35–40)."[7]

The Sermon on Humility and Forgiveness (Matt 18:1–35) [Aland §166, 168–173]

Not long before Jesus' climactic journey to Jerusalem, Matthew records (compiles?) another extended discourse of Jesus, again for the disciples only. Having already promised to build his church (Matt 16:16–19), he here elaborates on some of the foundational principles for this fledgling community. Jesus' "sermon" falls into two main parts: teaching on humility (vv. 1–14) and teaching on forgiveness (vv. 15–35).[8] Verses 1–9 outline the humility disciples need. They must imitate childlike dependence on God (vv. 1–5) but avoid anything that might cause even one of the seemingly most insignificant of Christians to stumble (vv. 6–9). Verses 10–14 turn to God's "humility"—what great steps he takes to try to save the wayward. In this context (diff. Luke 15:4–7), the parable of the lost sheep seems to apply primarily to straying church members.[9] Throughout this chapter and elsewhere, "little ones" is a favorite term of Matthew for fellow believers.

---

[4] See further J. M. McDermott, "Mt. 10.23 in Context," *BZ* 28 (1984): 230–40; Keener, *Matthew*, 324; Turner, *Matthew*, 277 (who also notes the other major interpretive options).

[5] For challenging applications of these verses to contemporary "family values," see Hauerwas, *Matthew*, 109–10.

[6] "Popular usage has sanitized the language of having 'a cross to bear' so that its challenge has evaporated. It is not of course true that every loyal disciple will be a martyr, but all must recognize and accept the possibility of dying for Jesus, and many who have not faced literal execution have nonetheless known well the social stigma implied in carrying the cross behind Jesus" (France, *Matthew*, 411).

[7] Keener, *Matthew*, 332.

[8] The most detailed modern treatment of this chapter, including an extended focus on its structure, is W. G. Thompson, *Matthew's Advice to a Divided Community: Mt 17,22–18,35* (Rome: BIP, 1970).

[9] Matthew's and Luke's versions of the lost sheep provide a classic test case for identifying a critic's presuppositions. If the similarities between the two versions demand that Matthew and Luke have each modified a common source, then clearly they felt free to take considerable liberties with their traditions. But, given two entirely different settings and applications, why not assume that Jesus himself

Verses 15–35 turn to the complementary topic of forgiveness. When a fla-grantly sinning Christian remains unrepentant, an increasingly rigorous process of intervention is needed to try to bring a change of heart (vv. 15–18). Here is the classic passage in the New Testament to which churches turn (or should turn) to understand the process of discipline. In extreme cases, excommunication may even be necessary, but it is still in hopes of rehabilitation. To treat someone as a "pagan or tax collector" (v. 17) means that they cannot be admitted to gather-ings designed for Christians only, but they should still be treated with the respect and love with which one would try to win a non-Christian to Christ.[10] Verses 19–20 clearly belong in this context. The "two or three" gathered in Jesus' name correspond to the person confronting a fellow Christian plus the "one or two" witnesses of verse 16 who should likewise be present. "Witness" here does not mean an eyewitness to the offense; that kind of witness often was never present. Rather these are the ones who will "testify" to what the aggrieved parties said and try to help bring reconciliation.[11] When in this context Jesus promises to be with the two or three gathered together in his name, then, he is teaching nothing here about his being present with every small prayer group, true as that may be, but everything about the fact that heaven is in accord with properly followed church discipline.[12]

By contrast, Jesus enjoins forgiveness seventy-seven-fold in verses 21–22. The only way not to see a contradiction with verses 15–20 is to assume that here true repentance has occurred. The alternating grace and severity of the king in the appended parable (vv. 23–35) confirms this conclusion (cf. also Luke 17:3–4). Together, verses 21–35 outline the lavishness of forgiveness that should be extend-ed to those who truly repent by changing their behavior rather than just apologiz-ing. Where professions of repentance do not produce a forgiving demeanor toward others, judgment may be severe indeed. Verses 34–35 have understandably been viewed as support for believing that God's grace and forgiveness can be retracted, but it may be more helpful to understand, with Ridderbos, that

> whoever tries to separate man's forgiveness from God's will no longer be able to count on God's mercy. In so doing he not merely forfeits it [*sic*], like the servant in the parable. Rather he shows that he never had a part in it. God's mercy is not something cut and dried that is received only once. It is a persistent power that pervades all of life. If it does not become manifest as such a power, then it was never received at all.[13]

---

used one basic plot in two different ways in two different contexts? See further C. L. Blomberg, "When Is a Parallel Really a Parallel? A Test Case: The Lucan Parables," *WTJ* 46 (1984): 78–103.

[10] Wilkins, *Matthew,* 619. An excellent handbook, biblically rooted with many practical guidelines, is J. C. Laney, *A Guide to Church Discipline* (Minneapolis: Bethany, 1985). On conflict resolution more generally, see esp. K. Sande, *The Peacemaker: A Biblical Guide to Resolving Conflict,* rev. ed. (Grand Rapids: Baker, 2004).

[11] Cf. Mounce, *Matthew,* 177; Witherington, *Matthew,* 351.

[12] Nolland, *Matthew,* 748.

[13] H. Ridderbos, *Matthew* (Grand Rapids: Zondervan, 1987), 346. Cf. Wilkins, *Matthew,* 625.

In other words, forgiven people will forgive others. It may not be easy, it may take time, it may require help from others. Those who absolutely refuse even to try cannot legitimately claim to have God's Spirit living in them.[14]

Tragically, Christian forgiveness is one of the most misunderstood and least practiced virtues in the contemporary church. A chapter like Matthew 18 makes it clear that it can*not* mean that one always returns to exactly the kind of relationship two people had before one sinned against the other. When true contrition and change in behavior occurs, it is the Christian's obligation to reconcile–to restore cordial interpersonal relationships. But there may need to be new kinds of boundaries drawn to minimize the temptation of a recurring offense. Where genuine repentance does *not* occur, there will invariably be a changed relationship that involves a certain distancing between the two parties. Believers are still called to forgive, in the sense that they must not harbor a grudge, be consumed with how they have been victimized, plot retaliation, and/or be unable to move on with their lives.[15]

Historicity

Whether "M" (see above, p. 103) is a distinct source or the apostle's memory, we must take seriously the likelihood of authentic material in Matthew's unparalleled sections. The Jewish particularism of Matt 10:1–16, much of it later rescinded, clearly shows that Matthew differentiated historical information from the changed circumstances of his day. Verse 23 is sufficiently cryptic and potentially embarrassing as to be almost certainly authentic. Verses 34–36 and 37–39 are obvious "hard sayings," particularly cutting against the grain of other Jewish and later Christian "family values." The topics and forms of Matthew 18 speak for the authenticity of an important core of that "sermon" as well: two "triadic" parables with Jesus' characteristic themes of forgiveness and repentance, each portrayed with distinctive twists, along with a focus on humility, not considered a virtue in most of the Hellenistic world and not well modeled in ancient Jewish or early Christian circles.[16]

Luke's Central Section (9:51–18:14) [Aland §174–237]

Chronology, Geography, and Outline

As noted in our discussion of the outlines of the Gospels (above, Part 3), Luke's central section, or travel narrative as it is sometimes called, is made up almost entirely of Q + L material. These comprise almost exclusively teachings of Jesus. Although the section begins as though it were going to trace Jesus' itinerary from Galilee to Jerusalem for the fate that he knows awaits him there (9:51),

---

[14] Cf. esp. A. J. Hultgren, "Forgive Us, As We Forgive (Matthew 6:12)," *WW* 16 (1996): 284–90.

[15] See further C. L. Blomberg, "On Building and Breaking Barriers: Forgiveness, Salvation and Christian Counseling with Special Reference to Matthew 18:15–35," *JPC* 25 (2006): 137–54, and the literature there cited. For implications from this process for the entire church, cf. S. E. Hylen, "Forgiveness and Life in Community," *Interpretation* 54 (2000): 146–57.

[16] Cf. esp. C. A. Evans, "Jesus' Ethic of Humility," *TJ* 13 (1992): 127–38.

there are fewer indications of chronology or geography in the subsequent nine chapters than in any other section of comparable length in any Gospel. What can be deduced is limited to three passages: (1) In 9:51–56 Jesus is rejected in Samaria and so goes "to another village." This departure has often been interpreted as implying that Jesus avoided Samaria altogether and followed the popular Jewish route of traveling along the Jordan's east bank through Perea. Yet this is sheer inference, and Jesus may well have proceeded simply to a different Samaritan village. (2) In 10:38–42 he is with Mary and Martha, who lived in Bethany, just outside Jerusalem (but we know this location only from John 11:1). (3) In 17:11 he is traveling along the border between Samaria and Galilee. Whatever else we conclude, this is certainly no straight-line journey from Galilee to Jerusalem![17]

Given the topical arrangement of these nine chapters, it is best to see them as Luke's way of gathering together teachings of Jesus, perhaps largely from the climactic phase of his public ministry, as he traveled about in numerous places, but all "under the shadow of the cross" that he knew loomed large in his future (9:51). Indeed, the most persuasive attempts to outline this section have virtually nothing to do with chronology at all. Several writers have seen parallels between the sequence of passages beginning in 9:51 and selected teachings from the book of Deuteronomy, proving further evidence that Luke wanted to portray Jesus as the eschatological prophet Moses predicted.[18] Even more compelling are outlines that see the "travel narrative" as an extended chiasmus, usually with the climactic center in Jesus' solemn pronouncement that he must journey to Jerusalem and be killed there (13:31–35).[19] The most consistently convincing parts of such an outline match pairs of closely parallel parables, thus suggesting a modification of this hypothesis: Luke used a chiastically arranged parables source (either oral or written), around which he grouped topically related teachings of Jesus to create a thematically organized section. The climactic center of this hypothetical source would then come in Luke's great banquet parable and related teachings in 14:7–24, which stress Luke's key themes of coming judgment on unrepentant Israel, the acceptance of the kingdom by the outcasts of Jewish society, and possibly also the foreshadowing of the Gentile mission:

---

[17] Older "lives of Christ" sometimes tried to reconstruct multiple journeys of Jesus up and down the Jordan valley during this period, but this too, while possible, goes beyond anything the meager evidence can actually demonstrate. For a full review of perspectives through 1975, see H. L. Egelkraut, *Jesus' Mission to Jerusalem: A Redaction-Critical Study of the Gospel of Luke 9:51–19:48* (Frankfurt: Peter Lang, 1976).

[18] See an influential hypothesis first proposed by C. F. Evans ("The Central Section of St. Luke's Gospel," in *Studies in the Gospels*, ed. D. E. Nineham [Oxford: Blackwell, 1955], 37–53), who found twenty-two separate parallels that he believed matched texts from Luke 10–18 with passages, in sequence, from Deuteronomy 1–26. Other scholars, noting that not all of these parallels prove equally close or convincing, have preferred to speak merely of key Deuteronomic themes permeating Luke's central section (see above, pp. 165–66).

[19] See esp. Bailey, *Poet and Peasant*, 80–82.

A Chiastic Source of Parables Unique to Luke's Central Section	
A. The Good Samaritan (10:25–37)	A.' The Pharisee and Publican (18:9–14)
(outcasts as heroes; Jewish leaders as bad role models)	
B. The Friend at Midnight (11:5–8)	B.' The Unjust Judge (18:1–8)
(rhetorical question form; bold, persistent prayer)	
C. The Rich Fool (12:13–21)	C.' The Rich Man and Lazarus (16:19–31)
(eternal danger due to misuse of riches)	
D. The Watchful Servants (12:35–38)	D.' The Unjust Steward (16:1–13)
(servant parables; right and wrong use of stewardship)	
E. The Barren Fig Tree (13:1–9)	E.' The Lost Sheep, Coin, Son (15:1–32)
(triad of parallel texts on repentance; two short and one long)	
F. The Great Banquet (14:7–24)	
(climactic center; key Lukan themes of reversal, poor/rich, Christ's return)[*]	
* Craig L. Blomberg, "Midrash, Chiasmus, and the Outline of Luke's Central Section," in *Gospel Perspectives*, vol. 3, ed. R. T. France and David Wenham (Sheffield: JSOT, 1983), 217–61. Cf. also Nolland, *Luke 9:21–18:34*, 530–31.	

Selected Comments on Individual Passages

Space prohibits consideration of every passage in Luke's central section, so we will concentrate here primarily on passages unique to Luke, and on the overall narrative flow of the text. Most of the Q-passages are already treated elsewhere in this book in comments on material in Matthew.

Contrasting Pictures of Discipleship (9:52–62) [Aland §175–176]. With all of the parallels between Jesus and Elijah earlier in Luke, we are not surprised to read that the disciples propose replicating Elijah's miracle of calling down fire from heaven in order to destroy their enemies (vv. 54–56; cf. 1 Kgs 18:38). But one who is journeying to the cross must be prepared to suffer without retaliation. Thus Jesus stresses the radical commitment required of would-be disciples (vv. 57–62). Burying one's father and saying good-bye to one's family could actually be euphemisms for waiting until relatives were dead before joining up with Jesus,[20] but the harshness of Jesus' call must not be overly muted. "Following him is not a task which is added to others like working a second job. . . . It is every-

---

[20] Or at least to the period of close to a year, after which the original coffin was exhumed and the deceased person's bones (which is all that would remain by that time) were reburied in a much smaller "ossuary."

thing. It is a solemn commitment which forces the disciples-to-be to reorder all their other duties."[21]

The Mission of the Seventy (-two) (10:1–24) [Aland §177–181]. In one of the rare narrative events of Luke's central section, Jesus sends out seventy (-two) disciples, corresponding to the number of nations listed in Genesis 10.[22] His charge closely parallels his earlier commissioning of the Twelve to preach and heal exclusively among the cities of Israel (Matt 10:5–15 pars.). But this time, especially if Jesus is in Perea, he would be commissioning an explicit Gentile mission; if not, the ministry of this larger band of disciples at least foreshadows it.[23] For this reason, Luke inserts various texts from Q that contrast Jesus' rejection in key Jewish cities with his acceptance by the "nobodies" of this world (vv. 13–16, 21–24). In between, he uniquely stresses how the successful exorcisms performed by his followers demonstrate the vanquishing of Satan, which the arrival of God's reign accomplishes (vv. 17–20). Though not yet completely executed, the devil's doom is assured.[24]

On Love of God and Neighbor (10:25–42) [Aland §182–184]. A lawyer trying to trap Jesus asks him about eternal life. Jesus initially gives a classically Jewish answer: love God and neighbor (cf. Deut 6:5; Lev 19:18). The lawyer, no doubt thinking ethnocentrically, asks how far the definition of "neighbor" extends, so Jesus tells the parable of the Good Samaritan (vv. 25–37). From the Samaritan's example we learn that we must show compassion to all who are in need. From the priest and Levite, we see that religious duty is no excuse for lovelessness. But the climactic and unifying theme of the passage that answers the lawyer's question and explains why the hero is a Samaritan, shocking Jesus' Jewish audience, is that even one's enemy is one's neighbor.[25]

Attempts at neighbor love, however, can degenerate into mere busywork and can squander appropriate love for God. So Luke juxtaposes the equally challenging encounter between Jesus and the two sisters, Mary and Martha. Flying squarely in the face of societal convention, Jesus proclaims that Mary, who is provocatively acting as though she were equal to the male disciples by sitting at her rabbi's feet to learn from him, has chosen the only thing needed on this occasion. Martha's "typically female" preoccupation with domestic chores, to provide

---

[21] R. J. Karris, *Invitation to Luke* (Garden City: Doubleday, 1977), 130.

[22] The textual evidence in Luke 10:1, 17 between "seventy" and "seventy-two" is relatively evenly balanced but slightly favors the latter. The same variations in number appear, respectively, between the Hebrew and Greek manuscripts of Genesis 10.

[23] Nolland, *Luke 9:21–18:34*, 558.

[24] Cf. esp. M. F. Bird, "Mission as an Apocalyptic Event: Reflections on Luke 10:18 and Mark 13:10," *EQ* 76 (2004): 117–34. Bird insists that mission thus "does not simply anticipate the final triumph of God, but it actually achieves it in embryonic form. . . .to be engaged in mission is not only a continuation of the mission of Jesus but is also a continual re-creation of the triumph of God" (132–33).

[25] Cf., e.g., P. F. Esler, "Jesus and the Reduction of Intergroup Conflict: The Parable of the Good Samaritan in the Light of Social Identity Theory," *BI* 8 (2000): 325–57.

the kind of hospitality for Jesus and his troupe that society expected, misses the point altogether.[26]

Teachings about Prayer (11:1–13) [Aland §185–187]. Distinctive in this context is the little parable of the friend at midnight (vv. 5–8). The imagery and language of this parable teach not so much persistence in prayer (that point will come in 18:1–8) but "boldness" (NIV) or "shameless audacity" (TNIV). Perhaps the best translation of the character trait commended here in verse 8 (*anaideia*) is chutzpah.[27] In the appended Q-passage (vv. 9–13 par.), Jesus promises that God will give only good gifts to his children in response to their requests. Unlike Matthew's version, Luke concludes by referring specifically to the Holy Spirit as the preeminent good gift that they will receive. This is probably a use of "synecdoche" (a figure of speech in which a part stands for the whole), in which the Spirit is the supreme example of the blessings God freely gives us.[28]

Controversy with the Pharisees (11:14–54) [Aland §188–194]. This section is almost exclusively Q-material and is dealt with in various other places in this book.

Preparing for Coming Judgment (12:1–13:9) [Aland §195–207]. The distinctively Lukan portions of this unit center on various parables. The rich fool (12:13–21) is not condemned for his wealth, but for covetousness (NIV "greed," v. 15), wholly self-centered accumulation and hoarding (vv. 16–20), and taking no thought for God (v. 21). Still, the danger for most affluent Westerners, including Christians, is that we do not see how much we still resemble this man, even after these various qualifications are made.[29] In 12:35–48, one L and two Q parables are grouped together to demonstrate the watchfulness that is needed for Christ's return. Every attempt to guess the time of the Parousia is misguided: he may come surprisingly late (vv. 35–38), wholly unexpectedly (vv. 39–40), or surprisingly soon (vv. 42–46). To this last parable, Luke adds two unparalleled verses that stress that the severity of judgment will vary according to an individual's knowledge (vv. 47–48). It would seem by this that Jesus is teaching degrees of punishment in hell, which is only fair, since condemnation is based on one's works.[30] Luke 13:1–9 is also unique to this Gospel. References to two recent national disasters lead to a parable about the impending judgment on the nation of Israel if it does not repent.

---

[26] Cf. C. F. Olson, *Mary, Martha, and Me: Seeking the One Thing That is Needful* (Salt Lake City: Deseret, 2006), a work all the more significant because it is from a Latter-day Saint perspective, which has at times recognized the proper role of women even less than historic Christianity.

[27] Young, *Parables*, 50. The KJV captured this well with "importunity," but this word is little known today. The NLT is good with "shameless persistence," as is the ESV with "impudence" (for those who know *that* word).

[28] E. Schweizer, *The Good News according to Luke* (London: SPCK; Atlanta: John Knox, 1984), 192. Cf. R. H. Stein, *Luke* (Nashville: Broadman and Holman, 1993), 328.

[29] D. E. Oakman, "The Radical Jesus: You Cannot Serve God and Mammon," *BTB* 34 (2004): 122–29. See further Blomberg, *Neither Poverty nor Riches*, 119–20.

[30] Cf. further C. L. Blomberg, "Eschatology and the Church: Some New Testament Perspectives," *Them* 23.2 (1998): 3–26 (esp. 5–6); repr. in *Solid Ground: 25 Years of Evangelical Theology*, ed. C. P. Trueman, T. J. Gray and C. L. Blomberg (Leicester: IVP, 2000), 84–107 (esp. 86–87).

Kingdom Reversals (13:10–14:24) [Aland §208–216]. This section falls into two closely parallel units (13:10–35; 14:1–24). Each begins with Jesus healing a person on the Sabbath, proceeds to present a pair of brief, parallel parables, and concludes with a longer discourse on who will and will not enter the kingdom. Put together, the dominant theme of this chapter and a half is the surprising reversal of contemporary expectation concerning kingdom participants, including a reasonably clear anticipation of many Gentiles taking part, especially in 13:28–29.[31] Standard practices of reciprocity are rebuked (14:7–14a), while Christ promises eternal reward only to those who follow him with no desire for repayment (v. 14b, illustrated by vv. 15–24).[32]

The Cost of Discipleship (14:25–35) [Aland §217–218]. Again, distinctively Lukan parables form the core of this short section (vv. 28–32). Matthew 10:37 is important in interpreting Luke 14:26—"hating" was a vivid Semitic hyperbole for "loving less."[33] Still, in a contemporary conservative Christianity that often seems to stress commitment to "family values" above radical service for Christ, there are strong warnings here. The medieval church was so challenged by the theme of "counting the cost" that at times it limited the application of these verses to clergy and monastic orders! We may also need to rethink the ease with which we declare people to be Christians who pray a simple prayer of invitation or raise a hand in response to an evangelistic appeal. Only those who persevere over the long haul demonstrate themselves truly to have been saved. Still, verses 28–30 balance the cost of following with the cost of not following (vv. 31–32), and it is clear that the second price is far higher.[34]

The Joy of Repentance (15:1–32) [Aland §219–221]. One might also label this section "three parables about lostness"—the lost sheep, lost coin, and lost sons. The three lessons become clear especially when one reads the parable of the prodigal through the eyes of each of the three characters. (1) Wayward individuals are always invited to repent, no matter how far they have fallen. There is no pit so deep that God is not deeper still. (2) God is always waiting, ready to welcome the sinner home. The father demonstrates lavish love by running in a socially undignified fashion and throwing a party rather than requiring penance. (3) The climactic point, however, again addresses conservative religious folk. Those who consider themselves more upright must never resent such "unworthy" recipients of God's

---

[31] M. F. Bird, "Who Comes from the East and West? Luke 13:28–29/Matt. 8:11–12 and the Historical Jesus," *NTS* 52 (2006): 441–57. For a broader catalogue and discussion of key texts, see G. Strathearn, "Jesus and the Gentiles," in *The Life and Teachings of Jesus Christ,* ed. Holzapfel and Wayment, vol. 2, 286–317.

[32] The three main points of the great banquet parable, associated with the three main (groups of) characters, are well captured by R. H. Stein, *An Introduction to the Parables of Jesus* (Philadelphia: Westminster, 1981), 89: "The point [sic] is that the kingdom of God has come and that those who would have been expected to receive it (the religious elite) did not do so, whereas the ones least likely to receive it (the publicans, poor, harlots, etc.) have."

[33] Stein, *Luke,* 397.

[34] Cf. further C. L. Quarles, "The Authenticity of the Parable of the Warring King," in *Authenticating the Words of Jesus,* ed. B. Chilton and C. A. Evans (Leiden: Brill, 1999), esp. 413–16.

grace. Luke 15:1–3 makes it clear that the father is a symbol for God (and indirectly for Jesus), that the prodigal stands for the tax collectors and sinners, and that the older brother represents the Pharisees and scribes criticizing Jesus. But this means that the shepherd and woman in the preceding two parables are also, in some sense, images for God—striking metaphors in a culture that often despised shepherds and considered women second-class citizens![35]

The Use and Abuse of Riches (16:1–31) [Aland §222–228]. The story of the unjust steward (16:1–13) is perhaps the most perplexing of all of Jesus' parables. Why does the master praise one who has squandered his possessions and then legally cheated him out of additional money? The simplest and probably correct answer is because of his shrewdness (v. 8). Jesus ironically comments that God's people are often not nearly as clever as fallen humanity. We must learn to be equally shrewd, without being unethical, particularly in the use of our finances. Verse 9 commands us to use our material resources for kingdom priorities so that the men and women who have benefited in their Christian lives from our stewardship will welcome us in the world to come.[36]

Luke 16:19–31 is also unique to this Gospel and furthers the theme of the right use of our riches. This sumptuous feaster is not condemned merely for being rich. The concern he expresses for his family members who have not repented (v. 30) shows he realized that he, too, had never become right with God. Yet the manifestation of that lack of repentance was his daily neglect of a hopelessly poor and suffering person on his doorstep. He had Moses and the prophets—the Hebrew Bible (v. 31)—and knew his responsibility to be generous to the needy, but he altogether ignored them. Similar behavior in any era falsifies any claim of faith in Christ a person may profess to make.[37]

Teachings about Faith (17:1–19) [Aland §229–233]. Unique to Luke here is the short parable of the unworthy servant (vv. 7–10), which excellently expresses in story form the biblical doctrine of salvation by grace through faith alone.[38] The episode of the ten lepers (vv. 11–19) furthers Luke's concern for society's

---

[35] Cf. B. E. Reid, "Beyond Pretty Pursuits and Wearisome Widows: Three Lucan Parables," *Int* 56 (2002): 284–94. On this whole chapter, see esp. K. E. Bailey, *The Cross and the Prodigal: Luke 15 through the Eyes of Middle Eastern Peasants*, rev. ed. (Downers Grove: IVP, 2005). On vv. 11–32, see G. Forbes, "Repentance and Conflict in the Parable of the Lost Son (Luke 15:11–32)," *JETS* 42 (1999): 211–29; and C. Brown, "The Parable of the Rebellious Son(s)," *SJT* 51 (1998): 391–405. For popular-level exposition from a very encouraging LDS perspective, cf. R. L. Millet, *Lost and Found: Reflections on the Prodigal Son* (Salt Lake City: Deseret, 2001).

[36] For this approach and for a full history of interpretation, see D. J. Ireland, *Stewardship and the Kingdom of God* (Leiden: Brill, 1992). Cf esp. D. L. Mathewson, "The Parable of the Unjust Steward (Luke 16:1–13): A Reexamination of the Traditional View in Light of Recent Challenges," *JETS* 38 (1995): 29–39. For an interesting twist on this view, in which the master has to learn what the steward did all along, namely that money is meant to be used for friendship and human need (including one's own!), see R. Dormandy, "Unjust Steward or Converted Master?" *RB* 109 (2002): 512–27.

[37] On *The Afterlife Imagery in Luke's Story of the Rich Man and Lazarus*, see the book so-entitled by O. Lehtipuu (Leiden and Boston: Brill, 2007).

[38] Esp. as a foil to cultural expectations of reciprocity in patron-client relationships. See M. P. Knowles, "Reciprocity 'Favour' in the Parable of the Undeserving Servant (Luke 17.7–10)," *NTS* 49 (2003): 256–60.

outcasts, including the Samaritans. It also upends expectations of reciprocity. All the Samaritan could do was return and give thanks; the Jews might not have given thanks because they assumed that they owed Jesus a favor in return. But there is nothing we can do to repay Christ for what he does for us, except express our gratitude. As a result, only the Samaritan experiences both physical and spiritual healing (recall above, p. 72).[39]

When and How the Kingdom Will Appear (17:20–18:8) [Aland §234–236]. Most of this section appears in Luke's sources, but Luke balances present and future eschatology by adding verses 20–21, which stress the kingdom's presence, to verses 22–25. The TNIV (cf. NIV margin) gives the more likely reading for verse 21: the kingdom is "among" (not "within") the Pharisees.[40] Thus this text cannot be used to support a merely spiritual or internal interpretation of the kingdom's arrival, as opposed to one that also includes an external or social dimension. In 18:1–8 Jesus returns to the theme of prayer, this time to argue *a fortiori* (from the lesser to the greater) that if even corrupt human judges can be badgered into granting justice, then surely one can expect God to vindicate his chosen children.[41]

The Pharisee and Tax Collector (18:9–14) [Aland §237]. In terms of Luke's overall outline, his central section probably extends a little beyond this passage. With 18:15 he returns to following Mark's narrative fairly closely, and we will pick up the story line there in our next chapter. The final passage entirely unique to Luke in his travel narrative is this parable with yet another striking reversal of expectation as to who is right with God. Unless we recognize the Pharisee as the one assumed to be godlier, we altogether miss the dynamic of Jesus declaring the tax collector justified rather than the religious leader. It is only the tax collector who understands the principle that justification comes solely by throwing oneself on the mercy of God.[42]

Historicity

The historicity of the Q-material in Luke's central section is treated elsewhere in this book. Many of these passages present us with the often unanswerable question: When did Jesus say something more than once, and when has Matthew or Luke (or both) relocated a given saying into a new context? As for Luke's distinctive material, we may observe that it is filled with Jesus' characteristic and challenging parables, along with other succinct, subversive sayings. The occasional miracles that occur cohere with Jesus' behavior elsewhere, as they involve healings on a Sabbath (13:10–17; 14:1–6) or praise for outcasts (17:11–19). Luke

---

[39] Cf. further F. J. Gaiser, "'Your Faith Has Made You Well': Healing and Salvation in Luke 17:12–19," *WW* 16 (1996): 291–301.

[40] Cf. J. Lieu, *The Gospel of Luke* (London: Epworth, 1997), 136.

[41] For a sense of how countercultural this narrative and its characters would have proved, see W. Cotter, "The Parable of the Feisty Widow and the Threatened Judge (Luke 18:1–8)," *NTS* 51 (2003): 328–43.

[42] Cf. T. A. Friedrichsen, "The Temple, a Pharisee, a Tax Collector, and the Kingdom of God: Rereading a Jesus Parable (Luke 18:10–14a)," *JBL* 124 (2005): 89–119.

9:57–62 furthers the theme of radical discipleship, while letting the (spiritually) dead bury the (physically) dead is almost universally agreed to be much too harsh to have been invented. The sending of the seventy (-two) (10:1–24) coheres with the sending of the Twelve (Mark 6:7–13 pars.). The reference to mighty works in Chorazin and Bethsaida (Luke 10:13–15) is probably historical because these miracles are not actually described anywhere that could have generated this reference. Jesus' commendation of Mary's learning as a rabbi's disciple at the expense of Martha's domesticity (10:38–42) almost entirely inverts both Jewish and early Christian practice. It, too, is thus surely authentic. Whether or not attested elsewhere, the gruesome event of 13:1 fits well with the ruthless behavior of Pilate described in Josephus. Luke 13:31–35 strikingly juxtaposes harshness and tenderness in Jesus' verbal assault on Herod and poignant lament over Jerusalem, both in the context of the most positive statement about the Pharisees as a group anywhere in the Gospels. None of these features, much less their combination, would have easily been invented. The theme of the "great reversal" that pervades Luke's central section, especially chapters 14–15, meshes well with the overall patterns of the historical Jesus, while 17:7–10, 17:11–19, and 18:9–14 narrate three illustrations of his characteristically radical grace. Luke 17:20–37 well balances Jesus' distinctive "already but not yet" approach to the arrival of the kingdom. These and similar passages support the hypothesis that Luke relied on tradition or source material even for his unparalleled passages. That tradition also shows numerous signs of historical reliability.[43]

John 5–11

The only full chapter in John's Gospel that presents material about Jesus' great Galilean ministry, and thus overlaps with the Synoptic accounts, is chapter 6 (see above, pp. 315–16). Chapters 5 and 7–11 all describe events in conjunction with Jesus' various trips to Jerusalem at festival time, in between his first and last Passovers there. Because John refers to the various feasts, we are able to develop a rough chronology of Jesus' ministry, but his primary purpose in giving these references is not to enable us to reconstruct a life of Christ. Rather, he wants to show how Jesus fulfills all the major institutions of Judaism.[44] In each case, too, Jesus' claims generate considerable controversy and opposition among his Jewish audiences. In chapter 5, John does not identify the feast at hand (5:1), perhaps because the major controversy here surrounds a healing on the Sabbath, which Jesus fulfills. Chronologically, though, this chapter records events either at Passover (spring) or at the Feast of the Tabernacles (fall), relatively early in Jesus' ministry. John 7:1–10:21 narrates material related to the Feast of the Tabernacles of Jesus' last year of ministry. John 10:22–39 is associated with Hanukkah

---

[43] See throughout D. L. Bock, *Luke 9:51–24:53* (Grand Rapids: Baker, 1996), in the sections entitled "Sources and Historicity."

[44] Cf. Moloney, *John*, 164; B. D. Johnson, "'Salvation Is from the Jews': Salvation in the Gospel of John," in *New Currents through John: A Global Perspective*, ed. F. Lozada, Jr. and T. Thatcher (Atlanta: SBL, 2006), 98.

(December) during Jesus' last year. As noted in our discussion of chronology above (pp. 226–27), Jesus' final trip to Jerusalem probably begins in between these two festivals because, in John 11, Jesus is still nearby in Bethany. With chapter 12, the final week of Jesus' life ensues, and overlaps between John's Gospel and the Synoptics resume.

Healing the Paralytic on a Sabbath (5:1–47) [Aland §140–141]

John 5:1–18 reminds the reader of Jesus' Capernaum miracle narrated in Mark 2:1–12 and parallels, particularly with Jesus' dramatic command, "Pick up your mat and walk" (John 5:8). But the circumstances vary. Jesus is passing by the Bethesda pool where invalids waited in hopes of a chance to bathe and receive divine healing (vv. 2–3, 7). Interestingly, Jesus singles out only one of many to be a recipient of his grace. He redirects the man's attention from the supposedly miraculous power in the water to that which resides in his own person.[45] He also presupposes a connection between the man's illness and his past sinful behavior (v. 14).[46] As with various Synoptic healings, however, the primary controversy that Jesus' actions generate deals with his "working" on the Sabbath (vv. 9–10, 16). Jesus' defense appeals to the continual working of God, whom he invokes as his Father. But for Jesus to be justified in breaking Sabbath by appealing to God's behavior, he must be tacitly claiming divine prerogatives.[47] More specifically, the charge is phrased as "making himself God," which may mean declaring an identity that is not his and/or not acknowledging his dependence on God.[48] The Jewish leaders, hence, again begin to plot his death (vv. 17–18).

As frequently happens in John, a miracle leads to a discourse. Verses 19–47 supply Jesus' more extended defense of his actions. Verse 19 has sometimes been supposed to have been a mini-parable all its own—about an apprentice's son who must always imitate his master—which Jesus is now applying to himself.[49] Beginning with this illustration, Jesus elaborates his "sermon" in two main sections: verses 19–30 and 31–47. Verses 19–30 articulate two key themes: (1) Jesus is completely dependent on and subordinate to his Father. (2) The Father entrusts Jesus with all judgment. Together these themes balance what has been called Jesus' ontological (or essential) equality with God and his functional subordination within the Godhead. "The Father initiates, sends, commands, commissions, grants; the Son responds, obeys, performs his Father's will, receives authority."[50] In his equality with God, Jesus stands over against us; in his subordination he

---

[45] S. M. Bryan, "Power in the Pool: The Healing of the Man of Bethesda and Jesus' Violation of the Sabbath (Jn 5:1–18)," *TynBul* 54 (2003): 7–22.

[46] A connection not always adequately grasped in the noncharismatic world. See J. C. Thomas, "'Stop Sinning Lest Something Worse Come Upon You'," *JSNT* 59 (1995): 3–20.

[47] J. W. Pryor, *John, Evangelist of the Covenant People* (London: Darton, Longman & Todd; Downers Grove: IVP, 1992), 26–27. Cf. Köstenberger, *John*, 185.

[48] Keener, *John*, vol. 1, 647–48.

[49] See esp. C. H. Dodd, "A Hidden Parable in the Fourth Gospel," in *More New Testament Studies* (Manchester: Manchester University Press, 1968), 30–40.

[50] Carson, *John*, 251.

stands with us, showing how we, too, must perform God's will in complete dependence on him. Verse 26 encapsulates both (1) and (2). On the one hand, the Son has life in himself, in the way no other human does. On the other hand, he received that from the Father in a fashion the Father did not have to follow.[51] Verses 31–47 proceed to present four witnesses to corroborate Christ's claims: John the Baptist (vv. 33–35), Jesus' "works" (v. 36), the Father himself (vv. 37–38), and Scripture (vv. 39–47).[52] However, the latter three are not particularly distinct from one another; it is precisely through Jesus' miracles and the Scripture that the Father speaks.

Jesus as Fulfillment of the Feast of Tabernacles (7:1–10:21)

Living Water (7:1–52) [Aland §238–241]. The introductory section of this chapter (vv. 1–13) reminds one of the prelude to the Cana miracle of turning water into wine (2:1–11). Jesus' family members urge him to reveal himself plainly; Christ seemingly refuses but then does so anyway, yet on his own timetable rather than theirs. From verse 14 on, we read of what happens when he does appear publicly in Jerusalem. His discourse takes up where he left off when he was last in town (chap. 5). Verses 14–24 raise again the issue of the origin of Jesus' astonishing teaching and defend the legitimacy of his healing on a Sabbath. The key to determining Jesus' identity is ultimately a moral rather than an intellectual issue.[53] As Jesus continues, he alludes to the hypocrisy of those who would try to take his life (recall 5:18, and cf. 7:1, 11, 13), a plot of which the crowds are ignorant (v. 20). Within the Law, the need to circumcise a child could overrule Sabbath regulations.[54] How much more should one who speaks for the Father himself be able to supersede them (vv. 22–24)?

Jesus' words leave the crowds divided. Verses 25–31 reflect this debate. Verse 27 alludes to a Jewish tradition that the Messiah would suddenly appear "out of nowhere,"[55] whereas the crowds know that this man comes from Nazareth. Verse 28 should be taken either as an ironic declaration, "You think you know me and where I am from," or as a question, "Do you know me. . . ?" Either way, it is clear that the crowds do not recognize his true heavenly origin. The Jewish leaders

---

[51] Cf. U. C. von Wahlde, "He Has Given to the Son to Have Life in Himself (John 5,26)," *Biblica* 85 (2004): 409–12.

[52] For elaboration, see idem., "The Witnesses to Jesus in John 5:31–40 and Belief in the Fourth Gospel," *CBQ* 43 (1981): 385–404.

[53] "This enunciates a very important fact: recognizing the truth of Jesus' teaching is not dependent upon intellectual ability or formal learning, nor is it a reward for the noble search for truth. It depends, rather, upon a person's willingness to do the will of God. The impediments to knowing the truth about God are more likely to be moral (lack of readiness to do God's will) than anything else" (Kruse, *John*, 185).

[54] In the Mishnah, circumcision on the eighth day of a baby's life *had* to be performed, even if that day fell on the Sabbath. See *Shabb.* 18.3; 19:1–2; *Ned.* 3.11. Elsewhere, even the "how much more" (*a fortiori* or *qal-wa-homer*–"from the lesser to the greater") form was employed on this issue. See *Mekilta Exodus* 31.13b; *b. Yoma* 85b.

[55] Justin Martyr (*Dial.* 8.7), e.g., refers to the Jewish belief "that the messiah would be born of flesh and blood yet would be wholly unknown until he appeared to effect Israel's redemption."

remain dead set against him too (v. 32). Jesus knows all this and predicts his coming departure (by death), though again in sufficiently enigmatic language that his
listeners fail to catch on (vv. 33–36).

Verse 37 brings us to the climactic claim of this chapter. For seven days the
festival-goers had observed the water-drawing ritual in which priests processed
from the pool of Siloam to the temple with a golden pitcher of water, proclaiming
with trumpet blasts the text of Isa 12:3: "With joy you will draw water from the
wells of salvation." All the participants then waved palm branches and praised
God joyfully. On the eighth and final day the ceremony was not enacted. How
dramatic and timely, then, for Jesus himself to come and proclaim that he was the
living water, the provider of salvation, for which the Jews longed![56] Many modern
commentators prefer the NIV margin to the text itself for verses 37–38 so that it is
clear that it is Christ alone who is the source of this metaphorical water: "If anyone is thirsty, let him come to me. And let him drink, who believes in me. As the
Scripture has said, streams of living water will flow from within him [i.e., Christ]"
(cf. NRSV, NLT, NET).[57] There is no one Old Testament passage that Jesus is
quoting here, but the themes he enunciates appear in such texts as Isa 58:11, Zech
14:8, and various passages throughout Nehemiah 8–9.[58] John explains, too, that
Jesus is speaking about the coming Spirit who will be dispensed, through Christ,
to his people after his coming "glorification"—death, resurrection, and exaltation
(v. 39). Once more a debate ensues among the crowd, again over Christ's origin
(vv. 40–44). They are apparently oblivious to his birth in Bethlehem, the city of
David from whose lineage Messiah must come. Once again, also, the Jewish leaders are incensed, though Nicodemus offers a minority defense on Jesus' behalf
(vv. 45–52).[59]

Light of the World and the Divine "I AM" (8:12–59) [Aland §243–247]. After
we realize that 7:53–8:11 was almost certainly not in what John originally wrote
(see above, p. 85), 8:12–59 follows naturally. Still at the Feast of Tabernacles,
Jesus now makes a second claim: "I am the light of the world." This pronouncement would also have electrified the crowds. Every night of the feast, four huge
lamps were lit to accompany joyful singing and dancing. On the last night, the
main candelabrum was deliberately left unlit as a reminder that Israel had not yet
experienced full salvation (*Sukk.* 5.2–4). Jesus is now declaring himself to be the
one who can provide that salvation (v. 12).[60]

Jesus' claim is immediately challenged by the religious leaders (v. 13). For
corroborating witness, he appeals again to his Father and to his coming departure

---

[56] See further Beasley-Murray, *John*, 113–14. For full details in the development of these festivities
over time, see H. M. Knapp, "The Messianic Water Which Gives Life to the World," *HBT* 19 (1997):
109–21.

[57] See esp. G. M. Burge, *John* (Grand Rapids: Zondervan, 2000), 227–29. Cf. Keener, *John*, vol.
2, 728–29.

[58] Carson, *John*, 326–38.

[59] For a good treatment of the narrative flow of chap. 7, see H. W. Attridge, "Thematic Development
and Source Elaboration in John 7:1–36," *CBQ* 42 (1980): 160–70.

[60] Cf. Ridderbos, *John*, 292.

(at his crucifixion and heavenly return) in verses 14–29.[61] An oddly worded reply to the question of Jesus' identity in verse 25 should perhaps be translated, "[I am] 'From the Beginning'!—precisely what I have been saying (speaking) to you."[62] Many in his audience at first apparently believe in him (v. 30), but, as the subsequent dialogue demonstrates (vv. 31–59), some have altogether misunderstood him (cf. the description of fickle faith in 2:23–25).[63] Adequate faith will continue to hold fast to Jesus' teaching and provide spiritual liberation (vv. 31–32). Particularly from the religious leaders among Jesus' listeners, however, some believe that their ancestral credentials as God's chosen people have already guaranteed that (v. 33), so Jesus and his audience debate who the true spiritual descendants of Abraham really are and who are, in fact, "children of the devil" (vv. 34–47).[64] As strong as the language is, and even though many would label it anti-Semitic, it is no worse than repeated "in-house" prophetic indictments of major segments of Israel in the Old Testament and intertestamental literature.[65]

When reason fails, the authorities resort to name-calling and abuse (v. 48). Tensions heighten as Jesus further defends his claims in language that makes him out to be, first, greater than Abraham; second, preexisting from before the time of Abraham; and, finally, worthy of the very divine name of Exod 3:14—"I AM" (vv. 49–58).[66] The authorities are so outraged that they initiate mob violence and attempt to stone Jesus (v. 59). Jewish law commanded the stoning of a blasphemer; under Rome, though, Jews were forbidden most forms of capital punishment (cf. John 18:31). In the emotion of the moment, the law apparently did not matter.

More Light for the World: The Healing of the Man Born Blind (9:1–41) [Aland §248]. Jesus' next miracle seems to occur shortly after the Feast of Tabernacles, before Jesus left Jerusalem with the rest of the festival pilgrims and returned home to Galilee one last time. The miracle invites comparison and contrast with 5:1–15. Again, Jesus deliberately selects a Sabbath on which to do his good work (v. 14) and employs an unusually elaborate method—mixing mud and saliva to put on

---

[61] Indeed, the entire chapter is couched as a trial in which Jesus judges his audience. The core of this process involves a five-fold cycle of statement, misunderstanding, and explanation in vv. 32–58. See J. H. Neyrey, "Jesus the Judge: Forensic Process in John 8.21–59," *Bib* 68 (1987): 509–42.

[62] C. C. Caragounis, "What Did Jesus Mean by τὴν ἀρχήν in John 8:25," *NovT* 49 (2007): 129–47.

[63] For the major approaches to the disjunction between one group of people having believed in Jesus and the polemic that ensues, see D. Hunn, "Who Are 'They' in John 8:33?" *CBQ* 66 (2004): 387–99. Hunn observes numerous unannounced partial changes of audience throughout chaps. 7–8, concluding that the "they" of v. 33 (indicated in the Greek only by the third-person plural suffix on the verb "replied") switches, at least in part, to the Jewish authorities who had *not* believed in Jesus.

[64] The best explanation of this and related charges in John in view of the relevant historical and literary contexts is S. Motyer, *Your Father the Devil? A New Approach to John and "The Jews"* (Carlisle: Paternoster, 1997).

[65] See the catalogue of references in Lincoln, *John*, 272–73.

[66] This accounts for the otherwise "bad grammar" in "Before Abraham was, I am" (v. 58). The Greek for "I am" (*egō eimi*) could also reflect dependence on passages like Isa 41:4—"I, the Lord—with the first of them and with the last—*I am he*" (italics added). See also esp. 43:10. Cf. further C. H. Williams, *I am He: The Interpretation of 'Ani Hu' in Jewish and Christian Literature* (Tübingen: Mohr, 1999).

the blind man's eyes (v. 6; recall the discussion on pp. 320–21). Thus he can be accused of violating the Pharisaic Sabbath laws against kneading and the use of spittle. Once again washing in a Jerusalem pool is instrumental in the healing. Rabbinic traditions about the eschatological dimensions of Siloam may suggest deliberate symbolism here.[67] On the other hand, this time Jesus makes it clear that no one's sin has directly caused this man's deformity; rather, "this happened so that the work of God might be displayed in his life" (v. 3).[68] We must beware of assuming either that disease or disaster is always a direct result of an individual's sin or that it can never be.

As in 8:12, Jesus declares himself to be the light of the world. Healing a blind man vividly illustrates that principle in the physical realm as well as the spiritual. After the miracle itself (9:1–12), the Pharisees investigate what has happened by interviewing the formerly blind man, then his parents, and finally the man himself again (vv. 13–34). They cannot believe that a Sabbath-breaker can be from God. The man cannot believe that one who has brought such great good into his life is not from God. In this case, experience disproves tradition. But again logic gives way to verbal abuse.

This twofold dimension of physical and spiritual sight vs. blindness runs throughout chapter 9 and has formed the basis for J. L. Martyn's influential thesis that John is writing to combat Jews who are excommunicating Christians from their synagogues (see esp. v. 22 and recall above, p. 195). Verse 22 has thus been seen as an anachronism that applied only to John's day, but that is to assume that it refers to an empire-wide pogrom. Probably only a short-lived policy within Jerusalem is in view. After all, it is the parents of the man rather than the man himself who fear expulsion, and they are not even described as believing in Jesus. Indeed, what is anachronistic is to imagine a unified, empire-wide verdict in first-century Judaism against Christian Jews at *any* time. To wrongly attribute to institutional Judaism widespread and wholesale persecution of Christians at *any* time in the century smacks far more of the anti-Semitism that scholars who support such theories otherwise want to avoid than to acknowledge smaller, informal hostilities much more sporadically at an earlier time, which are also more historically credible. Indeed, the substantial evidence for close relationships between Jews and Christians in many locations throughout the second through fifth centuries[69] combines with the evidence for intra-Jewish debates over Jesus' potential messianic identity to make it highly likely that the Gospel of John here reflects polemic

---

[67] B. Grigsby, "Washing in the Pool of Siloam—A Thematic Anticipation of the Johannine Cross," *NovT* 27 (1985): 227–35.

[68] A connection not always grasped in the charismatic world. "This happened" is not, in fact, in the Greek text, which is unusually elliptical here (v. 3 altogether reads literally, "Jesus replied, 'Neither this man sinned nor his parents, but in order that the works of God might be shown in him'"), as if to focus more on God's purposes in the healing than on the prior blindness. Cf. Ridderbos, *John*, 333. Burge (*John*, 272–73) takes this as a pointer to taking v. 3b as the introduction to v. 4 instead: "But so that the work of God might be displayed in his life, we must do the work of him who sent me. . ."

[69] For massive documentation, see O. Skarsaune and R. Hvalvik, eds., *Jewish Believers in Jesus: The Early Centuries* (Peabody: Hendrickson, 2007).

within Jewish circles rather than between Jews and a form of Christianity already clearly broken away from Judaism.[70]

The final segment of chapter 9 finds Jesus back with the healed man, eliciting a confession of faith from him while pronouncing judgment on his spiritually blind critics (vv. 35–41). Verse 39 recalls Jesus' reason for speaking in parables (Mark 4:11–12 pars.), and F. F. Bruce comments, "[Jesus'] presence and activity in the world themselves constitute a judgment as they compel men and women to declare themselves for or against him."[71] This is the only place in the whole Bible where a person *born* blind is described as being able to see again. This truly is evidence that demands a verdict.

The Good Shepherd (10:1–21) [Aland §249–250]. The chapter break indicates no change of time or place, and what follows may be an allegory of the preceding incident. Jesus now shifts to a different metaphor: he is the Good Shepherd. Verses 1–5 employ a quasi-parable (see v. 6), which verses 7–18 proceed to explain and elaborate. This entire section develops the contrast between Jesus, the true and noble leader of his people,[72] and the current Jewish regime that has proved false and misleading. Jesus alternates between contrasting himself (a) as the good shepherd, who enters the sheep pen by the gate, with robbers who would climb over the wall, and (b) as the actual gate, through whom the sheep enter by listening to their shepherd's voice, with hirelings whose words the sheep cannot recognize.[73] Behind these contrasts lies Ezekiel 34 with its prophecies of the messianic shepherd who would save his people from the false shepherds currently guiding them.

What makes Jesus so "good" or "noble" above all is his willingness to sacrifice his very life for his flock (vv. 11, 15, 17). Jesus also hints here at the coming ministry to the Gentiles when he adds that he has other sheep "not of this sheep pen" (v. 16). To all he offers abundant life (v. 10; NIV—"life . . . to the full"), but in context this involves no promises of earthly glory or prosperity but of rich, eternal life ("whoever enters through me will be saved"—v. 9). Once again, Jesus' audience is deeply divided over all his remarks (vv. 19–21).[74] Little wonder that 2

---

[70] E. W. Klink III, "Expulsion from the Synagogue? Rethinking a Johannine Anachronism," *TynBul* 59 (2008): 99–118.

[71] Bruce, *John*, 220.

[72] For a detailed defense of why *kalos* ("good") here implies "noble" (a well-established meaning of the word), in light of the Greco-Roman traditions about noble deaths, see J. H. Neyrey, "The 'Noble Shepherd' in John 10: Cultural and Rhetorical Background," *JBL* 120 (2001): 267–91.

[73] For a fascinating discussion of how realistic all this is, even by the practices of contemporary Middle Eastern peasant shepherds, see K. E. Bailey, "The Shepherd Poem of John 10: Their Culture and Style," *NESTTR* 14 (1993): 3–21. Allowing oneself to be killed merely to protect a few sheep, however, is very rare, and highlights the allegorical meaning and central thrust of Jesus' word pictures.

[74] On this chapter more generally, cf. J. Beutler and R. T. Fortna, eds., *The Shepherd Discourse of John 10 and Its Context* (Cambridge: CUP, 1991). On the ways in which Jesus aligns himself unique with God and uniquely with humanity in this section, see J. H. Neyrey, "'I Am the Door' (John 10:7–9): Jesus the Broker in the Fourth Gospel," *CBQ* 69 (2007): 271–91.

Baruch 77:11–16 will depict the Law as a shepherd, light, and water, but Jesus has now completed this Tabernacles celebration by claiming to be all three himself!

The Feast of Dedication (Hanukkah): Jesus and the Father Are One (10:22–42) [Aland §257–258]

The events of John 10:22–11:54 presumably take place after at least the start of Jesus' Judean ministry (see below, chap. 16), but it makes sense to comment on them here because of their thematic links with the preceding material in John. In December of AD 29 (or 32), Jesus is in Jerusalem for the last festival before the Passover in which he will lay down his life (vv. 22–23). Just as he has fulfilled the other main Jewish institutions, so he will provide the true spiritual liberation that corresponds to the physical liberation that Hanukkah commemorated. Jesus' audience, frustrated by his seemingly blasphemous claims during prior forays to Jerusalem, but realizing that all of them were susceptible to a variety of interpretations, demands him to disclose his identity plainly (v. 24). Still he refuses. If they had the eyes of faith, they would have found his words and works more than sufficient; for those who do belong to Jesus are already secure in that relationship with him (vv. 25–29). Again, he climaxes his reply with a claim that is taken as blasphemy (vv. 31–33), while still open to other explanations: "I and the Father are one" (v. 30).[75]

To refute the charge of blasphemy, Jesus in verse 34 makes one of his more enigmatic appeals to Scripture, citing Ps 82:6. In this passage, the psalmist refers to the corrupt evil judges of his day (or perhaps to Israel at the time of the giving of the Law) as "gods." If the authoritative Scriptures can call mere mortals "gods," in this limited sense of referring to earthly leaders, Jesus argues, then how much more is it not acceptable for him to apply the term to himself, who is God's unique agent on earth (vv. 35–36)?[76] *Contra* various cults or sects, this passage teaches nothing about Christians becoming deified.[77] Jesus again appeals to the testimony of his works, but to no avail. He leaves Jerusalem to avoid further troubles for the moment and goes back across the Jordan to where people will believe (vv. 37–42).

The Raising of Lazarus (John 11:1–54) [Aland §259–261]

The first "half" of John's Gospel climaxes with the most dramatic miracle in all of Jesus' ministry, excluding his own resurrection. He has previously brought people back to life shortly after their deaths, but never a person who had been dead four days and already entombed (11:17). Given the Jewish tradition that one's soul hovered near the body for up to three days after expiry (e.g., *Gen. Rab.* 100 [164a]), here is an individual who has truly "given up the ghost." Once again,

---

[75] See esp. J. C. O'Neill, "'Making Himself Equal with God' (John 5.17–18): The Alleged Challenge to Jewish Monotheism in the Fourth Gospel," *IBS* 17 (1995): 50–61.

[76] On the "from the lesser to the greater" logic of this passage and its various other implications, see J. H. Neyrey, "I Said 'You Are Gods': Psalm 82:6 and John 10," *JBL* 108 (1989): 647–63.

[77] C. B. Mosser, "The Earliest Patristic Interpretations of Psalm 82, Jewish Antecedents, and the Origin of Christian Deification," *JTS* 56 (2005): 30–74.

Jesus' behavior stresses God's sovereign timing: on hearing of Lazarus's illness, Jesus deliberately delays for two days before leaving for Bethany (v. 6).[78] The result is to magnify the miracle that much more, for the sake of God's glory (v. 4). "The tragedy is not by God's design, but God will use it for an opportunity to glorify his Son."[79] When the disciples protest that Jerusalem and its vicinity are too dangerous, Jesus explains that he is safe until the appointed time for his tragic destiny (vv. 9–10).

John 11:1–16 thus sets the stage for the miracle; verses 17–44 describe what happens when Christ arrives in town. Parallel conversations with Lazarus' sisters, Martha and Mary (vv. 17–37), highlight some of the same features noted about them in Luke 10:38–42. For example, bustling Martha hurries out to meet him, but reflective Mary stays at home (v. 20). A still more important difference characterizes this encounter with the two women. While Jesus elicits a profession of faith from Martha (v. 27), it remains well within conventional Jewish categories (v. 24). "Christ" and "Son of God" need mean no more than "nationalistic Messiah," as with Nathanael in 1:49. Even if for Martha the titles mean more than this, it is clear that she does not yet envision Lazarus's revivification (v. 24). Martha appears in John's Gospel only again in the context of providing domestic hospitality (12:2). Mary however seems to have understood more fully, as she reappears in the company of those Jews who see Lazarus's return to life and genuinely believe (11:45). In chapter 12 she will be the one to anoint Jesus' body in preparation for his burial, perhaps the first person to grasp completely what kind of Messiah Jesus would be (12:3–8).[80]

The central focus of John 11, of course, is the revivification miracle itself (vv. 38–44). Jesus has shown deep emotion upon arrival at the tomb (v. 35); now tears turn to anger (the more common meaning of the verb *embrimaomai* used in v. 38—"deeply moved"). His strong emotions are responding not only to death's apparent victory but also to his contemporaries' unbelief (v. 37). Jesus' sorrow and anger balance each other in crucial ways. "Grief and compassion without outrage reduce to mere sentiment, while outrage without grief hardens into self-righteous arrogance and irascibility."[81] Christ proceeds to corroborate his claim to be the resurrection and the life (v. 25) by calling Lazarus to come out of the tomb. This is the only miracle in which we have a record of Jesus' praying as a prelude, and he does so audibly. He also explains, however, that this is for the crowd's benefit, not his own (vv. 41–42).[82]

Verses 45–54 describe the aftermath of Lazarus' revivification. Here appear some of the most ironic words in all the Gospels. Caiaphas, the high priest, along

---

[78] Despite the NIV's "yet," the Greek reads, literally, "So thus when he heard. . ." (rightly TNIV). This "shows that Jesus' delay was not at odds with his love, but motivated by it" (Kruse, *John*, 247).

[79] Burge, *John*, 313.

[80] Cf. F. Moloney, "The Faith of Martha and Mary: A Narrative Approach to John 11, 17–40," *Bib* 75 (1994): 47–93.

[81] Carson, *John*, 476.

[82] For broader theological syntheses, see W E. Sproston North, *The Lazarus Story within the Johannine Tradition* (Sheffield: SAP, 2001).

with the Sanhedrin, determines that one who can bring someone back to life is too dangerous to be allowed to live. They act as if they could permanently lay Jesus to rest! In solidifying their plot against him, Caiaphas speaks better than he knows. For him, verse 50 would have meant merely that they must save the Jewish nation from Roman retribution by sacrificing Jesus before he stirred up the masses, but John sees in this statement an unwitting prophecy of Christ's atoning sacrifice.[83] The two perspectives together add up to a theology that views Jesus' followers as the true, restored remnant of Israel.[84] For the time being, however, Jesus retreats from the public eye to a small village, Ephraim, probably about twelve miles northeast of Jerusalem (v. 54).

Even at this late date in his ministry, even in this Gospel most concerned to stress the deity of Christ, Jesus' words and works are left to speak for themselves. There is always another way to explain who he is. God never coerces belief. The growing polarization of response to Jesus will soon erupt into violence and execution.

Historicity

It is very likely that Jesus the Jew would have made the required pilgrimages to Jerusalem at festival times. Contrary behavior would surely have cropped up in the Synoptic accounts of the debates between Jesus and the Jewish leaders. The Sabbath healings of chapters 5 and 9 cohere in contents and style with the Synoptic healing and conflict stories, most notably Mark 2:1–12 and parallels (cf. esp. Mark 2:9 with John 5:8). The healing of blind men and the use of spittle (John 9:6) also form striking parallels with what we have seen in the Synoptics. So, too, do specific teachings of Christ in these chapters (cf., e.g., John 5:30 with Luke 22:42; or John 9:39 with Matt 15:14) as well as general themes (e.g., Jesus' joint concern for both physical and spiritual wholeness and his subordination to the Father as one sent as the Father's agent). Nevertheless, the length and tenor of the dialogues and discourses in these chapters is clearly distinct. Perhaps an initial parable about a son's apprenticeship (5:19–20a) has been elaborated into a discourse (see above, p. 344); perhaps Jesus realized that the stakes were higher in his encounters with the Jerusalem officials so that more detailed discussion was needed. In choosing to leave out an entire portion of Jesus' ministry, namely, his frequent trips to Jerusalem at festival time and the public debates they triggered, the Synoptists may have omitted one distinctive form of debate and discourse in which Jesus engaged.

John 7 begins with Jesus at odds with his family, much as in Mark 3:31–35 and parallels. We have already noted that the "I am" sayings were probably more cryptic in their original contexts than they seem to us. If Jesus believed himself to be the Light of the World (John 8:12; 9:5), it would be natural for him

---

[83] Josephus repeatedly speaks of the belief that the high priest could exercise the gift of prophecy (*Ant.* 11.8.4. 13.10.3).

[84] J. A. Dennis, *Jesus' Death and the Gathering of True Israel: The Johannine Appropriation of Restoration Theology in Light of John 11,47–52* (Tübingen: Mohr Siebeck, 2006).

Jesus Fulfills Jewish Festivals (John 5–11)						
5	**6**	**7**	**8**	**9**	**10**	**11**
		——————Tabernacles———————				
"the Feast" (5:1) (Passover?) Sabbath	Passover (6:4)	(7:2)		Sabbath	Sheep Gate and Good Shepherd (10:7, 11)	The Resurrection and the Life
fulfilling water rituals of Judaism	Bread of Life	Living Water	Light of the World	Light of the World	Hanukkah	
(5:2)	(6:35)	(7:38)	(8:12)	(9:5)	(10:22)	(11:25)

to tell his disciples to reflect that light (Matt 5:14). John 7:23 contains the same kind of reasoning about the Sabbath as in Luke 13:15–16 and 14:5. The harsh accusations by Jesus' opponents (he has a demon—7:20; he is a Samaritan and demon-possessed—8:48; he is raving mad—10:20) are too unflattering to have been invented. The slave-son comparison of 8:35 mirrors much of the imagery of the Synoptic parables. Jesus' denial that Abrahamic descent guarantees spiritual freedom (8:37–58) matches John the Baptist's warnings (Matt 3:8–9 par.). Even Jesus' stunning identification of himself with the divine "I AM" in 8:58 simply makes explicit what is already implicit in Mark 6:50 (see above, p. 316). And the divided responses of the crowd throughout these chapters are exactly what one would expect a radical charismatic to elicit.

The metaphors of John 10 fit well with the Synoptics: Jesus' calling himself the good shepherd matches God's role in the parable of the lost sheep (Luke 15:3–7 par.), while calling himself the Door (i.e., gate for the sheepfold) reminds us of his command to enter by the correct gate (Matt 7:13–14). His promise to lay down his life for his sheep (John 10:11–18) meshes with his passion predictions in the Synoptics. The Jews' plea in 10:24 foreshadows Caiaphas' later question at Jesus' trial (Mark 14:61 pars.). Lazarus's revivification in John 11 is not the first such miracle in the Gospels, even if it may be the most dramatic. As with Jairus' daughter (Mark 5:21–43 pars.), Jesus is delayed in coming, but this serves only to magnify the miracle. The roles Mary and Martha play (e.g., in John 11:20) perfectly fit their characters as described in Luke 10:38–42. Jesus' very human emotions (John 11:35, 38) distinguish this narrative from later Christian apocrypha, while the wealth of circumstantial detail throughout the account reads like eyewitness testimony. The omission of this "greatest of all miracles" from the Synoptics is probably due to nothing more than their desire not to describe Jesus in or around Jerusalem until his final Passover.[85]

---

[85] For further discussion of all of these passages, see Blomberg, *Historical Reliability of John's Gospel*, 108–18, 131–75.

For Further Study

Matthew 10 and 18

Levine, Amy-Jill. *The Social and Ethnic Dimensions of Matthean Social History.* Lewiston: Mellen, 1988.

Park, Eung Chun. *The Mission Discourse in Matthew's Interpretation.* Tübingen: Mohr, 1995.

Thompson, William G. *Matthew's Advice to a Divided Community: Mt 17,22–18,35.* Rome: BIP, 1970.

Weaver, Dorothy J. *Matthew's Missionary Discourse: A Literary-Critical Analysis.* Sheffield: JSOT, 1990.

Luke's Central Section

Bailey, Kenneth E. *Poet and Peasant* and *Through Peasant Eyes.* 2 vols. Grand Rapids: Eerdmans, 1983.

Drury, John. *Tradition and Design in Luke's Gospel.* London: Darton, Longman & Todd; Atlanta: John Knox, 1976.

Egelkraut, Helmuth L. *Jesus' Mission to Jerusalem: A Redaction-Critical Study of the Gospel of Luke 9:51–19:48.* Frankfurt: Peter Lang, 1976.

Evans, Craig A. and James A. Sanders. *Luke and Scripture: The Function of Sacred Tradition in Luke-Acts.* Minneapolis: Fortress, 1993; Eugene, OR: Wipf & Stock, 2001.

McComiskey, Douglas S. *Lukan Theology in the Light of the Gospel's Literary Structure.* Waynesboro, GA, and Milton Keynes: Paternoster, 2004.

Moessner, David P. *Lord of the Banquet: The Literary and Theological Significance of the Lukan Travel Narrative.* Minneapolis: Fortress, 1989.

The Teaching of Jesus

Beck, James R. *The Healing Words of Jesus.* Grand Rapids: Baker, 1993; Eugene, OR: Wipf & Stock, 2001.

Bruce, F. F. *The Hard Sayings of Jesus.* London: Hodder & Stoughton; Downers Grove: IVP, 1983.

Chilton, Bruce and Craig A. Evans, eds., *Authenticating the Words of Jesus.* Boston and Leiden: 2002.

Flusser, David with R. Steven Notley. *The Sage from Galilee: Rediscovering Jesus' Genius.* Grand Rapids and Cambridge: Eerdmans, 2007.

Gempf, Conrad. *Jesus Asked: What He Wanted to Know.* Grand Rapids: Zondervan, 2003.

Manson, T. W. *The Sayings of Jesus.* London: SCM, 1957; Grand Rapids: Eerdmans, 1975.

McKnight, Scot. *The Jesus Creed: Loving God, Loving Others.* Brewster, MA: Paraclete, 2004.

Stein, Robert H. *The Method and Message of Jesus' Teachings.* Rev. ed. Louisville: WJKP, 1994.

Thatcher, Tom. *Jesus the Riddler: The Power of Ambiguity in the Gospels.* Louisville and London: WJKP, 2006.

Vanderlip, D. George. *Jesus of Nazareth: Teacher and Lord.* Rev. Ed. Valley Forge: Judson, 1994.

Young, Brad H. *Jesus the Jewish Theologian.* Peabody: Hendrickson, 1995.

Questions for Review

1. As you survey this potpourri of additional teachings of Jesus in Matthew, Luke, and John, review the distinctive theological emphases of each of these three evangelists. How many of them can you find in the material surveyed here? Which ones stand out in particular?

2. Are there any of the exegetical observations about specific passages that strike you as particularly new? as particularly relevant to contemporary Christian living? Itemize a few and explain.

3. Summarize the structure of Matthew 10 and how the outline proves relevant for important interpretive debates on key passages in this chapter. Do the same for Matthew 18.

4. How would you summarize Jesus' ethics as they emerge from the teachings largely unique to Luke in his "central section"? In other words, what are the key topics to which he keeps returning again and again?

5. Take each of the major events and/or discourses in John 5–11 and show how they demonstrate John's conviction that Jesus came to fulfill one of the key festival days or rituals of Judaism.

16

JESUS' JUDEAN MINISTRY

T HE SYNOPTICS GO their separate ways in describing the latter stages of Jesus' Galilean ministry, but they converge again as Jesus arrives in Judea for the final phase of his life. Closer verbal parallelism leads to fewer redactional distinctives among the Gospel writers. This chapter surveys Jesus' teaching immediately en route to Jerusalem, his final public ministry in Jerusalem during his last week, and his "sermon" to his disciples on the Mount of Olives overlooking the town.

In Judea on the Road to Jerusalem (Mark 10 pars.; John 11:55–12:11 pars.)

The episodes narrated in Mark 10 and parallels seem to unfold in mostly chronological order as Jesus draws ever nearer to Jerusalem. They are also united by reflecting (a) primarily teaching material; (b) a series of controversies, often "traps," generated by questioners who approach Jesus to engage him in dialogue; (c) Jesus' increasing focus on the demands of discipleship; and (d) his concern to reverse the patterns of privilege of the powerful, religious males in his society by expressing concern for women, children, the poor, and the sick. The anointing in Bethany (John 12:1–11 pars.) takes place the day before Jesus' "triumphal entry," inaugurating his final week in Jerusalem.

Teaching on Divorce (Mark 10:1–12 par.) [Aland §251–252][1]

A lively debate separated the Pharisaic schools of Shammai and Hillel, two leading rabbis a couple of decades older than Jesus. Deuteronomy 24:1 permitted a man to divorce his wife if he found "something indecent" about her. Was this limited to sexual unfaithfulness (so Shammai), or could it be applied much more widely (so Hillel)? The Mishnah would later attribute to Hillel the opinion that divorce could occur "for any good cause"—"he may divorce even if she spoil his cooking" (*Git.* 9:10)! What did Jesus think? These Pharisees may have hoped that he would incriminate himself on the topic the way John the Baptist had by criticizing Herod Antipas.

For once Jesus' reply is more conservative than both camps. In Mark, his prohibition against divorce seems absolute. In Matthew, he allows divorce in the case of adultery (19:9; recall 5:32), but he does not require it as both schools of Pharisaic law did. Many redaction critics argue that Matthew's "exception clauses" are later additions trying to tone down the seemingly impossible and idealistic demands of Christ. A few ultraconservatives have argued that neither Mark's nor Matthew's version permits divorce under any circumstances because the verb *apoluō* can also be translated "to separate."[2] But it is clear from the reference to Deut 24:1 that the Pharisees were debating divorce, not merely separation, and there is no contextual evidence that the meaning of the word changes in the middle of the passage. More likely, Mark does not spell out the exception to his rule because all Jewish and Greco-Roman opinion of the day recognized that adultery *de facto* severed a marriage, after which both divorce and remarriage were expected.[3] Matthew, writing to a more Jewish-Christian audience, preserves the fuller account of Jesus' words, to position him more explicitly in the midst of the Jewish debate. Yet both versions agree that the predominant pattern to be emphasized is lifelong faithfulness to marriage vows, in keeping with God's creation ordinances, and in contrast to a society in which divorce ran rampant.

Numerous other exegetical controversies surround Matt 19:9 and 5:32. Should *porneia* ("sexual immorality") be translated more broadly than "adultery" to include premarital sexual relations? Should it be translated more narrowly so as to limit it to marriages between close relatives prohibited by Leviticus 18 (as in 1 Cor 5:1)? Probably neither is correct in this context. Jewish women married so young that premarital sex was rarely a problem, and the word *porneia* is the stan-

---

[1] For details of the subsequent exposition, see C. L. Blomberg, "Marriage, Divorce, Remarriage and Celibacy: An Exegesis of Matthew 19:3–12," *TJ* 11 (1990): 161–96.

[2] E.g., J. C. Laney, "No Divorce and No Remarriage," in *Divorce and Remarriage: Four Christian Views*, ed. H. W. House (Downers Grove: IVP, 1990), 15–54. Another option is to translate *mē epi* in v. 9 a way so that it does not mean "except for." But A. R. Guenther ("The Exception Phrases: Except πορνεία, Including πορνεία or Excluding πορνεία? [Matthew 5:32; 19:9]," *TynBul* 53 [2002]: 83–96) shows how grammatically unlikely this is.

[3] See further W. A. Heth, "Jesus and Divorce: How My Mind Has Changed," *SBJT* 6 (2002): 4–29. For more detailed cultural background, see B. Rawson, ed., *Marriage, Divorce, and Children in Ancient Rome* (Oxford: Clarendon, 1996); and M. L. Satlow, *Jewish Marriage in Antiquity* (Princeton and Woodstock, Oxfordshire: Princeton University Press, 2001).

Marriage & Divorce in Matt. 19 & 1 Cor. 7

Leave	become
&	one
Cleave	flesh

physical | sexual
BUT
presence | infidelity

sexual | physical
BUT
fidelity | desertion

other items
? equivalent in ?
destructiveness

forming
a
marriage

rupturing
a
marriage

dard general term in the Greek for sexual sin, so one should not limit it to incest without immediate contextual support.[4] What does "except for adultery/sexual immorality" modify? Just "divorce" or both "divorce and remarriage"? Probably the latter, given that it is sandwiched in between the two and given the cultural assumptions already noted.[5] Admittedly, the majority view in the ancient church was against all remarriage. This prohibition included widows and widowers, whom the Bible at times encourages to remarry, and was heavily influenced by an unbiblical asceticism that increasingly crept into the Greek and Latin churches in sexual matters more generally (hence, the later Roman Catholic insistence that clergy and monastic orders be celibate).[6]

Application of Jesus' teaching on divorce for today requires a fair amount of exegetical sophistication and pastoral sensitivity. At least five points merit emphasis: (1) *God's primary intention for marriage remains no separation of any kind.* Christians who are contemplating marriage, or who are still married to their first spouse, should move heaven and earth to stay faithful to one another.[7] (2) In a radically countercultural move, *Jesus puts the husband's and wife's rights (and sins!) on an equal footing* (Mark 10:11–12). (3) *Some Christians may never marry, and they dare not be treated as second-class citizens.* Indeed, celibacy can be a gift

---

[4] Cf. further D. Janzen, "The Meaning of *Porneia* in Matthew 5.32 and 19.9: An Approach from the Study of Ancient Near Eastern Culture," *JSNT* 80 (2000): 66–80.

[5] For details, see P. H. Wiebe, "Jesus' Divorce Exception," *JETS* 32 (1989): 327–33; and cf. the caveats raised by S. E. Porter and P. Buchanan, "On the Logical Structure of Matt. 19.9," *JETS* 34 (1991): 335–39.

[6] See, in detail P. A. Harrell, *Divorce and Remarriage in the Early Church* (Austin: Sweet, 1967).

[7] See, e.g., the many helpful works by L. Parrott and L. Parrott, esp. *Love Talk: Speak Each Other's Language Like You Never Have Before* (Grand Rapids: Zondervan, 2004).

from God, like other spiritual gifts (Matt 19:10–12; 1 Cor 7:7).[8] ("This word" of verse 11 most likely refers back to verse 10; hence, not all have this gift but some do.) If Catholicism has historically overemphasized the value of celibacy, Protestantism has historically underemphasized the value of the holy, single life.[9]

(4) Additional, crucial teaching appears in 1 Corinthians 7, including *a second exceptional situation in which divorce may be permitted: desertion by an unbeliever* (vv. 15–16). It is instructive to note what this exception has in common with Matthew's. Each ruptures half of the marriage relationship as defined by Gen 2:24 ("A man will leave his father and mother and be united to his wife, and they will become one flesh"). Part one refers to intimate, interpersonal loyalty; part two, to the consummation of the bond with sexual intercourse. Desertion makes it impossible to continue the interpersonal allegiance; infidelity destroys the exclusivity of the sexual relationship.[10] Perhaps the way to answer the question if any other circumstances ever make divorce permissible in God's eyes is to ask if anything else so undermines an actual marriage. Decisions may need to be settled on a case-by-case basis but always leaning on the side of caution to help keep marriages intact.[11]

(5) Finally, where divorce is already an accomplished fact, we need *the right balance of compassion and firmness*. Where sorrow for sin and repentance for whatever fault one party had in the breakup of a marriage have not adequately occurred, consistent discipline requires that a Christian not be allowed to carry on with church membership or ministry as if nothing had happened. Where such contrition has occurred and where a person has demonstrated over time a proven track record of celibacy in singleness or faithfulness to a second spouse, divorce must not be treated as an unforgivable sin. Neither church membership in good standing nor opportunities for ministry are necessarily forfeited.[12]

---

[8] C. Bernabé ("Of Eunuchs and Predators: Matthew 19:1–12 in a Cultural Context," *BTB* 33 [2003]: 128–34) offers the intriguing suggestion that men who followed Jesus' countercultural teachings that place a greater priority on love than on patriarchy could have been viewed as "unmanly" enough by some to have been thought of as (metaphorical) eunuchs!

[9] For important contemporary applications, see K. Aune, *Single Women: Challenge to the Church?* (Carlisle and Waynesboro, GA: Paternoster, 2002); and L. F. Winner, *Real Sex: The Naked Truth about Chastity* (Grand Rapids: Brazos, 2006).

[10] Cf. esp. D. L. Atkinson, *To Have and To Hold* (London: Collins, 1979; Grand Rapids: Eerdmans, 1981).

[11] Cf. W. F. Luck, *Divorce and Remarriage* (San Francisco: Harper & Row, 1987); C. S. Keener, . . . *And Marries Another: Divorce and Remarriage in the Teaching of the New Testament* (Peabody: Hendrickson, 2001). It is not clear that abuse or neglect constitute biblical grounds for divorce, simply because a biblical marriage is described as not containing these elements (*contra* D. Instone-Brewer, *Divorce and Remarriage in the Bible: The Social and Literary Context* [Grand Rapids and Cambridge: Eerdmans, 2002], 189–212). At least a temporary separation for physical and/or mental protection should, however, be initiated whenever needed.

[12] "The husband of but one wife" in 1 Tim 3:2 cannot exclude the divorced unless it also excludes the widowed (i.e., if the verse refers to someone literally married only once, then it does not distinguish between reasons for a second marriage). Paul elsewhere counsels widows and widowers to remarry under certain circumstances (1 Tim 5:14; 1 Cor 7:9), and it is unlikely he would do this if he knew such people were thereby disqualifying themselves from church office. All the other criteria of

Jesus Blesses the Children (Mark 10:13–16 pars.) [Aland §253]

After discussing marriage and divorce, the topic of children follows naturally. Rabbis were often asked to bless boys and girls in the ancient Jewish world, and they would pray for God's favor to rest on them. Jesus' disciples reflect a common, low view of children in antiquity as they snub some who were seeking Jesus' blessing. The episode turns into a "pronouncement" or "controversy" story with Jesus' climactic declaration that one must enter the kingdom like these little children. As in Matt 18:3–4, Jesus is not commending childishness, but childlikeness. Just as children recognize their absolute dependence on the adult world, whether they like it or not, so would-be believers must come to God recognizing their utter dependence on him.[13] Jesus' blessing the children has sometimes been used to promote infant baptism, but it may suffice to point out that neither infants nor baptism appears anywhere in the passage. Instead, in its first-century context, "since it is disciples, and not the Pharisees or scribes who raise the objection, it is likely that the pericope reflects an internal issue in church life, namely exclusiveness and striving after status."[14]

The Rich Young Ruler and Related Incidents (Mark 10:17–31 pars.; Luke 19:1–27) [Aland §254–255, 265–266]

The next person to approach Jesus on the road is a well-to-do, young synagogue official (called a "ruler" in Luke 18:18).[15] The contrast with the little children just blessed could scarcely be greater. Like the lawyer in Luke 10:25, this man asks how to inherit eternal life. Jesus gives a strange rebuff. In Mark, he inquires as to why the man calls him a good teacher since only God is good (Mark 10:18). Is Jesus denying that he is good? Is he implying that he is God? Matthew's redaction makes it less likely that one would come to the former conclusion (Matt 19:17). Perhaps Jesus is merely diverting attention from the man's inadequate criterion ("What must I do?) to focus instead on the divine standard of goodness.[16] Christ goes on to quote key commandments from the Decalogue, but the man

---

1 Tim 3:1–7 refer to the settled, current behavior of candidates for the eldership, not to things they may have done a long time ago. "Husband of but one wife" should thus be understood as someone who is (and has been) faithful to his or her current spouse, if married—a mature, committed, family person—nothing more and nothing less. Cf., e.g., M. D. Owens, "Should Churches Ordain the Divorced and Remarried? An Examination of Μιᾶς Γυναικὸς Ἀνήρ in the Pastoral Epistles," *Faith and Mission* 22.3 (2005): 42–50; E. F. Glasscock, "'The Husband of One Wife' Requirement in 1 Timothy 3:2," *BSac* 140 (1983): 244–58.

[13] Cf. J. L. Bailey ("Experiencing the Kingdom as a Little Child: A Rereading of Mark 10:13–16," *WW* 15 [1995]: 58–67), who stresses the element of vulnerability; with S. Fowl ("Receiving the Kingdom of God as a Child: Children and Riches in Luke 18.15ff.," *NTS* 39 [1993]: 153–58), who highlights the characteristic of a single-minded, unrelenting pursuit of a desire.

[14] Cf. Boring, *Mark*, 289.

[15] In Mark's, probably oldest, account, it is not until the end of the narrative, as the man leaves grieving, that we are told that he was rich, i.e., that he had many possessions (10:22). S. E. Wheeler (*Wealth as Peril and Obligation: The New Testament on Possessions* [Grand Rapids: Eerdmans, 1995], 51) thus comments: "For Mark, the fact of the man's wealth is the least important thing about him, deservedly tacked on at the end of the account as a kind of afterthought."

[16] So already St. John Chrysostom in the fourth century in his *Homilies on Matthew* 63.1.

insists he has kept these (Mark 10:19–20). Yet he still senses a lack (Matt 19:20). Jesus puts his finger on it by commanding him to sell his many possessions, give to the poor, and follow him in discipleship (Mark 10:21). These commands must be taken as a package: altruism or humanitarian aid without commitment to Christ counts for nothing in eternity.

Does Jesus make so stringent a demand of all would-be followers? No, in fact, there is no other person in the entire Bible who is given a similar call. Luke's outline at this point reinforces this observation most explicitly. Luke will shortly juxtapose the story of Zacchaeus' conversion (Luke 19:1–10) and the parable of the pounds (vv. 11–7).[17] The former describes the about-face of a chief tax collector (one of the "publicans" who worked directly for Rome) who voluntarily gives up half his goods to the poor and restores fourfold to those he has cheated in his tax business.[18] Rabbinic law normally discouraged someone from ever giving away more than 20 percent. So Zacchaeus is clearly going well beyond the call of duty, but still he retains at least some of his wealth. The parable of the pounds commends the faithful servants who invest their wealth and make more money, but all of it reverts back to the master for his service and use.[19] Obviously, there are many different ways to be good stewards of the material possessions God gives us. However, if wealth ever stands in the way of our wholehearted allegiance to Christ, then we must divest ourselves of it.[20] As Gundry remarks, "That Jesus did not command all his followers to sell all their possessions gives comfort only to the kind of people to whom he would issue that command"![21]

After the rich young ruler goes away sorrowfully,[22] Jesus astonishes his audience by stressing how hard it is for rich people in general to enter the kingdom (Mark 10:23–24). Using a dramatic hyperbole, he likens the situation to a camel going through the eye of a needle—the largest Palestinian animal passing through the smallest common opening (v. 25)! The disciples recognize the literal impossibility involved. Given the prominent Old Testament mind-set that recognized

---

[17] On all three passages, cf. further Blomberg, *Neither Poverty nor Riches*, 124–25, 138–41.

[18] A vigorous debate has ensued over whether this is a *conversion* story (about behavior Zacchaeus was just about to begin) or a *defense* story (in which Luke 19:8 would be describing his *characteristic* practice). The former is more likely; cf. J. Nolland, *Luke 18:35–24:53* (Dallas: Word, 1993), 906.

[19] This parable is often seen as a later allegorical elaboration of Matt 25:14–30 and a conflation of the Matthean parable with a "throne claimant parable" (the story of the nobleman going to receive a kingdom opposed by an embassy of his citizens). But the Lukan context (increased opposition on the road to the cross) makes Jesus' parable here intelligible on its own. See esp. B. Schultz, "Jesus as Archelaus in the Parable of the Pounds (Lk. 19:11–27)," *NovT* 49 (2007): 105–27. In Matthew, moreover, the emphasis is on the appropriate response of disciples; in Luke, on the horrible fate of opponents.

[20] Cf. esp. A. P. Stanley, "The Rich Young Ruler and Salvation," *BSac* 163 (2006): 46–62. Keener (*Matthew*, 476) adds that "Jesus' sorrow over the unwilling disciple (Mk 10:23–25) indicates that he hoped not to turn disciples away but rather to make them *genuine* disciples, which they could do only by counting the cost and choosing the narrow way of following him."

[21] Gundry, *Matthew*, 388.

[22] Showing that he *knew* he was letting himself be deceived by wealth, for otherwise why would he grieve? Thus, D. O. Via, Jr., *The Ethics of Mark's Gospel—In the Middle of Time* (Philadelphia: Fortress, 1985), 138.

riches as a blessing from God for faithfulness, they wonder how anyone could ever be saved (v. 26). Jesus' reply makes it clear that by God's grace the humanly impossible becomes possible (v. 27). What then of the disciples who have left many of their possessions behind to go on the road with Christ (v. 28)? Jesus promises them a hundredfold recompense. It is illegitimate to spiritualize verses 29–30 or limit them to heavenly rewards since Jesus speaks also of persecutions. Rather, the hundredfold homes and fields the disciples receive come the same way they acquire more brothers, sisters, mothers, and children. All members of the community of God's people are family and share with each other as anyone has need.[23] Matthew's version adds a promise seemingly just for the Twelve: they will sit on

Luke on Wealth & Stewardship		
18:18–30	19:1–10	19:11–27
Jesus & the Rich Young Ruler	Zacchaeus's Conversion	The Parable of the Pounds
"Sell all that you have and distribute to the poor."	"The half of my goods I give to the poor, and if I have defrauded any one of anything, I restore it fourfold."	"Why then did you not put my money into the bank, and at my coming I should have collected it with interest?"
(v. 22)	(v. 8)	(v. 23)
		(RSV)

thrones judging Israel when the new age arrives in all its fullness (Matt 19:28). Because 1 Cor 6:2–3 speaks of all Christians judging the whole world and even angels, this privilege is somewhat relativized.

The Parable of the Laborers in the Vineyard (Matt 20:1–16) [Aland §256]

Matthew uniquely appends a parable of Jesus that stresses the equality of all disciples in a world preoccupied with privilege. The three points associated with the master, the first workers, and the last workers are aptly captured in Matt 20:13–16. From those hired first, we learn that God treats no one unfairly (vv. 13–14). From those hired last, we discover that he chooses to treat some quite generously (v. 15). From verse 16, interpreted in light of the imagery of the parable, we recognize the fundamental equality of all disciples in God's eyes. First are last and

---

[23] See D. M. May, "Leaving and Receiving: A Social-Scientific Exegesis of Mark 10:29–31," *PRS* 17 (1990): 141–54. J. H. Hellerman ("Wealth and Sacrifice in Early Christianity: Revisiting Mark's Presentation of Jesus' Encounter with the Rich Young Ruler," *TJ* 21 [2000]: 164) adds, "Jesus challenged the rich young ruler to do much more than simply divest himself of his wealth. Jesus offered him the opportunity to disentangle himself from the structural evil which characterized first-century Palestinian social relations in order to participate in a new spiritual and socio-economic reality which would someday turn the Roman Empire on its head."

last are first in this context because all roles are interchangeable.[24] This parable is one of the clearest teaching passages in Scripture against the notion of degrees of eternal reward in heaven. After all, what can improve on perfection?[25] The passage also convicts those who are entirely content with their God-given gifts in this life until someone else gets even more. "The grumblers are not reacting to injustice but to generosity, and about that they have no right to complain."[26]

The Third Passion Prediction and the Disciples' Misunderstanding (Mark 10:32–45 pars.) [Aland §262–263]

To further underline his commitment to servanthood rather than privilege, Jesus predicts his suffering, death, and resurrection yet once more (recall Mark 8:31; 9:31 pars.), this time in the greatest detail of all (10:32–34). Creating a striking contrast, Mark immediately juxtaposes the incident in which two of the disciples request positions of power in Jesus' kingdom (vv. 35–37). Jesus makes it plain that all he can share with them is the right to suffer (vv. 38–41) and proceeds to redefine true spiritual leadership as ruling through selfless service rather than authoritarian power-broking. The latter is a pagan, not a Christian approach, from which Christians should be liberated (vv. 42–45).[27] "If there is to be ambition in the service of God . . . it must be the ambition to serve others."[28] The passage culminates with a rare and important statement by Jesus about the vicarious, atoning nature of his coming death: "the Son of Man did not come to be served, but to serve, and to give his life as a ransom for many" (v. 45). The language of ransom mirrors that of the slave market—the price paid to buy a slave's freedom. An allusion to Isa 53:10, 12 about God's suffering servant is probably present, especially in light of Jesus' explicit use of verse 12 in Luke 22:37. The Greek word for "for" (*anti*) is probably best rendered here as "instead of" or "in place of," hence, the substitutionary nature of the sacrifice is mentioned here.[29]

---

[24] See further Blomberg, *Interpreting the Parables*, 221–25.

[25] Following Martin Luther, but *contra* John Calvin. See further C. L. Blomberg, "Degrees of Reward in the Kingdom of Heaven?" *JETS* 35 (1992): 159–72. I in no way deny that each believer will have a very unique experience with God on Judgment Day, some receiving much more praise than others. What I dispute is that there are any passages that clearly teach that such differences translate into varying statuses or privileges throughout all eternity. Damnation is by works, but salvation is by grace.

[26] Witherington, *Matthew*, 375.

[27] See esp. A. de M. Kaminouchi, *"'But It Is Not So among You': Echoes of Power in Mark 10.32–45* (London: T&T Clark, 2003).

[28] France, *Matthew*, 760.

[29] On the meaning and authenticity of this saying, see esp. R. E. Watts, "Jesus' Death, Isaiah 53, and Mark 10.45: A Crux Revisited," in *Jesus and the Suffering Servant: Isaiah 53 and Christian Origins*, ed. W. H. Bellinger, Jr. and W. R. Farmer (Harrisburg: Trinity, 1998), 125–41. On the current controversy over substitutionary atonement more generally, see esp. I. H. Marshall, *Aspects of the Atonement: Cross and Resurrection in the Reconciling of God and Humanity* (Milton Keynes and Waynesboro, GA: Paternoster, 2008), esp. 34–67.

Healing Blind Bartimaeus (Mark 10:46–52 pars.) [Aland §264]

By now Jesus is in Jericho, just fifteen miles from his destination in Jerusalem.[30] The final full-fledged healing-narrative of the Gospels ensues. Blind Bartimaeus cries out to the one he acknowledges as Messiah ("Son of David") to help him see.[31] Jesus cures him and, for the last recorded time in the Gospels, repeats the refrain, "your faith has healed you" (v. 52)—spiritually as well as physically. Previously, Jesus told the recipients of his miracles to say nothing or to return home and witness to their families. Now, however, the appropriate response is to follow Jesus along the road because it is the road to the cross. Bartimaeus' physical and spiritual sight contrasts with the disciples' continuing lack of vision, most recently evidenced in their jockeying for positions of power.[32]

The Anointing in Bethany (John 11:55–12:11; Mark 14:3–9 par.) [Aland §261, 267–268]

Only John gives an explicit statement of when this event happened—six days before the Passover (12:1)—that is, the Saturday before what we now call Palm Sunday. Mark and Matthew relocate this passage topically because of the symbolism of preparing Jesus for his burial, sandwiching the narrative between a reference to the later plot of the Jewish leaders to arrest Jesus (Mark 14:1–2 par.) and Judas' arrangement to betray him (vv. 10–11 par.). There are other noteworthy differences between John and Mark/Matthew, though none of them needs be viewed as a contradiction.[33] At any rate, Mary lavishes her affection on Jesus by pouring over him a jar of perfume worth about a year's wages (John 12:3). Judas protests at the "waste," but we are told that he was used to pilfering from the disciples' treasury (vv. 4–6).

Jesus' reply answers the similar objection even of a well-meaning individual with a developed social conscience. There are times for one-of-a-kind, unrepeatable, costly acts of devotion to Christ. But the words, "You will always have the poor among you" (v. 8), afford no excuse for general inaction. Mark's fuller

---

[30] Mark and Matthew place this story as Jesus is leaving Jericho (Mark 10:4; Matt 20:29). Luke seems to locate it before they arrive in town (Luke 18:35). But "drawing near" may refer more generally to "being in the vicinity" (see S. E. Porter, "'In the Vicinity of Jericho': Luke 18:35 in the Light of Its Synoptic Parallels," *BBR* 2 [1992]: 91–104). Or Luke may be simply abbreviating his material and re-arranging it topically, as Calvin suggested already in the sixteenth century in his *Harmony of the Gospels*, vol. 2, p. 278. See further Liefeld and Pao, "Luke," 284.

[31] As in Matt 9:27–31, Matthew's version refers to two blind men (Matt 20:30). Perhaps Bartimaeus was the primary speaker, or perhaps he was the one who most distinguished himself in subsequent discipleship.

[32] Cf. esp. I. U. Olekamma, *The Healing of Blind Bartimaeus (Mk 10,46–52) in the Markan Context: Two Ways of Asking* (Frankfurt and New York: Peter Lang, 1999). Cf. Kernaghan, *Mark*, 207: "If the healing of the blind man at Bethsaida (8:22–26) is a parable for Peter, then the healing of Bartimaeus may be a parable for James and John."

[33] Was the home Simon's or Lazarus's? Probably Simon's, with Lazarus and his family as the invited guests and servers. Was Jesus anointed on the head or on the feet? Probably both, since the quantity of spikenard involved could easily have covered his whole body. In John, moreover, Mary and Judas replace otherwise unnamed characters in Mark, and additional information is given about their motives. Cf. further Carson, *John*, 426–27.

account of Jesus' reply continues to explain, "and you can help them any time you want" (Mark 14:7). His words actually allude to Deut 15:11 ("There will always be poor people in the land"), a verse that immediately goes on to declare, "Therefore I command you to be openhanded toward your brothers and toward the poor and needy in your land." In this unique context, Mary's "waste" was appropriate. As Bruce explains, "Unusual expense at a funeral was not regarded as unseemly; why should anyone object if the ointment which would otherwise have been used to anoint his dead body in due course was poured over him while he was still alive and able to appreciate the love which prompted the action?"[34]

Historicity

Jesus' pronouncements in this section continue to differ from both Judaism and early Christianity: his stringent rejection of divorce by appealing to creation ordinances rather than legal casuistry, his exaltation of children as a paradigm of the humble, and his demanding teachings on stewardship of wealth. In addition, Mark 10:18 contains potentially embarrassing Christology; Mark 10:23–25, Jesus' characteristic hyperbole. Matthew 19:28 goes to the heart of Jesus' intentions to constitute a new or renewed Israel, despite being largely unparalleled.[35] Other distinctively Matthean material is primarily parabolic and generally held to be authentic. The saying about Jesus' death as a ransom (Mark 10:45) is more disputed. Still, like the passion predictions more generally, this verse seems to be a natural outgrowth of Jesus' meditation on Isaiah 52–53 and the model of the Maccabean martyrs, yet with a distinctive messianic application not characteristic of the Judaism of Jesus' day.[36] The healing of blind Bartimaeus coheres with other miracles of healing the blind we have previously discussed. At the anointing in the house of Simon the leper, both Mary's and Judas' behavior proves embarrassing, even if in different ways.[37] Interestingly, one of the Dead Sea scrolls confirms that the vicinity of Bethany was home to one of the leper colonies of that day (11QTemple 46:16–18).

Jesus in Jerusalem: Final Days of Public Ministry (Mark 11–12 pars.)

With Jesus' arrival in Jerusalem, anticipation and conflict both grow to a fever pitch. The events covered in this section span the Sunday through Tuesday prior to Christ's execution. Three prophetic "object lessons" all portend Israel's ominous

---

[34] Bruce, *John*, 257.

[35] See Sanders, *Jesus and Judaism*, 98–102.

[36] See esp. M. Wilcox, "On the Ransom-Saying in Mark 10:45c, Matt 20:28c," in *Geschichte—Tradition—Reflexion*, ed. H. Cancik, H Lichtenberger, and P. Schäfer (Tübingen: Mohr, 1996), 173–86. Cf. R. Riesner, "Back to the Historical Jesus through Paul and His School (The Ransom Logion—Mark 10.45; Matthew 20.28)," *JSHJ* 1 (2003): 171–99.

[37] On the authenticity of at least a substantial core of this event, see K. E. Corley, "The Anointing of Jesus in the Synoptic Tradition: An Argument for Authenticity," *JSHJ* 1 (2003): 61–72.

Jesus' Final Week								
Sat.	**Sun.**	**Mon.**	**Tues.**	**Wed.**	**Thur.**	**Fri.**	**Sat.**	**Sun.**
anointing in Bethany	triumphal entry	temple cleansing & fig tree (1)	fig tree (2) & teaching in temple/ Mt. of Olives	?	prep. for Passover, Last Supper & Gethsemane	trial(s), sentence, & execution		resurrection!

future. Then Jesus teaches in the temple, evading verbal traps set by the Jewish leaders, and concludes by pronouncing judgment on them instead.[38]

Actions of Judgment (Mark 11:1–26 pars; John 12:17–50)

Entrance into Jerusalem (Mark 11:1–10 pars.; Luke 19:41–44) [Aland §269–270, 302–304]. This story is usually called the "triumphal entry" and has been celebrated throughout Christian history on "Palm Sunday," one week before Easter. It might better be labeled the "a-triumphal entry." This ragtag band of followers accompanying a Galilean peasant riding a donkey would have looked like a parody of the standard welcome and fanfare for governors and generals astride their white horses with a retinue of soldiers. Still, Jesus is making deliberate messianic claims. His behavior enacts the prophecy of Zech 9:9, which both Matthew and John spell out (Matt 21:5; John 12:15). He orders the animal commandeered in kingly fashion (Mark 11:2–3). The colt must be unridden, thus still "pure" and suitable for sacred purposes.[39] Jesus is acknowledged by the crowds of Galilean pilgrims in a manner reminiscent of the greetings for rulers in Old Testament and intertestamental times (cf. 2 Kgs 9:13; 1 Macc 13:51). They line the road with their garments and palm branches from nearby Jericho (Mark 11:8; John 12:13) and cry "Hosanna" (Hb., "God save us"), using messianic language from the pilgrims' Psalm 118 (vv. 25–26), which was customarily sung during their ascent to the Temple Mount.

The crowds still do not understand, however, that Jesus has come to his nation's capital to die and that reigning as king must await a future day. Unlike the war horse, the donkey is an animal of peace and humility. No Romans will be conquered this week. Luke's immediately preceding parable of the pounds was told to dispel the notion that the kingdom would come in power at once (Luke

---

[38] On the connections among these events, as well as with those during the rest of Jesus' final week, see J. P. Heil, "The Narrative Strategy and Pragmatics of the Temple Theme in Mark," *CBQ* 59 (1997): 76–100.

[39] It is often alleged that Matthew has garbled the picture by speaking of Jesus astride two donkeys (Matt 21:5, 7), but v. 5 is a case of synonymous parallelism, while the antecedent in the Greek for the final "them" of v. 7 is more naturally the cloaks, not the animals. That a mother would be needed along with her colt to make the younger animal willing to be ridden (and the text does not say that the animal had never previously carried *any* kind of pack) is only to be expected. See Gundry, *Matthew*, 409; Witherington, *Matthew*, 391. Cf. also D. Instone-Brewer, "The Two Asses of Zechariah 9:9 in Matthew 21," *TynBul* 54 (2003): 87–98.

19:11). Luke also adds Jesus' lament that the people did not recognize his overtures for peace. As a result the city can look forward only to its coming destruction, in AD 70 (19:41–44), about which Jesus will have more to say later on the Mount of Olives. It is little wonder that some of these cheering Jesus would join the native Jerusalemites in their disenchantment only five days later and call for Jesus' crucifixion.[40] Overall, however, the makeup of the two crowds would have been substantially different.

As he often does, John makes it clear that even the disciples did not understand the significance of these events until after his resurrection (John 12:16). Typically, too, John appends a discourse of Jesus on the theme at hand: here, the glorification of the Son of Man (12:23–50). It is impossible to determine when this was given; any time between Sunday and Thursday would fit. For John, however, these words form an appropriate conclusion to Jesus' public ministry. They are triggered by the desire of some Greeks (i.e., Gentiles) to see Jesus (vv. 20–22). In essence, Jesus replies that now is not the time for an audience with them but rather for the event that would provide salvation for all peoples, Greeks included. After frequently declaring that his hour had not yet come (2:4; 7:30; 8:20), Jesus now climactically announces that it has arrived (12:23; cf. 13:1; 17:1). Death must precede victory, as it seems to do with seeds and as it will be for disciples (vv. 24–26). Jesus' message is accompanied by the divine voice of attestation (vv. 27–30), and his audible prayer recalls his language at Lazarus's tomb (11:41–42). His death will bring judgment against his opponents but the opportunity of salvation for all who will allow themselves to be drawn to him (12:31–32).[41] The "lifting up" in verse 32 suggests a classic Johannine double meaning: the crucifixion will also lead to Christ's exaltation. The crowds continue not to grasp Jesus' intent (vv. 33–36), which he recognizes as further fulfillment of Isa 6:10 (vv. 37–43). Verses 44–50 conclude the discourse by reiterating the twofold power of Christ's mission—both to judge and to save—in complete accordance with the Father's will.

The Withered Fig Tree (Mark 11:12–14, 20–25 par.) [Aland §271–272, 275]. Part of the anticlimax of Jesus' "triumphal entry" into Jerusalem is that he goes to the temple, looks around, and does nothing (Mark 11:11).[42] After lodging overnight in nearby Bethany, he heads again for the temple the next morning. En route, he finds a fig tree with leaves but no fruit and pronounces a curse on it (vv. 12–14).

---

[40] On this whole event, esp. with its various triumphal and a-triumphal elements, see B. Kinman, "Jesus' Triumphal Entry in the Light of Pilate's," *NTS* 40 (1994): 442–48; and P. B. Duff, "The March of the Divine Warrior and the Advent of the Greco-Roman King," *JBL* 111 (1992): 55–71. For a book-length treatment, cf. B. Kinman, *Jesus' Entry into Jerusalem: In the Context of Lukan Theology and the Politics of His Day* (Leiden: Brill, 1995).

[41] "There is no limit to Jesus' saving power—except the resistance of unbelief. In spite of the universalistic overtone and intent of the statement, faith is still included as a condition" (R. Schnackenburg, *The Gospel according to St. John*, vol. 2 [London: Burns & Oates; New York: Seabury, 1980], 393).

[42] Nor do the accompanying pilgrims try to force his hand in any way (contrast John 6:15). Little wonder the authorities take no action. "Jesus appears to be only a figure of some unspecified distinction against the background of the popular hope that God would save Israel by restoring David's kingdom" (Kernaghan, *Mark*, 213).

By the next day it has completely withered (vv. 20–21). This second miracle of destruction in the Gospels is clearly filled with symbolism. Mark deliberately sandwiches the two parts of its narrative around the story of the "temple cleansing" (vv. 15–19).[43] The two events are meant to be interpreted together. Just as the land producing no fig trees often stood for judgment against Israel in Jewish literature (esp. Mic 7:1; Jer 8:13), and just as Jesus had earlier told a parable of a fig tree threatened with destruction (Luke 13:6–9), so now he uses an enacted parable or object lesson to demonstrate the imminent doom of the current Jewish nation if it does not repent.[44]

The disciples marvel, and Jesus uses the occasion to teach a related point about faith (Mark 11:22–25). These verses are often taken out of context and generalized in ways that the text does not permit. Although language about faith moving mountains was proverbial in antiquity (cf. 1 Cor 13:2), here Jesus specifically promises that "if anyone says to this mountain" (NIV) that it be cast into the sea, it will occur (Mark 11:23, italics added). As the disciples walked from Bethany to the temple, "this" mountain would most naturally refer either to the Mount of Olives or to Zion, the Temple Mount. Given the eschatological symbolism of the Mount of Olives being split in two (Zech 14:4) and given the symbolism of the withered fig tree and the related incident in the temple, it is far more likely that Jesus is calling his disciples to trust in his promises that a new world order replacing the temple is imminent. Verses 24–25 are probably to be taken in this context, too, although it remains true theologically that "when prayer is the source of faith's power and the means of its strength, God's sovereignty is its only restriction."[45]

Clearing the Temple (Mark 11:15–19 pars.) [Aland §273–274]. Even though it is delayed by a day, Jesus does complete the prophesied coming of God to his temple to refine and to judge it (Mal 3:14).[46] Jesus' action in the temple has traditionally been called a "cleansing," on the assumption that, by ridding its precincts of the money changers and vendors of sacrificial animals, Jesus was purifying the building and restoring its original purpose as a house of prayer. An element of

---

[43] In his desire to create a neater literary narrative, Matthew puts both parts of the fig tree story together, creating the illusion that it all took place on one day (Matt 21:18–22). Still, Matthew never says this in so many words, and the language of "immediate" withering (v. 19) is still appropriate even if it took place over several hours. Trees normally take far longer to decay! Cf. Ridderbos, *Matthew*, 389–90.

[44] Cf. esp. W. R. Telford, *The Barren Temple and the Withered Tree* (Sheffield: JSOT, 1980). One "miracle of destruction" does not justify our rape of the environment any more than the loss of one herd of pigs earlier in Gerasa justifies systematic neglect of animal rights. Both incidents do remind us that humans are the unique "life form" created in God's image so that there are special occasions known at times only to God, when it is acceptable to prioritize human need (even for vivid object lessons!) over the needs of other parts of creation.

[45] Lane, *Mark*, 410. For a full study of *Prayer, Power, and the Problem of Suffering: Mark 11:22–25 in the Context of Markan Theology*, see the work so-entitled by S. E. Dowd (Atlanta: Scholars, 1988). On the link between Jesus' teaching on prayer here and the temple-clearing, see M. Moulton, "Jesus' Goal for Temple and Tree: A Thematic Revisit of Matt 21:12–22," *JETS* 41 (1998): 561–72.

[46] On the connections between the "Palm Sunday" activity, cursing the fig tree, and Jesus' subsequent temple ministry, see esp. S. G. Brown, "Mark 11:1–12:12: A Triple Intercalation?" *CBQ* 64 (2002): 78–89.

cleansing is no doubt intended, but it seems that it is too late in Jesus' ministry and that the Jewish leaders are too entrenched in their opposition to him for his behavior in the temple to have any enduring positive effect. He may, indeed, be offering one last chance at repentance, but the outcome is all but certain. Not surprisingly, this event becomes the final catalyst in prodding on those who are plotting his death (Mark 11:18; Luke 19:47–48). Quite likely, an element of prophetic symbolism is also present throughout. As with the fig tree, the temple and all it stands for will soon be destroyed.[47] The literal building will not fall until AD 70, but the sacrificial system will be outmoded and superseded as soon as Christ dies and is raised again (though Jesus' followers would not recognize that fact immediately). Only in Jesus will forgiveness of sins then be available. That explains why on the very next day Jesus will leave the temple for the last time, declaring "Your house is left to you desolate" (Matt 23:38).[48] There is also a contrast between the intended use of the court of the Gentiles and its Jewish transformation into a "nationalist stronghold," as Jesus appeals to Isa 56:7 and Jer 7:11 and their larger contexts.[49] God's salvation in Jesus will be equally accessible to all people.

Teaching in the Temple (Mark 11:27–12:44 pars.)

On Tuesday morning Jesus and his disciples return to the temple for the third straight day. All three Synoptics report how he encounters a series of questioners from among the Jewish leaders trying to make him incriminate himself.[50] Each question aptly fits the category of person who asks it. In Mark, these conflict stories create an inclusio with the similar set of conflicts narrated in 2:1–3:6. The four episodes in Mark 12:13–37 interestingly correspond to the four questions of the ancient Passover liturgy: (a) a question regarding a point of law (on paying taxes—vv. 13–17); (b) a question with a note of scoffing (on the resurrection—vv. 18–27); (c) a question by a person of "plain piety" (the scribe asking about the greatest commandment—vv. 28–34); and (d) a question by the father of the family at his own initiative (Jesus asking about David's son—vv. 35–37).[51] Do the evangelists by this device intend to point out Jesus as the true fulfillment of the Passover?

The Question about Jesus' Authority (Mark 11:27–33 pars.; Matt 21:28–32; Mark 12:1–12 pars.; Matt 22:1–14) [Aland §276–279]. The three groups comprising the temple authorities understandably approach Jesus first to ask by what

---

[47] See further J. B. Chance, "The Cursing of the Temple and the Tearing of the Veil in the Gospel of Mark," *BI* 15 (2007): 268–91.

[48] On the theme of messianic judgment in the temple clearing, cf. C. L. Wahlen, "The Temple in Mark and Contested Authority," *BI* 15 (2007): 248–67.

[49] On which, see H. J. Carey, "Teachings and Tirades: Jesus' Temple Act and His Teachings in Mark 11:15–19," *SCJ* 10 (2007): 93–105. Cf. Hagner, *Matthew 14–28*, 601.

[50] For a fascinating study of the dynamics of honor and shame that would have governed these interchanges, see J. H. Hellerman, "Challenging the Authority of Jesus: Mark 11:27–33 and Mediterranean Notions of Honor and Shame," *JETS* 43 (2000): 213–28.

[51] D. Daube, *The New Testament and Rabbinic Judaism* (London: Athlone, 1956; Peabody: Hendrickson, 1994), 158–69.

authority he created the previous day's chaos (Mark 11:27–28). In common rabbinic fashion, Jesus answers the question with a question. His ploy in forcing
them to respond to the issue of John the Baptist's identity is clear; his authority
comes from the same source as John's (God). The leaders cannot affirm this in
good conscience, yet they dare not deny it publicly. So the attempted trap gets
them nowhere (vv. 29–33).

Jesus, however, keeps talking. All three Synoptics narrate the parable of the
wicked tenants, which contains a clear jab at the leaders' own authority. Matthew
uniquely includes this as the middle of a series of three parables that narrate,
metaphorically, the trial—"verdict," "sentence," and "execution"—of the present
Jewish leadership.[52] The parable of the two sons portrays outcasts and sinners
entering the kingdom before (or "instead of") the religious authorities. Performance takes priority over promise (Matt 21:28–32). Here, too, appears a further
implicit answer to the Jewish leaders' question: Jesus' authority comes from God,
just as the ultimately obedient son's authority came from *his* father.[53]

The parable of the wicked tenants narrates the results of the leaders' disobedience: the kingdom will be taken away from them and given to a people (i.e., Jesus'
followers of any ethnic background) who do produce the appropriate fruit (Matt
21:33–46, see esp. v. 43). Three clear points associated with the main characters of this parable emerge: God's patience, the eventual destruction of the rebellious, and the replacement of Israel with the church as the locus of God's saving
activity. The role of the son suggests a fourth point, however muted. Like the
son, Jesus will soon be killed, but like the stone of Ps 118:22–23, he will subsequently be honored and inflict damage on those who oppose him.[54] Whether or
not Jesus' opponents understood this veiled Christological claim, they definitely
recognized their role in his allegory and left all the more convinced to do him in
(Mark 12:12).

Matthew 22:1–14 brings this triad of parables to a climax. (On the debate
about whether verses 6–7 are a "prophecy after the fact," see above, pp. 152–53).
Jesus may be looking beyond the Roman suppression of the Jewish rebellion in
AD 70 to final judgment. Again, three key points appear. Two are reminiscent of
Luke's great banquet parable (Luke 14:16–24): God invites all kinds of people
into his kingdom, and rejection of the invitation leads to exclusion for the origi-
nal guests and the invitation of replacements. The distinctive, climactic focus of
Matthew's parable involves the curious episode of a man without a wedding gar-

---

[52] Schweizer, *Matthew*, 402. W. G. Olmstead (*Matthew's Trilogy of Parables: The Nation, the
Nations and the Reader in Matthew 21.28–22.14* [Cambridge: CUP, 2003]) demonstrates that Matthew has more than *just* the leaders of Israel in view, since many other Jews rejected Jesus also, but it
is "supremely" the leaders on whom he focuses.

[53] G. R. Smillie, "Jesus' Response to the Question of His Authority in Matthew 21," *BSac* 162
(2005): 459–69.

[54] Blomberg, *Interpreting the Parables*, 247–51. By far the fullest study of this parable now is J.
S. Kloppenborg (*The Tenants in the Vineyard: Ideology, Economics, and Agrarian Conflict in Jewish
Palestine* [Tübingen: Mohr Siebeck, 2006). The best one, however, remains K. R. Snodgrass, *The Par-
able of the Wicked Tenants* (Tübingen: Mohr, 1983).

ment (vv. 11–13). Perhaps the ancient tradition of a host providing festive attire is presupposed; the man would thus have deliberately refused it. At any rate, Jesus seems to be stressing that all who would come to him must come on his terms and not their own.[55]

On Tribute to Caesar (Mark 12:13–17 pars.) [Aland §280]. Jesus' next group of interrogators is sure they have him trapped. Pharisees resented paying taxes to Rome, while Herodians supported the status quo. However Jesus answers their question, one group will be irate. He avoids their "catch-22" situation by affirming part of each of their views. Human governments have a legitimate but limited scope. The Jews are happy to use Roman coinage minted with the impression of Caesar's image when it serves their financial purposes, so they should pay the tribute even when those purposes seem not to be served. However, God demands the primary loyalty—if his mandates conflict with human regulations, the latter must always give way.[56] This passage has understandably been central in the Lutheran, Baptist, and later American convictions that political and religious "kingdoms" be kept separate. If Jesus could issue this command to oppressed peoples living under a foreign totalitarian regime, how much more ought Christians in modern democratic contexts work lawfully within the system whenever possible![57]

Ridiculing the Resurrection (Mark 12:18–27 pars.) [Aland §281]. The Sadducees did not believe in resurrection from the dead, for they did not find it taught in the five books of Moses (recall, above, pp. 51–52). To ridicule the doctrine and to try to trap Jesus where the other Jewish leaders failed, they imagine an unusual situation in which a woman has had seven different brothers for husbands. The scenario builds on the Old Testament levirate laws in which brothers were required to marry and raise up children for childless, widowed sisters-in-law (cf. Deut 25:5; Gen 38:8). Jesus' reply accomplishes two things: it refutes the Sadducees' mistaken notion that the age to come would preserve the institution of marriage and procreation as we know it, and it demonstrates the existence of resurrection life from the Torah. Jesus' appeal to the implicit present tenses of Exod 3:6 ("I *am* the God of Abraham," italics added) does not at first glance seem to demand his conclusion, at least by modern standards of exegesis, but it does closely parallel ancient Jewish methods of interpretation (cf. esp. *b. Sanh.* 90b, deriving the resurrection from Num 18:28). Perhaps the best explanation is

---

[55] Cf. R. Bauckham, "The Parable of the Royal Wedding Feast (Matthew 22:1–14) and the Parable of the Lame Man and the Blind Man (Apocryphon of Ezekiel)," *JBL* 115 (1996): 488: "Those who are unworthy of entering the Kingdom of God are not only those who spurn the Gospel invitation but also those who ostensibly accept it while rejecting what it really represents."

[56] Hauerwas (*Matthew*, 190) offers the indictment that "Christians are told that they should never let their loyalty to the state qualify their loyalty to God, but they never seem clear when and if such a conflict might actually happen. Christians are usually Herodians but lack the means to recognize themselves as such."

[57] Cf. Stein, *Luke*, 496; Evans, *Mark 8:27–16:20*, 247; Davies and Allison, *Matthew*, vol. 3 (1997), 216–17. The view that sees God's claims as so all-encompassing as to cancel out the first part of Jesus' statement ("give to Caesar . . .") is improbable, not least because it destroys the delicate balance of Jesus' answer in fully satisfying neither Pharisee nor Herodian. Nevertheless, it is certainly the case that what is owed to God is far more than what is owed to even the greatest of merely human rulers.

that he was presupposing the Jewish belief that death annulled a covenant. But if God was still keeping his covenant to the patriarchs by this kind of present tense self-description, then they must still be alive. Part of that covenant also involved giving them embodied life in the land of Canaan forever, so therefore they must be awaiting a resurrection in order to inherit that part of the promise.[58]

The Greatest Commandment (Mark 12:28–34 par.) [Aland §282]. A lawyer now takes his turn in the line of questioners. He naturally asks about the greatest law, a topic of lively Jewish debate already. Jesus' answer is thoroughly orthodox. Love of God was commanded immediately after the *shema* ("Hear, O Israel: The Lord our God, the Lord is one"—Deut 6:4–5) and seen as fundamental to all of life. Hillel had already summarized the Law via Lev 19:18, and Akiba would later agree (*b. Shabb.* 31a; *Sifra* 89b). Jesus fuses together the commands to love God and neighbor in a way that makes claims of doing one without the other nonsensical. Although the lawyer concurs with Jesus' summary, Christ still criticizes him as outside (though not far from) the kingdom (Mark 12:34). Because the man is not yet a disciple of Jesus, he cannot adequately fulfill either commandment. Those who do become his followers discover that the process of discipleship itself fulfills the whole Law (recall above, p. 289). But, "this does not mean, as some modern ethicists have argued, that 'all you need is love,' so that one can dispense with the ethical rules set out in the Torah. It is rather to say that those rules find their true role in working out the practical implications of the love for God and neighbor on which they are based."[59]

The Question about David's Son (Mark 12:35–37 pars.) [Aland §283]. The questioners have been silenced, so Jesus turns the tables on them. How can they view the Messiah as a merely human, royal, nationalist descendant of David?[60] To press home his point, he calls attention to Ps. 110, widely believed in his day to be Davidic. In it, two "lords" appear: Yahweh God and another "lord" (*adonai* in Hb.). Were the speaker anyone other than David, king of Israel, the second "lord" could be some earthly master. But there is no human higher than David in Israel. The lord must be the Messiah, and he must be higher than David. The logic seems irrefutable, and the crowds marvel. Not surprisingly, Psalm 110 came to be the most widely quoted Old Testament passage in all of the New Testament.[61]

Warnings and Woes against the Jewish Leaders (Matthew 23 pars.) [Aland §284–285]. Jesus culminates his teaching in the temple with vituperative denunciations of select Pharisees and scribes. Mark gives only a brief account of this

---

[58] B. R. Trick, "Death, Covenants, and the Proof of Resurrection in Mark 12:18–27," *NovT* 49 (2007): 232–56.

[59] France, *Matthew*, 847. On this whole passage, see further G. Keerankeri, *The Love Commandment in Mark: An Exegetico-Theological Study of Mk 12,28–34* (Rome: PIB, 2003).

[60] No one in ancient Judaism, including Jesus elsewhere, denied the Messiah's humanity or his descent from David, so we have to understand an implied "merely" in the question about how the Jewish leaders could view this "Lord" as David's "son." Cf. Witherington, *Mark*, 333; Evans, *Mark 8:27–16:20*, 274.

[61] On its various uses and their interrelationships in the church's developing Christology, see M. Hengel, *Studies in Early Christology* (Edinburgh: T&T Clark, 1995), 119–225.

invective; Matthew goes into gruesome detail. Jesus' woes at the beginning of the last sermon that Matthew records create an inclusio with the beatitudes at the beginning of his first sermon (Matt 5:3–12). Matthew 23 has been called the most anti-Semitic chapter in the New Testament, but this label is unfair: (1) Jesus and all his first disciples were also Jewish. (2) Jesus is not denouncing all Jews, not even all Jewish leaders. (3) Jesus' words are no harsher than long sections of Old Testament prophecy, most notably Jeremiah, in which God was particularly displeased with his people and their rulers.[62] (4) Jesus ends his polemic with a poignant lament, demonstrating how grieved he is about this state of affairs (vv. 37–39). (5) Matthew's application of this material to his community probably has conservative legalistic Christians *inside* his church primarily in view (cf. vv. 8–12).

There are hypocrites in every religious community, so Jesus' charges are not historically implausible. At the very beginning of his denunciations, he acknowledges that even these teachers should be followed when they promote that which is consistent with Torah (vv. 2–3).[63] But then he proceeds to castigate them for several serious inconsistencies. They are motivated by the desire for human praise and status (vv. 5–12)[64] and misguided in their proselytizing zeal (vv. 13–15).[65] They have inverted priorities in oath-taking and tithing (vv. 16–24)[66] and are more concerned for ritual cleanliness than moral purity (vv. 25–28). Worst of all, they reenact the behavior of their rebellious forefathers by condemning and murdering the spokesmen God sends them (vv. 29–36). These climactic verses are steeped in bitter irony. The Good News Bible captures the sense of verse 32: "Go on, then, and finish up what your ancestors started!" Yet, despite the fact that the sins of generations of Israelites are coming to a head at this moment in the first century, there is nothing here to suggest the permanent damnation of a race. From Jesus'

---

[62] Indeed, numerous allusions to Jeremiah's Lamentations appear in both Matthew 23 and 27. See D. M. Moffitt, "Righteous Bloodshed, Matthew's Passion Narrative, and the Temple's Destruction: Lamentations as a Matthean Intertext," *JBL* 125 (2006): 299–320. For a detailed catalogue of non-Christian Jewish texts at least as harsh in their indictment of Israel, see Davies and Allison, *Matthew*, vol. 3, 259–60.

[63] M. A. Powell, "Do and Keep What Moses Says (Matthew 23:2–7)," *JBL* 114 (1995): 419–35.

[64] R. F. Talbott ("Nazareth's Rebellious Son: Deviance and Downward Mobility in the Galilean Jesus Movement," *BTB* 38 [2008]: 112) labels Jesus' demand to call no one father or teacher "an incredible act of rebelliousness" in a patriarchal culture with a highly authoritarian structure. Perhaps an appropriate contemporization today would be to abandon all ecclesiastical and academic titles that some of us inappropriately value, and use first names only with our parishioners and students, as is, in fact, done in some parts of the world!

[65] A lively debate surrounding just how much proselytizing first-century Jews engaged in, based on the extra-canonical data, seems to be generating a consensus: energetic efforts to gain converts among initially disinterested Gentiles were relatively rare, but attempts to get "God-fearers" to "clinch the deal" through full-fledged conversion to Judaism was much more common. See esp. McKnight, *Light among the Gentiles.* Cf. M. F. Bird, "The Case of the Proselytizing Pharisees?—Matthew 23.15," *JSHJ* 2 (2004): 117–37.

[66] "This sanctioning of tithing is for Pharisees and perhaps for our Evangelist's Jewish Christian audience. It should not be seen as a blanket requirement of tithing for all followers of Jesus, including those not observing or choosing to be under the Mosaic covenant" (Witherington, *Matthew*, 430).

death to the fall of Jerusalem was forty years—exactly one generation. Does verse 36 imply that after that period, judgment is complete and restoration possible? Verse 39 at least hints at such a day, described as one in which Israel will finally honor Jesus as its Messiah.[67]

The Widow's Mites (Mark 12:41–44 par.) [Aland §286]. As a fitting contrast with the denunciation of the well-to-do and influential within Israel, Mark concludes Jesus' time in the temple with the praiseworthy example of a widow who gave an extraordinarily generous offering to the temple treasury. The quantity was miniscule, but the percentage of her gift enormous in comparison with the seeming generosity of the wealthy. Jesus is not impressed with how much we give but with how much we sacrifice.[68] There may also be an implied critique here of the system that tolerated such disparity.[69]

Historicity

The merely "implicit" Christology of this entire section speaks strongly for its authenticity.[70] Jesus acts out Zechariah's prophecy but makes no explicit messianic claims as he enters Jerusalem and, indeed, subverts conventional expectation concerning a "triumphal entry."[71] His enacted parables of the temple's coming destruction directly challenge prevailing Jewish beliefs, yet do not lead immediately to early Christian abandonment of the temple as a place of prayer and witness. His teaching in the temple involves further distinctive pronouncement stories in which he characteristically and cleverly evades the seemingly foolproof traps set for him. The parable of the wicked tenants suggests that he views himself as God's son, but that is only a subordinate motif in the story. The question about how David's son could also be his Lord points in the same direction but remains equally indirect. Jesus' praise for the widow's offering reflects a perspective on almsgiving little imitated in any ancient religion.

The extensive woes against the scribes and Pharisees prove more difficult, but the arguments for not seeing anti-Semitism here work well only if at least a substantial core of these sentiments are historical. If they are purely the invention of the later church to blindside the Jewish leaders in the second generation of Christianity, it is hard not to see them as a mere blanket condemnation of (non-Christian) Judaism. If they are limited to certain Jewish leaders and members of crowds on fixed historical occasions, they are more understandable.[72] Additional evidence that the Synoptists are constrained to write what actually happened here include the unusually positive acknowledgment of the scribes'

---

[67] On which, see esp. D. C. Allison, Jr., "Matt. 23:39 = Luke 13:35b as a Conditional Prophecy," *JSNT* 18 (1983): 75–84.

[68] Edwards, *Mark*, 378–82; and Collins, *Mark*, 586–90.

[69] A. G. Wright, "The Widow's Mites: Praise or Lament?—A Matter of Context," *CBQ* 44 (1982): 256–65, though Wright unnecessarily pits this interpretation against the traditional one.

[70] Cf. esp. Wright, *Jesus and the Victory of God*, 489–510.

[71] On the historical reliability of this whole incident, see B. Kinman, "Jesus' Royal Entry into Jerusalem," *BBR* 15 (2005): 223–60.

[72] Cf. further Carson, "Matthew," 32–36.

and Pharisees' authority in Matt 23:2–3a; the intra-Jewish nature of the debates over phylacteries, tassels, titles, proselytes, oaths, cups, tombs, and so on (vv. 5–30); the possibility of interpreting verse 39 as holding out a future hope for Israel; and Paul's seeming awareness of the tradition behind verses 31–36 in 1 Thess 2:14–16.

The latter part of John 12 includes another "parable" possibly expanded into a discourse (the "kernel of wheat" in vv. 24–26) and Jesus' inner turmoil, reminiscent of Gethsemane (vv. 27–28). The use of Isa 6:10 in verse 40 closely resembles Jesus' words in Mark 4:12 and parallels. The lack of any explicit context in which Jesus spoke verses 44–50 may suggest that this is John's own summary of Jesus' teaching from many occasions. In each of the above segments of the text, however, similarities with the Synoptic tradition enhance the case for the authenticity of the content, even if John has used his own idiom to narrate it.[73]

The Olivet Discourse (Mark 13; Matt 24–25; Luke 21:5–38)

Jesus leaves the temple and heads east across the Kidron Valley and up the slopes of the Mount of Olives. As they walk, the disciples understandably marvel at the temple's beauty. To their astonishment, Jesus predicts its coming destruction (Mark 13:1–2 pars.). The disciples reply by asking two questions: when will this be, and what will be the sign that it is imminent (vv. 3–4)? In light of Jesus' subsequent answer, it is clear that Matthew has interpreted these as separate questions: when will the temple be destroyed, and what will be the sign of Christ's coming and the end of this age (Matt 24:3)? In the disciples' minds, the two events were undoubtedly one and the same. Jesus' answer will make plain that they are different issues.

This answer, also known as the Eschatological Discourse, has received a myriad of interpretations through history. Some of the most popular approaches at the grassroots Christian level are among some of the least defensible via sound hermeneutics. The following brief exposition sketches a major, scholarly evangelical perspective that is not as well known as it should be.[74]

When Will the Temple Be Destroyed? (Mark 13:5–23 pars.) [Aland §287–291]

Events Which Must Not Be Interpreted as Overly Significant (vv. 5–13). Trying to calm the eschatological fervor of the day, Jesus answers this first question, in essence, by saying, "not immediately." Verses 5–13 itemize events which must take place without necessarily heralding the end (see 13:7, 8, 10, 13).[75] These

---

[73] See further Ellis, *Making of the New Testament*, 172.

[74] For elaboration, with minor variations in detail, see G. R. Beasley-Murray, *Jesus and the Last Days: The Interpretation of the Olivet Discourse* (Peabody: Hendrickson, 1993; Vancouver: Regent, 2005). Cf. also Keener, *Matthew*, 559–93; Witherington, *Matthew*, 444–56; Turner, *Matthew*, 568–90; Cranfield, *Mark*, 387–411; Lane, *Mark*, 444–82.

[75] Cf. esp. throughout T. J. Geddert, *Watchwords: Mark 13 in Markan Eschatology* (Sheffield: JSOT, 1989).

include: (1) the rise of false Messiahs (vv. 5–6, cf. vv. 21–23; "in my name" in v. 6 likely refers to "Christ," not necessarily "Jesus"); (2) wars and rumors of wars (v. 7); (3) earthquakes, famines, and related natural disasters (v. 8; cf. Luke 21:11); (4) persecution from governments and family members (vv. 9, 11–13); and (5) preaching the gospel to all nations (v. 10). Items (1) through (4) were clearly all fulfilled in the years between the crucifixion and the destruction of the temple (AD 30–70). Acts 5:36 mentions from this time period the messianic pretender Theudas, while Josephus narrates the rise of several other would-be Christs (*Ant.* 20.97–99, 160–72, 188). Sporadic fighting presaged the Jewish revolt in 67, which itself was the major war leading to the temple's downfall. Laodicea and Pompeii suffered devastating earthquakes in the early 60s, and a significant famine hit parts of the Roman empire, especially Judea, in the late 40s (cf. Acts 11:28). The Book of Acts repeatedly documents the persecution that dogged the early church (cf. also the poignant catalogue of Paul's sufferings in 2 Cor 11:23–12:10). Even (5) seems to have been fulfilled at least once, given Paul's comments in Rom 10:18; Col 1:6, 23; and 1 Tim 3:16, with "preaching to all the nations" being equivalent to "representative witness throughout the Roman empire" (the Gk. οἰκουμένη, often translated "whole world," in fact, regularly referred to the known limits of imperial domination).[76]

These five activities, of course, have recurred repeatedly throughout church history. The Book of Revelation depicts similar "end-time horrors." But the application of Jesus' words to the debate about the end of the age would be the same as to the disciples' questions about the timing of the temple's demise. "Such things must happen, but the end is still to come" (Mark 13:7). On the other hand, precisely because all these predictions were at least in some sense fulfilled by AD 70, the church in every subsequent generation has been able to believe that the end could come at any time. The challenge for believers, however short or long the interval before Christ's return, is to stand firm, avoid apostasy or lovelessness, be prepared even for martyrdom if necessary, and so be (spiritually) saved (Matt 24:9, 12–13).

Events Immediately Surrounding the Temple's Destruction (vv. 14–23). Verse 14 brings us to the threshold of AD 70. Appropriating the terminology of Dan 9:27; 11:31; 12:11; and 1 Macc 1:54; 6:7, Jesus alludes to the "abomination that causes desolation" (see above, p. 26). Something as bad as or worse than Antiochus Epiphanes' desecration of the temple will occur again. Mark adds parenthetically, "let the reader understand," indicating that the language is deliberately cryptic, perhaps to keep any government official who might read this Gospel from being able to accuse the Christians of anti-Roman propaganda! The awful conditions surrounding this "abomination" include uniquely first-century Jewish and Judean concerns—living on rooftops and traveling on the Sabbath (Mark 13:15; Matt 24:20). Luke makes it completely explicit that the event in view is the destruction of Jerusalem (Luke 21:20, 24), which will initiate a period of Jewish captivity

---

[76] See esp. Gundry, *Mark*, 739. Cf. Evans, *Mark 8:27–16:20*, 310.

and dispersion, during which the city itself will be overrun by Gentile inhabitants. This is exactly what happened after AD 70 for almost 1900 years.[77]

In this same context, Jesus speaks of unparalleled tribulation (Mark 13:19). It would be hard to prove, historically, that suffering in first-century Jerusalem eclipsed that of all the rest of human history (though recall above, p. 26). But it also makes no sense to limit this suffering to some event just prior to the return of Christ, for then it would be so obvious as to be silly for Jesus to have said there would never again be such suffering. Luke clearly sees this tribulation beginning in AD 70, but Matthew just as clearly sees the events portending Christ's return as happening "immediately" after the tribulation (Matt 24:29). It seems best to understand Jesus' prediction as referring to the entire period between the destruction of the temple and his return as the unequaled days of distress (v. 21). This does not mean that all true Christians have led unpleasant lives filled with persecution, but it does mean that Jesus, like the New Testament writers, does not see the earthly lot of believers, who faithfully follow their Lord and proclaim his message, to be one of acclaim and ease (cf. esp. 2 Tim 3:12)![78] It is arguable, historically, that the bold articulation and consistent application of the tenets of orthodox Christian faith tend to arouse more animosity than does the comparable practice of any other world religion or ideology.

What Will Signal the End of the Age? (Mark 13:24–32 pars.) [Aland §292–293]

Jesus' answer to this second question is, in essence, "nothing conclusive" or "Don't worry, when it comes you won't miss it!" At some unspecified time after the destruction of the temple, Christ will come back (vv. 24–27). The cosmic distress described is common in apocalyptic literature as metaphorical language for the dramatic, widespread, political and religious turmoil and upheavals that will be brought on by the shift in the ages of human history (cf. Isa 13:10; 34:4; Ezek 32:7; Dan 8:10; Joel 2:10; Hag 2:21).[79] The only time the word "sign" appears in Jesus' discourse is in Matt 24:30, but this "sign of the Son of Man" in heaven, whatever it may be, appears too late for those who want to interpret contemporary events and make confident predictions about the time of Christ's return. Rather it is part of the very return (*parousia*) of Jesus itself that is described in this paragraph.

---

[77] Bock (*Luke 9:51–24:53*, 1681) notes how this corresponds closely to the sequence of events in Rom 11:25–26.

[78] Cf. Davies and Allison, *Matthew*, vol. 3, 331. The language of Revelation and the frequent pattern in Scripture of multiple fulfillments of prophecy suggest that there may be a particular intensifying of "tribulation" at the very end of the church age. Jesus, *in this context*, is probably not limiting his use of the term just to that very last period of human history.

[79] Wright (*Jesus and the Victory of God*, esp. 360–67) goes even further, arguing that the return of the Son of man itself is equally metaphorical. T. R. Hatina ("The Focus of Mark 13:24–27: The Parousia or the Destruction of the Temple?" *BBR* 6 [1996]: 43–66) unpacks the most common application of this metaphorical interpretation, that Jesus was predicting his invisible coming in judgment on Israel in AD 70. At least for Luke, Acts 1:9 and 11 seem decisive in rebutting this view. See D. C. Allison, Jr., "Jesus and the Victory of Apocalyptic," in *Jesus and the Restoration of Israel*, ed. C. C. Newman (Downers Grove: IVP; Carlisle: Paternoster, 1999), 126–41.

This return will be a public, worldwide, universally visible event (Matt 24:30–31), disproving the claims of all who have pretended to be Christ incognito (recall Mark 13:21–23).

The second part of Jesus' remarks on the timing of the end of the age is the little parable of the budding fig tree (vv. 28–31). Its point is simply that as leaves on the tree show that summer is near, so the fulfillment of "all these things" demonstrates that Christ's return is near. But what does verse 30 mean by declaring that "this generation will certainly not pass away until all these things have happened"? Many have speculated that Jesus thought he would come back within his disciples' lifetime but was mistaken. Others have translated *genea* not as "generation" but as "race," referring to the Jews. One modern, dispensationalist alternative has been to suggest that "this generation" refers to the end-time generation: from start to finish the events portending Christ's return (sometimes taken to have begun with the reestablishment of the state of Israel in 1948) will last a generation.[80]

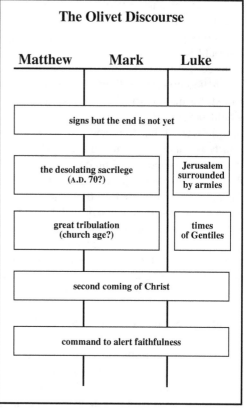

None of these options is plausible. In light of its consistent use elsewhere in the Gospels, "this generation" almost certainly refers to a roughly forty-year period of time beginning in Jesus' day (in Matthew alone, cf. 11:16; 12:39, 41, 42, 45; 16:4; 17:17; and esp. 23:36).[81] Careful attention to the immediate context demonstrates that Jesus is not claiming to be coming back in "this generation."

---

[80] No one has made this view more popular than H. Lindsey (*The Late Great Planet Earth* [Grand Rapids: Zondervan, 1970], 43), who notes how often fig trees represent Israel in Jewish literature. Lindsey goes on to equate a generation with a forty-year period of time, which suggests that 1988 should be about the longest one would have to wait for the Parousia. How much longer will Christians wait before recognizing Lindsey's approach as simply altogether misguided? The same questions should be asked about the enormously popular sixteen-volume *Left Behind* series of end-times fiction, written by T. LaHaye and J. B. Jenkins (Wheaton: Tyndale, 1995–2007). Contrast C. L. Blomberg and S. W. Chung, eds., *A Case for Historical Premillennialism: An Alternative to "Left Behind" Eschatology* (Grand Rapids: Baker, 2009).

[81] Carson, "Matthew," 507.

"All these things" in verse 30 must be the same as "these things" in verse 29. The things in question in verse 29 are those things that will show merely that the end is near. It makes no sense to say that Christ's return demonstrates that the end is near; by that time it will have already arrived! So "these things" must be all the events of verses 5–23, which, indeed, have already happened and did at least initially occur even before AD 70. In other words, nothing any longer stands in the way of Christ's return. But neither does Jesus give any "sign" by which we might be able to predict the time of his coming.

Mark 13:32 now makes that point explicitly. Not even the Son, in his voluntarily accepted limitations on his divine omniscience while a human being, knew the time of his return. How dare any of us claim to know what Jesus himself did not! Nor will it do to claim to know the week or month or year or era because Jesus said merely that he did not know "the day or hour." These are terms regularly used in Scripture for indefinite periods of time, and Acts 1:7 is even more general: "It is not for you to know the times or dates the Father has set by his own authority."[82]

The Appeal to Wakefulness (Mark 13:33–37 par.; Matt 24:37–25:46) [Aland §294–300]

How should we then live? If we are not to try to set dates, not to try to read the "signs of the times" from contemporary events, what do Christ's appeals to alert and wakeful living mean? Quite simply, they mean: be ready; be prepared. Be about the business of the kingdom so that whenever the end comes, however unexpectedly, you are ready.[83] Mark, briefly, and Matthew, in much greater detail, record how Jesus proceeded to make this point by means of a variety of parables.

The parable of the doorkeeper (Mark 13:33–37 par.) captures the concept succinctly: stay awake for the master's return, lest he come during any one of the four standard watches (three-hour divisions) of the night. Matthew 24:37–42 and 43–44 reinforce this command with illustrations about the unexpectedness of the flood in Noah's day and of burglars in any day.[84] The parables of 24:45–51 and 25:1–13 then contrast scenarios in which the master returns surprisingly early and surprisingly late. Clearly, disciples are being instructed to be ready for every eventuality. The parable of the talents elaborates what we are to be doing during the interval between Christ's advents, however long or short: we must use all the resources with which he has entrusted us for kingdom purposes. All persons will

---

[82] Cf. further the helpful popular-level work by B. J. Oropeza, *99 Reasons Why No One Knows When Christ Will Return* (Downers Grove: IVP, 1994).

[83] Cf. D. B. Deppe, "Charting the Future or a Perspective on the Present? The Parenetic Purpose of Mark 13," *CTJ* 41 (2006): 89–101 (though Jesus may have intended a "both-and" rather than an "either-or"); and France, *Matthew*, 939.

[84] Matt 24:40–41 (par. Luke 17:34–35) is often taken to teach a secret rapture: believers will suddenly disappear from this world as Christ returns before the tribulation and before his universal, public Parousia, leaving behind only unbelievers. But, in context, being "taken away" would have to mean taken away for judgment (parallel to the flood in Matt 24:39 that "took away" all the unrepentant). Whatever one's position on the rapture, it is best not derived from this passage. Cf. further J. F. Walvoord, *Matthew: Thy Kingdom Come* (Chicago: Moody, 1974; Grand Rapids: Kregel, 1998), 193.

be called to account for their behavior, and those who have done nothing for the
Lord demonstrate that they are no kind of disciple at all and, hence, are eternally
condemned (Matt 25:14–30).[85]

The Olivet Discourse ends with one more quasi-parabolic illustration. The
events of Judgment Day, already depicted in the parable of the talents, will resemble a flock herder who separates his sheep from his goats (Matt 25:31–46). Jesus,
the coming king, will divide his followers, who will enjoy his presence forever,
from those who are to be condemned to everlasting punishment. What is the criterion for making this separation? At first glance it seems to be good deeds done for
the poor and needy of this world (feeding the hungry, clothing the naked, etc.). Is
Jesus teaching salvation by works? Almost certainly not (recall Mark 5:34; 10:52;
Luke 7:50; 11:17–19; 18:10–14; etc). Is he then teaching that the true righteousness a disciple exhibits will include such works? This is the most popular contemporary interpretation, but it has not been the dominant view throughout church
history[86] nor is it the most plausible.

Every other use of "brother(s)" in Matthew, when not meaning biological
siblings, refers to spiritual kin—fellow Jews or fellow disciples of Jesus (Matt
5:22–24, 47; 7:3–5; 12:48–50; 18:15, 21, 35; 23:8; 28:10). The term "least" of
these (25:40, 45) uses the superlative form of the adjective "little one," which is
one of Matthew's unique ways of referring to Christians (10:42; 18:6, 10, 14; cf.
5:19; 11:11). Matthew 10:40–42 offers a close parallel with its promise of reward
for those who offer even small acts of kindness to itinerant disciples. So it seems
most likely that Jesus is referring to deeds of compassion done for suffering, persecuted Christian emissaries. Because one has accepted the message of the gospel, one is concerned to care for its messenger. Moreover, these "sheep" are not,
as it is sometimes alleged, surprised that they are accepted as Christ's followers
(the "anonymous Christian" theory); they are surprised only when they are told
that they ministered directly to Jesus, since he no longer lives on earth in incarnate
form. But Jesus assures them that he is present in every one of his followers to
whom they *have* ministered. None of this absolves us of the responsibility to care
for the *non*-Christian needy of our world; we simply have to turn to other texts for
that teaching.[87]

---

[85] The "talent" was a large unit of gold or silver currency. But applications go well beyond literal
money matters, and beyond "talents" in the modern sense of the term also (see, e.g., B. Chenoweth,
"Identifying the Talents: Contextual Clues for the Interpretation of the Parable of the Talents [Matthew
25:14–30]," *TynBul* 56 [2005]: 61–72). They nevertheless include talents and money. On the latter,
cf. M. S. Northcott, "The Parable of the Talents and the Economy of the Gift," *Theology* 107 (2004):
241–49.

[86] For a full history of interpretation, see S. W. Gray, *The Least of My Brothers: Matthew 25:31–
46—A History of Interpretation* (Atlanta: Scholars, 1989).

[87] For this line of interpretation, cf., e.g., J. P. Heil, "The Double Meaning of the Narrative of
Universal Judgment in Matthew 25.31–46," *JSNT* 69 (1998): 3–14; France, *Matthew*, 958; Wilkins,
Matthew, 811.

Historicity

Although it is usually assumed that this discourse is a composite created from the standard Synoptic sources, a good case can be made for a pre-Synoptic "sermon" that Matthew, Mark, and Luke have each in their own ways abbreviated.[88] The fact that Jesus never directly answers the questions with which the discourse begins (Mark 13:4 pars.) speaks for the sermon's authenticity, as does the generally cryptic nature of the discourse itself—most notably the reference to the desolating sacrilege (Mark 13:14 pars.). Jesus' insistence on preliminary signs—"but the end is still to come" (v. 7)—would be superfluous if this teaching were being created after or just before the destruction of the temple. Jesus' ignorance of the day and hour of his return (13:32 pars.) presents potentially embarrassing Christology. Yet, given the frequent refrain of the Old Testament prophets that the Day of the Lord was at hand and in light of the proliferation of apocalyptic speculation in first-century Judaism, it would be extraordinary if Jesus had never addressed the topic of the end-times in something like this fashion. First Thessalonians 4:16–17; 5:2; and 2 Thess 2:3–6 all betray awareness of similar early "Jesus-traditions."[89] The distinctively Matthean additions to the discourse, moreover, are virtually all parables, which cohere with the form and contents of the paralleled parables that are almost universally admitted to be authentic.

For Further Study

In Judea on the Road to Jerusalem

Jesus and Divorce

Atkinson, David. *To Have and to Hold.* London: Collins, 1979; Grand Rapids: Eerdmans, 1981.

Cornes, Andrew. *Divorce and Remarriage: Biblical Principles and Pastoral Practice.* London: Hodder & Stoughton; Grand Rapids: Eerdmans, 1993; Fearn, Scotland: Christian Focus, 2002.

Instone-Brewer, David. *Divorce and Remarriage in the Bible: The Social and Literary Context.* Grand Rapids and Cambridge: Eerdmans, 2002.

Keener, Craig S. *. . . And Marries Another: Divorce and Remarriage in the Teaching of the New Testament.* Peabody: Hendrickson, 1991.

Luck, William F. *Divorce and Remarriage.* San Francisco: Harper & Row, 1987.

Strauss, Mark L., ed. *Remarriage after Divorce in Today's Church: 3 Views.* Grand Rapids: Zondervan, 2006.

Jesus and Riches

Blomberg, Craig L. *Neither Poverty nor Riches: A Biblical Theology of Possessions.* Leicester: Apollos, 1999; Downers Grove: IVP, 2001.

---

[88] Wenham, *Rediscovery of Jesus' Eschatological Discourse.*

[89] Cf. esp. S. Kim, "The Jesus Tradition in 1 Thess 4.13–5.11," *NTS* 48 (2002): 225–42.

Hengel, Martin. *Property and Riches in the Early Church*. London: SCM; Philadelphia: Fortress, 1974; Mifflintown, PA: Sigler, 2005.

Hoppe, Leslie J. *There Shall be No Poor among You: Poverty in the Bible*. Nashville: Abingdon, 2004.

Moxnes, Halvor. *The Economy of the Kingdom: Social Conflict and Economic Relations in Luke's Gospel*. Philadelphia: Fortress, 1988; Eugene, OR: Wipf & Stock, 2004.

Schmidt, Thomas E. *Hostility to Wealth in the Synoptic Gospels*. Sheffield: JSOT, 1987.

Wheeler, Sondra E. *Wealth as Peril and Obligation: The New Testament on Possessions*. Grand Rapids: Eerdmans, 1995.

Other

Carter, Warren. *Households and Discipleship: A Study of Matthew 19–20*. Sheffield: JSOT, 1994.

Via, Dan O., Jr. *The Ethics of Mark's Gospel—In the Middle of Time*. Philadelphia: Fortress, 1985.

Jesus in Jerusalem: Final Ministry to, in, and from the Temple

Garland, David E. *The Intention of Matthew 23*. Leiden: Brill, 1979.

Grangaard, Blake R. *Conflict and Authority in Luke 19:47 to 21:4*. New York: Peter Lang, 1999.

Notley, R. Steven, Marc Turnage and Brian Becker, eds. *Jesus' Last Week: Jerusalem Studies in the Synoptic Gospels*, vol. 1. Leiden and Boston: Brill, 2006.

Olmstead, Wesley G. *Matthew's Trilogy of Parables: The Nation, the Nations and the Reader in Matthew 21.28–22.14*. Cambridge: CUP, 2003.

Telford, William R. *The Barren Temple and the Withered Fig Tree*. Sheffield: JSOT, 1980.

The Olivet Discourse

Balabanski, Vicky. *Eschatology in the Making: Mark, Matthew and the Didache*. Cambridge: CUP, 1997.

Beasley-Murray, George R. *Jesus and the Last Days: The Interpretation of the Olivet Discourse*. Peabody: Henrickson, 1993; Vancouver: Regent, 2005.

Geddert, Timothy J. *Watchwords: Mark 13 in Markan Eschatology*. Sheffield: JSOT Press, 1989.

Wenham, David. *The Rediscovery of Jesus' Eschatological Discourse*. Sheffield: JSOT Press, 1984.

17

PASSION, CRUCIFIXION, AND RESURRECTION

T HE FINAL EVENTS of the Gospel narratives quickly unfold. The plotting of Jesus' death by the Jewish leaders (Mark 14:1–2 pars.; Aland §305) probably takes place on Tuesday. They want to avoid conflict with the crowds, with whom Jesus is still popular. That they arrested him during the Passover feast anyway, though with stealth and by night, could reflect a change in plans—or else Mark 14:2a should be translated, "apart from the festal crowds."[1] Nothing that has been recorded can be confidently ascribed to Wednesday of Jesus' final week. We pick up the action on Thursday night with Jesus' last supper with the Twelve, their departure for the Garden of Gethsemane, and his arrest. His conviction, execution, and resurrection will follow shortly.

Thursday Night: The Upper Room and Gethsemane

The Last Supper (Mark 14:10–26 pars.) [Aland §307–16]

Preparation (vv. 10–16 pars.). Two plots are intertwined here. Judas is scheming with the Jewish leaders to betray Jesus (vv. 10–11), while Jesus himself, fully aware of what is going on, is preparing to celebrate his last meal, a Passover feast, with his disciples (vv. 12–16). Matthew characteristically adds information that enables us later to see a fulfillment of prophecy: Judas agrees to betray Jesus for

---

[1] J. Jeremias, *The Eucharistic Words of Jesus*, rev. ed. (London: SCM; New York: Scribner's, 1966), 71–73.

thirty pieces of silver (Matt 26:15; cf. 27:9). His motives are never explained. Suggestions have ranged from pure greed (but the price was not that high) to a desire to force Jesus' hand and make him act like the military king people hoped he would become. Neither of these is probable. Instead, it is likely that Judas had become disenchanted with the "suffering servant" focus of Christ's mission.[2] The first day of Unleavened Bread (Mark 14:12) informally marked the beginning of the week-long Passover festival, as Jews cleaned all yeast out of their homes. Jesus' directions about preparing for their meal suggest prearranged signals to avoid public scrutiny and the danger that was lurking so close behind (vv. 13–16).

The Passover Meal (vv. 17–26 pars.). For most Jews, the Passover was the favorite feast of the year. Commemorating their escape from Egypt (see Exodus 12), and performed according to the laws God had commanded them (cf. Lev 23:4–8; Num 9:1–14; Deut 16:1–8), this was the one annual festival celebrated primarily in family units. Jesus presides at table with his disciples like the father of a family. The men would have reclined on couches arranged in a square-cornered U-shaped configuration. Jesus, as host, would have been second from one end, with Judas on his left and John on his right. Peter may have sat directly across from John, in the position of the humble servant.[3] Together the thirteen men would have begun to reenact the Passover "haggadah" or liturgy. With each of four cups of wine, a portion of Exod 6:6–7a was recalled. The elements of the ceremony, in their probable sequence, would have included:

A blessing and the first cup of wine ("I will bring you out . . .")

The serving of the meal: unleavened bread, bitter herbs, greens, stewed fruit, and roast lamb, each symbolizing details of the first Passover

The youngest son asks, "Why is this night different from other nights?" and the story is retold

Second cup of wine ("I will free you from being slaves to them")

Hallel ("praise") Psalm 113 (or 113–114) sung

Breaking of bread and the eating of the meal

Third cup of wine at end of meal ("I will redeem you")

Hallel ("praise") Psalms 114 (or 115)–118 sung

Fourth cup of wine ("I will take you as my own people, and I will be your God")*

*G. N. Stanton, *The Gospels and Jesus,* rev. ed. (Oxford and New York: OUP, 2002), 277. Cf. esp. *Pesah.* 10.1–7. On the issue of what was likely to have developed already by Jesus' day, see R. Routledge, "Passover and Last Supper," *TynBul* 53 (2002): 203–21.

---

[2] Wilkins, *Matthew,* 831. On Judas more generally, see K. Paffenroth, *Judas: Images of the Lost Disciple* (Louisville and London: WJKP, 2001); and M. Meyer, *Judas: The Definitive Collection of Gospels and Legends about the Infamous Apostle of Jesus* (New York and London: Harper One, 2007). The fragmentary Gospel of Judas, so much in the news recently, reflects a late second-century Gnostic reversal in which Judas' betrayal is a necessary, heroic act. It contains no authentic information from the life of Christ where it diverges from the canonical texts. So even B. D. Ehrman, *The Lost Gospel of Judas Iscariot: A New Look at Betrayer and Betrayed* (Oxford and New York: OUP, 2006). Recall also above, p. 40.

[3] For the details of seating and conversation, see further Morris, *John,* 555–58.

The three Synoptic Gospels all clearly allude to various portions of this liturgy. Jesus is proclaiming that a new Passover will now be available through his coming death. John does not include the details of the meal or Christ's "words of institution," describing instead the "footwashing" that Jesus initiated on this occasion. The prediction of Judas' betrayal apparently occurred next, followed by the meal itself. By then appending Jesus' detailed Farewell Discourse (see below, p. 388), John may be contextualizing his story and describing it as a Greco-Roman "symposium"—an occasion of informal fellowship and serious conversation following a more formal banquet.[4]

John 13:1–20 narrates the footwashing. Verses 1–2 preface the account by describing this as an expression of Jesus' uttermost love.[5] Washing the grime from sandal-clad feet that had walked dusty roads was a common courtesy by a host for his meal guests, but it was normally assigned to the most menial of slaves. Jesus takes the initiative, despite his disciples' complaints, to teach a powerful object lesson about servant ministry,[6] all the more appropriate given the death he would soon die. He also wants to teach them about spiritual cleansing (v. 8). Impulsive Peter, when he catches on, then asks for an entire bath! But Jesus replies that one who has previously bathed needs only to wash one's feet. Most commentators recognize this as teaching that a person receives salvation (and possibly baptism) in Christ as a non-repeatable event, but then needs regular opportunities for confession and forgiveness of subsequent sin.[7] A few churches have made footwashing an ordinance or sacrament to be literally imitated in church from time to time. There is nothing inherently objectionable in this, and, in fact, the ceremony can be quite humbling and spiritually powerful, but footwashing does differ from baptism and the Lord's Supper by not building on preexisting religious rituals, merely on a commonplace household courtesy.

Already in verses 1–20, Jesus has recognized that not all of his disciples are spiritually clean (vv. 10, 18), and he proceeds to spell this out (vv. 21–30; cf. Mark 14:18–21 pars.). One of the Twelve will deliver him over to be crucified (the Greek word for "betray" and "deliver up" is identical). "Ancient hospitality customs were such that a guest sitting at table was sacrosanct and protected from harm from anyone else present. Thus in the most intimate setting we have the beginning

---

[4] Cf. Smith, *From Symposium to Eucharist*, 272–75.

[5] Here are the first of several verses that lead many scholars to think that John wants to portray Jesus spending his last night with his disciples *before* the Passover, with the crucifixion taking place on the day of the slaughter of the lambs, rather than one day afterwards, as in the Synoptics. But all v. 1 says is that before the Passover Jesus knew what was about to happen and was prepared to love his followers to the end. Without any further qualification, the meal described in v. 2 is most naturally understood *as* the main Passover meal, in light of the reference to Passover in v. 1 (Ridderbos, *John*, 455). When Jesus leaves in vv. 29–30 to buy provisions for the "feast," the rest of the week-long festival is in view (Carson, *John*, 475). The same is true of 18:28 (Köstenberger, *John*, 524).

[6] Cf. J. J. Kanagaraj, "Johannine Jesus, the Supreme Example of Leadership: An Inquiry into John 13:1–20," *Them* 29 (2004): 15–26.

[7] J. C. Thomas, *Footwashing in John 13 and the Johannine Community* (Sheffield: JSOT, 1991), 125.

of the gravest sort of betrayal."[8] Although Jesus knows exactly what is happening, and, indeed, it has been foreordained, still Judas remains fully culpable for his treachery. This sharp juxtaposition of divine predestination and human responsibility matches Scripture's consistent treatment of these two themes.[9] Although the disciples badger Jesus to tell them who the traitor is, all he replies is that it is one dipping his bread into the sauce with him, something all of the Twelve would have done during the course of the meal. Matthew adds that Judas asked if it was he (Matt 26:25), but the most literal translation of Jesus' reply is "you said it"—not an unambiguous affirmative! In John, the beloved disciple (i.e., probably John himself; recall above, pp. 197–200) is reclining next to Jesus and finds out specifically that Judas is the betrayer (John 13:26). This seems to have been a whispered conversation not overheard by anyone else, because, when Judas leaves, the rest of the disciples have no idea why he is going out (vv. 28–29).[10]

Luke gives a fuller account of the Passover meal itself than Mark or Matthew.[11] Twice Jesus takes a cup of wine and offers solemn pronouncements over it (Luke 22:17, 20). The "cup" in the Old Testament often symbolized the outpouring of God's wrath (e.g., Ps 75:8; Isa 51:17). Whether the first reference corresponds to the first or second cup of the liturgy, the second reference, which is paralleled in Mark and Matthew, drunk after the meal had begun, almost certainly corresponds to the third cup of the haggadah. Jesus speaks of his coming death by means of broken bread and spilled blood, in conjunction with the very cup of the Passover service meant to remind the celebrants of God's redemption. Later Christian theology would erect elaborate theological edifices on Jesus' simple words here, debating such issues as transubstantiation, consubstantiation, and so on (i.e., when and how the bread and wine actually become Christ's body and blood).[12] All of this is anachronistic in the historical context, however. No one seeing Jesus physically holding out a loaf of bread or cup of wine would have imagined him to be claiming that they were somehow a literal extension of his arms or hands![13] The Aramaic behind "this is my body" and "this is my blood" most likely would not have even used a verb for "is". Rather Jesus is offering an enacted parable about how these elements of the Passover meal now represent, symbolize, or depict

---

[8] Witherington, *Matthew*, 482. On the relevant customs more generally, see esp. A. Arterbury, *Entertaining Angels: Early Christian Hospitality in Its Ancient Mediterranean Setting* (Sheffield: Sheffield Phoenix, 2005).

[9] See esp. Carson, *Divine Sovereignty and Human Responsibility*. C. H. Talbert (*Reading John*, rev. ed. [Macon: Smyth & Helwys, 2005], 203), describes Jesus' overtures of table-fellowship intimacy with Judas here as "love's last appeal to one on the verge of perdition."

[10] Ridderbos, *John*, 471; Michaels, *John*, 235.

[11] A few ancient manuscripts omit Luke 22:19b–20, but the evidence for their inclusion is quite strong. See esp. B. S. Billings, *Do This in Remembrance of Me: The Disputed Words in the Lukan Institution Narrative (Luke 22.19b–20): An Historic-Exegetical, Theological and Sociological Analysis* (London and New York: T&T Clark, 2006).

[12] For a concise history, see D. Bridge and D. Phypers, *The Meal that Unites?* (London: Hodder & Stoughton, 1981 [= *Communion: The Meal that Unites* (Wheaton: Harold Shaw, 1983)]).

[13] Cf. S. McKnight, *Jesus and His Death: Historiography, the Historical Jesus, and Atonement Theory* (Waco: Baylor University Press, 2005), 283.

his coming substitutionary, sacrificial death.[14] "For many" (Mark 14:24) probably alludes to the suffering servant's role in Isa 53:4, 10, and 12. The "new covenant" clearly harks back to the one that was prophesied in Jer 31:31–34.

Mark 14:25 suggests that Jesus may not have drunk the fourth cup of wine; at any rate he knows he will not be celebrating this festival again until his second coming. The allusion to the future aspect of the kingdom gives each celebration of the Lord's Supper a forward-looking thrust as well as a backward-looking one. We not only memorialize and reenact Christ's atoning death in the Lord's Supper, but we long for and proclaim our belief in his return to establish his kingdom in all its fullness (cf. the reference to the messianic banquet in Rev 19:9, drawing on the imagery of Isa 25:6).[15] Luke inserts at this point a brief episode largely parallel to Mark 10:41–45 (cf. Matt 20:24–28; 19:28): Jesus' teaching on servant leadership in response to the disciples' dispute about greatness, teaching that was counter-cultural indeed in light of the prevailing authoritarian systems of leadership, particularly in Greco-Roman circles (Luke 22:24–30).[16] The little troupe then sings the closing *Hallel* ("Praise") Psalms and leaves the upper room of the Jerusalem house to head for the slopes of the Mount of Olives (Mark 14:26 pars.).

Prediction of Peter's Denial (Mark 14:27–31 pars.; Luke 22:35–38). About the time of their departure, Jesus also predicts that all the disciples will abandon him and that Peter will explicitly deny him three times during the coming night (before the rooster crows twice—Mark 14:30). Luke 22:31–32 sees this as Satan's doing, but, as consistently in Scripture, Satan's power is limited by God's sovereign permission. Jesus ensures Peter that his faith will later return, enabling him to lead God's people. Also distinctive to Luke is Jesus' "change of strategy" for the disciples in their post-resurrection missionary work (vv. 35–38). Previously, they were to go out peacefully, entirely dependent on others' hospitality (recall 9:1–6 pars.; 10:1–12). From now on they must be more self-sufficient, prepared for hostility and persecution. The disciples take Jesus' words overly literally and brandish two swords, to which Jesus replies with exasperation, "That is enough" (Luke 22:38)—almost equivalent to "Never mind; you just don't get it!"[17]

John's account of the prediction of Peter's denial also includes distinctive material: another reminder that the hour of Jesus' glorification is imminent (John 13:31–33) and the giving of a "new" commandment to love—new in the sense

---

[14] D. Wenham, "How Jesus Understood the Last Supper: A Parable in Action," *Them* 20 (1995): 11–16.

[15] We celebrate his spiritual presence with us in the current moment. Past, present, and future meanings all coalesce. See Davies and Allison, *Matthew*, vol. 3, 477. For good primers on what can and cannot fairly be derived from Scripture on the Eucharist more generally, see I. H. Marshall, *Last Supper and Lord's Supper* (Exeter: Paternoster; Grand Rapids: Eerdmans, 1980); and B. Witherington III, *Making a Meal of It: Rethinking the Theology of the Lord's Supper* (Waco: Baylor, 2007).

[16] On which see esp. P. K. Nelson, *Leadership and Discipleship: A Study of Luke 22:24–30* (Atlanta: Scholars, 1994).

[17] Cf. further Marshall, *Luke*, 827.

that in Christ they would have a new empowerment to obey it (vv. 34–35).[18] This love would offer a dynamic witness to a watching world. Roughly two centuries later, Tertullian confirms this effect by citing the pagan admiration for the character of Christian assemblies: "'Look,' they say, 'how they love one another' (for themselves hate one another); 'and how they are ready to die for each other' (for themselves will be readier to kill each other)" (*Apology* 39.7).

The Farewell Discourse (John 14:1–17:26)

Only John records Jesus' more extended remarks following the Passover meal. Formally, this "discourse" is introduced already at 13:31, but verses 31–38 have been treated in connection with the prediction of Peter's denial above. Despite this gloomy prophecy, Jesus now urges the disciples not to be troubled but to trust in God and in himself (14:1). Chapters 14–17 in various ways resemble the established genre in Jewish literature of a farewell discourse—a famous hero about to die, instructing his followers about how to prepare for life after his departure (cf. esp. the Testaments of the Twelve Patriarchs). Chapters 14–16 contain the body of the discourse proper, while chapter 17 appends a closing prayer. Chapters 14–16 divide naturally into four parts, which form an ABBA structure: on Jesus' departure and return (14:1–31), the disciples' responsibility to love (15:1–17), contrasted with the world's hatred for the disciples (15:18–16:4), and more on Jesus' departure and return (16:5–33).[19]

Jesus' Departure and Return (14:1–31) [Aland §317–319]. This section of Jesus' discourse is unified by the pattern of four questions from four different disciples, each of which elicits a somewhat oblique answer from Jesus that in turn triggers the next question. Peter has already asked where Jesus is going in 13:36; Jesus continues his answer in 14:1–4. He is returning to the Father to prepare a place for his followers. Verse 2a is better translated as "in my Father's house are many rooms" (NIV) or "dwelling places" (HCSB), not as "mansions" (KJV). The most prominent multi-room dwelling in ancient Israel was, of course, the temple.[20] Jesus' language in verses 2–3 also suggests that the life in the presence of the Father to which his disciples can look forward is a spacious home and involves

---

[18] The Latin for "new commandment" (*mandatum novum*) led to this day being called "Maundy" Thursday in the Christian calendar.

[19] It is common in scholarly circles to speak of "two farewell discourses" (or more!) because of the apparent literary seam at 14:31—Jesus says, "Come now; let us leave," but keeps on talking as if they are all still in the upper room. But an even more elaborate chiasmus may well mark these three chapters out as a unified whole (Brouwer, *Literary Development of John 13–17*). Stylistic and structural features further unite these chapters (L. S. Kellum, *The Unity of the Farewell Discourse: The Literary Integrity of John 13.31–16.33* [London and New York: T&T Clark, 2004]). Perhaps they may even be outlined according to the conventional subsections of Greco-Roman rhetoric (J. C. Stube, *A Graeco-Roman Rhetorical Reading of the Farewell Discourse* [London and New York: T&T Clark, 2006]).

[20] For a survey of the temple motif throughout John, in defense of the thesis that Jesus has temple imagery in mind here, too, see J. McCaffrey, *The House with Many Rooms: The Temple Theme of John 14, 2–3* (Rome: BIP, 1988). Cf. also S. M. Bryan, "The Eschatological Temple in John 14," *BBR* 15 (2005): 187–98.

a welcoming fellowship. By claiming that they know the way, he elicits the next question, this time from Thomas.

Verses 5–7 address the issue of the way to the Father. Jesus replies that he is the true and living way (v. 6). In context, the point is that one cannot have the Father without the Son. Those who reject Jesus turn their back on God also. This passage does not address the question of whether anyone who has never heard of Jesus can be saved.[21] If anyone can, however, it would be only on the basis of the cross-work of Christ. Philip, nevertheless, insists that Jesus show them the Father (v. 8). Jesus' answer comes in two parts. He again calls the Twelve to look at him (vv. 9–14). Then he promises the Holy Spirit as the one to come to replace him (vv. 15–21). Verses 9–14 make four points: (1) The Father and the Son are so closely related that Jesus can talk of each as being "in" the other (vv. 9–10). (2) If people will not believe Jesus' own claims, they should believe on the basis of his miracles (v. 11). (3) Those who do believe will do even greater works than Christ—not so much qualitatively as quantitatively (v. 12).[22] The Spirit will enable Christians to reach far more people and influence the world in far greater ways than Jesus could during his lifetime, with his human limitations and a ministry largely restricted to Israel. (4) Requests based on Christ's power and authority (the meaning of "name"), and hence in accordance with his desires, will be granted (vv. 13–14).

Verses 15–21 introduce the first of five "Paraclete" passages in the Farewell Discourse. The Greek *paraklētos* is a term that can mean comforter, counselor, advocate, strengthener, or exhorter. In these passages we see the Holy Spirit introduced as just such a person, a replacement for Jesus ("*another* advocate"—v. 16, italics added), who functions as a helper (14:16), interpreter (14:26), witness (15:26), prosecutor (16:7), and revealer (16:13).[23] In 14:15–21, the Paraclete helps the disciples by not leaving them "orphaned" when Jesus departs. The Spirit is currently with them, as he was with Jesus and believers throughout Old Testament times, but from Pentecost on, he will be in them (v. 17), permanently indwelling and empowering his people to demonstrate their love through obedience to Christ's commands (v. 21).

The final question of chapter 14 comes from Jude. Why such exclusivity that God, in Jesus and the Spirit, reveals himself only to believers (v. 22)? Jesus' answer basically affirms that people must choose for themselves, but that the Triune God will make his "home" with anyone willing to love and obey him (vv. 23–24). Verses 25–31 summarize the chapter. The purpose of this discourse is to help the disciples make sense of coming events, particularly Jesus' death and resurrection,

---

[21] On which see the excellent survey of historic Christian options in J. Sanders, *No Other Name: An Investigation into the Destiny of the Unevangelized* (Grand Rapids: Eerdmans, 1992; Eugene, OR: Wipf & Stock, 2001). On 14:6, Whitacre (*John*, 352) observes, "This verse does not address the ways in which Jesus brings people to the Father, but what it does say is that no one who ends up sharing God's life will do so apart from Jesus, the unique Son of God who *is*, not just who conveys, truth and life."

[22] Cf. Ridderbos, *John*, 497. But their empowerment by the Spirit, now given in his fullness in the new covenant age, creates some of the former as well (Köstenberger, *John*, 433).

[23] Bruce, *John*, 302. Recall above, p. 191 .

after they have happened. The Spirit will help them interpret his ministry (v. 26) so that they can experience an inner peace different from the mere cessation of external hostility that the world tries to promise (v. 27). Verse 28 offers a balance to the previous statements that stressed the equality of Father, Son, and Holy Spirit. There is still a hierarchy of persons that is irreversible.[24] The Son proceeds from the Father and the Spirit proceeds from both Father and Son. "Fallen human society can understand hierarchy and equality separately, but to have them both at the same time is a concept found rarely if ever in fallen humanity."[25] The puzzling reference at the end of verse 31 may refer to the time at which the disciples followed Jesus out of the Upper Room and headed toward Gethsemane. The rest of the discourse could well have been spoken en route; certainly the imagery of vine and branches might easily have been suggested as they passed the vineyards near the temple and headed for the slopes of the mount covered with olive trees.[26]

The Vine and the Branches (15:1–17) [Aland §320–321]. This section falls into two parts. Verses 1–8 exhort Jesus' followers to remain in him. Verses 9–17 command them to love each other. This love flows organically from abiding in Christ, just as a branch must remain attached to the vine in order to keep growing and bearing fruit. Verses 1–8 present only two alternatives: remaining (growing and bearing fruit) or not remaining at all. Certain branches (faithful believers) are pruned (disciplined) so as to bear more fruit (all the marks of Christian obedience). They receive whatever they ask for (but, by remaining in Christ, such requests by definition fit in with his will—v. 7; cf. v. 10). Others are cut off and burned (vv. 2, 6). The language here is too strong to refer simply to immature, carnal, or less rewarded Christians. This category of person is best interpreted by another Johannine passage: "They went out from us, but they did not really belong to us. For if they had belonged to us, they would have remained with us; but their going showed that none of them belonged to us" (1 John 2:19).[27] In this context, Judas is the most obvious example of someone who did not "remain" (John 13:18). Jesus' use of the vine metaphor may also suggest that he is presenting himself here as the new Israel.

---

[24] See esp. C. K. Barrett, *Essays on John* (London: SPCK; Philadelphia: Westminster, 1982), 19–36.

[25] Whitacre, *John*, 368.

[26] Kellum (*Unity of the Farewell Discourse*, 238) agrees, noting that 18:1 would then mark the time they left Jerusalem to cross the Kidron ravine for the Garden of Gethsemane. But he also believes the device slows down the narrative "immediately before the peak of the discourse." Parsenios (*Departure and Consolation*, 49–76) calls attention to parallels in Greek tragedies to "the delayed exit," in which speakers recognize their need to go to face opposition but then wait, highlighting the significance of the occasion.

[27] D. A. Carson, *The Farewell Discourse and Final Prayer of Jesus* (Grand Rapids: Baker, 1980) [= *Jesus and His Friends: His Farewell Message and Prayer in John 14 to 17* (Leicester: IVP, 1986)]), 98. Cf. Bass, "A Johannine Perspective of the Human Responsibility to Persevere in the Faith," 315–19; Köstenberger, *John*, 451–52. *Contra* the view popularized by B. Wilkerson, *Secrets of the Vine* (Sisters, OR: Multnomah, 2001).

John 15:9–17 elaborates on the theme of love.[28] It functions for John much as 1 Corinthians 13 does for Paul. By loving obedience, Christians' joy will be perfected (v. 11). The greatest example of love is willingness to die for a friend, as Jesus will soon do for his (v. 13). By no longer calling them servants but friends, he is indicating their privileged position with respect to receiving the Father's revelation (v. 15). But this privilege is nothing in which they can boast, for it was entirely initiated by God (v. 16).

Hatred from the World (15:18–16:4) [Aland §322–324]. The disciples may love each other, but they can expect at least some outsiders to hate them. This thought is unpacked via four subpoints: (1) They will be hated because Jesus was hated (15:18–21). This is the context for the proverb, "A slave is not greater than the master" (v. 20 NLT), which in other contexts might prove false. In any era, no loyal follower of the one who was crucified by hatred can expect lifelong exemption from opposition. (2) Such hatred is inexcusable because people can know about Jesus' good teachings and mighty deeds (15:22–25). Nevertheless it will often persist, typologically fulfilling Scripture, much like King David was hated irrationally (v. 25; cf. Ps 35:19; 69:4). (3) The Spirit will empower them for bold testimony in the midst of persecution (15:26–27). Acts 5:29–32 narrates one dramatic fulfillment of this promise. (4) All these warnings are prophylactic so that the disciples can be ready for what happens (16:1–4). Persecution for Jewish Christians will extend even to excommunication from the synagogue (v. 2; recall 9:22). This policy at first developed only sporadically, but by the end of the first century it was more widespread throughout the empire (see above, p. 348).

More on Jesus' Departure and Return (16:5–33) [Aland §325–328]. Again, four subsections may be identified. To begin with, Jesus outlines further work of the Holy Spirit (vv. 5–15). This section begins with a puzzling apparent contradiction, as Jesus chastises the disciples for not asking where he is going (v. 5; but see 13:36; 14:5). Perhaps his point is that, after all this talk of hatred, *now* is the more appropriate time to ask the question, as they grieve over his departure (v. 6).[29] Unless Jesus leaves, the Spirit cannot replace him (v. 7). The Spirit's ministry will be powerful, indeed. He will convict unbelievers of their sin, sham righteousness, and coming judgment (vv. 8–11).[30] Through his disciples, the Holy Spirit will guide believers "into all truth" (vv. 12–15; see esp. v. 13). No doubt, this included the writing of the Gospel of John itself and the other New Testament documents, but there is nothing in the context to limit this prophecy to the canon of Scripture.

---

[28] Cf. esp. F. F. Segovia, *Love Relationships in the Johannine Tradition* (Chico: Scholars, 1982).

[29] Cf. Barrett, *John*, 485; Burge, *John*, 436; Lincoln, *John*, 418.

[30] D. A. Carson ("The Function of the Paraclete in John 16:7–11," *JBL* 98 [1979]: 547–66) stresses that it is most natural to take all three adjectives as attributes of the fallen world. Cf. also J. Aloisi, "The Paraclete's Ministry of Conviction: Another Look at John 16:8–11," *JETS* 47 (2004): 55–69; Kruse, *John*, 331. An alternate, more common interpretation takes the middle term (righteousness) as referring to what Christ bestows on believers.

God may not grant revelation today on a par with Scripture, but the Spirit is still in the business of illuminating his Word and his will for his people.[31]

Second, the disciples' grief will turn to joy (vv. 16–22). This section revolves around Jesus' enigmatic declaration that in a little while the Twelve would no longer see him, but then, shortly afterwards, they would see him again (v. 16). Jesus' departure and return can be interpreted as referring to his death and resurrection but also to his ascension and second coming. In each case, happiness will follow the sorrow produced by the temporary "absence" of Christ.[32] Third, even in his absence the disciples can ask and receive many things from the Father in Christ's "name" (vv. 23–28). Now they can make requests of Jesus directly; later they will ask more indirectly. Asking through Christ and by his power and authority (and so, again, in accordance with his desires) will have a mighty effect.

Finally, and fourthly, the disciples claim to understand. But Jesus' response shows the claim to be premature (vv. 29–33).[33] They are still not prepared for his departure, but, with God's presence, they will "rebound." Despite the persecutions the church age will inflict, they will have peace with God. Knowing that he has overcome the world and made their eventual victory certain, they will persevere.

The True "Lord's Prayer" (17:1–26) [Aland §329]. Jesus closes his Farewell Discourse with a poignant prayer for himself (vv. 1–5), for his disciples (vv. 6–19), and for coming generations of followers (vv. 20–26).[34] Because of its intercessory function, it has often been called Jesus' high-priestly prayer. Had the prayer he modeled for his disciples not have come to be known as the Lord's Prayer, that label might have stuck here instead. Once again, Jesus acknowledges that the hour for his departure has come (v. 1). His prayer for himself is that he might complete the work for which the Father sent him. This would bring glory to him, but he would merely reflect that glory back to the Father (vv. 1, 4–5).

The main request for his disciples is for spiritual protection in the midst of the predicted adversity. On the basis of their eternal security (vv. 6–14), Jesus prays that they might be shielded from being overpowered by the devil in this life, and be sanctified (growing in holiness) instead (vv. 15–19). Verse 9 surprises us as Jesus says he is not praying for unbelievers. That does not mean he never prays for them, merely that he is not praying for them here. As he prays for his followers who will spread his message, he is clearly demonstrating concern for the lost.[35] Verse 12 is not an exception to the principle of eternal security, but it stresses that the one who would betray Christ was a "son of perdition" from the start. Verse 15

---

[31] Cf. Bruce, *John*, 320: "As the Messiah was expected to bring out plainly the fuller implications of the revelation that had preceded his coming, so the Paraclete will bring out plainly the fuller implications of the revelations embodied in the Messiah and apply them relevantly to each succeeding generation."

[32] The comfort a surrogate would provide in the Greco-Roman world after the loss of a loved one to death or departure forms important background to this theme here. See P. A. Holloway, "Left Behind: Jesus' Consolation of His Disciples in John 13,31–17,26," *ZNW* 96 (2005): 1–34.

[33] Köstenberger, *John*, 479–80; Lincoln, *John*, 428.

[34] On the careful, thematic parallelism among the three sections, see Brown, *John*, vol. 2, 750.

[35] Cf. Beasley-Murray, *John*, 298; Whitacre, *John*, 410; Kruse, *John*, 342.

has massive implications for Christian living in any culture. Jesus never promoted isolationism or monasticism, nor did he promise relief from great tribulation. He did pray for, and we can be assured of, protection in the midst of the sin and suffering of the world.[36] It is from verses 14–16 that we derive the abbreviated paraphrase that Christians are to be "in the world but not of it."

Included in Jesus' prayer for his disciples is the request for unity (v. 11). In his intercession for those who would come to belief through the apostles' ministry, unity becomes the dominant theme (vv. 21–23). An important reason for desiring unity is its evangelistic impact (vv. 21b, 23b). How impotent much subsequent Christianity has become through its rampant factionalism and/or isolationism! The evangelical parachurch movement of our day has demonstrated the potential of Bible-believing Christians of numerous theological traditions working together for kingdom objectives. Established churches and denominations are, in some settings, beginning to follow suit, but they still have a long way to go to catch up.[37] But "unless [believers] are unified, how can they expect to give authentic, credible testimony to the Father, who is united with the Son and the Spirit in revealing himself and his salvation in Christ?"[38] As amazing as anything in this section of Jesus' prayer is this concern that our unity in some sense would reflect the unity of the Triune Godhead (vv. 21a, 22, 24). This does not mean that believers are deified, but it means we have access to the very revelation of God (vv. 25–26). 1 Corinthians 2:10–16 offers an apt commentary.

Prayer and Arrest in the Garden (Mark 14:32–52 pars.) [Aland §330–331]. Eventually, Jesus and the disciples arrive at the Garden of Gethsemane (from Hb. "oil press") on the western slopes of Olivet, overlooking the Kidron ravine and the temple in Jerusalem (Mark 14:32–42 pars.). Jesus asks all his followers to wait for him but takes the inner three to a separate place and commissions them to pray fervently that they might not succumb to temptation. As he goes a little further on, he prays for himself, "Abba, Father . . . Take this cup from me. Yet not what I will, but what you will" (v. 36). Here we see Jesus' close personal intimacy with the Father (on Abba, see above, p. 293). Jesus' full humanity is disclosed, conjoined

---

[36] Interestingly, the identical two Greek words for "protect . . . from" (the verb *tēreō* plus the preposition *ek*) recur in Rev 3:10, in which John quotes Jesus as promising the faithful church of Philadelphia that he will "keep them from" the hour of trial about to come on the whole world. Therefore, if this verse refers to the great tribulation at the end of the church age (and it may not), it fits a posttribulational view (protection in the midst of trial) better than a pretribulational one (exemption from the tribulation altogether). Cf. further C. L. Blomberg, "The Posttribulationism of the New Testament: Leaving 'Left Behind' Behind," in *A Case for Historic Premillennialism*, ed. Blomberg and Chung, 100–37.

[37] Witherington (*John's Wisdom*, 274) notes: "Protestantism has tended to hold up Truth, with a capital *T*, while intoning unity with a lowercase *u*, with the end result that Protestant churches and denominations have proved endlessly divisive and factious. On the other hand, Catholicism and Orthodoxy have held up Unity with a capital *U*, and at least from a Protestant viewpoint this has been at the expense of Truth. In other words, no part of the church has adequately gotten the balance between truth and unity right, it would seem."

[38] Köstenberger, *John*, 499. See also J. E. Staton, "A Vision of Unity—Christian Unity in the Fourth Gospel," *EQ* 69 (1997): 291–305.

with his perfect obedience to God. No one should ever want to endure the agony Christ knew lay ahead, but he was prepared to submit to God if there was no other way. This is also a perfect example of a prayer not answered in the manner preferred by the person making the request, but through no fault of the one praying! Heb 5:7 will later reflect on this text and insist that Christ "was heard because of his reverent submission." But the answer to Jesus' prayer was resurrection after death, not exemption from it. God may often answer our most fervent prayers to be spared hard times in the same way.[39]

After a while, Judas arrives leading Jewish (and perhaps Roman) authorities to seize Jesus (Mark 14:43–52 pars.). Christ has had to rouse his sleeping disciples who were unable to stay awake and pray (vv. 41–42). Judas greets him with the conventional sign of friendship—a kiss (vv. 43–46).[40] Why did Jesus need to be identified at all to the authorities? Perhaps because it was dark, and perhaps Jesus looked very much like several others in his little group. The presence of people with clubs and swords shows that they feared the disciples might be numerous and armed. Peter, in fact, does briefly resist, cutting off the ear of the high priest's slave, Malchus (John 18:10), but Jesus rebukes him, demonstrates forgiveness for his enemies by healing the ear (Luke 22:51), and reiterates that this is not the time for violent rebellion (Matt 26:52–56). John, more than any of the other Gospels, highlights how Jesus is in control of the situation. At first, the soldiers fall to the ground in his presence, unable to arrest him (John 18:4–9), but he proceeds to submit, because this is their "hour"—they who belong to the power of darkness (Luke 22:53). In stark contrast, the disciples all flee, including a young man who leaves behind his linen undergarment and runs away naked (Mark 14:51–52). This latter reference, unique to Mark, has often been viewed as his ignominious signature to the Gospel. (We know from Acts 12:12 that the disciples later met in Mark's home in Jerusalem; could this have been the site of the Last Supper as well?) Whoever the young man was, he, too, abandoned Christ. All of his followers had now left.[41]

---

[39] The view that Christ prayed in the garden to be spared premature death on the spot seems improbable. Mark 14:34 reflects hyperbole (M. M. Culy, "Would Jesus Exaggerate? Rethinking Matthew 26.38//Mark 14.34," *BT* 57 [2006]: 105–9). Luke 22:43–44 maintains merely that Jesus' sweat was so profuse that it was "*like* drops of blood falling on the ground" (italics mine) not that he actually bled, or bled from every pore, as some have imagined, thus putting his life in immediate, grave jeopardy. Moreover, these two verses do not even appear in several of the oldest and most reliable manuscripts and may therefore not be original to Luke or historically reliable, but it is very hard to be sure. For a judicious discussion, see Bock, *Luke 9:51–24:53*, 1763–64.

[40] "Disciples may betray Jesus with the very sort of acts that outwardly symbolize devotion" (Keener, *Matthew*, 641).

[41] This may be the only point that Mark is trying to stress here. For the full range of suggested options, see Collins, *Mark*, 688–94. For a vigorous defense of the perspective that this is the climax to the emotion, fear, flight and shame of Jesus' followers' failure in the garden, see H. M. Jackson, "Why the Youth Shed His Cloak and Fled Naked: The Meaning and Purpose of Mark 14:51–52," *JBL* 116 (1997): 273–89.

Historicity

The unusually close similarities between John and the Synoptics from here on in the Gospel accounts have suggested to many the concept of an early, written source containing most or all of the passion narrative.[42] The betrayal, denial, and flight of the disciples are all too embarrassing to have been invented.[43] The same is true of the temptation of Jesus in the Garden of Gethsemane, an episode that is also attested in Heb 5:7–10. Jesus' submission to his Father's will nicely matches the petition from the Lord's Prayer, "Your will be done." The Last Supper finds detailed corroboration in the "words of institution" passed on as sacred tradition by Paul in 1 Cor 11:23–26. The rest of the events of that Passover meal fit perfectly into the details of the Jewish ceremony, yet they receive Jesus' characteristic and surprising reinterpretations. The entire account also has an unusual concentration of Semitisms.[44]

John 13–17, as with most passages in the Fourth Gospel, proves more complex. It contains overlaps with the Synoptic accounts of Thursday night, most notably the predictions of Peter's denial and Judas's betrayal. We have already noted that John would have had reason to omit the words of institution over the bread and wine (see above, p. 192). The footwashing scene that he describes instead fits well with the emphases of that evening on humility, self-sacrifice, and selfless love (cf. Luke 22:24–27 in particular), however much John's idiom may have transformed it. Various other individual verses find close parallels in the Synoptics (e.g., John 13:20 with Matt 10:40; John 14:13–14 and 16:23–24 with Matt 7:7–11). Jesus' advance predictions of his death, resurrection, and return permeate both the Farewell Discourse and the Synoptic narratives. John 14:6 ("I am the way") could explain why the first Christians were called "the Way" (e.g., Acts 9:2), while John 15 again seems to rely on parable-like sayings for its core imagery (vine, vinedresser, fruitbearing, etc.). The warnings about the world's hatred, especially prominent in 15:18–16:4, echo many of the predictions of Matt 10:17–42. John 13:16 and Matt 10:24 parallel each other particularly closely in this respect. The theme of coming tribulation also ties in with the Olivet Discourse (cf. esp. the repeated imagery of a woman in labor in John 16:21 and Mark 13:8).[45] As noted previously (p. 180), the promises about the ministry of the coming Paraclete (14:26; 15:26) may explain some of the freedom John felt to write his Gospel the way he did. The very fact that he distinguishes this role of the Spirit as future from what Jesus was saying on the last night of his life further confirms that the past and present ministries of the Spirit are not being confused with each other.[46]

---

[42] For a detailed survey of the relevant source-critical theories, with judicious hypotheses, see R. E. Brown, *The Death of the Messiah*, (New York and London: Doubleday, 1994), 1:36–93.

[43] Eusebius and Chrysostom both made the point in the ancient world that Mark "must have had an extraordinarily high standard of truth telling to record" these stories (Witherington, *Mark*, 387, n.121).

[44] Jeremias, *Eucharistic Words of Jesus*, 101–5.

[45] On John 14–16, see esp. Blomberg, *Historical Reliability of John's Gospel*, 195–218.

[46] See esp. Witherington, *John's Wisdom*, 253. Cf. Ridderbos, *John*, 509; Pryor, *John*, 62; Carson, *John*, 505.

John 17, finally, may be read as an expansion of the main thoughts of the Lord's Prayer in Matt 6:9–13.[47]

Friday: The Trials and Crucifixion of Jesus

Jesus before the Sanhedrin (Mark 14:53–15:1 pars.) [Aland §332–35]

After his arrest, Jesus is brought before the Jewish leaders in three phases: an informal hearing before Annas, a more formal trial before Caiaphas and the Sanhedrin while it is still dark, and a brief early morning "rubber-stamping" of the nighttime verdict by the same court, perhaps to create an aura of legality.

Before Annas (John 18:12–14, 19–23). Though Caiaphas had been legally installed as high priest in AD 15, Annas, his father-in-law and predecessor in office (AD 6–15), would still have been considered by Jews as the rightful man for the position because Jewish law declared it a role to be held for life. It is not at all implausible, therefore, that the arresting leaders would pay respect to Annas by granting him this brief hearing of the celebrated Jesus.[48] If Annas thought he might learn something new and surprising, Jesus assured him that what he stood for was nothing that he had not regularly proclaimed in the open. For his blunt uncooperativeness he is struck, but he quickly points out the injustice of the slap. In John's Gospel especially, even though Jesus is literally on trial before both Jewish and Roman authorities, it repeatedly becomes clear at a spiritual level that they are on trial before him![49]

Before the Sanhedrin at Night: The Scene Inside—Jesus' Confession (Mark 14:53–65 pars.). All four Gospels agree that Jesus was next arraigned before Caiaphas (although in John the episode is merely implied in 18:24, 28a).[50] The Synoptics make it clear that the Sanhedrin had no legitimate charge against Jesus; they could not even get false witnesses to agree (Mark 14:56)! The closest they come is a garbled accusation that Jesus had claimed he would destroy the temple: either a reference back to his prophecies of its coming destruction (by others) or an allusion to John 2:19 ("Destroy this temple, and I will raise it again in three days").[51] Caiaphas finally has to put the question to Jesus directly, "Are you the Messiah, the Son of the Blessed One?" (Mark 14:61). He wants to know what Jesus really claims to be. All this is strong evidence that Jesus had not previously made regular unambiguous affirmations of his messiahship among his opponents.

---

[47] W. O. Walker, Jr., "The Lord's Prayer in Matthew and John," *NTS* 28 (1982): 237–56; Lincoln, *John*, 432.

[48] Barrett, *John*, 524. That five of Annas' sons held the high priesthood after him and before Caiaphas also shows the continuing, informal authority he would have wielded. See also Ridderbos, *John*, 578–80.

[49] Carson (*John*, 585) adds: "Jesus did not call anyone names; he had nothing for which to apologize. Nor was he refusing to 'turn the other cheek': that ought to be clear from the cross itself. But turning the other cheek without bearing witness to the truth is not the fruit of moral resolution but the terrorized cowardice of the wimp."

[50] On whom, see esp. Bond, *Caiaphas*.

[51] See esp. Robinson, *The Priority of John*, 127–31.

At last he answers. Mark records his words as simply, "I am" (v. 62a). Matthew and Luke give more evasive replies (Matt 26:64; Luke 22:67, 70). "You say that I am" or "You have said it" may be the more literal translation of what was a cautious or circumlocutory affirmative.[52] Jesus may even be indicting his interrogators by this way of phrasing things, but he does not stop here. He goes on to add, "and you will see the Son of Man sitting at the right hand of the Mighty One, and coming on the clouds of heaven" (Mark 14:62b, RSV). This reply combines allusions to Dan 7:13 and Ps 110:1. In this context, "Son of Man" means far more than a simple human being. Jesus is describing himself as the "one like a son of man, coming with the clouds of heaven" who "approached the Ancient of Days and was led into his presence" and given authority and power over all humanity, leading to universal worship and everlasting dominion (Dan 7:13–14). This claim to be far more than a mere mortal is probably what elicited the verdict of blasphemy from the Jewish high court. Notwithstanding the diversity of expectation, they could not automatically condemn every messianic pretender or they would never get a Messiah! But, in their eyes, one who too closely associated himself with God the Father in this fashion had blasphemed and was worthy of death.[53]

Jesus' Final Hours

Thursday

after sundown	Last Supper
	Prayer in garden
	Betrayal and arrest

Thurs.-Friday

nighttime	Custody
	Hearing before Annas
	Trial before Caiaphas
	Peter's denial

Friday

early morning	Sanhedrin completes deliberations
	Jesus sent to Pilate
	Hearing before Pilate
	Jesus sent to Herod
	Return to Pilate
late morning/noon	Jesus nailed to cross
midafternoon	Jesus dies
near sundown	Jesus buried

The language of sitting at God's right hand echoes Ps 110:1, which Jesus had already utilized in his previous teaching in the temple (Mark 12:35–37 pars.). Perhaps that is why Luke adds Jesus' words that, "If I tell you, you will not believe me, and if I asked you, you would not answer" (Luke 22:67–68). That Jesus "sits"

---

[52] See esp. D. R. Catchpole, "The Answer of Jesus to Caiaphas (Matt. XXVI.64)," *NTS* 17 (1970–71): 213–26.

[53] Ironically, popular Christian usage today regularly assumes that 'Son of Man' means Jesus in his complete humanity and 'Son of God' refers to his full deity. In this context, the usage is almost exactly the opposite. "Son of Man" makes Jesus so divinely exalted a Messiah that the Sanhedrin is scandalized, whereas "Son of God" (Matt. 26:63) is simply another expression for the military-political ruler many people were awaiting. Cf. the similar use of this title in fragment 4Q246 from Qumran. See also below, pp. 473–74.

before he "comes" makes it highly probable that he has in mind his exaltation to the Father followed by his return to earth, not some other kind of "coming" (such as coming to the Father to receive authority or coming invisibly in judgment on Jerusalem in AD 70).[54] Once the Sanhedrin has passed its death sentence, some begin to revile him. They blindfold him and ask him to "prophesy" who is striking him (Mark 14:65), possibly drawing on an interpretation of Isa 11:3. There the Messiah will not judge by what he sees or hears but will "delight in the fear of the Lord."[55]

Before the Servants near the Fire: The Scene Outside—Peter's Denial (Mark 14:66–72 pars.). As is his custom elsewhere, Mark starkly juxtaposes two events in sandwich fashion, this time inserting the story of Jesus' confession between the two parts of the account of Peter's denial (Mark 14:54, 55–65, 66–72). The contrast between episodes could scarcely be harsher: Jesus courageously admitting his identity, even though he would be condemned to die vs. Peter timidly fearing to admit his identity as a disciple of Jesus even to the lowliest of servants.[56] In so doing, Peter fulfills Jesus' earlier prophecy (vv. 27–31). Hearing the rooster crow, he remembers Christ's words and weeps bitterly (Matt 26:75). We are meant to understand these as tears of repentance, particularly in Matthew, who alone goes on to add the story of Judas' suicide (27:3–10; though cf. Acts 1:18–19). Judas, too, is filled with remorse and even seemingly confesses his sin (v. 4).[57] Yet instead of returning to Jesus, he appeals to Christ's enemies who can offer him no help. So Peter contrasts unfavorably with Jesus but favorably with Judas. There are no unforgivable sins except refusing to come (or come back) to Christ.

Before the Sanhedrin in the Morning: Jesus Is Taken Away (Mark 15:1 pars.). In Luke it appears as if the entire trial before the Sanhedrin takes place after daybreak (Luke 22:66). However, Mark and Matthew clearly locate the proceedings during the night, with merely a final "consultation" occurring in the morning before Jesus is taken to Pilate (Mark 15:1; Matt 27:1–2). This latter chronology would seem to be the more precise, for it appears legal verdicts could not be reached during the night. Luke may have streamlined the story for literary purposes and even recognized that the more elaborate nighttime proceedings would

---

[54] Davies and Allison, *Matthew*, vol. 3, 531.

[55] The word for "delight" could also mean "smell," so the tradition arose that the Messiah would be able by smell to detect who was doing what to him (*b. Sanh.* 93b).

[56] It would seem from comparing the parallel accounts that more than three people asked Peter if he were one of Jesus' followers. But there are no grounds for assuming Peter replied more than three times. For the redactional and stylistic elements illustrated in the diversity of the four accounts, see esp. N. J. McEleney, "Peter's Denials—How Many? To Whom?" *CBQ* 52 (1990): 467–72.

[57] Some translations of Matt 27:3 read that Judas even "repented." But the verb is *metamelomai,* not *metanoeō* (the standard New Testament word for "repent"), so the NIV/TNIV "seized with remorse" seems better in this context. The ESV's "changed his mind," however, is too weak. Matthew, characteristically, finds in Judas' death a fulfillment of Scripture. While referring only to Jeremiah, he obviously has texts from both Jeremiah 19 (vv. 1, 4, 6, 11) and Zechariah (11:12–13) in mind. Cf. further D. J. Moo, "Tradition and Old Testament in Matt. 27.3–10," in *Gospel Perspectives*, vol. 6, 157–75; Keener, *Matthew*, 657.

have had to be repeated, however perfunctorily, come daylight.[58] France cites *m. Sanh.* 7:5 to the effect that "when blasphemy has been proven using euphemisms in open court, the chief witness is asked to repeat the offending words verbatim in a closed session so that the people as a whole do not hear them, and then 'the judges stand up on their feet and rend their garments, and they may not mend them again'."[59]

All this raises the question of other seeming illegalities surrounding the Sanhedrin's proceedings. A comparison with Mishnaic law on capital trials (in the tractate Sanhedrin) discloses so many irregularities that many scholars find it impossible to accept the historicity of the Gospel accounts.[60] These include a trial on the eve of a Sabbath, on a feast day at night, without witnesses on behalf of the accused, and with the high priest speaking before those of lesser authority. Some of these details may have been present but not narrated; others are clear violations. On the other hand, (1) there is no evidence that all of these later laws for the second- and third-century Jewish court, the *beth din*, were in force in Jesus' day. (2) Those that were current would have been supported by Pharisees but not necessarily by the Sadducees who dominated the council. (3) Even the later Jewish literature allows for trials during festivals in the cases of seducers to idolatry or false prophets (*t. Sanh.* 10:11 and 11:7). (4) Desperate people will often manipulate the law if they perceive a higher cause is at stake.[61] Craig Keener concludes that "the Gospel writers probably intended to convey breach of procedure, not to pretend that the mock trial and abuse they depict were standard Jewish custom."[62]

Closely related is the question of whether the Gospels are anti-Semitic in their assigning the primary blame for Jesus' execution to Jewish hands. Surely, this charge is unfounded. Jesus and all his first followers were Jews too. The Gospels describe an intra-Jewish debate, at least at the earliest stages. Even as strong and severe a statement as the Jerusalem crowd's cry, "His blood is on us and on our children" (Matt 27:25) does not indict all Jews for all time. It merely means that one group of Jewish leaders in Jerusalem and the followers they whipped up into a temporary frenzy accepted responsibility for Jesus' death. Matthew may well have seen in the addition, "and on our children," a reference to the generation from AD 30–70, culminating in the destruction of Jerusalem. We must also remember

---

[58] Cf. further A. N. Sherwin-White, "The Trial of Christ," in *Historicity and Chronology in the New Testament*, ed. D. E. Nineham, et al. (London: SPCK, 1965), 97–116. See also D. R. Catchpole, *The Trial of Jesus: A Study in the Gospels and Jewish Historiography* (Leiden: Brill, 1971), 153-203.

[59] France, *Mark*, 614.

[60] For a succinct catalogue, see Brown, *Death of the Messiah*, vol. 1, 358–59. The fullest defense of the historicity of numerous elements of the trial narrative often thought suspect remains J. Blinzler, *The Trial of Jesus* (Cork: Mercier; Westminster, MD: Newman, 1959).

[61] For a detailed list of every possible illegality in all stages of Jesus' trials, on the assumption that all later rabbinic laws were already in force, see L. L. Berg, "The Illegalities of Jesus' Religious and Civil Trials," *BSac* 161 (2004): 330–42. She concludes, "Legally the trial was a sham. The accusation was changed twice. There were no bona fide witnesses or testimony. No defense was presented. Jesus' innocence was repeatedly declared . . . ." (340).

[62] Keener, *John*, vol. 2, 1087. Cf. idem., "Mistrial of the Millennium," *Christian History* 59 (1998): 38–40.

that the very death for which these crowds clamored made possible their later forgiveness, at least for those who accepted the offer (cf. Acts 2:37; 6:7; 21:20).[63] Although Pilate will try to excuse himself, he, representing Rome, must take equal responsibility for the crucifixion. Furthermore, from a more theological perspective, every one of us must admit that, because of our sins, we crucified Christ.

Jesus before the Roman Authorities (Mark 15:2–20a) [Aland §336–42]

John 18:31 explains that, under Rome at this time, the Sanhedrin does not have the right to inflict capital punishment.[64] Therefore, the Jewish authorities must contextualize their complaints against Jesus in a way that will catch the Roman governor's attention.[65] Since in many Jewish hopes the Messiah would be an earthly king, this is the natural charge to bring before Pilate—it would then imply a threat against Rome. Jesus replies to Pilate as circuitously as he did to the Sanhedrin (Mark 15:2), and later he remains altogether silent. In all four Gospels, Pilate is not convinced that Jesus has done anything deserving of death. Luke, in particular, highlights the theme of Jesus as innocent sufferer (Luke 23:4, 13–16, 22). Only Luke explains that Pilate pawns Jesus off on Herod Antipas (in town from Galilee for the Passover) in hopes that he will render a verdict and get Pilate off the hook (vv. 6–12). Matthew uniquely adds the dream that Pilate's wife had, warning her against dealing with "that innocent man" (Matt 27:19). John arranges his account in seven scenes so that Pilate alternates between interrogating Christ inside his palace and going outside to try to dissuade the Jews of their heinous plot (John 18:28–19:16). Only in John does Jesus clarify that his kingship is not of this world (18:36). This does not mean that God's reign has no sociopolitical effect on the authorities of this age. Rather, "John certainly expects the power of the inbreaking kingdom to affect this world," but "theirs is the sort of struggle, and victory, that cannot effectively be opposed by armed might."[66]

Pilate tries to find a final way out by offering to release one prisoner to the crowd, according to a Passover custom. He pits Jesus against Barabbas, a notorious terrorist (Mark 15:7). An early scribal tradition in Matt 27:17 calls Barabbas "Jesus Barabbas," which may reflect his actual name (esp. since "Barabbas" is not a proper name but a nickname, meaning "son of a father"—*bar-abba*). How ironic

---

[63] Cf. esp. C. S. Hamilton, "'His Blood Be upon Us': Innocent Blood and the Death of Jesus in Matthew," *CBQ* 82 (2008): 82–100.

[64] Possible striking corroboration of this claim appears in *p. Sanh.* 1:1, 7:2, where it is said that this privilege was taken from Israel forty years before the destruction of the temple. For details of this and other disputed elements unique to John's trial narrative, see F. F. Bruce, "The Trial of Jesus in the Fourth Gospel," in *Gospel Perspectives*, vol. 1, 7–20.

[65] Still, Mark 15:10 asserts that Pilate recognized the Jewish leaders' envy of the honor Jesus had been accruing at their expense. On the probable socio-cultural dynamics of this dimension, see A. C. Hagedorn and J. H. Neyrey, "'It Was Out of Envy that They Handed Jesus Over' (Mark 15.10)," *JSNT* 69 (1998): 15–56.

[66] Carson, *John*, 594. Cf. Lincoln, *John*, 462: "though it will not be achieved by political means, it will have political implications, as this trial itself reveals. Religious and political dimensions of the kingdom are inextricably interwoven, since for both 'the Jews' and Pilate acknowledgement of Jesus' kingship is shown to clash with loyalty to Caesar's rule."

that the crowds opted for crucifying the true Son of their heavenly Father and called for the freedom of this murderous Barabbas. Because Pilate recognizes that he dare not alienate the Jews too much and risk a riot that would discredit him in Rome's eyes (cf. esp. John 19:12), he finally accedes to the mob's requests. Jesus is flogged, traditionally understood to be the wretched Roman *verberatio*—an unspecified number of lashes with a metal-tipped rope that opened gaping wounds in the skin and muscles of a victim's back and so weakened the accused criminal that it was itself at times fatal.[67] Then Jesus is delivered over to be nailed to a cross. Before they lead him off, they add insult to injury by dressing him up with a mock crown, royal robe, and scepter (Mark 15:17–20a).[68]

Crucifixion (Mark 15:20b–47 pars.) [Aland §343–51]

The Nature of the Punishment. Death by crucifixion was one of the cruelest forms of execution humanity has ever devised. It was also one of the most shame-filled punishments of antiquity.[69] Roman citizens were mostly exempt from this kind of torture; it was generally reserved for the worst of slaves and criminals. Someone condemned to die in this way typically carried his own crossbar, onto which his arms were eventually affixed either with nails through his wrists or by tying them with ropes. The ankles could be similarly attached to the vertical wooden beam. Sometimes footrests or seats were added, not for comfort but to keep the individual alive longer and prolong the torture. Crosses were occasionally X-shaped but usually resembled either a capital or lowercase "t" in form. The earliest Christian testimony is divided as to which of these last two was employed for Jesus, although later Christian art has almost unanimously opted for the latter.

Death usually proceeded slowly, often over a period of several days, and the typical cause was suffocation. The victim eventually became so weakened as to be unable to lift his chest and breathe. Meanwhile, in addition to the torture inflicted by all his wounds, the victim could not ward off birds and bugs that might attack, nor prevent his "bodily wastes from coming out while hanging naked."[70] Jesus died unusually quickly, perhaps because of his previous flogging and perhaps because of the use of nails rather than ropes. The Gospels also suggest that he died voluntarily, at his chosen time. After all, he had enough strength at the end to cry out with a loud voice and enough will to entrust himself to God. Jews interpreted

---

[67] Köstenberger, *John*, 531.

[68] For more historical background on the Jewish and Roman trial procedures, respectively, see D. M. Pike, "Before the Jewish Authorities," and E. D. Huntsman, "Before the Romans," in *From the Last Supper through the Resurrection: The Savior's Final Hours*, ed. R. N. Holzapfel and T. A. Wayment (Salt Lake City: Deseret, 2003), 210–68 and 269–317.

[69] For a thorough study, see M. Hengel, *Crucifixion: In the Ancient World and the Folly of the Message of the Cross* (London: SCM; Philadelphia: Fortress, 1977). Cf. also D. Tombs, "Crucifixion, State Terror, and Sexual Abuse," *USQR* 53 (1999): 89–109. For a modern scientific analysis, see W. D. Edwards, W. J. Gabel, and F. E. Hosmer, "On the Physical Death of Jesus Christ," *Journal of the American Medical Association* 255 (1986): 1455–63.

[70] Keener, *Matthew*, 679.

death by crucifixion as equivalent to "hanging on a tree" and thus concluded that anyone so punished was accursed by God (Deut 21:22–23). This explains why the Christian message of a crucified Messiah later scandalized so many Jews (1 Cor 1:23).

Exegetical Observations. Sometime between midmorning and noon on the eve of the Sabbath of Passover week, Pilate delivers Jesus to the soldiers to have him crucified.[71] They take him through the narrow, crowded streets of Jerusalem, memorialized today as the *Via Dolorosa* ("Sorrowful Way"). The "parade" becomes a macabre parody of the triumphal marches of visiting emperors.[72] Because he was already weak and close to death, he is unable to carry his crossbeam far, so a passerby, Simon of Cyrene, is conscripted to take it the rest of the way for him (Mark 15:20–21). Various women in the crowd bewail his fate, but he musters enough strength to warn them to bemoan God's coming judgment on Jerusalem instead (Luke 23:27–31). When the entourage arrives at Golgotha,[73] probably by a busy intersection chosen to heighten the effect of the execution as a public deterrent to similar "crimes," Jesus is hoisted onto his cross between two *lēstai* (insurrectionists—not thieves—Mark 15:27) and left to die.

The Gospels recount the roughly three hours Jesus hung alive on the cross, by means of two primary narrative devices: the reactions of those who saw him and Jesus' final remarks. Putting all the Gospels together reveals seven sayings of Jesus from the cross, made famous in the history of Christian liturgy as Christ's seven last "words." The reactions of the onlookers all add to the indignity of Jesus' fate.[74] The soldiers offer him an exotic perfumed wine (Mark 15:23). To remain drinkable at all, any possible pain-killing effect would have been minimal, and as a dehydrator it would have increased Jesus' suffering.[75] In any event, this is a continuing part of the mockery of the one whom they believe traitorously claimed to be king (cf. v. 26). They gamble for his clothes; he may well have been left to hang naked, a major disgrace in Jewish eyes (v. 24). John 19:24 finds in this a typological fulfillment of Ps 22:18. In fact, echoes of Psalm 22 and various other

---

[71] Mark's "third hour" (9:00 A.M.; Mark 15:25) and John's "about the sixth hour" (12:00 P.M.; John 19:14) are probably best taken as approximate designations in a culture that often did not refer to time more precisely than by quarters of the day or night. John 19:14 and 31a both refer to "the day of Preparation" of the Passover, which probably does not contradict the Synoptics by implying Passover Eve. Instead, given the explicit language of 31b, it must mean the day of preparation *for the Sabbath* in Passover week. Cf. Köstenberger, *John*, 537–38, 551.

[72] T. E. Schmidt, "Mark 15.16–32: The Crucifixion Narrative and the Roman Triumphal Procession," *NTS* 41 (1995): 1–18.

[73] Quite likely the site currently occupied by the Church of the Holy Sepulcher, but in those days very similar in appearance to the skull-shaped rocks visible in the hillside at the location known today as Gordon's Calvary.

[74] Nolland (*Matthew*, 1135) well captures a probable motive from the perception of these who watched: "Cruel and vindictive belittlement is often the fate of a person of influence who has been discredited. Sadistic pleasure is found in the fall of the mighty, and perhaps even more in the fall of those who have reached too high."

[75] E. Koskenniemi, K. Nisula and J. Toppari, "Wine Mixed with Myrrh (Mark 15.23) and *Crucifragium* (John 19.31–32): Two Details of the Passion Narratives," *JSNT* 27 (2005): 379–91.

Old Testament texts appear throughout the Passion narratives.[76] The *titulus* affixed above the cross in three languages for all to read refers to the kingship that his death so ingloriously appears to discredit (John 19:20). Various passersby taunt him to demonstrate his power and come down off the cross (Mark 15:29–32). Ironically, if he saved himself, he would be unable to save anyone else, including his tormenters. The criminals crucified with him revile him as well, though one apparently has a change of heart when he sees the noble way in which Jesus is dying (Luke 23:39–42).[77]

The significance of Jesus' death, however, is arguably best brought out by a focus on what Jesus spoke while he died. In the probable order of their utterance, Jesus' seven last words were: (1) "Father, forgive them, for they do not know what they are doing" (Luke 23:34). He who had taught love for one's enemies models it even as they kill him. Jesus' prayer does not mean that all the Jewish and Roman leaders involved in his death will be saved, but it paves the way for their forgiveness should they repent.[78] (2) "Truly I tell you, today you will be with me in paradise," he declares to the criminal on the cross (Luke 23:43). The doctrine of the descent into hell is a later Christian creation, not conclusively supported by any text of the New Testament.[79] Here Jesus affirms that heaven is available to believers immediately upon death and that he will go there at once in spirit to be with this one "deathbed" convert. (3) Speaking first to Mary and then to John, Jesus declares, "Woman, here is your son," and "Here is your mother" (John 19:27). These words strongly suggest that Joseph has died. Jesus demonstrates a concern for those closest to him (just as he did for his enemies) and a commitment to incorporating his biological family into his spiritual family.

(4) "My God, my God, why have you forsaken me?" (Mark 15:34; cf. Ps 22:1). The best interpretation of these words is the most literal. Jesus senses divine abandonment.[80] The close, unbroken communion with the Father he had experienced throughout his life has been suddenly interrupted. Other New Testament writers understood this as the moment that he bore the sins of the world and experienced the wrath of God that we deserved instead (e.g., 2 Cor 5:21). Later Christian theo-

---

[76] See esp. D. J. Moo, *The Old Testament in the Gospel Passion Narratives* (Sheffield: Almond, 1983).

[77] On this theme, see esp. J. J. Pilch, "Death with Honor: The Mediterranean Style Death of Jesus in Mark," *BTB* 25 (1995): 65–70.

[78] E. E. Ellis, *The Gospel of Luke* (London: Oliphants, 1974; Grand Rapids: Eerdmans, 1981), 267–68. Ellis also deals well with the textual question of why this saying was omitted in a number of early mss.

[79] First Peter 3:18–22 is the most commonly cited passage in support of a descent into hell, but it probably teaches Jesus' announcement of victory over the demonic realm as part of his ascension. For this understanding, along with a full history of interpretation, see W. J. Dalton, *Christ's Proclamation to the Spirits*, rev. ed. (Rome: BIP, 1989). The clause in the Apostles' Creed, "{Jesus] descended into hell," was not part of the creed when it was first fashioned in the fourth century, and not officially added until the middle of the eighth century.

[80] The hearers mistake Jesus' (slurred?) speech for a cry for Elijah, the prophet who was to prepare the way of the Lord. "Ironically, while Elijah will not intervene on Jesus' side, soon God will, and in a very visible way that all shall see" (Brown, *Death*, vol. 2, 1063).

logians wrestled with numerous other questions about the relationship between Christ's human and divine natures that this text refuses to answer. Suffice it to say, Jesus died as still the same psychosomatically whole individual that he had been throughout his life. John, writing against incipient Gnosticism and docetism (see above, pp. 195–96), stressed this by describing the spear thrust that proved that a truly human Jesus had expired (John 19:34–35). Against those today who would accuse God of "divine child abuse," we must stress that, as Jesus' divine nature remained even as he was crucified, it was God himself paying the price for us.[81] Father and Son are not independent beings or separate gods.[82]

(5) "I am thirsty" (John 19:28). No doubt literally true, this statement probably struck John as even more significant in its spiritual sense. One more attempt at offering a mild sedative is rebuffed; Jesus will endure the worst until the end. (6) "It is finished" (John 19:30). Christ will drink little if any of the wine vinegar, so his need for the beverage is quickly ended. Again, the spiritual import of Jesus' words proves more crucial. His life is over, but so is the crowning accomplishment of his career—dying an atoning death for the sins of humanity.[83] (7) "Father, into your hands I commit my spirit" (Luke 23:46; cf. Ps 31:5). Strikingly, he who has just experienced divine abandonment echoes this prayer of trust in his seemingly absent heavenly Father that would later become the standard Jewish child's bedtime prayer. With these words, he breathes his last.

The Events Immediately after Jesus' Death. The Synoptics tell us that already from noon until 3 PM on the day we now know as Good Friday a preternatural darkness had fallen upon the land (Mark 15:33 pars.). Whatever its cause, it is clear that "nature" was in sympathy with the horror of the Son of God being put to death. Apocalyptic signs continue as the veil of the temple is torn from top to bottom (v. 38). It is impossible to resolve every question surrounding these symbolic actions (Did the veil rip just before or just after Jesus' expiry? Was it the inner or outer veil? Are the later ideas of Eph 2:14–16 and Heb 4:14–16 implied—with people now having immediate access to God?).[84] But the veil's splitting fits the whole scene. The temple, the city, and all those loyal to its corrupt alliance with Rome are being condemned, even as they think they are condemning Jesus.[85]

The Gentile centurion supervising the proceedings, observing these signs and how Jesus died, becomes convinced of Christ's innocence.[86] Further apocalyptic

---

[81] "By delivering himself to his creatures, God delivers himself up to experience his own wrath. Now what does this tell us about God?" (P. G. Bolt, *The Cross from a Distance: Atonement in Mark's Gospel* [Leicester: Apollos; Downers Grove: IVP, 2004], 141).

[82] As, e.g., in some forms of Latter-day Saint thought. For some good steps in more orthodox directions, however, see R. L. Millet, *What Happened to the Cross?* (Salt Lake City: Deseret, 2007).

[83] The fear of death was pervasive in the ancient world. "This is the problem that was dealt the decisive blow by Jesus" (Bolt, *Jesus' Defeat of Death*, 278).

[84] For a thorough study, see D. M. Gurtner, *The Torn Veil: Matthew's Exposition of the Death of Jesus* (Cambridge: CUP, 2007).

[85] The key point stressed throughout M. J. Borg and J. D. Crossan, *The Last Week: The Day-by-Day Account of Jesus' Final Week in Jerusalem* (San Francisco: HarperSanFrancisco, 2006).

[86] Luke 23:47 has him say, "Surely this was a righteous (or innocent) man." Mark 15:39 and Matt 27:54 are quite different, making him proclaim Jesus as a S/son of God. Perhaps his literal words

portents shake the area, most notably a significant earthquake (Matt 27:51). Probably the strangest episode of all appears only in Matthew (vv. 52–53)—tombs were opened and certain "saints" were raised to life. The punctuation of some translations makes it appear as if these resurrections occurred before Jesus' own, but the text should probably be rendered as in the TNIV (*contra* the NIV), "the tombs broke open. The bodies of many holy people who had died were raised to life. They came out of the tombs after Jesus' resurrection and went into the Holy City."[87] Again, there are many unanswerable questions surrounding this mysterious scene (Who were the holy people? How long did they make appearances? What happened to them next?). Matthew's point is similar to Paul's: the new age is here; the general resurrection has begun. Jesus being raised is the "firstfruit" of the resurrection of all believers of both old and new covenant times (cf. 1 Cor 15:20). A few got to be raised not at the end of the world but with Jesus as a dramatic testimony to that fact.[88]

The Passion accounts in the Gospels conclude with the story of Jesus' burial. Joseph of Arimathea, a member of the Sanhedrin, asks Pilate for permission to inter the corpse (Mark 15:42–47). The story is credible, if only because of Jewish scruples that the land not be defiled with a dead body during the Sabbath that began with nightfall.[89] Luke, however, adds that Joseph was a good man who had not consented to the council's verdict (Luke 23:50–51), while Matthew and John describe him as a (secret) disciple of Jesus (Matt 27:57; John 19:38). In John, Nicodemus accompanies Joseph as well, although his motives are never spelled out (v. 39). Later Christian legends insist that he, too, had become a believer, but we really have no way of knowing. At any rate, the men give Jesus the honorable burial he deserved in a newly-hewn rock tomb with a massive quantity of embalming spices.[90] A group of women, including Jesus' mother who had been watching the public events all day long, sees where he is laid so that they can return after the Sabbath and complete the process of caring for the body (Mark 15:40–41, 47 pars.).

Unique to Matthew is the account of the Jewish leaders securing permission from Pilate to seal the tomb and set a guard lest Jesus' disciples should come, steal his body, and declare that he had been raised as he had predicted would happen (Matt 27:62–66). This episode clearly prepares the reader for a second paragraph found only in Matthew, as part of the resurrection narrative, that explains how the

---

were something like, "He was a good man, and quite right in calling God his Father" (A. Plummer, *A Critical and Exegetical Commentary on the Gospel according to S. Luke* [Edinburgh: T&T Clark, 1896], 539). But Mark and Matthew see a second level of meaning as well—a confirmation of Jesus' true divine sonship.

[87] J. W. Wenham, "When Were the Saints Raised?" *JTS* 32 (1981): 150–52.

[88] Cf. A. G. van Aarde, "Matthew 27:45–53 and the Turning of the Tide in Isaiah's History," *BTB* 28 (1998): 16–26; Davies and Allison, *Matthew*, vol. 3, 639.

[89] On Joseph's actions as consistent with those of a pious Jew, see W. J. Lyons, "On the Life and Death of Joseph of Arimathea," *JSHJ* 2 (2004): 29–53.

[90] On the burial itself, see further C. M. Peek, "The Burial," in *From the Last Supper through the Resurrection*, ed. Holzapfel and Wayment, 338–77.

same authorities later tried to use the story of a stolen body as their explanation for the empty tomb (28:11–15). For now, disciples and opponents alike think Jesus is gone for good. To their astonishment, they will soon learn how wrong they are.

Historicity

Jesus' lack of resistance at his arrest and his concern for his enemies (most notably Malchus) both pass the double dissimilarity test. Even John's more dramatic threefold, "I am he" (John 18:5, 6, 8) coheres with similar Synoptic statements suggestive of a double meaning—"It is I" and the divine "I AM" (Mark 6:50; 13:6). The trial before Annas, unique to John, gains plausibility from the Lukan reference to this former high priest in conjunction with his son Caiaphas (Luke 3:1). We have already responded to charges of illegalities (or historical improbabilities) at the trial before the Sanhedrin (above, p. 399). Here we may add, positively, that the later Talmudic tradition confirms that Jesus was condemned by the Jewish leaders for blasphemy (*b. Sanh.* 43a)—probably not for explicitly pronouncing the divine name but for equating himself with the Son of Man who could enter into the divine presence.[91] This could have been taken as equivalent to entering the Holy of Holies on earth and thus would have placed Jesus above the Jewish leaders. That Jesus refers to the Son of Man sitting at God's right hand first and then coming on the clouds (rather than the reverse sequence as in Dan 7:13) makes it clear that the Old Testament was not simply mined to create a saying of Jesus.

The whole picture of subsequent abuse—mockery, flogging, and crucifixion, culminating in the cry of divine abandonment—is far too humiliating for early Christians to have invented, especially without widespread Jewish precedent for a crucified Messiah. The flogging of Christ closely resembles that unleashed on Jesus ben Ananias a generation later (Josephus, *War* 6.5.3).[92] Pilate's ruthlessness combined with a certain cowardice also fits Josephus's description of his behavior elsewhere (*Ant.* 18.3.1; 18.3.2; 18.4.1–2). The release of Barabbas based on an annual Passover custom has not been conclusively documented elsewhere but resembles offerings of amnesty described in *Pesah.* 8:6a and later texts commenting on this passage,[93] as well as partially parallel accounts from the Roman world.[94] The crucifixion itself, of course, is amply attested by non-Christian writers (Josephus, *Ant.* 18.3.3; Tacitus, *Ann.* 15.44; *b. Sanh.* 43a [referring to the death as a hanging]). The atoning significance of Jesus' death was accepted early in

---

[91] On which, see esp. D. L. Bock, *Blasphemy and Exaltation in Judaism: The Charge against Jesus in Mark 14:53–65* (Tübingen: Mohr; 1998; Grand Rapids: Baker, 2000); idem., "Jewish Expressions in Mark 14:61–62 and the Authenticity of the Jewish Examination of Jesus," *JSHJ* 1 (2003): 147–59; idem., "Blasphemy and the Jewish Examination of Jesus," *BBR* 17 (2007): 53–114.

[92] As indeed do several other details of the trials of the two men. See C. A. Evans, "Jesus and the 'Cave of Robbers': Toward a Jewish Context for the Temple Action," *BBR* 3 (1993): 93–110.

[93] Blinzler, *The Trial of Jesus,* 218–21. Robert L. Merritt ("Jesus, Barabbas and the Paschal Pardon," *JBL* 104 [1985]: 57–68) adduces parallel Assyrian, Babylonian, and Greek customs.

[94] See Keener, *Matthew,* 669 and n. 181, for references. Cf. esp. C. A. Evans, *Fabricating Jesus: How Modern Scholars Distort the Gospels* (Downers Grove: IVP, 2006), 174–75.

Christian history, as witnessed by its presence in a pre-Pauline creedal formula (1 Cor 15:3). Johannine distinctives also demonstrate Jewish backgrounds—the Aramaic expression *Gabbatha* (John 19:13), a testamentary disposition from the cross (19:26–27),[95] the expression "the day of Preparation of Passover Week" (19:14)—and reflect even more directly on eyewitness testimony (19:35).

Other events accompanying Jesus' death also show signs of historical trustworthiness. Judas' death (Matt 27:3–10) fits the Old Testament fulfillment quotations attached to it so awkwardly that the details must have been accurately narrated. The same is true of the proliferation of Old Testament quotes throughout the Passion narratives more generally.[96] Darkness and an earthquake are cited by the Roman historian Thallus, as quoted by Julius Africanus (*Gk. Pap.* 10.89). Possible allusions to the torn veil appear in *The Lives of the Prophets (Habbakuk)* 10.12–13, a pseudepigraphal work from very close to the time of Jesus' life that prophesies the tearing of the curtain separating the Holy Place from the Holy of Holies, and in later (garbled?) Talmudic traditions that refer to the temple doors opening on their own forty years prior to the destruction of Jerusalem (*p. Yoma* 6:3; *b. Yoma* 4:1).[97] The burial of Jesus' corpse by Joseph of Arimathea seems probable on several counts,[98] especially in light of Jewish scruples against desecrating the Sabbath. That it was an unused tomb would make it unlikely that Jesus' followers would mistakenly go anywhere else after the Sabbath, especially since the same women who had observed the burial went first. The story about the posting of a guard at the tomb cannot plausibly be ascribed to Christian invention since it has a built-in loophole in it: had the disciples wanted to steal Jesus' body and falsely claim him to be resurrected they still would have had all night to do so before the guard ever arrived (cf. Matt 27:57–61 with 62–66).

Theological Distinctives

Redactional distinctives again come to the fore in the passion narratives. For *Mark*, Jesus' crucifixion culminates his ministry as suffering servant; he gives his life as a ransom for many (recall Mark 10:45; 14:22–25). The theme of the disciples' failure and misunderstanding also comes to a climax: they deny, betray, and flee, all as Jesus predicted. For the Jews, the temple and the system for which it stands are now doomed, awaiting imminent judgment and destruction. The crucifixion, however, confirms Jesus as the Son of God (15:39). Anyone who wants

---

[95] E. Stauffer, *Jesus and His Story* (London: SCM; New York: Knopf, 1960), 136–38.

[96] See the articles on each of the four Gospels in Carson and Beale, eds., *Commentary on the New Testament Use of the Old Testament.* Cf. also C. A. Evans, "The Passion of Jesus: History Remembered or Prophecy Historicized?" *BBR* 6 (1996): 159–65.

[97] R. L. Plummer, "Something Awry in the Temple? The Rending of the Temple Veil and Early Jewish Sources That Report Unusual Phenomena in the Temple around AD 30," *JETS* 48 (2005): 301–16.

[98] A point repeatedly stressed by W. L. Craig. See, e.g., his "Opening Address," in *Will the Real Jesus Please Stand Up? A Debate between William Lane Craig and John Dominic Crossan*, ed. P. Copan (Grand Rapids: Baker, 1998), 26–27.

to follow Jesus and receive similar vindication must also first follow the road of suffering and rejection.[99]

Matthew gives the Jewish leaders a higher profile and the Jewish people in general a greater responsibility for Jesus' death, highlighting the motif of bloodguilt (Matt 26:3, 57; 27:25). Rome, on the other hand, is more clearly portrayed as recognizing Jesus' innocence (27:19–24). This is the moment of the passing of the kingdom from the Jewish leadership to those in any nation who will follow Jesus (recall 21:43). Additional Scriptures are fulfilled, most notably with respect to Judas (26:14–25, 50; 27:3–10). The crucifixion itself is narrated, first by successive scenes of mocking (27:39–40, 41–43, 44) and then by a heightened emphasis on the cosmic signs that vindicate an apocalyptic interpretation of Christ's death (27:51–53).[100]

For *Luke*, the passion is a time of the resumption of intense demonic activity (Luke 22:3, 31, 53b; recall 4:13). The innocence of Jesus is heightened; he is a righteous sufferer who forgives his enemies (23:2, 4, 6–16, 34, 43, 47). Jesus eschews violence (22:38, 51–53) and weeps over Jerusalem, lamenting her fate (23:27–31; recall 19:41–44). He trusts completely in God, right up to his death, and he is the "prophet-martyr" who fearlessly proclaims God's justice even in the face of rejection and execution.[101] Overall, it is Jesus' role as the righteous and innocent martyr that characterizes Luke's presentation more than any explicit focus on the atonement.[102]

In *John*, Jesus is consummately in charge, nowhere more strikingly than when he is arrested (John 19:4–6). He speaks the truth, which various authorities reject (19:23, 37).[103] He dies as a fully human being, refuting every form of docetism (19:31–37). His death is the ultimate act of self-revelation, mutual glorification of the Father and the Son, and love for others (chaps. 13–17). It is also the shepherd's sacrifice. On the cross, he triumphs over the cosmic powers of darkness, manifest in the world, whose "hour" has temporarily held sway. In returning to the Father who sent him, he makes a similar "homegoing" possible for all who will be his disciples.[104]

---

[99] Cf. further D. P. Senior, *The Passion of Jesus in the Gospel of Mark* (Wilmington: Glazier, 1984).

[100] Cf. further idem., *The Passion of Jesus in the Gospel of Matthew* (Wilmington: Glazier, 1985).

[101] Cf. further idem., *The Passion of Jesus in the Gospel of Luke* (Wilmington: Glazier, 1989).

[102] E.g., G. Sterling, "Mors Philosophi: The Death of Jesus in Luke," *HTR* 94 (2001): 383–402.

[103] Not all the authorities and certainly not all the people. See L. C. Boughton, "The Priestly Perspective of the Johannine Trial Narratives," *RB* 110 (2003): 517–51. On the truth theme, see esp. A. J. Köstenberger, "'What Is Truth?' Pilate's Question in Its Johannine and Larger Biblical Context," *JETS* 48 (2005): 33–62.

[104] Cf. further D. P. Senior, *The Passion of Jesus in the Gospel of John* (Collegeville: Liturgical, 1991).

Resurrection

Philosophical and Historical Issues

The resurrection brings us to the heart and climax of the Gospel stories. Jesus of Nazareth was seen alive again after his crucifixion! In the Book of Acts, it is consistently the resurrection that forms the central topic of early Christian preaching (e.g., 2:22–36; 17:18; 26:6–8). Although Paul can be viewed as focusing more on the crucifixion than Luke does (see esp. 1 Cor 2:2), he can also devote lengthy teaching passages to the resurrection as the necessary sequel to the cross (1 Cor 15; cf. Eph 1:15–2:10; Col 3:1–4; and 1 Thess 4:13–18). The resurrection vindicates the claim that Jesus is both Christ (Messiah) and Lord (Acts 2:36). It gives meaning and purpose to his life and death—a successful revelation of God to the world (the thrust of John) and an atoning sacrifice for its sins (the thrust of the Synoptics). It ensures that God's plan and purposes for the cosmos will ultimately triumph, among them the resurrection and glorification of all of God's people throughout history (1 Cor 15:20–28).[105] If Christ's bodily resurrection should turn out not to be true, Christians, Paul declares, would be of all people most to be pitied (v. 19).

But can the resurrection stories be believed? It is often claimed that modern, scientific people know full well that dead people are never again raised to life. In fact, the ancients knew that resurrections were seemingly impossible also, and many early Christian apologists had to address the same skepticism that remains in our age. The nineteenth century saw the rise of many rationalistic explanations of the resurrection, which occasionally reappear in popular-level writings today. Some argued that Christ never fully died on the cross, but revived in the tomb, managed to escape, and appeared to his disciples before dying some time later. Others echoed the original counterclaim of the Jewish authorities that Jesus' disciples stole the body (Matt 28:13). Or perhaps they went to the wrong tomb, thus finding it empty. Or maybe all the witnesses to the resurrection experienced some kind of mass hallucination.[106]

Most contemporary scholars rightly reject these explanations as harder to believe than the resurrection itself. The gruesome details of the crucifixion, the length of time of burial, and the size of the stone covering the tomb all preclude the idea that Jesus somehow survived this ordeal and escaped from his burial chamber. If the disciples stole the body, then their entire lives (and in many cases their deaths by martyrdom) were in the cause of a known fraud—a highly unlikely hypothesis, psychologically speaking. Had the disciples or the women originally

---

[105] For a good study of the theme of resurrection in the various NT writers, see J. F. Jansen, *The Resurrection of Jesus Christ in New Testament Theology* (Philadelphia: Westminster, 1980). For a concise synthesis, cf. W. W. Willis, Jr., "A Theology of Resurrection: Its Meaning for Jesus, Us, and God," in *Resurrection: The Origin and Future of a Biblical Doctrine,* ed. J. H. Charlesworth, C. D. Elledge, J. L. Crenshaw, H. Boers, and W. W. Willis, Jr. (London and New York: T&T Clark, 2006), 187–217.

[106] For an exhaustive survey of these and similar theories in the current landscape, see G. R. Habermas, "The Late Twentieth-Century Resurgence of Naturalistic Responses to Jesus' Resurrection," *TJ* 22 (2001): 179–96.

gone to the wrong tomb, Christianity's opponents could easily have produced the right one, with body intact.[107] Mass hallucinations have never elsewhere occurred over a forty-day period (Acts 1:3), in different places, to more than five hundred people (1 Cor 15:6) who are known to be defeated in outlook and not expecting anything miraculous to happen (John 20:19).[108]

It is far more common, therefore, among scholarly skepticism to promote the idea that the Gospel stories of the resurrection are primarily legendary. Many posit that the disciples had some kind of spiritual experience of God in which they became convinced that the cause of Christ lived on.[109] A number are willing to grant that Jesus' immortal *spirit* did continue to live and may even have been experienced by his followers, even perhaps in concrete yet visionary fashion.[110] It is a literal *bodily* resurrection that continues to be the stumbling block for most. Not surprisingly, it is often postulated that only at a late stage of the tradition did the story of Jesus' continuing to live in some spiritual fashion become "mythologized" in the garb of a bodily resurrection.[111] Sometimes parallels in other religions and religious fiction of the day are cited as support for this line of development: the Gnostic redeemer myth of a descending and ascending heavenly Man, belief in the resurrection of the bull-god Mithras, or the fertility cults' myths of nature gods who die and rise annually.

But the relevant Gnostic myths and Mithraic beliefs are too late to have influenced early Christianity (see above, pp. 36, 39–40), and the parallels with pagan fertility rites are really quite remote.[112] In fact, there are *no* known accounts from the ancient world of a human being who was believed to have been raised to an eternal, embodied existence emerging during the lifetimes of many who had known that individual. Had Christianity been born in Greece and later migrated

---

[107] *Contra* the sensationalized claims that archaeologists in 2007 had discovered the tomb containing ossuaries (small coffins or bone boxes), complete with DNA residue, of Jesus and numerous family members, see C. L. Quarles, ed., *Buried Hope or Risen Savior? The Search for the Jesus Tomb* (Nashville: B & H, 2008).

[108] See further J. J. Johnson, "Were the Resurrection Appearances Hallucinations? Some Psychiatric and Psychological Considerations," *Churchman* 115 (2001): 227–38. In response to this whole barrage of alternate explanations, see G. R. Habermas and M. R. Licona, *The Case for the Resurrection of Jesus* (Grand Rapids: Kregel, 2004), 81–119.

[109] E.g., J. D. Crossan, in his various chapters in *The Resurrection of Jesus: John Dominic Crossan and N. T. Wright in Dialogue*, ed. R. B. Stewart (Minneapolis: Fortress, 2006) takes "resurrection" as a metaphor for the continuing presence of Jesus in the new form of living modeled by the communities of his followers.

[110] See esp. D. C. Allison, *Resurrecting Jesus: The Earliest Christian Tradition and Its Interpreters* (London and New York: T&T Clark, 2005), 198–375. *Contra* the view that claims that stories of empty tombs pointed merely to the spiritual deification of a Greco-Roman hero, see P. G. Bolt, "Mark 16:1–8: The Empty Tomb of a Hero?" *TynBul* 47 (1996): 27–37.

[111] The most recent and sophisticated example of these trends is P. M. Fullmer, *Resurrection in Mark's Literary-Historical Perspective* (London and New York: T&T Clark, 2007).

[112] See Finegan, *Myth and Mystery*, 203–12; Tripolitis, *Religions of the Hellenistic Roman Age*, 47–57; Nash, *The Gospel and the Greeks*, 133–38. Cf. esp. T. N. D. Mettinger, *The Riddle of the Resurrection: "Dying and Rising Gods" in the Ancient Near East* (Stockholm: Almqvist & Wiksell, 2001).

to Israel, one might find more credible the story of a spiritual rebirth later being reclothed in the language of a bodily resurrection. But most Jews had always believed in a very literal reenfleshment of skeletons (cf., e.g., Ezek 37), while it was the Hellenistic world that accepted only the immortality of the soul.[113] So for a religion born in Judaism and later transplanted into the Greco-Roman world, the hypothesis of development from spirit to body reverses the only plausible order of development What a truly mythological account of a resurrection would look like is amply illustrated in the docetic, apocryphal *Gos. Pet.* 10:39–40: Christ appears striding across the earth with his head towering above the clouds of heaven!

Numerous other details suggest that the earliest accounts of the resurrection were not fictitious. Deuteronomy 21:23 demonstrated to first-century Jews that anyone executed by crucifixion was accursed by God, so it would have been enormously difficult for them to create the story of the resurrection of a "crucified Messiah" unless it had really happened. All four Gospels agree that the first primary witnesses to the resurrection were women, another detail unlikely to have been invented, inasmuch as their testimony, because of their gender, would have normally been inadmissible in a court of law.[114] The empty tomb seems almost certainly to be a historical fact, for no one ever produced a body and no gravesite was ever venerated in early Christianity. Further, something dramatic must have happened on that first Sunday to cause Christians to stop resting and worshiping on the Sabbath (Saturday), the day commanded by God from the time of the Ten Commandments onward to be set aside as holy, and to replace it with Sunday observance (Acts 20:7; 1 Cor 16:2; Rev 1:10). Indeed, it is arguable that nothing short of the bodily resurrection of Jesus can adequately explain the rise of "post-Easter" Christian faith more generally.

We may also point to the diversity of witnesses in a variety of places over a forty-day period, the relative anonymity of many of those witnesses (Cleopas and an unnamed disciple, five hundred otherwise unknown), the apparent aimlessness of the disciples even after several appearances (John 21:2–3), the lack of immediate recognition and acceptance by the various observers in numerous resurrection accounts, the early pre-Pauline tradition of several of those appearances (1 Cor 15:4–8), the use of "the first day of the week" in Mark 16:2 (rather than the later, more conventional "after three days"), and the virtual impossibility of proclaiming the resurrection in Jerusalem in the face of unbelieving Jewish opposition if the grave (identifiable by the Sanhedrin through Joseph of Arimathea) were not in fact

---

[113] For thorough documentation, see N. T. Wright's magisterial work, *The Resurrection of the Son of God* (London: SPCK; Minneapolis: Fortress, 2003), 85–206. Cf. J. D. Levenson, *Resurrection and the Restoration of Israel: The Ultimate Victory of the God of Life* (New Haven and London: Yale University Press, 2006); and R. Bauckham, "Life, Death, and the Afterlife," in *Life in the Face of Death: The Resurrection Message of the New Testament*, ed. R. N. Longenecker (Grand Rapids and Cambridge: Eerdmans, 1998), 80–95.

[114] Cf. C. Setzer, "Excellent Women: Female Witness to the Resurrection," *JBL* 116 (1997): 259–72.

empty.[115] In addition, of all the sign prophets and self-styled Messiahs of the first century, only Jesus remained the spiritual leader of his followers after his death. In every other case, either the movement died out or leadership was transferred to a different family member.[116] An account of Christian origins that rejects Jesus' bodily resurrection must account for this anomaly; to date none has done so.

But what of the scientific and philosophical objections? Of course, if one refuses to believe in the possibility of miraculous occurrences altogether, the resurrection will seem an absurdity. But large numbers of "modern, scientific" people recognize that science itself is merely descriptive rather than prescriptive. If a God exists, it is only natural to expect him to have powers beyond that which science has discovered or can explain, and to be able to use them for his purposes.[117] It is also arguable that of all the alleged miracles in ancient history, the resurrection is actually the one with by far the most historical support.

A different kind of objection argues that the Bible does not claim that Jesus rose bodily. Here, scholars often appeal to 1 Cor 15:35–58. Paul talks of a "spiritual" body (vv. 44, 46) and insists that "flesh and blood cannot inherit the kingdom of God" (v. 50). Perhaps what the disciples first saw was, indeed, real, but a real vision, not a real physical resurrection. This, of course, is hard to square with Jesus' insistence that Thomas touch him and see his scars (John 20:27) or with his ability to eat fish as a demonstration of the corporeality of his presence (Luke 24:40–43). In fact, Paul's language in 1 Corinthians 15 should be understood differently. "Spiritual" is best taken as "supernatural," not "noncorporeal," while "flesh and blood" (*not* "flesh and bones" as in Luke 24:39) was a Semitic idiom for frail, fallen, mortal humanity.[118] At the same time, it is clear that the resurrection involved far more than a resuscitated corpse. Jesus could appear and disappear, pass through locked doors, and not be recognized for some time. We should hope that glorified, perfected bodies will be considerably different than our present ones! There will be substantial discontinuity of form as well as significant continuity of personal identity.

---

[115] For these and related arguments, see esp. W. L. Craig, *Assessing the New Testament Evidence for the Historicity of the Resurrection of Jesus* (Lewiston: Mellen, 1989). Cf. R. Dudrey, "What the Writers Should Have Done Better: A Case for the Resurrection of Jesus Based on Ancient Criticism of the Resurrection Reports," *SCJ* 3 (2000): 55–78.

[116] For full details, one must read large stretches of Josephus' *Jewish Antiquities*, books 18–20. For an overview of the key individuals in these movements, see Evans, *Jesus and His Contemporaries*, 53–81.

[117] On the scientific question, see esp. P. Medawar, *The Limits of Science* (San Francisco: Harper & Row, 1984; Oxford: OUP, 1985). Cf. J. C. Polkinghorne, *The Faith of a Physicist* (Princeton: Princeton University Press, 1994). For a philosophical apologetic for the resurrection, given the presuppositions of a theistic worldview, see A. Gibson, "Logic of the Resurrection," in *Resurrection*, ed. Porter, Hayes and Tombs, 166–94.

[118] Cf. further A. C. Thiselton, *The First Epistle to the Corinthians* (Carlisle: Paternoster; Grand Rapids: Eerdmans, 2000), 1275–81. Cf. K. R. MacGregor, "1 Corinthians 15:3b–6a, 7 and the Bodily Resurrection of Jesus," *JETS* 49 (2006): 225–34.

Exegetical Issues (Mark 16; Matthew 28; Luke 24; John 20–21) [Aland §352–367]

Chronology of Events. The four Gospels prove remarkably divergent as to what they include about Jesus' resurrection. Still, they agree on the basics to such an extent that they constitute considerable corroboration of the historicity of the event itself.[119] A plausible harmony of the accounts and sequence of events is as follows: (1) A group of women come to the tomb near dawn, with Mary Magdalene possibly arriving first (Matt 28:1; Mark 16:1–3; Luke 24:1; John 20:1). (2) Mary and the other women are met by two young men who in reality are angels, one of whom acts as the spokesman and announces Jesus' resurrection (Matt 28:2–7; Mark 16:4–7; Luke 24:2–7). (3) The women leave the garden with a mixture of fear and joy, at first unwilling to say anything but then resolving to report to the Eleven remaining apostles (Matt 28:8; Mark 16:8). Mary Magdalene may have dashed on ahead, telling Peter and John in advance of the arrival of the other women (John 20:2). (4) Jesus meets the remaining women en route and confirms their commission to tell the disciples, with the reminder of his promise of meeting them in Galilee. The women obey (Matt 28:9–10; Luke 24:8–11).

(5) Peter and John meanwhile have returned to the tomb, having heard the report by Mary Magdalene, and discover it to be empty (John 20:3–10; Luke 24:12). (6) Mary also returns to the tomb after Peter and John have left. She sees the angels and then Jesus, although at first supposing him to be a gardener (John 20:11–18). (7) Later that afternoon, Jesus appears to Cleopas and his unnamed companion on the road to Emmaus and, in a separate incident, to Peter (Luke 24:13–35). (8) That same Sunday evening, Jesus appears to the Ten (the Eleven minus Thomas) behind locked doors in Jerusalem (Luke 24:36–43; John 20:19–23). (9) A week later he appears to the eleven at the same venue, with Thomas now present (John 20:24–29). (10) Further appearances take place over a forty-day period, including in Galilee, with over five hundred seeing him altogether (Acts 1:3; John 21; 1 Cor 15:6). (11) A climactic commissioning in Galilee instructs the disciples to spread the news throughout the world (Matt 28:16–20). (12) Perhaps only shortly thereafter, Jesus gives his parting instructions to await the coming Holy Spirit and ascends into heaven (Luke 24:44–53; Acts 1:4–11).[120]

Redactional Emphases. Each evangelist, of course, did not have a harmony of the Gospels in mind but was concerned to communicate distinctive theological interests. Perhaps nowhere do these emerge more clearly than in the resur-

---

[119] Cf. the comments of German classical historian H. E. Stier, cited and trans.in H. Staudinger, *The Trustworthiness of the Gospels* (Edinburgh: T&T Clark, 1981), 77: "The sources for the resurrection of Jesus, with their relatively big contradictions over details, present for the historian for this very reason a criterion of extraordinary credibility. For if that were the fabrication of a congregation or a similar group of people, then the tale would be consistently and obviously complete." We would wish to insert the word "apparent" before Stier's use of the term "contradiction."

[120] For a similar harmony with elaboration, see G. E. Ladd, *I Believe in the Resurrection of Jesus* (Grand Rapids: Eerdmans; London: Hodder & Stoughton, 1975), 91–93. In great detail, cf. J. Wenham, *Easter Enigma: Are the Resurrection Accounts in Conflict?* (Exeter: Paternoster; Grand Rapids: Zondervan, 1984; Eugene, OR: Wipf & Stock, 2005).

rection narratives. *Mark*'s brief account focuses on the women's discovery of the empty tomb and the announcement by the young man that the disciples will meet Jesus in Galilee. Perhaps Mark thinks of them as beginning again. "They have failed Jesus, failed to take up their crosses and follow him to crucifixion, but now they are being summoned once again to follow him, and to learn once again what discipleship means."[121] More striking is Mark's abrupt ending in 16:8 on what seems to be a very discordant and unsatisfying note.[122] Some once argued that it is a grammatically impossible ending, but parallels have since been discovered.[123] In fact, this conclusion fits with Mark's portrayal of Jesus' disciples throughout his Gospel. As Lane explains, "Fear is the constant reaction to the disclosure of

... therefore

(1) having gone

Make all the nations disciples

(2) baptizing them

in the name

of {
the Father
and
the Son
and
the Holy
Spirit
}

(3) teaching them to keep all

that I have commanded you

Matthew 28:19–20a

Jesus' transcendent dignity in the Gospel of Mark." Again, "the focus upon human inadequacy, lack of understanding and weakness throws into bold relief the action of God and its meaning."[124]

But verse 8 must be kept together with verse 7. The resurrection has been repeatedly predicted, and Jesus has proven himself to be a reliable predictor.

---

[121] Hooker, *Mark*, 386, in the context of suggesting multiple explanations for this phenomenon.

[122] On the unlikelihood that what Bible translations usually label vv. 9–20 stood in what Mark original wrote, see above, pp. 83–86. The view that Mark's original ending was lost (perhaps literally "ripped off" of the open end of the scroll) has become noticeably more popular among recent commentators than it used to be. See Evans, *Mark 8:27–16:20*, 539; Edwards, *Mark*, 501–4; Witherington, *Mark*, 417–18; and France, *Mark*, 673, 684. But a sizable majority still agrees that Mark intended to end with v. 8. Later scribes, not understanding his reasons, supplied what they believed was a more appropriate and detailed ending. See further J. A. Kelhoffer, "The Witness of Eusebius' *ad Marinum* and Other Christian Writings to Text-Critical Debates Concerning the Original Conclusion to Mark's Gospel." *ZNW* 92 (2001): 78–112; cf. Boring, *Mark*, 451–53..

[123] I.e., ending with a postpositive *gar* ("*For* they were afraid," in which the "for" (*gar*) comes after the verb "they were afraid" (*ephobounto*). See esp. N. Denyer, "Mark 16:8 and Plato, *Protagoras* 328d," *TynBul* 57 (2006): 149–50. Cf. also K. R. Iverson, "A Further Word on Final Γάρ (Mark 16:8)," *CBQ* 68 (2006): 79–94.

[124] Lane, *Mark*, 591, 592.

Even someone entirely unfamiliar with the Gospel story, having read this much of Mark, should recognize that Mark believed verse 7 would be fulfilled. The original Christian readers would of course have already heard the story of the resurrection as the core of the preaching that brought them to faith; Mark does not need to tell the story again here. The reason he does not may be to keep in balance the tension of Christian living before Christ's return: ". . . the word of promise and the failure of the disciples, and yet the word of promise prevailing despite human failure."[125]

Matthew begins with material largely parallel to Mark, though heightening the cosmic signs a bit, as in the Passion narrative—here appears another earthquake; the young man becomes an angel; the white robe is like snow (Matt 28:2–3). But Matthew, who consistently portrays Jesus' followers somewhat more positively than Mark, has the women conquer their fear and report back to the disciples (v. 8), even meeting Jesus himself en route (vv. 9–10). Verses 11–15 further the theme of Jewish apologetic, countering the earliest Jewish attempt to explain away the resurrection. Verses 16–20 bring Matthew's resurrection narrative, and indeed the whole Gospel, to a climax with the well-known Great Commission. Here appear in summary form several of Matthew's key themes: the universal mission of the church, the importance of discipleship, Jesus' followers' mixture of faith and doubt, his commandments as the center of God's will for Christians, and the abiding and authoritative presence of Jesus as teacher.[126]

The words "go and make disciples" (v. 19) have been the subject of countless expositions. It is important to realize that the only imperative verb in the Greek is "make disciples." Nevertheless, the attendant adverbial participle "go," by modifying the main verb, functions derivatively as a mild imperative. The main command is to duplicate Christian followers wherever one is, but there is a subordinate emphasis on going into the whole world. "All nations" could also be translated "all the Gentiles," and some see here an end to the Jewish mission. But the Greek word (*ethnē*) has been used in the more inclusive sense of "ethnic (or people) groups," including Jews, in the most recent occurrences of the term (24:9, 14; 25:32) and should be viewed similarly here.[127] Making disciples is defined as "baptizing them" and "teaching them to obey everything" Christ had commanded. This makes it clear that Jesus' commission is not primarily about initial evangelism but about the lifelong process of bringing people to faith and nurturing them in the will of God. Baptism, according to Jesus, is a crucial and foundational part

---

[125] A. T. Lincoln, "The Promise and the Failure: Mark 16:7, 8," *JBL* 108 (1989): 292. Similarly J. F. Williams, "Literary Approaches to the End of Mark's Gospel," *JETS* 42 (1999): 21–35, after a thorough survey of the interpretive options.

[126] Cf. E. Krentz, "Missionary Matthew: Mt 28:16–20 as a Summary of the Gospel," *CTM* 31 (2004): 24–31; Davies and Allison, *Matthew*, vol. 3, 687–89. The Great Commission may even be reinterpreting the Pentateuchal theme of Israel's literal conquest of the nations, with its negative consequences for them, in terms of the church's spiritual conquest of the nations, with the gospel's positive consequences for them. See K. L. Sparks, "Gospel as Conquest: Mosaic Typology in Matthew 28:16–20," *CBQ* 68 (2006): 651–53.

[127] France, *Matthew*, 1114–15; Keener, *Matthew*, 719–20.

of this obedience. The Trinitarian expression used here is the only appearance of this wording ("Father, Son, and Holy Spirit") in the Gospels and probably has not yet become a technical formula (cf. Acts 2:38, in which baptism is commanded "in the name of Jesus"). What is significant is that Matthew uses one definite article to cover all three names; at least by his day, the concept of one God in three persons had already taken root in Christian thinking.[128]

Luke's account is longer still. At least six distinctive themes emerge: (1) Jesus is the fulfillment of all of the Hebrew Scriptures (Luke 24:26–27, 44–48). Indeed, Luke's central emphasis on the fulfillment of prophecy in the gospel offer of salvation and forgiveness for those who repent appears here, too (v. 47). (2) Jesus is made known in table fellowship among his people (vv. 30–35). In these references to the breaking of the bread may also be an allusion to the Lord's Supper. (3) The reality of Christ's humanity and bodily resurrection is stressed, perhaps against incipient docetic trends in Luke's day (vv. 36–43). (4) Luke's interest in the Holy Spirit continues as the Spirit's role in empowering the disciples at Pentecost is predicted (vv. 48–49). (5) All of Luke's resurrection appearances take place in Jerusalem, and the disciples return to the temple, highlighting the central role of this city in God's plans for his people (cf. v. 47, 52–53; Acts 1:8). (6) Only Luke narrates the ascension (vv. 50–51), which Acts will describe in more detail as taking place forty days after the resurrection (Acts 1:9–11).[129] We have commented already on the chiastic outline of Luke-Acts with the central role of the resurrection and ascension for Luke's entire two-volume work (see above, p. 162). Unifying all of these items in Luke is a distinctive emphasis on the exaltation of Christ.[130]

John has the longest resurrection narrative of all, a full two chapters. The beginning and end of these chapters frame John's account by comparing and contrasting Peter and the beloved disciple. Together they run to the tomb and find it empty (20:3–7), but only John (if we take the beloved disciple to be the son of Zebedee) is explicitly said to believe (v. 8). At the end of the Gospel, after a seemingly ignominious fate is predicted of Peter, we learn that John may be let off more lightly (21:20–23). In between, attention falls more exclusively on three scenes: Jesus and Mary in the garden (20:10–18); Jesus and the disciples, first without and then

---

[128] G. Sharp's rule of Greek grammar observes that two or more singular, personal, non-proper nouns governed by only one article *always* refer to the same entity. Hagner (*Matthew 14–28*, 883) notes that this formula is credible on the lips of Jesus precisely because this is after the resurrection and he is now en route to his re-exalted role, leaving behind the limitations of his incarnation.

[129] Verses 50–53 form a classic benediction to Jesus' ministry. Perhaps, like the priest's blessing in the temple, we are also meant to understand this as a sign that God has accepted the sacrifice, in this case of Jesus himself. See K. M. Kapic, "Receiving Christ's Priestly Benediction: A Biblical, Historical, and Theological Exploration of Luke 24:50–53," *WTJ* 67 (2005): 247–60.

[130] A. Johnson, "Our God Reigns: The Body of the Risen Lord in Luke 24," *WW* 22 (2002): 133–43. On this chapter, cf. further D. T. Prince, "The 'Ghosts' of Jesus: Luke 24 in Light of Ancient Narratives of Post-Mortem Apparitions," *JSNT* 29 (2007): 287–301. She argues that Luke combines a variety of elements from Greco-Roman narratives of after-death appearances of individuals to show how Jesus' resurrection surpasses all of them.

with Thomas, in the locked room (20:19–29); and Jesus' reinstatement of Peter by the shore of the Sea of Galilee (21:1–19).[131]

The key words in Jesus' disclosure to Mary, "Do not hold on to me" (20:17), are better rendered, "Stop clinging to me." Jesus has not yet ascended; the period of the resurrection appearances is not yet one of permanent reunion.[132] In the meantime, Mary must be a witness for her Lord (v. 18). In the upper room when Thomas is absent, Jesus breathes the Spirit on the disciples (v. 23) and commissions them in language reminiscent of Matt 16:19.[133] But without Thomas, and without any dramatic new ministry of the disciples immediately afterwards, this is not likely to be John's equivalent of Pentecost, as some have claimed. Still, it seems to be more than just a foreshadowing of that later event; it indicates the fulfillment of John's previous promises about the Paraclete. We should probably imagine a two-stage event (combining John 20 and Acts 2), somewhat analogous to the reception of the Spirit followed by the filling of the Spirit.[134] Because these are transitional, nonrepeatable experiences at the time of the shift from old to new covenants, nothing can be deduced from the apostles' experiences here regarding how the Spirit empowers believers today.

A week later when Thomas is with the ten, Jesus demonstrates the reality of his resurrection. Thomas cries out, "My Lord and my God!" (John 20:28). Here is another key text in support of Jesus' deity. Jesus' reply also reminds us of John's twofold emphasis on the role of signs—they should stimulate faith but they should not be necessary for faith: "Because you have seen me, you have believed; blessed are those who have not seen and yet have believed" (v. 29). John 20:30–31 reads as if the Gospel is coming to an end and clearly articulates John's purpose in writing. But the manuscripts are evenly divided between a present and aorist subjunctive for the verb "you may believe." The former would imply continued belief and point to a Christian readership; the latter would leave the door open to first-time belief and an evangelistic purpose for the Gospel. It may well be that John had some of both functions in mind (cf. above, p. 196).[135]

The importance of Peter's reinstatement in chapter 21 makes it unnecessary to attribute this chapter to a later redactor, as is commonly done, even if its literary genre is something of an "appendix." This chapter creates an inclusio with Peter's threefold denial of Jesus (18:15–18, 25–27) as well as with his original

---

[131] Recent attempts to find some rivalry between Mary and the male disciples, or an elevation of her or them above the other(s), read into the text comparisons and competition not actually present.

[132] Cf. Moloney, *John*, 526: "Associated with this confession is a desire to cling to Jesus (v. 17). Jesus' words, *mē mou haptou*, instruct her that she must desist from her attempt to reestablish the relationship she once had with him."

[133] Cf. also S. E. Hansen, "Forgiving and Retaining Sin: A Study of the Text and Context of John 20:23," *HBT* 19 (1997): 24–32.

[134] Bruce, *John*, 397, n. 18. Cf. T. R. Hatina, "John 20,22 in Its Eschatological Context: Promise or Fulfillment," *Bib* 74 (1993): 196–219; and, with some nuancing, C. Bennema, "The Giving of the Spirit in John's Gospel—A New Proposal?" *EQ* 74 (2002): 195–213.

[135] Cf. K. S. O'Brien, "Written That You May Believe: John 20 and Narrative Rhetoric," *CBQ* 67 (2005): 284–302. For numerous thematic inclusios between John 1 and 20, see D. Tidball, "Completing the Circle: The Resurrection According to John," *ERT* 30 (2006): 169–83.

calling (1:41–42).[136] The accompanying miracle (21:4–14) is strikingly reminiscent of the astonishing fish catch that accompanied Peter's original call (Luke
5:1–11); we may aptly label the second event his "recall." Jesus solicits a threefold affirmation of Peter's love (21:15–19), balancing out his earlier threefold
denial. Despite many popular sermons distinguishing between Jesus' word for
love (*agapaō*) and Peter's (*phileō*), this is probably mere stylistic variation. John
also uses two different Greek words for "sheep" in this passage and two for
"tend," without implying any significant distinctions. While in certain contexts
biblical writers use *agapaō* for a divine love and *phileō* for a brotherly love, in
other places the distinction is not observed (e.g., 2 Sam 13:4; John 5:20; 2 Tim
4:10; 1 John 2:15).[137] With nothing in this context to demand the distinction, it is
risky to assume it is present.

The Gospel closes with testimony to the veracity of the book's author (vv.
24–25). On the implications of these verses for the Gospel's composition, see
above (p. 200). The change of person (to "we" and then to "I") shows that at least
some minimal final redaction of the Gospel has occurred. This leaves the door
open for theories of more widespread editing, however unverifiable they may be.
The suggestion that this editing occurred just after John's death, which had neces-
sitated the clarification of verse 23, remains an attractive hypothesis but is also
unprovable.[138]

For Further Study

The Upper Room and Gethsemane

The Last Supper

Jeremias, Joachim. *The Eucharistic Words of Jesus*. Rev. ed. London: SCM; New York:
    Charles Scribner's, 1965.

Marshall, I. Howard, *Last Supper and Lord's Supper*. Grand Rapids: Eerdmans; Exeter:
    Paternoster, 1980.

Perry, John M. *Exploring the Evolution of the Lord's Supper in the New Testament*. Kansas
    City: Sheed and Ward, 1994.

Smith, Dennis E. *From Symposium to Eucharist: The Banquet in the Early Christian World*.
    Minneapolis: Fortress, 2003.

Thomas, J. Christopher. *Footwashing in John 13 and the Johannine Community*. Sheffield:
    JSOT, 1991.

Witherington, Ben, III. *Making a Meal of It: Rethinking the Theology of the Lord's Supper*.
    Waco: Baylor University Press, 2007.

Wright, Tom. *The Meal Jesus Gave Us*. Louisville and London: WJKP, 2003.

---

[136] P. S. Minear, "The Original Functions of John 21," *JBL* 102 (1983): 85–98.

[137] D. A. Carson, *Exegetical Fallacies*, rev. ed. (Grand Rapids: Baker, 1996), 31–32, 51–53; Keener,
John, vol. 2, 1236; A. G. Brock, "The Significance of φιλέω and φίλος in the Tradition of Jesus Sayings and in the Early Christian Communities." *HTR* 90 (1997): 393–409.

[138] See further Burge, *John*, 581; Pryor, *John*, 93; Beasley-Murray, *John*, 412.

The Farewell Discourse (John 14–17)

Brouwer, Wayne. *The Literary Development of John 13–17: A Chiastic Reading*. Atlanta: SBL, 2000.

Carson, D. A. *The Farewell Discourse and Final Prayer of Jesus*. Grand Rapids: Baker, 1980 [= *Jesus and His Friends: His Farewell Message and Prayer in John 14 to 17*. Leicester: IVP, 1986].

Kellum, L. Scott. *The Unity of the Farewell Discourse: The Literary Integrity of John 13.31–16.33*. London and New York: T&T Clark, 2004.

Parsenios, George L. *Departure and Consolation: The Johannine Farewell Discourses in Light of Greco-Roman Literature*. Leiden and Boston: Brill, 2005.

Segovia, Fernando F. *The Farewell of the Word: The Johannine Call to Abide*. Minneapolis: Fortress, 1991.

Stube, John C. *A Graeco-Roman Rhetorical Reading of the Farewell Discourse*. London and New York: T&T Clark, 2006.

Trials and Crucifixion of Jesus

Introductory

Borg, Marcus J. and J. Dominic Crossan. *The Last Week: The Day-by-Day Account of Jesus' Final Week in Jerusalem*. San Francisco: HarperSanFrancisco, 2006.

Bovon, François. *The Last Days of Jesus*. Louisville and London: WJKP, 2006.

Hengel, Martin. *Crucifixion: In the Ancient World and the Folly of the Message of the Cross*. London: SCM; Philadelphia: Fortress, 1977.

Kiehl, Eric H. *The Passion of our Lord*. Grand Rapids: Baker, 1990; Eugene, OR: Wipf & Stock, 2003.

Stott, John R. W. *The Cross of Christ*. Rev. ed. Leicester and Downers Grove: IVP, 2006.

Intermediate

Blinzler, Josef. *The Trial of Jesus*. Cork: Mercier; Westminster, MD: Newman, 1959.

Bock, Darrell L. *Blasphemy and Exaltation in Judaism: The Charge against Jesus in Mark 14:53–65*. Tübingen: Mohr; 1998; Grand Rapids: Baker, 2000.

Bolt, Peter G. *The Cross from a Distance: Atonement in Mark's Gospel*. Leicester: Apollos; Downers Grove: IVP, 2004.

Sherwin-White, A. N. *Roman Society and Roman Law in the New Testament*. Oxford: OUP, 1963; Eugene, OR: Wipf & Stock, 2004.

Sloyan, Gerard S. *The Crucifixion of Jesus: History, Myth, Faith*. Minneapolis: Fortress, 1995.

Advanced

Brown, Raymond E. *The Death of the Messiah*. 2 vols. New York and London: Doubleday, 1994.

Carroll, John T. and Joel B. Green. *The Death of Jesus in Early Christianity*. Peabody: Hendrickson, 1995.

Catchpole, David R. *The Trial of Jesus: A Study in the Gospels and Jewish Historiography*. Leiden: Brill, 1971.

Green, Joel B. *The Death of Jesus: Tradition and Interpretation in the Passion Narrative.* Tübingen: Mohr, 1988.

McKnight, Scot. *Jesus and His Death: Historiography, the Historical Jesus, and Atonement Theory.* Waco: Baylor University Press, 2005.

Bibliography

Garland, David E. *One Hundred Years of Study on the Passion Narratives.* Macon: Mercer, 1989.

Resurrection of Jesus

General

Davis, Stephen T., Daniel Kendall and Gerald O'Collins, eds. *The Resurrection: An Interdisciplinary Symposium on the Resurrection of Jesus.* Oxford and New York: OUP, 1997.

Harris, Murray J. *From Grave to Glory: Resurrection in the New Testament.* Grand Rapids: Zondervan, 1990.

Ladd, George E. *I Believe in the Resurrection of Jesus.* Grand Rapids: Eerdmans; London: Hodder & Stoughton, 1975.

Lapide, Pinchas. *The Resurrection of Jesus: A Jewish Perspective.* Minneapolis: Augsburg, 1983.

Porter, Stanley E., Michael A. Hayes and David Tombs, ed. *Resurrection.* Sheffield: SAP, 1999.

Perkins, Pheme. *Resurrection: New Testament Witness and Contemporary Reflection.* Garden City: Doubleday, 1984; London: Geoffrey Chapman, 1985.

Philosophical-Apologetic

Carnley, Peter. *The Structure of Resurrection Belief.* Oxford: Clarendon, 1987.

Copan, Paul, ed. *Will the Real Jesus Please Stand Up? A Debate between William Lane Craig and John Dominic Crossan.* Grand Rapids: Baker, 1998.

Craig, William L. *Assessing the New Testament Evidence for the Historicity of the Resurrection of Jesus.* Lewiston: Mellen, 1989.

Davis, Stephen T. *Risen Indeed: Making Sense of the Resurrection.* Grand Rapids: Eerdmans, 1993.

Habermas, Gary R. and Michael R. Licona. *The Case for the Resurrection of Jesus.* Grand Rapids: Kregel, 2004.

Stewart, Robert B., ed. *The Resurrection of Jesus: John Dominic Crossan and N. T. Wright in Dialogue.* Minneapolis: Fortress, 2006.

Wenham, John. *Easter Enigma: Are the Resurrection Accounts in Conflict?* Exeter: Paternoster; Grand Rapids: Zondervan, 1984; Eugene, OR: Wipf & Stock, 2005.

Theological-Exegetical

Allison, Dale C., Jr. *Resurrecting Jesus: The Earliest Christian Tradition and Its Interpreters.* London and New York: T&T Clark, 2005.

Charlesworth, James H., Casey D. Elledge, James L. Crenshaw, Hendrikus Boers, and W. Waite Willis, Jr. *Resurrection: The Origin and Future of a Biblical Doctrine.* London and New York: T&T Clark, 2006.

Harris, Murray J. *Raised Immortal: Resurrection and Immortality in the New Testament.* London: Marshall, Morgan & Scott, 1983; Grand Rapids: Eerdmans, 1985.

Osborne, Grant R. *The Resurrection Narratives: A Redactional Study.* Grand Rapids: Baker, 1984.

Peters, Ted, Robert J. Russell and Michael Welker, eds. *Resurrection: Theological and Scientific Assessments.* Grand Rapids and Cambridge: Eerdmans, 2002.

Wright, N. T. *The Resurrection of the Son of God.* London: SPCK; Minneapolis: Fortress, 2003.

Questions for Review

1. How does interpreting the Last Supper against its Passover background illumine this event?
2. What are the key themes that John stresses in John 13–17?
3. What is the theological significance of Jesus' time in the Garden of Gethsemane?
4. What are the most acute historical problems surrounding Jesus' trial and execution? What are some possible solutions to these problems?
5. What are the main theological distinctives of each evangelist in the Passion narratives?
6. What are the most acute historical problems surrounding Jesus' resurrection? What are some possible solutions to these problems?
7. What are the main theological distinctives of each evangelist in the Resurrection narratives?

Part Five

HISTORICAL AND
THEOLOGICAL SYNTHESES

I T IS TIME to draw together the many threads of this study. We have already
commented in numerous places on the historicity of the gospel tradition in
general and of specific passages and themes in particular. We must briefly
review these discussions and then proceed to deal with additional external evidence for the Gospels' reliability. This will occupy our attention in chapter 18. But
a theological synthesis is needed as well. If the main contours of the gospel data
surveyed here can be trusted, what do they disclose about the primary themes and
intentions of Jesus? What was the heart of his message, and how may we categorize the kind of religious teacher that he represented? Answers to these questions
will form the core of chapter 19.

18

THE HISTORICAL TRUSTWORTHINESS OF THE GOSPELS

A N INVESTIGATION OF the historicity of any ancient document must begin with the discipline of *textual criticism*. Do we even have reliable copies of what the original author of that document wrote? We have already noted briefly above that the evidence in the case of the Gospels is overwhelming in this respect (see pp. 83–86). More than 5700 ancient Greek manuscripts, from fragments to whole books, contrast dramatically with the available material for any other document from antiquity. The works of three main Roman historians whose lives overlapped with the first century (Suetonius, Livy and Tacitus) remain in about 200, 27 and 3 manuscripts, respectively. The oldest manuscripts of both Suetonius and Tacitus date from no earlier than the ninth century, while the oldest of Livy comes from the fourth century. The two most prolific pre-Christian Greek historians (Herodotus and Thucydides), who both wrote in the fifth century BC, have only 75 and 20 surviving manuscripts, respectively, and the oldest for each dates only to the first century AD. Even Homer, with a nine-century headstart on the New Testament, and whose *Iliad* and *Odyssey* were the closest documents pre-Christian Greeks had to a "Bible," with their epic narratives used to teach countless schoolchildren the main lessons of life, is preserved in less than 2500 Greek manuscripts.[1] In short, "the New Testament is far and away the best-attested work of Greek or Latin literature in the ancient world."[2]

Second, we must consider questions of *authorship and date*. We have argued in chapters 6 through 9 that a good case can still be made for Matthew, Mark, Luke, and John as the authors of the Gospels that have traditionally been attributed to them, and that at least the three Synoptics may have been completed by the decade of the 60s, little more than thirty years after Jesus' life and death. These conclusions would clearly put the Gospel authors in touch with eyewitness data within one generation of the events they narrate. The presence of hostile opposition that also witnessed many of the public events of Jesus' life makes it unlikely that widespread fabrication of gospel tradition could have survived without refutation. But even the critical consensus places all four Gospels in the first century and assumes authorship by orthodox Christians who were in touch with apostolic tradition, which by ancient standards gives them outstanding credentials (recall above, pp. 93–97).

Third, we must ask questions of *intention and genre*. Again, we have given reasons why the early church probably wanted to preserve accurate history, was in a position to do so (given the emphasis on memorization in the oral culture), and used literary genres that express such a historical intention, though obviously with theological motivations as well (see above, pp. 121–22). Throughout our survey of Christ's life, in the "historicity" sections, we have pointed to a variety of arguments that suggest the evangelists were concerned to distinguish the events of Jesus' lifetime from later theological convictions of the church and, indeed, generally succeeded in keeping these periods separate in their thought and writing. The so-called "contradictions" among Gospel parallels all turn out to have plausible harmonizations or resolutions, and we have highlighted some of the most significant of these as well.[3]

Fourth, we have applied the *criteria of authenticity* to each of the main stages of Jesus' ministry, showing how numerous themes and details demonstrate dissimilarity from ancient Jewish or early Christian thought, are multiply attested, fit an early first-century Palestinian environment, and so on. Indeed, the first and the third of these combine to create a criterion of double similarity and dissimilarity or historical plausibility (recall above, pp. 220–21) that can be a very powerful tool for authenticating major segments of the Gospel tradition.[4]

But what of specific *external evidence*? What archaeological evidence impinges on the historicity of the gospel traditions? Or again, what do other ancient

---

[1] For all these statistics, see Komoszewski, Sawyer and Wallace, *Reinventing Jesus* , 71–72.

[2] Ibid., 71.

[3] Additional, excellent works on these and related questions include Eddy and Boyd, *The Jesus Legend;* and, at a more popular level, idem., *Lord or Legend? Wrestling with the Jesus Dilemma* (Grand Rapids: Baker, 2007). Cf. also M. D. Roberts, *Can We Trust the Gospels: Investigating the Reliability of Matthew, Mark, Luke, and John* (Wheaton: Crossway, 2007).

[4] See further Blomberg, *Historical Reliability of the Gospels*, 303–31, and the literature there cited.

writings besides the four Gospels say about these events? We may divide this latter question into three parts: (1) What evidence is there for the life of Jesus from ancient *non-Christian writers*? (2) How are our assessments affected by early *noncanonical Christian writers*? (3) What about the evidence of *the rest of the New Testament* itself, apart from the four Gospels? For some, question (1) is the most significant of the three. It is argued that only writers not already committed to the Christian movement can be trusted to be objective in their presentations. This argument, however, is seriously flawed. There is no necessary connection between supporting a movement and one's ability to tell the truth. We have already drawn attention to the modern analogy of Jewish historians of World War II and noted that in the ancient world *all* history and biography was narrated for ideological purposes (above, p. 105). Detached objectivity was largely unknown and would have been considered pointless. But historians still distinguished between reliable and unreliable reports.[5] We must also remember that many early Christians converted to this fledgling religion from Jewish or Greco-Roman backgrounds precisely because they were convinced by the evidence supporting it. So we insist on the importance of surveying both non-Christian and Christian testimony outside the Gospels.

Archaeology

In a world without photography or tape recorders, the vast majority of the deeds and sayings of Jesus disappeared without any physical remains. It is unrealistic, therefore, to turn to archaeology for corroboration or refutation of most of the Gospel data. Nevertheless, a remarkable amount of circumstantial detail does receive support of one kind or another from the excavations that dot the Middle Eastern landscape. Most of these serve merely to enhance our understanding of the historical, religious, cultural, and social background of the world of Jesus, as discussed in our opening three chapters—Herod's building projects, the layout and function of the temple, the size and contents of the typical Palestinian home, the nature of Roman roads, and so on.[6]

Some findings give insights into specific imagery Jesus used in his teaching. For example, the millstone was a huge, round rock attached by a pole to a beast of burden (like a donkey) which repeatedly walked around a stone birdbath-shaped structure into which grain or olives were poured. As the heavy wheel was dragged in circles, the produce was easily crushed. Little wonder, then, that putting a millstone around someone's neck and throwing that person into the open sea would insure instant drowning (cf. Matt 18:6). Or again, foundation stones still standing in the Herodian parts of the outer wall surrounding the temple precincts in Jerusalem measure up to 40 feet long, 3 feet high, and 8 feet thick, estimated at

---

[5] See esp. Hemer, *Acts*, 63–100.

[6] For voluminous detail, see J. McRay, *Archaeology and the New Testament* (Grand Rapids: Baker, 1991), 37–222; and J. Finegan, *The Archeology of the New Testament: The Life of Jesus and the Beginning of the Early Church*, rev. ed. (Princeton: Princeton University Press, 1992), 3–291.

50 tons apiece.[7] If Jesus referred to himself as a cornerstone (Mark 12:10 [TNIV/ NIV mg]), there would have been little doubt as to how solid a foundation he was describing! Still other findings have disclosed the Jewish practice of baptism by immersion (the *mikveh* pools), "Moses' seat" in the Chorazin synagogue (cf. Matt 23:2), houses with thatched roofs that a person might dig through (cf. Mark 2:4), and the style of ancient winepresses (cf. Luke 6:38).

In some instances, however, actual sites described in the Gospels seem likely to have been unearthed—the synagogue in Capernaum, possibly Peter's home there (recall above, p. 63), Jacob's well at Sychar where Jesus met with the Samaritan woman, the pool of Bethesda with its five porticoes near the Sheep Gate in Jerusalem, the pool of Siloam also in Jerusalem, and possibly the paving stones (*Gabbatha* or *Lithostrotos*—see John 19:13) outside Pilate's Jerusalem headquarters (assuming this to have been the Antonia Fortress).[8] The same is true for the location of cities. A first-century mosaic of a fishing boat with the inscription "Magdala" helped lead to the discovery of the hometown of Mary the Magdalene. Ruins of an ancient Byzantine church east of the Sea of Galilee may point to the site of Khersa, near which the demon-possessed pigs ran over the cliff. Still other natural features of the landscape remain above ground—a garden with olive trees on the ancient site of Gethsemane on the western slopes of the Mount of Olives, the rugged Judean wilderness where one can easily imagine the need for an ascetic lifestyle like that of John the Baptist, or Mt. Gerizim in the center of Israel, still home to a small Samaritan sect. Present-day tourists can quite literally eat lunch in "hell"—*Gehinnom* (Hb.) and *Gehenna* (Gk.)—the valley to the west and south of Mt. Zion, which later traditions described as a perpetually burning garbage dump, and which was the site of child sacrifice by Canaanites to the god Molech in Old Testament times.[9]

Some finds are comparatively recent. Ossuaries (small coffins or bone boxes), apparently of the family of Simon of Cyrene (cf. Mark 15:21) were discovered in 1941.[10] Not until 1961 was inscriptional evidence unearthed (at Caesarea Maritima) corroborating Pilate as prefect of Judea during Tiberius' reign. In 1968 an ossuary (bone box) of a crucified man named Johanan confirmed for the first time that nails could be driven through the feet or anklebones of executed victims. A first-century fishing boat from the mud beneath the Sea of Galilee was found as recently as 1986, when a drought caused the coastline to recede more than at any time in recent memory. In 1990, the tomb of what seems likely to be that of

---

[7] Finegan, *The Archeology of the New Testament*, 205.

[8] The last of these is the most disputed, in view of a strong case that can be made for Pilate staying at Herod's palace on the west side of town near the present-day Jaffa Gate. See U. C. von Wahlde, "Archaeology and John's Gospel," in *Jesus and Archaeology*, ed. Charlesworth, 572–73. This would then locate the *Via Dolorosa* and Christ's "stations of the cross" in almost the exact opposite direction from where they have traditionally been identified.

[9] For most all of these and numerous similar examples, see throughout Pixner, *With Jesus in Jerusalem*; and idem., *With Jesus in Galilee according to the Fifth Gospel*.

[10] A. C. Skinner, *Golgotha* (Salt Lake City: Deseret, 2004), 112.

the high-priest Caiaphas was first discovered.[11] A recent center of archaeological activity has been Bethsaida. Although to date nothing dramatic has emerged, many small artifacts, including numerous items relating to the fishing industry, have been dug up.[12] The apparent discovery of the ossuary of James the (half-) brother of Jesus in 2002 has been fraught with sufficient controversy that we may simply not know for sure if it is authentic without additional evidence.[13] Less dramatically, we *can* now say with greater confidence than prior to new discoveries in 2007 that we have correctly identified the full site of the pool of Siloam. Who knows what yet lies buried in the places Jesus walked or nearby, awaiting excavation that will shed further light on the Gospels?

Frequently, archaeology provides good "object lessons" for the interested Bible reader. In other words, sites that are not the actual locations of biblical events closely resemble what the real sites probably looked like. Thus, with respect to the Gospels, the location now occupied by the Church of the Holy Sepulcher in Jerusalem is far more likely to be the actual place of the crucifixion than "Gordon's Calvary." Yet the latter, a skull-shaped outcropping of rock just above the modern-day Jerusalem city bus station, is so characteristic of the terrain that it probably looks something like the original site of Golgotha. So, too, a circular tomb entrance—complete with sloping pathway and (sideways) rolling stone—discovered near Bethphage may resemble the very gravesite of Jesus, even though it is several miles from any place Joseph of Arimathea is likely to have used. Or again, tourists are regularly shown a small plateau a few hundred feet up from the northwest shore of Galilee and beneath the traditional "Mount of Beatitudes," where the natural acoustics allow one speaker standing on the slopes to be heard by a large crowd. This could be where Jesus preached his great sermon, but we simply have no way of telling.

Other discoveries of this nature include caves under and around the Church of the Nativity in Bethlehem (was one of these where Jesus was born?) and a decree in Nazareth threatening capital punishment for grave robbers (similar to the seal placed over Jesus' tomb outside Jerusalem?). Or one can imagine Jesus looking across to the east of the sea of Galilee to the hilltop city of Hippos, whose torch lights at night could be seen around the entire lake, when he declared, "A city on a hill cannot be hidden" (Matt 5:14). Was he looking down into the Kidron Valley to many of the beautifully ornate graves and mausoleums there, relatively

---

[11] The identification was disputed by W. Horbury, "The 'Caiaphas' Ossuaries and Joseph Caiaphas," *PEQ* 126 (1994): 32–48. For a confident affirmation, see W. R. Domeris and S. M. S. Long, "The Recently Excavated Tomb of Joseph Bar Caipha and the Biblical Caiaphas," *JTSA* 89 (1994): 50–58. C. A. Evans ("Excavating Caiaphas, Pilate, and Simon of Cyrene: Assessing the Literary and Archaeological Evidence," in *Jesus and Archaeology*, ed. Charlesworth, 329) calls the identification "tenuous."

[12] Ibid., 145–66.

[13] But those who would dismiss it out of hand need to read H. Shanks' (first) half of H. Shanks and B. Witherington III, *The Brother of Jesus: The Dramatic Story and Meaning of the First Archaeological Link to Jesus and His Family* (San Francisco: HarperSanFrancisco, 2003).

recently built in his day, when he compared the hypocritical scribes and Pharisees to "whitewashed tombs" (Matt 23:27)?

Excavated artifacts can often give insights into specific words or customs. The single word *corban*—dedicated to God—has been found on a Jewish sarcophagus as a guard against grave robbers. We know from the shape of the temple mount in Jerusalem that it had no "pinnacles," only "porticoes"—flat, porch-shaped structures. Yet, the southeast portico overlooking the Kidron valley would still have been a sufficiently fear-inspiring location for the devil to tempt Jesus to jump off (Matt 4:5–6). Coins in abundance confirm the custom of minting Caesar's image on them and also help archaeologists date other items in which they are embedded. The discovery of the enigmatic words Jesus spoke to Judas just before his betrayal (*eph ho parei*—literally, "for what you are here"—Matt 26:50) also inscribed on an early first-century Israelite drinking beaker, following the word, "Rejoice," make it natural to interpret them as, "That's why you are here" in both contexts.[14] James Charlesworth, finally, goes so far as to say that "perhaps the new discoveries of a vineyard with walls, a winepress, and a tower just to the west of first-century Nazareth should be considered among the most important archaeological discoveries for Jesus Research" (confirming the accuracy of the imagery of Mark 12:3).[15]

Ancient traditions, perhaps as old as the fourth or fifth century, often equate certain sites with events from the Gospels, even though there are good reasons for doubting the locations. For example, Mount Tabor was probably not remote or high enough for the Transfiguration; modern-day Cana is in the wrong place to be the ancient city by that name; and the traditional site of Caiaphas's headquarters is built over ancient Jewish graves—not where a high priest would have made his home. The feeding of the five thousand was not likely near Tabgha on the west bank of Galilee, as some tour guides allege, because John 6:17 describes the disciples departing from the site of that miracle by boat to head "across the lake" for Capernaum, which was also on the western shore. In other cases there is simply not enough information, inside or outside the Gospels, to prove or refute certain traditions—Ain Karim in the Judean hill country as John the Baptist's birthplace, the alleged tomb of Lazarus in Bethany, the supposed "upper room" on Mt. Zion, the *Dominus Flavit* chapel as the place Jesus wept over Jerusalem on the Mount of Olives, or the Church of the Annunciation in Nazareth as the place of Gabriel's appearance to Mary. Indeed, doubts of various kinds surround even many of the locations we have mentioned above as probably authentic. This simply reflects the uncertainty that characterizes the disciplines of archaeology and historical geography in general.

A different kind of uncertainty results when archaeology provides multiple options in trying to resolve a thorny historical problem. There are at least two, possibly three plausible locations for Emmaus. We have still not solved the prob-

---

[14] W. Klassen, "Judas and Jesus: A Message on a Drinking Vessel of the Second Temple Period," in *Jesus and Archaeology*, ed. Charlesworth, 506.

[15] J. H. Charlesworth, "Jesus Research and Archaeology: A New Perspective," in ibid., 38.

lem of Quirinius' census, even though we have discovered some ambiguous evidence that may suggest censuses on fourteen-year cycles throughout the Roman empire, a possible joint-governorship of some kind for Quirinius before his one clearly documented term beginning in AD 6, and evidence from Egypt that those who were residing away from property of their family of origin had to return to their homes for a census (see above, pp. 222–23). It seems premature, therefore, to accuse Luke of a definite error in attributing a census to a reign of Quirinius in about 6 BC, as so many have, even though we have no demonstrable vindication of Luke's accuracy either.[16]

Archaeology further holds the potential for illuminating the silences of the Gospels. Much recent excavation has centered on Sepphoris, the original Herodian capital of Galilee before the construction of Tiberias in the mid-20s, and a center of much building and trade during Jesus' youth and early adulthood. As it was less than five miles from Nazareth, can we imagine Jesus not having visited this center of Greek culture, complete with its theater? Might he have been employed in town? Is that where he learned about "hypocrites" (Gk. for "play actors"), a term he later used with such rhetorical power against various Jewish leaders? Conversely, may we assume from the silence of the Gospels about Sepphoris that Jesus' later adult ministry deliberately avoided this least Jewish of Galilean locales precisely because of his commitment to go to the Jew first (cf. our discussion above, p. 149)? But the pendulum recently has been swinging from the initial emphasis by archaeologists on the Hellenized elements of Sepphoris to the still predominantly Jewish culture that appeared there. Perhaps it was more that Jesus wanted to avoid a premature confrontation with the authorities that explains his absence from the two centers of political power in Galilee.[17]

Archaeological evidence can, however, be abused. Implausible harmonizations of difficult problems can be too easily proposed. For example, it is well known that there are ruins of two different cities within two miles from each other: Old Testament Jericho and New Testament Jericho. A popular solution to the problem of Mark having Jesus heal blind Bartimaeus as he was leaving Jericho (Mark 10:46), while Luke seems to think this happened en route to Jericho (Luke 18:35), has been to postulate that Jesus was in between the two Jerichos. But there is no evidence that any reader of a New Testament account of an otherwise unspecified Jericho would ever assume it to be the old city then in ruins, so other solutions to this problem will have to be sought (as we did above, p. 364, n. 30). Nor is it always remembered that the parable of the Good Samaritan was precisely that—a parable—so that debates over the authenticity of ruins of an inn on the Jericho road prove irrelevant. Jesus may have had no real-life site in mind at all as he told his story!

---

[16] Similarly, G. R. Habermas, *The Historical Jesus: Ancient Evidence for the Life of Christ,* rev. ed. (Joplin, MO: College Press, 1996), 172–73.

[17] See further J. L. Reed, *Archaeology and Galilean Jesus* (Harrisburg, Trinity, 2000); Freyne, *Jesus, a Jewish Galilean. Contra* significant portions of R. A. Horsley, *Archaeology, History and Society in Galilee: The Social Context of Jesus and the Rabbis* (Harrisburg: Trinity, 1996).

One ancient artifact of a quite different nature deserves brief comment. Small fragments of the Shroud of Turin, carefully guarded for centuries by Italian Catholic authorities, and traditionally believed to be the very grave clothes of Jesus, were subject to a battery of scientific tests in 1988 at three different laboratories around the world. All the results independently concurred that this was an eleventh or twelfth-century piece of cloth, much too recent to have belonged to Christ. There is still no convincing explanation of the origin of the striking impression of a crucified man imprinted on this cloth, but nothing is to be gained by arguing any longer for its authenticity, unless new evidence emerges.[18] Notwithstanding "reversals" of this nature, the ancient physical remains that impinge on the life of Jesus as narrated in the canonical Gospels continue to vindicate its substantial historicity time and again in those areas that can be tested. We should welcome all further investigations with the confidence that such corroboration will continue to emerge.

Other Ancient Sources

Non-Christian Writers

It is occasionally doubted if Jesus even existed. This claim can be decisively refuted without once appealing to Christian evidence.[19] The non-Christian testimony from antiquity may be divided into Greco-Roman and Jewish sources.

Greco-Roman Sources. Four ancient Roman historians of whom we are aware referred to Jesus.[20] The briefest and least significant reference comes from the early third-century historian Julius Africanus, who cites a certain Thallus who wrote a chronicle of world history in Greek in the first century. In that document, Thallus referred to the darkness that occurred at the time of the crucifixion (*Chronography*, frag. 18), attributing it to an eclipse of the sun, an interpretation Africanus disputes. Pliny the younger, a Roman legate from the early second century, wrote to the emperor Trajan requesting advice on how to deal with Christians who refused to worship the emperor. Pliny noted that these Christians met regularly and sang hymns "to Christ as if to a god" *(Ep.* 10.96.7). This expression suggests that Pliny knew Jesus was a historical figure and so was reluctant to call him divine.[21] Arguments that Pliny is simply reporting an erroneous Christian claim

---

[18] See further Stanton, *Gospel Truth?* 119–20; M. J. Harris, *From Grave to Glory: Resurrection in the New Testament* (Grand Rapids: Zondervan, 1990), 125–28.

[19] The most thorough treatment appears in R. E. van Voorst, *Jesus outside the New Testament: An Introduction to the Ancient Evidence* (Grand Rapids and Cambridge: Eerdmans, 2000). See also C. A. Evans, "Jesus in Non-Christian Sources," in *Studying the Historical Jesus: Evaluations of the State of Current Research*, ed. Chilton and Evans, 443–78.

[20] Cf. esp. M. J. Harris, "References to Jesus in Early Classical Authors," in *Gospel Perspectives*, vol. 5, 343–68.

[21] From the larger contexts of the quotation it may also be inferred that worship of Christ was both central to these services and distinctive in form from both pagan and Jewish antecedents. See G. N. Stanton, "Aspects of Early Christian and Jewish Worship: Pliny and the *Kerygma Petrou*," in *Worship, Theology and Ministry in the Early Church*, ed. M. J. Wilkins and T. Paige (Sheffield: JSOT, 1992),

fail on the grounds that he explains that he received this information from those who had denied their Christian faith.[22]

The third Roman source is Suetonius, also an early second-century writer, who describes the expulsion of Jews from Rome under the emperor Claudius as due to rioting "at the instigation of *Chrestus*" (*Claud.* 25:4), a remark usually interpreted as a garbled reference to Jewish followers of Christ (Lat., *Christus*). The reference nevertheless points to Jesus as the leader of a group of Jewish dissidents and perhaps even the founder of Christianity.[23] The one really substantive and decisive piece of Roman testimony, however, comes from a contemporary of Suetonius, the historian Tacitus. In *Ann.* 15:44, he wrote that Christians received their name from "Christ who had been executed by sentence of the procurator Pontius Pilate in the reign of Tiberius," details which mesh perfectly with the information found in the New Testament.[24]

Two additional scraps of testimony come from the ancient Greek-speaking world. Lucian of Samosata, a satirist writing in the mid-second century describes a recently deceased philosopher Peregrinus, who apparently made some profession of Christian faith. Lucian likens him to "that other whom they still worship, the man who was crucified in Palestine because he introduced this new cult into the world." Later he calls Jesus the Christians' "first lawgiver," who persuaded his followers that they were all "brothers of one another," as well as "that crucified sophist" (*Peregr.* 11, 13). Categories of law and wisdom are exactly what one would expect a non-Christian Hellenist to use in describing Jesus.[25] Mara bar Serapion, a non-Christian Syrian probably from the second century, twice refers to a "wise King" whom the Jews executed, which led to their recent exile from the land. Probably he has Jesus' crucifixion and the aftermath of the war with Rome in mind.[26] It is interesting to recall how Jesus himself linked his rejection and demise to the coming Roman invasion of Jerusalem (esp. Matt 23–25).

Jewish Sources. Of slightly more help are scattered references throughout the voluminous rabbinic literature.[27] It is difficult to know where, if ever, these references represent independent or accurate historical information. Rabbinic literature progressively excised mention of Jesus and Christianity and became increasingly polemical against its rival faith.[28] None of the references comes in the Mishnah or early midrashim (late first- through early–third century) but only in later Jewish

84–98. For the broader meaning and significance of Pliny's testimony, see Cassidy, *John's Gospel in New Perspective*, 17–26.

[22] M. J. Harris, *3 Crucial Questions about Jesus* (Grand Rapids: Baker, 1994), 18.

[23] See further ibid., 22–24; van Voorst, *Jesus outside the New Testament*, 29–39.

[24] See further van Voorst, *Jesus outside the New Testament*, 39–53.

[25] Harris, "References to Jesus in Early Classical Authors," 356.

[26] Habermas, *The Historical Jesus*, 206–8.

[27] For "Jesus in Jewish Traditions," see esp. the article so-entitled by G. H. Twelftree in *Gospel Perspectives*, vol. 5, 289–341.

[28] See esp. the passages tabulated in Schäfer, *Jesus in the Talmud*, 131–44. R. Kalmin ("Christians and Heretics in Rabbinic Literature of Late Antiquity," *HTR* 87 [1994]: 155–69) shows how the Babylonian Talmud turned earlier, more disparate traditions about Jesus into ones that made him just another (apostate) rabbi.

sources. Nevertheless, their contents are intriguing. In the Palestinian Talmud, the third-century Rabbi Abbahu says, "If a man says to you 'I am (a) God,' he is a liar; 'I am (a) Son of Man,' he will regret it; 'I go up to heaven,' he has said it but he will not be able to do it" (*p. Ta'anith* 65b). However derivatively, the passage reflects Christian claims about who Jesus said he was. Interestingly, no attempt is made to deny the claims, only a person's power to fulfill them. Equally intriguing is the account of the blasphemous messianic claim, trial and execution of bar Kochba in *b. Sanh.* 93b. None of the details fits any of the other known traditions about this early second-century rabbi whom various *other* Jews hoped might be the Messiah, but they all fit the Gospels' account of Jesus' demise. Has the desire to excise references to Jesus led to traditions originally about him to be ascribed to a later "failed Messiah"?[29]

As already noted above (p. 280), the same situation recurs with rabbinic commentary on Jesus' miracles and exorcisms. Plenty of ancient writers knew how to dispute claims of extraordinary ability, but the consistent Jewish witness was merely to question the source of Jesus' admitted powers. Thus *b. Sanh.* 103a likens a rebellious disciple to one "who publicly burns his food like Jesus of Nazareth"—a metaphor for distorting Jewish teaching. In the same tractate, we read that "Jesus the Nazarene practiced magic and led Israel astray" (43a; cf. 107b).[30] Several sources refer to Jesus as the son of Pandera (or Pantera or Panthera), a Roman soldier, hinting at the unusual circumstances surrounding his birth. As already suggested in the Gospels (John 8:41), Jewish polemic against Christ's virginal conception argued that he was merely an illegitimate child. Actually, Pand/t/thera may be a corruption of the Greek *parthenos* or virgin.

Yet, another rabbinic tradition speaks of Jesus as having five disciples named Matthai, Naqai, Nezer, Buni, and Todah (*b. Sanh.* 43a). Matthai, Naqai, and Todah could be corrupt spellings of Matthew, Nicodemus, and Thaddaeus, while Nezer probably refers to an unnamed "Nazarene." Buni might just be a corruption of the Hebrew for John, but all this is guesswork. The most substantial testimony in a later Jewish source probably remains the statement in this same section of the Babylonian Talmud that Jesus was hanged on the eve of the Passover. But this section also contains a reference to his being stoned and to a herald who announced the execution for forty days before it took place. Since both of these statements seem historically groundless, it is hard to know whether any of the text relies on accurate tradition.[31]

Other information is of even more dubious worth. One possible reference to Jesus (but the individual in question is referred to only as a well-known heretic

---

[29] So J. C. O'Neill, "The Mocking of bar Kokhba and of Jesus," *JSJ* 25 (1994): 39–41.

[30] On the pervasiveness and significance of this latter tradition, see G. N. Stanton, "Jesus of Nazareth: A Magician and False Prophet Who Deceived God's People?" in *Jesus of Nazareth*, ed. Green and Turner, 164–80. J. W. Welch ("Miracles, *Maleficium*, and *Maiestas* in the Trial of Jesus," in *Jesus and Archaeology*, ed. Charlesworth, 349–83) adds that fear of evil powers may be an important, though often neglected factor in the desire of the Jewish authorities to do away with Christ.

[31] See further R. E. Brown, "The Babylonian Talmud on the Execution of Jesus," *NTS* 43 (1997): 158–59.

like Balaam) states that he was thirty-three or thirty-four when he died (*b. Sanh.* 106b). Another describes a dialogue between a putative disciple of Jesus and Rabbi Eliezer, in which Jesus is quoted as having taught that a latrine could be bought with the wages of a harlot (*b. Abod. Zar.* 16b–17a). Numerous passages refer to anonymous heretics, some of which could be speaking of Jesus. A widely read medieval Jewish source, perhaps as old as the eighth century, called the *Toledoth Jesu* ("The Generations of Jesus"), describes the illegitimate child Jesus growing up to disrespect his teachers, performing miracles, attracting a following, and eventually being executed. The story then describes the discovery of an empty tomb followed by the recovery of Jesus' corpse. All in all the work is nothing but a late, polemical revisionist attempt by certain Jews to discredit the classic claims of Christian origins.

The only truly valuable Jewish testimony to the life of Christ thus comes not from the rabbinic literature but from the first-century Pharisee and defeated freedom-fighter-turned-historian, Josephus. In *Ant.* 20.9.1, Josephus describes the martyrdom of James, "the brother of Jesus—the one called Christ." This passing reference alone serves to substantiate the historicity of Jesus per se, but it seems to presuppose more detailed, prior knowledge of this individual. This information was in fact provided in 18.3.3. The text as it stands reads:

> About this time there lived Jesus, a wise man, if indeed one ought to call him a man. For he was one who wrought surprising feats and was a teacher of such people as accept the truth gladly. He won over many Jews and many of the Greeks. He was the Messiah. When Pilate, upon hearing him accused by men of the highest standing amongst us, had condemned him to be crucified, those who had in the first place come to love him did not give up their affection for him. On the third day he appeared to them restored to life, for the prophets of God had prophesied these and countless other marvellous things about him. And the tribe of the Christians, so called after him, has still to this day not disappeared.

Because the rest of his writings make it clear that Josephus never became a Christian, it seems impossible that he (1) should have questioned Jesus' humanity, (2) called Jesus the Messiah, or (3) affirmed the resurrection. As a result some scholars have wondered whether or not this entire passage is a later Christian "interpolation" into the works of Josephus, especially because it was largely in Christian circles that his writings came to be preserved. But if we excise these three parts, the rest of Josephus' testimony flows smoothly, fits his style, and seems likely to be authentic. Perhaps, as in section 20, he originally wrote "the one called Messiah." A later Arabic version of Josephus, in fact, closely resembles this abridged reconstruction of his original text, with the latter two supposed interpolations combined at the end of the paragraph. This would seem to confirm our hypothesis about the original form of Josephus's testimony.[32] Other passages

---

[32] Meier, *A Marginal Jew*, vol. 1, 56–88. For the most thoroughgoing recent defense of this position, see J. C. Paget, "Some Observations on Josephus and Christianity," *JTS* 52 (2001): 539–624. For a full survey of approaches to this text, see A. Wheatley, *Josephus on Jesus: The Testimonium Flavianum Controversy from Late Antiquity to Modern Times* (New York: Peter Lang, 2003).

in *Antiquities* describe the ministry and execution of John the Baptist,[33] and the lives and times of the various Herods, the Roman governors, and the Jewish high priests, including Pilate and Caiaphas, respectively.

To some this may all seem like precious little non-Christian corroboration of the Gospel narratives. But we have to remember that in the ancient world, history was almost exclusively the chronicle of the deeds of politicians, warriors, and holders of high religious office. Other figures were mentioned only if they spawned widespread, long-term, public followings. Jesus and Christianity fit none of these categories at this early date. So it is arguable that it is both surprising and significant that they even got as much press as they did![34]

Post–New Testament Christian Writers

Unorthodox Sources. We have already noted how the Coptic *Gospel of Thomas* has been alleged to preserve reliable, independent tradition about the sayings of Jesus, even though its origin cannot be demonstrated to predate the mid-second century and even though it contains numerous sayings attributed to Jesus that are thoroughly Gnostic in character (above, p. 39). While Thomas is by far the most commonly cited heterodox Christian document that some think may illuminate the gospel tradition, other works have at times been appealed to in this respect as well. From the Nag Hammadi collection of primarily Gnostic texts comes also the Apocryphon of James, with various new parables and kingdom sayings attributed to Jesus. A large number of "Gospels" are made up primarily of lengthy dialogues attributed to the resurrected Jesus, who imparts secret (i.e., Gnostic) revelation to various disciples. Two that occasionally have sayings more akin to the canonical Gospels are the *Gospel of Philip* and the *Gospel of Truth.*Yet careful studies have demonstrated that all these works are in fact later than and most likely dependent on the collected canonical Gospels and add nothing to our knowledge about the historical Jesus.[35]

Other Apocrypha. A very different type of document that some have appealed to as a primitive Gospel source is the *Gospel of Peter*, a narrative that deals largely with the passion and resurrection of Christ. This work is clearly "docetic" in nature, that is, Christ only seems (Gk. *dokeō*) to be human. Thus 4:10b states that during his crucifixion Jesus "was silent, as if having no pain." As already noted above (p. 412), in the account of Christ's resurrection, even more obviously legendary elements appear: three men emerge from the tomb, "two sustaining the one, and a cross following them, and the heads of the two reaching to heaven, but that of him who was led by them by the hand going beyond the

---

[33] On which, see esp. C. A. Evans, "Josephus on John the Baptist and Other Jewish Prophets of Deliverance," in *The Historical Jesus in Context*, eds. A.-J. Levine, D. C. Allison, Jr., and J. D. Crossan (Princeton and Oxford: Princeton University Press, 2006), 55–63.

[34] Cf. further P. Barnett, *Is the New Testament History?* (London: Hodder & Stoughton, 1986; Milton Keynes and Waynesboro, GA: Authentic Media, 2002), 159–63.

[35] See esp. C. M. Tuckett, *Nag Hammadi and the Gospel Tradition* (Edinburgh: T&T Clark, 1986). Cf. also G. P. Luttikhuizen, *Gnostic Revisions of Genesis Stories and Early Jesus Traditions* (Leiden and Boston: Brill, 2006).

heavens" (10:39–40). Notwithstanding this ethos, Dominic Crossan has attempted
to reconstruct an underlying "Cross Gospel" behind the *Gospel of Peter,* which he
postulates as the sole pre-Markan source for the canonical passion narratives.[36]
Far more brief and fragmentary is Papyrus Egerton 2, the so-called "Unknown
Gospel," which comprises four scraps of Gospel-like accounts, including a dialogue between Jesus and the Jewish rulers similar to those in John 5 and 9–10,
the story of a cleansing of a leper, the question for Jesus about paying taxes, and
an apparent miracle of quickly growing seed that has no exact canonical parallel.
With both the *Gospel of Peter* and the Unknown Gospel, however, painstaking
comparisons with the canonical narratives make it far more probable that the New
Testament accounts generated the later additions and "revisions" than that the
reverse sequence obtained.[37]

Even more blatantly legendary are the apocrypha that try to fill in the gaps
in the canonical Gospels concerning Christ's "hidden years"—his childhood
and young adulthood. The *Protevangelium of James* is important as the source
for Roman Catholicism's dogma of *Mary's* sinlessness, describing among other things Jesus' emerging from the womb without breaking Mary's hymen (see
above, p. 243). The *Infancy Gospel of Thomas*, not to be confused with the Coptic
Gnostic document by the same name, describes Jesus the child miracle-worker
and carpenter prodigy (p. 242). But neither document shows any signs of preserving independent historical traditions about Christ.[38]

Jewish-Christian Gospels. This category of literature is known to us solely
from quotations that have been preserved in the various Church Fathers. Apparently there were at least three different documents, all perhaps bearing some
resemblance to the Gospel of Matthew—an Ebionite Gospel, the *Gospel of the
Nazarenes*, and an Egyptian *Gospel of the Hebrews*. These traditions are of interest because of the recurring testimony within early Christianity that Matthew
compiled something in the Hebrew language before the appearance of the canonical Greek Gospel that bears his name. Certain patterns emerge in the scattered
references to these Gospels that remain: Jesus is cast in terms of Wisdom and Law,
there are ascetic tendencies, and James the brother of Jesus plays a prominent
role. All of these fit with what we know of second-century Jewish Christianity.
As with the Coptic *Gospel of Thomas*, it is possible that in isolated places these
documents preserve otherwise unknown but authentic sayings of Jesus. Still, as
with the other documents surveyed in this section, there is also plenty of evidence
of dependence on the canonical tradition.[39]

[36] J. D. Crossan, *The Cross That Spoke: The Origins of the Passion Narrative* (San Francisco: Harper & Row, 1988; Eugene, OR: Wipf & Stock, 2008).

[37] D. F. Wright, "Apocryphal Gospels: 'The Unknown Gospel (Pap. Egerton 2) and the *Gospel of Peter*," in *Gospel Perspectives*, vol. 5, 221–27.

[38] See further C. L. Quarles, "The *Protevangelium of James* as an Alleged Parallel to Creative Historiography in the Synoptic Birth Narratives," *BBR* 8 (1998): 139–49; and T. Chartrand-Burke, "Authorship and Identity in the *Infancy Gospel of Thomas*," *TJT* 14 (1998): 27–43.

[39] For the fullest analysis and presentation of texts, see A. F. J. Klijn, *Jewish-Christian Gospel Tradition* (Leiden: Brill, 1992).

Later Legends (of Christian and Non-Christian Origin). The unsuspecting modern reader may pick up "New Age" or similar literature that refers to still more extracanonical documents. Often, this literature does not disclose that the works it treats were not even composed until the Middle Ages or later. In such works, one can read about Pilate's correspondence, Jesus as an Essene, or Christ traveling to India to study with the great gurus there. Muslims often appeal to the *Gospel of Barnabas*, a document that has Judas replacing Jesus on the cross at the last minute and that denies Christ's divinity, even though it was not composed until well after the birth of Islam. Indeed, the oldest known copies are an eighteenth-century Spanish manuscript and a sixteenth-century Italian one.[40] Modern-day forgeries even pass off Jesus as an alien from outer space! All of this literature is worthless for an analysis of the Jesus of history, regardless of the misleading claims of some of the books that reproduce this material.[41]

The Apostolic Fathers. Substantially more valuable testimony comes from the second-century orthodox Christian writers known as the Apostolic Fathers.[42] Within less than a hundred years from the completion of the books we now know as the New Testament, quotations and allusions from sizable portions of those books were showing up in other Christian literature. Polycarp, Ignatius, and Clement alone betray awareness of twenty-five of the twenty-seven New Testament documents. Ignatius recognizes, too, that the end of an era has come. In his early second-century letter to the Trallians, for example, he admits, "I did not think myself competent for this, that . . . I should order you as though I were an apostle" (*Trall.* 3:3). The Gospels, and the sayings of Jesus in particular, were the most popular part of the New Testament documents to be cited by these early Church Fathers, and Matthew was the most popular Gospel of all. (John would later receive the special attention of the heterodox or Gnostic works because of passages that could be twisted or taken out of context to support that theological system.[43])

Indeed, it is important to stress that one of the significant contributions of the Apostolic Fathers is to corroborate the widespread influence of a substantial portion of the Gospel tradition. Clearly, all four canonical Gospels, circulating together by at least the early second century, had a profound influence on the developing church. But whereas various critics have put forward relatively specious arguments for the Nag Hammadi and other heterodox literature relying on early, independent tradition, the case is different with the Apostolic Fathers. The

---

[40] See further O. Leirvik, "History as a Literary Weapon: The Gospel of Barnabas in Muslim-Christian Polemics," *ST* 54 (2001): 4–16; J. Joosten, "The Gospel of Barnabas and the Diatessaron," *HTR* 95 (2002): 73–96.

[41] For representative samplings of this material, see P. Beskow, *Strange Tales about Jesus: A Survey of Unfamiliar Gospels* (Philadelphia: Fortress, 1983); and D. Groothuis, *Jesus in an Age of Controversy* (Eugene, OR: Harvest House, 1996; Eugene, OR: Wipf & Stock, 2002), 119–51.

[42] A standard edition of their collected works is *The Apostolic Fathers: Greek Texts and English Translations*, trans. J. B. Lightfoot and J. R. Harmer, ed. and rev. M. W. Holmes (Grand Rapids: Baker, 2007).

[43] See esp. C. E. Hill, *The Johannine Corpus in the Early Church* (Oxford and New York: OUP, 2004), 205–93.

Coptic *Gospel of Thomas* discloses parallels to every single canonical Gospel and every putative Gospel layer of tradition or redaction, even the relatively rare material unique to Mark. But several of the Apostolic Fathers are far less balanced in their use of canonical Gospel material. The *Didachē* (or "Teaching of the Twelve Apostles"), written probably as early as the 90s, is filled with references to teachings of Jesus paralleled in Matthew's Gospel but never when Matthew is identical to Mark. Given Matthew's widespread dependence on Mark, this is a striking coincidence if this document were relying on the final form of the Gospel. But it could be evidence that the *Didachē* knew and used something like Q—an underlying Gospel source. So, too, Ignatius also cites texts from Matthew in abundance, but *three*-fourths of his quotations or allusions come from "M" (uniquely Matthean) material, whereas "M" comprises no more than *one*-fourth of the overall Gospel. In some cases these references involve material previously thought to be Matthew's own redaction (e.g., Matt 3:15 in Ignatius's *Smyrn.* 1.1). So perhaps there is actually evidence here for the persistence of underlying oral or written source material to which later Christian writers referred. First Clement and Polycarp independently reproduce collections of gospel traditions that resemble one another in ways that also suggest common, noncanonical source material. None of this proves the historical trustworthiness of the details cited, but it all suggests that early sources continued to influence Christian writers even after the four Gospels were compiled. The earlier the source, the more likely it was in touch with authentic tradition.[44]

Authentic Agrapha? When we amass all of the evidence of these post-canonical Christian writers, do we discover potentially reliable information about Jesus that we would not have known from Matthew, Mark, Luke, or John? The question is legitimate, for even the Book of Acts quotes a saying of Jesus not found in any of the Gospels ("It is more blessed to give than to receive"—Acts 20:35). John reminds us, however hyperbolically, that many other things Jesus said and did were never written down (John 21:25). A famous study called *Unknown Sayings of Jesus*, by the relatively conservative German scholar Joachim Jeremias, identified eighteen such *agrapha* (from the Greek for "unwritten things"—i.e., not written down in the canonical Gospels but found in other early Christian literature).[45] More recent studies have been skeptical of accepting even this many.[46] A sample of those that might conceivably pass the standard criteria of authenticity, and the sources in which they are found, include:

---

[44] For more on all of these points, see Blomberg, *Historical Reliability of the Gospels*, 258–63, and the literature there cited.

[45] Rev. ed. (London: SPCK, 1964). The texts of 266 agrapha appear in W. D. Stroker, *Extracanonical Sayings of Jesus* (Atlanta: Scholars, 1989). The vast majority of these stand no chance of reflecting independent authentic information about or from the historical Jesus.

[46] O. Hofius, "Unknown Sayings of Jesus," in *The Gospel and the Gospels*, ed. Stuhlmacher, 336–60; and J. H. Charlesworth and C. A. Evans, "Jesus in the Agrapha and Apocryphal Gospels," in *Studying the Historical Jesus*, ed. Chilton and Evans, 479–545.

On the same day Jesus saw a man working on the sabbath, and said to him, "Man, if you know what you are doing, you are blessed; but if you do not know, you are cursed and an offender against the law." (an addition to Luke 6:5 in Codex Bezae [D])

No one will reach the kingdom of heaven without being tempted. (Tertullian, *On Baptism*, 20)

Ask for great things, and the little things will be added to you. (Clement of Alexandria, *Stromateis* 1.24)

Be approved money-changers. (Origen, *Commentary on John*, 19.7; and several other sources)

But the rich man began to scratch his head, and it pleased him not. And the Lord said to him: "How can you say, 'I have kept the law and the prophets?' For it is written in the law: 'You shall love your neighbor as yourself,' and lo, many of your brothers, sons of Abraham, are clad in filth, dying of hunger, and your house is full of many good things, and nothing of it goes out to them." (*Gospel of the Nazoreans* 16, as quoted by Origen, *Commentary on Matthew* 15.14)

Whoever is near me is near the fire; whoever is far from me is far from the kingdom. (*Gospel of Thomas* 82)

And never be joyful, save when you look upon your brother in love. (*Gospel of the Hebrews* 5, as quoted by Jerome, *Commentary on Ephesians* 3)

Woe to you blind who see not! You have washed yourself in water that is poured forth, in which dogs and swine lie night and day, and washed and scoured your outer skin, which harlots and flute girls also anoint, bathe, scour, and beautify to arouse desire in men, but inwardly they are filled with scorpions and with all manner of evil. But I and my disciples, of whom you say that we have not bathed, have bathed ourselves in the living and clean water, which comes down from the father in heaven. (*pOxyrhynchus* 840.2)

Whether or not any of these sayings is authentic, the overwhelming conclusion at the end of this survey of post–New Testament Christian writers is that very little if anything emerges to supplement or alter the picture of Jesus we receive from the canonical Gospels. On the other hand, widespread citation of the canonical tradition demonstrates that the early Christian church was convinced of the truthfulness and relevance of at the very least a quite sizable portion of the contents of Matthew, Mark, Luke, and John.

The Testimony of the Rest of the New Testament

It is sometimes argued that the rest of the New Testament shows so little awareness of the Jesus-tradition that it could not have been well known in the first generation of Christianity. In extreme instances, Paul and not Jesus is treated as the founder of this new religion![47] On the one hand, it is true that the Acts and

---

[47] One of the most famous examples is the essay by the celebrated English writer and outspoken critic of Christianity, G. B. Shaw, "The Monstrous Imposition on Jesus," in *The Writings of St. Paul*, ed. W. A. Meeks, rev. ed. (New York: Norton, 2007 [orig. 1913]), 296–302. Among recent scholars, see esp. G. Lüdemann, *Paul: The Founder of Christianity* (Amherst, NY: Prometheus, 2002).

the epistles do not regularly quote sayings of Jesus and that episodes from his life are rarely mentioned, but there are several plausible reasons for this. None of these documents represents the initial evangelistic outreach of the church; all are written to well-established Christian communities for specific reasons (usually "in-house" concerns) that do not require a first-time presentation of the life of Christ. Luke, of course, has already narrated his Gospel when he writes the Acts. Paul and the other epistle writers may equally presume that the core *kerygma* (proclamation) of the church is well known, so that they can proceed to build upon it. After all, the author of the epistles of John almost certainly knew the Gospel of John (and most likely wrote it), yet there are only vague allusions to the actual teachings of Jesus in these epistles. Moreover, Christian theology became quickly convinced that the most important things about Jesus' life were his death and resurrection. Important as his teachings and other deeds were, they did not put into effect God's plan of atonement for the sins of the world, and so they came to take second place in overtly theological presentations of Christ's significance.[48]

On the other hand, it is easy to underestimate the extent to which the Jesus-tradition *did* influence Acts and the epistles. There are actually quite a number of places where direct quotations or references to various sayings or events from Jesus' life appear, and numerous additional allusions, although it becomes difficult to know when certain references actually allude to teachings of Jesus rather than referring to common illustrative material in ancient religious thought more generally. We will briefly survey some of the more secure and significant quotations and allusions here. Because most of these predate the written form of the Gospels, they provide evidence for the conservative nature of the earlier, collective oral tradition.[49]

Acts. In Acts 13:24–25, Paul's sermon in Pisidian Antioch includes reference back to John the Baptist and specific teaching from John about his unworthiness even to untie the sandals of the one coming after him. In 20:35, as noted above, we have an otherwise unknown saying of Jesus, but the most important reference in Acts back to the Gospel tradition is the summary of Jesus' life in Peter's words to Cornelius in 10:36–41:

> This is the message God sent to the people of Israel, telling the good news of peace through Jesus Christ, who is Lord of all. You know what has happened throughout Judea, beginning in Galilee after the baptism that John preached— how God anointed Jesus of Nazareth with the Holy Spirit and power, and how he went around doing good and healing all who were under the power of the devil, because God was with him. We are witnesses of everything he did in the country of the Jews and in Jerusalem. They killed him by hanging him on a tree, but God raised him from the dead on the third day and caused him to be seen. He was not seen by all the people, but by witnesses whom God had already chosen—by us who ate and drank with him after he rose from the dead.

---

[48] See further C. L. Blomberg, *Making Sense of the New Testament: Three Crucial Questions* (Grand Rapids: Baker; Leicester: IVP, 2004), 84–88, and the literature there cited.

[49] Cf. further G. M. Keightley, "Christian Collective Memory and Paul's Knowledge of Jesus," in *Memory, Tradition, and Text: Uses of the Past in Early Christianity*, eds. A. Kirk and T. Thatcher (Atlanta: SBL, 2004), 129–50.

A summary like this was what led C. H. Dodd to suggest that the Gospels themselves fleshed out the outline of early Christian preaching (see above, p. 131). On the other hand, the paucity of more detailed references to the Jesus tradition combines with regular reference to guidance by the Holy Spirit to show that it was by no means necessary to relate doctrinal or ethical decision-making directly to words of the historical Jesus.[50]

Paul.[51] Because most, if not all, of the Pauline epistles were written before the first Gospel was ever published, Paul's testimony proves even more significant, demonstrating the existence of information being circulated about the life of Christ within the first twenty years or so of Christian history. Upon careful inspection, a fairly full summary of the main contours of Jesus' life can, in fact, be pieced together from Paul's writings: his descent from Abraham and David (Gal 3:16; Rom 1:3); upbringing in the Jewish Law (Gal 4:4); gathering together disciples, including Cephas (Peter) and John; having a brother named James (Gal 1:19; 2:9); an impeccable character and exemplary life (Phil 2:6–8; 2 Cor 8:9; Rom 15:3, 8); the Last Supper and betrayal (1 Cor 11:23–25); and numerous details surrounding his death and resurrection (Gal 3:1; 1 Thess 2:15; 1 Cor 15:4–8).[52]

Even more noteworthy are various quotations of or references to Jesus' teaching. Romans 12:17–19 includes a cluster of allusions to the Sermon on the Mount and the principles of enemy love (cf. esp. Matt 5:38; Luke 6:27, 33). Romans 13:7 seems familiar with Jesus' famous teaching on paying taxes (cf. Mark 12:17 pars.). Romans 14:20 apparently relies on Jesus' abolition of the kosher laws (cf. Mark 7:19).[53] 1 Corinthians contains three direct references: 7:10 on marriage and divorce (cf. Matt 19:1–12), 9:14 (cf. also 1 Tim 5:18) on a worker deserving his wages (cf. Luke 10:7), and 11:23–25 with its detailed knowledge of the teaching of Jesus about the Passover bread and wine (cf. esp. Luke 22:19–20). Other probable allusions include 9:18 (on Paul's preaching the gospel free of charge) to Matt 10:8, and 13:2 (on faith moving mountains) to Mark 11:23 and parallels.[54] Second Corinthians 1:17 seems to hark back to Matt 5:37—letting one's yes be yes and one's no be no. 1 Thessalonians again contains three clear clusters of references to Jesus' teachings: 2:14–16 resembles selections of Matt 23:29–38, with its invective against the Jewish leaders; 4:15–17 refers to a word of the Lord concerning his return and contains several echoes of the Olivet Discourse (Mark

---

[50] W. A. Strange, "The Jesus-Tradition in Acts," *NTS* 46 (2000): 59–74.

[51] By far and away the most important study and collection of possible citations and use of the Jesus-tradition in Paul is D. Wenham, *Paul: Follower of Jesus or Founder of Christianity?* (Grand Rapids and Cambridge: Eerdmans, 1995). See also idem., *Paul and Jesus: The True Story* (Grand Rapids and Cambridge: Eerdmans, 2002).

[52] These are simply the most secure details. Awareness of numerous other traditions remains probable. See Blomberg, *Making Sense of the New Testament*, 81–84. Cf. J. P. Arnold, "The Relationship of Paul to Jesus," in *Hillel and Jesus: Comparative Studies of Two Major Religious Leaders*, ed. J. H. Charlesworth and L. L. Johns (Minneapolis: Fortress, 1997), 256–88.

[53] On Romans' use of the Jesus tradition, see esp. M. B. Thompson, *Clothed with Christ: The Example and Teaching of Jesus in Romans 12.1–15.13* (Sheffield: JSOT, 1991).

[54] Cf. esp. A. Eriksson, *Traditions as Rhetorical Proof: Pauline Argumentation in 1 Corinthians* (Stockholm: Almqvist and Wiksell, 1998).

13 pars.); and 5:2–4 refers specifically to the Day of the Lord coming like a thief, in dependence on the parable in Matt 24:43–44 and Luke 12:39–40. More generally, 2 Thess 2:3–4 refers to belief in a coming Antichrist reminiscent of Jesus' teaching about the "abomination that causes desolation" (Mark 13:14 pars.).[55]

Other references are less definite and yet seem still to betray some awareness of the Jesus-tradition. Paul's mention of the Jerusalem apostles as "pillars" of the church (Gal 2:9) could allude back to Jesus' promises to Peter and his companions in Matt 16:17–19 and 18:19–20. Echoes of the parable of the sower may be heard in Col 1:6 or 1 Thess 1:6 and 2:13. It would be striking for Paul to have described God the Father as Abba (almost "Daddy") in Gal 4:6 and Rom 8:15 had he not known about Jesus' own distinctive use of the term (see esp. Mark 14:36). Paul's understanding of Christ's redemptive death (e.g., Rom 3:24) may well depend in part on Jesus' ransom saying in Mark 10:45 and parallel texts. Key themes in Paul's theology, as different as it superficially seems to be from Jesus' own thought, also suggest stronger lines of continuity: several references to "kingdom," though substantially diminished in frequency from the Gospels; the sequence of going first to Jew and then to Gentile with the gospel; Jesus as the fulfillment of the Law, implying freedom from slavish obedience to its "letter," coupled with the need to adhere to its abiding moral demands; the summary of the Old Testament in the love-command; the flesh-Spirit contrast as in Mark 14:38; and justification by grace through faith as in Luke 18:10–14.[56]

The General Epistles. James and 1 Peter, too, seem to rely on a form of the Jesus-tradition that would have circulated prior to the first written Gospels. The evidence from James may prove particularly significant if, as many scholars suspect, that letter was the earliest New Testament document written, perhaps in the late 40s. Then the oral tradition on which James relied would be barely more than fifteen years removed from the events themselves. James has one direct quotation of Jesus' words (again on letting one's yes be yes and one's no, no—James 5:12; cf. Matt 5:37) but numerous allusions, especially to the Sermon on the Mount. Compare, for example, 1:2 with Matt 5:11–12; 1:4 with Matt 5:48; 1:5 with Matt 7:7; 1:6 with Mark 11:23; and so on.[57] First Peter, on the other hand, even if dated as early as about 64 (during Peter's lifetime and just at the onset of Nero's persecution), could have known the final forms of Matthew, Mark, or Luke. But interestingly, some of Peter's clearest allusions to Gospel tradition resemble uniquely Johannine material, perhaps not written down until the 90s. Thus, 1:3 speaks of being born anew (cf. John 3:3); 1:8, of loving Jesus without having seen him (cf. John 20:29); and 2:9, of being called out of darkness into light (cf. John 8:12).

---

[55] On allusions to the Olivet Discourse throughout Paul, see D. Wenham, "Paul and the Synoptic Apocalypse," in *Gospel Perspectives*, vol. 2, 345–75. Cf. also S. Kim, "The Jesus Tradition in 1 Thess 4.13–5.11," *NTS* 48 (2002): 225–42.

[56] Cf. further S. Kim, "Jesus, Sayings of," in *DPL*, esp. 481.

[57] For the dating of James and for a list and discussion of allusions to the Jesus tradition, see esp. P. H. Davids, *The Epistle of James* (Exeter: Paternoster; Grand Rapids: Eerdmans, 1982), 2–22, 47–51. Cf. also V. V. Porter, "The Sermon on the Mount in the Book of James," *BSac* 162 (2005): 344–60; 470–82.

Again, there may be evidence for the oral transmission at an earlier date of what was only later written down in our canonical Gospels.[58]

Early Christian Creeds. A final piece of evidence may push back the existence of the oral traditions about Jesus to an astonishingly early date. There are various passages in the epistles that have frequently been identified as poetic, even hymnic, in structure and form, which are filled with Christological teaching in a style reminiscent of later Christian creeds.[59] There are often signs, too, that these predate the New Testament authors who use them, because of key words or phrases reflecting those authors' distinctive theologies that interrupt the structure or symmetry of the "creeds." If this is the case, then we have evidence in these passages for what Christians confessed about Jesus at a very early date. Remarkably, these passages include some of the "highest Christology"—the most lofty and exalted statements about the person and work of Christ—found anywhere in the New Testament (e.g., Phil 2:5–11; Col 1:15–20; Rom 1:3–4; and 1 Tim 3:16). Peter clearly makes reference to the exemplary life and redemptive death of Jesus in similar confessional passages (1 Pet 1:20–21; 2:21–25; 3:18–22). In perhaps the most significant creed of all, Paul cites tradition that had been passed on to him about the eyewitnesses to Jesus' resurrection (1 Cor 15:3–7). The language here is technical Jewish terminology for the transmission of sacred tradition. Given that the reality and significance of Jesus' death and resurrection would have no doubt been one of the first things other Christians would have taught Paul as a new convert, it is plausible to date this information to the year of Paul's conversion, perhaps as early as AD 32. Thus, based on all these lines of evidence, within at least two years of Jesus' death, Jewish Christians may well have been confidently proclaiming his bodily resurrection.[60] What a far cry from revisionist reconstructions of Christian origins that assign all this to late, second-generation Hellenistic perversions of the story of Jesus!

Conclusion

In various places in this book we have seen evidence for (1) the general care the early Christians took to preserve accurate information about Jesus and (2) the authenticity of a broad cross-section of selections from the Gospel texts themselves. In this chapter we have focused primarily on (3) the testimony of other evidence outside the Gospels—the physical remains of archaeology or historical geography and the written references in other Christian and non-Christian

---

[58] Cf. further R. H. Gundry, "'Verba Christi' in 1 Peter: Their Implications Concerning the Authorship of 1 Peter and the Authenticity of the Gospel Tradition," *NTS* 13 (1966–67): 366–50; idem., "Further Verba on *Verba Christi* in First Peter," *Bib* 55 (1974): 211–32.

[59] For the most common proposals, see R. J. Karris, *A Symphony of New Testament Hymns* (Collegeville: Liturgical, 1996). For critical analysis, see throughout Hurtado, *Lord Jesus Christ;* and idem., *How On Earth Did Jesus Become a God? Historical Questions about Earliest Devotion to Jesus* (Grand Rapids and Cambridge: Eerdmans, 2005).

[60] Cf. further P. J. Kearney, "He Appeared to 500 Brothers (1 Cor. XV 6)," *NovT* 22 (1980): 264–84.

authors. None of this adds up to proof for the total trustworthiness of the Gospel tradition. Neither does it demonstrate their inspiration or inerrancy. Those who believe these theological affirmations of faith *deduce* them from other convictions about the nature of God and his revelation. There is a proper time and place for such affirmations, but they cannot be of much help in discussion with those who do not already share certain common presuppositions. This book has focused primarily on more *inductive* observations about the nature of the Gospel texts themselves, interpreted in light of a wide diversity of other ancient historical, theological, and literary data. Whatever else one may or may not believe by faith, on sheer historical grounds alone, there is substantial reason to believe in the *general* trustworthiness of the Gospel tradition. Those who then go on by a "leap of faith" to accept the *entire* trustworthiness of that material do so not by flying in the face of the bulk of the evidence but by moving in a direction in which the evidence was already pointing.[61]

For Further Study

Archaeology

Introductory

Blaiklock, E. M. *The Archaeology of the New Testament.* Rev. ed. Nashville: Thomas Nelson, 1984.
Blaiklock, E. M. and R. K. Harrison, eds. *The New International Dictionary of Biblical Archaeology.* Grand Rapids: Zondervan, 1983.
Lewin, Ariel. *The Archaeology of Ancient Judea and Palestine.* Los Angeles: Getty, 2005.

Intermediate

Arav, Rami, and John J. Rousseau. *Jesus and His World: An Archaeological and Cultural Dictionary.* Minneapolis: Fortress, 1995.
Pixner, Bargil. *With Jesus in Galilee according to the Fifth Gospel.* Rosh Pina, Israel: Corazin, 1992; Collegeville: Liturgical, 1996.
Pixner, Bargil. *With Jesus in Jerusalem: His First and Last Days in Judea.* Rosh Pina, Israel: Corazin, 1996.
McRay, John. *Archaeology and the New Testament.* Grand Rapids: Baker, 1991.

Advanced

Charlesworth, James H., ed. *Jesus and Archaeology.* Grand Rapids and Cambridge: Eerdmans, 2006.
Finegan, Jack. *The Archeology of the New Testament.* Rev. ed. Princeton: Princeton University Press, 1992.
Reed, Jonathan L. *Archaeology and the Galilean Jesus.* Harrisburg: Trinity, 2000.

---

[61] See esp. Barnett, *Jesus and the Logic of History.* Cf. also Jenkins, *Hidden Gospels;* and D. L. Bock, *Dethroning Jesus: Exposing Popular Culture's Quest to Unseat the Biblical Christ* (Nashville: Nelson, 2007).

Other Ancient Sources

Introductory

Bock, Darrell L. *The Missing Gospels: Unearthing the Truth Behind Alternative Christi-anities.* Nashville: Nelson, 2006.

Bock, Darrell L. *Dethroning Jesus: Exposing Popular Culture's Quest to Unseat the Bibli-cal Christ.* Nashville: Nelson, 2007.

Evans, Craig A. *Fabricating Jesus: How Modern Scholars Distort the Gospels.* Downers Grove: IVP, 2006.

France, R. T. *The Evidence for Jesus.* Vancouver: Regent College Press, repr. 2006.

Habermas, Gary R. *The Historical Jesus: Ancient Evidence for the Life of Christ.* Rev. ed. Joplin, MO: College Press, 1996.

Jeremias, Joachim. *Unknown Sayings of Jesus.* Rev. ed. London: SPCK, 1964.

Still, Todd D., ed. *Jesus and Paul Reconnected: Fresh Pathways into an Old Debate.* Grand Rapids and Cambridge: Eerdmans, 2007.

Intermediate

Barnett, Paul W. *Jesus and the Logic of History.* Leicester: Apollos; Downers Grove: IVP, 1997.

Jenkins, Philip. *Hidden Gospels: How the Search for Jesus Lost Its Way.* Oxford and New York: OUP, 2001.

Mason, Steve. *Josephus and the New Testament.* Peabody: Hendrickson, 1992.

Stroker, William D. *Extracanonical Sayings of Jesus.* Atlanta: Scholars, 1989.

van Voorst, Robert E. *Jesus outside the New Testament: An Introduction to the Ancient Evidence.* Grand Rapids and Cambridge: Eerdmans, 2000.

Wenham, David, ed. *Gospel Perspectives.* Vol. 5: *The Jesus Tradition outside the Gospels.* Sheffield: JSOT, 1985; Eugene, OR: Wipf & Stock, 2004.

Wenham, David. *Paul: Follower of Jesus or Founder of Christianity?* Grand Rapids and Cambridge: Eerdmans, 1995.

Advanced

Akenson, Donald H. *Saint Saul: A Skeleton Key to the Historical Jesus.* Oxford and New York: OUP, 2000.

Klijn, A. F. J. *Jewish-Christian Gospel Tradition.* Leiden: Brill, 1992.

Luttikhuizen, Gerard P. *Gnostic Revisions of Genesis Stories and Early Jesus Traditions.* Leiden and Boston: Brill, 2006.

Meier, John P. *A Marginal Jew: Rethinking the Historical Jesus.* Vol. 1. New York and London: Doubleday, 1991.

Schäfer, Peter. *Jesus in the Talmud.* Princeton and Oxford: Princeton University Press, 2007.

Tuckett, Christopher M. *Nag Hammadi and the Gospel Tradition.* Edinburgh: T&T Clark, 1986.

Index

Evans, Craig A., Robert L. Webb, and Richard A. Wiebe. *Nag Hammadi Texts and the Bible: A Synopsis and Index.* Leiden: Brill, 1993.

Bibliography

Evans, Craig A. *Jesus. IBR Bibliographies #5*. Grand Rapids: Baker, 1992.

Questions for Review

1. Itemize each of the main steps in constructing a case for the general historical trustworthiness of the Gospels.
2. Which of these steps seem most persuasive to you? least persuasive? Why? (Give reasons for each evaluation.)
3. What kinds of details in the Gospels can archaeology illuminate? What strikes you as some of the most significant findings discussed in this section? What makes them significant?
4. Summarize the composite picture that results from all the non-Christian evidence for Jesus' existence and life from the earliest centuries of the Common Era (AD).
5. What is the nature of the testimony of post-New Testament Christian sources to Jesus? Break it down in terms of the different main categories of literature?
6. Why does the rest of the New Testament seemingly have so few direct references to the information about Jesus found in the four Gospels? What kind of references do appear and what is their significance?

19

THE THEOLOGY OF JESUS

W E HAVE HAD neither the space nor adequate comparative data to assess the authenticity of every portion of the Gospel tradition by conventional historical criteria. But based on the evidence for the general trustworthiness of the major contours of the Gospels, particularly the Synoptics, and based more specifically on those sayings, deeds, and themes of Jesus' ministry for which good arguments for their reliability can be marshaled, what may we conclude with reasonable probability about Jesus' own agenda and intentions? The answers to this question fall into several broad headings: Jesus announced the arrival of the kingdom, promoted high ethical standards for those who would be his followers, particularly in the area of social concern; and challenged many prevailing interpretations of the Law with a gospel ("good news") that was based fundamentally on his direct understanding of God's will rather than the written Scriptures of Israel (see below, pp. 457–61). While resembling other Jews of his day in a variety of ways, the specific mix of views and claims he put forward meshes neatly with no other known sect or party from the first century. Central to Jesus' distinctives were his convictions that he must die for the sins of the world and be vindicated by a subsequent resurrection and future return to earth in glory. Jesus' self-understanding is disclosed both by implicit claims and actions— suggesting a very high view of himself as God's unique agent mediating God's will to humanity—and by his use of and response to various Christological titles, most notably Son of Man, Son of God, Lord, and Messiah. His reticence to accept acclamation with several of these does not diminish his exalted self-image but reflects conventional stereotypes attached to the titles that did not characterize Jesus' own understanding of his mission. Whether as a historian or as a believer, the diligent student of this first-century Jew from Nazareth is confronted with a man who fits no conventional religious categories.[1] It quickly becomes clear why the Gospel writers (most notably John) and Christians in the next several centuries came to the conviction that Jesus was the unique God-man who made salvation available for all, but who required a response from every person, on which his or her eternal destiny would hinge.

Kingdom

It is widely agreed that the heart of Jesus' authentic message centers on the *kingdom of God* (recall above, pp. 270–71). The expression never appears in the Old Testament, but the concept of God as king and sovereign is pervasive throughout it, especially among the promises to David and in the Book of Daniel. In the intertestamental period, the phrase was frequently used to refer to God's regal power, often in the context of some kind of hope for the restoration of a literal Davidic kingship to Israel. Jesus developed the idea of the kingdom as *the in-breaking of God into history to realize his redemptive purposes* but dissociated his current ministry from the establishment of a politically free Israel. As we have already noted, for Jesus the kingdom was a reign more than a realm, a power rather than a place. Yet, inasmuch as he created a community of his followers, one may speak of the kingdom particularly manifested in the group of disciples that would form the nucleus of the church. Perhaps the English word "dominion" best captures the implied combination of sovereign authority with a group of subjects confessing allegiance to their sovereign.[2]

Jesus' teachings about the kingdom can be variously categorized. E. P. Sanders identifies six groups of sayings, with the kingdom described as (a) a covenant into which one enters; (b) a future entity yet to be fully established; (c) an unexpected coming event separating the righteous from the wicked; (d) the establishment of a recognizable social order; (e) a present experience of Jesus' words and deeds; and (f) a characteristic of God and his reign as kingly.[3] Most scholars simplify the discussion, comparing and contrasting merely *the present and future aspects of God's reign*. This consensus has emerged after several previous periods of scholarship. The nineteenth century's various sociopolitical interpretations of the kingdom gave way to Albert Schweitzer's "consistent eschatology"—the kingdom as entirely future—at the beginning of the twentieth century. In the 1930s, C. H. Dodd swung the pendulum to the opposite extreme, arguing for an entirely "realized eschatology"—the kingdom as fully present. Today, most follow Joachim Jeremias' "eschatology in the process of being realized," and admit both present

---

[1] R. T. France, *Jesus the Radical: A Portrait of the Man They Crucified* (Vancouver: Regent College Press, 1989); idem., *I Came to Set the Earth on Fire: A Portrait of Jesus* (London and Downers Grove: IVP, 1975).

[2] Witherington, *Christology of Jesus*, 197–98.

[3] Sanders, *Jesus and Judaism*, 141–50.

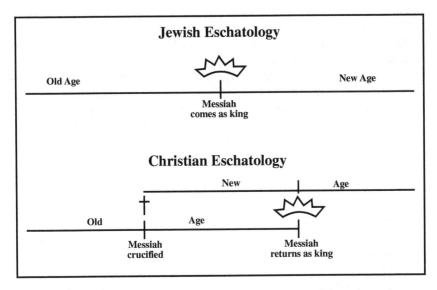

and future dimensions to the kingdom. "Already but not yet" is perhaps the most commonly cited slogan that encapsulates this combination of perspectives.[4]

The future dimensions of the kingdom for Jesus most closely match previous Jewish expectation. The Last Supper foreshadows the messianic banquet envisioned in Isa 25:6–9, which is also depicted in Jesus' parables of feasting (Matt 22:1–14; Luke 14:15–24) and foreshadowed in his table fellowship with sinners.[5] Jesus teaches his disciples to pray for the coming kingdom (Matt 6:10). He promises to give his "little flock" a kingdom, when they will judge the twelve tribes of Israel (Luke 12:32; 22:28–30) and warns the crowds against a belief in its immediate appearance (19:11). He contrasts entering the kingdom with being thrown into hell as two possible future destinies (Mark 9:47). Enjoying God's reign is likened to an inheritance (Matt 5:20) or a future state into which one enters (Matt 25:31–46). It is part of what happens at Judgment Day (Matt 7:21–23; 25:1–13; Luke 21:31).

More striking, however, are the present dimensions of Jesus' teaching on the kingdom, which would have stood out against his Jewish background. The "headline" of his entire ministry is the call to repent because the kingdom of God is at hand or has drawn near (Mark 1:15; Matt 4:23; Luke 4:43). It is bound up with Jesus' ministry of exorcism and the vanquishing of Satan (Luke 9:1; 10:18–19), demonstrating that the kingdom has come upon those in Jesus' audience (Matt 12:28 par.). In Jesus' person, God's reign appears even in the midst of his enemies

---

[4] See the first three chapters in Willis, ed., *The Kingdom of God in 20th Century Interpretation*, 1–52.

[5] See Blomberg, *Contagious Holiness*, 97–163. Cf. also Corley, *Private Women, Public Meals*; P.-B. Smit, *Fellowship and Food in the Kingdom: Eschatological Meals and Scenes of Utopian Abundance in the New Testament* (Tübingen: Mohr Siebeck, 2008).

(Luke 17:20–21). One can enter it, in part at least, already in the present (Luke 16:16), by humbling oneself as a child (Mark 10:15 pars.).[6] Indeed, the kingdom era has been present ever since the ministry of John the Baptist (Matt 11:11–12 par.). More general statements speak also of the fulfillment of prophecy in the ministry of Jesus as a pointer to the arrival of a new era (Luke 4:21; Matt 11:4–6 par.), into which certain Pharisees and scribes prevent many from entering (Matt 23:13). In short, with the coming of Jesus, a new stage of God asserting his power over the cosmos had arrived. God's people, namely Jesus' disciples, were thus given a greater and more permanent empowerment than Israel of old had received. Still, the full purposes of God for us and for the universe await future fulfillment.

Understanding this combination of future and present elements of the kingdom gives us both hope and a certain realism about the Christian life and task. On the one hand, we dare not underestimate how much we can accomplish for God when yielded to his Spirit. He wants to create an outpost or colony of heaven— of the world to come—in our lives individually and corporately now in this age. Thus, we become the salt of the earth and light of the world (Matt 5:14–16). On the other hand, we dare not underestimate the strength of the opposition. We will not Christianize the earth or establish God's righteousness in any wholesale way in this life; that remains for Jesus himself to do after his return.[7]

A related topic involves the expression Jesus uses in Mark 4:11–12 and parallels—the "mystery" of the kingdom. A popular old-line dispensationalist approach that still has widespread influence at the grassroots level imagines that Jesus came to offer a literal, earthly, sociopolitical kingdom to Israel. When the nation rejected that offer, God fell back on "plan B," as it were—the "mystery form of the kingdom"—that is, the multiethnic church. From this point on, Jesus spoke to the crowds only in parables so that they might not understand (Matt 13). But one day, after his return, Jesus will again literally establish Israel as a nation under his kingship.

This view, however, does not do justice to the data of the Gospels, as most contemporary dispensationalist scholars today admit.[8] Jesus came, first of all, to die a redemptive death for humanity; establishing an earthly kingdom for Israel would have short-circuited this necessary prerequisite. In context, the mystery of the kingdom is elucidated by the parables of Mark 4 and Matthew 13 that describe the surprising endings that come from inauspicious beginnings (the so-called parables of growth). Jesus does not speak in parables for the first time here (cf. Matt 7:24–27), while as late as the last week in his life his opponents are still

---

[6] On the recurring theme of "entering the kingdom," see esp. J. Marcus, "Entering into the Kingly Power of God," *JBL* 107 (1988): 663–75. Marcus shows how frequently this expression refers to human participation in God's already present activity in the world.

[7] Remarkably balanced in this respect remains A. Kirk, *A New World Coming* (London: Marshall, Morgan & Scott [= *The Good News of the Kingdom Coming* (Downers Grove: IVP)], 1983).

[8] Se esp. Blaising and Bock, *Progressive Dispensationalism*; R. L. Saucy, *The Case for Progressive Dispensationalism* (Grand Rapids: Zondervan, 1993). For a move back to a more traditional form of dispensationalism on this topic, see M. Saucy, *The Kingdom of God and the Teaching of Jesus: In 20th Century Theology* (Dallas: Word, 1997).

understanding his parabolic claims quite well, at least at the cognitive level (Mark 12:12). Jesus' calling of twelve apostles suggests that he intended to create a "new Israel" out of the community of his followers from the outset. It is best, therefore, to recognize the mystery of the kingdom—the secret now revealed—as nothing more and nothing less than the fact that *the kingdom of God is present in the ministry of Christ but not with irresistible power* (recall above, p. 305).[9]

A final reminder that the kingdom does not refer primarily to a future Jewish realm comes with Paul's use of the expression in letters to predominantly Gentile Christians about the blessings of the Christian life presently available: righteousness, peace, and joy in the Holy Spirit (Rom 14:17); spiritual power (1 Cor 4:20); departure from the kingdom of darkness (Col 1:13); and cooperative work with the apostles (Col 4:11). Yet, to the extent that the vision of the kingdom continues to espouse "utopian" and "theocratic" ideals—a state of perfection in which God reigns fully as king—it must, of course, retain a future dimension as well.[10]

The old supposed distinction between "kingdom of God" and "kingdom of heaven" can no longer withstand careful exegetical scrutiny either. "Heaven" was a well-known Jewish euphemism for "God" (cf., e.g., Luke 15:21). The two expressions are used interchangeably (along with inheriting "eternal life" and being "saved") in Matt 19:23 and 24 (cf. vv. 16, 25). Numerous passages in Matthew (the only Gospel to use "kingdom of heaven") are exactly paralleled in Mark or Luke with no substantive differences save the expression "kingdom of God" (cf., e.g., Matt 4:17 with Mark 1:14–15; Matt 5:3 with Luke 6:20; Matt 8:11 with Luke 13:29; Matt 13:11 with Mark 4:11; Matt 13:31 with Mark 4:30; Matt 19:14 with Mark 10:14; and Matt 19:23 with Mark 10:23).[11]

The kingdom of God (or heaven) is thus not identical to the church—*the kingdom is a power; the church is a people*. That explains how Jesus can describe the field in the parable of the wheat and the weeds alternately as the "world" and the "kingdom" (Matt 13:38, 41). God's sovereign power extends over all the cosmos, even though not all persons and powers in the universe yet acknowledge that fact. But there remains substantial overlap between the two entities, inasmuch as the church is the collection of persons who individually submit to God's reign. "Until Christ returns, every local church is a visible manifestation of the kingdom, a precursor to his rule and reign over all creation," while each "believer is an example and ambassador of the kingdom to the world, and this responsibility should guide his conduct accordingly."[12] Ladd aptly summarizes the relationship between church and kingdom under five headings: the church is not the kingdom;

---

[9] Against the postponed kingdom theory more generally, see G. E. Ladd, *Crucial Questions about the Kingdom of God* (Grand Rapids: Eerdmans, 1952), 101–17.

[10] M. A. Beavis, "The Kingdom of God, 'Utopia' and 'Theocracy'," *JSHJ* 2 (2004): 91–106.

[11] Indeed, in 19:16–30 five different expressions are used virtually interchangeably: "kingdom of heaven," "kingdom of God," "eternal life," being "perfect," and being "saved." See Turner, *Matthew*, 472–73.

[12] K. Keathley, "The Work of God: Salvation," in *A Theology for the Church*, ed. D. L. Akin (Nashville: B & H, 2007), 763. Cf. I. H. Marshall, "The Hope of a New Age: The Kingdom of God in the New Testament," *Them* 11 (1985): 5–15.

the kingdom creates the church; the church witnesses to the kingdom; the church is the instrument of the kingdom; and the church is the custodian of the kingdom. He also notes the resultant picture of the God of this kingdom: a father who seeks, invites, and yet judges.[13]

Ethics

General Principles

The combination of petitions in the Lord's Prayer, "Thy kingdom come, thy will be done," shows how closely the topics of kingdom and ethics are related. God's kingly rule is fully established on earth precisely when his righteous standards are implemented. The ethics of the kingdom thus refer to *the accomplishment of God's will in every area of life*. The believers' task is to seek first his kingdom and its righteousness (or justice);[14] then all their needs will be met (Matt 6:33 par.).

Does this then lead to works-righteousness? There are two seemingly competing strands of thought in Jesus' teaching about his followers' behavior. On the one hand, many passages command us to do good—to pursue righteousness, live a life of discipleship, and imitate Jesus. The Sermon on the Mount is summed up in the righteousness demanded of us that is greater than that exhibited by the Jewish leaders (Matt 5:20). We are told to enter by the narrow gate, anticipating the stringency of this life of discipleship (Matt 7:13). God's forgiveness of us is in some way contingent on our forgiveness of others (Matt 6:12, 14–15). We must be prepared to sacrifice everything (Matt 13:44–46) in unqualified commitment to the gospel (Luke 14:25–33).

On the other hand, Jesus makes it equally clear that a life of discipleship is a life of faith. The starting point is repentance that leads to belief in the good news Jesus preaches (Mark 1:15). We confess this belief publicly (Luke 12:3) and receive God's kingdom as a gift (v. 32). Frequently, Jesus praises the faith of those who come in trust to him—most notably the centurion with a sick servant (Matt 8:10), but also several others who believe Jesus can heal them or their loved ones (Matt 9:22, 29; 15:28). Indeed, the refrain "your faith has made you whole" appears in four different contexts in the Gospels to refer to a combination of physical and spiritual healing (Mark 5:34 pars.; Mark 10:52 par.; Luke 7:50; 17:19).[15] The little parable of the unprofitable servant beautifully summarizes a theology of grace (Luke 17:7–10), while the story of the Pharisee and tax collector anticipates Pauline language about justification by faith (18:9–14). The parable of the laborers in the vineyard makes it clear that believers do not work for a wage and that heavenly reward is the great equalizer, but it is the equality of perfection!

---

[13] Ladd, *A Theology of the New Testament*, rev. and ed. D. A. Hagner, 109–17, 80–88. Cf. also R. Bauckham, "Kingdom and Church according to Jesus and Paul," *HBT* 18 (1996): 1–26.

[14] On the frequent interchangeability of these terms as translations for one and the same Greek word, see E. Tamez, *The Amnesty of Grace: Justification by Faith from a Latin American Perspective* (Nashville: Abingdon, 1993).

[15] For elaboration, see Blomberg, "'Your Faith Has Made You Whole'," 75–93.

Conversely, "we are all the eleventh-hour workers; to change the metaphor, we are all honored guests of God in the kingdom. . . . The point of the parable—both at the level of Jesus and the level of Matthew's Gospel—is that God saves by grace, not by our worthiness."[16] Finally, the thief on the cross stands as the crowning example of one who didn't have time to do good works by which he might try to merit salvation.

How do we resolve the potential tension between these two strands of texts from Jesus? Precisely by recognizing the context of the demands Jesus makes. In most instances, as with the Sermon on the Mount, these are addressed primarily to those who have already begun to follow him in discipleship. Character precedes conduct (Matt 7:16–20). Recognition of the forgiveness God gives enables us to forgive others (Luke 6:36; Matt 18:23–35). The greater righteousness Christ demands is not an entrance requirement to get into the kingdom but *a lifestyle characteristic that God enables those who come to him in Christ increasingly to approximate.*[17] Thus, paradoxically, he can speak of his requirements as an easy yoke and a light burden (Matt 11:30). The foundational motive for obeying Jesus thus becomes one of profound gratitude for what he has done for us that we could never have performed or deserved on our own. This leads to a radical commitment, a renunciation of our own rights (Mark 8:34–38 pars.), where the only rewards that are given are to those who are not looking for them (Luke 14:7–14).

The centerpiece of Jesus' ethic is love: the twofold command to love God and neighbor (Mark 12:29–31 par.) and the reminder that neighbors include even our enemies (Luke 10:25–37; cf. Luke 6:35). The gospel calls us to confront all tribalism, nationalism, or ethnocentrism that would value allegiance to human groups above cross-cultural *agapē* for all people and especially all fellow Christians. Unlike various negative prohibitions, the positive command to love can never be said to have been perfectly kept. Modeling our love upon God's leads us to reject every form of judgmentalism (Matt 7:1) and to treat others exactly as we, in our best moments, would want to be treated (v. 12). Whether or not enemy-love leads to full-fledged pacifism, it certainly should stir us to move heaven and earth proactively to promote "just peacemaking," that is, doing everything within our power to reconcile alienated persons to God and to one another, and to prevent interpersonal and inter-group alienation in the first place.[18] In short, our lives are lived in loving service for others, at the risk of suffering and, if necessary, to the point of death (John 15:12–13).

Numerous topics receive concentrated focus in Jesus' ethical teaching. One involves "family values."[19] On the one hand we are commanded to unswerving,

---

[16] Hultgren, *Parables of Jesus*, 43.

[17] Cf. esp. A. P. Stanley, *Did Jesus Teach Salvation by Works? The Role of Works in Salvation in the Synoptic Gospels* (Eugene, OR: Pickwick, 2006).

[18] Again, see esp. Stassen, *Just Peacemaking: Transforming Initiatives for Justice and Peace*. Cf. also M. Volf, "Christianity and Violence," in *War in the Bible and Terrorism in the Twenty-First Century*, ed. R. S. Hess and E. A. Martens (Winona Lake, IN: Eisenbrauns, 2008), 1–17.

[19] See esp. Barton, *Discipleship and Family Ties in Mark and Matthew*. Cf. also Westfall, "Family in the Gospels and Acts."

lifelong loyalty and faithfulness to our spouses and children if we have them. Jesus gives wives and children a dignity unparalleled in his culture (Mark 10:1–16 pars.). On the other hand, our love for our families is to seem like hate in comparison with our love for God (Luke 14:26 par., Mark 3:31–35 pars.), and singleness may also be a gift from God (Matt 19:10–12). Other topics that receive extended attention include personal integrity (Matt 5:33–37; 7:1–6; 23:1–39); bold, persistent, faith-filled prayer (Luke 11:1–13; 18:1–14; Mark 11:22–25); humility, considered more a vice than a virtue in Greco-Roman society (Matt 18:1–5; Mark 9:33–37; 10:13–16; Luke 17:7–10);[20] paying taxes, though neither Jewish nor Roman claims may be considered absolute (Matt 17:24–27; Mark 12:13–17 pars.); and rejecting the Jewish rituals that served as badges of national identity (see below, p. 458). Eclipsing all these is a cluster of topics united under the theme of social concern: mercy, justice, stewardship, and the like.

Social Concern

Jesus was never overtly political in the sense that he attempted to wield or usurp earthly power or promote a particular political party or socioeconomic program. When his followers tried by force to make him king, he fled (John 6:15). When his teachings about preparation for danger were misinterpreted in Gethsemane, he healed the wound that Peter's sword had inflicted (Luke 22:51). Although he cleared the temple, this was a small-scale protest with no lasting effect, intended more to portend the temple's doom than create systemic change. Hence, he was neither a social revolutionary nor a reformer in the contemporary senses of those terms.[21] Partly, this was because he knew the climactic focus of his mission was to die for the sins of the world, but partly it was also because he was too radical to settle for a merely structural reform. He knew regenerated hearts were the prerequisite to lasting social or economic redistribution of resources. Nevertheless, he called his listeners to observe the weightier matters of the Law, which he defined, as in Mic. 6:8, as justice, mercy, and faithfulness (Matt 23:23)—the epitome of social concern. We misrepresent his ethic of nonviolence and nonretaliation if we label it one of passivity; he is better likened to the Old Testament prophets whose strong denunciations of the injustice they saw called on others to practice God's righteous standards.[22]

In rejecting institutional power, Jesus called on his followers to lead, not in the authoritarian fashion of the Roman world around them but as servants (Luke 22:25–27). He promoted "the upside-down kingdom,"[23] seeking to save the lost and outcast of his society and calling his followers to do the same. Nevertheless, he never endorsed the state uncritically (cf. his two major injunctions on the Jew-

---

[20] Evans, "Jesus' Ethic of Humility," 127–38.

[21] M. F. Bird, "Jesus and the Revolutionaries: Did Jesus Call Israel to Repent of Nationalistic Ambitions?" *Colloquium* 38 (2006): 127–39.

[22] See, e.g., W. Wink, "Neither Passivity nor Violence: Jesus' Third Way (Matt. 5:38–42/Luke 6:29–30)," *Forum* 7 (1991): 5–28.

[23] The title of an outstanding little book on the topic by D. B. Kraybill rev. ed. (Scottdale. PA: Herald, 2003).

ish and Roman tax just noted). He saw the possibility of lasting change for the better in this world not through government, not even through individuals, but through the collective body of his followers that came to be known as the church. Hauerwas and Willimon put it succinctly: "The church does not have a social strategy, the church is a social strategy."[24] In the history of Protestantism, we have seen attempts at creating a Christian state (esp. through Calvinism) and a focus on individual repentance and Christian living (esp. through Lutheranism), but it is the Anabaptist vision of *the church corporately as the model of implementing the ethics of God's kingdom* that may best approximate the contexts and intentions of Jesus' teachings.[25]

In his world, Jesus' position was a *via media* between the pietistic retreatism of the Essenes and the revolutionary fervor of the Zealots. In his objectives he was probably closest to the Pharisees—wanting people to live their entire lives by God's will—but Jesus' methods differed sharply. Although the categories are Paul's, they fit Jesus' life as well: empowerment not by the Law but by the Spirit. When any community catches the vision for the possibilities of living this way, the established political and religious leaders will often be threatened because their impotence to create similar improvements is highlighted by contrast.[26]

Mercy and justice were key concerns throughout Christ's life. John's and Jesus' ministries had been predicted to be ones of reconstituting Israel along the lines of these attributes (Luke 1:17, 50, 72), and John's own teaching on these topics ultimately cost him his life (Luke 3:10–14, 19). Jesus' inaugural sermon in Nazareth outlined his manifesto: good news to the poor, release to the captives, sight to the blind, liberty to the oppressed, and a declaration of the year of jubilee (Luke 4:16–21). His holistic ministry of healing spirit and body concentrated in particular on the social outcast, the poor, Samaritans, Gentiles, women, children, and the sick (especially the "untouchable" lepers). His parables highlighted God's grace and mercy (Luke 15:1–32) but also God's desire for social justice (Luke 18:1–8) that transcends all cultural distinctions (Luke 10:25–37; John 4:1–42).[27]

Yet the area about which he taught most was that of *stewardship of our material possessions.*[28] One cannot serve both God and money (Matt 6:19–34 par.).

---

[24] S. Hauerwas and W. H. Willimon, *Resident Aliens: Life in the Christian Colony* (Nashville: Abingdon, 1989), 43.

[25] In addition to works cited earlier in the volume, see esp. A. Trocmé, *Jesus and the Nonviolent Revolution*, rev. and ed. C. E. Moore (Maryknoll: Orbis, 2004); and W. Swartley, *Covenant of Peace: The Missing Peace in New Testament Theology and Ethics* (Grand Rapids and Cambridge: Eerdmans, 2006).

[26] A key theme, e.g., throughout the works of R. A. Horsley. See esp. his *The Kingdom of God and the New World Disorder* (Minneapolis: Fortress, 2003).

[27] See further Herzog, *Jesus, Justice and the Reign of God.*

[28] On which, see further Blomberg, *Neither Poverty nor Riches*, 111–46. Cf. esp. S. E. Wheeler, *Wealth as Peril and Obligation: The New Testament on Possessions* (Grand Rapids: Eerdmans, 1995), 39–72; A. J. Köstenberger, "Will a Man Rob God? (Malachi 3:8): A Study of Tithing in the Old and New Testaments," *BBR* 16 (2006): 53–77; and A. J. Köstenberger and D. A. Croteau, "Reconstructing a Biblical Model for Giving: A Discussion of Relevant Systematic Issues and New Testament Principles," *BBR* 16 (2006): 237–60.

Blessed are those materially poor whose poverty drives them to utter dependence on God (Luke 6:20; Matt 5:3). Beware of covetousness or needless accumulation of wealth (Luke 12:13–21) and of living in luxury while the poor of the world go begging (Luke 16:19–31). Use worldly wealth for eternal purposes (Luke 16:1–13). No fixed percentage for giving is established (recall the trio of passages in Luke 18:18–30; 19:1–10, 11–27), but in every instance all possessions are ultimately the Lord's. Doubtless the most haunting question of all comes in Mark 8:36: "What good is it for a man to gain the whole world, yet forfeit his soul?" (NIV).

Implementing Jesus' kingdom ethics, especially his ethics of social concern, particularly in a modern democratic society unlike the first-century Roman world, requires considerable sensitivity and sophistication. Surely, we have the right and responsibility as much as anyone to pursue what we believe will promote our "common good," but we dare never count on legislation or political parties to accomplish what only God's people functioning as the church can do. We must seek a completely pro-life agenda, trying to prevent abortion and to avoid endorsing sexual sin or glamorizing dysfunctional family life, but at the same time we must work for the best quality of life for those already born, including adequate health care for the poor, housing for the homeless, jobs for the unemployed, fair treatment for immigrants, and positive alternatives for those lured by a life of crime.[29] We must demonstrate genuine concern for the rape of the environment, which is also God's creation. In societies, including our own, where racism, sexism, classism, and ethnocentrism still alienate millions of people from one another and do not give everyone equal opportunities for basic human rights, we must oppose injustice and promote the liberation of the oppressed. But we dare never assume that these are ends in themselves, lest people gain earthly freedoms without being prepared for eternity by being followers of Jesus Christ.[30]

In short, implementing Jesus' ethics requires walking the fine line between legalism and license. Too often those who would apply Jesus' moral instruction fall down on one side or the other—"teaching a rigorist ethic with extreme demands which seem condemnatory and alienate people from the church" or "having an open acceptance of sinners and being accused of having no ethics at all!" Instead, "seeking to follow Jesus" requires the uneasy balance between "becoming both 'perfect' and 'merciful' as God is perfect and merciful."[31]

---

[29] Cf. R. J. Sider, *Completely Pro-Life* (Downers Grove: IVP, 1987); idem., *The Scandal of Evangelical Politics: Why Christians Are Missing the Chance to Really Change the World* (Grand Rapids: Baker, 2008); D. P. Gushee, *The Future of Faith in American Politics: The Public Witness of the Evangelical Center* (Waco: Baylor University Press, 2008).

[30] Cf. R. J. Sider, *One-Sided Christianity? Uniting the Church to Heal a Lost and Broken World* (Grand Rapids: Zondervan, 1993); and B. J. Nicholls and B. R. Wood, eds., *Sharing the Good News with the Poor: A Reader for Concerned Christians* (Carlisle: Paternoster; Grand Rapids: Baker, 1996).

[31] R. A. Burridge, *Imitating Jesus: An Inclusive Approach to New Testament Ethics* (Grand Rapids and Cambridge: Eerdmans, 2007), 79.

Law and Gospel

It is clear from our discussions throughout this book that all of Jesus' ethical teachings need to be understood in their historical context. All contain timeless principles, but not all may be applied in our world today in the identical way they were in his. But what of the relationship between Jesus' teaching and the Old Testament Scriptures? Here, too, radical changes took place. Although Jesus clearly stands for various abiding moral absolutes, he has not given us a new Law. Although many of the principles of the Torah carry over into the New Testament age, we cannot take any command of Moses and assume that it applies to believers until we understand how it has been fulfilled in Christ (recall above, p. 289).[32] It is striking how rarely Jesus ever invokes the Hebrew Scriptures as his authority; indeed, most of the time he cites the Old Testament merely as a foil or contrast for his own teaching! All of these observations now require some unpacking.

The relationship between Jesus' teaching and Old Testament Law has been variously categorized. Some have, indeed, spoken of him creating a new law; others, of him abrogating the old. Mediating positions suggest that Jesus transcends, expounds, obeys, radicalizes, intensifies, or internalizes the Law. All of these approaches can find support in certain passages but run afoul of others. The most consistent and valid approach would seem to follow from Jesus' own words in Matt 5:17: *he came to fulfill the Law*—"by teaching the eschatological will of God which the Law anticipated."[33] For the Christian to apply any passage of the Old Testament today requires filtering it through the grid of how Jesus' teaching and ministry did or did not change the nature of God's demands on his people.[34]

Jesus' appeals to the Old Testament are neither systematic nor anything like a representative cross-section of its contents. We have noted above that in the six antitheses of the Sermon on the Mount (Matt 5:21–48), he internalizes and intensifies the commands about murder, adultery, and enemy love, yet seemingly abrogates certain parts of the stipulations about divorce, oaths, and retaliation (pp. 290–91). In every case, however, Jesus shows himself to be the Law's sovereign and authoritative interpreter (cf. 7:28–29). There is no evidence that Jesus ever actually broke one of the written laws of the Pentateuch or taught others to do so, but still the impression we get is more one of discontinuity than of continuity between the Law and the gospel. Certainly he challenged the better part of the "traditions of the elders," so dear to the Pharisees. Those areas in which he seemingly kept various parts of the oral law—specific features of synagogue attendance and festival pilgrimage, the wearing of the fringes, and various prayers and postures at mealtimes—seem to involve standard Jewish custom more than adherence to dis-

---

[32] In addition to the literature already cited, see F. Thielman, *The Law and the New Testament: The Question of Continuity* (New York: Crossroad, 1999), 47–110; T. Holmén, *Jesus and Jewish Covenant Thinking* (Leiden: Brill, 2001); and P. G. Nelson, "Christian Morality: Jesus' Teaching on the Law," *Them* 32 (2006): 4–17.

[33] Moo, "Jesus and the Authority of the Mosaic Law," 3–49.

[34] Cf. also D. A. Dorsey, "The Use of the Old Testament Law in the Christian Life: A Theocentric Approach," *EJ* 17 (1998): 1–19; and J. P. Meier, "The Historical Jesus and the Historical Law: Some Problems within the Problem," *CBQ* 65 (2003): 52–79.

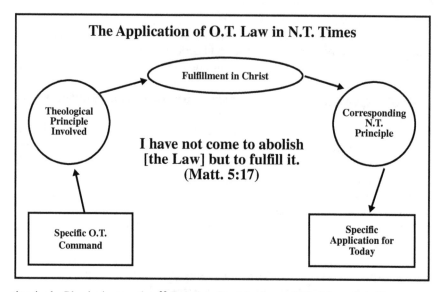

The Application of O.T. Law in N.T. Times

Fulfillment in Christ

Theological
Principle
Involved

Corresponding
N.T.
Principle

**I have not come to abolish
[the Law] but to fulfill it.
(Matt. 5:17)**

Specific O.T.
Command

Specific
Application for
Today

tinctively Pharisaic practice.[35] But the ritual badges of Jewish nationalism came under strong attack, particularly the Sabbath and kosher laws, along with other traditions that ostracized certain persons and kept them as second-class citizens.

Jesus' teachings concerning the Sabbath are particularly important because this command was one of the "Ten Commandments" on which all the others rested. It will not do simply to say that Jesus complained about the abuse of the spirit of the Sabbath by the nitpicking Pharisaical halakah, for he appeals to more foundational principles in his criticism: "The Sabbath was made for humankind" (Mark 2:27 NRSV), "The Son of Man is Lord even of the Sabbath" (v. 28), and "It is lawful to do good on the Sabbath" (Matt 12:12). Christians in the coming generation would interpret Jesus as having abolished the need for a mandatory day of the week in which they had to stop working. The Sabbath was fulfilled as they rested "in Christ" throughout their Christian lives (Col 2:16–17; Heb 4:1–11). Matthew 11:28–30 may well have set the precedent for this perspective. *Christian* Sabbatarianism—the legislated cessation of work one day in seven—would not emerge until after Constantine made Christianity a legal religion three centuries later; earlier Christian writers often referred to Sabbath observance as Judaizing![36]

The same kind of far-reaching implications stem from Jesus' treatment of handwashing, kosher, and corban laws (Mark 7:1–23 par.). Mark clearly believed that the later Christian conviction that all foods (and therefore all people) were

---

[35] Jesus' observation of customary Jewish ritual did not arise from an attitude of reverence or lack of reverence to the practices themselves. It derives from the compatibility or incompatibility of each with the purposes of his mission. See Banks, *Jesus and the Law in the Synoptic Tradition*, 237.

[36] See further C. L. Blomberg, "The Fulfillment View," in *Perspectives on the Sabbath*, ed. C. Donato. Cf. idem., "The Sabbath as Fulfilled in Christ," in *The Sabbath in Jewish and Christian Traditions*, ed. T. Eskenazi, D. Harrington, and W. Shea (Denver: Denver University Center for Judaic Studies, 1991), 122–28.

now clean stemmed from Jesus' own mandate in these controversies with the Jewish leaders, however poorly understood the implications may have been at the time (v. 19b).[37] Jesus seems even to go out of his way to provoke such controversies, deliberately healing people on the Sabbath whose lives were not at risk (Mark 3:1–6 pars.; Luke 13:10–17; 14:1–6; John 5:1–18; 9:1–41), associating and eating with the ritually unclean in ways that scandalized the scribes and Pharisees (Mark 2:13–17 pars.; Luke 7:36–50; 19:1–10), and touching a leper to heal him when a spoken word might have sufficed (Mark 1:40–45 pars.). The attitude that enabled Jesus to act in such a "cavalier" fashion was apparently a very exalted self-image: "one greater than the temple is here" (Matt 12:6).

The Gospel writers, too, regularly see the events of Jesus' life as the fulfillment of Scripture, particularly in the clusters of details surrounding his birth and death. Occasionally, these are the relatively direct fulfillments of straightforward prediction (the birth in Bethlehem or the triumphal entry), but more often than not they employ typology (see above, p. 234). Jesus is likened—though viewed as superior—to Jonah, Solomon, David, the priesthood, Elijah and Elisha, and Israel as a whole (esp. in his temptations, suffering, and resurrection on the third day). Disciples are viewed typologically, too, as in the employment of Ps 37:11 in Matt 5:5; the same is true of Jesus' opponents (cf. Mark 4:12 with Isa 6:9–10). Jesus' messianic image is taken from Scripture as well—the Good Shepherd, the Son of Man, the Suffering Servant.[38]

At least some of the inspiration for the evangelists' use of Scripture came from Jesus himself. Among the more indisputably authentic parts of the Jesus-tradition are the parable of the wicked tenants (Mark 12:1–12, reapplying Isaiah's vineyard metaphor—Isa 5:1–7), his question about how David's son could also be his lord (Mark 12:35–37, based on Ps 110:1), and his summary of the heart of the Law with the double love-command (Mark 12:28–34, citing Deut 6:4–5 and Lev 19:18). Often his use of the Old Testament is creative and polemical—finding the resurrection in the Pentateuch (Mark 12:26–27, citing Exod 3:6), labeling the temple a den of robbers (Mark 11:17, citing Jer 7:11), or reapplying Daniel's "abomination of desolation" to the destruction of that very edifice (Mark 13 pars.).[39]

So, too, the *form* of Jesus' teaching often closely approximates standard Jewish conventions, even while the *contents* may vary noticeably.[40] Thus Christ uses

---

[37] "In vv. 6–13 Jesus equated the Mosaic law with God's word and scolded the Pharisees for nullifying God's Word with their tradition. Now Jesus himself is nullifying God's word with regard to food. But it is the prerogative of Jesus as God's Son to change the Law. Such a change does not count as human tradition, for Jesus' word is divine." (Gundry, *Mark*, 356).

[38] For a classic treatment of the various direct and typological uses of the Old Testament, see R. T. France, *Jesus and the Old Testament* (London: Tyndale; Downers Grove: IVP, 1971; Grand Rapids: Baker, 1982; Vancouver: Regent College Press, 1992). Cf. also the articles on the various Gospels in S. E. Porter, ed., *Hearing the Old Testament in the New Testament* (Grand Rapids and Cambridge: Eerdmans, 2006).

[39] See further E. B. Powery, *Jesus Reads Scripture: The Function of Jesus' Use of Scripture in the Synoptic Gospels* (Leiden and Boston: Brill, 2003).

[40] See, e.g., Gerhardsson, *Reliability of the Gospel Tradition*, 42–46.

a large array of Jewish exegetical techniques, prefers parables and related meta-phors, and interprets Scriptures as messianic that usually have some Jewish prec-edent of being taken this way, even if only among a minority of interpreters. Yet, the heart of his message is not the exegesis of Scripture but the announcement of the arrival of God's reign and his Messiah. And the nature of his ethical teach-ings differs radically from law, which is characterized by apodictic or casuistic rules and regulations.[41] Strikingly, it is seldom possible to claim that (or even to know if) one has obeyed one of Jesus' mandates because of its open-ended, wide-ranging, principial nature—love your enemies, do good on the Sabbath, use your money for kingdom purposes, and so on. To the extent that Jesus has brought a new covenant "written on the heart," formerly external statutes have been internal-ized. To the extent that Jesus brought a new empowerment—the Holy Spirit—the laws have become personalized. Thus Douglas Moo can define the "law of Christ" (as in Gal 6:2) as not "legal prescriptions and ordinances," but "the teaching and example of Jesus and the apostles, the central demonstration of love, and the guid-ing influence of the indwelling Holy Spirit."[42]

Yet, although no teaching of Jesus is ever called *nomos* (law) in the Gospels, his ethical instructions are referred to, especially in John, as *entolai* (command-ments). Jesus still believes in moral absolutes. As Stephen Westerholm explains, Jesus "found the will of God not in statutes but in a heart in tune with the divine purposes." Nevertheless, "certain activities are in themselves so utterly opposed to the divine intention that it is impossible for one whose heart is sensitive to it to engage in them."[43] Still, these activities are not the external dos and don'ts of so many contemporary "Christian" lists, but foundational principles such as spouses loving each other their whole lives long, consistent stewardship of one's treasures, and reconciling previously estranged groups of people, especially within Chris-tian fellowship.

It is clear, finally, that Jesus' attitude to the Law cannot be summed up *merely* in the popular Christian categorization that alleges he kept the moral law while abolishing the ceremonial or civil law, good as those subdivisions may be for a start. But Jesus continues to be concerned for every arena of life—he, too, pro-moted rituals or ceremonies (baptism and the Lord's Supper) and recognized a legitimate role for governments (in levying taxes). In overturning a literal imple-mentation of the Sabbath, he challenged a cherished portion of Israel's moral law, yet the gospel is fundamentally moral itself. On the other hand, one can, with Jesus, speak of weightier matters of the Law that should be given priority—jus-tice, mercy, and faithfulness (Matt 23:23). So, in the end, there is profound truth to

---

[41] Apodictic laws are the "thou shalts" and "thou shalt nots"—straightforward, generalized com-mands and prohibitions. Casuistic laws, usually phrased in conditional sentences, refer to what to do in specific cases—"if such-and-such happens, then do this-or-that."

[42] D. J. Moo, "The Law of Christ as the Fulfillment of the Law of Moses: A Modified Lutheran View," in *Five Views on Law and Gospel*, ed. W. G. Strickland, rev. ed. (Grand Rapids: Zondervan, 1996), 343. This book, more generally, is an outstanding tool for comparing five major Christian approaches to the relationship between law and gospel.

[43] Stephen Westerholm, *Jesus and Scribal Authority* (Lund: Gleerup, 1978), 91, 124.

the saying made famous by Augustine, Luther, and many others that the demands of the gospel boil down to "love God and do as you please." When one truly loves God, having been born again and choosing to yield oneself to the empowerment of the Spirit, the instruction of the believing community, and the voice of conscience, one will do what pleases him.[44]

Jesus and Judaism

The previous section has already pointed out several similarities and differences between Jesus and other Jews of his day. The topic deserves further attention, however. The last generation of scholarship has seen a considerable resurgence of interest by both Christian and Jewish scholars in the topic, "Jesus the Jew."[45] A renewed scrutiny of ancient Jewish literature, coupled with a flurry of archaeological discoveries, has increasingly demonstrated the diversity of Judaism in the time of Jesus. On the one hand, it has become clear just how thoroughly Jewish Jesus and his disciples were. Hebrew or Aramaic idiom can be reconstructed behind a substantial percentage of Jesus' teachings. Christ used many of the identical teaching methods and observed many of the same customs of his culture. Parallels to numerous individual teachings of Jesus can be found in other Jewish literature, and, as noted above (p. 211), his itinerant ministry of healing resembled that of various other "charismatic" Jewish miracle-workers and exorcists of his day.[46] Our appreciation of how previous Christian portrayals of the Pharisees and other Jewish leaders have often relied on caricature and overgeneralization (above, pp. 50–51) also helps to narrow the gap between Jesus and other Jewish teachers of his time.

A considerable amount of Jesus-scholarship narrows this gap further, however, by jettisoning substantial portions of the Gospels as inauthentic. If one accepts the general trustworthiness of the gospel tradition, we must admit significant differences between Jesus and his contemporaries as well. Not only did he make indirect and direct messianic claims, in and of themselves not always unique, but he also linked himself with God as his Father more closely than most of the religious leadership could tolerate (see below, pp. 467–77). Yet Jewish monotheism was defined flexibly enough at that stage to permit even this, in principle, which explains how Jesus came to have any Jewish followers at all (recall p. 46).

The way for scholarship to progress in this arena is to recognize that one can accept the Gospels' portrait of Jesus as it stands and still see Jesus as thoroughly Jewish, however unconventional or surprising a form of Judaism he at times mani-

---

[44] See further W. C. Reuschling, *Reviving Evangelical Ethics: The Promises and Pitfalls of Classic Models of Morality* (Grand Rapids: Brazos, 2008).

[45] In addition to literature cited in earlier footnotes, see D. A. Hagner, *The Jewish Reclamation of Jesus* (Grand Rapids: Zondervan, 1984; Eugene, OR: Wipf & Stock, 1997); J. H. Charlesworth, *Jesus' Jewishness* (New York: Crossroad, 1991); and B. H. Young, *Jesus the Jewish Theologian* (Peabody: Hendrickson, 1995).

[46] I. Zeitlin (*Jesus and the Judaism of His Time* [Oxford: Blackwell, 1988], 61) uses the label "charismatic religious virtuoso." Cf. further G. Vermes, *Jesus in His Jewish Context*, rev. ed. (Minneapolis: Fortress, 2003).

fested. There is no evidence that Jesus ever intended to found a new religion. But he certainly did intend to shatter the ethnocentric boundaries of his day, to set the stage for the Gentile mission, in keeping with the Old Testament theme of Israel as a light to the nations (Isa 42:6), which began already with the promise to Abraham that by his seed all nations would be blessed (Gen 12:1–3).[47] Indeed, a considerable impetus for the "parting of the ways" between Judaism and early Christianity came after the destruction of the temple—as Rabbinic Judaism began to emerge from the Pharisaic movement as the sole, main survivor among the much greater diversity of pre-70 Judaisms, and was noticeably less willing to accept the Jesus-movement as an authentic expression of Judaism than many pre-70 Jews (including Christian Jews) had been.[48]

How did Jesus compare with the various Jewish sects? There are similarities and differences with each, as well as scholars who have attempted to identify Jesus with each. Possible links with *Essenism* include Jesus' techniques of biblical interpretation, apocalyptic focus, rejection of the rest of Judaism as corrupt, dissociation from the temple, and formation of a new community as the true Israel carrying out the will of God. Yet Jesus' emphases directly opposed the Essenes' austerity, monasticism, and passion for the Law.[49]

Was Jesus a *Zealot*?[50] It is true he gathered his followers in the wilderness, had a Zealot (Simon) as a follower, staged a triumphal entry to Jerusalem, and told them to take up swords and expect opposition, but too many differences remain for this identification to work either. His ethic was one of nonviolence: he healed Malchus' wound after Peter attacked him in Gethsemane, adopted no overtly political strategies or agendas (see above, p. 454), taught consistently about suffering and self-renunciation, and gave his life rather than fight back.

What about the *Sadducees*? In common with them, Jesus rejected the oral Torah and believed in the abiding authority of the written Scriptures. Presumably, this is why later Christians (esp. the author of Hebrews) saw the need for a literal sacrifice for sins when Pharisaism/early Rabbinic Judaism substituted prayer, repentance, and good works. Christ also saw the coming demise of the current temple, which no Sadducee could have welcomed, and sought to abolish nationalism (esp. in John 4) and the badges of religious ethnocentrism that went along with it.

---

[47] See esp. M. F. Bird, *Jesus and the Origins of the Gentile Mission* (London and New York: T&T Clark, 2006); Schnabel, *Early Christian Mission*, vol. 1: *Jesus and the Twelve*.

[48] See esp. J. D. G. Dunn, *The Parting of the Ways between Christianity and Judaism and Their Significance for the Character of Christianity* (London: SCM; Philadelphia: Trinity, 1991); idem., ed., *Jews and Christians: The Parting of the Ways, A.D. 70–135*, rev. ed. (Grand Rapids and Cambridge: Eerdmans, 1999); and D. Klinghoffer, *Why the Jews Rejected Jesus: The Turning Point in Western History* (New York and London: Doubleday, 2005).

[49] See further H. Stegemann, *Library of Qumran: On the Essenes, Qumran, John the Baptist, and Jesus* (Grand Rapids: Eerdmans; Leiden: Brill, 1998).

[50] By far and away the most famous attempt to make this case remains S. G. F. Brandon, *Jesus and the Zealots* (Manchester: Manchester University Press, 1967).

Paradoxically, it was probably the *Pharisaic* movement, with whom Jesus was most at odds, that he also most closely resembled.[51] Both Jesus and the Pharisees had a passionate commitment to apply God's will to every area of life. Jesus' teachings focused on the same topics the Pharisees debated. Sometimes he resembled the more conservative Shammai (as on the divorce question); other times he echoed the words of the more liberal Hillel (as with the double love-command and "golden rule"). With the Pharisees and against the Sadducees, he believed in the resurrection and in angels. But again, Jesus' ethics were not Law-centered. Against all the major Jewish sects, Jesus focused far more on morality than on ritual, announced the arrival of the kingdom, stressed love for *all* peoples, even one's enemies, and claimed that he was the Messiah who was one with God.[52]

In this post-holocaust age, Christians and Jews are (or should be) very sensitive about anything that smacks of anti-Semitism. Was Jesus (or any Gospel writer) anti-Semitic? There are certainly harsh invectives against various Jewish individuals and even wholesale broadsides against "the Jews," especially in the Fourth Gospel. We have already commented on this problem in conjunction with specific texts and themes above (e.g., p. 373). By way of review and synthesis, however, it is important to stress that: (1) Nothing in the Gospels is any stronger than the denunciatory polemic canonized in the Hebrew Scriptures, particularly in the Prophets, by various Jewish spokesmen against their own people. (2) Jesus and the evangelists are in-house critics; this is an *intra*-Jewish debate as to which forms of religion may or may not still call themselves Jewish and comprise the true people of God. (3) It is not anti-Semitic to claim Jesus as the one, true fulfillment of Old Testament promises; rather, it is *exclusivist*. Jesus and the Gospels were clearly making claims of uniqueness for Jesus, but that is quite different from expressing hostility against an entire people. (4) Even the seemingly sweeping references to "the Jews" in various pejorative contexts never embrace every ethnically Jewish person in Jesus' day, because Jesus and all his first followers were Jews. Rather, as noted above (p. 193), depending on the context, they may refer to all Jews who rejected Jesus, a prevailing group of opponents among the crowds, certain Jewish leaders, various Judeans, or select Jerusalemites.[53]

Genuine Christians must surely denounce the past atrocities that have been committed against Jews, often in the name of Christ, and do their best to see that they are never replicated. Ecumenical dialogue can help ensure that we avoid perpetuating the false stereotypes and sweeping generalizations that most conservative Christian preaching still puts forward about "the Jews." As simple a move as remembering every time one is talking about Jesus and his first-century

---

[51] An excellent illustration, though overstated, is H. Falk, *Jesus the Pharisee: A New Look at the Jewishness of Jesus* (New York: Paulist, 1985; Eugene, OR: Wipf & Stock, 2003).

[52] For a helpful nuancing of these various "transformations," see J. K. Riches, *Jesus and the Transformation of Judaism* (London: Darton, Longman & Todd, 1980; New York: Seabury, 1982).

[53] See further C. A. Evans and D. A. Hagner, eds., *Anti-Semitism and Early Christianity* (Minneapolis: Fortress, 1993); P. Richardson, D. Granskou, and S. G. Wilson, eds., *Anti-Judaism in Early Christianity*, 2 vols. (Waterloo, ON: Wilfrid Laurier, 1986); and A.-J. Levine, *The Misunderstood Jew: The Church and the Scandal of the Jewish Jesus* (San Francisco: Harper One, 2007).

opposition to say something like, "certain Jews" or "many of the Jewish leaders" can go a long way toward this end (and toward ensuring historical accuracy). Still, it is questionable whether a Christian can remain faithful to the biblical data or to history without at some point raising the problem of exclusivity. If Jesus claimed that he was the only way to the Father (John 14:6), then we dare not categorize non-Christian Jews as any more *soteriologically* privileged than any other non-Christians.[54] We can still carry on irenic dialogue, but we accomplish little by sidestepping altogether the most foundational issues that separate us.[55] Indeed, if the historic Christian claim is true that Jesus is the unique agent of God by whom anyone is saved, then it would be a gross act of anti-Semitism to *withhold* from Jews the announcement of that good news![56] But we also dare not lose sight of the future hope for Israel that Jesus holds out in texts like Matt 23:39 and Luke 21:24, after the time of Gentile dominance has run its course (esp. in light of Rom. 11:25–26). Finally, we must remember to apply Jesus' harsh polemic in a similar "in-house" fashion in our day and age—to those who corrupt and pervert *Christianity* in a legalistic direction.

Redemption and Vindication

We have thus far focused primarily on Jesus' teaching—his announcement of God's reign, the ethics that follow for his disciples, the comparison between Law and gospel, and the resulting similarities and differences between Jesus and the rest of Judaism. The first generation of Christians was profoundly convinced that the most important elements of Jesus' life were his death and resurrection. Given our conviction of the general trustworthiness of the Gospel tradition, what can we learn from it about Jesus' own understanding of these crucial events in his ministry?

To begin with, they were long anticipated. From the outset of his ministry, the devil tempted Jesus to bypass the way of the cross, but Christ remained unyielding. In an early pronouncement story, Jesus acknowledged that the days were coming when the "bridegroom" would be taken away (Mark 2:20 pars.). Ominous portents appear elsewhere when Jesus speaks of the violence surrounding the arrival of the kingdom (Matt 11:12 par.), the struggle between God and Satan (Mark 3:27 pars.), and the "sword" that would divide families (Matt 10:34 par.).[57]

---

[54] As, e.g., in the "two covenants" theology, espoused esp. by M. S. Kinzer, *Postmissionary Messianic Judaism: Redefining Christian Engagement with the Jewish People* (Grand Rapids: Brazos, 2005), which holds that Jesus is Savior for the Gentile world, while Jews may still be saved by faithfulness to the Mosaic covenant.

[55] For excellent examples of irenic dialogue that *do* deal with foundational issues in Jewish-Christian interchanges, see P. Copan and C. A. Evans, ed., *Who Was Jesus? A Jewish-Christian Dialogue* (Louisville and London: WJKP, 2001); P. Lapide and U. Luz, *Jesus in Two Perspectives: A Jewish-Christian Dialogue* (Minneapolis: Augsburg, 1985).

[56] D. G. Bloesch, "'All Israel Will Be Saved': Supersessionism and the Biblical Witness," *Int* 43 (1989): 140–41.

[57] Of course, this is violence initiated *against* him and his followers. Jesus does not promote attacking others, despite many Messianic hopes in his day for precisely such a revolt, except in the invis-

The key turning point in Jesus' career comes after Peter's confession on the road to Caesarea Philippi. Then Jesus speaks explicitly of his coming death and resurrection in his three passion predictions, using the language of divine necessity (Mark 8:31; 9:31; 10:33–34 pars.). Then Jesus "sets his face" to go to Jerusalem (Luke 9:51), knowing full well the fate that awaits him there (13:32–33).[58]

As the time draws close, he speaks of having to drink "the cup," a common Old Testament metaphor for judgment and God's wrath (Mark 10:38; cf. Luke 12:50). The cup image appears again as Jesus struggles in Gethsemane to come to grips with God's will. In Mark 10:45 and parallel appear a cluster of concepts that disclose Jesus' understanding of his death in even more detail. It will be a "ransom"—the price paid for a slave's freedom, "in the place of" (Gk. *anti*) many—a substitutionary sacrifice,[59] alluding to language from Isaiah's suffering servant prophecies (cf. Isa 53:12). John 10:11–18 refers to a similar sacrificial death—Jesus is the Good Shepherd who lays down his life for his sheep. Jesus predicts the demise of the current temple and seems to imply that his resurrected body will function as a new temple (John 2:19), providing further support for his death as an atoning sacrifice.

The Lord's Supper repeats a number of these concepts. As a Passover meal, it suggests the typology of Jesus as the Paschal lamb. The broken bread and poured out cup reiterate the allusions to life-bringing death and God's wrath being placated. The "blood" also symbolizes a life for a life, and Jesus declares it to be "poured out *for many*" (Mark 14:24), again a probable allusion to Isa 53:12.[60] His death inaugurates a new covenant for the forgiveness of sins (Luke 22:20, echoing the prophecy of Jer 31:31–34), and the memorial of that death in the Lord's Supper also looks forward to the coming of the kingdom in all its fullness (Mark 14:25 pars.).[61] The Passion narrative itself poignantly illustrates Jesus' selfless, suffering love as he forgives his persecutors, tends to his family and followers, senses divine abandonment, and yet entrusts himself to his Father in his dying gasps. Second Corinthians 5:21 is the natural interpretive outgrowth of these scenes: "God made him who had no sin to be sin for us, so that in him we might become the righteousness of God."[62]

---

ible domain of spiritual warfare. Cf. several of the chapters in M. Bockmuehl and J. C. Paget, eds., *Redemption and Resistance: The Messianic Hopes of Jews and Christians in Antiquity* (London and New York: T&T Clark, 2007).

[58] Cf. B. Pitre, *Jesus, the Tribulation, and the End of the Exile: Restoration Eschatology and the Origin of the Atonement* (Tübingen: Mohr, 2005; Grand Rapids: Baker, 2006).

[59] See further D. J. Antwi, "Did Jesus Consider His Death to Be an Atoning Sacrifice?" *Int* 45 (1991): 17–28.

[60] This allusion is disputed, but Jesus' use of this text and concept overall seems secure. See P. Stuhlmacher, "Isaiah 53 in the Gospels and Acts," in *The Suffering Servant: Isaiah 53 in Jewish and Christian Sources*, ed. B. Janowski and P. Stuhlmacher (Grand Rapids and Cambridge: Eerdmans, 2004), 153.

[61] On the authenticity and significance of all these elements, see esp. I. H. Marshall, *Last Supper & Lord's Supper*.

[62] On which, see esp. M. Harris, *The Second Epistle to the Corinthians* (Milton Keynes: Paternoster; Grand Rapids: Eerdmans, 2005), 449–56.

But what of the aftermath? In every one of Jesus' Passion predictions he also promised a resurrection. He consistently said this would take place "on the third day," a probable allusion to Hos 6:2 (and the experience of Jonah), enabling Paul later to stress that this chronology was "according to the Scriptures" (1 Cor 15:4). Jesus clearly believed in the general resurrection of "saints" at the end of time (Mark 12:18–27 pars.; cf. Luke 14:14), as well as the personal presence of believers with himself immediately upon their deaths (Luke 23:43). Belief in the resurrection of a single individual in advance of the general resurrection at Judgment Day, however, was unheard of. Almost certainly, then, at the very least, Jesus viewed his resurrection as *inaugurating* the last days, bringing in the new age to overlap with the old, even if all of God's plans for history were not yet fulfilled. He would have also seen it as *vindication* of his life and death, validating his claims to be the divine Messiah (see below, pp. 476–77) who offered the atoning sacrifice for the sins of humanity.[63] Jesus' ministry with his disciples during the forty-day period of resurrection appearances offered opportunity for further instruction on how the Scriptures were fulfilled in him and on the nature of the kingdom (Luke 24:45–49; Acts 1:3). It gave all the disciples a chance to be forgiven, reinstated (John 21:15–23), and recommissioned (Matt 28:16–20). Jesus' vindication was not complete until after his ascension, exaltation, and return to the right hand of the Father (Acts 1:9–11). The decisive moment for the empowerment of the disciples for their mission would not come until Pentecost (Acts 2).

What would come after that? Did Jesus really anticipate a prolonged interval between his resurrection and his return? Three texts have convinced many that he anticipated his return within the lifetimes of his disciples but was mistaken (Matt 10:23; Mark 9:1 pars.; Mark 13:30 pars.). We have seen that none of these texts is best taken as teaching this. Rather they most likely refer, respectively, to the perennially incomplete mission to the Jews, to the transfiguration as a foretaste of the Parousia, and to events preceding Christ's return that would, in fact, take place by AD 70. Parables like the pounds (see esp. Luke 19:11) and the ten bridesmaids (Matt 25:1–13) do indeed anticipate a possible delay, and the "bottom line" is that we simply cannot know when Christ will come back, for he himself in the limitations of his incarnation did not know (Mark 13:32 pars.).[64]

What we can know about the interval between Christ's first and second comings is that there will be a period of unspecified length for the church to carry out its work, most notably evangelizing the nations (Matthew 28:18–20), and that tribulations will intensify near the end, culminating in a reenactment of some kind of desecration reminiscent of the sacrilege of Antiochus Epiphanes (see above, pp. 15–16) that Jesus called "the abomination that causes desolation" (Mark 13:14

---

[63] See further Wright, *The Resurrection of the Son of God*, 719–38.

[64] The detailed analysis of A. L. Moore (*The Parousia in the New Testament* [Leiden: Brill, 1966]) still stands, which concludes that the end for Jesus "was *in some sense* near but that the evidence is lacking that he held to a delimited hope" (p. 190). Cf. also C. E. B. Cranfield, "Thoughts on New Testament Eschatology," *SJT* 35 (1982): 497–512; and Blomberg, "Eschatology and the Church".

par.). It is conceivable that there will be an influx of Jewish believers after this period. Christ will then return in a universal, visible, glorious fashion (vv. 24–27 pars.; cf. 14:62 pars.), gathering together his elect and assembling all humankind for the final judgment (Matt 25:31–46). People will be assigned to one of two fates—everlasting, conscious bliss with God or unending, conscious agony separate from him (cf. also Matt 19:28; John 5:24–30). The perfect fellowship and intimacy of believers with one another and with God in Christ is frequently depicted as a joyous banquet (Matt 8:11 par.; Matt 22:1–14; Luke 14:16–24), while "hell" is consistently described as a place of "weeping and gnashing of teeth" (Matt 8:12; 13:42, 50).[65] Questions about a rapture or a millennium are not clearly addressed in any texts from the Gospels; they will have to be answered by analysis of other parts of Scripture. Instead of speculating about the details and timing of the end, Christ calls us to vigilant obedience whenever the end may come (Matt 24:37–25:46).

Christology

What was Jesus' self-understanding? Did it progress? Was it consistent with the evangelists' later Christology? With questions like these we come to the most important issues of all concerning Jesus' theology as we attempt to answer for ourselves the question of his identity.

Indirect Evidence

We will look below at the specific titles that Jesus or others used to speak of him, but it is important not to neglect what is often called "nontitular" or "implicit" Christology. Precisely because these data often emerge in contexts that are not explicitly addressing the question of who Jesus is, they prove all the more valuable in the quest for the historical Jesus' self-understanding. We may cite twelve such categories of data here.

1. Jesus' Relationships. In the ways Jesus interacted with and spoke about others, the impression one gets is that he was always "in charge." Even while speaking humbly, he makes statements that disclose a remarkable self-estimation. Jesus declares that John the Baptist was the greatest of all previous people, yet Jesus ushers in the kingdom that will make its subjects greater still (Matt 11:11–12 par.). He calls John the Elijah who was to come (Matt 17:11–13 par.), but that leaves only a messianic "job description" open for Jesus, his successor. Jesus similarly challenges the Jewish leaders with an authority that transcends even the written Law, and he calls his disciples to form the nucleus of a new, spiritu-

---

[65] The other two primary metaphors for hell in the Gospels—unquenchable fire and outer darkness—if taken literally, contradict one another. Cf. Ladd, *Theology of the New Testament*, rev. and ed. Hagner, 196. But the fact that Jesus uses symbols rather than a literal description of eternal punishment should not lead us to play down the awfulness of the reality so depicted (W. V. Crockett, "The Metaphorical View," in *Four Views on Hell*, ed. W. Crockett [Grand Rapids: Zondervan, 1992], 43–76). For Jesus' treatment of judgment more broadly, cf. M. Reiser, *Jesus and Judgment: The Eschatological Proclamation in Its Jewish Context* (Minneapolis: Fortress, 1997).

ally liberated Israel, tasks traditionally reserved for God or at least his appointed spokespersons.[66]

2. Accepting Worship, Prayer, and Faith. Repeatedly, people fall down before Jesus with their requests. English translations may at times translate *proskuneō* with the term "worship," but *proskuneō* also means to "prostrate" oneself before an individual, a customary posture in the ancient world for someone to use when beseeching an authority figure. Still, there are times when more seems implied. After Jesus walks on the water and climbs into the disciples' boat, they "worship" him, saying, "Truly you are the Son of God" (Matt 14:33). Jesus commands his followers to pray to the Father in his name—that is, by his power or authority (John 16:23–24; 14:13–14), and it is faith in him that repeatedly brings people physical and spiritual healing (Mark 5:34 pars.; 10:52 par.; Luke 7:50; 17:19). Later the disciples (and even angels!) would rebuke people who treated them that way (e.g., Acts 14:14–15; Rev 22:8–9), but Jesus actually encourages such behavior (cf. also John 14:1).[67]

3. God's Final Eschatological Agent. In Mark 8:38 and parallels, Jesus declares that one's response to him determines his or her eternal destiny. Luke 12:8–9 puts it even more bluntly: "I tell you, whoever publicly acknowledges me, the Son of Man will also acknowledge before the angels of God. But whoever publicly disowns me will be disowned before the angels of God." Apparently, Jesus thinks he will be God's helper on Judgment Day (cf. also Matt 7:21–23; 25:31–46)! Even now, actions done to him are equivalent to those done to God (Matt 10:40; Mark 9:37).[68]

4. Authority to Forgive Sins. Mark 2:10 and parallels astounded its original audience as Jesus claimed to forgive the paralytic's sins. Of course, priests in a variety of religions have claimed to mediate forgiveness, although Jesus was not of priestly lineage. His reply suggests something more, a heavenly origin: "But I want you to know that the Son of Man has authority *on earth* to forgive sins" (italics added). Why add "on earth" unless he was more than an ordinary earth-dweller? His miraculous cure of the man demonstrates the power to back up his claim (cf. Luke 23:43 for Jesus' ability to promise the crucified "robber" immediate forgiveness and presence in Paradise).[69]

---

[66] For full detail, see Meier, *A Marginal Jew*, vol. 3.

[67] No doubt accounting for the extraordinarily widespread and rapid proliferation of worship of Jesus by his followers in the first generation after his death. See esp. throughout Hurtado, *Lord Jesus Christ*. Cf. also R. Bauckham, *God Crucified: Monotheism and Christology in the New Testament* (Carlisle: Paternoster, 1998; Grand Rapids and Cambridge: Eerdmans, 1999).

[68] Cf. throughout de Jonge, *God's Final Envoy*.

[69] The point may be not so much that the mere declaration of the forgiveness of sins was itself a veiled claim to deity; the temple priests, after all, regularly spoke on behalf of God pronouncing those who offered sacrifices forgiven of their sins. But Jesus was no priest, and he made these claims nowhere near the temple. Who but one who spoke more directly for God could justifiably make those changes? On Jesus' high priesthood in the Gospels, see C. H. T. Fletcher-Louis, "Jesus as the High Priestly Messiah," *JSHJ* 4 (2006): 155–75; 5 (2007): 55–79.

5. *Metaphors Applied to Yahweh in the Old Testament.* In a series of passages, particularly in the Synoptic parables, Jesus applies to himself metaphors from the Old Testament that were often reserved for God. Any one of these by itself is scarcely conclusive, but the cumulative effect is significant: Jesus refers to himself, often indirectly, as bridegroom, rock, director of the harvest, sower, shepherd, father, giver of forgiveness, vineyard owner, and king. The combined effect goes even beyond indicating Jesus as Messiah to pointing out one who is God himself, a theme which otherwise only John, among the Gospels, introduces explicitly. Other ways in which Jesus associates himself with functions of Yahweh include receiving children's praise (Matt 21:16; cf. Ps 8:2), seeking the lost (Luke 19:10; cf. Ezek 34), and experiencing rejection as the cornerstone that becomes a stumbling stone (Luke 20:17–18; cf. Isa 8:14–15).[70]

6. *Miracles and the Kingdom.* We have noticed above how Jesus' miracles were not arbitrary or capricious but dovetailed with his announcement of the arrival of God's kingdom and fulfilled Old Testament and intertestamental Jewish expectation of what would happen when the messianic age arrived (p. 318). But if the kingdom or messianic age has arrived, then the king or Messiah must also be present.[71]

7. *Abba.* Although its significance can be exaggerated, Jesus' sense of filial consciousness should not be ignored (see further below, pp. 473–74). The intimate Aramaic Abba (not exactly but almost "Daddy") is not quite as unparalleled in Jewish literature as once was thought, but it is still highly provocative. Found in transliteration in the Gospels in Mark 14:36, it presumably lies behind other uses of the Gk. *patēr* ("father") and explains Paul's use of the term in Rom 8:15 and Gal 4:6 for the new intimacy all believers can have with God through Christ.[72]

8. *Amēn.* A second Semitic term preserved in Greek transliteration is *Amēn*, often translated into English as "verily" or "truly." Jesus begins numerous solemn pronouncements with this forceful introduction (in John, it is often doubled— "truly, truly"), followed by "I say to you" (e.g., Matt 5:18, 26; 6:2, 5, 16; 8:10; Mark 3:28; 8:12; 9:1, 41; Luke 4:24; 11:51; 13:35; cf. John 1:51; 3:3, 5; 5:19, 24, 25; etc.). Unlike the prophets, Jesus does not declare what the Lord God says, but what he himself says, yet in contexts of equally authoritative claims.[73]

9. *The Messianic Demonstrations of the Final Week.* The "triumphal" entry consciously reenacts messianic prophecy (Zech 9:9); the cursed fig tree and "cleansed temple" portend the dissolution of "the Old Testament age"; and Jesus' teaching in and concerning the temple during the last week of his life reinforces the conviction that the last chance for repentance for the current regime in Israel

---

[70] Payne, "Jesus' Implicit Claim to Deity in His Parables." Cf. also D. Doriani, "The Deity of Christ in the Synoptic Gospels," *JETS* 37 (1994): 333–50.

[71] See esp. throughout Seccombe, *The King of God's Kingdom.*

[72] Cf. esp. McKnight, *A New Vision for Israel*, 49–65.

[73] Dunn, *Jesus Remembered*, 700–1.

will soon pass. But who can declare without further support that such apocalyptic upheavals have actually begun, who is not much more than a typical prophet?[74]

10. "Something Greater" Is Here. The same kind of logic lies behind several statements of Jesus that show him to be greater than David or the temple or Solomon or Jonah (Matt 12:3–6, 41–42). There are no obvious intermediate categories short of "the Messiah" for which such labels can qualify. The same is true of other "quasi-titles" in the Gospels such as John the Baptist's reference to "the coming one" (Mark 1:7 pars.) or Jesus as "wisdom" (Matt 11:19 par.).[75]

11. Shaliach. In the Synoptics, Jesus often uses the expression, "I have come to . . ." (e.g., Matt 5:17; 9:13; 10:34–35; cf. Luke 19:10). In John, his speech often refers to "[the one] who sent me" (John 4:34; 5:23–24, 36–37; 6:38–40; 7:16; etc.). Both forms suggest that he is on a mission from God. The language hints at, though does not require, the idea that his origin is otherworldly. It also conforms to one of the clusters of concepts at times associated with the Jewish Messiah— the *shaliach* (Gk. *apostolos* or apostle—cf. John 13:16)—the one sent out from Yahweh on a mission to reveal himself to and redeem his people.[76]

12. Jesus' Seemingly Supernatural Insight. On several occasions, Jesus appears to be able to read people's minds or sense their deepest needs (e.g., Mark 10:21; 12:24 pars.). He can predict the future (his passion, resurrection, the coming destruction of Jerusalem). He can refer to seemingly incidental details of coming events in ways that leave it unclear if he has supernatural knowledge or is simply staging somewhat cryptic or secretive activities (e.g., in his instructions to the disciples to find a man carrying a water jar as the rendezvous person for arranging the final Passover—Mark 14:13–15 pars.; cf. also the episode with the colt for "Palm Sunday" in Mark 11:2–3 pars.).[77]

Son of Man

From implicit Christology, we turn to the explicit titles used of Jesus. The most common one that he himself employed was "Son of Man." The term is used eighty-two times, well distributed among the four Gospels. It is always on the lips of Jesus, except in John 12:34 where the crowd uses the term in reply to Jesus' previous use of it. Outside the Gospels, however, it appears as a title only in Acts 7:56 when the dying Stephen addresses Jesus (cf. also the uses without the definite article in Rev 1:13 and 14:14). Jewish backgrounds are abundant, but which ones are most relevant is greatly disputed since there is no exact parallel to Jesus'

---

[74] Cf. esp. Wright (*Jesus and the Victory of God*, 489–539), who highlights how this is simply the beginning of the climax of a whole succession of such implicit Christological demonstrations throughout Jesus' public ministry. Cf. S. McKnight, "Jesus and Prophetic Actions," *BBR* 10 (2000): 197–232.

[75] On which, see esp. Witherington, *Jesus the Sage.*

[76] Cf. A. E. Harvey, "Christ as Agent," in *The Glory of Christ in the New Testament*, ed. L. D. Hurst and N. T. Wright (Oxford: Clarendon, 1987), 239–50.

[77] For a succinct list and discussion of several of the above implicit indicators of Christology, see R. T. France, "The Worship of Jesus: A Neglected Factor in Christological Debate?" in *Christ the Lord*, ed. H. H. Rowdon (Leicester: IVP, 1982), 28.

uses of the term. The expression thus passes the double dissimilarity and similarity criterion of authenticity with flying colors.

But what did Jesus mean by it? An older view, often associated with Bultmann and some of his followers, postulated that Jesus, at times at least, was talking about someone other than himself—a *coming* Son of Man or Messiah. But this view is now largely abandoned. In recent years, much linguistic study has given rise to hypotheses that the expression evolved from the frequent Old Testament use of the address "son of man" as an equivalent to "mortal human" (e.g., Ps 8:2 and throughout Ezekiel). Based on various later Aramaic usages of *bar (e)nash(a)*, it has thus been taken generically to mean "a man," or as a circumlocution for "I," or as a categorical reference to "a man like me" or "a man in my position."[78] These interpretations work reasonably well in texts like Matt 8:20 ("The Son of Man has no place to lay his head") or 12:32 ("Anyone who speaks a word against the Son of Man will be forgiven"), but less so in those that depict Jesus as more exalted. Proponents of this view usually argue, therefore, that a core of authentic "Son of Man" texts has been elaborated with additional, inauthentic ones. They are hard pressed, however, to explain how the expression became titular (or at least articular) in all its Greek references in the Gospels: *ho huios tou anthrōpou* ("*the* Son of Man"). Still, it is obvious that in certain texts the Gospel writers did recognize the interchangeability of Son of Man with "I" (cf., e.g., Luke 6:22 with Matt 5:11; Mark 8:27 with Matt 16:13; or within Luke 12:8).[79]

It is not likely, though, that this explanation can account for all or even a majority of the uses of this term.[80] Daniel 7:13 probably provides more directly relevant background.[81] In his vision, Daniel sees "one like a son of man," that is, one who is apparently human, yet, this individual was "coming with the clouds of heaven." He approached the Ancient of Days and was led into his presence (v. 13). "He was given authority, glory and sovereign power; all nations and people of every language worshiped him. His dominion is an everlasting dominion that will not pass away, and his kingdom is one that will never be destroyed" (v. 14).

On the basis of verse 18 ("The holy people of the Most High will receive the kingdom and will possess it forever"), many scholars have interpreted this vision as a prophecy of the collective future and glory of Israel.[82] But verses 13–14

---

[78] For a survey of the full range of interpretations in the twentieth century, see D. Burkett, *The Son of Man Debate: A History and Evaluation* (Cambridge: CUP, 1999).

[79] Too recent for Burkett's survey and in keeping with this non-exalted interpretation, W. Wink (*The Human Being: Jesus and the Enigma of the Son of Man* [Minneapolis: Fortress, 2002]) argues for Jesus claiming to be the archetypal human; cf. also M. Casey, *The Solution to the 'Son of Man' Problem* (London and New York: T&T Clark, 2007). E. E. Lemcio ("'Son of Man,' 'Pitiable Man,' 'Rejected Man': Equivalent Expressions in the Old Greek of Daniel," *TynBul* 56 [2005]: 43–60) argues that the stress is on Jesus' vulnerability and shame; while J. Marcus finds "son of man" merely equivalent to a descendant of Adam in "Son of Man as Son of Adam," *RB* 110 (2003): 38–61.

[80] See esp. P. Owen and D. Shepherd, "Speaking Up for Qumran, Dalman and the Son of Man: Was *Bar Enasha* a Common Term for 'Man' in the Time of Jesus?" *JSNT* 81 (2002): 81–122.

[81] J. J. Collins, "The Son of Man in First-Century Judaism," *NTS* 38 (1992): 448–66; C. A. Evans, "Defeating Satan and Liberating Israel: Jesus and Daniel's Visions," *JSHJ* 1 (2003): 161–70.

[82] E.g., T. Kazen, "The Coming Son of Man Revisited," *JSHJ* 5 (2007): 155–74.

seem to suggest more than this—that Israel will be led by a representative who is described as a heavenly figure worthy of universal worship (an unlikely attribute for monotheistic Jews to ascribe to themselves as a whole!). In 1 Enoch and 4 Ezra, Jewish pseudepigraphal works completed no later than the end of the first century,[83] the Son of Man appears clearly as an individual and a messianic figure. Demonstrably pre-Christian works also point to at least a minority voice within Judaism that would have agreed (cf. esp. Ezekiel the Tragedian and 11QMelchizedek from Qumran).[84] The Greek definite article may function as a demonstrative: "this 'Son of Man'," that is, "the one described in Daniel."[85]

Most scholars have grouped Jesus' Son of Man sayings into three categories: those that refer to his earthly ministry, those that portend his coming suffering, and those that allude to his future, exalted state. Seeing a Danielic background for the title allows one to accept sayings in all three categories as authentic. The vision of a heavenly man clearly fits the exalted sayings (e.g., Matt 10:23; 19:28; Mark 8:38; 9:1). The references to oppression and war against the saints in Dan 7:21, 25 could have suggested the link with suffering (as in Mark 8:31; 14:21; or Luke 12:40). Even in the sayings that seem least dependent on a Danielic background, hints of either suffering or exaltation seem present. For example, when the Son of Man has nowhere to lay his head, the ignominy of Jesus' itinerant ministry is highlighted. When he demonstrates authority to forgive sins on earth (Mark 2:10) or shows that he is Lord of the Sabbath (2:28), a certain transcendence seems present. If it is difficult to see how Ezekiel's "son of man" (a mere mortal) could have given rise to the exalted titular passages in the Gospels, it is not hard to see how a Danielic, messianic, suffering Son of Man could lurk in the background of even the less explicitly titular Gospel references.[86]

The upshot of all of this is that, contrary to popular contemporary Christian (mis)conceptions, "Son of Man" winds up being a very exalted title for Jesus. *It does not primarily focus on his true humanity but on his heavenly enthronement* (cf. also the plural "thrones" of Dan 7:9). It is more of a synonym than an antonym of "Son of God." But it remains ambiguous enough that Jesus was able to invest

---

[83] And the majority of 1 Enoch is clearly pre-Christian. The section, sometimes called the Parables of Enoch, containing the Son of Man references, was not found in the copies discovered at Qumran, so many scholars have assumed that it was a post-Christian addition to the document. But the scholarly pendulum is starting to swing back in the direction of a pre-Christian origin even if this section is not as old as the rest of the document. For an anthology of options, see G. Boccaccini, ed., *Enoch and the Messiah Son of Man: Revisiting the Book of Parables* (Grand Rapids and Cambridge: Eerdmans, 2007).

[84] See already W. Horbury, "The Messianic Associations of the 'Son of Man'," *JTS* 36 (1985): 34–55.

[85] This is the central point of S. Kim, *The Son of Man as the Son of God* (Tübingen: Mohr, 1983; Grand Rapids: Eerdmans, 1985).

[86] See further M. B. Shepherd, "Daniel 7:13 and the New Testament Son of Man," *WTJ* 68 (2006): 99–111; K. A. Kuhn, "The 'One like a Son of Man' Becomes the 'Son of God'," *CBQ* 69 (2007): 22–42.

the term with his own meaning and clarifications.[87] It was not susceptible to the political misunderstandings surrounding the term "Messiah" itself (see below, pp. 476–77). The possibility of linking it with suffering was not one that pre-Christian Jews had unambiguously exploited. Whereas Daniel's Son of Man travels on the clouds to the very throne room of God, Jesus uses this imagery to describe his return from heaven to earth in glory (Mark 14:62 pars.).

Son of God

The title "Son of God" is much less common in the Gospels than "Son of Man." It is used mostly by others to identify Jesus. The angels predict that Jesus will be called Son of the Highest and Son of God (Luke 1:32, 35). The voice from heaven declares Jesus to be his Son, alluding to Ps 2:7, at both Christ's baptism and his transfiguration (Mark 1:11; 9:7 pars.). Frequently the devil and his demons acknowledge Jesus as God's Son, as part of spiritual warfare (e.g., Matt 4:3, 6; Mark 3:11; 5:7). The centurion at the cross recognizes Jesus as the Son of God (Mark 15:39), but this need mean nothing more than a "divine man"—a human deified upon death—after the typical Greco-Roman conception (cf. the parallel in Luke 23:47 in which the centurion declares Jesus merely to be innocent). Indeed, even in Jewish backgrounds the term "son of God" could refer to powerful influential humans, charismatic teachers and rabbis, angelic or demonic beings, or the Messiah (see now esp. the recently translated Dead Sea fragment 4Q246; and cf. 1QSa 11–12 and 4QFlor 10–14 on 2 Sam 7:11–14).[88]

In several strategic places, however, the stakes seem to be higher. Gabriel tells Mary that the child she will conceive will be called "the Son of God" (Luke 1:35). After Jesus walks on the water, the disciples, at least in Matthew's account, worship him and declare him to be Son of God (Matt 14:33). Yet this understanding is apparently still not as appropriately nuanced as Peter's later confession of Jesus as "Son of the living God," a recognition which Jesus attributes to divine revelation (Matt 16:16). Even here the immediate context makes it clear that Peter does not understand as he will after the death and resurrection about the need for the Son of God to suffer. Since neither of these passages uses the title "Son of God" in their Markan parallels (the earliest written forms of the tradition), it is not until we get to Jesus' trial before the Sanhedrin that we can get a secure read on Jesus' own estimation of the label. There he replies with an affirmative, however qualified, to the question of his identity as "Christ, the Son of the *Blessed One*" (a Jewish euphemism for God). Still, he immediately redefines his role in terms of the heavenly Son of Man (Mark 14:61–62 pars.), the expression which, in this context, is the more blasphemous (recall above, p. 397).[89]

---

[87] F. F. Bruce, "The Background to the Son of Man Sayings," in *Christ the Lord*, ed. Rowdon, 50–70. See also C. M. Tuckett, "The Son of Man and Daniel 7: Inclusive Aspects of Early Christologies," in *Christian Origins: Worship, Belief, and Society*, ed. K. J. O'Mahony (London and New York: SAP, 2003), 164–90.

[88] Cf. further J. J. Collins, "The Background of the 'Son of God' Text," *BBR* 7 (1997): 51–62.

[89] On "Son of God" more generally, cf. esp. M. Hengel, *Son of God: The Origin of Christology and the History of Jewish-Hellenistic Religion* (London: SCM; Philadelphia: Fortress, 1976; Eugene, OR:

More helpful perhaps are references where Jesus speaks of the "son" without qualification. In Matt 11:27 he uses language very similar to numerous references to the Son or Son of God in John's Gospel when he declares, "All things have been committed to me by my Father. No one knows the Son except the Father, and no one knows the Father except the Son and those to whom the Son chooses to reveal him." Here is a clear expression of Jesus' awareness of a uniquely intimate and revelatory relationship with God as his heavenly Father.[90] This is the logical corollary of his use of *Abba* to address God.[91] In the parable of the wicked tenants, the "son" of the landlord emerges as a Christ-figure, anticipating Jesus' crucifixion (Mark 12:6 pars.; cf. the image of the king's son in the parable of the wedding banquet—Matt 22:2). In his Olivet Discourse, Jesus describes the limitations of his present knowledge in terms of what the "Son" does not know about his return (Mark 13:32 par.). Only after the resurrection is the term used approximately as in later confessional formulas in which Jesus becomes Son of God in the sense of being God's ontological equal and of existing as one part of the very Triune Godhead (Matt 28:19). Even in John's Gospel, where sonship throughout seems more exalted, there are also statements of functional subordination as radical as Jesus' words, "The Father is greater than I" (John 14:28).

Ironically, therefore, Son of God may often be a slightly less exalted title for Jesus, especially in the Synoptics, than Son of Man. A. E. Harvey's conclusions aptly summarize this "functional" sense of sonship:

> Jesus had indeed shown that absolute obedience to God, had spoken of God with that intimate authority, and had acted with the unique authorization which belonged to God's representative and agent on earth, which would be characteristic of one who was (in the sense usually ascribed to "sonship" in antiquity) in very truth "Son of God"; and the reversal of the world's judgment upon him, which was implied by the event his followers called "the Resurrection," enabled them to describe Jesus with absolute confidence as "the Son," a title which would certainly have been correct in his lifetime, and was presumably acknowledged by supernatural beings, but was too momentous to be openly acknowledged even by those of his followers who had found their way to faith in him.[92]

Still, even this functional sonship was impressive and unparalleled.

Lord

In the Greco-Roman world, "lord" (Gk. *kurios*) was a title applied to gods, emperors, other human masters, and anyone a person wanted to address respectfully. In the Jewish world, it was one of the titles for Yahweh, God himself (Hb., *adonai*) but could similarly apply to various human masters and authority figures. In most of the uses in the Gospels when somebody addresses Jesus as "lord," therefore, we dare not infer more than a title of respect that recognizes his charis-

---

Wipf & Stock, 2007).

[90] See further A. Denaux, "The Q-Logion: Mt 11,27/Lk 10,22 and the Gospel of John," in *John and the Synoptics*, ed. A. Denaux (Leuven: Leuven University Press and Peeters, 2005), 163–99.

[91] R. Bauckham, "The Sonship of the Historical Jesus in Christology," *SJT* 31 (1978): 245–60.

[92] Harvey, *Jesus and the Constraints of History*, 167–68.

ma or authority. Mark 11:3 is a bit more suggestive when Jesus tells his disciples to respond to anyone questioning them about taking the colt for "Palm Sunday" by saying, "The Lord needs it." The average Jew would assume the disciples were speaking of God, but is Jesus thus implicitly linking himself with God by using this title? In Mark 2:28 and parallels, the Son of Man is "Lord" even over the Sabbath. But who has the right to transcend Sabbath law but God? Most significant of all is 12:35–37 and parallels, in which Jesus questions the Jewish leaders in the temple about how David's son (the Messiah) can also be his "Lord." He quotes Ps 110:1, in which David declares, "The Lord [*Yahweh*] says to my Lord [*adonai*] . . ." But who is this second "Lord" who is above even the king of Israel if not a Messiah who is more than a mere man?[93]

Still, it is primarily only after the resurrection that "Lord" in its strongest sense can be applied to Jesus. Hence, Acts 2:36 climaxes Peter's Pentecostal sermon with the conclusion that on the basis of the resurrection and exaltation Jesus can be designated "both Lord and Christ." Among the Gospel writers it is only Luke who then retrojects this understanding into his Gospel account, not in settings where people approach Jesus but in his larger narrative framework. Elizabeth refers to Mary, before she has given birth, as "the mother of my Lord" (Luke 1:43). The angels proclaim to the shepherds that a Savior is born who is "Christ the Lord" (Luke 2:11). From time to time Luke refers to Jesus simply as "the Lord" (Luke 7:13, 19; 10:39, 41; 11:39; 12:42; etc.).[94]

Nevertheless, we must not underestimate the significance of the use of "Lord" as a title for Jesus. Even when it means only "master," we are reminded that *we must not conceive of worshiping Jesus as Lord (God) without simultaneously making him our master*.[95] Matthew 7:21 puts it pointedly, "Not everyone who says to me, 'Lord, Lord,' will enter the kingdom of heaven, but only he who does the will of my Father who is in heaven." On the other hand, the use of "Lord" for Jesus as God must have developed quite early in Christian circles because already by the time of the mid-50s Paul could quote the Aramaic *Maranatha* without explanation as a closing prayer for the return of Christ (1 Cor 16:22). Depending on how the compound word is divided, it means either "Come, O Lord!" or "Our Lord has come" (the former seems more probable). But *mar* was the Aramaic word that regularly was substituted for the Hebrew Yahweh in Old Testament texts and paraphrases. That a title used for God could be applied to Jesus so early in Jewish Christianity suggests it has roots in Jesus' own usage and self-understanding, particularly in light of Mark 12:35–37.[96]

---

[93] Cf. esp. Hengel, *Studies in Early Christology*, 119–25.

[94] Cf. further J. A. Fitzmyer, "New Testament Kyrios and Maranatha and Their Aramaic Backgrounds," in *To Advance the Gospel: New Testament Studies,* rev. ed. (Grand Rapids and Cambridge: Eerdmans, 1998), 218–35.

[95] With respect to the "lordship salvation" controversy, particularly helpful and balanced are D. L. Bock, "Jesus as Lord in Acts and in the Gospel Message," *BSac* 143 (1986): 146–54; and idem., "A Review of *The Gospel according to Jesus*," *BSac* 146 (1989): 21–40.

[96] See also Hurtado, *Lord Jesus Christ*, 53–64, 288–89.

Messiah

We have saved the most well-known of all the titles of Jesus for last. "Christ" (Gk. *christos*), even within the later New Testament writers, seems to become a virtual second name for Jesus. Yet it never entirely loses its titular sense as the translation of the "Messiah" (Hb. *Meshiach*) or *anointed one*.[97] The English word "Messiah" itself appears in most translations of the Old Testament only in Dan 9:25–26. But prophets, priests, and kings were all anointed at various times throughout the Old Testament period. The concept of Messiah came to be associated particularly with the kingly line that Nathan had promised would occupy David's throne in perpetuity (2 Sam 7:14). Old Testament kings, both in prophecy and in historical narrative, are regularly called "the Lord's anointed." Other influential texts describing this kingship include 1 Sam 2:10; Isa 7:1–9:7; 11:1–9; Mic 5:1–5; Zech 9:9–12; and Pss 2, 45, and 110. Even a pagan Persian ruler could be called God's *meshiach* (Cyrus in Isa 45:1) when he fulfilled God's purposes in repatriating God's people.

In intertestamental Judaism, one may distinguish at least six different strands of messianic expectation: (1) The Maccabean revolt initially did away with the need in some people's minds for a literal Messiah. As the Hasmonean dynasty moved further away from its original ideals, others came to the conviction that God would no longer bless his people as previously anticipated. We can speak of this strand of thought as the messianic hope *fulfilled or forfeited*. (2) In the sectarian Judaism represented at Qumran, both *priestly and kingly* Messiahs were anticipated. This hope reflected both the dissatisfaction with the corrupt Hasmonean regime that had combined the two offices and the realization that priest (tribe of Levi) and king (tribe of Judah) could not normally be joined in the same person. (3) A substantial portion of mainstream Judaism looked for a *warrior* king who would help the Jews shake off the shackles of Rome (recall the discussion of the Psalms of Solomon above, p. 18). Hence, we read of the various prophets, bandits, and would-be Messiahs that characterized the initial ragtag stages of the Zealot movement (p. 54).

(4) The parables or similitudes of 1 Enoch equate the Messiah, portrayed as an *apocalyptic* Davidic king, with titles such as "Holy" or "Elect one" and "Son of Man." So, too, does the post-Christian 4 Ezra. Questions about the dating of these documents have led many scholars to wonder whether such expectation was present in Christ's day, but, as we have noted, increasing analysis of the Qumran and other little-known pseudepigraphal literature is making this assumption probable.[98] (5) The Samaritans looked for a *Taheb* (a "*restorer*"), who would fulfill the prophecy of a new Moses outlined in Deut 18:18. While having certain charac-

---

[97] For full details, see C. L. Blomberg, "Messiah in the New Testament," in *Israel's Messiah in the Bible and the Dead Sea Scrolls*, ed. R. S. Hess and M. D. Carroll R. (Grand Rapids: Baker, 2003), 111–41.

[98] See esp. J. J. Collins, *The Scepter and the Star: The Messiahs of the Dead Sea Scrolls and Other Ancient Literature* (New York and London: Doubleday, 1995; New Haven: Yale University Press, 2007).

teristics of a political deliverer, he was viewed more as a teacher than in some of the other traditions. (6) This concept of *teacher or sage* became prominent in the post-Christian rabbinic literature; it is probable that its seeds were at least beginning to germinate in the first century.

Thus we must beware of any glib generalizations about what all or most Jews were looking for at the time of Jesus. Messianic expectations were diverse and in some circles virtually nonexistent. Where they were present, they were often politicized.[99] This probably explains Jesus' reticence to accept the term without qualification (Mark 8:29; 14:62 pars.), the relative scarcity of occasions in which he uses the term himself, and his concern to silence others at times when they do use it (the "messianic secret" motif, on which see above, pp. 132–33). One must also take into account belief in certain Jewish circles that it was inappropriate for the Messiah to identify himself as such until after he had fulfilled his ministry.

Nevertheless, there are references to the title "Christ" attributed to Jesus in the Gospels that indicate indirectly that he was prepared to accept the designation, however overlaid those references may be with the evangelists' redaction. In Mark 9:41 he promises a reward to any who give a cup of water "in my name because you belong to the Messiah." In Mark 12:35 he asks how the Christ can be merely the Son of David. In Matt 23:10, he reminds the Pharisees that there is only one who is the Christ, and in 24:5, 23, he predicts the coming of false Christs who would imitate him. In John 4:25, he discloses himself more directly to the Samaritan woman as the Messiah. All of these texts set the stage for his post-resurrection question, "Did not the Christ have to suffer these things and then enter his glory?" Luke immediately adds, "And beginning with Moses and all the Prophets, he explained to them what was said in all the Scriptures concerning himself" (Luke 24:26–27). Little wonder that the title became the most all-embracing in subsequent Christian thought. But it probably originated with Jesus. As de Jonge explains,

> In view of the fact that David was not only portrayed as a king, and thereby as a political figure, but also as a prophet, a singer of psalms, and an exorcist, it does not seem impossible that Jesus regarded himself as a true Son of David who could properly be called the Lord's anointed—not only in view of his future role when God's rule would reveal itself with power, but already in the present while the kingdom of God manifested itself in his words and actions.[100]

Other Titles

Closely related to Messiah but even more susceptible to political misunderstandings was the title *king*. Jesus is the one (unlike Herod) who is *born* "king of the Jews" (Matt 2:2). He comes as humble messianic king at the triumphal entry

---

[99] For an even fuller range of options than is listed here, see J. H. Charlesworth, ed., *Messiah: Developments in Judaism and Earliest Christianity* (Minneapolis: Fortress, 1992), although he probably somewhat overestimates the diversity of expectation; for balance, cf. I. H. Marshall, "The Messiah in the First Century: A Review Article," *CTR* 7 (1995): 67–83.

[100] M. de Jonge, *Christology in Context: The Earliest Christian Response to Jesus* (Philadelphia: Westminster, 1988), 211.

(Matt 21:5) and as kingly judge at the end of history (25:34, 40). Jesus is crucified as "king of the Jews" (Mark 15:9, 12, 18, 26, 32), a charge which is accurate but misunderstood. Christ's kingdom is not of this world (John 18:36), but that does not mean it has no sociopolitical overtones (see above, p. 400).

Jesus is also *servant of the Lord* (Mark 10:45; Matt 12:18–21), interpreting Isaiah's suffering servant prophecies to apply to his own ministry of substitutionary, atoning death (recall above, p. 363).[101] He is a *prophet*, particularly the eschatological prophet *par excellence* like Moses (Deut 18:18). The crowds hail him as such (Mark 6:15; 8:28; Luke 7:16, 39; 24:19), but his followers generally find it to be inadequate as a full description of his identity. He is called *teacher* (Hb. *rabbi*), but particularly in Matthew and John this title is usually used in contexts by people who do not grasp Jesus' full identity. His own attitude to the title is reflected in Matt 23:10—"Nor are you to be called 'teacher,' for you have one Teacher, the Messiah." Other titles are more distinctive of particular Gospels— Matthew's "Son of David," Luke's "Savior," John's "Lamb of God," "Word," and the Divine "I Ams," and have already been treated above in the chapters on those individual Gospels.

Conclusion

No matter what level of Gospel tradition one examines—the evangelists' redaction, the developing oral tradition, or the bedrock core of what can securely be assigned to the historical Jesus—one impression remains the same. Jesus, like his earliest followers, was convinced that how one responded to him was the most important decision anyone could make in his or her life. On this response hinges one's eternal destiny. We are called to become Christ's followers, to be subjects of the kingdom, to practice the "greater righteousness" that he demands but also makes possible for those who declare their allegiance to him. We must mirror his compassion for the outcasts and disenfranchised of our world. We dare not turn his teaching into a new law or legalism, but we must be prepared to carry our own crosses, experiencing rejection, hostility, and even martyrdom if necessary. Simply admiring and imitating Jesus, however, is not adequate, unless it stems from our faith in his person as the unique God-man and our reception of the forgiveness of sins that he offers. If this book has enabled its readers to progress towards these goals, in the myriad of fascinating and controversial details that it has explored, then it will have more than accomplished its goals.

For Further Study

Kingdom of God
Beasley-Murray, George R. *Jesus and the Kingdom of God.* Grand Rapids: Eerdmans; Exeter: Paternoster, 1986.

---

[101] See esp. Janowski and Stuhlmacher, eds., *The Suffering Servant.* Cf. also several of the essays in Bellinger and Farmer, eds., *Jesus and the Suffering Servant.*

Beavis, Mary Ann. *Jesus and Utopia: Looking for the Kingdom of God in the Roman World.* Minneapolis: Fortress, 2006.

Chilton, Bruce D. *Pure Kingdom: Jesus' Vision of God.* Grand Rapids: Eerdmans; London: SPCK, 1996.

Ladd, George E. *The Presence of the Future.* Grand Rapids: Eerdmans, 1974; London: SPCK, 1980.

Marcus, Joel. *The Mystery of the Kingdom of God.* Atlanta: Scholars, 1986.

Song, C. S. *Jesus and the Reign of God.* Minneapolis: Fortress, 1993.

Willis, Wendell, ed. *The Kingdom of God in 20th Century Interpretation.* Peabody: Hendrickson, 1987.

Ethics

Jesus' Ethics in General

Burridge, Richard A. *Imitating Jesus: An Inclusive Approach to New Testament Ethics.* Grand Rapids and Cambridge: Eerdmans, 2007.

Chilton, Bruce, and J. I. H. McDonald. *Jesus and the Ethics of the Kingdom.* London: SPCK, 1987; Grand Rapids: Eerdmans, 1988.

Harvey, A. E. *Strenuous Commands: The Ethics of Jesus.* London: SCM; Philadelphia: Trinity, 1990.

Matera, Frank J. *New Testament Ethics: The Legacies of Jesus and Paul.* Louisville and London: WJKP, 1999.

Stassen, Glen H. and David P. Gushee, *Kingdom Ethics: Following Jesus in Contemporary Context.* Downers Grove: IVP, 2003.

Wiebe, Ben. *Messianic Ethics: Jesus' Proclamation of the Kingdom of God and the Church in Response.* Scottdale, PA and Kitchener, ON: Herald, 1992.

Social Concern

Bammel, Ernst, and C. F. D. Moule, eds. *Jesus and the Politics of His Day.* Cambridge: CUP, 1984.

Blomberg, Craig L. *Contagious Holiness: Jesus' Meals with Sinners.* Leicester: Apollos; Downers Grove: IVP, 2005.

Cassidy, Richard J. *Jesus, Politics and Society: A Study of Luke's Gospel.* Maryknoll: Orbis, 1978.

Hengel, Martin. *Victory over Violence* and *Was Jesus a Revolutionist?* Philadelphia: Fortress 1971; Eugene, OR: Wipf & Stock, 2003.

Herzog, William R. II. *Jesus, Justice and the Reign of God: A Ministry of Liberation.* Louisville: WJKP, 2000.

Ringe, Sharon H. *Jesus, Liberation and the Biblical Jubilee.* Philadelphia: Fortress, 1985; Eugene, OR: Wipf & Stock, 2004.

Segundo, Juan L. *The Historical Jesus of the Synoptics.* Maryknoll: Orbis, 1985.

Stassen, Glen H. *Just Peacemaking: Transforming Initiatives for Justice and Peace.* Louisville: WJKP, 1992.

Witherington, Ben, III. *Women in the Ministry of Jesus.* Cambridge: CUP, 1984.

Yoder, John H. *The Politics of Jesus.* Rev. ed. Grand Rapids: Eerdmans; Carlisle: Paternoster, 1994.

Law and Gospel

Banks, Robert. *Jesus and the Law in the Synoptic Tradition.* Cambridge: CUP, 1975.

Dodd, C. H. *Gospel and Law: The Relation of Faith and Ethics in Early Christianity.* Cambridge: CUP, 1951; New York: Columbia University Press, 1963.

France, R. T. *Jesus and the Old Testament.* London: Tyndale; Downers Grove: IVP, 1971; Grand Rapids: Baker, 1982; Vancouver: Regent College Press, 1992.

Holmén, Tom. *Jesus and Jewish Covenant Thinking.* Leiden and Boston: Brill, 2001.

Loader, William. *Jesus' Attitude Towards the Law: A Study of the Gospels.* Tübingen: Mohr, 1997; Grand Rapids and Cambridge: Eerdmans, 2002.

Powery, Emerson B. *Jesus Reads Scripture: The Function of Jesus' Use of Scripture in the Synoptic Gospels.* Leiden and Boston: Brill, 2003.

Westerholm, Stephen. *Jesus and Scribal Authority.* Lund: Gleerup, 1978.

Jesus and Judaism

Charlesworth, James H., ed. *Jesus' Jewishness.* New York: Crossroad, 1991.

Evans, Craig A., and Donald A. Hagner, eds. *Anti-Semitism and Early Christianity.* Minneapolis: Fortress, 1993.

Fredriksen, Paula and Adele Reinhartz, eds. *Jesus, Judaism, and Christian Anti-Judaism: Reading the New Testament after the Holocaust.* Louisville: WJKP, 2002.

Hagner, Donald A. *The Jewish Reclamation of Jesus.* Grand Rapids: Zondervan, 1984; Eugene, OR: Wipf & Stock, 1997.

Levine, Amy-Jill. *The Misunderstood Jew: The Church and the Scandal of the Jewish Jesus.* San Francisco: Harper One, 2007.

Sanders, E. P. *Jesus and Judaism.* London: SCM; Philadelphia: Fortress, 1985.

Sandmel, Samuel. *Judaism and Christian Beginnings.* Oxford: OUP, 1978.

Vermes, Geza. *Jesus in His Jewish Context.* Rev. ed. Minneapolis: Fortress, 2003.

Young, Brad H. *Jesus the Jewish Theologian.* Peabody: Hendrickson, 1995.

Zeitlin, Irving. *Jesus and the Judaism of His Time.* Oxford: Blackwell, 1988.

Redemption and Vindication

Redemption

Hengel, Martin. *The Atonement: The Origins of the Doctrine in the New Testament.* London: SCM; Philadelphia: Fortress, 1981; Eugene, OR: Wipf & Stock, 2007.

McKnight, Scot. *Jesus and His Death: Historiography, the Historical Jesus, and Atonement Theory.* Waco: Baylor University Press, 2005.

Pitre, Brant. *Jesus, the Tribulation, and the End of the Exile: Restoration Eschatology and the Origin of the Atonement.* Tübingen: Mohr, 2005; Grand Rapids: Baker, 2006.

Reiser, Marius. *Jesus and Judgment: The Eschatological Proclamation in Its Jewish Context.* Minneapolis: Fortress, 1997.

Stott, John R. W. *The Cross of Christ.* Rev. ed. Leicester and Downers Grove: IVP, 2006.

Vindication

Allison, Dale C., Jr. *The End of the Ages Has Come: An Early Interpretation of the Passion and Resurrection of Jesus.* Philadelphia: Fortress, 1985.

Beasley-Murray, George R. *Jesus and the Last Days: The Interpretation of the Olivet Discourse.* Peabody: Hendrickson, 1993.

Conyers, A. J. *The End: What Jesus Really Said about the Last Things.* Downers Grove: IVP, 1995.

Hill, Craig C. *In God's Time: The Bible and the Future.* Grand Rapids and Cambridge: Eerdmans, 2002.

Moore, Arthur L. *The Parousia in the New Testament.* Leiden: Brill, 1966.

Pate, C. Marvin and Douglas W. Kennard. *Deliverance Now and Not Yet: The New Testament and the Great Tribulation.* New York: Peter Lang, 2003.

Witherington, Ben, III. *Jesus, Paul, and the End of the World.* Downers Grove: IVP, 1992.

Christology

In General

Brown, Raymond E. *An Introduction to New Testament Christology.* New York: Paulist, 1994.

Dunn, James D. G. *Christology in the Making.* Rev. ed. London: SCM, 1989; Grand Rapids: Eerdmans, 1996.

Longenecker, Richard N., ed. *Contours of Christology in the New Testament.* Grand Rapids and Cambridge: Eerdmans, 2005.

Marshall, I. Howard. *The Origins of New Testament Christology.* Rev. ed. Leicester and Downers Grove: IVP, 1990.

Matera, Frank J. *New Testament Christology.* Louisville: WJKP, 1999.

Moule, C. F. D. *The Origin of Christology.* Cambridge: CUP, 1977.

Reymond, Robert L. *Jesus: Divine Messiah.* Phillipsburg, N.J.: Presbyterian & Reformed, 1990.

Witherington, Ben, III. *The Christology of Jesus.* Minneapolis: Fortress, 1990.

Son of Man

Burkett, Delbert. *The Son of Man Debate: A History and Evaluation.* Cambridge: CUP, 1999.

Caragounis, Chrys C. *The Son of Man.* Tübingen: Mohr, 1986.

Casey, Maurice. *The Solution to the 'Son of Man' Problem.* London and New York: T&T Clark, 2007.

Hare, D. R. A. *The Son of Man Tradition.* Minneapolis: Fortress, 1990.

Kim, Seyoon. *The Son of Man as the Son of God.* Tübingen: Mohr, 1983; Grand Rapids: Eerdmans, 1985.

Lindars, Barnabas. *Jesus Son of Man.* London: SPCK; Grand Rapids: Eerdmans, 1983.

Wink, Walter. *The Human Being: Jesus and the Enigma of the Son of Man.* Minneapolis: Fortress, 2002.

Son of God

Gathercole, Simon J. *The Pre-existent Son: Recovering the Christologies of Matthew, Mark, and Luke.* Grand Rapids and Cambridge: Eerdmans, 2006.

Gieschen, Charles A. *Angelomorphic Christology: Antecedents and Early Evidence.* Leiden: Brill, 1998.

Hengel, Martin. *The Son of God*. London: SCM; Philadelphia: Fortress, 1976.

Lord

Hengel, Martin. *Studies in Early Christology*. Edinburgh: T&T Clark, 1995.
Hurtado, Larry W. *Lord Jesus Christ: Devotion to Jesus in Earliest Christianity*. Grand Rapids and Cambridge: Eerdmans, 2003.
Hurtado, Larry W. *One God, One Lord: Early Christian Devotion and Ancient Jewish Monotheism*. Philadelphia: Fortress, 1988.

Messiah

Charlesworth, James H., ed. *The Messiah: Developments in Earliest Judaism and Christianity*. Minneapolis: Fortress, 1992.
Chester, Andrew. *Messiah and Exaltation: Jewish Messianic and Visionary Traditions and New Testament Christology*. Tübingen: Mohr Siebeck, 2007.
Collins, John J. *The Scepter and the Star: The Messiahs of the Dead Sea Scrolls and Other Ancient Literature*. New York and London: Doubleday, 1995.
Dahl, Nils A. *Jesus the Christ: The Historical Origins of Christological Doctrine*. Ed. Donald Juel. Minneapolis: Fortress, 1990.
Fitzmyer, Joseph A. *The One Who Is to Come*. Grand Rapids and Cambridge: Eerdmans, 2007.
Hess, Richard S. and M. Daniel Carroll R., eds. *Israel's Messiah in the Bible and the Dead Sea Scrolls*. Grand Rapids: Baker, 2003.
Horbury, William. *Messianism among Jews and Christians*. London and New York: T&T Clark, 2003.
Porter, Stanley E., ed. *The Messiah in the Old and New Testaments*. Grand Rapids and Cambridge: Eerdmans, 2007.

God

Bauckham, Richard. *God Crucified: Monotheism and Christology in the New Testament*. Grand Rapids and Cambridge: Eerdmans, 1999.
Bowman, Robert M., Jr. and J. Ed Komoszewski. *Putting Jesus in His Place: The Case for the Deity of Christ*. Grand Rapids: Kregel, 2007.
Harris, Murray. *Jesus as God: The New Testament Use of* Theos *in Reference to Jesus*. Grand Rapids: Baker, 1992.
Hurtado, Larry W. *How on Earth Did Jesus Become a God? Historical Questions about Earliest Devotion to Jesus*. Grand Rapids and Cambridge: Eerdmans, 2005.

Questions for Review

1. What are the major topics about which Jesus taught? How would you summarize his main emphases on each topic?
2. What are the categories of data available to us for constructing a Christology of Jesus?
3. What did each of the main Christological titles in the Gospels mean in its primary, original contexts?
4. As a result of this chapter (and this book), how would you summarize the mission and identity of Jesus of Nazareth? How are these conclusions relevant to our contemporary world? to your life personally?

Name Index

SUBJECT INDEX

SCRIPTURE INDEX